Lecture Notes in Artificial Intelligence   3071

Edited by J. G. Carbonell and J. Siekmann

Subseries of Lecture Notes in Computer Science

Andrea Omicini   Paolo Petta
Jeremy Pitt (Eds.)

Engineering Societies in the Agents World IV

4th International Workshop, ESAW 2003
London, UK, October 29-31, 2003
Revised Selected and Invited Papers

 Springer

Series Editors

Jaime G. Carbonell, Carnegie Mellon University, Pittsburgh, PA, USA
Jörg Siekmann, University of Saarland, Saarbrücken, Germany

Volume Editors

Andrea Omicini
Università di Bologna a Cesena
Dipartimento di Elettronica, Informatica e Sistemistica
Via Venezia 52, 47023 Cesena, Italy
E-mail: andrea.omicini@unibo.it

Paolo Petta
Austrian Research Institute for Artificial Intelligence
Freyung 6/2, 1010 Vienna, Austria
E-mail: paolo@oefai.at

Jeremy Pitt
Imperial College
Intelligent Systems and Networks Group
Electrical and Electronic Engineering Department
Exhibition Road, London, SW7 2BT, UK
E-mail: j.pitt@imperial.ac.uk

Library of Congress Control Number: 2004108441

CR Subject Classification (1998): I.2.11, I.2, C.2.4, D.1.3, D.2.2, D.2.7, D.2.11

ISSN 0302-9743
ISBN 3-540-22231-6 Springer-Verlag Berlin Heidelberg New York

This work is subject to copyright. All rights are reserved, whether the whole or part of the material is
concerned, specifically the rights of translation, reprinting, re-use of illustrations, recitation, broadcasting,
reproduction on microfilms or in any other way, and storage in data banks. Duplication of this publication
or parts thereof is permitted only under the provisions of the German Copyright Law of September 9, 1965,
in its current version, and permission for use must always be obtained from Springer-Verlag. Violations are
liable to prosecution under the German Copyright Law.

Springer-Verlag is a part of Springer Science+Business Media

springeronline.com

© Springer-Verlag Berlin Heidelberg 2004
Printed in Germany

Typesetting: Camera-ready by author, data conversion by DA-TeX Gerd Blumenstein
Printed on acid-free paper   SPIN: 11012399   06/3142   5 4 3 2 1 0

Preface

The fourth international workshop, "Engineering Societies in the Agents World" (ESAW 2003) was a three-day event that took place at the end of October 2003. After previous events in Germany, the Czech Republic, and Spain, the workshop crossed the Channel, to be held at the premises of Imperial College, London.

The steady increase in the variety of backgrounds of contributing scientists, fascinating new perspectives on the topics, and number of participants, bespeaks the success of the ESAW workshop series. Its idea was born in 1999 among members of the working group on "Communication, Coordination, and Collaboration" of the first lease of life of the European Network of Excellence on Agent-Based Computing, AgentLink, out of a critical discussion about the general mindset of the agent community. At that time, we felt that proper considerations of systemic aspects of agent technology deployment, such as acknowledgement of the importance of the social and environmental perspectives, were sorely missing: a deficiency that we resolved should be addressed directly by a new forum.

A first focal point was the vision that to tackle the issues inherently connected to the emergent complexity of multi-agent systems (MAS) it would be inevitable to introduce the notion of a *society of agents* as a first-class entity in the modeling and engineering of MAS. In particular, paying attention to software infrastructure as a location to provide intelligence in MAS, and the notion of social intelligence drove the first ESAW workshop, co-located with ECAI 2000 in Berlin. ESAW 2001, held in Prague together with the by now renowned European Agent Systems Summer School (ACAI'01), reinforced the line of research relating to the design of agent society and underlined further the necessity for methodologies to properly guide the increasingly popular use of social and cognitive concepts in agent theories and technologies. The third workshop in Madrid took advantage of co-location with the workshop series on Cooperative Information Agents (CIA 2002) to set itself apart and gain further in identity by opening up to a yet a wider range of contributing technologies, while maintaining its central focus on theoretical and methodological aspects applied by this direction of research.

ESAW 2003 was the first workshop neither connected to nor co-located with any other scientific event. Even so, the stand-alone workshop proved the most vivid and rich one to date: this stands to testify, on the one hand, that the community aggregating around ESAW is by now sufficiently large and mature to sustain an autonomous scientific event, and, on the other hand, that the original intent to define and extend this community beyond the traditional (and already outdated) borders of computer engineering has definitely been met. Following the tradition of this workshop, the structure of the event developed around a few main themes constituting the pivotal elements of the sessions, as well as two invited talks that provided further topics of high relevance and prompted stimulating discussions.

In particular, the sessions addressed the following themes over the three days of the workshop:

- *Agent-Oriented Software Engineering and Formal Methods.* Two sessions covered methodological aspects of AOSE as well as formal methods in the analysis and planning of agent systems.
- *MAS Protocols and Interaction Management.* This session hosted presentations and discussions on communication and coordination between agents, focusing in particular on social aspects.
- *MAS Organization and Workflow.* Presentations in this session concentrated on organizational aspects, as well as related technologies and applications.
- *MAS Architectures, Cooperation and Teamwork.* In this session we discussed agent architectures, team and coalition formation, and economies of interaction in agent societies.
- *Artificial Intelligence Techniques in MAS.* This session covered more traditional (in a certain sense) topics in MAS research, such as planning and collective forms of intelligence.
- *Agent Society Dynamics and Engineering.* This session developed a series of notions from as heterogeneous backgrounds as sociology, political philosophy, and organizational theories, to serve as sources for foundational concepts for agent societies and their construction.
- *Agent Applications: Services, User Modeling, and E-Commerce.* In this session, different applications of agent technologies were presented, including user profiling, intelligent and dynamic service integration, and the realization of models of trust.

Two invited presentations rounded off the program in a most worthy manner. Dr. André P. Meyer, of the Command & Control and Simulation group of the Dutch TNO FEL, spoke about "Privacy-Aware Mobile Agents: Protecting Privacy by Modeling Social Behavior in Open Systems of Software Agents," examining the problem of privacy in open systems where a multitude of different MAS may interact. The presentation by Dr. Jean-Pierre Müller, now senior researcher at the French LIRMM, entitled "Emergence of Collective Behavior; Simulation and Social Engineering," examined the different notions of emergent behavior in complex systems and the correlation with concepts such as agent orientated and environment oriented programming. Techniques discussed in the analysis phase have been applied to resource management tasks – in particular, social engineering and ecological modeling.

It is useful to underline how the tradition of ESAW differs from other scientific workshops: here, the selection process includes the very meeting event, to which in particular the typical borderline paper submissions are also invited: The workshop allows the presenters to utilize the open atmosphere of discussion (promoted as much as possible by the organizers) to get their own innovative contributions into focus and make them stand out as deserved, whilst, at the same time, offering the organizers in their role as curators of the event the possibility to catalyze and encourage original approaches and judge individual efforts in a more comprehensive way. The constructive quality of the workshop – in particular, of this most recent event – thus contrasts decidedly with the dry and meticulous climate that all too often characterises analogous events, and it thereby promotes a typically broader and more collaborative scientific development of presented work.

The complete range of contributions that were collected in the working notes of the event are available online – along with the presentation slides – at the ESAW 2003 workshop site. The present post-proceedings continue the series published with Springer-Verlag (ESAW 2000: LNAI 1972, ESAW 2001: LNAI 2203, and ESAW 2002: LNAI 2577). This volume contains reworked and extended versions of selected papers and also includes contributions by the two invited speakers.

The organizers gratefully acknowledge financial support granted by the following institutions:

- Polo Scientifico-Didattico di Cesena, Università degli Studi di Bologna
- Imperial College London
- the Austrian Society for Artificial Intelligence (ÖGAI)
- Whitestein Technologies

as well as the scientific support by ACM SIGART and AgentLink II. Our thanks also go to Springer-Verlag's Alfred Hofmann for his essential background role in helping ESAW through its infancy. The Austrian Research Institute for Artificial Intelligence is supported by the Austrian Federal Ministry for Education, Science and Culture and by the Austrian Federal Ministry for Transport, Innovation and Technology.

The next ESAW workshop is scheduled to be hosted in France by the University of Toulouse in October 2004, with Marie-Pierre Gleizes, Andrea Omicini, and Franco Zambonelli as organizers. We look forward to an ever broader and larger attendance, an even more lively interaction, and a still higher level of originality and innovation.

April 2004   Andrea Omicini
                                                                    Paolo Petta
                                                                    Jeremy Pitt

Organization

ESAW 2003 Workshop Organizers

Andrea Omicini	DEIS, Università degli Studi di Bologna, Cesena (Italy)
Paolo Petta	Austrian Research Institute for Artificial Intelligence, Vienna (Austria)
Jeremy Pitt	Department of Electrical & Electronic Engineering, Imperial College London (UK)

ESAW 2003 Local Organizing Committee

Jeremy Pitt	(Local Chair)
Alexander Artikis	Department of Electrical & Electronic Engineering,
Lloyd Kamara	Imperial College London (UK)
Dimosthenis Kaponis	
Brendan Neville	

ESAW 2003 Program Committee

Makoto Amamiya	School of Information Science & Electrical Engineering, Kyushu University, Fukuoka (Japan)
Alexander Artikis	Department of Electrical & Electronic Engineering, Imperial College London (UK)
Federico Bergenti	Dipartimento Ingegneria dell'Informazione, Università degli Studi di Parma (Italy)
Jeffrey Bradshaw	Institute for Human & Machine Cognition, University of West Florida (USA)
Monique Calisti	Whitestein Technologies (France/Switzerland)
Cristiano Castelfranchi	Institute of Cognitive Sciences and Technology, CNR (Italy)
Paolo Ciancarini	Dipartimento Scienze dell'Informazione, Università degli Studi di Bologna (Italy)
Helder Coelho	Department of Informatics of the Faculty of Sciences, University of Lisbon (Portugal)
R. Scott Cost	Department of Computer Science and Electrical Engineering, University of Maryland Baltimore County (USA)
Paul Davidsson	Department of Software Engineering & Computer Science, Blekinge Institute of Technology (Sweden)
Keith Decker	Department of Computer & Information Sciences, University of Delaware (USA)
Rino Falcone	Institute of Cognitive Sciences and Technology, CNR (Italy)
Stephan Flake	C-LAB, Cooperative Computing & Communication Lab (Germany)
Alessandro Garcia	TecComm, PUC-Rio (Brazil)
Marie-Pierre Gleizes	IRIT, Université Paul Sabatier, Toulouse (France)
Andrew Jones	Department of Computer Science, King's College, London (UK)
Paul Kearney	Intelligent Agents, BT Exact (UK)

Barbara Keplicz — Institute of Computer Science of the Polish Academy of Sciences, Warsaw (Poland)

Manolis Koubarakis — Department of Electronic & Computer Engineering, Technical University of Crete (Greece)

Yannis Labrou — Fujitsu Laboratories of America (USA)

Lyndon C. Lee — Intelligent Agents, BT Exact (UK)

Michael Luck — Department of Electronics & Computer Science, University of Southampton (UK)

Antoni Mazurkiewicz — Institute of Computer Science of the Polish Academy of Sciences, Warsaw (Poland)

Pablo Noriega — Spanish Scientific Research Council, Campus Universitat Autónoma de Barcelona (Spain)

Eugenio Oliveira — Department of Computer and Electrical Engineering, University of Porto (Portugal)

Sascha Ossowski — Universidad Rey Juan Carlos, Madrid (Spain)

H. Van Dyke Parunak — Altarum Institute, Ann Arbor, MI (USA)

Michal Pechoucek — Faculty of Electrical Engineering, Czech Technical University Prague (Czech Republic)

Agostino Poggi — Dipartimento di Ingegneria dell'Informazione, Università degli Studi di Parma (Italy)

Omer Rana — Department of Computer Science, University of Cardiff (UK)

Alessandro Ricci — DEIS, Università degli Studi di Bologna, Cesena (Italy)

John R. Rose — Department of Computer Science & Engineering, University of South Carolina (USA)

Giovanni Sartor — CIRSFID, Università degli Studi di Bologna (Italy)

Ken Satoh — National Institute of Informatics, Tokyo (Japan)

Marek Sergot — Department of Computing, Imperial College London (UK)

Onn Shehory — IBM Haifa Research Laboratories (Israel)

Christophe Sibertin-Blanc — IRIT, Université Paul Sabatier, Toulouse (France)

Munindar Singh — Department of Computer Science, North Carolina State University (USA)

Kostas Stathis — Department of Computer Science, City University, London (UK)

Robert Tolksdorf — Institut für Informatik, Freie Universität Berlin (Germany)

José M. Vidal — Department of Computer Science & Engineering, University of South Carolina (USA)

Gerhard Weiß — Institut für Informatik, Technische Universität München (Germany)

Steve Wilmott — LSI, Universitat Politècnica de Catalunya, Barcelona (Spain)

Bin Yu — Information Technology & Engineering, North Carolina State University (USA)

Franco Zambonelli — Department of Computer Science, Università degli Studi di Modena and Reggio Emilia (Italy)

Table of Contents

Multi-disciplinary Models for Agent Societies

Coordination, Organization and Security of Agent Societies

Abstractions, Methodologies and Tools for Engineering Agent Societies

Applications of Agent Societies

Emergence of Collective Behaviour and Problem Solving

Jean-Pierre Müller*

CIRAD-TERA-REV-GREEN**
73, av. Jean-François Breton
34398 Montpellier cedex 5 - France
jean-pierre.muller@cirad.fr

Abstract. The goal of this paper is to explore the notion of complex system and, in particular the emergence phenomenon, in order to see which lessons could be learned for both understanding and designing complex software systems. Complex systems are described as sets of non-linearly interacting components making multi-agent systems particularly suitable for modelling and designing such systems. The notion of emergence is explicited and used to derive ways of understanding and designing such complex systems. We conclude by discussing the pros and cons of the emergentist approaches and the research perspectives.

1 Introduction

As explicited in the aims and scope of the "Engineering Societies in the Agents World" workshop, software systems are undergoing drastic changes in scale and complexity, making them more resemble natural systems and societies than mechanical systems and traditional software architectures. The goal of this paper is to explore the notion of complex system and, in particular the emergence phenomenon, in order to to see which lessons could be learned for both understanding and designing such software systems.

A traditional approach in computer science is to decompose the system in manageable components (functions, objects or coarser grain components) with clear interfaces, i.e. manageable way of handling the interactions, most often carried out by a middleware (as discussed in [1]). Artificial Intelligence and Multi-Agent Systems are proposing problem solving methods inspired by the strategies developed by the natural systems (from ant colonies to human beings conceived as thinkers). Nevertheless these methods mostly rely on an *a priori* formalisation of the problem domain. In dynamic and uncertain domains, this *a priori* formalisation becomes difficult and requires an increased adaptive capability. Nature seems to have solved this problem by emergence of collective

---

* I would like to thank the program committee of the ESAW'03 workshop for inviting me to this very stimulating event.
** Also associate researcher to LIRMM, 161, rue Ada, 34392 Montpellier cedex 5 - France.

A. Omicini, P. Petta, and J. Pitt (Eds.): ESAW 2003, LNAI 3071, pp. 1–21, 2004.
© Springer-Verlag Berlin Heidelberg 2004

behaviours self-organising from the dynamics of entities in interaction between themselves and with an environment. Unfortunately, the notion of emergence itself is problematic for the modeller as well as for the designer, being most often defined by an absence of "something" as composability, predictability, and so on when the notion itself is not criticised.

The notion of emergence is usually associated with a misunderstanding or with an intuition facing some phenomena observed in nature; it is therefore rejected for a reductionist interpretation. For example, Daniel Memmi [2] limits emergence to a problem of description or explanation and assumes that emergent phenomena are examples among others of the variety of scientific explanations. In this sense, emergence is not in nature but in the change of observation focus on the phenomena. However, even if emergence can be characterised epistemologically, these phenomena have to pre-exist to our observation. In other terms, the emergence of an entity, a structure, a function or a process is in the system independently of our observation even if it is a change of the point of view of the observer, which reveals the emergence.

To better understand and exploit these emergent phenomena, one should provide an alternative approach not only to computer modelling, but also to problem solving. This approach principle is to build a society of agents, immersed in an environment, which by their interactions will evolve towards a stable state representing a solution. This approach, initiated by R.Brooks in robotics [3], is opposed to the classical problem solving approach where the global resolution task is decomposed into subtasks. The program then codes the resolution steps; while executing, the process follows the predefined path until the solution is reached. In the "emergentist" approach, the program codes the agents, the environment and the interactions; while executing, the process self-organises and builds a solution.

Another characteristic of the emergentist approach is the adaptative capability of emergent phenomena or structures to the changes of the environment. These phenomena are in dynamic interaction with the environment, but are not totally dependent on it. Generic regularities and properties are abstracted away through self-organisation and are applicable in other environments. In reality, the environment instantiates behavioural and structural rules, raising the emergence of a global phenomena. For example, a bacteria following a sugar gradient can go towards a sugar source or follow such a source without modifying the "program" controlling the behaviour of the bacteria. This adaptability to external changes is immediate because it does not rely on internal representations nor internalisation of paths. Therefore it does not necessitate updating or modification of the representation.

In the french multi-agent community, the concept of emergence for problem-solving has gained considerable interest. We can cite the teams at LIRMM [4, 5], LIP6 [6], LEIBNIZ [7, 8], CASCAD [9] or IRIT [10]. It is less used in the anglo-saxon community with the important exception of the work by Van Parunak around industrial applications [11]. The notion of emergence is better explored in the artificial life domain where we can cite the work of Deneubourg [12],

E. Bonabeau [13], J.L. Dessalles, L. Steels [14]. The two papers of [13] : "Characterizing emergent phenomena", give a number of examples of phenomena considered as emergent and propose a frame of study for a better understanding of these phenomena. Finally, we have to make reference to the seminal work of S. Forrest [15, 16] in the domain of emergent computation, we shall come to later on.

In the following, we will first introduce the notion of complex system, pointing out the importance of emergence in this definition. Several approaches to cope with complex systems shall be reviewed and illustrated. We shall conclude that multi-agent systems are good candidates for modelling and designing complex systems. The next section will introduce the notion of emergence, which is of outmost importance to understand complex systems. We shall propose a definition, which can be operational for understanding and for designing multi-agent systems. In section 4, we will discuss how we can use this definition to derive a methodology for designing emergentist multi-agent systems. Section 5 will conclude on the interest of the advantages and limits of using an emergentist approach to multi-agent systems and open research perspectives.

2   Complex Systems

It is hard to find a definition of what a complex system is but a mere list of properties (as is the case for intelligence, life, etc.). We can cite the exception of the definition of complex adaptive systems in [17] with a bias towards darwinian adaptiveness. Roughly speaking (and almost tautologically), a complex system is:

A System: a set of interacting components composing a whole (which whole to consider is dependent on the observer, hence on the question being asked) creating, *de facto*, a distinction between the system to be considered and the rest (the environment or outside);

Which is Complex: the interactions among the components are non-linear, such that the global behaviour of the system cannot be compositionaly deduced from the components' behaviours.

The second property makes the distinction between a complex system and a mere complicated system, which may have up to a huge number of components and still be compositionaly understood (like the digital electronic circuits, for example).

This definition exhibits most of the properties generally ascribed from complex systems [18], i.e.:

- the need of multi-scale descriptions, because it minimaly implies the articulation of the level of the components, the level of the whole and the level of the underlying environment;
- the multiplicity of view points because the wholes to consider are intrinsically related to the question being asked and therefore give rise to interacting view points (in addition to interacting components!);

- the intricacy of whole and component behaviours both by the reciprocal relationship of the global behaviour and the local behaviours and by the relative autonomy of the global behaviour with respect to the local behaviours;
- the emergence of the whole organisation because of the non-linearity of the underlying interactions.

In order to model complex systems, three approaches can be sketched:

Analytical Approaches: by analysing the system component by component as advocated by the classical rational approach. In such models, the focus is on the individual behaviours rather than on the interactions;

Holistic or Systemic Approaches: by analysing the system as a whole by isolating aggregated variables and their interactions (rather than the interactions between the components) as is done in most dynamical models as compartment, statistical or eulerian models;

Constructivist Approaches: by trying to articulate the individual behaviours of the components with the global behaviour of the system as is done in lagrangian dynamical models, individual-based approaches, microsimulation or multi-agent systems depending on the scientific domain in which such inquiries take place. In such models, the focus is on the interactions rather than on the individual behaviours.

As transdisciplinary considerations, it is not a surprise that these kinds of approaches can be found in most scientific fields in a form or another. For example, in sociology, we find the distinction between methodological individualism (the first approach), methodological holism (the second category) and constructivist approaches (see [19]).

As an example, fluid dynamics can be described from:

- the behaviour of water molecules: the analytical approach;
- the Navier-Stockes equations: the holistic approach;
- the interaction among micro-level entities (as droplets or vortices) and the resulting structure of the fluid dynamics: the constructivist approach.

Each approach has its own domain of validity as negligible non linear interactions for the analytical approaches, and sufficiently stable systems for the second approach (when the system does not undergo changes, which can result in a change of the equations themselves). The constructivist approach can be used in several cases:

- when one knows the individual behaviour and one wants to explore the resulting global dynamics. It is particularly the case for negociation support where the various actors are not always conscious of the joined effect of their current and future actions;
- when one knows or intends (when designing) the global behaviour and one seeks an explanation or design from local behaviours. It is the case in science where an explanation (rather than a description) must always relate on underlying phenomena[20] (a stone does not fall *because* of the gravity law but because of the gravitational interaction between two bodies). In this case, the constructivist approach has a heuristic role in the scientific inquiry;

– when one knows both behaviours but the relationship is hard to articulate as
it is the case when the whole behaviour emerges from the local interactions
and when the global behaviour can qualitatively change over time (requiring
new sets of equations to describe it). In general, the constructivist approach
is related to any understanding building process.

As it can be seen, the notion of emergence is at the core of the notion of complex systems and multi-agent systems at the core of constructivist approaches
to complex systems. It is the reason why we shall explore the notion of emergence more deeply, mostly based on the work of a special interest group called
"COLLINE"[1] [21].

3   Notion of Emergence

As we shall see, the notion of emergence is multiply defined rather than ill-
defined and covers two aspects : the static aspect (emergence as a result or
observable) and the dynamic aspect (emergence as a process). Focusing on the
former aspect, we shall present the history and some of the most interesting
definitions without being exhaustive. After discussing these definitions, we shall
propose a new one opening the possibility to derive a methodology for designing
multi-agent systems, in particular for problem solving.

The British Emergentism The first mention of the term "emergence" comes
from the so-called *british emergentism*. It initialy took place in the debate between various accounts of life as: the *substantial vitalism*, which states that it
exists a substance linked to the living called entelechy; the *mechanistic theory*
for which we are only machines (life is reducible to biochemical processes);
and finally the theory of emergentism (Lewes, S.Alexander, Broad, Stuart Mill:
book of Broad "the mind and its place in nature", 1923). This last theory is
based on the work by Stuart Mill, which distinguishes between two types of laws
organising nature :

– the *homopathic or resultant* modality, we can explain by causal laws or composition of them ;
– the *heteropathic or chemical or emergent* modality, we cannot explain by
causal laws as the acquisition of the properties of water out of the properties
of oxygen and hydrogen respectively.

The debate is on the existence of these heteropathic laws, which raises the problem of relating specific sciences (chemistry, biology, etc.) to physics.
    The argumentation of the emergentists uses a vision of nature in levels artic-
ulated on top of one another, the physical level being the most fundamental, and

---

[1] "COLLINE" stands for "COLLective, INteraction, Emergence", SIG of the Multi-
agent System chapter of AFIA "Association Franìaise d'Intelligence Artificielle" (Artificial Intelligence French Association).

on the ontological existence of the entities at a given level, emerging from the level immediately under it. For the british emergentist, the entities at a certain level $n + 1$ emerging from a level n exist if and only if they have a causal power and therefore allows the explanation of the phenomena at their level. If we can find a cause between n and $n + 1$, we do not have emergence but reducibility. If there is only a cause between n and $n + 1$, it is an epiphenomenon (e.g. the shadow of the hand). In this argumentation, the nature and the existence of a descending causality is fundamental.

Recent Definitions of Emergence

Emergent Computation. A definition of Stephanie Forrest [16] of the notion of emergent computation is particularly interesting because it is conceptually closer to what we want to formalise in multi-agent systems. Emergent computation is defined as:

- a set of entities in interaction: the process;
- an epiphenomenon produced by this process: a stable state, an invariant or an execution trace;
- the interpretation of this epiphenomenon as a computation or the result of a computation.

A first remark concerns the distinction between an epiphenomenon and an emergence. What is emergent is not the stable state, the invariant or the trace but its interpretation in a given vocabulary distinct from the vocabulary in which the process is programmed. For example with the ants, the emergent phenomenon is not the pheromone trace but its identification by the observer as a path between the nest and the food source.

As a second remark, an epiphenomenon is not an emergence because it as been created by the process, but does not interact with the process itself (no feedback from the level $n + 1$ on the level n). Automatically, we can create an emergence precisely when this feedback takes place. In order to do that, it is enough that the trace (it is the only physical reality, the stable state or the invariant can only be potentially perceivable when they let a trace) interacts with the process. At this moment something new is produced, which is neither in the process (because we need the trace) nor in the trace (because we need the process) and, if it stabilises, it becomes emergent simultaneously as a structure (the trace) and as a dynamics (the process). We have an illustration of the duality structure/dynamics.

Emergence in Cognitive Science. John Searle [22] writes : "Some characteristics of the system can be deduced or conceived, or computed from the characteristics of [its components] on the simple basis of their arrangement or of their composition (and sometimes from the relations they have with their environment) for example the form, the weight, the speed. But other characteristics cannot be conceived only from the composition of its elements or their environmental relations; they must be explained in terms of causal interactions produced between the elements. Let us call them the "causally emergent characteristics of the system". Solidity, liquidity and transparency are some examples. From these definitions, consciousness is an emergent property of the system. This conception of causal emergence, we will call "emergence 1", must be distinguished from a more adventurous conception, we will call "emergence 2". A characteristics F is emergent 2 if F is emergent 1 and F has causal power, which cannot be explained by the causal interactions $a, b, c \ldots$. If consciousness is emergent 2, consciousness could cause things, which would not be explained by the causal behaviour of the neurons."

For Minsky, the careful analysis of emergent phenomena "makes generally apparent that these phenomena can completely be explained when one take into account the interactions between the parts as well as the particularities and limitations of the perception and expectations of the observer" [23]. It is the precise position of Bertalanffy when he is talking about emergent properties: "the knowledge of the set of parts contained in the system and of the relations linking them allows to deduce from the behaviour of the parts, the behaviour of the whole" [24]. Finally, [25] makes a very interesting contribution to the role of non-reductionist concepts in psychology and cognitive science.

Emergence in Sociology. Without being exhaustive, it is worth mentioning the use of the concept of emergence in sociology in particular with the paper of [19] and more recently the work of Castelfranchi [26] and of Keith Sawyer [27, 28] where important discussions about the various approaches can be found.

3.1   Towards a Definition of Emergence in MAS

At the light of the various definitions, in philosophy, in computer science, and in cognitive science, it seems essential to come up with a positive, temporal (where time appears explicitly) and constructive definition of emergence, especially for multi-agent systems.

The first essential feature of a multi-agent system is that no agent controls entirely the dynamics of the population. The agents act only locally and therefore modify the environment by interpreting it given his limited means (using the distinctions it is able to make). The agents are limited and there are differences of the global system they are unaware of. Therefore, there is an exteriority relative to each agent: an environment. The second feature is that the exterior of each agent contains other agents. There are several agents in a common environment (they are exterior to each other). The interpretation of the environment by the various agents can possibly be different. In the case of reactive agents, the environment contains the objects and the other agents. In the case of cognitive agents, the environment can also contain messages. Therefore, the dynamics proceeds by iteration of interpretation of the local environment by the agents, action of the agents on this environment, new interpretation of the modified environment and new actions, etc.

When such a dynamics (or some of its components) stabilises, we can talk of emergence of a structure or of a global function. Notice that at any moment, it is the environment possibly modified by all the other agents (and itself) that each agent submits to its interpretation. It is the condition for the global dynamics to be by more than a simple sum of independent dynamics. In this definition, the dynamics of interaction is postulated as a basic condition for emergence of phenomena, structures, etc.. Also notice the importance of the link whole-parts, which characterises the various kinds of emergent phenomena.

In the following, we will derive a more operational definition by caracterising the whole and the parts, and most importantly the feedback whole-parts. This definition is inspired by the preceding definitions and moreover the one by S. Forrest. A phenomenon is emergent if and only if we have:

- a system of entities in interaction whose expression of the states and dynamics is made in an ontology or theory D;
- the production of a phenomenon, which could be a process, a stable state, or an invariant, which is necessarily global regarding the system of entities;
- the interpretation of this global phenomenon either by an observer or by the entities themselves via an inscription mechanism in another ontology or theory D'.

The non-linearity of the interactions guarantees the irreducibility of D' to D. In other words, D' is not just another way to talk about D.

The inscription mechanism is essential for two reasons. First, it endows the global phenomenon of a causal power (feedback of the level $n+1$ on the level n), producing more than a mere epiphenomenon. Second, it allows the global phenomenon to be perceived and interpreted as a whole by the observer, otherwise it would just occur without anybody able to notice it.

This definition also introduces a distinction depending on the considered observers. When the observer is outside of the system, we talk of *weak emergence* because the emergence only exists for the external observer. This notion of emergence corresponds to the notion of emergence 1 by Searle, or to the first order organisation in system theory. As an example of weak emergence, we can take the ants that produce a path between a food source and their nest. An ant transporting food deposits pheromones. These pheromones diffuse, producing a gradient attracting other ants. As a result, a collective back and forth movement is produced between the source and the nest as long as there is food available. The global phenomenon, i.e. the path, is identified as such by an external observer (most probably, the ants are not aware of the path itself). The three conditions are satisfied:

- a set of agents interacting in terms of pheromones (and not in terms of paths);
- the production of a stable global phenomenon (as long as there is remaining food): i.e. the ants going back and forth between the nest and the food source;

- the observation of this global phenomenon in terms of a path (geometrically speaking) through an inscription, which is the pheromone trace, or more easily observable, the ants themselves along the trace.

Notice that the system is flexible because its behaviour is related to the pheromone gradient and not to the produced path. The path, being a side product, can dynamically change depending on new obstacles or change of food source position; If the dynamics would depend on the path and then of a representation in the ants heads, the decision process to change both the path and its representations would be much heavier. It is this advantage of emergence we would like to exploit in emergentist approaches of problem solving and not only the intrinsic efficacy of parallelism.

If the observer is within the system, we obtain a *strong emergence*, which corresponds to the emergence 2 of Searle or to the second order organisation in system theory. In this case, the global phenomenon interacts with the entities as a whole. As a counter-example, the pheromone path does not interact as a path with the ants but only locally by the diffusion mechanism. It would be the case if the ants would have a map in their heads. Nevertheless, we have a lot of examples of strong emergence in human societies where, for example, the produced collective behaviours find explicit representations in the institutions, constraining further the individual behaviours.

From this definition we can derive a number of consequences:

- the environment plays an important role as an inscription medium. At the micro level, it not only provides the ressources for the agents but also the interaction medium between the agents. As such, the environment structure and properties shape and therefore constrain and coordinate the interactions at various time scales depending on the dissipation rate of the substrate (from very volatile as the sound to almost permanent like stone buildings). At the macro level, as a collective memory recording the historical evolution of the individual agent actions and as the inscription medium from which most global phenomena can be observed and interpreted at the collective level;
- any individual agent can participate to several theories D, corresponding to multiple points of view it can have, and consequently multiple individual roles. But in the case of strong emergence, it can can also react to various interpretations D' of the global phenomena it participates to, resulting in multiple collective roles;
- in highly complex system, there is co-existence of both weak and strong emergence. It is especially the case in social systems because the collective necessarily produces social order, which is out of its awareness, but nevertheless impacts its functioning. It simultaneously produces representations of parts of its global functioning through institutions and more generally what Castelfranchi calls *cognitive emergence* [26].

4   Designing Emergentist Multi-agent Systems

4.1   Introduction

Designing multi-agent systems is distinct from designing other types of classical computer systems, in particular distributed systems, by at least two dimensions:

- the importance of the interactions among the agents, which should exceed the importance of the agent architecture itself if we want the whole to be more than the sum of its constituents;
- the role of the environment simultaneously as a place of inscription and a set of constraints on the multi-agent system dynamics. In distributed systems, the environment is often reduced to the communication channels among the processes. However, if these channels can be dynamically reconfigured, it is essential to introduce spatiality and not only connectivity, in order for the connectivity to be deduced from the spatiality and not the converse.

The design of multi-agent systems raises new challenges and becomes a major issue after a somewhat exploratory phase necessary to any new and expanding domain. We shall distinguish three types of design approaches:

- the agent-oriented approaches, which focus on the individual agents and propose specification formalisms of their behaviours with various tools (agent-oriented programming by [29] or Rao [30], temporal logics approach by Wooldridge [31]. These approaches are distinct from pure mono-agent approaches by the introduction of communication up to complex negotiation protocols;
- the organisational approaches, which deal with the specification of interactions through the notions of roles, relations among roles and groups either to statically specify interaction networks as in [32] or dynamically as, more recently, in [33] and [34];
- the emergentist approaches, distinguishing a micro-level of interacting agents from a macro-level where the desired global phenomenon is produced, which could be either an organisational structure, or the realisation of a task or the building of a solution to a problem. These approaches must therefore articulate these two levels thanks to a positive definition of emergence as proposed earlier and, for example, used in [35, 9].

These various approaches are in fact complementary in the sense that the agent-oriented approaches specify the entities in interaction, the organisational approaches are an important tool to specify what we want to obtain at a macro-level, et finally, the emergentist approaches insist on the interactions and on the micro/macro articulation, making the link with organisational structures (at the global level) using the interactions (at the local level). Separately, they suffer limitations because the agent-oriented approaches can hardly take into account group dynamics, the direct implementation of organisational structures hardly grasps reorganisation dynamics and the emergent approaches still lack sufficiently general methodologies to articulate the micro-level and the macro-level.

To go towards a design methodology of multi-agent systems for problem solving by emergence (excluding multi-agent systems for simulation or cooperative work as with software agents and CSCW), one can start either from the proposed definitions of emergence, or from an analysis of existing systems, natural or artificial, exhibiting emergent properties in order to determine their common features and to deduce a heuristic methodology if not a systematic one. This last approach is proposed in this section taking the definition of emergence developed earlier as a reading grid.

After having fixed the vocabulary on problem solving, we shall present a number of multi-agent systems obeying the following criteria:

- their aim is to perform problem solving, and even optimisation;
- the structure of the state space, as well as the search process, are not explicitly manipulated but emerge from the MAS dynamics ;
- the solution that results can adapt dynamically to changes of the problem data.

We shall present a synoptic table of their common structure and derive a systematic methodology.

4.2   Problem Solving

In order to fix the vocabulary, we shall define formally what problem solving is (see, for example, [36]). This clarification will allow us to compare more easily the classical algorithmic approaches with the multi-agent approaches in general and emergentist ones in particular. A problem is specified by a search space E constituted by an finite or infinite, discrete (combinatorial) or continuous set of states $\{e_i\}$, and a subspace S in E called the space of solutions (or admissible states). The problem is dynamic if the state space and/or the solution space evolve over time.

The search space must be described by a set of components, the parametrisation and the composition operators allowing to generate the search space (i.e. the set of states represented as structures made of these components). This structure is often given as a set of variables v_i and their domain of definition D_i. We will call S the structure of the search space.

The set of solutions is generally expressed in intention by a set of constraints. When the definition does not allow to directly build one or several solution states, we need a search method. One distinguishes two classes of search methods:

- restriction search consists in reducing the search space by incrementally fixing the parameters, the components and their composition until one obtains a state or a sub-space of the solution set. When one obtains a subspace in which no state can be a solution, a backtrack is performed (see, for example, CHIP or PrologIII);

- repair search consists in building a random state and to modify it whenever it does not satisfy the solution criteria (i.e. whenever it is not in the solution space) (see [37]).

Notice that the process goes along a trajectory in the search space and therefore can be reformulated as a control problem [38], optimal if we want to optimise the search time and stochastic if the search is stochastic. Any combination of these two methods is possible.

One can define on the search space an objective function F and search a state that is the best solution state in the sense that it optimises this function F (minimum or maximum). In such a case, we have an optimisation problem.

Classical methods are based on an explicit representation of the current state of the search and an algorithm to compute the next state. In our case, we want the search process to emerge from interactions among agents in such a way that when the system stabilises, the solution can be read as the global state of the multi-agent system. It means that the search state representation is distributed and also is the computation of the next state. In the following examples, we have therefore to identify the structure of the search space, the agents, which have been chosen and their interactions.

4.3   Some Emergentist Multi-agent Systems

Among the first multi-agent systems to make explicitly reference to the emergence of a solution to a problem by side-effect of the interaction dynamics, we must cite the eco-resolution of Ferber [39] from ethological inspiration. It has been applied to a number of problems among which:

- the blocks world whose problem consists in finding a sequence of executable actions to go from an initial configuration to a final configuration. In the proposed solution, the agents are the blocks themselves that interact on the basis of their relationships. These interactions produce movements whose succession will generate a plan and even an executable and acceptable plan. In this case, the search space is the space of possible configurations of the blocks and the emergent solution is the trajectory in the search space [39];
- the magic square consists in putting the tiles in a final configuration by moving one tile at a time. In this case, the agents are the tiles that will push one another in order to go to their final place and, hence, generate the necessary movement sequence [40].

This approach is also applied to chess, to show the possibility to have the emergence of a global strategy from the local interactions of the chess pieces [41].

Another kind of emergentist multi-agent systems relies on dynamical systems like PACO [42] and SMARPS [43], which have been applied to:

- contrast line detection in computer vision. The agents are located on the pixels of the image and will climb the local intensity gradient, trying to keep a given distance from a given number of agents (in general, two) and being influenced by their movements. Lines of agents will eventually stabilise on the contrast lines and even follow them if the image changes sufficiently slowly with respect to the agent own dynamics. It is one of the rare examples where we have an explicit environment, i.e. the image [42];

- cartographic generalisation in which the agents are geographic entities (houses, trees, road segments, rivers, etc.), which will enter a competition to appear on a map of a given resolution. The place occupied by the graphism (lines, icons, etc.) will constrain the other agents to move slightly and/or to reduce the size and shape of their graphism up to invisibility if there is not enough place. The search space is constituted of all the possible positions with all the possible graphisms. The actual position and graphical representation will emerge from the interactions under the resolution constraint [44];
- production of a set of possible positions of linear structures (roads, power lines, etc.) under multi-criteria constraints in land planning. Here, we have multiple environments describing the spatial constraints from various points of view [43].

We can also cite AMROSE [45], a multi-agent system to control an articulated robot to sold steel "plaques". In this case, the rigid parts of the robot are the agents trying to go to a certain position without touching the obstacles or the other parts of the robot. The result is a trajectory of the end tool of the robot resulting from a sequence of commands to the joints.

We can also mention more applied multi-agent systems using optimisation processes as:

- MARSA is a dynamic scheduling system for flow-shop workplant [46]. This system is coupled with a workplant simulator providing various events as: command arrivals, the beginning and end of lot treatments, setup and breaks. The scheduler provides back the next lots to produce. The agents are the commands trying to by produced in accordance with their associated deadlines and the machines trying to minimise their setup time. The interactions are formulated in terms of allocation (and not of temporal order) with an implicit gradient produced by the optimisations to realise. The result is a schedule of the commands as produced for a production campaign. Similar systems have been deployed by Daewoo in Corea [47] and in other industrial applications [48];
- AMACOIA is a design system of assembly lines. Given the description of a product to assemble and contract cycle time (time between the finishing of two parts), the system computes a functional description of an assembly line with minimal cost. Two multi-agent systems are coupled: one to explore the space of assembly sequences taking into account the product constraints, the other one to explore the space of possible assembly lines taking into account the production constraints. In the first system, the agents are the links between the sub-assemblies (and not the sub-assemblies themselves) trying to place themselves into the assembly sequence. In the second system, the agents are the operations instantiating the movement axes competing to be placed on assembly posts, themselves into cells, and the latter into the

assembly line. In each case, the dynamics is in term of assignment, but the result is respectively a temporal and a topological structure.

These cases easily allow to see how emergence can provide a better adaptivity of the multi-agent system as a whole. Now we shall make the synthesis of these examples on the basis of the definition of emergence and problem solving as defined earlier.

4.4   Towards a Methodology

The definition of emergence suggests a number of steps to defined a multi-agent system:

- the formal description of the global phenomenon the multi-agent system must realise;
- the projection of this global phenomenon on the interaction structure at the micro-level to determine the identities of the agents and the interaction dynamics;
- the specification of individual behaviours of the agents to produce the interactions generating the global phenomenon we want to observe.

The lack of direct connection between the macro and the micro levels calls for validation tools to guarantee effectively the emergence of the desired global behaviour. This methodology has been entirely developed in [35] and [49].

The preceding examples allows to detail further this methodology. In effect, all the case have been described as search processes of a solution in search space. The structure S of the search space can be either spatial as a path, a map or contrast lines, or relational as a schedule or any relational configuration as a logical proof considered as a deduction relation on formulas, or spatio-temporal as the tasks to be performed by a collective of robots [35]. This structure is a composition of elementary entities C:

Spatial: pheromones deposits, graphisms, proximity links;
Relational: relations, assignments;
Spatio-temporal: movements, force applications, etc..

In classical programming, we would represent a state of the search space as a data structure to be built and modified by a given algorithm. This algorithm would depend implicitly or explicitly on all the constraints, initial hypotheses and state to elaborate its solution. The problem has to be closed. Any modification would require to stop computing or even to change the algorithm itself. If the initial data change over time and that new constraints are added or removed dynamically, the approach becomes extremely difficult to solve because the problem becomes open.

In the multi-agent systems we just described, the state is not explicitly manipulated by the agents. The agents interact with one another and with the environment in a way, which is indirectly related to the state we want to manipulate. For example, the agents "task" or "command" are seeking to be placed

Table 1. Comparisons between emergentist cases

MAS	Structure	Components	Agents	Interactions
Ants	Path	Pheromone deposits	Ants	Pheromones
Termites	Nest	Ground deposits	Termites	Pheromones
Allocation	Global assignment	Individual assignment	Tasks and resources	Availability
MARSA	Total order	Temporal position	Commands and machines	Deadline and setup time
AMACOIA	Assembly sequence	Relative position	Link	Product constraints
	Assembly line	Posts	Operations	Production
Blocks world	Configuration	Block relations	Blocks	Freedom
Magic square	Configuration	Tile positions	Tiles	Freedom
PACO	Contrast lines	Points positions	Points	Intensity
	Map	Positions and graphisms	Geographic entities	Freedom
AMROSE	Trajectory	Parts positions	Parts	Gravity, obstacles

with given criterion as the availability of the resource and their deadline and not to placed before or after another one. Therefore, the schedule is only an indirect outcome of these interactions. The ants follow the pheromone gradients and bring food. The resulting pheromone deposits, which constitute the path are only an indirect effect that feedbacks locally on the ant behaviours. In AMA-COIA, the agents are the links between the parts when the result is the order on the operation. In a similar way, the assembly line is a structure imposed on the tools, stations and cells and not the tools, stations and cells themselves (which are the agents). The same rationale can be seen in the case of AMROSE, where the agents are the rigid parts and the joint angles are resulting from their positioning.

We have systematically reported these observations on the described multi-agent systems in the table 1. The first column is the search space structure S, the second are the components C, the third column exhibits the chosen agents, and the last one on what they interact.

We would like to comment further on the role of the environment and the distinction to make between agents and processes:

1. we have two distinct roles of the environment in the described systems. One is to contain the state of the search during the solving process such that it can indirectly feedback on the multi-agent system dynamics. The other

is to provide exogeneous constraints on this dynamics as the time line in the scheduling systems, the obstacles in the ants paths and, more generally, restrictions on the search space. Notice that the agents are themselves situated in the environment and this "physical" presence is also source of interaction and constraints. For example, in the blocks world or the magic square interactions take place because the agents are in the way of other agents;

2. We have to know whether we have to really specify an agent or just a dynamical process taking place in the environment (because the environment can have his own dynamics). It is enough to refer to the definitions of agents (as, for example in [4]), which insist on the autonomy of the agents in the form or more or less explicit representation of their goals. In the case of problem solving, it is enough to identify the choice points, i.e. the components of the search space structure, which allows to potentially explore the whole search space (it does not mean we will have to do it exhaustively). These choices must result from the interactions among the agents. The rest of the search space structure can be processes propagating the consequences of theses choices if necessary. For example, in dynamic scheduling the choice is a date of production. Recomputing the dates of the other jobs placed before or after is just the computation of the consequences of this choice and should not be taken in charge by an agent. In the case of simulation we are not talking about in this paper, what is a process and what is an agent is less clear and is more related to the interpretation of the observer of the system [50].

We are now at the position to propose a methodology derived from this analysis:

1. to specify the search space and the structure of its possible states S;
2. to determine the elementary components C from which the states of the search space are made and among them the choice points determining the change from a state to another and potentially guaranteeing the exhaustive search through the search space (ergodicity condition);
3. to determine the entities whose interaction will produce these components. We obtain the agents of the system as a kind of negative image of the structure to produce;
4. to determine the objectives and the dynamics of these entities allowing to go through the search space. We obtain the production mechanisms of the interactions, which will go through the search space and possibly converge towards a solution by side-effect ;
5. to determine the exogeneous constraints guiding the trajectory and to potentially forbid some parts of the search space. This allows to completely define the environment with the inscription of the search space ;
6. to determine the processes propagating the consequences of the actions of the agents, defining the dynamics of the environment itself. It is also possible that the exogeneous constraints are directly linked to the world external to the multi-agent system (for example in the workplant scheduling, to the

workplant itself), in which case the proper dynamics becomes more than a simple reaction to the agents interactions;

7. to validate the design either experimentally if the multi-agent system is too complex. For example, by exploration of the topology of the phase space as in [11] or theoretically by using either non-linear dynamics, Markov chains [51] or statistical dynamics.

This methodology demonstrates clearly why a multi-agent system is more adaptable and flexible than a classical algorithm. In effect, the solution is not computed explicitly by the multi-agent system but emerges from the interactions among the agents, which are in dynamical relationship with the problem data and the constraints on the possible solutions. This dynamic formulation of accounting for the data and the constraints allows the multi-agent system to react spontaneously to the modifications either while trying to find a solution, or after a solution has already been found. In reference to the section on problem solving, we are in a logic of search by repair and therefore in the paradigm of control. In effect, a solution appears as an invariant or a stable state of the dynamics of the multi-agent system. However, this formulation raises the problem of the observability of the stable state, which represents the solution we are looking for. It is the reason why the notion of emergence puts forward the notion of observer. We shall detail two reasons to this:

– the multi-agent system may not know that he found the solution (as it is the case for contrast lines), in the sense that no single agent can locally decide it but only a global observer of the system.
– The medium and the inscription process takes all its importance because it is this way the observer will be able to observe the solution (as the drawing of the links among the agents on the image to visualise the contrast lines). The inscription process can also constitute a discretisation process, allowing to observe a stable state where the multi-agent with a continuous dynamics is in a chaotic attractor.

This last remark justifies the conclusion of the part on the notion of emergence [21] that suggests that a theory of emergence has to use a theory of inscription and interpretation and, therefore, calls for semiotic thinking.

5   Conclusion

From the definition of complex systems and emergence, we have provided argumentations for using multi-agent systems for modelling and designing the complex systems, the current computer systems are becoming to be. More than a decade of research and developpement of multi-agent problem solving using emergentist approaches give us enough experience to be able to outline a methodology for the conception of such systems. The methodology presented in this paper relies directly on the definition of emergence as proposed. Surprisingly enough, it is a top-down design methodology of an emergentist system, while emergence is intuitively associated to bottom-up production of results.

Few other methodologies exist to systematically build emergentist multiagent systems. We have to cite in particular the ADELFE [52] approach based on the AMAS theory [53], which is not based directly on the definition of emergence and is typically a bottom-up approach. The idea is to specify what each agent should locally not do (i.e. be non-cooperative), the correct global behaviour emerging accordingly.

This approach raises a number of perspectives:

- there is a clear need for software engineering tools to support the design process as it exists for ADELFE;
- the multiplicity of points of view both at the local (D) and the global (D') levels suggests a strong relationship among roles, norms, institutions and so on which is until now situated in more cognitive and agent oriented approaches of multi-agent systems. This direction should be further exploited with the perspective to link cognitive specifications with actual implementations;
- the problem of validation of emergentist multi-agent systems is very important because a part of the achieved flexibility makes it hard to control. Two directions could be pursued: either an incremental process through exploratory simulation and correction, or formal approaches coming from dynamical systems and statistical mechanics. Adaptive systems could also be foreseen with an interaction between the local behaviours and an assessment of the distance between the actual global behaviour and the expected outcome. It is already partially the case in optimising systems when the optimality criterion remains global.

References

[1] Bergenti, F.: Formalizing the reusability of software agents. In: Engineering Societies in the Agents World IV. (2003) 1
[2] Memmi, D.: Emergence et niveaux d'explication. In: Journées thématiques de l'ARC (émergence et explication). (1996) 2
[3] Brooks, R. A.: Intelligence without reason. In: IJCAI'91. (1991) 2
[4] Ferber, J.: Les systèmes multi-agents. InterEditions (1995) 2, 16
[5] Beurier, G., Simonin, O., Ferber, J.: Un modèle de système multi-agents pour l'émergence multi-niveaux. In: JFSMA'03, Hermès (2003) 2
[6] Drogoul, A., Ferber, J. In: Multi-agent simulation as a tool for studying emergent processes in societies. North-Holland (1994) 2
[7] Demazeau, Y.: La plate-forme paco et ses applications. In: 2èmes Journée Nationale du PRC-IA sur les Systèmes Multi-Agents. (1993) 2
[8] Ferrand, N., Demazeau, Y., Baeijs, C.: Systèmes multi-agents réactifs et résolution de problèmes spatialisés. Revue d'Intelligence Artificielle (1997) 2

[9] Müller, J. P.: Vers une méthodologie de conception de systèmes multi-agents émergents. In: Proceedings of JFIADSMA'98, Hermès (1998) 2, 10

[10] Bernon, C., Camps, V., Gleizes, M. P., Picard, G.: Designing agents' behaviours within the framework of adelfe methodology. In: Engineering Societies in the Agents World IV. (2003) 2

[11] Brueckner, S., Parunak, V. D.: Resource-aware exploration of the emergent dynamics of simulated systems. In: Proceedings of AAMAS'03. (2003) 2, 17

[12] Deneubourg, J. L., Theraulaz, G., Beckers, R.: Swarm-made architectures. In Varela, F., Bourgine, P., eds.: Toward a practice of autonomous systems, MIT Press (1992) 123–133 2

[13] Bonabeau, E., Dessalles, J. L., Grumbach, A.: Characterizing emergent phenomena (1) and (2),: A critical review. Revue internationale de systémique 9 (1995) 327–346,347–371 3

[14] Steels, L.: Towards a theory of emergent functionality. In Meyer, J., Wilson, S., eds.: From Animals to Animats (SAB'91), MIT Press (1992) 451–461 3

[15] Forrest, S., Miller, J. H.: Emergent behavior in classifier systems. In: Emergent computation, MIT Press (1990) 3

[16] Forrest, S.: Emergent computation: Self-organizing, collective, and cooperative phenomena in natural and artificial computing networks. In: Emergent computation, MIT Press (1990) 3, 6

[17] Holland, J.: Hidden Order: How Adaptation Builds Complexity. Perseus Publishing (1996) 3

[18] Bar-Yam, Y.: Dynamics of complex systems. Perseus press (1997) 3

[19] Nigel, G. In: Emergence in social simulation. UCL Press (1995) 144–156 4, 7

[20] Maturana, H.: Ontology of observing : the biological foundations of self-consciousness and the physical domain of existence. In: American society for Cybernetics Conference. (1988) 4

[21] (collective name), M. J.: Emergence et sma. In: Journées Francophones IAD et SMA. (1997) 5, 17

[22] Searle, J. R.: The rediscovery of the mind. MIT Press (1992) 6

[23] Minsky, M.: La société de l'esprit. Ed. Intereditions (1988) 7

[24] von Bertalanffy, L.: General System Theory. Foundations, Development, Applications. (1968) 7

[25] Sawyer, R. K.: Emergence in psychology: Lessons from the history of non-reductionist science. Human Development 45 (2002) 2–28 7

[26] Castelfranchi, C.: Emergence and cognition: Towards a synthetic paradigm in ai and cognitive science. In: Progress in AI - IBERAMIA'98. Number 1484 in LNAI, Springer Verlag (1998) 7, 9

[27] Sawyer, R. K.: Emergence in sociology: Contemporary philosophy of mind and some implications for sociological theory. American Journal of Sociology 107 (2001) 551–585 7

[28] Sawyer, R. K.: Artificial societies: Multi-agent systems and the micro-macro link in sociological theory. Sociological Methods and Research 31 (2003) 325–363 7

[29] Shoham, Y.: Agent-oriented programming. Artificial Intelligence 60 (1993) 51–92 10

[30] Rao, A.: Agentspeak(l): Bdi agents speak out in a logical computable language. In de Velde, W. V., Perram, J., eds.: Agents Breaking Away. Number 1038 in LNAI. Springer Verlag (1996) 42–55 10

[31] Wooldridge, M.: Time, knowledge, and choice. In Wooldridge, M., Müller, J. P., Tambe, M., eds.: Intelligent Agents II. Number 1037 in LNAI. Springer Verlag (1996) 79–96 10

[32] Durand, B.: Simulation multi-agents et épidémiologie opérationnelle. PhD thesis, Université de Caen (1996) 10

[33] Gutknecht, O., ferber, J.: A meta-model for the analysis and design of organizations in multi-agent systems. In: 3rd International Conference on Multi-Agent Systems. (1998) 10

[34] Amiguet, M., Müller, J. P., Baez-Barranco, J., Nagy, A.: The MOCA platform: Simulating the dynamics of social networks. In: MABS'02, Springer Verlag (2002) 10

[35] Labbani, O.: Contribution à une méthodologie de conception de comportements collectifs émergents dans une colonie de robots miniatures et autonomes. PhD thesis, ENSMM (1998) 10, 14

[36] Papadimitriou, C. H., Steiglitz, K.: Combinatorial optimization: algorithms and complexity. Prentice Hall (1982) 11

[37] Ghedira, K.: MASC: une approche multi-agents des problèmes de satisfaction de contraintes. PhD thesis, Ecole Nationale Supérieure de l'Aéronautique et de l'Espace (1993) 12

[38] Dean, T., Wellman, M.: Planning and Control. Morgan Kaufmann (1991) 12

[39] Ferber, J., Jacopin, E.: The framework of eco-problem solving. In Demazeau, Y., Müller, J. P., eds.: Decentralized AI 2. North-Holland (1991) 12

[40] Drogoul, A., C.Dubreuil: Eco-problem-solving model: results of the n-puzzle. In Demazeau, Y., Müller, J. P., eds.: Decentralized AI 2. North Holland (1992) 12

[41] Drogoul, A.: When ants play chess (or can strategies emerge from tactical behaviours?). In Castelfranchi, C., Müller, J. P., eds.: From reaction to cognition. Number 957 in LNAI. Springer Verlag (1993) 12

[42] Demazeau, Y.: La plate-forme paco et ses applications. In: 2èmes Journée Nationale du PRC-IA sur les Systèmes Multi-Agents. (1993) 12, 13

[43] Ferrand, N.: Modèles multi-agents pour l'aide ê la décision et la négociation en aménagement du territoire. PhD thesis, Université Joseph Fourier (1997) 12, 13

[44] Baeijs, C., Demazeau, Y., Alvares, L.: Application des systèmes multi-agents à la généralisation cartographique. In: 3èmes Journées Francophones sur l'Intelligence Artificielle Distribuée et les Systèmes Multi-Agents. (1995) 13

[45] Overgaard, L., Petersen, H., Perram, J.: Motion planning for an articulated robot: a multi-agent approach. In: Proceedings of MAAMAW'94, Springer Verlag (1994) 13

[46] Daouas, T., Ghedira, K., Müller, J. P.: A distributed approach for the flow shop scheduling problem. In: Third International Conference on Artificial Intelligence Applications. (1995) 13

[47] Chung, K., Wu, C. H.: Dynamic scheduling with intelligent agents: an application note. Technical Report 105, Metra (1997) 13

[48] Yoo, M. J., Müller, J. P.: Using multi-agent system for dynamic job shop scheduling. In: ICEIS 2002. (2002) 517–525 13

[49] Labbani, O., Müller, J. P., Bourjault, A.: Conception de comportements collectifs: l'étape d'analyse. In: Journées Francophones IAD et SMA. (1997) 14

[50] Batard, E.: L'agent comme signe. In Müller, J. P., Quinqueton, J., eds.: JFI-ADSMA'96. Hermès (1996) 16

[51] Labbani, O., Müller, J. P., Bourjault, A.: Cirta: An emergentist methodology to design and evaluate collective behaviours in robots'colonies. In: Collective Robotics Workshop. (1998) 17

[52] Bernon, C., Gleizes, M. P., Peyruqueou, S., Picard, G.: ADELFE: A methodology for adaptive multi-agent systems engineering. In: ESAW 2002. (2002) 156–169 18

[53] Capera, D., George, J. P., Gleizes, M. P., Glize, P.: The AMAS theory for complex problem solving based on self-organizing cooperative agents. In: WETICE 2003. (2003) 383–388   18

Social Order and Adaptability
in Animal and Human Cultures
as Analogues for Agent Communities:
Toward a Policy-Based Approach

Paul J. Feltovich, Jeffrey M. Bradshaw, Renia Jeffers,
Niranjan Suri, and Andrzej Uszok

Institute for Human and Machine Cognition/University of West Florida
40 S. Alcaniz, Pensacola, FL 32501
{pfeltovich,jbradshaw,rjeffers,nsuri,auszok}@ihmc.us

Abstract. In this paper we discuss some of the ways social order is maintained in animal and human realms, with the goal of enriching our thinking about mechanisms that might be employed in developing similar means of ordering communities of agents. We present examples from our current work in human-agent teamwork, and we speculate about some new directions this kind of research might take. Since communities also need to change over time to cope with changing circumstances, we also speculate on means that regulatory bodies can use to adapt.

1   Introduction

As computational systems with increasing autonomy interact with humans in more complex ways—and with the welfare of the humans sometimes dependent on the conduct of the agents—there is a natural concern that the agents act in ways that are acceptable to people [7,51]. In addition to traditional concerns for safety and robustness in such systems [12], there are important social aspects relating to predictability, control, feedback, order, and naturalness of the interaction that must be attended to [8,10,50]. In this paper we investigate just some of the ways social order is maintained in animal and human realms (sections 2 and 3), with the goal of enriching our thinking about mechanisms that might be employed to enhance order in mixed human-agent teams.[1] We present examples of such systems that have been created to support agent-based applications (section 4), and we speculate about new directions this kind of research might take (section 5). Since enduring communities also need to change over time to cope with changing circumstances, we speculate briefly on means that regulatory bodies can utilize for supporting adaptation (section 6). Finally, we present some concluding observations (section 7).

---

[1] In this sense, we agree with the conjecture of Norman: "Technology recapitulates phylogeny" [50, p. 134].

A. Omicini, P. Petta, and J. Pitt (Eds.): ESAW 2003, LNAI 3071, pp. 21-48, 2004.
© Springer-Verlag Berlin Heidelberg 2004

2   Some Sources of Order in the Animal World

We start by examining some of the ways that animals cooperate and maintain order. Why would individuals ever choose to cooperate with others to pursue their aims, rather than "going it alone"? In the animal realm, ethnologists and evolutionary biologists have taken a fairly common stance with regard to this question. Speaking of the process of mutual "attunement" (roughly, "getting to know one another") among individuals, a component process of cooperation, biologist W.J. Smith states:

> *Such attunement is necessary when no single individual can fully control an encounter—when participants in encounters must depend on each other for a useful outcome. The value of that outcome need not be equal for each participant, but it must exceed for each the average payoff that would come from eschewing the interaction [61, p. 366].*

Smith goes on to discuss two main benefits that accrue from such processes of cooperation or "joint activity." The first is that certain tasks get accomplished that could not have been accomplished by any individual. The second is that these kinds of activities, over time, yield increased *inter-predictability* among the parties; they come to know each other's ways. This can have constructive benefits: for instance, knowledge of the other's capabilities might be tapped during future cooperation. It can also yield protective benefits: for example, learning the other's "hot buttons" that tend to invoke hostility. But the main benefit of predictability is the social order it contributes to the group. Gross, mutual unpredictability is almost definitional of *disorder*. Predictability and order are so important to animals that they seem to go to great lengths to build but also maintain it: For instance:

> *[Some male birds] remember how to recognize previous neighbors by their individually distinctive songs and remember the location in which each neighbor belongs. Relationships with known neighbors are valuable and those with strangers are problematic. Known mutual boundaries can be reestablished with much less effort and uncertainty than goes into the task of working out relationships with new neighbors [61, p. 365].*

Animals engage in joint activities, in which they get to know each other, in part through processes of signaling and display that are associated with predictable kinds of behaviors. That is, display and signaling behavior among animals supports joint activity by providing more or less rough clues to others concerning what each individual is about to do. Displays and signals can range widely in form (e.g., vocalizations, body posture, facial expressions):

> *Each individual has a repertoire of behavior made up of all the many kinds of acts it can perform. It can be thought of as continuously choosing among these acts, even at times when its behavior is unchanging (among the choices available at any instant is to do whatever was done in the previous instant). Any choice can be called a 'behavioral selection.'*

> *Each kind of display has a consistent and specifiable relationship to certain choices. It is performed in correlation with some kinds of behavior and not others. Thus, to know that an individual is performing a particular display is*

to learn something about the behavior it may select—every display can thus be described as encoding messages about behavioral selections [60, p. 87].

Hence, display behavior has an anticipatory, predictive (but only a *probabilistically predictive*) function. It is a clue, sometimes highly indicative, sometimes much less so,[2] to what an individual is about to do. It also decouples actual action from a kind of notice that it is about to happen.[3] This decoupling both invites and enables others to participate in coordination, support, or avoidance with respect to what might occur. This joint engagement in an activity would not be possible if the activity were merely executed and not signaled in advance. In this sense, display is an important ingredient in enabling things like coordination and teamwork.

While signaling and display can take many and complicated forms, even in the animal world, biologist Smith has advanced ten signal-behavior couplings that appear to be pervasive in almost all vertebrates, although they might manifest different physical forms in different species [60, pp. 87-126]. The fact that these are so pervasive suggests they may be particularly fundamental. We will briefly describe each of these types of displays and signals along with possible functions they could serve within agent communities.

2.1 Interactional Displays

Interactional displays indicate availability or unavailability to participate in joint activity. These displays "primarily provide information about the communicator's readiness or lack of readiness, to join in acts that involve other individuals" [60, p. 88]. Since they may be associated with more than one kind of interaction, they do not specify any one kind. They might indicate readiness to copulate, associate, attack an intruder, and so forth. Hence, they are anticipatory to various kinds of intended joint activity, simply signaling a readiness (or lack thereof) to join in association with others.

This category also includes displays indicating *absence of opportunity to interact*. These displays essentially signal that an individual is alone and has nobody else to interact with, for example, when an individual is the last remaining at the nest or territory. This category also includes signals of *shunning interaction*. These are simply signals that the initiator does not want interaction with others, and this intention can range from mild to fierce.

Example Interactional Forms. Kinds of chirping. Various forms of bowing. "Tidbitting"—offering a morsel of food. Forms of touching. Signals from a subordinate to a dominant, the purpose of which is to test the dominant's willingness to interact, to tolerate interaction.

---

2 Sometimes the ambiguity of the signal itself serves an important function, for example as an indicator that the signaler's next move may depend on the response its current move evokes.

3 To see why this may be useful, consider the signaling functions of the lights on the back of a car: "[W]e use turn signals and brake lights to tell others of our actions and intentions. In the case of brake lights, we signal actions as we carry them out. In the case of turn signals, we signal our intentions before we actually commit them into action. In either case, we allow others to know our future actions so that we can ensure that there is no conflict" [50, p. 129].

Absence of opportunity: Loud sounds, loud singing, howling (e.g., one jackal howls, and all the rest in the area howl in response), assuming high, visible physical positions, special kinds of flight patterns or displays.

Shunning: Interestingly, various forms of displaying the tongue. Chittering barks. Vocalizations at special, unusual frequencies.

Possible Functions in Agent Communities. Displays in this general category clearly have benefits for coordination among groups of agents by providing information about which are or are not in a position to interact with others, in what ways, when, and so forth, e.g.: Call me. I am open for calls. I need to talk to someone. May I interject, may I say something?

Absence of opportunity: I am out of touch. I am working all alone. I have no help. I have lost contact with everybody.

Shunning: Do *not* attempt to communicate with me for whatever reason, e.g., my line is bugged, or I am involved in something that cannot be interrupted. Leave me alone.

While the general interactional displays just discussed are non-specific in the activity they portend, others are more specific.

2.2 Seeking Displays

Displays indicating that one is *seeking* joint activity are similar to the interactional ones in that they indicate a readiness to participate in some kind joint activity but differ in that they indicate *active attempt* at engaging in a particular kind of activity rather than just a general state of availability or receptiveness:

> *"Animals may display while seeking the opportunity to perform some kind of activity during what ethnologists call 'appetitive' behavior as distinguished from 'consummatory' behavior in which activity is completed. The behavioral selection about which a display provides information if it is done only in this way can be termed 'seeking.' What a communicator is seeking to do is encoded in the same display by a second behavioral selection message. The display is interpreted as providing not just the information that a communicator is ready to do this second selection, but that its behavior includes seeking or preparing to seek an opportunity"* [60, p. 118].

The seeking display can be associated with many kinds of activities, seeking, for example, to interact, associate, copulate, attack, or escape.

Example Forms. These are associated with so many kinds of behaviors that their particular forms vary widely.

Possible Functions in Agent Communities. Agents that indicate to others what they are trying to do can elicit the right form of aid from others, can contribute to possible coordination among tasks, and the like.

2.3 Receptiveness Displays

Displays indicating *receptiveness* are the inverse of seeking displays, i.e., they indicate a specific response to the seeking of particular kinds of activities by others:

"Some displays indicate the behavioral selections that a communicator will accept, not those it is prepared to perform. At least two behavioral selection messages must be provided by such a display, one indicating that the communicator will behave receptively and another indicating the class of acts to which it is receptive. Effectively, the communicator adopts the role of soliciting acts from another individual; it does not offer them" [60, p. 122].

The display indicating receptiveness indicates that the communicator is willing to engage in a behavior, or set of behaviors, initiated by another. An interesting form of soliciting has to do with being receptive to "aid or care" and is common among infants who indicate receptiveness to feeding, grooming, shading, and so forth. Although often associated with the young, these displays sometimes carry over into adult relationships, as when a female mate solicits various forms of "help with the nest" from her male partner [60, p. 125].

Example Forms. As with seeking displays, receptivity displays are so diverse that they defy general description.

Possible Functions in Agent Communities. As with the seeking displays, receptivity displays can contribute to cooperation in the conduct of activity and to the coordination among activities.

2.4 Attack and Escape Displays

Displays indicating *attack* and *escape*:

"are said to encode either, or both, of attack and escape messages when all their occurrence is correlated with a range of attack- or escape-related behavior. Behavioral indices of attack differ among and within species, but include acts that, if completed, will harm another individual. Escape behavior can be any appropriate form of avoidance, ranging from headlong fleeing to turning aside, or even freezing and other ways of hiding" [60, p. 93].

Attack and escape displays may differ, but they are sometimes more or less the same display, differing only in degree or subtle nuance. They have value both between and within groups, for instance, to muster help against an intruder or to avoid inadvertent flare-ups (e.g., one group member coming upon another by surprise). Various choreographies of interactive displays relating to attacking and escaping can more often than not serve to avoid actual combat. Actual fighting is more likely to happen among relatively unfamiliar groups [60, p. 94], partly because they have less mutual predictability, including prediction of each other's reaction to display activities that can fend off real fighting.

Example Forms. Body posture and orientation. Head bobbing. Forms of jumping. Baring teeth.

Possible Functions in Agent Communities. Displays in this category have increased importance when agents are acting in adversarial environments, such as those found in military or information intelligence applications. They can be used on the one hand to frighten or warn, or on the other hand to signal defeat or flight.

2.5 Copulation Behavior Displays

There are displays indicating *copulation behavior*:

> *"Some displays are performed only before or during the social interactions in which eggs are fertilized. These interactions involve either copulation or some behavioral analogue such as the amplexus behavior of frogs" [60, p. 97].*

Possible Function in Agent Communities. This class of social display would seem to have little to do with agents—at least at their current stage of development. However, analogues to these displays may be pertinent when certain forms of intricate inter-coordination are occurring among agents, involving the need for complex cooperation and coordination to carry out the task successfully, e.g., exchanging ontologies. The copulatory displays are, after all, cues to the parties involved in complex, interdependent operations designed to get an important job done. In a simple fashion, a Palm PDA demonstrates this kind of display when it beeps and lights up after successful docking in its cradle.

2.6 Association Maintenance Displays

There are displays associated with *maintaining, staying-in* association:

> *"Some displays correlate with the behavior involved in remaining with another individual. When individuals so associate they remain together because one, both, or all will follow, will not leave when the other may not follow, and because each permits the others to be nearby.... These displays are not common when animals can maintain their association with ease, but are used primarily when other behavior may disrupt the group. For instance, disruption may result when an individual has just attacked a companion, or flees from an approaching predator before the rest of the group reacts, or even when an individual that has been absent approaches to resume peaceful associating with the group... or when an individual [is] about to move some distance from its group in seeking another foraging site, or by an animal able to maintain contact with its associates only auditorily" [60, p. 104].*

These displays appear to provide a kind of reassurance to other group members that, despite some possible indications to the contrary, the individual has not broken ranks with the group. Such assurances are particularly useful when salient events may raise doubt about the continued association. For example, "the likelihood that a group will remain together after one or more have fought with each other or with outsiders can also be increased by displays encoding an association message" [60, p. 104]. Activities, such as foraging or other societal maintenance activities that require an emphasis on individual effort and perhaps separation from the group, are also prominently associated with association displays. For example, mates who are about to be separated for some time exhibit association displays upon leaving and maintain these messages during the period of separation to the extent possible (e.g. by special vocalizations or gestures—"kissing good-bye and calling home every night," so to speak) [60, p. 104].

Example Forms. Special (often oblique) body orientations toward group members. Various kinds of vocalizations—clearly, signals that can operate over a distance are important in this function.

Possible Functions in Agent Communities. Ways of indicating allegiance to the team and team goals would seem to have a useful place in agent groups and teamwork, especially when some agent is temporarily stepping beyond normal bounds of location or activity for whatever reason. When agents exercise physical mobility, the reporting of location, continued association, and continued commitment to group intent would seem to have a potentially beneficial role.

2.7 Indecisiveness Displays

Displays indicating *indecisiveness* signal that the individual is in a state of indecision about what to do next. Indicators of indecision are various, ranging from simply adopting a static, frozen stance, as if waiting for the situation to provide greater cues, to variations on displays that usually indicate action but are modified to increase the range of choice. An example of the latter would be moving back-and-forth laterally ("pacing") with respect to a pertinent stimulus, as opposed to approaching it or backing away. Displays for indecisiveness can include behaviors irrelevant and inappropriate to the situation, e.g., suddenly, unexpectedly initiating grooming or eating [60, p. 107].

Example Forms. Irrelevant behavior. Moving back-and-forth laterally in relation to a stimulus.

Possible Functions in Agent Communities. It may be useful for an agent to signal that it does not know what to make of some situation, that it is "confused," or cannot figure out what to do next as a means for eliciting help from humans or other agents.

2.8 Locomotion Displays

Displays indicating *locomotion* simply signal that the animal is moving or is about to move:

> *"[These] displays provide information about a communicator's use of flight (or other locomotive) behavior, but not about functional categories of flight such as approach, withdrawal, attack, or foraging. The displays correlate with all these acts and more...some [animals] extend the performance of the displays to correlate with hopping or running when they forage on the ground. Thus the behavior is viewed as 'locomoting' rather than as 'flying...'" [60, p. 108].*

Example Forms. These displays appear to consist primarily of various forms of vocalizations. However, signals indicating that an animal is *about* to move can be more diverse, for example, dances in honeybees, head-tossing in geese.

Possible Functions in Agent Communities. Signals that indicate that an agent is moving or is about to move would seem particularly germane in teams containing mobile agents. As an example of such a display as a warning, think of the distinctive sound that large trucks make when they are about to move in reverse.

2.9 Staying-Put Displays

Displays indicating *remaining with a site* are the opposite of the locomotion displays:

> *"Displays performed only when a communicator is remaining at a fixed site encode the information he will remain at a single point, in the vicinity of such a locus, or in an area that allows considerable movement within fixed boundaries. The behavioral selection referred to is simply "staying-put," defined with respect to a site" [60, p. 115].*

Example Forms. Song vocalizations, in particular, are associated with remaining in a territory. Birds that do not sing can have special vocalizations for remaining in place, e.g., the "ecstatic" vocalization of the Adelie penguin [60, p. 115]. Also included are wing-beating, and various specialized postures and movements.

Possible Functions in Agent Communities. As with displays of locomotion, displays of "staying put" are pertinent to mobile agents.

2.10   Attentiveness Displays

Displays indicating *attentiveness to a stimulus* simply convey that the communicator is attending to something and monitoring it.

Example Forms. Three distinct barks of a prairie-dog, indicating three different phases of monitoring. Such barks might indicate, for example, that a predator is in the vicinity.

Possible Functions in Agent Communities. For agents, these signals could portend that something important might be happening. It would be useful in agent communities to have a general indicator of alert, that something significant might be transpiring at a particular location or involving a particular agent. Appropriate response, of course, would require additional information. In the animal world, for instance, this additional information sometimes indicates the location of the stimulus.

3   Some Sources of Order in the Human World

It is not surprising that joint activity—and the "getting to know each other" both necessary for it and engendered by it—are also important to humans. Additionally, many of the same benefits are accrued—in particular, inter-predictability and its relationship to coordination and an orderly society. Moreover, the same basic components are involved, including signals understood by both parties to be an invitation to engage in joint activity. However, because of our wider behavioral repertoire, the greater complexity of our communication processes, and our reduced dependence on biological determinism, human cooperation and regulatory processes take on an even greater variety of forms.[4]

In fact, *because* of our vast behavioral repertoire, and because we are so underdetermined in our biology, the argument has been made that a very large portion of what humans do and create is constituted to "control ourselves"! In this view, the role of human culture is that of a vast, fabricated self-regulatory mechanism [29]:[5]

> *I want to propose two ideas: The first of these is that culture is best seen not as complexes of concrete behavior patterns—customs, usages, traditions, habit clusters—as has, by and large, been the case up to now, but as a set of control mechanisms—plans, recipes, rules, instructions (what computer engineers call 'programs')—for the governing of behavior. The second idea is that man is precisely the animal most desperately dependent upon such extragenetic, outside-the-skin mechanisms, such cultural programs, for ordering his behavior...* (p. 44)

> *Man is in need of such symbolic sources of illumination [i.e., human-created cultural control mechanisms—addition ours] to find his bearings in the world because the non-symbolic sort that are constitutionally engrained in his body cast such a diffuse light. The behavior patterns of lower animals are, at least to much greater extent, given to them with their physical structure: genetic sources or information order their actions within much narrower ranges of variation, the narrower and more thouroughgoing the lower the animal. For man, what are innately given are extremely general response capacities, which, although they make possible far greater plasticity, complexity, and, on the scattered occasions when everything works as it should, effectiveness of behavior, leave it much less precisely regulated. This then, is the second face of our argument: Unregulated by cultural patterns—organized systems of significant symbols—man's behavior would be virtually ungovernable, a mere chaos of pointless acts and exploding emotions, his experience virtually shapeless. Culture, the accumulated totality of such patterns, is not just an ornament of human existence but—the principal basis of its specificity—an essential condition for it.* (pp. 45-46)

In summary, according to this argument people create and have created cultures and social conventions—albeit in many disparate forms across mankind that can be hard for outsiders to understand—to provide order and predictability. This is also the main reason we claim, following Smith's arguments above that animals cooperate at all, when they do—that is, in order to make themselves better known and more predictable to each other. Furthermore, it would seem to follow from Geertz's argument that the more autonomous the agents involved, the more need there is for such regulation and the wider the variety of forms it might take.

Order and predictability may have a basis in the simple cooperative act between two people, in which the parties "contract" to engage together in a set of interlinked,

---

4 For a comprehensive and interesting treatment of these kinds of issues regarding joint activity in humans, see[15].

5 We recognize that Geertz represents only one of many views of culture, but a discussion of competing views is beyond the scope of this paper.

mutually beneficial activities. From this simple base, in humans at least, there are constructed elaborate and intricate systems of regulatory tools, from formal legal systems, to standards of professional practice, to norms of proper everyday behavior (along with associated methods of punishment or even simple forms of shaming for violations of these).

4   The Problem of Adaptability

While the discussion so far has dealt mainly with the maintenance of order, change is also necessary in perpetuating healthy societies, especially if those societies are expected to adapt to new circumstances and endure over long periods of time. While we cannot investigate adaptation mechanisms in depth in this paper, we feel it important to point out that such mechanisms of change are recognized as critical in both animal and human societies.

For instance, while animal and human signals carry a certain core nature and meaning in a given community, this meaning is not completely rigid or mechanical, and may be very different in different contexts.[6] Such interaction can often best be described as a kind of "improvisation"—embodying considerable novelty while respecting the rules of the form [53].

Take for example two different cases of a human signaling a call to joint activity with another, in fact, signaling the *same* call in the two cases, "help me." In the first instance, the solicitor is sinking in quicksand, and in the other case the solicitor is posed at one end of a heavy table that needs moving. The particulars of what might ensue will depend on the nature of the two different circumstances but also on the particular individuals involved. In the first case the party responding to the request for help may try to throw a rope. However, if there were a history of bad will between himself and the person in the quicksand, he might also just lay back and watch him slowly sink [lack of will]. In the second case, the party responding to the request for help might, on the one hand, go to the unmanned end of the table and try to help lift (and he would not throw a rope—due to the basic circumstantial difference). On the other hand, he might not—his response may depend on how strong he thinks he is or if he has sustained an injury (degree of capability) or depending on his personal history of experienced helpfulness from the individual making the request [(lack of will)—"He never helps me!"] [after[60, p. 224]].

Thus the elements of consistency, but also potential novelty, may both be necessary to signaling activity in the real world, because the world is never static:

> *"In all social events, the behavior of participants must engender considerable predictability. Without predictability, events falter and their orderliness*

---

6   Norman [50, p. 130] gives the following example of this phenomenon from traffic behavior in different countries: "In Mexico, one wins by aggression. In Britain, one wins by politeness and consideration. [In Mexico, when two cars approach a narrow bridge from different directions, flashing your headlights means, 'I got here first, so keep out of my way.' However] in Britain, in a similar situation, the car that flashes its lights first is signaling, 'I see you, please go ahead and I will wait.' Imagine what happens when a Mexican driver encounters a British driver."

dissipates... [But] the dilemma addressed in this volume is that development of shared signals and codes necessarily leads to conformity in signaling, but conformity cannot cope well with changing or novel events and, when rigid, is maladaptive" [61, p. 366].

Hence, all signaling must accommodate elements of variation in the pertinent core joint activity conveyed by the signal. These variations are sensitive at least to the particulars of the circumstances and parties involved; that is, the variation on the core activity is context-sensitive:

"Another crucially important aspect of all communication is that it is context-dependent. That is, although the information made available by a formalized signal is largely consistent, the significance or 'meaning' of that information in any event, its interpretation by the individual responding to the signal is affected by information in addition to the signal. This is another form of openness in communication and an important means of dealing with novelty. This requisite ability to alter responses to signals as circumstances change is also the basis of our calibration of individual signalers. Clues to their identities become clues to the specific significances of their signals, although only for individuals who are sufficiently familiar with them" [61, p. 368].

With regard to change and adaptation in *culture* and its regulatory role, modern biologists have increasingly emphasized that the natural selection process includes not only basic biology but also the equally complex elements of culture, cultural change and cultural selection. For instance Mayr has emphasized that "a person is a target of selection in three different contexts: as an individual, as a member of a family... and as a member of a social group." [44, p. 251]. The latter two, at least, implicate culture in the sense we have been addressing it in this essay. Geertz has gone farther, essentially arguing that humanity and culture are so tightly intertwined that the human-culture system is the unit of selection [29, p. 67]. In short, in enduring societies, culture is not static.

Although such nuanced tailoring of communication and culture to circumstance may not always prove necessary in the working interactions of pure agent teams, the need for such tailoring and adjustment will almost surely arise in mixed human-agent teams, as their work together becomes increasingly consequential and as they sustain their interactions for long periods. This is another key element of making agents acceptable to humans. To be acceptable to humans, agents must conform to certain standards of predictability, but they also must not exhibit bald, naïve-looking rigidity.

While recognizing the importance of adaptation, because of the tremendous challenges currently involved in machine learning, our own work has been initially focused on understanding and enabling various forms of order in agent communities. We will briefly address adaptation again in section 6.

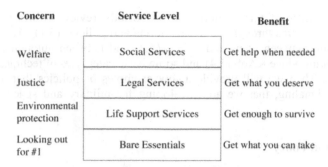

Fig. 1. Required elements of future infrastructure for agents

5   Building Cultures for Agent Communities: Sources of Order

Our agent research and development efforts over the past decade have maintained a consistent trend. We have been progressively off-loading selected classes of knowledge, some aspects of decision-making, and various kinds of specialized reasoning and problem solving from individual agents into a common environment shared by all agents of a given community, regardless of the nature or sophistication of their internals or the platform on which they are running.[7] This has taken the form, for instance, of the creation of various types of services and various bodies of policy that help regulate conduct across communities of heterogeneous agents running on various platforms. It is in this sense that what we have been doing might be thought of as creating "cultures" for agent communities, especially communities that might endure for long periods of time. We have termed this kind of approach "terraforming cyberspace" (referring to the aspect of the effort that aims to make networked environments a more habitable place for agents) and "cyberforming terraspace" (referring to the aspect of the effort that aims to embed socially-competent agents in the physical world) [12]. To support sustainability of groups of agents over long periods, we have envisioned basic types of services that will be needed (Fig. 1.). At a minimum, future infrastructure must go beyond the bare essentials of support to provide pervasive *life support services* (relying on mechanisms such as orthogonal persistence [36] and strong mobility [62,63]) that help ensure the survival of agents designed to live for long periods of time. Beyond the basics of individual agent protection, these communities will depend on *legal services*, based on explicit policies, to ensure that rights and obligations are monitored and enforced. Benevolent *social services* might also be provided to proactively avoid problems and help agents fulfill their obligations. Although some of these elements exist in embryo within specific agent systems, their scope and effectiveness has been limited by the lack of underlying support at both the platform and application levels.

---

[7] It could also be said that we have been moving elements from the "sharp end" to the "blunt end" of agents' activity, as these two terms have been characterized by David Woods and colleagues [20].

In the remainder of this section, we will briefly review efforts to create and regulate agent cultures through the use of norms and policies (5.1)[8]. We will discuss the relationship between plans and policy (5.2) and between autonomy and policy (5.3). We will introduce KAoS (5.4) and some basic categories of technical and social policies (5.5). Then we will provide a few examples of policies that address joint activity and signaling, that we are developing for military and space applications (5.6).

5.1 Norms and Policy

In the early 20th century, a legal theorist named Wesley Newcomb Hohfeld developed a theory of fundamental legal concepts [32] from which most of current work on theories of normative positions have taken at least some degree of inspiration (see e.g., [40,57]).

The idea of building strong social laws into intelligent systems can be traced at least as far back as the 1940s to the science fiction writings of Isaac Asimov [3]. In his well-known stories of the succeeding decades he formulated a set of basic laws that were built deeply into the positronic-brain circuitry of each robot so that it was physically prevented from transgression. Though the laws were simple and few, the stories attempted to demonstrate just how difficult they were to apply in various real-world situations. In most situations, although the robots usually behaved "logically," they often failed to do the "right" thing— typically because the particular context of application required subtle adjustments of judgments on the part of the robot (e.g., determining which law took priority in a given situation, or what constituted helpful or harmful behavior).[9]

Shoham and Tennenholtz [58] introduced the theme of social laws into the agent research community, where investigations have continued under two main headings: *norms* and *policies*. Drawing on precedents in legal theory, social psychology, social philosophy, sociology, and decision theory [71], *norm-based* approaches have grown in popularity [6,21,41,42]. In the multi-agent system research community, Conte and Castelfranchi [19] found that norms were variously described as constraints on

---

[8] We have concentrated first on mechanisms for establishing order and predictability in agent communities because at the current state of agent development these seem to be the greatest concerns of both producers and consumers of agent technologies. Others have focused on issues of "democracy," micro-economics, and other forms of relative freedom in open societies of agents e.g. [14][45][49]

[9] In an insightful essay, Roger Clarke explores some of the implications of Asimov's stories about the laws of robotics for information technologists [16]. Weld and Etzioni [72] were the first to discuss the implications of Asimov's first law of robotics for agent researchers. Like most norm-based approaches described below (and unlike most policy-based approaches) the safety conditions are taken into account as part of the agents' own learning and planning processes rather than as part of the infrastructure. In an important response to Weld and Etzioni's "call to arms," Pynadath and Tambe [52] develop a hybrid approach that marries the agents' probabilistic reasoning about adjustable autonomy with hard safety constraints to generate "policies" governing the actions of agents. The approach assumes a set of homogeneous agents, which are motivated to cooperate and follow optimally generated policies

behavior, ends or goals, or obligations. For the most part, implementations of norms in multi-agent systems share three basic features:

- they are designed offline; or
- they are learned, adopted, and refined through the purposeful deliberation of each agent; and
- they are enforced by means of incentives and sanctions.

Interest in *policy-based* approaches to multi-agent and distributed systems has also grown considerably in recent years (http://www.policy-workshop.org) [22,37,67]. While sharing much in common with norm-based approaches, policy-based perspectives differ in subtle ways. Whereas in everyday English the term *norm* denotes a practice, procedure, or custom regarded as typical or widespread, a *policy* is defined by the American Heritage Online dictionary as a "course of action, guiding principle, or procedure considered expedient, prudent, or advantageous." Thus, in contrast to the relatively descriptive basis and self-chosen adoption (or rejection) of norms, policies tend to be seen as prescriptive and externally imposed entities. Whereas norms in everyday life emerge gradually from group conventions and recurrent patterns of interaction, policies are consciously designed and put into and out of force at arbitrary times by virtue of explicitly recognized authority.[10] These differences are generally reflected in the way most policy-based approaches differ from norm-based ones with respect to the three features mentioned above. Policy-based approaches:

- support dynamic runtime policy changes, and not merely static configurations determined in advance;
- work involuntarily with respect to the agents, that is, without requiring the agents to consent or even be aware of the policies being enforced; thus aiming to guarantee that even the simplest agents can comply with policy; and
- wherever possible they are enforced preemptively, preventing buggy or malicious agents from doing harm in advance rather than rewarding them or imposing sanctions on them after the fact.

5.2 Plans and Policy

Policy management should not be confused with planning or workflow management, which are related but separate functions. Planning mechanisms are generally *deliberative* (i.e., they reason deeply and actively about activities in support of complex goals) whereas policy mechanisms tend to be *reactive* (i.e., concerned with simple actions triggered by some environmental event) [27, pp. 161-162]. Whereas plans are a unified roadmap for accomplishing some coherent set of objectives, bodies of policy collected to govern some sphere of activity are made up of diverse constraints imposed by multiple potentially-disjoint stakeholders and enforced by mechanisms that are more or less independent from the ones directly involved in planning. The independence of policy, reasoning, and enforcement mechanisms from

---

10 While it is true that over time norms can be formalized into laws, policies are explicit and formal by their very nature at the outset.

planning capabilities helps assure that, wherever possible, key constraints imposed by the humans are respected even in the face of buggy or malicious agents on the one hand, and poorly designed or oversimplified plans on the other. Plans tend to be strategic and comprehensive, while policies, in our sense, are by nature tactical and piecemeal. In short, we might say that while policies constitute the "rules of the road"—providing the stop signs, speed limits, and lane markers that serve to coordinate traffic and minimize mishaps—they are not sufficient to address the problem of "route planning."[11]

5.3 Autonomy and Policy[12]

Some important dimensions of the relationship between autonomy and policy can be straightforwardly characterized by reference to figure 1. [13]

The outermost rectangle, labeled *potential actions,* represents the set of all actions defined in some ontology under current consideration.[14] In other words, it contains the union of all actions for all actors currently known to the computational entities that are performing reasoning about adjustable autonomy and mixed-initiative interaction. Note that there is no requirement that all actions that an agent may take be represented in the ontology; only those which are of consequence for policy representation and reasoning need be included.

The rectangle labeled *possible actions* represents the set of potential actions whose achievement by some agent is deemed sufficiently imaginable in the current context. Of these possible actions, any given actor[15] (e.g., Agent A) will likely only be deemed to be *capable of* performing some subset. Capability is a function of the *abilities* and *resources* available to an actor attempting to undertake some action. An actor's ability is the sum of its own knowledge and skills, whereas its resources consist of all other assets it can currently draw on in the performance of the action. Two actors, Agent A

---

11 We are exploring the relationship between policy and planning in new research with James Allen [2][9].

12 More detail on this topic can be found in [9].

13 We can make a rough comparison between some of these dimensions and the aspects of autonomy described by Falcone and Castelfranchi [25]. Environmental autonomy can be expressed in terms of the possible actions available to the agent—the more the behavior is wholly deterministic in the presence of a fixed set of environmental inputs, the smaller the range of possible actions available to the agent. The aspect of self-sufficiency in social autonomy relates to the ranges of what can be achieved independently vs. in concert with others; deontic autonomy corresponds to the range of permissions and obligations that govern the agent's choice among actions.

14 The term *ontology* is borrowed from the philosophical literature, where it describes a theory of what exists. Such an account would typically include terms and definitions only for the very basic and necessary categories of existence. However, the common usage of ontology in the knowledge representation community is as a vocabulary of representational terms and their definitions at any level of generality. A computational system's "ontology" defines what exists for the program—in other words, what can be represented by it.

15 For discussion purposes, we use the term *actor* to refer to either a biological entity (e.g., human, animal) or an artificial agent (e.g., software agent, robotic agent).

and Agent B, may have both overlapping and unique capabilities.[16] If a set of actors is *jointly capable of* performing some action, it means that it is deemed to be possible for it to be performed by relying on the capabilities of both actors. Some actors may be capable of performing a given action either individually or jointly; other actors may not be so capable.

In addition to the *descriptive* axis describing various dimensions of capability, there is a *prescriptive* axis that is defined by policies specifying the various *permissions* and *obligations* of actors. *Authorities* may impose or remove involuntary policy constraints on the actions of actors. Alternatively, actors may voluntarily enter into *agreements* that mutually bind them to some set of policies so long as the agreement is in effect. The *effectivity* of an individual policy is the set of conditions that determine when it is in or out of force.

The set of *permitted actions* is defined by *authorization policies* that specify which actions an actor is allowed (*positive authorizations* or *A+* policies) or not allowed (*negative authorizations* or *A-* policies) to perform in a given context. The intersection of what is possible and what is permitted to a given set of actors defines a set of *available actions*.

Of those actions that are available to a given actor, some subset may be judged to be *independently achievable* by it in the current context. Some actions, on the other hand, would only be *jointly achievable*.

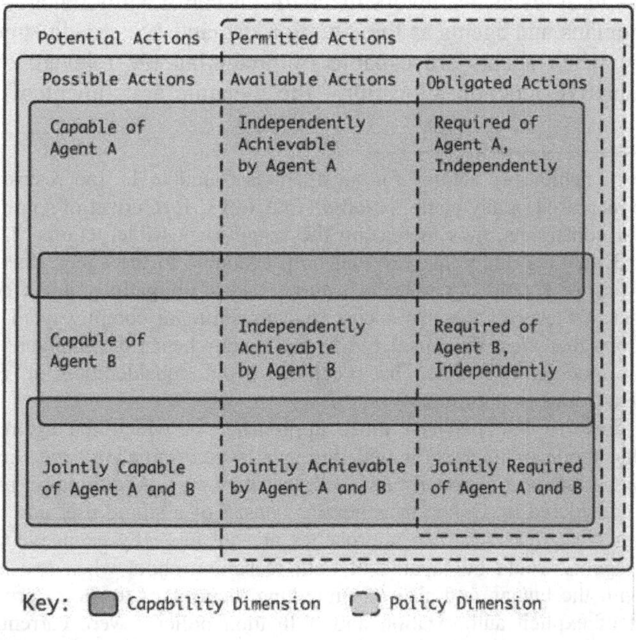

Potential Actions	Permitted Actions	
Possible Actions	**Available Actions**	**Obligated Actions**
Capable of Agent A	Independently Achievable by Agent A	Required of Agent A, Independently
Capable of Agent B	Independently Achievable by Agent B	Required of Agent B, Independently
Jointly Capable of Agent A and B	Jointly Achievable by Agent A and B	Jointly Required of Agent A and B

Key: ▮ Capability Dimension   ⬚ Policy Dimension

Fig. 2. Basic dimensions of adjustable autonomy and mixed-initiative interaction

---

[16] Note that although we show A and B sharing the same set of possible actions in figure 2, this is not necessarily the case.

Finally, the set of *obligated actions* is defined by *obligation policies* that specify actions that an actor is required to perform (*positive obligations* or *O+* policies) or for which such a requirement is waived (*negative obligations* or *O-* policies). Positive obligations commit the resources of actors, reducing their current overall capability accordingly. *Jointly obligated actions* are those that two or more agents are explicitly required to perform.

A major challenge is to ensure that the degree of autonomy is continuously and transparently adjusted to be consistent with explicitly declared policies which themselves can, ideally, be imposed and removed at any time as appropriate [48]. For example, one goal of the agent or external entity performing such adjustments should be to make sure that the range of permissible actions do not exceed the range of those that are likely to be achievable by the agent.[17] While the agent is constrained to operate within whatever deontic bounds on autonomy are currently enforced as authorization and obligation policies, it is otherwise free to act.

Thus, the coupling of autonomy with policy gives the agent maximum opportunity for local adaptation to unforeseen problems and opportunities, while assuring humans that agent behavior will be kept within desired bounds.

In principle, the actual adjustment of an agent's level of autonomy could be initiated either by a human, the agent, or some other software component.[18] To the extent we can adjust agent autonomy with reasonable dynamism (ideally allowing handoffs of control among team members to occur anytime) and with a sufficiently fine-grained range of levels, teamwork mechanisms can flexibly renegotiate roles and tasks among humans and agents as the situation demands. Such adjustments can also be anticipatory when agents are capable of predicting the relevant events [5,25]. Research in adaptive function allocation—the dynamic assignment of tasks among

---

17 If the range of achievable actions for an agent is found to be too restricted, it can, in principle, be increased in any combination of four ways: 1. removal of some portion of the environmental constraints, thus increasing the range of possible actions; 2. increasing its permissions; 3. making additional external help available to the agent, thus increasing its joint capabilities; or 4. reducing an agent's current set of obligations, thus freeing resources for other tasks. Of course, there is a cost in computational complexity to increasing the range of actions that must be considered by an agent—hence the judicious use of policy where certain actions can either be precluded from consideration or obligated with confidence in advance by a third party.

18 Cohen [18] draws a line between those approaches in which the agent itself wholly determines the mode of interaction with humans (mixed-initiative) and those where this determination is imposed externally (adjustable autonomy). Additionally, mixed-initiative systems are considered by Cohen to generally consist of a single user and a single agent. However, it is clear that these two approaches are not mutually exclusive and that, in an ideal world, agents would be capable of both reasoning about when and how to initiate interaction with the human and also of subjecting themselves to the external direction of whatever set of explicit authorization and obligation policies were currently in force to govern that interaction. Additionally, there is no reason to limit the notion of "mixed initiative" systems to the single agent-single human case. Hence we prefer to think of mixed-initiative systems as being those systems that are capable of making context-appropriate adjustments to their level of social autonomy (i.e., their level or mode of engagement with the human), whether a given adjustment is made as a result of reasoning internal to the agent or due to externally-imposed policy-based constraints.

humans and machines—provides some useful lessons for implementations of adjustable autonomy in intelligent systems [31].

When evaluating options for adaptively reallocating tasks among team members, it must be remembered that dynamic role adjustment comes at a cost. Measures of expected utility can be used to evaluate the tradeoffs involved in potentially interrupting the ongoing activities of agents and humans in such situations, in order to communicate, coordinate, and reallocate responsibilities [18,33,34]. It is also important to note that the need for adjustments may cascade in complex fashion: interaction may be spread across many potentially-distributed agents and humans who act in multiply-connected interaction loops. For this reason, adjustable autonomy may involve not merely a shift in roles among a human-agent pair, but rather the distribution of dynamic demands across many coordinated actors.[19] Defining explicit policies for the transfer of control among team members and for the resultant required modifications to coordination constraints can prove useful in managing such complexity [54]. Whereas in the past goal adoption and the commitment to join and interact in a prescribed manner with a team have sometimes occurred as part of a single act in early teamwork formulations, researchers are increasingly realizing the advantages of allowing the respective acts of goal adoption, commitment to work jointly with a team, and the choice of specific task execution strategies to be handled with some degree of independence [4,48]. Over the last few years, we have been developing a set of services within a framework called KAoS to accomplish just these kind of goals.

5.4 Overview of KAoS

KAoS is a collection of componentized agent services compatible with several popular agent frameworks, including Nomads [63], the DARPA CoABS Grid [38], the DARPA ALP/Ultra*Log Cougaar framework (http://www.cougaar.net), CORBA (http://www.omg.org), and Voyager (http://www.recursionsw.com/osi.asp). While initially oriented to the dynamic and complex requirements of software and robotic agent applications, KAoS services are also being adapted to general-purpose grid computing (http://www.gridforum.org) and Web services (http://www.w3.org/2002/ws/) environments as well [35].

KAoS domain services provide the capability for groups of agents, people, resources, and other entities to be structured into organizations of agent domains and subdomains to facilitate agent-agent collaboration and external policy administration.

KAoS policy services allow for the specification, management, conflict resolution, and enforcement of policies within domains. The KAoS Policy Ontologies (KPO), represented in OWL [69], distinguishes between *authorizations* (i.e., constraints that permit or forbid some action) and *obligations* (i.e., constraints that require some action to be performed, or else serve to waive such a requirement) [22].

---

19 As Hancock and Scallen [31] rightfully observe, the problem of adaptive function allocation is not merely one of efficiency or technical elegance. Economic factors (e.g., can the task be more inexpensively performed by humans, agents, or some combination?), political and cultural factors (e.g., is it acceptable for agents to perform tasks traditionally assigned to humans?), or personal and moral considerations (e.g., is a given task enjoyable and challenging vs. boring and mind-numbing for the human?) are also essential considerations.

5.5 Technical and Social Policy Categories

To increase the likelihood of human acceptance of agent technology, successful systems must attend to both the technical and social aspects of policy [51]. From a *technical perspective*, we want to be able to help ensure the protection of agent state, the viability of agent communities, and the reliability of the resources on which they depend [12]. To accomplish this, we must guarantee, insofar as is possible, that the autonomy of agents can always be bounded by explicit enforceable policy that can be continually adjusted to maximize the agents' effectiveness and safety in both human and computational environments. From a *social perspective*, we want agents to be designed to fit well with how people actually work together and otherwise interact. Explicit policies governing human-agent interaction, based on careful observation of work practice and an understanding of current social science research, can help assure that effective and natural coordination, appropriate levels and modalities of feedback, and adequate predictability and responsiveness to human control are maintained [11,26,50]. These and similar technical and social factors are key to providing the reassurance and trust that are the prerequisites to the widespread acceptance of agent technology for non-trivial applications.

We currently classify *technical policies* into six categories:

- *Authentication policies.* This category of policies is concerned with assuring that identification of proper users is associated with various agent commands and actions.
- *Data and resource access and protection policies.* These policies control access to resources, information, and services, and specify any constraints on data protection (e.g., encryption).
- *Communication policies.* Communication policies govern message passing among individuals and groups, including forms of content filtering and transformation [64,65].
- *Resource control policies.* Going beyond simple access control, these policies control the amount and rate of resource usage (e.g., CPU, memory, network, hard disk, screen space) [62,63].
- *Monitoring and response policies.* These policies typically represent obligations for the system to perform specific monitoring and response actions (e.g., logging, response to authorization failures or changes to global system defense postures).
- *Mobility policies.* Mobility policies govern the physical movement of software or hardware agents [39].

We are also currently developing *social policies* within six categories:[20]

---

20 The motivation for such policies is eloquently expressed by Norman [50, p. 126-127]: "One of the reasons that modern technology is so difficult to use is because of [its] silent, invisible operation [when compared with mechanical devices]. The videocassette recorder, the digital watch, and the microwave oven—none is inherently complicated. The problem for us is their lack of communication. They fail to interact gracefully. They demand attention and services, but without reciprocating, without providing sufficient background and context. There is little or no feedback.... The modern information-processing machine fits the

- *Organization policies.* This category of policies includes those that specify relationships among classes of agents, e.g., policies about delegation of responsibilities and agent registration in domains.
- *Notification policies.* It is important that important information be conveyed to the appropriate people at the appropriate time and with an appropriate modality. Based on the work of [55,56], we are building ontologies supporting policies for categories of agents, roles, notifications, latency, focus of attention, and presence as a foundation for policies governing context-sensitive notification.[21]
- *Conversation policies.* Explicit conversation policies simplify the work of both the agent and the agent designer [30]. Such policies include, for example, constraints on conversation message sequencing, termination conditions, and timeouts.
- *Nonverbal expression.* These policies govern signaling and display behavior of agents. Detailed examples are given below.
- *Collaboration policies.* Policies governing team coordination are classed in this category, including the formation and discharge of joint goals as is central in traditional multi-agent teamwork theory [17,66].
- *Adjustable autonomy policies.* These policies regulate levels of, and adjustments to, levels of agent autonomy [23].

A fuller discussion of examples from each of these categories may be found in [7].

We now discuss a few simple examples of policy relating to the theme of display and signaling behavior. The policy examples are drawn from our studies of the Personal Satellite Assistant (PSA), currently under development at NASA Ames. The PSA is a softball-sized flying robot, designed to help astronauts, that is being developed to operate onboard spacecraft in pressurized micro-gravity environments [1,10,24,28,59].

For clarity's sake, we will present example policies in ordinary English rather than in DAML. For brevity's sake, the policies will be presented in an incomplete form. Each example is preceded by A+, A-, O+, or O- to indicate whether it is respectively a positive authorization, negative authorization, positive obligation, or negative obligation.

---

stereotype of an antisocial, technological nerd. It works efficiently, quietly, and autonomously, and it prefers to avoid [social] interactions with the people around it.".

21 Of course the important point in context-sensitive notification in our day of information and sensory overload is sometimes not helping the information get through but rather blocking, filtering, or rechanneling it in appropriate ways: "Most instrument panels [use lights, buzzers, and alarms to] tell us when something is wrong and needs immediate attention. No social protocols, no etiquette. No checking to see whether we are busy at some other activity, usually not even a check to see if other alarms or warnings are also active. As a result, all the alarms and warnings scream in their self-centered way... In places that have large control panels,... the first act of the human operators is to shut off the alarms so they can concentrate upon the problem" [50, p. 128].

5.6 Nonverbal Expression Policy: Examples

Where possible, agents usually take advantage of explicit verbal channels for communication in order to reduce the need for relying on current primitive robotic vision and auditory sensing capabilities [47, p. 295]. On the other hand, animals and humans often rely on visual and auditory signals in place of explicit verbal communication for many aspects of coordinated activity. As part of our work on human-robotic interaction for NASA, the Army, and the Navy, we are developing policies to govern various nonverbal forms of expression in robotic and software agents. These nonverbal behaviors will be designed to express not only the current state of the agent but also—importantly—to provide rough clues about what it is going to do next.

Maes and her colleagues were among the first to explore this possibility in her research on software agents that continuously communicated their internal state to the user via facial expressions (e.g., thinking, working, suggestion, unsure, pleased, and confused) [43]. Breazeal has taken inspiration from research in child psychology [68] to develop robot displays that reflect four basic classes of preverbal social responses: affective (changing facial expressions), exploratory (visual search, maintenance of mutual regard with human), protective (turning head away), and regulatory (expressive feedback to gain caregiver attention, cyclic waxing and waning of internal states, habituation, and signals of internal motivation) [13]. Norman has investigated the role of signaling, not only in effective coordination and communication, including the communication of emotion, but also with regard to the role of deception in human and agent affairs [50]. Books on human etiquette [70] contain many descriptions of appropriate behavior in a wide variety of social settings. Finally, in addition to this previous work, we think that display and signaling behavior among people [46] and groups of animals will be one of the most fruitful sources of policy for effective nonverbal expression in agents. Our initial study indicates that there are useful agent equivalents for each of Smith's ten categories of widespread vertebrate animal cooperation and coordination displays [60, pp. 84-105]. Some examples are discussed below.

```
O+: IF the current task of the PSA is of type
uninterruptible
THEN the PSA must blink red light until the current
task is finished
PRECEDENCE: A-: The PSA is forbidden from performing
any tasks but the current one
```

This policy would require the PSA to blink a red light while it is busy performing an uninterruptible task. During this time, it is also forbidden from performing any tasks but the current one. Related messages it may want to give with a similar signal might include: "I am unable to make contact with anybody," "Do not attempt to communicate with me (for whatever reason, e.g., 'my line is bugged')." On the positive side, various uses of a green light might signal messages such as: "I am open for calls," "I need to talk to someone," or "May I interject something into this conversation?" Displays in this general interactional category clearly have benefits for coordination among groups of agents by providing information about which are or are not in a position to interact with others, in what ways, when, and so forth.

```
O+: IF a conversation has been initiated with someone
THEN the PSA must face the one with whom it is
conversing, so long as they are within the line of
sight, until the conversation has finished
```

This policy implements a kind of display associated with maintaining a previously established association. This display might be especially useful when the PSA is moving around the room and needs to let a person know that it is still attending to the ongoing conversation and/or task.

```
O+: IF the current task of the PSA is to move some
distance greater than D
THEN the PSA must signal its intention to move for S
seconds
PRECEDENCE: A-: The PSA is forbidden from executing its
move
```

It's no fun being hit in the head by a flying robot that suddenly decides it's got to be on the move. This policy prevents the PSA from moving until it has first signaled for some number of seconds its intention to move. Besides the pre-move signaling, some kind of signaling could also take place during the move itself.

In addition to this policy regarding movement, other policies should be put in place to, for instance, require the PSA to stay at a safe and comfortable distance from people, other robotic agents, and space station structures and equipment. Of course the policies would take into account that different social distances may be appropriate in different cultures, as will be pertinent in, for example, multinational operations of the International Space Station.

As our new phases of research proceed, we hope to verify the effectiveness of KAoS policies and services through a series of tests assessing *survivability* (ability to maintain effectiveness in the face of unforeseen software or hardware failures), *safety* (ability to prevent certain classes of dangerous actions or situations), *predictability* (assessed correlation between human judgment of predicted vs. actual behavior), *controllability*(immediacy with which an authorized human can prevent, stop, enable, or initiate agent actions), *effectiveness* (assessed correlation between human judgment of desired vs. actual behavior), and *adaptability* (ability to respond to changes in context). We briefly address some aspects of adaptation next.

6 Building Cultures for Agent Communities: Potential Sources of Adaptation

There are two sorts of adaptation we believe will be critical to capture if communities of agents are to be enduring. The first has to do with the adaptation of policy to accommodate diverse contexts over which it must be applied. For example, we have seen an example of the need for this kind of adaptation in the last section, in which the comfortable distance a PSA should keep from its partner invokes cultural considerations.

The limited progress we have made with regard to adaptation to context has been mostly in the area of adjustable autonomy and the capability it provides for functions like dynamic handoff of control among team members and flexible renegotiation of roles and tasks among humans and agents when new opportunities arise or when breakdowns occur [see section 5.3 and [9]].

The second type of adaptation involves changes in policy, either in response to experience, for example, in realizing that enforcing a policy or set of policies has consistently resulted in untoward outcomes, or by recognizing that the nature of the operational world had changed in consequential ways. This second kind of adaptation has been even less explored. From the perspective of this paper, such adaptation might involve a sort of "cultural learning" that might prove challenging to current machine learning approaches.

7 Conclusion

In this paper, we have attempted to encourage an expansion of thinking about the sources, nature, and diversity of regulatory systems that can be utilized to achieve acceptable levels of order when groups of agents or mixed agent-human groups are engaged in consequential work. Interestingly, one impetus for this direction has been a desire to "make agents acceptable to humans," for example, to make communication with agents natural, to make agents seem trustworthy (and actually be trustable) in their participation in important affairs, and perhaps most importantly, to ensure, as in human societies, a kind of predictability—agents will not be acceptable to humans if they unexpectedly keep running amok.

In addition, recognizing that societies need to adapt to changing conditions in addition to maintaining order, we have examined elements of adaptation in animal and human groups. Since healthy order can lapse into ineffective and unacceptable rigidity, we have made some brief speculations about ways elements of useful adaptation might coexist with those enforcing order.

While we have focused primarily on animal signaling and order, we anticipate, especially in situations in which agents are embodied (e.g., physical robots), and move around, and act in the world, that there will be considerable benefit from expanding our repertoire of agent-cultural devices even farther, to include, for example, concrete instantiations such as "lines on the highway" or more subtle codes of "good manners."

Some years ago, Paul Wohlmuth, a philosopher of law, wrote the introductory chapter to an interdisciplinary special issue of the *Journal of Contemporary Legal Issues* focused on the "constitution of authority" [73]. Roughly interpreted, the constitution of authority refers to how things of various sorts come to have regulatory power over human conduct.

In his introductory chapter, Wohlmuth used the simple example of an automobile navigating a bend in the road[22] to illustrate the ubiquity and wide variety of authoritative forms that come to bear on human activity. Even the basic laws of physics are involved. That is, there are limits to the speed with which a particular sort of car, on a particular sort of road, can navigate the turn without crashing, and people who do not want to get hurt will honor these constraints as they are able. The laws of

---

22 Interestingly, Smith [60] and Norman [50] also draw extensively on analogies to highway traffic to illustrate their discussion of signaling and coordination.

basic physiology are in place, for instance, the eyesight, reaction time, and degree of alertness of the driver. Beyond these more physical constraints, all sorts of cultural artifacts are imparting regulatory influence. Stripes on the road demarcate the lanes and boundaries of the highway and whether or not the lanes may be traversed. Regional custom determines which side of the highway the driver should be on at all. Signs containing both words (e.g., "slow down") and symbols (e.g., a twisting portrayal of the road section) are present. There are also inter-vehicular signalings of intent and disposition, and processes of coordination taking place, if there are multiple vehicles present. Furthermore, the appearance of a law-enforcement official, for example a patrolling police car, emerging on the scene, has dramatic effect on the behavior of the drivers. At much greater degrees of abstraction from the scene, there is the Motor Vehicle Code and other formal statutes that, for instance, prescribe the amount of certain substances that the driver may have in his or her body. In addition, there are entire culturally constructed deliberative bodies (e.g., the courts) empowered, if needed, to bridge the gap between pertinent statutes and the particulars of any one instance of traveling this bend. And, not much, if any, of this is static. For instance, if a particularly high rate of accidents results at this bend, many changes may take place, ranging from the physical to the more abstract. The road banking on the curve may be increased. The posted speed limit may be decreased. More ominous, scarier symbols may be posted. Consequences of violations of pertinent rules of the road may be made harsher.

Societies must maintain a degree of continuity and stability; this represents a kind of historical memory of practices that have been effective in the past and have supported survival. On the other hand, the world is ever-changing; continued survival requires adaptations in practice to address novelty and surprise. The complexity of this interplay makes us realize even more that we are only at the beginning in addressing the dual problems of order and change in agent communities (let alone the optimal delicate balance between them), and it is hard not to feel a bit overwhelmed. But we are convinced that even little steps in understanding how to better incorporate the content and mechanisms of culture into agent societies will be both interesting and fruitful.

Acknowledgements

The authors gratefully acknowledge the sponsorship of this research by the NASA Cross-Enterprise and Intelligent Systems Programs, and a joint NASA-DARPA ITAC grant. Additional support was provided by DARPA's CoABS, Ultra*Log, EPCA, and Augmented Cognition programs, by the Army Research Lab's Advanced Decision Architectures program (ARLADA), and the Office of Naval Research. A special thanks is due to the following individuals for their valuable contributions to the ideas developed in this paper: Alessandro Acquisti, James Allen, Guy Boy, Kathleen Bradshaw, Maggie Breedy, Larry Bunch, Murray Burke, Nate Chambers, Bill Clancey, Greg Dorais, Joan Feltovich, Ken Ford, Lucian Galescu, Mark Greaves, Jack Hansen, Pat Hayes, Robert Hoffman, Matt Johnson, Hyuckchul, Jung, Shri Kulkarni, Henry Lieberman, Cheryl Martin, Cindy Mason, Robin Murphy, Nicola Muscettola, Don Norman, Jerry Pratt, Anil Raj, Dylan Schmorrow, Debra Schreckenghost, Mike

Shafto, Maarten Sierhuis, Austin Tate, Milind Tambe, William Taysom, Ron Van Hoof, the late Paul Wohlmuth, and Tim Wright.

References

[1]   Acquisti, A., Sierhuis, M., Clancey, W. J., Bradshaw, J. M. (2002). Agent-based modeling of collaboration and work practices onboard the International Space Station. *Proceedings of the Eleventh Conference on Computer-Generated Forces and Behavior Representation*. Orlando, FL, USA.

[2]   Allen, J. F., Ferguson, G. (2002). Human-machine collaborative planning. *Proceedings of the NASA Planning and Scheduling Workshop*. Houston, TX, USA.

[3]   Asimov, I. (1942/1968). Runaround. In I. Asimov (Ed.), *I, Robot*. (pp. 33-51). London, England: Grafton Books. Originally published in *Astounding Science Fiction*, 1942, pp. 94-103.

[4]   Barber, K. S., Gamba, M., Martin, C. E. (2002). Representing and analyzing adaptive decision-making frameworks. In H. Hexmoor, C. Castelfranchi, R. Falcone (Ed.), *Agent Autonomy*. (pp. 23-42). Dordrecht, The Netherlands: Kluwer.

[5]   Boella, G. (2002). Obligations and cooperation: Two sides of social rationality. In H. Hexmoor, C. Castelfranchi, R. Falcone (Ed.), *Agent Autonomy*. (pp. 57-78). Dordrecht, The Netherlands: Kluwer.

[6]   Boman, M. (1999). Norms in artificial decision-making. *Artificial Intelligence and Law*, 7, 17-35.

[7]   Bradshaw, J. M., Beautement, P., Raj, A., Johnson, M., Kulkarni, S., Suri, N. (2003). Making agents acceptable to people. In N. Zhong J. Liu (Ed.), *Intelligent Technologies for Information Analysis: Advances in Agents, Data Mining, and Statistical Learning*. (pp. in press). Berlin: Springer Verlag.

[8]   Bradshaw, J. M., Boy, G., Durfee, E., Gruninger, M., Hexmoor, H., Suri, N., Tambe, M., Uschold, M., Vitek, J. (Ed.). (2003). *Software Agents for the Warfighter. ITAC Consortium Report*. Cambridge, MA: AAAI Press/The MIT Press.

[9]   Bradshaw, J. M., Jung, H., Kulkarni, S., Taysom, W. (2004). Dimensions of adjustable autonomy and mixed-initiative interaction. In M. Klusch, G. Weiss, M. Rovatsos (Ed.), *Computational Autonomy*. (pp. in press). Berlin, Germany: Springer-Verlag.

[10]   Bradshaw, J. M., Sierhuis, M., Acquisti, A., Feltovich, P., Hoffman, R., Jeffers, R., Prescott, D., Suri, N., Uszok, A., Van Hoof, R. (2003). Adjustable autonomy and human-agent teamwork in practice: An interim report on space applications. In H. Hexmoor, R. Falcone, C. Castelfranchi (Ed.), *Agent Autonomy*. (pp. 243-280). Kluwer.

[11]   Bradshaw, J. M., Sierhuis, M., Gawdiak, Y., Jeffers, R., Suri, N., Greaves, M. (2001). Adjustable autonomy and teamwork for the Personal Satellite Assistant. *Proceedings of the IJCAI-01 Workshop on Autonomy, Delegation, and Control: Interacting with Autonomous Agents*. Seattle, WA, USA.

[12]   Bradshaw, J. M., Suri, N., Breedy, M. R., Canas, A., Davis, R., Ford, K. M., Hoffman, R., Jeffers, R., Kulkarni, S., Lott, J., Reichherzer, T., Uszok, A. (2002). Terraforming cyberspace. In D. C. Marinescu C. Lee (Ed.), *Process Coordination and Ubiquitous Computing*. (pp. 165-185). Boca Raton, FL: CRC Press. Updated and expanded version of an article that originally appeared in IEEE Intelligent Systems, July 2001, pp. 49-56.

[13]   Breazeal, C., Scassellati, B. (1999). How to build robots that make friends and influence people. *IROS*. Kyonjiu, Korea.

[14]   Calmet, J., Daemi, A., Endsuleit, R., Mie, T. (2004). A liberal approach to openess in societies of agents. In this volume.

[15]   Clark, H. H. (1996). *Using Language*. Cambridge, UK: Cambridge University Press.

[16]   Clarke, R. (1993-1994). Asimov's laws of robotics: Implications for information technology, Parts 1 and 2. *IEEE Computer*, December/January, 53-61/57-66.

[17]   Cohen, P. R., Levesque, H. J. (1991). *Teamwork*. Technote 504. Menlo Park, CA: SRI International, March.

[18]   Cohen, R., Fleming, M. (2002). Adjusting the autonomy in mixed-initiative systems by reasoning about interaction. In H. Hexmoor, C. Castelfranchi, R. Falcone (Ed.), *Agent Autonomy*. (pp. 105-122). Dordrecht, The Netherlands: Kluwer.

[19]   Conte, R., Castelfranchi, C. (1995). *Cognitive and social action*. London, England: UCL Press.

[20]   Cook, R. I., Woods, D. D. (1994). Operating at the sharp end: The complexity of human error. In S. U. Bogner (Ed.), *Human Error in Medicine*. Hillsdale, NJ: Lawrence Erlbaum.

[21]   d'Inverno, M., Luck, M. (2001). *Understanding Agent Systems*. Berlin, Germany: Springer-Verlag.

[22]   Damianou, N., Dulay, N., Lupu, E. C., Sloman, M. S. (2000). *Ponder: A Language for Specifying Security and Management Policies for Distributed Systems, Version 2.3*. Imperial College of Science, Technology and Medicine, Department of Computing, 20 October 2000.

[23]   Dorais, G., Bonasso, R. P., Kortenkamp, D., Pell, B., Schrekenghost, D. (1999). Adjustable autonomy for human-centered autonomous systems on Mars. *Proceedings of the AAAI Spring Symposium on Agents with Adjustable Autonomy. AAAI Technical Report SS-99-06*. Menlo Park, CA, Menlo Park, CA: AAAI Press.

[24]   Dorais, G., Desiano, S. D., Gawdiak, Y., Nicewarmer, K. (2003). An autonomous control system for an intra-vehicular spacecraft mobile monitor prototype. *Proceedings of the Seventh International Symposium on Artificial Intelligence, Robotics, and Automation in Space (i-SAIRAS 2003)*. Nara, Japan.

[25]   Falcone, R., Castelfranchi, C. (2002). From automaticity to autonomy: The frontier of artificial agents. In H. Hexmoor, C. Castelfranchi, R. Falcone (Ed.), *Agent Autonomy*. (pp. 79-103). Dordrecht, The Netherlands: Kluwer.

[26]   Feltovich, P., Bradshaw, J. M., Jeffers, R., Uszok, A. (2003). Order and KAoS: Using policy to represent agent cultures. *Proceedings of the AAMAS 03 Workshop on Humans and Multi-Agent Systems*. Melbourne, Australia.

[27]   Fox, J., Das, S. (2000). *Safe and Sound: Artificial Intelligence in Hazardous Applications*. Menlo Park, CA: AAAI Press/The MIT Press.

[28]   Gawdiak, Y., Bradshaw, J. M., Williams, B., Thomas, H. (2000). R2D2 in a softball: The Personal Satellite Assistant. H. Lieberman (Ed.), *Proceedings of the ACM Conference on Intelligent User Interfaces (IUI 2000)*, (pp. 125-128). New Orleans, LA, New York: ACM Press,

[29]   Geertz, C. (1973). *The Interpretation of Cultures*. New York, NY: Basic Books.

[30]   Greaves, M., Holmback, H., Bradshaw, J. M. (1999). What is a conversation policy? M. Greaves, J. M. Bradshaw (Ed.), *Proceedings of the Autonomous Agents '99 Workshop on Specifying and Implementing Conversation Policies*, (pp. 1-9). Seattle, WA, USA.

[31]   Hancock, P. A., Scallen, S. F. (1998). Allocating functions in human-machine systems. In R. Hoffman, M. F. Sherrick, J. S. Warm (Ed.), *Viewing Psychology as a Whole*. (pp. 509-540). Washington, D.C.: American Psychological Association.

[32]   Hohfeld, W. N. (1913). Fundamental legal conceptions as applied in judicial reasoning. *Yale Law Journal*, 23.

[33]   Horvitz, E. (1999). Principles of mixed-initiative user interfaces. *Proceedings of the ACM SIGCHI Conference on Human Factors in Computing Systems (CHI '99)*. Pittsburgh, PA, New York: ACM Press.

[34]   Horvitz, E., Jacobs, A., Hovel, D. (1999). Attention-sensitive alerting. *Proceedings of the Conference on Uncertainty and Artificial Intelligence (UAI '99)*, (pp. 305-313). Stockholm, Sweden.

[35]   Johnson, M., Chang, P., Jeffers, R., Bradshaw, J. M., Soo, V.-W., Breedy, M. R., Bunch, L., Kulkarni, S., Lott, J., Suri, N., Uszok, A. (2003). KAoS semantic policy and domain services: An application of DAML to Web services-based grid architectures. *Proceedings of the AAMAS 03 Workshop on Web Services and Agent-Based Engineering*. Melbourne, Australia.

[36]   Jordan, M., Atkinson, M. (1998). *Orthogonal persistence for Java—A mid-term report*. Sun Microsystems Laboratories.

[37]   Kagal, L., Finin, T., Joshi, A. (2003). A policy language for pervasive systems. *Proceedings of the Fourth IEEE International Workshop on Policies for Distributed Systems and Networks,* (pp. http://umbc.edu/~finin/papers/policy03.pdf). Lago di Como, Italy.

[38]   Kahn, M., Cicalese, C. (2001). CoABS Grid Scalability Experiments. O. F. Rana (Ed.), *Second International Workshop on Infrastructure for Scalable Multi-Agent Systems at the Fifth International Conference on Autonomous Agents.* Montreal, CA, New York: ACM Press.

[39]   Knoll, G., Suri, N., Bradshaw, J. M. (2001). Path-based security for mobile agents. *Proceedings of the First International Workshop onthe Security of Mobile Multi-Agent Systems (SEMAS-2001) at the Fifth International Conference on Autonomous Agents (Agents 2001),* (pp. 54-60). Montreal, CA, New York: ACM Press.

[40]   Krogh, C., Herrestad, H. (1999). Hohfeld in Cyberspace and other applications of normative reasoning in agent technology. *Artificial Intelligence and Law,* 7(1), 81-96.

[41]   Lopez y Lopez, F., Luck, M., d'Inverno, M. (2001). A framework for norm-based inter-agent dependence. *Proceedings of the Third Mexican Internation Conference on Computer Science.*

[42]   Lopez y Lopez, F., Luck, M., d'Inverno, M. (2002). Constraining autonomy through norms. *Proceedings of the Conference on Autonomous Agents and Multi-Agent Systems,* (pp. 674-681). Bologna, Italy.

[43]   Maes, P. (1997). Agents that reduce work and information overload. In J. M. Bradshaw (Ed.), *Software Agents.* (pp. 145-164). Cambridge, MA: AAAI Press/The MIT Press.

[44]   Mayr, E. (1997). *This Is Biology.* Cambridge, MA: Belkamp Press of Harvard University Press.

[45]   McBurney, P., Parsons, S. (2004). Engineering democracy in open agent systems. In this volume.

[46]   Morris, D. (2002). *Peoplewatching.* London, England: Vintage.

[47]   Murphy, R. R. (2000). *Introduction to AI Robotics.* Cambridge, MA: The MIT Press.

[48]   Myers, K., Morley, D. (2003). Directing agents. In H. Hexmoor, C. Castelfranchi, R. Falcone (Ed.), *Agent Autonomy.* (pp. 143-162). Dordrecht, The Netherlands: Kluwer.

[49]   Neville, B., Pitt, J. (2004). A computational framework for social agents in agent-mediated e-commerce. In this volume.

[50]   Norman, D. A. (1992). Turn signals are the facial expressions of automobiles. In *Turn Signals Are the Facial Expressions of Automobiles.* (pp. 117-134). Reading, MA: Addison-Wesley.

[51]   Norman, D. A. (1997). How might people interact with agents? In J. M. Bradshaw (Ed.), *Software Agents.* (pp. 49-55). Cambridge, MA: The AAAI Press/The MIT Press.

[52]   Pynadath, D., Tambe, M. (2001). Revisiting Asimov's first law: A response to the call to arms. *Proceedings of ATAL 01.*

[53]   Sawyer, R. K. (2001). *Creating Conversations: Improvisation in Everyday Discourse.* Cresskill, NJ: Hampton Press.

[54]   Scerri, P., Pynadath, D., Tambe, M. (2002). Adjustable autonomy for the real world. In H. Hexmoor, C. Castelfranchi, R. Falcone (Ed.), *Agent Autonomy.* (pp. 163-190). Dordrecht, The Netherlands: Kluwer.

[55]   Schreckenghost, D., Martin, C., Bonasso, P., Kortenkamp, D., Milam, T., Thronesbery, C. (2003). Supporting group interaction among humans and autonomous agents. *Submitted for publication.*

[56]   Schreckenghost, D., Martin, C., Thronesbery, C. (2003). Specifying organizational policies and individual preferences for human-software interaction. *Submitted for publication.*

[57]   Sergot, M. (2001). A computational theory of normative positions. *ACM Transactions on Computational Logic,* 2(4), 581-622.

[58]   Shoham, Y., Tennenholtz, M. (1992). On the synthesis of useful social laws for artificial agent societies. *Proceedings of the Tenth National Conference on Artificial Intelligence,* (pp. 276-281). San Jose, CA, USA.

[59]   Sierhuis, M., Bradshaw, J. M., Acquisti, A., Van Hoof, R., Jeffers, R., Uszok, A. (2003). Human-agent teamwork and adjustable autonomy in practice. *Proceedings of the Seventh International Symposium on Artificial Intelligence, Robotics and Automation in Space (i-SAIRAS).* Nara, Japan.

[60]   Smith, W. J. (1977). *The Behavior of Communicating.* Cambridge, MA: Harvard University Press.

[61]   Smith, W. J. (1995). The biological bases of social attunement. *Journal of Contemporary Legal Issues,* 6.

[62]   Suri, N., Bradshaw, J. M., Breedy, M. R., Groth, P. T., Hill, G. A., Jeffers, R. (2000). Strong Mobility and Fine-Grained Resource Control in NOMADS. *Proceedings of the 2nd International Symposium on Agents Systems and Applications and the 4th International Symposium on Mobile Agents (ASA/MA 2000).* Zurich, Switzerland, Berlin: Springer-Verlag.

[63]   Suri, N., Bradshaw, J. M., Breedy, M. R., Groth, P. T., Hill, G. A., Jeffers, R., Mitrovich, T. R., Pouliot, B. R., Smith, D. S. (2000). NOMADS: Toward an environment for strong and safe agent mobility. *Proceedings of Autonomous Agents 2000.* Barcelona, Spain, New York: ACM Press.

[64]   Suri, N., Bradshaw, J. M., Burstein, M. H., Uszok, A., Benyo, B., Breedy, M. R., Carvalho, M., Diller, D., Groth, P. T., Jeffers, R., Johnson, M., Kulkarni, S., Lott, J. (2003). DAML-based policy enforcement for semantic data transformation and filtering in multi-agent systems. *Proceedings of the Autonomous Agents and Multi-Agent Systems Conference (AAMAS 2003).* Melbourne, Australia, New York, NY: ACM Press.

[65]   Suri, N., Carvalho, M., Bradshaw, J. M., Breedy, M. R., Cowin, T. B., Groth, P. T., Saavendra, R., Uszok, A. (2003). Mobile code for policy enforcement. *Policy 2003.* Como, Italy.

[66]   Tambe, M., Shen, W., Mataric, M., Pynadath, D. V., Goldberg, D., Modi, P. J., Qiu, Z., Salemi, B. (1999). Teamwork in cyberspace: Using TEAMCORE to make agents team-ready. *Proceedings of the AAAI Spring Symposium on Agents in Cyberspace.* Menlo Park, CA, Menlo Park, CA: The AAAI Press.

[67]   Tonti, G., Bradshaw, J. M., Jeffers, R., Montanari, R., Suri, N., Uszok, A. (2003). Semantic Web languages for policy representation and reasoning: A comparison of KAoS, Rei, and Ponder. In D. Fensel, K. Sycara, J. Mylopoulos (Ed.), *The Semantic Web—ISWC 2003. Proceedings of the Second International Semantic Web Conference, Sanibel Island, Florida, USA, October 2003, LNCS 2870.* (pp. 419-437). Berlin: Springer.

[68]   Trevarthen, C. (1979). Communication and cooperation in early infancy: A description of primary intersubjectivity. In M. Bullowa (Ed.), *Before Speech.* (pp. 321-348). Cambridge, England: Cambridge University Press.

[69]   Uszok, A., Bradshaw, J. M., Hayes, P., Jeffers, R., Johnson, M., Kulkarni, S., Breedy, M. R., Lott, J., Bunch, L. (2003). DAML reality check: A case study of KAoS domain and policy services. *Submitted to the International Semantic Web Conference (ISWC 03).* Sanibel Island, FL, USA.

[70]   Vanderbilt, A. (1952/1963). *Amy Vanderbilt's New Complete Book of Etiquette: The Guide to Gracious Living.* Garden City, NY: Doubleday and Company.

[71]   Verhagen, H. (2001). Norms and artificial agents. Sixth Meeting of the Special Interest Group on Agent-Based Social Simulation, ESPRIT Network of Excellence on Agent-Based Computing. Amsterdam, Holland, http://abss.cfpm.org/amsterdam-01/abssnorms.pdf.

[72]   Weld, D., Etzioni, O. (1994). The firsts law of robotics: A call to arms. Proceedings of the National Conference on Artificial Intelligence (AAAI 94), (pp. 1042-1047).

[73]   Wohlmuth, P. C. (1995). Traveling the highway: Sources of momentum in behavioral regulation. Journal of Contemporary Legal Issues, 6, 1-9.

Using Swarm Intelligence in Linda Systems*

Robert Tolksdorf[1] and Ronaldo Menezes[2]

[1] Freie Universität Berlin
Institut für Informatik
AG Netzbasierte Informationssysteme
Takustr. 9, D-14195 Berlin, Germany
research@robert-tolksdorf.de
[2] Florida Institute of Technology
Department of Computer Sciences
150 W. University Blvd., Melbourne, FL 32901, USA
rmenezes@cs.fit.edu

Abstract. Natural forming multi-agent systems can grow to enormous sizes and perform seemingly complex tasks without the existence of any centralized control. Their success comes from the fact that agents are simple and the interaction with the environment and neighboring agents is local in nature. We describe how swarm intelligence can be used in the implementation of a Linda-based system called *SwarmLinda*. We argue that SwarmLinda achieves many desired characteristics such as scalability, adaptiveness and even some level of fault-tolerance.

1 Introduction

In the past 20 years, coordination models, and in particular Linda, have proven to be quite successful in tackling the intricacies of medium-to-large-scale open systems. Yet, Linda systems may not scale well with the number of tuple spaces and processes. One of the reasons for the poor scalability is that the design of these systems still inherits ideas from early Linda systems [1, 2] which were focused on parallel computing.

In the quest for identifying systems that are scalable we turned away from standard techniques and looked in the field of Biology, more specifically Zoology where one can find several examples of scalable natural forming multi-agents systems (aka Swarms). Swarms are notorious for their organization despite their enormous sizes. Their activities are based on simple rules that can be easily implemented as computer programs. Their interaction involves only local communications.

We focus on the use of swarm-based techniques (such as approaches based on ant-colonies [3]) in tuple space systems. Our goal is to tackle the scalability problem studying how to improve the current scenario using techniques adapted from models originating from biological collective organisms.

---

* This work has been partially funded by the DAAD (Germany) and the NSF (USA) contract numbers D/03/34491 and INT-0337161 respectively.

A. Omicini, P. Petta, and J. Pitt (Eds.): ESAW 2003, LNAI 3071, pp. 49–65, 2004.
© Springer-Verlag Berlin Heidelberg 2004

Fig. 1. Centralized tuple spaces

1.1 Scalability of Linda Systems

Scalability of tuple space systems is a well studied topic. Studies range from theoretical works [4] to implementations of tuple-space systems that claim to be scalable [5, 6], to studies on the suitability of these systems to wide-area computing [7].

Theoretical works tend to formalize the concept of tuple spaces and use the formalism as a way to show how tuples should be distributed. For instance, Obreiter and Gräf [4] argue that scalability can be achieved by organizing tuples in servers based on the tuples' structure. In the practical arena, Rowstron did several works attempting to make Linda systems more scalable [8, 6]. His approach is based on the idea of configuring tuple spaces hierarchically and classifying them into local and global tuple spaces.

As an illustration of the communication overhead in existing Linda implementations, consider the problem of retrieving a tuple (based on a given template) from a set of remote servers. A common approach is to ask a set of servers for matching tuples by some multicast. Each server searches, matches and locks the candidate tuples while it offers them to the requestor. This scheme establishes a state "tuple under request" which is global to the set of servers and the requestor.

The above approaches assume that improved scalability depends solely on the way the data is distributed. To be of use to Linda systems, these data-oriented techniques need to be augmented with other concepts to minimize the communication overhead.

1.2 Distributing Linda

The literature on describes a plethora of approaches for distributing tuple spaces:

- *Centralization* is a simple client-server distribution strategy where one specific server-machine operates the complete tuple space (as in TSpaces [9]). The tuple space can be accessed by clients that are arbitrarily located on a network (see Fig. 1).
  The centralized tuple-space server has the advantage of an easy implementation that basically attaches a network interface to an otherwise non-distributed tuple-space. However, it carries all the disadvantages of any centralization of services.
- *Partitioning* of tuple spaces is the strategy to co-locate tuples with common characteristics in one of a set of tuple-space servers; requests with the same characteristics are then routed towards that node (see Fig. 2). While simple

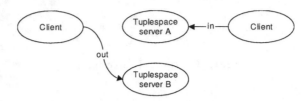

Fig. 2. Partitioned tuple spaces

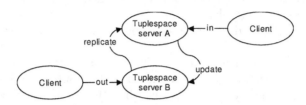

Fig. 3. Full replication

partitioning might lead to unbalanced partitions, a carefully chosen hashing function on tuples can do better [10].

Partitioning provides a distributed management of tuple spaces including concurrent execution of operations on the partitions. But it does include centralization for certain sets of tuple and handles reconfigurations very poorly.

- *Full replication* places complete copies of tuple spaces on several nodes at different locations. Any addition and removal of data has to be replicated to all nodes so that searches for data can be performed locally (see Fig. 3). It distributes the load for data-searches and offers some support for fault-tolerance. However, the cost of keeping the replicas consistent is high and it requires locking protocols or equivalents [11].
- *Intermediate replication* is a schema that uses a grid of nodes formed by logical intersecting "busses" [12]. Each node is part of exactly one *outbus* and one *inbus*. Data is replicated on all nodes of the outbus, whereas searches are performed on the inbus. As inbusses intersects all outbusses, they provides a complete view of the tuple space (see Fig. 4).

  This scheme allows for as many concurrent replications and searches for data as there are out- and inbusses respectively. The removal of some data, however, requires a consistent update on all nodes on the respective outbus.

None of these approaches are long-term solutions. Our proposal is SwarmLinda.

2   Concepts of a SwarmLinda

Over the past few years, new models originating from biology have been studied in the field of computer science [13, 14, 15, 16]. The primary interest lies on using these models as techniques for finding feasible solutions to NP-hard problems.

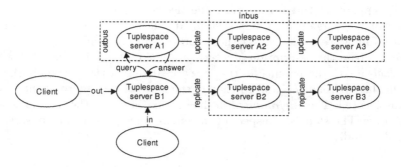

Fig. 4. Intermediate replication

In these models, actors (ants, termite, etc.) sacrifice individual goals (if any) for the benefit of the collective. They act extremely decentralized. The work is carried out by making purely local decisions and by taking actions that require only very small computations. These characteristics alone enable these systems to scale very well. This *swarm intelligence* is an interesting opportunity to rethink scalability of tuple spaces.

The use of such principles as an alternative to data-oriented schemes could simply consist of a system where templates are modeled as ants that search for food (the matching tuples). One can understand the "world" of Linda servers as a two-dimensional space in which ants search for food, leaving trails to successful matches.

With an ant-based optimization of the trails, shortest tuple-producer/-consumer paths can be found and used to optimize system performance: instead of querying sets of replicas, the "template-ant" goes directly to where it expects a match. Technically, this accounts to a single message interchange between the producing and consuming sites.

The above is just an illustration. A more realistic SwarmLinda should consider a few principles that can be observed in most swarm systems [3]:

Simplicity: Swarm individuals are simple creatures that perform simple tasks. They do no deep reasoning and implement a small and set of simple rules. The execution of these rules leads to the emergence of complex behavior. Active entities in a SwarmLinda should also obey the principle of simplicity and be "small" in terms of resource usage.

Dynamism: Natural swarms adapt to dynamically changing environments. In open distributed systems, the configuration of running applications and services changes over time. If a tuple is found in a given location it does not necessarily mean that other similar tuples will exist in the same location in the future.

Locality: Swarm individuals observe their direct neighborhood and take decisions based on their local view. As the key to scalability in SwarmLinda, active entities have to perform only local searches and inquire only to direct neighbors.

To fully appreciate these principles, one needs to understand how a Swarm-Linda should be organized. Linda systems do not have the idea of ants or food. A SwarmLinda needs to abstract these concepts in the Linda world.

We will base the description of a SwarmLinda on the following abstractions. *Individuals* are the active entities that are able to observe their neighborhood, to move in the environment, and to change the state of the environment in which they are located. The *environment* is the context in which the individuals work and observe. The *state* is an aspect of the environment that can be observed and changed by individuals.

3   Algorithms for a SwarmLinda

We can now focus on bringing the concepts above to life by defining the concrete environment and its state, and the individuals and the rules they apply (based on [14, 3]). The description here is succinct. For a full description refer to [17].

3.1   Searching for Tuples

Ants look for food in the proximity of the ant hill. Once found, the food is brought to the ant hill and a trail is left so that other ants can know where food is. The ants know the way back to the ant hill because they have a short memory of the last few steps they took and also because the ant hill has a distinctive scent that can be tracked by the ants. One could view tuples as food, the locations where the tuples are stored can be seen as the terrain while the templates are seen as ants that wander in the locations in search of tuples. The ant hill is the process that executed the operation.

The individuals are the template-ants, the environment consists of tuple-space nodes whose state is composed by the tuples stored and "scent" of different kinds of templates indicating the likelihood that matches for that template are available. The scents are volatile and disappear slowly. The tuple-searching ants follow the properties below:

1. The first step is to spread the scent of the process in the node it is connected and that node's neighborhood to represent the ant hill.
2. Check for a matching tuple at the ant's current location. If a match is found, return to the origin location and leave scent for the template matched at each step. If no match is found, check the direct neighborhood for traces of the desired scent.
3. If there are no desired scents in the direct neighborhood of the ant's location around the current location, randomly choose a direction from the neighboring nodes to look for a tuple.
4. If there is a scent that indicates a direction for next step (matching scent), move one step towards that scent and start over. We achieve non-determinism by adding a small random factor in a range of $[-\xi, \xi]$ to each scent. This enables paths other that the one with the strongest scent to be chosen.

5. After each unsuccessful step without a match, the ant stops its search with a probability γ. γ is initially 0 and it is increased by some Γ with each unsuccessful step. Γ itself also increases over time. When the ant decides to stop searching, it takes one of three actions:

   (a) Sleep for some time and then continue.
   (b) Die and be reborn after some time at the location the search started.
   (c) Materialize in some other random location and continue to search for tuples.

   Which action to take depends on the age of the ant. After it has slept several times, it tries a rebirth. After some re-births, it decides to rematerialize elsewhere.

The result of the above is the emergence of application specific paths between tuple producers and consumers. Given that scents are volatile, the paths found can dynamically adapt to changes in the system – when consumers or producers join, leave or move within the system.

An additional concept needs to be mentioned: ants do not tend to change their direction radically – given no influence of scents. If an ant comes from one direction, the opposite direction has the highest probability to be chosen.

Compare this searching approach with a hashing mechanism. Tuples are normally searched based on a hash function that takes the template as the input and generate a location where the tuple can be found. Hashing is definitely fast but unfortunately not very adaptive. The determinism that exist in hash functions forces tuples with the same template to *always* be placed in the same location no matter the size of the system, thus causing bottleneck problems if tuples matching such template are highly demanded.

In SwarmLinda, tuples matching the same template rather *tend* to stay together. However, if such tuples are being produced in locations that are far enough from each other the tuples will remain separated and clusters across the system will be created. This should avoid the creation of bottlenecks when tuples of a certain template are required by several processes. As searches will be started from various locations, tuples should be retrieved from the closest cluster of tuples.

Another problem with hashing approaches is that they are not fault tolerant. When using swarming, failures are just another change in the environment – they behave like ants trying to search for food in a food supply that was suddenly destroyed.

3.2 Distribution Mechanism

Another area of SwarmLinda where swarming abstractions may be used is in the distribution of tuples amongst the nodes. Historically, tuples have been distributed using various *static* mechanisms (see Section 1.2). In SwarmLinda the partitioning of tuple spaces can be dynamic using the ants concept of brood sorting.

Ants are able to sort different kinds of things kept in the ant hill such as food, larvae, eggs, etc. In an ant hill these are normally sorted by their type. More importantly, ants do this process in spite of the amount of each type, thus being very scalable. The individuals that operate here are tuple-ants (as opposed to template-ants). The environment is unchanged – it remains as a network of nodes. The state is the set of tuples stored.

A SwarmLinda implementation may use brood sorting for tuple distribution. In this process, tuples are the food and the ant is the active process representing an out:

1. Upon the execution of an out primitive, start visiting the nodes.
2. Observe the kind of tuples (the template they match) the nodes store. Each out-ant should have a limited memory to base that decision on local information.
3. Store the tuple in the node if nearby nodes store tuples matching the same template. Again this decision also considers a small random factor $[-\xi, \xi]$.
4. If nearby nodes do not contain similar tuples, randomly choose (using the random factor) whether to drop or continue to carry the tuple to another node.

To guarantee that the steps above work well, certain conditions must be satisfied. The out-ant should be able to store the tuple eventually. For each time the process decides *not* to store the tuple, the random factor will tend to ξ. This increases the chance of storing the tuple in the next step. Also the likelihood to store the tuple is calculated stochastically based on the kinds of objects in memory – if most of the objects in memory are similar to the one being carried out the likelihood to store the tuple becomes very high.

The power of this approach shows when it is compared with the partitioning scheme from Section 1.2 since it can improve the availability of the system without counting on costly techniques such data replication. In the ant-based approach, there are no assumptions about the behavior of applications, there are no pre-defined distribution schema, and there are no special scenarios implemented to deal with failures in the node.

3.3   Dealing with Openness

Openness is known to be one of the main challenges in distributed systems – the ability of a system to deal with changes can be a great asset. For SwarmLinda to show adaptive behavior for collections of similar tuples, we again use tuple-ants as the individuals and the environment as the terrain of nodes that has scents as the state.

For a SwarmLinda, we want tuples matching the same template to be kept together (as described in Section 3.2) but we do not want them to be fixed to a given location. Consider a function $Sc : T \to S$ on templates and tuples and a relation $C : S \times S$ on scent that defines similarity of scent. When template te and tuple tu match, then $Sc(te), Sc(tu) \in C$.

1. A new tuple-ant that carries a tuple tu emits $Sc(tu)$ at its origin. A new template-ant that carries a template te emits $Sc(te)$ at its origin.
2. Template-ants remain at that position and never move.
3. Tuple-ants sense their environment for a scent similar to $Sc(tu)$ – as given by C. If there is such scent, then other template- or tuple-ants are around.
4. Based on the strength of the detected scent plus the small random factor $[-\xi, \xi]$, the tuple-ant decides to move into that direction or to stay where it is.

The above properties causes tuples to stay closer to where other similar tuples are needed or are being produced even if this consists of migrating from one node to another. This would affect on the distribution mechanism explained in Section 3.2. When a tuple is being stored, the scent left by in and out primitives should also be considered when deciding to drop the tuple in the current node or to keep "walking" through the nodes searching for a good place to drop the tuple.

3.4   Balancing Tuple- and Template Movement

So far, we always identified either the tuple-ants or the template-ants as individuals that move and perform a continued search. Here we describe an intermediate approach where ants can be both tuples and templates. Every tuple- and template-ant decides after its birth whether it goes out to other nodes seeking matches or stays at its origin until it is found by some other ant.

Consider an application where a node consumes a lot of tuples that are generated on other nodes. If trails from the producers to the consumer are found, it makes no sense to have the consumer start template-ants that seek the producers. Based on the system history (of scents), it is known where a consumer is and what the path is, so tuple-ants should be started there while the template-ants at the consumer should remain stationary and wait for a matching tuple-ant. But if the former consumer starts to be a producer after the calculation of some results, it becomes reasonable to start template-ants from the former producers to search for the result.

For the algorithm, the individuals are tuple- and template-ants. The environment is the terrain of nodes. Their states include two scents: The *visitor scent* indicates whether the location is visited successfully by other ants (it is an attraction) or not (it is an outsider). Success means that the visiting ant found matches at this location. The *producer-consumer scent* ranges over $[-\phi, \phi]$. Positive values indicate that the matches that took place were such that a visiting template-ant retrieved a tuple from that location – showing that the location is a producer of information. A negative scent indicates that visiting tuple-ants were matched with a template – the location is a consumer of tuples.

Tuple- and template-ants follow the algorithms from Section 3.1 to find matching templates resp. tuples. If a tuple-ant finds a match, it neutralizes a bit of producer-consumer scent at the location. When a template-ant finds a match, it adds a bit of this scent at the location. Both kinds of ants leave a bit of visitor scent in the case of success.

New ants are either tuple- or a template-ants depending on the kind of operation requested. A new tuple-ant emits a bit of producer-consumer scent at the location of its birth, a template-ant neutralizes some. These ants can behave in two different ways: Either they are active and move around following the search algorithms as described above, or they are passive and remain at their origin to be found by others.

The further fate of a new ant depends on the current state of their location based on the visitor- and producer-consumer-scent:

	Producer	Consumer
Attraction	Passive tuple-ant	Passive/active template-ant
	Active/passive tuple-ant	Passive template-ant
Outsider	Active tuple-ant	Passive template-ant
	Passive tuple-ant	Active template-ant

If a producer is visited by many ants, there is no need to send out tuple-ants. Template-ants can be passive too as many visitors satisfy them, but also active to establish a global balance. The ratio passive/active could be adjusted. For an attractive consumer, template-ants can remain passive. Tuple-ants might be active with the same argument on a global balance. If a producer is only rarely visited, it will send out its tuples-ants to find matches. Its template-ants can remain passive as they are not many.

If a consumer is not visited by many other ants, it will send out active template-ants to find matches and generate passive tuple-ants to attract other active template-ants to improve the chance of becoming an attraction.

3.5   Analysis

The algorithms described in this demonstrate the power of swarm abstractions in the context of Linda systems. In particular, SwarmLinda appears to be efficient dealing with (at least) the following issues:

Scalability: The decisions taken by ants are based on local observations like sensing the direct environment or asking the currently visited node for a match. State changes are also purely local like changing the scent at the current or directly surrounding locations. There are no global states like locking at a set of nodes. With that, the activities of the algorithms are independent of the number of active ants.

Adaptiveness: The decisions taken by ants are based on the current state of the system. This state is changed based on decisions of individuals in the system by leaving fresh scent at locations. The influence of prior decisions becomes smaller over time with the evaporation of old scent. The state therefore reflect the current configuration of the system in terms of where and what kind of tuples are produced and consumed. The behavior of the ants dynamically adapts to this configurations.

Fault-Tolerance: The influence of wrong decisions of ants are only temporary. Changes in scent based on wrong decisions also vanish over time with the evaporation. In a traditional Linda-system, specialized processes have to take care of fault-detection and correction and often even the coordination language is extended. A SwarmLinda is fault-tolerant through adaptiveness, which also improves the availability of the system. Failures in nodes are treated by the ants as changes in the system's configuration.

Load Balancing: Adaptation to the current configuration of tuple production and consumption does not lead to bottlenecks in the system. As shown, the load in terms of activity of ants can also be dynamically adjusted by simple local decisions.

4   Implementing SwarmLinda

This section breaks down the issues one faces when given a task of implementing a SwarmLinda and discusses how the current prototype has been implemented and some of the alternatives that can be used to implement what we refer to as a *full* SwarmLinda.

4.1   Network Topology

In all the algorithms defined in Section 3, it is assumed that SwarmLinda nodes are organized in a terrain in which tuple- and template-ants can walk. However, a particular network topology is never mentioned. This was not by chance. The *swarming* only requires the nodes to be connected but their degree of connectivity (ie. how many other nodes they are directly connected to) is not specified. The connectivity of the nodes creates a *neighborhood* for each node.

In the current implementation of SwarmLinda, the topology is fixed and the degree of connectivity of each node is uniform across all nodes. The nodes are organized in a two-dimensional grid as this reasonably represents a terrain used in ant-based algorithms. In practice though, the actual topology may not be as well organized with exactly N × M nodes since the system has to work with any number of nodes.

A full SwarmLinda is not restricted to a N-dimensional grid nor to a uniform number of neighbors – nodes can keeps a dynamic list of neighbors. For a random walk, ants choose one of the entries in the list at random and use it as the direction for a next step.

There is a tradeoff between the number of neighbors and the performance of the algorithms, since more neighbors lower the probability of taking the "right" direction by random. In a full SwarmLinda, this could be subject to another adaptation mechanism. The mentioned tradeoff can be quantified by introducing a notion of "fitness" of nodes. It is calculated from factors such as how often a node simply routes ants through to other nodes – slowing them down and lowering the fitness of the node – or how many matches occur at the node –

more matches raise the fitness factor. Based on such a factor, a node could for example tell its neighbors about shortcuts.

This can be easily integrated to the dynamic update of routine entries. When a substantial number of ants coming from node A always go to node B but find no match there and go on to node C, node B can detect this and establish a shortcut from A to C. To do so, it tells the ants to change their origin information for the walk from B to C. If they carry A as the origin information, node C learns about A. When a first ant goes from C to A, node A will learn about C and a shortcut can develop.

The maintenance of the neighbor list is essential for the algorithms and the method utilized must reflect the adaptiveness of the system and also take into consideration that nodes may be down or not working properly. Currently SwarmLinda implements something that is very similar to the algorithms used to keep routing tables in networks up-to-date. Each node maintains a list of nodes in its neighborhood. When a new node is started, it connects to another node which is already part of the current network and request its neighbor list. The new node then picks the node it connected to and N-1 of its neighbors to build its own neighbor list. A neighbor list is also broadcasted to each of the neighbors when changes in the list need to be propagated.

For a full SwarmLinda, the routing lists would also underlie the principles of dynamic adaptation. First of all, the neighborhood relation does not have to be implemented as symmetric. It can well be that node A knows of node B as a neighbor while B does not know about A. The movement of tuples itself would distribute the neighborhood information by carrying a reference to the node they came from. If an ant moves from A to B, it will tell B that it came from A. Then, B updates its neighborhood information accordingly. The benefit from this is the relaxation of consistency requirements among the neighborhood lists. Given a uniform tuple/ant-movement, the lists will converge finally.

The neighborhood information should not be fixed. An entry to A in the neighborhood list of B should vanish slowly over time unless it is refreshed by another ant/tuple coming from A. Also, at the system level, failed attempts to contact A should lead to an even stronger evaporation of the entry. Thereby the routing tables adapt to both failure and system communication structures.

The details of the scheme and their calibration remain open. Critical is the initialization of the routing tables. One approach would be to have a new node N contact exactly one node M, being entered as a neighbor of M and copying its neighborhood list. N would be eventually entered into the neighborhood tables of the surrounding nodes. Another important issue is the control of lower and upper bounds in the number of neighbors of a node. Although it is desirable for the neighborhood configuration to be adaptable to changes, the general conditions of swarming may have to be relaxed to avoid undesirable extremes.

4.2 Dealing with Separation of Concerns

The algorithms described in Section 3 do not assume the existence of multiple tuple spaces in the system – at no point the algorithms refer to the logical location of tuples. Does this mean that SwarmLinda is moving away from a known improvement to Linda systems? Not necessarily, although an implementation where multiple tuple spaces do not exist would be more straightforward, on the implementation level the use of multiple tuple spaces is not a complex task.

The options available on how to implement multiple tuple spaces in the context of SwarmLinda are more limited than in standard implementation. Clearly, Linda process cannot (for certain) tell whether a tuple space is physically created. If the uniqueness of the handles is guaranteed one could easily implement a Linda system were all tuples are just prefixed with the tuple spaces handle instead placing them into a physical data structure representing the tuple space.

Given that the swarm algorithms assume that all food is distributed in a flat structure, SwarmLinda would not be able to implement multiple tuple spaces by physically creating tuple spaces. The option then is to utilize the concept of prefixing all tuples with a handle – a process that is completely transparent to users. Therefore, in the implementation of SwarmLinda physical tuple spaces are not present. This is a consequence of the tuple distribution algorithm used in SwarmLinda which attempts to be adaptive and independent of any clustering imposed by the user such as the definition of tuple spaces.

In a full SwarmLinda, however, the adaptation might take advantage of the fact that tuples in the same logical subspace "belong" together for some application specific reason. Therefore, it might be a useful optimization to use the handle when placing tuples or template. For example, the algorithm from section 3.2 can be extended by weighting the handle-field very strong when determining the similarity of tuples.

4.3   Movement of Ants

All algorithms described earlier depend on the movement of tuple- and template-ants. The prime question here is how a decision can be made with regards to how ants decide their next step. In the currently prototype, the ants interact with the environment to decide what is the best suited neighbor node to move to. The suitability of the neighbor is computed based on two aspects:

Scent strength of the neighbor: The scent strength for a particular tuple type (template) is kept as a characteristic of each node. When an ant decides to move to another node, it exchanges local messages with the neighboring nodes. The scent strength for that type is then used as a probability that the ant will choose to move to that location.

Direction system: In some cases the scent alone may not have the desired effect. In fact, it is known that real ants also have an internal direction system. That is, even when scents are not available, ants *tend* to walk in straight lines – if an ant is moving towards direction D it is least likely to choose for the next step the direction $-D$ (minus D).

Since the environment of the current implementation is a two-dimensional grid, the direction system and the scent level can also be seen as a grid of values around

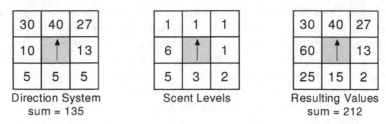

Fig. 5. Scent levels in the neighborhood

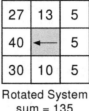

Fig. 6. Rotated direction system

the current position of the ant (shown as shaded in Figures 5 and 6). Figure 5 is an example of the direction system and scent levels currently implemented in SwarmLinda.

The idea is simple, a direction system is pre-determined and fixed for the entire system. In swarming terms, this represents a system where all ants belong to the same species and therefore follow the same direction system. Currently, we are using a system of values that (under the absence of a scent) make an ant less likely to change its direction radically. For instance, observe the leftmost picture in Figure 5 and assume that the current direction of the ant is as indicated in by the arrow. Given these conditions, the direction system indicates that the ant has a 40/135 chance of keeping the same direction as opposed to 5/135 chance of choosing the exactly opposite direction.

This system is always augmented with the information about the scent level of the neighborhood (middle picture in Figure 5). Once combined, they produce the final direction system which will be used for the next step of that particular ant. For instance in the scenario depicted, the ant has a 60/212 change of moving west and only 40/212 chance of keep moving in the same direction (north).

Once the ant decides about the next move, the direction system may have to rotate to represent the initial idea correctly. In Figure 5 we argued that the reason for the higher chance of an ant moving north was due the fact that ants *tend* to keep the same direction. However, if it decides to take a different direction, the direction system must remain consistent with the change. For instance, assume that after the resulting values were calculated the ant indeed moved west. In this new position the direction system should reflect the fact that for the next step the ant will have a 40/135 chance of keep moving west. The direction system rotates to the configuration shown in Figure 6.

The relaxation of the approach to allow as many directions as necessary may hinder the use of the direction system idea as described above. Following the "swarming" idea, one could adapt the direction system to a system of success. Note that the scent is not an indication of the path taken by the previous ants but rather the path used by returning ants. So if we assume no evaporation of scents, a scent of value S indicates that S ants returned via that node after successfully finding the tuple/template they looked for. This does not necessarily mean that S ants took that path *before* finding the tuple/template.

Indeed the scent has an influence on the decision of an ant but we also want to have a secondary value that indicates the probability of an ant to move in situations where scent values are inexistent or too similar. A secondary scent-like value can be stored in the environment keeping track on the number of ants that took that particular direction. This should be represented using a delta vector (see description in the next section). For instance, a vector could have the values $(12, 5, 1, 3, 4)$ indicating that 12 ants that reached that node decided to go to neighbor 1, 5 ants decided to go to neighbor 2, and so on. These values can now be used in a similar fashion as the direction system described above – used as probabilities. In this example ant ant would have 12/25 chance of going to neighbor 1, 5/25 chance of going to neighbor 2, and so on.

4.4   Ant Activity and the Environment

The environment keeps a state which can be sensed by the ants. It has several dimensions, making it possible to drop different kinds of scents for different information. The state observable at a place in the neighborhood of an ant is a vector consisting of intensity values of different scents. We currently assume a fixed dimension of this vector.

Every ant operates in a cycle: *(i)* observe environment, *(ii)* plan change of environment and *(iii)* change environment. The observation results in a vector for each neighborhood environment location. A complete observation leads to a matrix of vectors which represents the environment-matrix at the time of observation.

The ant then has to generate a delta-vector that reflects the changes planned to the environment. To drop a unit of scent of kind 2 at the current location, the respective delta vector could be $(0, 1, 0, 0)$ for a four dimensional state. All delta-vectors together form a delta-matrix. In the final step, the change is applied by adding the delta-matrix to the environment matrix in an atomic step.

While in the current algorithms described ants always add one unit of scent to their environment, we do not restrict our change system to that. Ant that follow other algorithms could also drop five units of scent with a vector $(0, 5, 0, 0)$ for example when they perform a `collect` operation and carry more than one tuple.

The atomic addition of the delta matrix ensures that ants can operate concurrently. In some future algorithms they can even neutralize changes, for example when another ant adds the delta vector $(0, -5, 0, 0)$ to the current location.

The evaporation of scent is implemented by periodic application of vectors on each location, for example $(-1, -1, -1, -1)$ if all scents are greater that 0. Spreading scent can be implemented by a similar delta-matrix.

4.5   Lifecycle of Ants

The description above makes it clear how ants communicate with the environment but one still needs to discuss when they are created and why do they cease to exist (die).

One can consider ants as mobile agents (or mobile processes). Although this is an implementation choice, it is not necessarily the only one. In fact, in the current implementation ants are messages transmitted between the nodes of the network.

Tuple-ants are messages created when "storing" primitives are executed (eg. out). Once a tuple-ant is created, it is inserted in the network from some initial node. From that point onwards, the node will decide whether the ant should drop its food (the tuple contained in the message) locally or whether the message should be transmitted to one of the neighbor nodes. The decision follows the algorithms described in Section 3.

Each tuple-ant has a delta value that is incremented every time the ant is routed to a new node. The larger this delta value becomes the greater is the likelihood the tuple will be stored at that location. Template-ants on the other hand, are created when a "retrieving" primitive is executed (eg. in, rdp). Similarly to tuple-ants, these are also implemented as messages that are routed through the nodes. The difference here is the consequence of the delta value. Unlike the case with tuple-ants, template-ants cannot just be abandoned (or stored in the case of tuples). In Linda-systems, a request for a tuple must be fulfilled (or fail in the case of non-blocking primitives).

In the current implementation, the delta-value is used to determine failure. If a template-ant dies, it reports the failure to the originating process which uses the failure message as the return value for the primitive executed (in the case of inp, rdp).

For the case of primitives that must be fulfilled the template-ant behaves as in the algorithm described in Section 3.1. If a template-ant reaches a failure mode, the node places the message in a "sleep list". This represents the templates-ants that could not find a matching tuple. The sleep time may allow the status of the system to change and matching tuples to be stored. After a few unsuccessful sleeps, the template-ant is destroyed and the message is recreated in the original source. Another option after several recreations is for the template-ant to "warp" to a completely random node somewhere and restart the search algorithm there. This last step has not yet been implemented in SwarmLinda as its benefits are not yet clear since it can create "false" paths.

In future implementations, we want to deal better with Linda specific characteristics such as blocking. Currently blocking is "simulated" but not really implemented. As described in above ants will keep searching until a matching tuple is found. A problem that might happen with this approach is that if a tuple does not really exist in the system, the approach where templates keep looking for it may be naive and costly. A possible approach is to use the aging mechanism embedded in template-ants to decide that the template should, instead of keep searching, stop and diffuse its scent at that location (characterizing the blocking) thus not wasting the system's resources. Future tuple-ants should then be able to track the scent of the template-ants and unblock them if a match takes place.

5   Conclusion

This paper described approaches for implementing a Linda systems using swarm intelligence, SwarmLinda. The paper demonstrated that organized behavior in SwarmLinda can be implemented based on a few simple rules that mimic naturally forming multi-agents systems. We claimed that the use of swarm abstractions in an implementation of SwarmLinda would not only be simple but will improve its scalability and adaptiveness.

The algorithms presented here provide an alternative to the standard approaches used in various Linda implementations. The algorithms follow three principles that can be observed in most swarm-based systems: simplicity, dynamism and locality.

Implementations and other publications related to SwarmLinda will be made available in the SwarmLinda Project website [18].

References

[1] Gelernter, D.: Generative Communication in Linda. ACM Transactions on Programming Languages and Systems **7** (1985) 80–112   49
[2] Gelernter, D.: Multiple tuple spaces in Linda. In Odijk, E., Rem, M., Syre, J.C., eds.: PARLE '89, Vol. II: Parallel Languages. LNCS 366 (1989) 20–27   49
[3] Parunak, H.: "Go to the ant": Engineering principles from natural multi-agent systems. Annals of Operations Research **75** (1997) 69–101   49, 52, 53
[4] Obreiter, P., Gräf, G.: Towards scalability in tuple spaces. In: Proceedings of the 2002 Symposium on Applied Computing, ACM (2002) 344–350   50
[5] Zambonelli, F., Corradi, A., Leonardi, L.: A scalable tuple space model for structured parallel programming. In: Proc. of the 1995 2nd Int'l Conf. on Programming Models for Massively Parallel Computers. (1995)   50
[6] Rowstron, A.: WCL: A co-ordination language for geographically distributed agents. World Wide Web **1** (1998) 167–179   50
[7] Menezes, R., Tolksdorf, R., Wood, A.: Coordination and scalability. In Omicini, A., Zambonelli, F., Klusch, M., Tolksdorf, R., eds.: Coordination of Internet Agents: Models, Technologies, and Applications. Springer Verlag (2001) 299–319   50

[8] Rowstron, A., Wood, A.: Bonita: a set of tuple space primitives for distributed coordination. In: Proc. HICSS30, Sw Track, Hawaii, IEEE Computer Society Press (1997) 379–388 50

[9] Wyckoff, P., McLaughry, S., Lehman, T., Ford, D.: T spaces. IBM Systems Journal **37** (1998) 454–474 50

[10] Bjornson, R.: Linda on Distributed Memory Multiprocessors. PhD thesis, Yale University Department of Computer Science (1992) Technical Report 931 51

[11] Corradi, A., Leonardi, L., Zambonelli, F.: Strategies and protocols for highly parallel linda servers. Software: Practice and Experience **28** (1998) 51

[12] Carriero, N., Gelernter, D.: The s/net's linda kernel. ACM Transactions on Computer Systems **4** (1986) 110–129 51

[13] Resnick, M.: Turtles, Termites, and Traffic Jams. MIT Press (1994) 51

[14] Bonebeau, E., Dorigo, M., Theraulaz, G.: Swarm Intelligence: From Natural to Artificial Systems. Oxford Press (1999) 51, 53

[15] Dorigo, M., Maniezzo, V., Colorni, A.: The ant system: Optimization by a colony of cooperating agents. IEEE Transactions on Systems, Man, and Cybernetics Part B: Cybernetics **26** (1996) 29–41 51

[16] Kennedy, J., Eberhart, R.C.: Swarm Intelligence. Morgan Kaufmann (2001) 51

[17] Menezes, R., Tolksdorf, R.: A new approach to scalable Linda-systems based on Swarms (extended version). Technical Report CS-2003-04, Florida Institute of Technology, Department of Computer Sciences (2003) http://www.cs.fit.edu/ tr/cs-2003-04.pdf 53

[18] Menezes, R., Tolksdorf, R.: The SwarmLinda Project Website. (2003) http://cs.fit.edu/˜rmenezes/SwarmLinda 64

Engineering Democracy in Open Agent Systems

Peter McBurney[1] and Simon Parsons[2]

[1] Department of Computer Science
University of Liverpool
Liverpool L69 7ZF UK
p.j.mcburney@csc.liv.ac.uk
[2] Department of Computer and Information Science
Brooklyn College, City University of New York
Brooklyn NY 11210 USA
parsons@sci.brooklyn.cuny.edu

Abstract. How should open agent societies be organized? Should they
be democracies, and, if so, what types of democracy? We present three
normative models of democracy from political philosophy and consider
their relevance for the engineering of open multi-agent systems: democracy as wise rule by an elite; democracy as the exercise of rational consumer choices by voters; and democracy as deliberative decision-making
by citizens. We consider the implications of these different models for the
design of open systems, in terms of the communications language, the
interaction protocol, and the conflict-resolution mechanism used by the
agents involved. We also consider the issue of verifiability of the internal
semantics of communications languages, and argue that a model of agent
democracy based on deliberative democracy provides the basis for a form
of verifiability which is stronger than a social semantics.

1 Introduction

Open agent systems are multi-agent systems with open admissions policies and
therefore potentially fluid membership. Entry may require compliance with particular stated conventions, such as use of an agent communication language and
interaction protocol, or the making of a financial deposit. However, subject only
to such conventions, any agent may join. Because such agents may represent
different human principals and typically will have been constructed by different
software design teams, they may, in general, have conflicting goals, interests,
beliefs and values. In these circumstances, which agent's goals or beliefs prevail
in the interaction will depend on the nature of the social and political relationships between the participants. In situations where the agents adhere to some
hierarchical relationship inside the agent system, that agent or agents at the top
of the hierarchy may have final decision-making authority. For example, in an
auction interaction, the auctioneer may have the explicit power to determine the
final allocation of the scarce resources being sought by the bidders. Power such

A. Omicini, P. Petta, and J. Pitt (Eds.): ESAW 2003, LNAI 3071, pp. 66–80, 2004.
© Springer-Verlag Berlin Heidelberg 2004

as this may not reside in particular agents, but accrue to certain roles within the agent system, as in the electronic institutions of [1].

However, if human interaction is any guide, in many open environments there will either be no such hierarchy, or what hierarchies there are may be contested by some participants. Indeed, this is already true of existing agent societies on the Internet. What structures are appropriate for agent societies in these circumstances? The absence of hierarchy means that the relationship between the participants is closer to one of equality; this in turn suggests that some form of democracy is appropriate when we consider the structure of these agent systems. Within the discipline of political philosophy, human democracy is a notion much debated, and there are several alternative normative theories of democracy [2]. In this paper, we explore these alternatives from political theory, in order to identify what structures they provide for, and what constraints they place on, designers of multi-agent systems. A designer of an open agent system intending to permit democratic participation by the agents in the system therefore has a choice of forms of democracy to encode in the system; indeed, an agent society may encode forms other than those studied by political philosophers. In Section 2 we present the three primary normative theories of democracy developed by political philosophers, and then discuss, in Section 3, their implications for the design of open agent systems. It happens that one theory, the Deliberative Model of democracy, stresses the joint and discursive nature of decision-making in a democracy, with participants exchanging arguments for and against various policy proposals, and forming preferences on the basis of these exchanges. The structure that this model provides to the agent system designer creates the means necessary to develop a strong form of social semantics, thereby increasing the extent to which a mentalistic semantics of an agent communications languages can be verified. This view is explained in Section 4. The paper concludes with a summary in Section 5.

2   Three Models of Democracy

Political philosophers have articulated several normative models of democracy, and we present here the three most influential. The problem they confront was first formulated in an abstract form by philosopher Jean-Jacques Rousseau [3], who viewed a polity as comprising just two entities: *Society* and *the State*. Society is the collection of individuals, organizations and companies in a polity, together with the panoply of relationships between them, while the State is the apparatus of public-sector administration. The key question for political theory is then: *What should be the process of formation of political will?* or *How should Society program the State?*[1] Supporters of democracy believe that these questions should be answered with the use of democratic procedures, such as elections based on universal adult suffrage. But if such procedures are used, what is the nature of the relationship between citizens and their elected representatives? Rousseau

---

[1] Note that use of the word "program" in this context is not due to our computational perspective, but is the usage of political philosophers [4, p. 239].

had assumed that the people have a single "general will" which their elected representatives should seek to implement, but this is at best only a high-level approximation to the multifarous cacophony which is modern democracy.[2]

The first modern political theory of democracy which sought to answer this question was proposed in 1942 by Austrian-American economist Joseph Schumpeter [5]. Schumpeter's theory, possibly in reaction to the mass populism of Nazism and Communism and to his own failed political career, was disdainful of ordinary people and their views: *"Thus the typical citizen drops down to a lower level of mental performance as soon as he enters the political field. He argues and analyzes in a way which he would readily recognize as infantile within the sphere of his real interests. He becomes a primitive again."* [5, p. 262]. Consequently, Schumpeter proposed that elected officials should act as a technocratic elite, making decisions on behalf of the general public and in accordance with what the elite believes are the public's best interests. Apart from voting, the people are entirely passive in Schumpeter's model of democracy, which has rightly acquired the label *elitist* [2, p. x]. We call this the *Wise Elite Model* of democracy.

In contrast to Schumpeter's hierarchical view of democracy, Anthony Downs proposed an economic-theoretic model of political will-formation in a democracy in which citizens were more than simply passive objects [6]. This model has since been called a *rational-choice* or *liberal* model [4], and it views democracy as akin to the operation of an economic market. Downs proposes a theory of democracy where political parties and interest groups act as entrepreneurs, offering alternative "products" in the form of bundles of state-instructions (or equivalently, ideologies, which are philosophies of bundle-formation), to voters who then "purchase" their preferred bundle when they vote. That bundle with the greatest "market-share" — in the form of popular votes — becomes the set of instructions used to program the State. Downs explicitly assumed that voter-consumers in a free and democratic society make their political choices on the basis of their perceived self-interest, and act according to the now-standard definition of rational economic behavior, e.g., [7, 8]. In other words, voters are assumed to always vote so as to maximize their perceived expected utility from the outcome of the election. In addition to consuming bundles of state-instructions, citizens also consume information about policies, ideologies, political parties and candidates to the extent necessary to make their voting decisions. And, as for any other good, such consumption may be subject to time-, resource-, or processing-constraints, and cost-benefit trade-offs.

The rational-choice model affords citizens a greater role than does the wise elite model, namely that of consumers of relevant political information and of recipients of the effects of policies enacted by their representatives. But citizens, in the rational-choice model of democracy, are not regarded as *producers* of political information or public policies. This viewpoint ultimately stems, we believe, from Downs' adoption of Kenneth Arrow's operational definition of economic

---

[2] Rousseau gave no procedures for identifying the general will, nor for reconciling competing interpretations of it. Accordingly, we do not discuss his model further here.

rationality [7], which assumes that a decision-maker's preferences and utilities are given and precede the task of selection of a decision-option. In many, if not all, public policy determinations, however, the preferences and utilities of voters may only be formed in the very process of decision-making, as participants learn about feasible decision-options and about the effects of various decision-options on one another and on others not involved in the decision process, as argued in [9] . Moreover, to the extent that one person's utility depends on the welfare or preferences of others, a rational, resource-unconstrained, voter would not finally determine his or her preferences until hearing from those others about their own utilities and preferences.[3] Insofar as preferences can only be determined jointly, or require information not available to everyone, multi-party deliberation therefore cannot be undertaken by individuals reasoning alone, as the rational-choice model assumes.

In contrast, the *deliberative democracy* model of political will-formation emphasizes the manner in which beliefs and preferences of participants are formed or change through the very process of interacting together [11, 12]. In this model, citizens do not merely interact to exchange their preferences at election time, and to consume political information, as is the case with the rational-choice model. Rather, they are also producers of political information and policies, as they participate in political processes and debate, identify and publicize issues of personal or social concern, exchange arguments for and against various policy options, and generally seek to influence the outcomes of political decision processes. Seeking to influence and persuade other participants means that they must themselves be open to persuasion, and thus undergo what has been called *self-transformation* [13, p. 184]. Although few studies have been conducted, there is evidence that deliberative decision-processes lead to better decision outcomes [14, 15].

The rational-choice and deliberative models of democracy embody different notions of rationality. As mentioned above, Downs' economic theory of democracy was based explicitly on Arrow's [7, Chapters 1 and 2] definition of rational behaviour as the maximization of expected perceived utility. This in turn was an operationalization of Lange's notion of rationality [8, p. 30]: *"A unit of economic decision is said to act rationally when its objective is the maximization of a magnitude."* This notion of rationality, although predominant in economics,[4] is not how the word is understood in the philosophy of argumentation [19, 20]. For example, Ralph Johnson [20, p. 14] gives this definition: *"Rationality is the ability to engage in the practice of giving and receiving reasons."* The deliberative model of democracy, because it construes democracy as the joint determination of public policy by the citizenry through debate and exchanges of views, embod-

---

[3] For example, one person's utility from a so-called network good, such as a fax machine, depends on whether or not other people have them. In so far as a purchase by one consumer sends signals to others [10], all products may be viewed as network goods to some extent.

[4] And influential in AI. It has been subject to much criticism, however; e.g., [16, 17]. Indeed, a winner of the Nobel Memorial Prize in Economics, Amartya Sen, has recently argued for a notion of rationality in economic theory which is closer to that used in the philosophy of argumentation [18].

ies the philosophers' notion of rationality rather than the economists', although the latter is not precluded. For agents who know the reasons for their own actions, the maximum-expected-utility notion of rationality is a special case of argumentation-theoretic rationality, since the method used to select an action-options can be advanced as a reason for the option by a speaker in a debate. However, the converse is not true: there may be many reasons for selecting an option which does not maximize expected utility, e.g., that it avoids catastrophic downside loss.[5]

These three models of political will-formation in a democracy can be seen as offering alternative roles to the citizens who comprise the Society. In the Wise Elite model, the people are seen as completely passive, except when choosing the Elite. In the Rational-Choice model, the people are viewed as consumers of policies, ideologies and information. In the Deliberative model, the people are viewed as both consumers and producers of policies, ideologies and political information.

3   Design Implications for MAS

Which of these theories of democracy is appropriate for the design of open multi-agent systems? The answer, of course, depends on the intended objectives of the system, and the nature of the application. In systems with differentiated agent roles and an explicit hierarchy some version of the Wise Elite model of democracy may be appropriate. An example here are public auction sites, in so far as the auctioneer makes decisions on behalf of the agents comprising the auction. Bidders have the freedom to join or not any given auction site, and so may be viewed as "electing" the elite in the form of the auctioneer. Once the auction is underway, however, bidders express preferences through their bids, and the rules of the auction mechanism may resolve these into a collective decision, rather than leaving the resolution to the wisdom of the auctioneer. Another example of the Wise Elite model is the use of agents for security and access-policing functions, similar to the space-administration objects of [21]. One can readily imagine the participants in an open agent system agreeing to delegate a limited amount of their joint power to a group of policing agents, who exercise that power in pursuit of collective aims of security and confidentiality which all agree are essential. For example, the interaction protocol rules may permit any participant to speak at any time, but a policing agent could prevent participants monopolizing the microphone by limiting usage from verbose (or badly-coded) agents. Thus, the collective goal of fair distribution of microphone access takes precedence over an individual agent's goal of exclusive use of the microphone, and the policing agents act to ensure this on behalf of all agents.

However, in most open agent systems, such voluntary ceding of power will not occur on matters of concern to the participants. Participants are likely to disagree with one another over such issues, and will wish to express their own

---

[5] Habermas [19, p. 10] calls these two notions of rationality *cognitive-instrumental* and *communicative*, respectively.

beliefs, preferences and intentions. Agent autonomy means that software agents cannot in general be *ordered* to fulfill requests; they may be requested and, at best, *persuaded* to do so. If their beliefs, preferences and intentions are pre-determined and fixed, no amount of persuasion will change these, and so the Rational Choice model of democracy would be appropriate. Here the only sensible interaction mechanism between the participating agents would be some form of preference aggregation or voting, since the exchange of reasons for beliefs or preferences would not alter decision outcomes. Auction mechanisms are examples of open multi-agent societies where agents are usually assumed to have pre-determined (although not necessarily fixed) preferences, and where no party seeks to persuade another to change these. In this case, democracy as the expression of preferences, as in the Rational Choice model, is sufficient to represent the relationships between the agents concerned.

In other domains, however, agents may well seek to influence the beliefs, preferences or intentions of others. Whenever the relationship between agents in a multi-agent system is one of equality, and where agents seek to influence the beliefs, preferences or intentions of one another, then a Deliberative model of democracy will be the most appropriate model for the design of the system. Adoption of a particular model of democracy for a multi-agent system has a number of design implications, which we explore in the next three subsections.

3.1 Communications Languages

The different models of democracy place different requirements on the communications language required for agent interaction. The Wise Elite Model requires that agents have some means to select the elite. But, other than this, no other expressions of beliefs, preference, intentions, etc, need be expressed by the participants, since all decisions are made by the elite. Under the Rational Choice model, participants express preferences for or between policy options but not necessarily arguments for these preferences. Thus, the communications language needs to be able to support the expression of preferences, either directly or by means of acceptance or rejection of particular proposals. Auction protocols, such as the FIPA ACL English auction protocol [22], typically permit the expression of preferences through utterances of acceptance of particular proposals.

Adoption of a deliberative model for democracy in a multi-agent system requires that the communications language allows each agent to express, not only its beliefs, intentions or preferences, but also its arguments for or against these. Participants require the ability to question or challenge the statements of others, and to defend and justify their own statements. Thus, the communications language needs to be able support the expression of arguments for statements, as well as expression of the statements themselves. There have been a number of proposals for agent communications languages providing this capability in recent years, e.g., [23, 24, 25].

In addition, if participants are to engage in debate with the potential to persuade one another to adopt new beliefs, intentions or preferences, then agents need to be able to withdraw prior statements and utter replacements in their stead. If one agent's goal in an interaction is to persuade a second agent of some belief which that other currently does not endorse, then the communications language should enable the second to express any changes of belief it makes as a result of the interaction; otherwise, why would the first agent seek to persuade the second? This self-transformation capability has not typically been a feature of agent communications languages or interaction protocols. In recent work [26], we proposed expression of self-transformation as a design criterion for multi-agent systems using dialogue game protocols, and assessed various interaction protocols and languages against this criterion (among others). As noted there, the FIPA Agent Communications Language FIPA ACL [27] provides only limited capability for participants to question one another and to express any changes in beliefs. Because FIPA ACL lacks retraction illocutions, changes in agent opinions can only be expressed by successive, and possibly contradictory, utterances of belief. An agent who believes the sky is blue utters an *inform* illocution to this effect; if it subsequently comes to believe the sky is red, it can only express this with a second, contradictory, *inform* illocution. How is a listener to such a sequence of contradictory utterances to interpret it? The sequence may be evidence of updated beliefs by the speaker, or it may be due to malice, whimsy, or simply faulty code. Explicit retraction locutions can ensure no such ambiguity of interpretation. Agent languages based on formal dialogue games have a better record in this regard [26], perhaps due to their origin as protocols for the conduct of debates in philosophy. However, there is still much work to be done in this area, particularly for dialogues over action rather than belief [28, 29].[6]

3.2   Interaction Protocols

We distinguish between the communications language used by the agents in an agent society to make utterances, and any rules which govern the combination of utterances, which, when combined with the language, we call the interaction protocol [31]. The FIPA ACL [27], for example, has no such rules, with the result that any utterance by any agent may follow any other by any agent. Of course, such rules may defined to overlay the FIPA ACL, as with the various auction protocols defined by FIPA, e.g., [22]. As with the communications language, the requirements placed on any interaction protocol will differ according to which model of democracy is used. Because the Wise Elite model does not require any expression of opinions or of arguments, there are no requirements on the inter-action protocol. The Rational Choice model only requires expression of opinions or preferences, and so any interaction protocol would need to enable expression of these in an orderly fashion. Auction protocols, for example, typically proceed through a series of rounds, with constraints on what can be uttered at each round [22].

The Deliberative model, by contrast, leads to the most extensive requirements on any interaction protocol. If participants are able to question and challenge

---

[6] We note in passing that threats and rewards may be used effectively to change a person's proposed actions, but not their sincere beliefs, a situation called Pascal's Law by Cristiano Castelfranchi [30].

one another's statements, and to defend their own statements when challenged, then an orderly interaction will require rules relating one type of utterance to another, and specifying when particular utterances are required or prohibited. For instance, the rules may specify the circumstances under which a question seeking the reasons for some claim must be answered by the agent which made the claim; without such a rule, the questioner would have no guarantee that the question would receive a response. Interaction rules such as these have received considerable attention from philosophers of argumentation, e.g., [32, 33, 34], work which has, in turn, influenced the design of agent interaction protocols, e.g., [23, 35]. Recent work, for example, has considered the formal specification [31] and verification [36] of agent interaction protocols.

3.3   Resolution Mechanisms

Agents in a multi-agent system may have different beliefs and intentions; accordingly, agent researchers have designed mechanisms to enable agents to share their opinions and justifications, and to engage in persuasion and negotiation dialogues, e.g., [25]. However, differences of opinion may persist even after exchanges of justifications and attempts at persuasion. In circumstances where a collective judgment must be made, such as where a group of agents need to agree a joint course of action, then the agents require some mechanism for resolving their differences. The mechanisms which are feasible and appropriate differ according to the model of democracy used.

Under the Wise Elite model, all decisions are taken by the elite so, as far as the other participants concerned, there is no need for a conflict-resolution mechanism.[7] In an auction with one seller and many potential buyers, for example, the auctioneer determines the winner, usually (but not necessarily) on the basis of previously-published rules; the auctioneer thus resolves the difference of opinion between the buyers unilaterally. Under the Rational Choice Model, agents choose between policies as if the agents were consumers and the policies were products. Although agents may receive information about policy options, the Rational Choice model does not assume they necessarily engage in debate or argument about these. The final resolution of any differences is made by each agent choosing whichever policy it most favors. If these choices differ, then the appropriate resolution mechanism is a vote by the agents, selecting that policy, for example, with the greatest numerical support. For instance, Hunsberger and Zancanaro propose a voting procedure for pooling agent judgements over alternative partial plans in undertaking joint planning activities [37].

Under the Deliberative Model, however, it is assumed that agents may engage in debate over policy choices, and so there may be an exchange of arguments prior to determination of a collective judgment. As with the Rational Choice Model, a voting mechanism may be used to make this final determination. But the exchange of arguments means that other mechanisms are also feasible, relying on the argument-aggregation procedures from argumentation theory, e.g., [38, 39].

---

[7] The Elite itself, if comprised of more than one agent, may require such a mechanism.

An example of such a procedure may make this clear. In [39], claims are classified into one of several mutually-exclusive classes on the basis of the arguments presented for or against them. In this framework, one argument B rebuts another A if B is an argument for the claim $\neg\theta$ and A is an argument for the claim θ. An argument C undercuts A if C is an argument for a claim $\neg\gamma$, where γ is a premise of argument A. We can then define the argument-status of a claim θ at time t as follows:

- If there have been no arguments uttered for or against θ up to time t, then the claim is *Open*.
- If there has been at least one argument uttered for θ up to time t, then the claim is *Supported*.
- If there has been at least one argument with consistent premises uttered for θ up to time t, then the claim is *Plausible*.
- If there has been at least one argument whose premises are consistent uttered for θ up to time t, and no undercutting or rebutting arguments have been uttered against θ by this time, then the claim is *Probable*.
- If there has been at least one argument whose premises are consistent uttered for θ up to time t, and any undercutting or rebutting arguments uttered against θ by this time have themselves been rebutted or undercut, then the claim is *Confirmed*.

The motivation for this approach is that the more and the stronger are the arguments for a claim, then the more support it has among the participants. The labels used, *Open*, *Supported*, etc, are entirely arbitrary and any set of qualitative labels could be defined in this way. Such a classification of arguments can be used as a conflict-resolution mechanism when the agents concerned are unable to agree on a claim. In [35], we explored the formal properties of such an argument-based resolution mechanism, particularly the circumstances under which the labels assigned to a claim would converge over time.[8]

Some political theorists claim that being open to persuasion requires participants with conflicting views to see each other as adversaries rather than as enemies, engaged in argument in particular interactions in the joint knowledge that every interaction may be followed by others [40, 41]. Participants therefore need to achieve a feasible middle ground between striving for an impossible consensus and refusing to interact with one another. Accordingly (these theorists argue), democratic political institutions and processes need to be able to permit participants to express what may be very different preferences and goals, and to participate in joint political processes despite such differences. Argument-classification systems, such as the one above, facilitate this by incorporating *all* the views and arguments expressed, even those which are not in the majority.

In summary, the model of democracy adopted has implications for the types of mechanisms which are feasible for resolving conflicts of agent opinion. Such

---

[8] There is still work to be done, however, on the rate of convergence, so as to better understand when in a dialogue it is appropriate to deploy a resolution mechanism.

differences of opinion are ignored under a Wise Elite model. Voting is essentially the only mechanism possible under a Rational Choice model, while the exchange of arguments under a Deliberative Model enables the additional use in these systems of resolution mechanisms based on argument classification from argumentation theory.

4   Semantic Verifiability

Verification of semantic requirements of agent communications languages and interaction protocols is problematic [42, 43]. This is essentially because a sufficiently-clever agent can always simulate insincerely any required mental state. In response to this problem, Munindar Singh [44] proposed a *social semantics* for agent communications languages, in which each participant to an interaction makes a public statement of its beliefs and intentions. Other agents can then use these public declarations to ensure that each agent is consistent in its utterances in an interaction. Of course, an agent may still make insincere declarations, but at least it can be called to account for inconsistencies between its declarations and its subsequent statements, as one of us has formalized in [45]. In the vernacular: *Liars need good memories.*

If a deliberative model of democracy forms the basis of an open agent system with a social semantics, then we are able to obtain a stronger form of semantic verifiability. Under a deliberative model, agents making claims may be questioned and challenged by other agents about the reasons for those claims; these reasons could be arguments for a belief of the agent, or reasons for an intention. Consequently, not only can the consistency of declarations and other utterances in the interaction be verified, but also the degree to which the declarations themselves — beliefs or intentions — are justified. We call this form of verification *contestability*, since social semantic declarations may be contested or challenged by other agents.[9] Of course, insincere declarations are still possible, but agents making false declarations may also need to fabricate a set of arguments for them. To be convincing to others, an insincere agent needs to create a set of inter-locking arguments for its statements, and other agents may only accept these arguments in defined circumstances, as is the case with the formal argumentation systems of [45, 46]. For example, if the listeners are skeptical regarding what arguments they accept [46], then they will only accept those arguments which defeat (in a precise sense) any attacking argument. Creating a set of interlocking arguments which convince a skeptical agent will usually not be easy for an insincere agent. In the words of Walter Scott [47, Canto 6, Stanza 17]: *"Oh what a tangled web we weave, when first we practice to deceive!"*

---

[9] We also use this word because of the analogy with its meaning in economics. A contestable market is one to which new entrants may join at any time, a prospect which should lead existing self-interested suppliers to act as if competitors were already present. Thus a monopolist in a contestable market may behave as if in a competitive market.

One might view this approach as fine for beliefs and intentions which have a reasoned basis. But what of agent mental states such as preferences or values, which (some would argue) have no rational basis. The first point to make is that many more of these may have a rational basis than is commonly perceived; for example, a consumer may justify a preference for a white-colored motor car on the basis that he or she lives in a hot climate, and light-colored cars are generally cooler inside than dark-colored cars. Secondly, some philosophers argue that rational debate is possible even on matters of profound disagreement over fundamental values, e.g., [48].[10] Indeed, it is possible to show that some arguments may defeat all others [11] regardless of the values of the participants [50]. Thus, even when participants disagree over fundamental values, there can be non-trivial claims which are accepted by everyone. However, even if an agent's mental states resist justification, the possibility of facing contestation may still reduce the likelihood that the agent declares them falsely. Of course, there are situations where agents may wish to declare their mental states insincerely, as in a negotiation where an agent provides false or misleading information about its preferences or intentions in order to gain an advantage.

Our argument in this Section can be summarized as follows: The Deliberative Model of democracy emphasizes the joint and discursive nature of decision-making in a society, with participants exchanging arguments for and against various policy proposals, and forming preferences on the basis of these exchanges. The structure provided by this model to the designer of an agent system creates the means necessary to develop a strong form of social semantics. This is because every assertion by an agent may be questioned or contested by others, thereby making insincere utterances harder to sustain. We call this feature of a dialogue system *contestability*. One agent can never finally verify the mental states of another, and thus can never verify semantic compliance with an Agent Communications Language defined in terms of such states, such as the Semantic Language SL of the FIPA ACL [27]. However, the use of a social semantics increases the extent to which compliance with the semantics of the agent communications language can be verified; the use of a deliberative democracy model providing contestability of utterances increases the degree of verifiability again, above that provided by a social semantics. Auction mechanism designers in economics have traditionally dealt with this situation by aiming to design the interaction mechanism so that insincere declarations by an agent are not in that agent's best interest. The use of a social semantics and contestability can be viewed as analogous to this goal in the context of agent conversations, interactions which are generally far less structured than are auctions.

---

[10] Habermas has explored how different types of utterances — e.g., statements of fact, statements of preference or value, and statements of social relations – may be contested by others [19, 49].

[11] In the sense of argumentation theory [38].

5   Conclusions

This paper has considered the problem of how to structure open agent societies. Open multi-agent systems are those where participation is open to any agent (possibly satisfying some conventions), and thus, in particular, to agents designed by a different design team to that responsible for the system itself. Because of this diversity, agents in an open agent system are likely to incorporate very different beliefs, goals, preferences, decision-processes and decision-constraints. In some such systems, social decision-making processes may be hierarchical and uncontested. In many systems, however, the relationship between the participating agents will be one of equality, and the question arises as to what organizing structures are appropriate in these domains. As a step towards answering this question, we have explored, for the first time in the agent literature, alternative normative models of democracy taken from political philosophy and considered their implications for open agent societies.

We considered the three most influential normative models of democracy for their relevance to the design of open agent systems. In particular, we considered their implications for the design of agent communications languages, for interaction protocols, and for any mechanisms for the resolution of conflicts. The different models place very differing requirements on the design of these aspects of an agent system, and thus allow for different ways of structuring open agent societies. Following this, we also discussed the notion of rationality in deliberative models of democracy, which we argued could provide a form of semantic verifiability of the communications language used by agents in an interaction.

Our paper does not discuss many other issues of relevance to this topic. For example, in large agent systems, issues of scalability become paramount. With large numbers of agents all attempting to express their own opinions and to contest those of others, it it not obvious that deliberative democracy is feasible. As with human societies, flexible large-scale agent systems should see the emergence of subsidiary dialogues, communities of interest, lobby groups, etc. Consequently, a thorough treatment of scalability would need a discussion of social organizations and of power relationships between agents in the context of agent democracy, both areas we have not yet tackled.

We believe the primary value of this paper is to raise awareness among designers of open agent systems of the availability of alternative conceptualizations of the notion of democracy, and the possibilities they provide for engineering open societies. Without such awareness, system designers are likely to encode one or other model implicitly, which may subsequently limit the functionality of the agent system. Indeed, as stated earlier, the development of agent societies may lead to new conceptualizations of democracy, in addition to those studied in political philosophy. A second value of this paper is our notion of contestability, which provides a form of semantic verifiability for agent communications languages stronger than previous forms. In future work, we hope to formalize the argument we have made here regarding the relative verification effectiveness of contestable and social semantics.

Acknowledgements

We are grateful to William Rehg and Paul Dunne for discussions and comments on these ideas. We also thank the anonymous referees and the lively participants at the ESAW 2003 meeting for their comments and suggestions.

References

[1] Noriega, P., Sierra, C.: Towards layered dialogical agents. In Müller, J.P., Wooldridge, M.J., Jennings, N.R., eds.: Intelligent Agents III. Lecture Notes in Artificial Intelligence 1193, Berlin, Germany, Springer (1997) 173–188 67

[2] Bohman, J., Rehg, W.: Introduction. [12] ix–xxx 67, 68

[3] Rousseau, J.J.: The Social Contract. Oxford University Press, Oxford, UK (1994) Published 1762. Translated by Christopher Betts, in a volume entitled: *"Discourse on Political Economy* and *The Social Contract"* 67

[4] Habermas, J.: The Inclusion of the Other: Studies in Political Theory. MIT Press, Cambridge, MA, USA (1998) Edited by C. Cronin and P. De Greiff 67, 68

[5] Schumpeter, J.: Capitalism, Socialism, and Democracy. Third edn. Harper, New York, USA (1950) First edition 1942 68

[6] Downs, A.: An Economic Theory of Democracy. Harper and Row, New York, NY, USA (1957) 68

[7] Arrow, K.J.: Social Choice and Individual Values. Wiley, New York (1951) 68, 69

[8] Lange, O.: The scope and method of economics. The Review of Economic Studies **13** (1945–1946) 19–32 68, 69

[9] Rehg, W.: The argumentation theorist in deliberative democracy. Controversia: An International Journal of Debate and Democratic Renewal **1** (2002) 18–42 69

[10] Beasley, R., Danesi, M.: Persuasive Signs: The Semiotics of Advertising. Mouton de Gruyter, Berlin, Germany (2002) 69

[11] Bessette, J.: Deliberative Democracy: The majority principle in republican government. In Goldwin, R.A., Schambra, W.A., eds.: How Democratic is the Constitution? American Enterprise Institute, Washington, DC, USA (1980) 102–116 69

[12] Bohman, J., Rehg, W., eds.: Deliberative Democracy: Essays on Reason and Politics. MIT Press, Cambridge, MA, USA (1997) 69, 78

[13] Forester, J.: The Deliberative Practitioner: Encouraging Participatory Planning Processes. MIT Press, Cambridge, MA, USA (1999) 69

[14] Fiorino, D.J.: Environmental risk and democratic process: a critical review. Columbia Journal of Environmental Law **14** (1989) 501–547 69

[15] Webler, T., Tuler, S., Krueger, R.: What is a good public participation process? Five perspectives from the public. Environmental Management **27** (2001) 435–450 69

[16] Jaeger, C.C., Renn, O., Rosa, E.A., Webler, T.: Risk, Uncertainty, and Rational Action. Earthscan Publications, London, UK (2001) 69

[17] Mandler, M.: A difficult choice in preference theory: rationality implies completeness or transitivity but not both. In Millgram, E., ed.: Varieties of Practical Reasoning. MIT Press, Cambridge, MA, USA (2001) 373–402 69

[18] Sen, A.: Rationality and Freedom. Harvard University Press, Cambridge, MA, USA (2002) 69

[19] Habermas, J.: The Theory of Communicative Action: Volume 1: Reason and the Rationalization of Society. Heinemann, London, UK (1984) Translation by T. McCarthy of: *Theorie des Kommunikativen Handelns, Band I, Handlungsrationalitat und gesellschaftliche Rationalisierung*. Suhrkamp, Frankfurt, Germany. 1981 69, 70, 76

[20] Johnson, R.: Manifest Rationality: A Pragmatic Theory of Argument. Lawrence Erlbaum Associates, Mahwah, NJ, USA (2000) 69

[21] Ducasse, S., Hofmann, T., Nierstrasz, O.: OpenSpaces: an object-oriented framework for reconfigurable coordination spaces. In Porto, A., Roman, G.C., eds.: Coordination Languages and Models. Lecture Notes in Computer Science 1906. Springer, Berlin, Germany (2000) 1–19 70

[22] FIPA: English Auction Interaction Protocol Specification. Experimental Standard XC00031F, FIPA (2001) 71, 72

[23] Amgoud, L., Maudet, N., Parsons, S.: Modelling dialogues using argumentation. In Durfee, E., ed.: Proceedings Fourth International Conference on Multi-Agent Systems (ICMAS 2000), Boston, MA, USA, IEEE Press (2000) 31–38 71, 73

[24] McBurney, P., Eijk, R., Parsons, S., Amgoud, L.: A dialogue-game protocol for agent purchase negotiations. Journal of Autonomous Agents and Multi-Agent Systems **7** (2003) 235–273 71

[25] Parsons, S., Sierra, C., Jennings, N.R.: Agents that reason and negotiate by arguing. Journal of Logic and Computation **8** (1998) 261–292 71, 73

[26] McBurney, P., Parsons, S., Wooldridge, M.: Desiderata for agent argumentation protocols. In Castelfranchi, C., Johnson, W.L., eds.: Proceedings First International Joint Conference on Autonomous Agents and MAS (AAMAS 2002), Bologna, Italy, New York, USA, ACM Press (2002) 402–409 72

[27] FIPA: Communicative Act Library Specification. Standard SC00037J, Foundation for Intelligent Physical Agents (2002) 72, 76

[28] Greenwood, K., Bench-Capon, T., McBurney, P.: Towards a computational account of persuasion in law. In Sartor, G., ed.: Proceedings of the Ninth International Conference on AI and Law (ICAIL-03), New York, NY, USA, ACM Press (2003) 22–31 72

[29] Hitchcock, D., McBurney, P., Parsons, S.: A framework for deliberation dialogues. In Hansen, H.V., Tindale, C.W., Blair, J.A., Johnson, R.H., eds.: Proceedings of the Fourth Biennial Conference of the Ontario Society for the Study of Argumentation (OSSA 2001), Windsor, Ontario, Canada (2001) 72

[30] Castelfranchi, C.: Guarantees for autonomy in cognitive agent architectures. In Wooldridge, M.J., Jennings, N.R., eds.: Intelligence Agents — Theories, Architectures, and Languages. Lecture Notes in Artificial Intelligence 890. Springer, Berlin, Germany (1995) 56–80 72

[31] McBurney, P., Parsons, S.: Games that agents play: A formal framework for dialogues between autonomous agents. Journal of Logic, Language and Information **11** (2002) 315–334 72, 73

[32] Alexy, R.: A theory of practical discourse. In Benhabib, S., Dallmayr, F., eds.: The Communicative Ethics Controversy. MIT Press, Cambridge, MA, USA (1990) 151–190 Published in German 1978 73

[33] Hitchcock, D.: Some principles of rational mutual inquiry. In Eemeren, F., et al., eds.: Proceedings Second International Conference on Argumentation, Amsterdam, The Netherlands, SICSAT (1991) 236–243 73

[34] Krabbe, E.C.W.: The problem of retraction in critical discussion. Synthese **127** (2001) 141–159 73

[35] McBurney, P., Parsons, S.: Representing epistemic uncertainty by means of dialectical argumentation. Annals of Mathematics and AI **32** (2001) 125–169 73, 74

[36] Artikis, A., Sergot, M., Pitt, J.: An executable specification of an argumentation protocol. In Sartor, G., ed.: Proceedings of the Ninth International Conference on AI and Law (ICAIL-03), New York, NY, USA, ACM Press (2003) 1–11 73

[37] Hunsberger, L., Zancanaro, M.: A mechanism for group decision making in collaborative activity. In: Proceedings 17th National Conference on AI (AAAI-2000), Menlo Park, CA, USA, AAAI Press (2000) 30–35 73

[38] Dung, P.M.: On the acceptability of arguments and its fundamental role in non-monotonic reasoning, logic programming and n-person games. Artificial Intelligence **77** (1995) 321–357 73, 76

[39] Krause, P., Ambler, S., Elvang-Gørannson, M., Fox, J.: A logic of argumentation for reasoning under uncertainty. Computational Intelligence **11** (**1**) (1995) 113–131 73, 74

[40] Ivie, R.L.: Rhetorical deliberation and democratic politics in the here and now. Rhetoric and Public Affairs **5** (2002) 74

[41] Mouffe, C.: The Return of the Political. Verso, London, UK (1993) 74

[42] Pitt, J., Mamdani, A.: Some remarks on the semantics of FIPA's Agent Communications Language. Journal of Autonomous Agents and Multi-Agent Systems **2** (1999) 333–356 75

[43] Wooldridge, M.J.: Semantic issues in the verification of agent communication languages. Journal of Autonomous Agents and Multi-Agent Systems **3** (2000) 9–31 75

[44] Singh, M.P.: A social semantics for agent communications languages. In Dignum, F., Chaib-draa, B., Weigand, H., eds.: Proceedings of the Workshop on Agent Communication Languages, IJCAI-99. (1999) 75–88 75

[45] Amgoud, L., Maudet, N., Parsons, S.: An argumentation-based semantics for agent communications languages. In Harmelen, F., ed.: Proceedings 15th European Conference on AI (ECAI 2002), Toulouse, France (2002) 75

[46] Parsons, S., Wooldridge, M., Amgoud, L.: Properties and complexity of some formal inter-agent dialogues. Journal of Logic and Computation **13** (2003) 347–376 75

[47] Scott, W.: Marmion: A Tale of Flodden Field. A. Constable, Edinburgh, Scotland (1808) 75

[48] Richardson, H.S.: Practical Reasoning about Final Ends. Cambridge University Press, Cambridge, UK (1994) 76

[49] Habermas, J.: On the Pragmatics of Communication. Studies in Contemporary German Social Thought. MIT Press, Cambridge, MA, USA (1998) Edited by Maeve Cooke 76

[50] Bench-Capon, T.: Agreeing to differ: modeling persuasive dialogue between parties with different values. Informal Logic **22** (2003) *In press* 76

A Liberal Approach to Openness in Societies of Agents*.

Jacques Calmet, Anusch Daemi, Regine Endsuleit, and Thilo Mie

Institute for Algorithms and Cognitive Systems (IAKS)
University of Karlsruhe (TH)
Germany
{calmet,daemi,endsuleit,mie}@ira.uka.de

Abstract. We outline a model for a society of agents based upon one of the classical theories of sociology: The Weber's model. We first investigate its links to agent technology through its relationship with the modeling of micro economy and the concept of expected utility. Then, some of the features of an agent society are enhanced by imposing security and validation requirements. We show that a societal concept from Sociology can be implemented through methods of Computer Science and thus is made feasible.

Keywords: Society of agents, sociology, security, knowledge society, legal validation.

1   Introduction

It is well known that agents interact with their environment. This interaction ranges from a simple link to a more involved reactive process. This implies that the concept of a society of agents is already valid for a system with a few agents. Indeed, formally speaking this interaction defines a concept of society. A possible organization of agents is thus achieved through the concept of a society of agents. This is well-recognized and different models have been proposed along the years [1]. For instance, social dependence networks were introduced quite early to formalize an environment for agents (see [2]). Social network analysis, established in social science, is the mapping and measuring of relationships and flows between people, groups, organizations, computers or any processing entity. The nodes are the people and groups while the links show relationships or flows between the nodes. The analysis is both a visual and a mathematical analysis of human relationships.

This is however fully different from the classical concepts upon which sociology is based. It is better defined as social awareness. In general, social concepts in agent methodologies are seldom set in the framework of sociology. An example is [3] where social communication is seen as commitments set by agents. We set

---

* Work partially supported by the Calculemus Research Training Network, HPRN-CT-2000-00102

A. Omicini, P. Petta, and J. Pitt (Eds.): ESAW 2003, LNAI 3071, pp. 81–92, 2004.
© Springer-Verlag Berlin Heidelberg 2004

social communication in the context of sociology. We propose an approach that relies on the very basic ideas of sociology. Our society of agents is governed by rules similar to those enabling to govern a human society. We will quickly see that this implies to view a society of agents as a decision making system, again a well accepted idea. We adopt Weber's approach to sociology [4, 5]. This leads to a formulation that has many similarities with the rules and concepts that facilitate the design of mathematical models for the economy [6]. We ascertain, that the resulting actions of the agents, viewed as a society, are the result of individual actions and not imposed by the society to the individual agents.

What does it mean for a society of agents to be open? A possible answer is to be neutral with respect to the architecture of the system [7]. Another one is that from the prospect of agent technology, we may have agents without an assigned goal and the goals assigned to agents are, in general, loose. This society is open to new agents either with no definite goal or with goals not exceedingly relevant to the society, which is fully compatible with the sociological decision we made. This openness signifies that the architecture of the system is not driven by goals imposed to the collective of agents, but that general goals arise from the collective actions of agents. Also, the adjunction of new agents must be as easy as required. In other words, the architecture of the society can exhibit some dynamical features rather than being solely static or bounded.

At this stage we may already state that such a society can be said to be liberal. We do not provide a formal definition for the term liberal, we only say that it refers to a society which offers some specific features such as Openness, Security, Usability and Feasibility.

To design a usable, secure and feasible society we may set some basic conditions on top of the sociological requirements.

(i) To identify and eliminate intruders that would, purposely or not, destroy the society without altering the efficiency of action.

(ii) To let the agents achieve their goals and purposes. This is a function based on the number of intruders detected and on counting the number of goals reached.

(iii) Let the agents speak a common language. This must be interpreted as sharing a common semantics, not necessarily a same language. If the society is open, it is probably heterogeneous and shares all available different paradigms for knowledge.

(iv) Conflicts ought to be solved. This is a mostly technical requirement that must follow from the previous point when the architecture of the society is cleverly designed. In the language of agents, this means that the agents are intelligent.

(v) The society is a knowledge society. Translated into more technical terms, this implies, besides the previous two points, that a context for any action is available. When a semantic is not directly available, one may, for instance, rely on ontologies. We can also state that the society has features similar to those a semantic web would possess.

(vi) Let the actions of the agents be legally validated. Any society is governed by laws or at least their individuals must obey the laws. They can be real laws, whether national or international ones or internal laws set by the designer. In both cases, they amount to a cluster of legal ontologies. They must be validated as some form of legal syntax. This means, that besides a semantic meaning and validation, we introduce a legal validation. Examples of such clusters could be given for privacy, property rights, ciphering, authentication or authorization, just to quote a few.

The paper is structured as follows: We first present the sociological theory on which the organization and management of the type of society we propose is based. In the same section we outline how we can formally model such a society. The next sections address issues of security of agent systems, knowledge requirements and legal validation respectively.

2 Sociology and Societies of Agents

2.1 A Societal Organization of Agents

It is well-known that agents interact with their environment. When the number of agents in a system becomes very large, it makes sense to speak of a society of agents. The different relationships that do exist among individuals in a human society can simulate those existing in an agent society. This is probably why a literature search tends to demonstrate that research in this area is centered more on social simulation than on sociology itself [8, 9, 10, 11, 12]. We adopt the point of view that we can organize a society of agents as the main sociological entity: the Society. A question then immediately arises: what are the basic theories or models in sociology that can serve as a model to organize a society of agents?

In sociology, two of the main ideas were set at the beginning of the previous century. There are two main entities in human science, the individuals and the society. Two primary approaches are possible. According to the first one, the society imposes or influences the actions of agents. The main reference for this line of thoughts is the book of Emile Durkheim [13] called "Suicide". It shows that even a very personal decision, such as deciding to commit suicide, has in fact its root in the society and not in the individual. The opposite approach of Max Weber ([4] and [5] that is a late translation of the German edition published posthumously in the early 1920s) states, that the behavior of the society is the result of the individual actions of the agents. The first cited reference is usually considered to be the founding stone of this theory. It is probably not necessary to remind that Durkheim is at the origin of collectivism (from socialism to communism) and Weber of what is called today liberalism.

From these early ages and until 1996 new theories have been mainly centered on social awareness. The link to computer science is illustrated by works such as [14]. A possible breakthrough occurs when Manuel Castells published his three books [15, 16, 17]. Castells' goal is to make sense of the global social dynamics of the transformations at the end of the century. It seems that it is still a topic of discussion among sociologists to decide whether this is the third founding piece of work after Durkheim and Weber ones or a modern adaptation to the information society of classical social awareness approaches.

To base a sociological organization of a society of agents on Castells' model is probably worthwhile but in our approach we adopt Weber's theory. This explains partly the word "liberal" in the title. The approaches of Durkheim and Weber have influenced the social, administrative and political organizations of societies during the last century and still do. We simply forget this facet of the problem and notice two facts. First, the goals of a multiagent system are the results of specific goals of the constituting agents which is closely tied to the design decision adopted when defining the architecture of the system. This seems pretty obvious when the number of agents is limited: they are designed with local goals that ought to ensure that the global goals are reached. When increasing the number of agents we extrapolate this concept. We have thus a conceptual continuity between a system of agents and a society of agents. The second fact is that the approach of Weber is at the basis of the mathematical modeling of economy [6]. We can learn from it to design some decision making mechanisms in agent systems.

2.2   A Brief History of Mathematical Modeling in Economy

We take the brief introduction here-under mostly from [6]. More precisely, this approach is at the heart of micro economy where individual agents take decisions that shape up the macro economy. This leads, by the way, to very challenging, still unsolved mathematical problems [18]. As a first approximation, this implies that we consider a society of agents to be a decision making system. This may look contradictory, but both are facets of the same thing. The actions done by the agents in the society are leading inevitably to discussions and we should be ready to accept such a constraint, as the price to pay to consider agents without a proper goal. At least collectively they will contribute to the community's actions and goals.

To proceed we must investigate whether we have a feasible model of the behavior of the agents. We aim at introducing the model of expected utility. It is widely accepted and used in economy. It was first proposed independently by the two famous economists Walras (founder of a school that is often opposed to Keyne's school of thoughts) and Pareto and finalized mathematically by von Neumann and Morgenstern [19]. It can be sketched as follows. Each agent is described through the following parameters or functions:

- a set of possible actions: $a \in \mathcal{A}$,
- a probabilistic measure on future events, $(x \in X)$, depending on the pending action, $a \in \mathcal{A} : d_{\mu_a}(x)$,
- a utility function $U(x) \in \mathbb{R}$,

– this utility function leads to the expected utility $E_a[U]$ defined through the integral

$$E_a[U] = \int U(x)d_{\mu_a}(x)$$

A decision making system then simply amounts to the following optimization problem:

$$\underset{a \in \mathcal{A}}{\text{Maximize}} \, E_a[U]$$

2.3 Utility Function in Agent Systems

A preliminary remark is that the idea of defining a concept of utility for agent systems is not new, it is for instance, mentioned in the book of Wooldridge [9], but never as a von Neumann-Morgenstern axiomatization of expected utility. Let us try to specialize the above model to multiagent societies. First, what is the meaning of this expected utility model of von Neumann and Morgenstern? The key idea is that when probabilities are associated to some lotteries, then in this theory, preferences over lotteries logically precede preferences over outcome. In an agent society, this means that the choice of the "next" agent to fulfill a task logically precedes the choice of the possible decision. The simplest model is when there is no uncertainty regarding the future (assignment of a task to an agent for instance). The problem is then simply to select some available decisions

$$x = (x^1, \ldots, x^K) \in \mathbb{R}^K,$$

where x^K is the number of possible actions. The utility function will be $U(x)$ and is associated to the cost (for us the complexity)

$$px = \sum_{k=1}^{K} p_k x^k,$$

where the coefficients p_k are not set by the agent but by the environment (individual complexities). Complexities could be space or time complexities. Assuming that we set w as upper limit of the total complexity, we get in first approximation the decision problem

$$\underset{\substack{x \\ px \leq w \\ \forall k: \, x^k \geq 0}}{\text{Maximize}} \, U(x)$$

At this stage we must raise the question of the correctness of the model and of the existence of utility functions. Economists and mathematicians have investigate thoroughly these questions that have no easy solution. The reason is that this framework is set in function theory. Some references can be found in [18].

In the context of agent societies, we may investigate some other ways of identifying other types of functions. A first approach is fuzzy logic. Decision making systems based upon fuzzy logic have been designed in economy [20] or for environmental applications [21] and can most probably be investigated in our domain, too. Another approach amounts to use social network analysis [2]. Functions ought to be the outcome of such network descriptions.

However, there is a more straightforward approach for computer scientists. Instead of formulating the expected utility in terms of functions we can rely on a logic formulation of the actions performed by agents. We get a set of clauses that we resolve through resolution algorithms. This is fully suitable with the tools (see the section on KOMET) we have already designed and is under investigation.

A general comment regarding decision making implied by our approach is as follows. As pointed out by Wooldridge decision making processes can be affected by different properties of the environment around the agent thus leading to different architectures. We assume that decision making processes arise from the actions performed by agents. This is both a simpler and a more generic requirement.

3   Security in an Open Society

There are two very general and complementary approaches to the problem of security of multiagent systems or societies. First, we may assess that we have a software system as any other and can rely on tools from cryptography or system security. For instance, we can work under the protection of a firewall. This is well acknowledged and the FIPA standardization effort suggests to have such a security level in the architecture of agent systems. References can be found, among many other relevant for multiagent systems, in the Road Map published by the AgentLink network of excellence [10]. For a very recent survey of provable security we refer to the work of Stern [22] that is based on cryptography. We assume that this aspect is covered by experts and that available software products provide satisfactory solutions.

The second approach deals with mobile agents and is required in case of open agent societies. Prototypical computations with systems encompassing a huge number of agents are to collect, filter and process large amounts of information either when available bandwidths or computing resources are limited or when a more suitable technology such as the GRID can be implemented. The broad range of such applications includes for instance mobile computing, information retrieval in large repositories and e-commerce applications. In such applications security means to identify and eliminate intruders and to secure the agents' functionality. Although there are some links to security issues arising in virus protection, the scope of this problem is different. To identify viruses is mainly seen as an overall protection of the system and essentially belongs to the first approach.

Until recently there was no satisfactory solution to the security problems in open multiagent systems without relying on a known trusted party (which means either regular communication with the agent's originator or a trusted third party). Indeed, for stand-alone agents it seems to be hard to provide any security guarantee without controlling them from time to time. This includes protection of data and execution integrity as well as prevention from malicious routing, deletion etc. More promising is the use of agent groups like those presented by Endsuleit and Mie in [23] where a new methodology is investigated that does not require a trusted party.

By using a group of n collaborating agents which we call an Alliance, it is possible to guarantee the reliability of the community's functionality as long as no more than $t < \frac{n}{3}$ agents have been corrupted at any time. This property is achieved by using Canetti's mathematical model for secure multi-party computation (see [24]). This model has been selected because it is tailored to represent communication networks like the Internet. The main idea is to distribute the computational state and all data redundantly over all Alliance members. All computations are performed jointly on data shares and bear up to t dishonest inputs (this includes missing ones as well as wrong ones). Those computations follow a suitable protocol ([23] uses the one of Ben-Or, Goldwasser and Wigderson [25], but [26] is more efficient with a linear communication complexity in each node) which maintains the $t < \frac{n}{3}$ requirement. Thus, we do not have to demand all hosting servers to be trustworthy. This is another reason to label our approach "liberal".

For the technical description of the approach see [23]. Recently, an analysis about possible attacks on violating the $t < \frac{n}{3}$ requirement has been done in the framework of [23] and showed that this is only possible by Denial-of-Service attacks (DoS). The model is a first step in the direction of achieving security for mobile multiagent systems. In its present state of development, this approach is fully suitable for societies of agents. It ought to be clear that it takes care of the requirements listed under the points i and ii in the introduction.

4   Knowledge Requirements

We set our definition of a society of agents in the context of knowledge societies. Indeed, every piece of information is a piece of knowledge. A trivial consequence is that we deal with heterogeneous knowledge which can be structured, semi-structured, unstructured, complete or incomplete. Our answer to this challenge is the KOMET (Karlsruhe Open Mediator Technology) system that we developed for several years [27].

The goal is to incorporate multiple knowledge sources into one system, regardless of where the information is located and how the information is stored. Such a system needs to be intelligent in the sense, that it is able to choose and access appropriate knowledge sources for answering an agent's request. It is supposed to completely hide the process of query processing, network access, data conversion and data processing which might be necessary to answer a user's question.

Sources can not only be traditional databases with different data models, but any information source such as web pages, software systems or spreadsheet calculators – using a common data model. Even humans can be considered as information source in the mediator context. A mediator *contains integration knowledge*

1. to compile new information which can only be obtained by combining information from different sources (horizontal value-addition)
2. to solve conflicts and contradictions between the sources using domain-dependent rules (vertical value-addition)

In the context of societies of agents we assume that we must deal with any available kind of knowledge society. In the context of agent technology information retrieval and processing, mediator systems are nowadays labeled intelligent agents. KOMET looks suitable to process knowledge in a wide variety of forms. This is due to its main design ideas that, without going into technical details (see [27] for a general description, [28] for an in-depth presentation or [29] for some recent theoretical issues) are as follows.

1. The KOMET language is a declarative language which implements a many-sorted annotated logic with a high degree of flexibility. This is known as the generalized annotated programming (GAP). It provides a set of basic data types and truth value sets which can be extended. The KOMET language extends GAP and defines the common data model.
2. The heart of the system is an efficient engine for annotated logic programs using SLG-resolution for evaluating the well-founded semantic, enhanced with constraints for integrating external knowledge sources. Therefore a KOMET mediator can be used like a deductive database.

In order to give uniform, integrated access to heterogeneous information sources, schema integration and conflict resolution needs to be done. Those conflicts, that can be solved, are the classical ones found in database or knowledge technology. Specifically KOMET allows to solve Knowledge Inconsistencies, Semantic Similarities, Domain Incompatibilities, Data Representation Conflicts, Default Value Conflicts, Schema Conflicts or Missing Data Item Conflicts among other problems.

Here once again the handling of heterogeneous knowledge sources is a prerequisite when defining a liberal and open society of agents. Although GAP enables efficient programming, it is true that the methodology is not always the most efficient for some applications. This is always possible when implementing resolution algorithms. However, the main results concerns the feasibility of the method and the solution of conflicts.

Another benefit of KOMET is to address the problem of the validation of queries/actions. In [30] we show how we can design and implement the syntactical validation of queries in a mediator system. We do not rely on a protocol of communication as it is often the case in multiagent systems. Instead, we plan to extend the syntactic validation to include a semantic validation to ensure consistency among the agents. This is more challenging since when dealing with heterogeneous knowledge bases a common semantic is only possible after the wrappers have transformed the source schema into the mediator one. In KOMET the latter one is soundly defined but there is no method to check that the source is semantically sound. A method under investigation is to define a context for such an external source when ontologies are available. The structure that must be part of any ontology leads indeed to a notion of context. Then, from the context, one may define some sort of semantic.

5   Legal Validation of Societies of Agents

One of the basic features of any society is the existence of laws governing its behavior at the individual as well as at the societal level. In addition to laws there are a number of rules that set a code of conduct for any agent belonging to the society. In a first approximation we may say, that a society must be law obedient when it is open. The extent of such a statement can be discussed but it must exist. This applies also to societies of agents.

Such a society ought to be labeled a knowledge society since each agent is going to represent or simulate some sort of knowledge. We are very familiar in artificial intelligence with such concepts. A knowledge society relies on representing knowledge through several paradigms. This knowledge can be validated somewhat easily through the syntax of the representations. It is already much more difficult to validate it through the semantics. This is for instance the case of most of the projects that are labeled "semantic web". We claim that legal knowledge is a new sort of knowledge paradigm and thus must be investigated. There are at least two levels at which to assess laws. The first level is the usual one; we are governed by national and international laws that can be similar or different. Any software system must face such laws. Problems to be addressed are for instance those dealing with privacy, property rights or patents. For example, protocols for a multiagent system in mobile communication are patterned but if we wish to enforce some sort of privacy or install silencing devices, we must modify the communication protocols and check the implications arising from property rights. If we send ciphered messages through the Internet, we must investigate whether this is legally allowed and/or authorized throughout the network or in restricted sections only.

The second level is internal. It deals with the internal rules set by the system designer. They can be explicit or implicit but always do exist. This is in fact the level with which we are familiar and we refer to when speaking of system security. This level may simply reflect the technology in use at a given time. It is well known that, besides semantic webs, our knowledge society will rely on the GRID technology to process large amount of data circulating at high speed. Such a technology is producing its own standards that amounts to laws to obey. For instance, we are all too familiar with standards in mobile communication when they are regulated through patents. We claim that besides the usual validation techniques that we master when designing software systems, we must introduce a new level of validation: the legal validation of societies of agents. At present, lawyers do use computer science technology to design tools aiming at making their trade easier. Conversely computer science uses, often reluctantly, law as a tool to provide a legal security net to many of its activities. None of these approaches look able to perform a continuous legal validation of a knowledge society. This is a pioneering domain at present although many projects are investigating related topics such as property rights or privacy to quote only two of them. A collaborative effort to investigate the main research directions in this new field is under construction.

6   Conclusion

We have presented a schema to define what a liberal, open society of agents could be. The model we propose is the result of works either performed or on-going. Their collection into a global framework delivers a concept for a society of agents. It is only one model among many possible ones and is a challenge that will be met in future research. For now, we only claim that we can offer some kind of consistency in establishing this model. More precisely, KOMET enables to tackle a large scope of knowledge problems and is under development for several years. Innovative results on the security of mobile agents have already been obtained and this topic is still under investigation. They fit well with the societal approach we propose. Although the main and only credits must be given to Weber and von Neumann-Morgenstern respectively, to use such methods in the framework of agent systems looks to be new. The relevant section concludes by giving some directions for research that are in fact well advanced. The first one relies on the classical approach within function theory. In [31] relevant functions are distance functions coming from basic principles. The second approach is basically a usual resolution problem as learned by any CS student. It looks like that once again a problem expressed through logics has a much simpler complexity than when expressed through functions.

It is amusing to remark that the model of Weber is nowadays present in what can be called common sense reasoning. Some authors (see for instance [6]) have noticed indeed, that this way of thinking about the organization of societies has been adopted, without even noticing that anything must be proven "by politicians introducing their agenda or religious leaders preaching for their faith". It is also questionable to know whether these persons were at all aware of the common origin of their agendas.

A concluding remark is that we start from a model for a societal organization. But, we may also think of starting from architectures for societies of agents to validate models in sociology. It looks like there is no such example in the literature.

This last paragraph is required to outline the links to the other presentations at the workshop. Since we propose a generic approach to the concept of a society of agents we could link it to all of the papers in the workshop proceedings including the invited one of Müller [32]. For instance, the expected utility function of von Neumann and Morgenstern subsumes the concept of Pareto optimality found in [33]. Our approach to security goes beyond the classical approaches reviewed in [34].

Beyond these obvious links we would like to point out to other links that are less obvious: The modelisation of engineering democracy in agent systems (see [35]) is a natural extension of our definition of a society. There is a hidden link to [36] where the object oriented methodology plays a key role. Our approach implies a vision of the concepts of agents and of objects that are not easily seen in this paper but are explained in [37].

References

[1] Dautenhahn, K., Bond, A., Cañamero, L., Edmonds, B., eds.: Socially Intelligent Agents. Kluwer Academic Publishers (2002) 81

[2] Wasserman, S., Faust, K.: Social network analysis: Methods and applications, Structural analysis in the social sciences. Cambridge University Press (1994) 81, 86

[3] Singh, M., Huhns, M.: Social Abstractions for Information Agents. Kluwer Academic Publishers (1999) 81

[4] Weber, M.: L'éthique protestante et l'esprit du capitalisme. Online available at www.uqac.uquebec.ca/zone30/Classiques_des_sciences_sociales/index.html (1904) 82, 83

[5] Weber, M.: Economy and Society. University of California Press (1986) 82, 83

[6] Ekeland, I.: La modélisation mathématique en économie. Gazette des Mathématiciens **78** (1998) 51–62 82, 84, 90

[7] Artikis, A., Pitt, J.: A formal model of open agent societies. Preprint (2002) 82

[8] Weiss, G., ed.: Multiagent Systems: A Modern Introduction to Distributed Artificial Intelligence. Cambridge, MA, USA, MIT Press (1999) 83

[9] Wooldridge, M.: Introduction to Multiagent Systems. John Wiley and Sons, New York (2002) 83, 85

[10] Luck, M., et al.: Agent technology: Enabling next generation computing (2003) Online available at http://www.agentlink.org/. 83, 86

[11] Petta, P., Tolksdorf, R., Zambonelli, F., eds.: Proc. of ESAW 2002: Engineering Societies in the Agents World III. Volume 2577 of Lecture Notes in Artificial Intelligence. Springer Verlag (2002) 83

[12] d'Inverno, M., Luck, M.: A formal view of social dependence networks. In Zhang, C., Lukose, D., eds.: Proc. of the First Australian Workshop on Distributed Artificial Intelligence. Volume 1087 of LNAI., Springer Verlag (1996) 115–129 83

[13] Durkheim, E.: Suicide: A study in sociology. The Free Press of Glenco (New York) (1951) 83

[14] Széll, G.: The social history of computers. Preprint, Univ. of Osnabrück (2003) 83

[15] Castells, M.: The Information Age: Economy, Society and Culture — The Rise of the Network Society. Volume 1. Cambridge, MA: Blackwell (1996) 83

[16] Castells, M.: The Information Age: Economy, Society and Culture — The Power of Identity. Volume 2. Cambridge, MA: Blackwell (1997) 83

[17] Castells, M.: The Information Age: Economy, Society and Culture — The End of the Millenium. Volume 3. Cambridge, MA: Blackwell (1998) 83

[18] Momi, T.: Excess demand functions with incomplete markets - a global result. Preprint (2002) 84, 85

[19] von Neumann, J., Morgenstern, O.: Theory of Games and Economic Behavior. Princeton University Press (1980) 84

[20] Ott, N.: Unsicherheit, Unschärfe und rationales Entscheiden - Die Anwendung von Fuzzy-Methoden in der Entscheidungstheorie. Physica-Verlag (2000) 85

[21] Wagner, U.: Entscheidungsfindung mit unscharfen Mengen. PhD thesis, Univ. of Karlsruhe (2003) 85

[22] Stern, J.: Why provable security matters? In: Advances in Cryptology — Eurocrypt '03. Volume 2656 of LNCS. (2003) 86

[23] Endsuleit, R., Mie, T.: Secure multi-agent computations. In: Proc. of the 2003 Int. Conf. on Security and Management (SAM'03). Volume 1., CSREA (2003) 149–155 87

[24] Canetti, R.: Universally composable security: A new paradigm for cryptographic protocols. Technical Report 2000/067, Cryptology ePrint Archive (2000) 87

[25] Ben-Or, M., Goldwasser, S., Wigderson, A.: Completeness theorems for non-cryptographic fault-tolerant distributed computation. In: Proc. 20th ACM Symposium on the Theory of Computing (STOC). (1988) 1–10 87

[26] Hirt, M., Maurer, U.: Robustness for free in unconditional multi-party computation. In: Proceedings of Advances in Cryptology - CRYPTO 2001. Volume 2139 of Lecture Notes in Computer Science., Springer Verlag (2001) 101–118 87

[27] Calmet, J., Jekutsch, S., Kullmann, P., Schü, J.: KOMET - a system for the integration of heterogeneous information sources. In: International Syposium on Methodologies for Intelligent Systems. Volume 1325 of LNAI., Springer Verlag (1997) 318–327 87, 88

[28] Kullmann, P.: Wissensrepräsentation und Anfragebearbeitung in einer logik-basierte Mediatorumgebung. PhD thesis, Univ. of Karlsruhe (2001) 88

[29] Calmet, J., Kullmann, P., Taneda, M.: Composite distributive lattices as annotation domains for mediators. Annals of Math. and AI 36 (2002) 263–277 88

[30] Calmet, J., Kullmann, P., Mann, Z.: Testing access to external information sources in a mediator environment. In Schieferdecker, I., König, H., Wolisz, A., eds.: Proc. of 14th IFIP International Conf. on Testing of Communicating Systems, Kluwer Academic Publisher (2002) 111–126 88

[31] Calmet, J., Daemi, A.: From entropy to ontology. Accepted for publication at AT2AI-4, Fourth International Symposium "From Agent Theory to Agent Implementation" (2004) 90

[32] Müller, J.P.: Emergence of collective behaviour and problem solving. (2004) In this volume 90

[33] Endriss, U., Maudet, N.: Welfare engineering in multiagent systems. (2004) In this volume 90

[34] Meyer, A.: Privacy-aware mobile agent: Protecting privacy in open systems by modelling social behaviour of software agents. (2004) In this volume 90

[35] McBurney, P., Parsons, S.: Engineering democracy in open agent systems. (2004) In this volume 90

[36] Henderson-Sellers, B., Giorgini, P., Bresciani, P.: Supporting tropos concepts in agent OPEN. (2004) In this volume 91

[37] Calmet, J., Maret, P.: Agent oriented abstraction. Forthcoming (2004) 91

Welfare Engineering in Multiagent Systems

Ulle Endriss[1] and Nicolas Maudet[2]

[1] Department of Computing
Imperial College London
180 Queen's Gate, London SW7 2AZ, UK
ue@doc.ic.ac.uk
[2] LAMSADE
Université Paris-Dauphine
75775 Paris Cedex 16, France
maudet@lamsade.dauphine.fr

Abstract. A multiagent system may be regarded as an artificial society of autonomous software agents. Welfare economics provides formal
models of how the distribution of resources amongst the members of
a society affects the well-being of that society as a whole. In multiagent
systems research, the concept of social welfare is usually given a utilitarian interpretation, i.e. whatever increases the average welfare of the
agents inhabiting a society is taken to be beneficial for society as well.
While this is indeed appropriate for a wide range of applications, we
believe that it is worthwhile to also consider some of the other social
welfare orderings that have been studied in the social sciences. In this
paper, we put forward an engineering approach to welfare economics in
multiagent systems by investigating the following question: Given a particular social welfare ordering appropriate for some application domain,
how can we design practical criteria that will allow agents to decide locally whether or not a proposed deal would further social welfare with
respect to that ordering? In particular, we review previous results on
negotiating Pareto optimal allocations of resources as well as allocations
that maximise egalitarian social welfare under this general perspective.
We also provide new results on negotiating Lorenz optimal allocations,
which may be regarded as a compromise between the utilitarian and the
egalitarian approaches. Finally, we briefly discuss elitist agent societies,
where social welfare is tied to the welfare of the most successful agent,
as well as the notion of envy-freeness.

1 Introduction

Multiagent systems have been successfully applied in a variety of different areas,
ranging from electronic commerce [1], over collaborative planning [2], to the
fair sharing of resources provided by an earth observation satellite [3]. We may
think of a multiagent system as a "society" of autonomous software agents.
Given a "solution" to a problem generated by such a society, we may assess the
quality of that solution using tools from formal economical sciences. A typical
example would be the notion of Pareto optimality: A situation (or state of the

A. Omicini, P. Petta, and J. Pitt (Eds.): ESAW 2003, LNAI 3071, pp. 93–106, 2004.
© Springer-Verlag Berlin Heidelberg 2004

system) is called Pareto optimal iff there is no other situation that would make at least one of the agents in the society happier without making any of the others worse off. Besides Pareto optimality, many other notions of *social welfare* have been put forward in philosophy, sociology, and economics. In the context of multiagent systems, on the other hand, only Pareto optimality and the utilitarian programme (where only increases in average utility are considered to be socially beneficial) have found broad application.

In this paper, we shall argue that also notions such as egalitarian social welfare, Lorenz optimality, or envy-freeness may be usefully exploited when designing multiagent systems. In particular, we are going to discuss scenarios in which autonomous agents negotiate with each other in order to agree on the redistribution of a number of resources. We put forward an engineering approach to welfare economics in multiagent systems by showing how we can design criteria that will allow agents to decide locally whether or not a proposed deal would further social welfare according to the metric chosen by the system designer. Here, we do not use the word engineering in the sense of constructing a physical (or a software) artefact, but rather to characterise the process of providing practical guidelines for designing artificial societies that exhibit particular properties we are interested in. This involves manipulating the decision making capacity of the agents inhabiting such a society appropriately. While classical welfare economics is concerned with the characterisation of the property of economic well-being with respect to the allocation of resources in a society, in this paper, we promote *welfare engineering* as the process of "engineering" appropriate behaviour profiles for individual agents in such a way that particular desirable properties can be guaranteed to emerge at the level of society.

The remainder of this paper is structured as follows. After motivating the need for different social welfare orderings in Section 2, we are going to define our basic negotiation framework in Section 3. In Section 4, we discuss previous results for two particular instances of this framework, namely for *utilitarian* systems (where a society of agents should at least be able to achieve a Pareto optimal allocation of resources) and for *egalitarian* systems (where society should aim at improving the individual welfare of its weakest member). We then move on to Section 5 and the case of artificial societies where *Lorenz optimal* allocations of resources are desirable (a compromise between the utilitarian and the egalitarian agenda). Before concluding, we briefly discuss *elitist* agent societies, where social welfare is tied to the welfare of the happiest agent, and *envy-free* allocations of resources in Section 6.

2   The *Veil of Ignorance* in Multiagent Systems

In the introduction to this paper we have claimed that multiagent systems research could benefit from considering notions of social welfare that go beyond the utilitarian agenda which aims solely at maximising the sum of the utility levels enjoyed by the individual agents in a system. The question what social welfare ordering is appropriate has been the subject of intense debate in philosophy and the social sciences for a long time. This debate has, in particular, addressed the respective benefits and drawbacks of utilitarianism on the one hand and egalitarianism on the other [4, 5, 6]. While, under the utilitarian view, social welfare is identified with average utility (or, equivalently, the sum of all individuals' utilities), egalitarian social welfare is measured in terms of the individual welfare of a society's poorest member. Precise definitions of the respective social welfare orderings are given in Section 4.

Different notions of social welfare induce different kinds of social principles. For instance, in an egalitarian system, improving one's personal welfare at the expense of a poorer member of society would be considered inappropriate. A famous argument put forward in defence of egalitarianism is Rawls' *veil of ignorance* [5]. This argument is based on the following thought experiment. To decide what form of society could rightfully be called *just*, a rational person should ask herself the following question:

Without knowing what your position in society (class, race, sex, ...) will be, what kind of society would you choose to live in?

The idea is to decide on a suitable set of social principles that should apply to everyone in society by excluding any kind of bias amongst those who choose the principles. The argument goes that behind this *veil of ignorance* (of not knowing your own future role within the society whose principles you are asked to decide upon), any rational person would choose an egalitarian system, as it insures even the unluckiest members of society a certain minimal level of welfare.

One may or may not agree with this line of reasoning. What we are interested in here is the structure of the thought experiment itself. As far as *human* society is concerned, this is a highly abstract construction (some would argue, *too* abstract to yield any reliable social guidelines). However, for an *artificial* society it can be of very practical concern. Before agreeing to be represented by a software agent in such a society, one would naturally want to know under what principles this society operates. If the agent's objective is to negotiate on behalf of its owner, then the owner has to agree to accept whatever the outcome of a specific negotiation may be. That is, in the context of multiagent systems, we may reformulate the central question of the *veil of ignorance* as follows:

If you were to send a software agent into an artificial society to negotiate on your behalf, what would you consider acceptable principles for that society to operate by?

There is no single answer to this question; it depends on the purpose of the agent society under consideration. For instance, for the application described in [3], where agents need to agree on the access to an earth observation satellite which has been funded jointly by the owners of these agents, it is important that each one of them receives a "fair" share of the common resource. Here, a society governed by egalitarian principles may be the most appropriate. In an electronic commerce application running on the Internet where agents have no commitments to each other, on the other hand, egalitarian principles seem of little relevance. In such a case, it may be in the interest of the system designer to ensure at least Pareto optimal outcomes.

3   Resource Allocation by Negotiation

The general framework within which we are going to investigate welfare engineering is that of *resource allocation by negotiation*, where a number of agents negotiate the redistribution of a number of discrete (i.e. non-divisible) resources in order to benefit either themselves or the artificial society they inhabit. A negotiation scenario consists of a finite set of *agents* $\mathcal{A}$ and a finite set of *resources* $\mathcal{R}$. Within such a scenario, a resource *allocation* A is a partitioning of $\mathcal{R}$ amongst the agents in $\mathcal{A}$. For example, for an allocation A with $A(i) = \{r_3, r_7\}$ it would be the case that agent i owns resources r_3 and r_7. Given a particular allocation of resources, agents may agree on a *deal* to exchange some of the resources they currently hold. In general, a single deal may involve any number of resources and any number of agents. It transforms an allocation of resources A into a new allocation A', i.e. we can define a deal as a pair $\delta = (A, A')$ of allocations. We also define the set of agents involved in δ as $\mathcal{A}^\delta = \{i \in \mathcal{A} \mid A(i) \neq A'(i)\}$.

Every agent $i \in \mathcal{A}$ is equipped with a *utility function* $u_i : 2^\mathcal{R} \to \mathbb{R}$ to measure its individual welfare with respect to the set of resources it currently holds. We abbreviate $u_i(A) = u_i(A(i))$ for the utility value assigned by agent i to the set of resources it holds for allocation A. An agent may or may not find a particular deal *acceptable*. Here are some examples for possible acceptability criteria:

- A purely *selfish* agent may only accept deals $\delta = (A, A')$ that strictly improve its personal welfare: $u_i(A) < u_i(A')$.
- A *selfish but cooperative* agent may also be content with deals that do leave its own welfare constant: $u_i(A) \leq u_i(A')$.
- A *demanding* agent may require an increase of, say, 10 units for each and every deal it is asked to participate in: $u_i(A) + 10 \leq u_i(A')$.
- A *masochist* agent may insist on losing utility: $u_i(A) > u_i(A')$, etc.

The above are all examples where agents' decisions are based entirely on their own utility functions. This need not be the case:

- A *disciple* of agent *guru* may only accept deals $\delta = (A, A')$ that increase the welfare of the latter: $u_{guru}(A) < u_{guru}(A')$.
- A *team worker* may require the overall utility of a particular group of agents to increase:

$$\sum_{j \in Team} u_j(A) < \sum_{j \in Team} u_j(A')$$

Besides the acceptability criteria adopted by individual agents, the *negotiation protocol* in operation may also restrict the range of possible deals $\delta = (A, A')$:

- For instance, a particular protocol may not allow for more than two agents to be involved in any one deal: $|\mathcal{A}^\delta| \leq 2$.

A social welfare ordering formalises the notion of a society's "preferences" given the preferences of its members (the agents) [7, 8]. We are going to see several examples in the following sections. A particular deal may affect social welfare either positively or negatively. Our objective is to design criteria for the acceptability of deals that will guarantee positive or even optimal outcomes of negotiations.

We should stress here that we have made a number of simplifying assumptions in the definition of our negotiation framework. For instance, we do not take into account the possible costs incurred by trading agents when they redistribute bundles of resources (neither when measuring social welfare nor when modelling the utility functions of individual agents). Furthermore, our framework is static in the sense that agents' utility functions do not change over time. In a system that also allows for the modelling of agents' beliefs and goals in a dynamic fashion, this may not always be appropriate. An agent may, for instance, find out that a particular resource is in fact not required to achieve a particular goal, or it may simply decide to drop that goal for whatever reason. In a dynamic setting, such changes should be reflected by a revision of the agent's utility function. Still, while assuming constant utility functions for the entire life time of an agent may be unrealistic, it does indeed seem reasonable that utility functions do not change for the duration of a particular negotiation process. It is this level of abstraction that our negotiation framework is intended to model.

The most widely studied mechanisms for the reallocation of resources in multiagent systems are *auctions*. We should stress that our scenario of resource allocation by negotiation is *not* an auction. Auctions are mechanisms to help agents agree on a price at which an item (or a set of items) is to be sold [9]. In our work, on the other hand, we are not concerned with this aspect of negotiation, but only with the patterns of resource exchanges that agents actually carry out.

4   Results for Utilitarian and Egalitarian Systems

In this section, we summarise and discuss previous results for the cases of agent societies that are governed by either *utilitarian* or *egalitarian* principles [10, 11].

Definition 1 (Utilitarian Social Welfare). *The utilitarian social welfare* $sw_u(A)$ *of an allocation of resources* A *is defined as follows:*

$$sw_u(A) = \sum_{i \in A} u_i(A)$$

In systems without explicit utility transfers (i.e. in systems where agents cannot pay each other in order to accept otherwise disadvantageous deals), it is not always possible to negotiate an allocation of resources that maximises utilitarian social welfare without individual agents having to accept a loss in utility. A simple example would be a system with two agents 1 and 2 and a single resource r with $u_1(\{r\}) < u_2(\{r\})$. If agent 1 initially owns the resource, then giving r to agent 2 would increase utilitarian social welfare, but agent 1 may not be prepared to do this. This is why, for utilitarian systems, it is more realistic to aim for allocations that are at least *Pareto optimal:*

Definition 2 (Pareto Optimality). *An allocation of resources A is Pareto optimal iff there is no other allocation A' such that $sw_u(A) < sw_u(A')$ and $u_i(A) \leq u_i(A')$ for all $i \in \mathcal{A}$.*

In [10], agents that are selfish but cooperative have been identified as appropriate for utilitarian systems without explicit utility transfers. Such agents will be prepared to accept a deal whenever it is *cooperatively rational:*

Definition 3 (Cooperatively Rational Deals). *A deal $\delta = (A, A')$ is called cooperatively rational iff $u_i(A) \leq u_i(A')$ for all $i \in \mathcal{A}$ and there exists an agent $j \in \mathcal{A}$ such that $u_j(A) < u_j(A')$.*

The second part of this definition ensures that at least one agent (say, the one proposing the deal) will have a strictly positive payoff for every cooperatively rational deal. This condition is required to ensure the termination of a negotiation process. The following result is proved in [10]:

Theorem 1 (Pareto Optimal Outcomes). *Any sequence of cooperatively rational deals will eventually result in a Pareto optimal allocation of resources.*

The importance of this result lies in the fact that *any* sequence of deals will lead to a Pareto optimal allocation as long as agents only agree to deals that are cooperatively rational. This means that agents can arrange cooperatively rational deals locally, as they come up; they do not need to plan ahead for society to be able to eventually reach an optimal situation.

On the downside, deals involving any number of resources as well as agents may be *necessary* to reach an optimal allocation provided agents will only agree to deals that are cooperatively rational [10]. Realising such a negotiation protocol seems highly challenging and complex. However, in some cases we can get more favourable results, where a simpler class of deals is sufficient to guarantee an optimal outcome. This is, in particular, the case for so-called *0-1 scenarios* where every agent assigns a utility value of either 1 or 0 to each single resource (thereby specifying whether it does or does not *need* that resource) and where the utility value assigned to a set of resources is simply the sum of the single utilities (i.e. utility functions are additive). In this case, so-called *one-resource-at-a-time* deals (i.e. deals only involving a single resource and two agents) are sufficient to guarantee optimal outcomes in utilitarian systems [10]:

Theorem 2 (Maximising Utilitarian Welfare in 0-1 Scenarios). *In 0-1 scenarios, any sequence of cooperatively rational one-resource-at-a-time deals will eventually result in an allocation of resources with maximal utilitarian welfare.*

As an aside, we remark here that in cases where we are interested in maximising social welfare in a utilitarian agent society with general utility functions, a framework that includes a monetary component that allows (selfish) agents to compensate their trading partners for otherwise disadvantageous deals would be more appropriate. A discussion of such a negotiation framework *with* money

Table 1. Utility functions for Bob and Mary

$u_{bob}(\{\,\}) = 0$	$u_{mary}(\{\,\}) = 0$
$u_{bob}(\{glass\}) = 3$	$u_{mary}(\{glass\}) = 5$
$u_{bob}(\{wine\}) = 12$	$u_{mary}(\{wine\}) = 7$
$u_{bob}(\{glass, wine\}) = 15$	$u_{mary}(\{glass, wine\}) = 17$

(i.e. with explicit utility transfers), as well as proofs for sufficiency and necessity results similar to those reported here, may be found in [10].[1]

We now turn our attention to *egalitarian agent societies* [11]. The first goal of an egalitarian society should be to increase the welfare of its weakest member [8, 5, 6]. In other words, we can measure the social welfare of such a society by measuring the welfare of the agent that is currently worst off:

Definition 4 (Egalitarian Social Welfare). *The egalitarian social welfare* $sw_e(A)$ *of an allocation of resources A is defined as follows:*

$$sw_e(A) = min\{u_i(A) \mid i \in \mathcal{A}\}$$

When searching the economics literature for a class of deals that would benefit society in an egalitarian system we soon encounter *Pigou-Dalton transfers* [8]. In the context of our framework, a Pigou-Dalton transfer (between agents i and j) can be defined as follows:

Definition 5 (Pigou-Dalton Transfers). *A deal $\delta = (A, A')$ is called a Pigou-Dalton transfer iff it satisfies the following criteria:*

- *Only two agents i and j are involved in the deal: $\mathcal{A}^\delta = \{i, j\}$.*
- *The deal is mean-preserving: $u_i(A) + u_j(A) = u_i(A') + u_j(A')$.*
- *The deal reduces inequality: $|u_i(A') - u_j(A')| < |u_i(A) - u_j(A)|$.*

The second condition could be relaxed to $u_i(A) + u_j(A) \leq u_i(A') + u_j(A')$, to also allow for inequality-reducing deals that increase overall utility. Pigou-Dalton transfers capture certain egalitarian principles; but are they sufficient as acceptability criteria to guarantee optimal outcomes of negotiations for society?

Consider a scenario with two agents, Bob and Mary, and two resources, a bottle of wine and an empty glass. The utility functions for the two agents are given in Table 1. Bob attributes a high utility value to the wine and a low value to the glass. Furthermore, the value of both resources together is simply the sum of the individual utilities for Bob (no synergy effects). Mary ascribes a medium value to either resource and a very high value to the full set. Now suppose the initial allocation of resources is A with $A(bob) = \{glass\}$ and $A(mary) = \{wine\}$. The "inequality index" for this allocation is $|u_{bob}(A) - u_{mary}(A)| = 4$. We can easily check that inequality is in fact minimal for allocation A. However, allocation A'

---

[1] See also the work by Sandholm on the closely related subject of sufficient and necessary contract types for optimal allocations of tasks [12].

with $A'(bob) = \{wine\}$ and $A'(mary) = \{glass\}$ would result in higher egalitarian social welfare (namely 5 instead of 3). Hence, Pigou-Dalton transfers alone are not sufficient to guarantee optimal outcomes of negotiations in egalitarian agent societies. We need a more general acceptability criterion. To this end, we have put forward the class of *equitable* deals in [11]:

Definition 6 (Equitable Deals). *A deal $\delta = (A, A')$ is called equitable iff we have $min\{u_i(A) \mid i \in \mathcal{A}^\delta\} < min\{u_i(A') \mid i \in \mathcal{A}^\delta\}$.*

As shown in [11], this is a sufficient acceptability criterion for deals to guarantee optimal negotiation results in egalitarian systems:

Theorem 3 (Maximising Egalitarian Welfare). *Any sequence of equitable deals will eventually result in an allocation with maximal egalitarian welfare.*

Again, the connections between the local acceptability criterion and the global welfare ordering are not that surprising. The importance of the theorem lies in the fact that it allows agents to converge towards a global optimum by agreeing on exchanges of resources *locally*, without having to consider the welfare of agents not involved into a particular deal. In the literature on multiagent systems, the *autonomy* of an agent (one of the central features distinguishing multiagent systems from other distributed systems) is sometimes equated with pure selfishness. Under such an interpretation of the agent paradigm, our notion of equitability would, of course, make little sense. We believe, however, that it is useful to distinguish different degrees of autonomy. An agent may well be autonomous in its decision in general, but still be required to follow certain rules imposed by society (and agreed to by the agent on entering that society).

From a purely practical point of view, our results for egalitarian agent societies may be of a lesser interest than those for utilitarian systems, because in the former case it has not been possible to define a deal acceptability criterion that only depends on a *single* agent. Of course, this coincides with our intuitions about egalitarian societies: maximising social welfare is only possible by means of cooperation and the sharing of information on agents' preferences.

5   Negotiating Lorenz Optimal Allocations of Resources

We are now going to introduce a welfare ordering that combines utilitarian and egalitarian notions of social welfare. The basic idea is to endorse deals that result in an improvement with respect to the utilitarian welfare function without causing a loss in egalitarian welfare, and vice versa. An appropriate welfare ordering for this kind of agent society is given by the notion of Lorenz domination [8].

For a society with n agents, let $\{u_1, \ldots, u_n\}$ be the set of utility functions for that society. Then every allocation A determines a utility vector $\langle u_1(A), \ldots, u_n(A) \rangle$ of length n. If we rearrange the elements of that vector in increasing order we obtain the *ordered utility vector* for allocation A, which we are going to denote by $\boldsymbol{u}(A)$. The number $\boldsymbol{u}_i(A)$ is the ith element in that ordered utility vector (for $1 \leq i \leq n$). That is, $\boldsymbol{u}_1(A)$ for instance, is the utility value assigned to allocation A by the currently weakest agent.

Table 2. A situation that is not Lorenz optimal

Agent 1	Agent 2	Agent 3
$A(1) = \{\}$	$A(2) = \{\}$	$A(3) = \{r_1, r_2\}$
$u_1(\{\}) = 0$	$u_2(\{\}) = 0$	$u_3(\{\}) = 0$
$u_1(\{r_1\}) = 6$	$u_2(\{r_1\}) = 1$	$u_3(\{r_1\}) = 1$
$u_1(\{r_2\}) = 1$	$u_2(\{r_2\}) = 6$	$u_3(\{r_2\}) = 1$
$u_1(\{r_1, r_2\}) = 7$	$u_2(\{r_1, r_2\}) = 7$	$u_3(\{r_1, r_2\}) = 10$

Definition 7 (Lorenz Domination). *Let A and A' be allocations of resources for a society with n agents. Then A is Lorenz dominated by A' iff we have*

$$\sum_{i=1}^{k} u_i(A) \;\leq\; \sum_{i=1}^{k} u_i(A')$$

for all k with $1 \leq k \leq n$ and that inequality is strict in at least one case.

For any k with $1 \leq k \leq n$, the sum referred to in the above definition is the sum of the utility values assigned to the respective allocation of resources by the k weakest agents. For $k = 1$, this sum is equivalent to the egalitarian social welfare for that allocation. For $k = n$, it is equivalent to the utilitarian social welfare.

An allocation of resources is called *Lorenz optimal* iff it is not Lorenz dominated by any other allocation. When moving from one allocation of resources to another such that the latter Lorenz dominates the former we also speak of a *Lorenz improvement*.

We are now going to try to establish connections between the global welfare measure induced by the notion of Lorenz domination on the one hand, and various local criteria on the acceptability of a proposed deal that individual agents may choose to apply on the other. For instance, it is an immediate consequence of Definitions 3 and 7 that, whenever $\delta = (A, A')$ is a cooperatively rational deal, then A must be Lorenz dominated by A'. As may easily be verified, any deal that amounts to a Pigou-Dalton transfer will also result in a Lorenz improvement. On the other hand, it is not difficult to construct examples that show that this is not the case for the class of equitable deals anymore (that is, while some equitable deals will indeed result in a Lorenz improvement, others will not).

Our next goal is to find a class of deals that captures the notion of Lorenz improvements in as so far as, for any two allocations A and A' such that A is Lorenz dominated by A', there exists a sequence of deals (or possibly even a single deal) belonging to that class leading from A to A'. Given that both cooperatively rational deals and Pigou-Dalton transfers always result in a Lorenz improvement, the union of these two classes of deals may seem like a promising candidate. In fact, according to a result reported by Moulin [8, Lemma 2.3], it is the case that any Lorenz improvement can be implemented by means of a sequence of Pareto improvements and Pigou-Dalton transfers.[2] It is important to stress that

---

[2] Note that every Pareto improvement corresponds to a cooperatively rational deal [10].

this seemingly general result does *not* apply to our negotiation framework. To
see this, consider the example shown in Table 2. The ordered utility vector for
allocation A, which assigns both resources to agent 3, is $u(A) = \langle 0, 0, 10 \rangle$, i.e.
utilitarian social welfare is currently 10. Allocation A is Pareto optimal, because
any other allocation would be strictly worse for agent 3. Hence, there can be no
cooperatively rational deal that would be applicable in this situation. We also
observe that any deal involving only two agents would at best result in a new
allocation with a utilitarian social welfare of 7 (this would be a deal consisting
either of passing both resources on to one of the other agents, or of passing the
"preferred" resource to either agent 1 or agent 2, respectively). Hence, no deal
involving only two agents (and in particular no Pigou-Dalton transfer) could
possibly result in a Lorenz improvement. However, there *is* an allocation that
Lorenz dominates A, namely the allocation assigning to each one of the first two
agents their respectively preferred resource. This allocation A' with $A'(1) = \{r_1\}$,
$A'(2) = \{r_2\}$ and $A'(3) = \{\}$ has got the ordered utility vector $\langle 0, 6, 6 \rangle$. The
reason why Moulin's result is not applicable to our domain is that we cannot use
Pigou-Dalton transfers to implement arbitrary utility transfers here. Any such
transfer has to correspond to a move in our (discrete) negotiation space.

While this negative result emphasises, again, the high complexity of our
negotiation framework, we can get better results for scenarios with restricted
utility functions. Recall our definition of 0-1 scenarios where utility functions can
only be used to indicate whether an agent does or does not need a particular
resource: In such a scenario, $u_i(\{r\})$ is required to be either 0 or 1 for every
agent $i \in \mathcal{A}$ and every (single) resource $r \in \mathcal{R}$. Furthermore, utility functions
are required to be additive, i.e. we have $u_i(R) = \sum_{r \in R} u_i(\{r\})$ for every set of
resources $R \subseteq \mathcal{R}$. As we shall see next, for 0-1 scenarios, the aforementioned
result of Moulin *does* apply. In fact, we can even sharpen it a little by showing
that only Pigou-Dalton transfers and cooperatively rational deals involving just
a single resource and two agents are required to guarantee negotiation outcomes
that are Lorenz optimal. We first give a formal definition of this class of deals:

Definition 8 (Simple Pareto-Pigou-Dalton Deals). *A deal* $\delta = (A, A')$ *is
called a simple Pareto-Pigou-Dalton deal iff it only involves a single resource and
it is either cooperatively rational or a Pigou-Dalton transfer.*

We are now going to show that this class of deals is sufficient to guarantee Lorenz
optimal outcomes of negotiations in 0-1 scenarios:

Theorem 4 (Lorenz Optimal Outcomes in 0-1 Scenarios). *In 0-1 scenarios, any sequence of simple Pareto-Pigou-Dalton deals will eventually result
in a Lorenz optimal allocation of resources.*

Proof. As pointed out earlier, any deal that is either cooperatively rational or
a Pigou-Dalton transfer will result in a Lorenz improvement (not only in the
case of 0-1 scenarios). Hence, given that there is only a finite number of different allocations, after a finite number of deals the system will have reached an
allocation A where no more simple Pareto-Pigou-Dalton deals are possible (that
is, negotiation must terminate).

Now, for the sake of contradiction, let us assume this terminal allocation A is not optimal, i.e. there exists another allocation A' that Lorenz dominates A. Amongst other things, this implies $sw_u(A) \leq sw_u(A')$, i.e. we can distinguish two cases: either (i) there has been a strict increase in utilitarian welfare, or (ii) it has remained constant. In 0-1 scenarios, the former is only possible if there are (at least) one resource $r \in \mathcal{R}$ and two agents $i, j \in \mathcal{A}$ such that $u_i(\{r\}) = 0$ and $u_j(\{r\}) = 1$ as well as $r \in A(i)$ and $r \in A'(j)$, i.e. r has been moved from agent i (who does not need it) to agent j (who does need it). But then the deal of moving only r from i to j would be cooperatively rational and hence also a simple Pareto-Pigou-Dalton deal. This contradicts our assumption of A being a terminal allocation.

Now let us assume that utilitarian social welfare remained constant, i.e. $sw_u(A) = sw_u(A')$. Let k be the smallest index such that $\boldsymbol{u}_k(A) < \boldsymbol{u}_k(A')$. (This is the first k for which the inequality in Definition 7 is strict.) Observe that we cannot have $k = |\mathcal{A}|$, as this would contradict $sw_u(A) = sw_u(A')$. We shall call the agents contributing the first k entries in the ordered utility vector $\boldsymbol{u}(A)$ the *poor* agents and the remaining ones the *rich* agents. Then, in a 0-1 scenario, there must be a resource $r \in \mathcal{R}$ that is owned by a rich agent i in allocation A and by a poor agent j in allocation A' and that is needed by both these agents, i.e. $u_i(\{r\}) = 1$ and $u_j(\{r\}) = 1$. But then moving this resource from i to j would constitute a Pigou-Dalton transfer (and hence also a simple Pareto-Pigou-Dalton deal) in allocation A, which again contradicts our earlier assumption of A being terminal. □

In summary, we have shown that (i) any allocation of resources from which no simple Pareto-Pigou-Dalton deals are possible must be a Lorenz optimal allocation and (ii) that such an allocation will always be reached by implementing a finite number of simple Pareto-Pigou-Dalton deals. As with our earlier sufficiency results, agents do not need to worry about which deals to implement, as long as they are simple Pareto-Pigou-Dalton deals. The convergence to a global optimum is guaranteed by the theorem.

6 Further Examples: Elitism and Envy-Freeness

In this section, we are going to briefly discuss two further notions of social welfare: *elitism* and *envy-freeness*. The former may be motivated by the fact that, for certain applications, a distributed multiagent system may merely serve as a means for helping a single agent in that system to achieve its goal. However, it may not always be known in advance which agent is most likely to achieve its goal and should therefore be supported by its peers. The welfare of such a society would be evaluated on the basis of the happiest agent (as opposed to the unhappiest agent, as in the case of egalitarian welfare):

Definition 9 (Elitist Social Welfare). *The elitist social welfare $sw_{el}(A)$ of an allocation of resources A is defined as follows:*

$$sw_{el}(A) = max\{u_i(A) \mid i \in \mathcal{A}\}$$

In an *elitist agent society*, agents would cooperate in order to support their champion (the currently happiest agent). While such an approach to social welfare may seem somewhat unethical as far as human society is concerned, we believe that it could indeed be very appropriate for certain societies of artificial agents. A typical scenario could be where a system designer launches different agents with the same goal, with the aim that *at least one* agent achieves that goal—no matter what happens to the others. As with the egalitarian agent societies, this does not contradict the idea of agents being *autonomous* entities. Agents may be physically distributed and make their own autonomous decisions on a variety of issues whilst also adhering to certain social principles, in this case elitist ones.

From a technical point of view, designing a criterion that will allow agents inhabiting an elitist agent society to decide locally whether or not to accept a particular deal is very similar to the egalitarian case [11]. In analogy to the case of equitable deals defined earlier, a suitable deal would have to increase the maximal individual welfare amongst the agents involved in any one deal.

Our final example for an interesting approach to measuring social welfare in an agent society is the issue of envy-freeness [13]. For a particular allocation of resources, an agent may be "envious" of another agent if it would prefer that agent's set of resources over its own. Ideally, an allocation should be envy-free:

Definition 10 (Envy-Freeness). *An allocation of resources A is called envy-free iff we have $u_i(A(i)) \geq u_i(A(j))$ for all agents $i, j \in \mathcal{A}$.*

We should stress that envy-freeness is defined on the sole basis of an agent's private preferences; that is, there is no need to take other agents' utility functions into account. On the other hand, whether an agent is envious or not does not only depend on the resources it holds, but also on the resources it *could* hold and whether any of the other agents currently hold a preferred bundle. As we shall see, this somewhat paradoxical situation makes envy-freeness far less amenable to our methodology than any of the other notions of social welfare we have discussed in this paper.

Envy-freeness is desirable (though not always achievable) in societies of self-interested agents in cases where agents have to collaborate with each other over a longer period of time. In such a case, should an agent believe that it has been ripped off, it would have an incentive to leave the coalition which may be disadvantageous for other agents or the society as a whole. In other words, envy-freeness plays an important role with respect to the stability of a group. Unfortunately, envy-free allocations do not always exist. A simple example would be a system with two agents and just a single resource, which is valued by both of them. Then, whichever agent holds that single resource, will be envied by the other agent. To be able to measure different degrees of enviness, we could, for example, count the number of agents that are envious for a given allocation. However, it is not possible to define a *local* acceptability criterion in terms of the utility functions of the agents involved in a deal (and only those) that indicates whether the deal in question would reduce envy according to such a metric.

7 Conclusion

We have argued that a wide spectrum of social welfare orderings (rather than just those induced by the well known utilitarian social welfare function and the concept of Pareto optimality) can be of interest to agent-based applications. In an artificial society where agents negotiate over the allocation of resources, different social principles induce different local criteria on the acceptability of a proposed deal. Both in previous work [10, 11] and in the present paper, we have exemplified the idea of *welfare engineering* by designing such local criteria for different social welfare orderings, which in turn are motivated by different types of applications. In particular, we have shown that, for the relatively simple 0-1 scenarios, Lorenz optimal allocations can be achieved using one-to-one negotiation by implementing deals that are either inequality-reducing or that increase the welfare of both agents involved. We have also discussed the case of elitist agent societies and we have pointed out some of the difficulties associated with designing agents that would be able to negotiate allocations of resources where the degree of envy between the agents in a society is minimal.

Acknowledgements

We would like to thank the ESAW referees for their helpful comments. This work has been supported by the European Union as part of the SOCS project (IST-2001-32530) and has been carried out while the second author was employed at City University, London.

References

[1] Sandholm, T.W.: Distributed Rational Decision Making. In Weiss, G., ed.: Multiagent Systems: A Modern Approach to Distributed Artificial Intelligence. MIT Press (1999) 201–258 93
[2] Grosz, B.J., Kraus, S.: Collaborative Plans for Complex Group Action. Artificial Intelligence **86** (1996) 269–357 93
[3] Lemaître, M., Verfaillie, G., Bataille, N.: Exploiting a Common Property Resource under a Fairness Constraint: A Case Study. In: Proceedings of the 16th International Joint Conference on Artificial Intelligence, Morgan Kaufmann Publishers (1999) 206–211 93, 95
[4] Harsanyi, J.C.: Can the Maximin Principle Serve as a Basis for Morality? American Political Science Review **69** (1975) 594–609 95
[5] Rawls, J.: A Theory of Justice. Oxford University Press (1971) 95, 99
[6] Sen, A.K.: Collective Choice and Social Welfare. Holden Day (1970) 95, 99
[7] Arrow, K.J.: Social Choice and Individual Values. John Wiley and Sons (1963) 97
[8] Moulin, H.: Axioms of Cooperative Decision Making. Cambridge University Press (1988) 97, 99, 100, 101
[9] Kersten, G.E., Noronha, S.J., Teich, J.: Are All E-Commerce Negotiations Auctions? In: Proceedings of the 4th International Conference on the Design of Cooperative Systems. (2000) 97

[10] Endriss, U., Maudet, N., Sadri, F., Toni, F.: On Optimal Outcomes of Negotiations over Resources. In: Proceedings of the 2nd International Joint Conference on Autonomous Agents and Multiagent Systems, ACM Press (2003) 177–184   97, 98, 99, 101, 105

[11] Endriss, U., Maudet, N., Sadri, F., Toni, F.: Resource Allocation in Egalitarian Agent Societies. In: Secondes Journées Francophones sur les Modèles Formels d'Interaction, Cépaduès-Éditions (2003) 101–110   97, 99, 100, 104, 105

[12] Sandholm, T.W.: Contract Types for Satisficing Task Allocation: I Theoretical Results. In: AAAI Spring Symposium: Satisficing Models. (1998)   99

[13] Brams, S.J., Taylor, A.D.: Fair Division: From Cake-cutting to Dispute Resolution. Cambridge University Press (1996)   104

Dynamics of Collective Attitudes during Teamwork

Barbara Dunin-Kęplicz[1,2] and Rineke Verbrugge[3]

[1] Institute of Informatics
Warsaw University
Banacha 2, 02-097 Warsaw, Poland
[2] Institute of Computer Science
Polish Academy of Sciences
Ordona 21, 01-237 Warsaw, Poland
keplicz@mimuw.edu.pl
[3] Department of Artificial Intelligence
University of Groningen
Grote Kruisstraat 2/1, 9712 TS Groningen, The Netherlands
rineke@ai.rug.nl

Abstract. In this paper we aim to describe dynamic aspects of social and collective motivational attitudes in teams of agents involved in Co-operative Problem Solving (CPS). Particular attention is given to the strongest attitude, collective commitment, and its evolution in a course of teamwork. During team action, the collective commitment leads to the execution of agent-specific actions. A dynamic and unpredictable environment may, however, cause the failure of some of these actions, or present the agents with new opportunities. The abstract reconfiguration algorithm, presented in a previous paper, is designed to handle the replanning needed in such situations in an efficient way. In this paper, the dynamic logic component of the logical framework addresses issues pertaining to adjustments in collective commitment during reconfiguration.

1 Introduction

Teamwork is a vital aspect of BDI system expressing its dynamics. In recent systems it is modelled explicitly, allowing the team to monitor its performance and especially to replan based on the present situation. The dynamic and unpredictable environment poses the problem that team members may fail to bring their tasks to a good end or new opportunities may appear. This leads to the *reconfiguration problem*: during plan execution, it is crucial that agents replan properly and efficiently when the situation changes. A generic solution of this problem in BDI systems is presented by us in [1]. We base our solution on the four-stage model of [2], containing the consecutive stages of *potential recognition*, *team formation*, *plan formation* and *team action*. The processes of potential recognition and team formation, including the role of dialogue, have been extensively discussed in [3]. Ultimately, the *reconfiguration algorithm*, showing the

A. Omicini, P. Petta, and J. Pitt (Eds.): ESAW 2003, LNAI 3071, pp. 107–122, 2004.
© Springer-Verlag Berlin Heidelberg 2004

phases of construction, maintenance, and realization of collective motivational attitudes, is formulated in terms of these levels and their (complex) interplay.

The algorithm is a departure point to describe the dynamics of social and collective attitudes in a team of agents involved in CPS. *Collective commitment* is defined on the basis of collective intention and social commitments: the ongoing collective intention is split up into sub-actions, according to a given social plan. Next, the action allocation is reflected in social (i.e. bilateral) commitments between pairs of agents. During the phase of team action, agents aim to realize actions they are committed to in order to achieve the overall goal of a team. Their individual success completes the solution. Otherwise, in the case of failure of some action performance, the realization of the collective commitment by the whole team is threatened. It means that some effects of the previous stages of teamwork, sometimes rather complex and expensive, may be wasted. However, in some cases a minor correction of the plan, and then the collective commitment based on it, suffices to save the situation.

In the reconfiguration algorithm, an *evolution* of collective commitment during reconfiguration is shown in a dynamically changing environment. In this paper we will characterize the properties of this process using dynamic logic notation, which allows to precisely describe the results of complex actions involved in reconfiguration. The new contribution of this paper as compared to [1] is that the process of motivational and informational attitude change during reconfiguration is made transparent. The dynamic logic description will provide a basis for implementation of the system, as well as for formal verification methods. Thus, we will adopt a computer science point of view, that is the perspective of a system developer, rather than the one of an agent. We will focus on generic properties ensuring a correct behaviour of the system as a whole. This enables a system designer to construct a program from the existing specification, even though this specification is rather complex.

The paper is organized in the following way. In section 2, the logical language and semantics are introduced. Section 3 defines the social and collective motivational attitudes that come to the fore during teamwork. Section 4 gives a short overview of the four levels of CPS. The central section 5 presents in a multi-modal language how collective commitments evolve during reconfiguration. Finally, section 6 focuses on discussion and options for further research. The reader may skip section 2 and instead start reading from section 3, only jumping back when needing more background about the language and semantics.

2   The Logical Framework

The language $\mathcal{L}$ is based on a denumerable set $\mathcal{P}$ of *propositional symbols*, and a finite set $\mathcal{A}$ of *agents*, denoted by numerals $1, 2, \ldots, n$. Below follows a simplified version of the full logical language presented in a forthcoming journal paper; the present version is geared towards expressing the dynamics of attitudes in CPS and does not include temporal operators, for example.

Definition 1 (Formulas).
We inductively define a set of formulas $\mathcal{L}$ as follows.

F1 each atomic proposition $p \in \mathcal{P}$ is a formula;
F2 if φ and ψ are formulas, then so are $\neg\varphi$ and $\varphi \wedge \psi$;
F3 if φ is a formula, α is an individual action, $i, j \in \mathcal{A}$, $G \subseteq \mathcal{A}$, σ a finite sequence of formulas, τ a finite sequence of individual actions, and P a social plan expression, then the following are formulas:
   Epistemic: $\mathrm{BEL}(i, \varphi)$, $\mathrm{E\text{-}BEL}_G(\varphi)$, $\mathrm{C\text{-}BEL}_G(\varphi)$;
   Motivational: $\mathrm{GOAL}(i, \varphi)$, $\mathrm{INT}(i, \varphi)$, $\mathrm{C\text{-}INT}_G(\varphi)$, $\mathrm{COMM}(i, j, \alpha)$,
      $\mathrm{C\text{-}COMM}_{G,P}(\varphi)$;
   Temporal Action and Dynamic: $done(P)$, $succ(P)$, $failed(P)$, $do(P)$,
      $[P]\varphi$;
   Level Results: $div(\varphi, \sigma)$, $means(\sigma, \tau)$, $all(\tau, P)$, $cons(\varphi, P)$;

Next, we define the class of social plan expressions $\mathcal{S}p$, based on a set of individual actions $\mathcal{A}c$, which are application-dependent and will not be defined here. An example is given in subsection 3.2.

Definition 2 (Social Plan Expressions).
The class $\mathcal{S}p$ of social plan expressions is defined inductively as follows:

SP1 if $\alpha \in \mathcal{A}c$ and $i \in \mathcal{A}$, then $\langle \alpha, i \rangle$ is a social plan expression;
SP2 if $\varphi \in \mathcal{L}$ and $G \subseteq \mathcal{A}$, then $\mathtt{conf}_G\, \varphi$ is social plan expression (of which the subscript G is often left out);
SP3 if φ is a formula, α is an individual action, $a \in \mathcal{A}$, $G \subseteq \mathcal{A}$, σ a finite sequence of formulas, τ a finite sequence of individual actions, and $P \in \mathcal{S}p$, then $\mathtt{PotR}(\varphi, a)$, $\mathtt{TeamF}(\varphi, a, G)$, $\mathtt{PlanG}(\varphi, P)$, $\mathtt{div}(\varphi, \sigma)$, $\mathtt{means}(\sigma, \tau)$, $\mathtt{all}(\tau, P)$, $\mathtt{succ}$, and $\mathtt{fail}$ are social plan expressions;
SP4 If α and β are social plan expressions, then $(\alpha; \beta)$ (sequential composition) and $(\alpha \parallel \beta)$ (parallellism) are social plan expressions.

Here, elements of SP3 refer to the respective stages of CPS described in section 4. Next, Kripke models are defined, but only including elements relevant to this paper.

Definition 3 (Kripke Model).
A Kripke model is a tuple
$\mathcal{M} = (W, \{B_i : i \in \mathcal{A}\}, \{I_i : i \in \mathcal{A}\}, \{R_P : P \in \mathcal{S}p\}, Val, perf, agents)$ such that

1. W is a set of possible worlds, or states;
2. For all $i \in \mathcal{A}$, it holds that $B_i, I_i \subseteq W \times W$. They stand for the accessibility relations for each agent w.r.t. beliefs and intentions, respectively. For example, $(w_1, w_2) \in B_i$ means that w_2 is an epistemic alternative for agent i in state w_1;
3. For all $P \in \mathcal{S}p$, $R_P \subseteq W \times W$. They stand for the dynamic accessibility relations, e.g. $(w_1, w_2) \in R_{(i,\alpha)}$ means that w_2 is a possible resulting state from w_1 by agent i executing action α; for example, $R_{\mathtt{conf}_G(\varphi)} = \{(w, w) \in W \mid \mathcal{M}, w \models \varphi\}$ (see definition 4 for $\mathcal{M}, w \models \varphi$);

4. $Val : \mathcal{P} \times W \rightarrow \{0,1\}$ is the function that assigns truth values to propositional atoms in states;
5. ag: $\mathcal{S}p \times W \rightarrow 2^{\mathcal{A}}$ is the agents function that indicates for each social plan in each world which set of agents is involved in it, e.g., $ag(\langle\alpha, i\rangle, w) = \{i\}$;
6. $perf$: $2^{\mathcal{A}} \times \mathcal{S}p \rightarrow (W \rightarrow \{0,1,2\})$ is the social plan performance function such that $perf(G,P)(w)$ indicates the result in world w of the performance of social plan P by a group of agents G (here 0 stands for failure, 1 for success, and 2 stands for "undefined", e.g. for states w that are not an endpoint of accessibility relation R_P);
7. $next$: $2^{\mathcal{A}} \times \mathcal{S}p \rightarrow (W \rightarrow \{0,1\})$ is the next moment social plan performance function such that $next(G,P)(w) = 1$ indicates that in world w the group of agents G will next start performing social plan P.

The accessibility relations for the epistemic and motivational operators may obey some restrictions corresponding to appropriate axioms (see [4, 5, 6, 7]). The accessibility relations R_P are built up from accessibility relations for individual actions in an appropriate way (see [8]).

Definition 4 (Semantics).
Below, we give non-standard parts of the truth definition.

- $\mathcal{M}, v \models succ(P) \Leftrightarrow perf(ag(P,v),P)(v) = 1$;
- $\mathcal{M}, v \models failed(P) \Leftrightarrow perf(ag(P,v),P)(v) = 0$;
- $\mathcal{M}, v \models done(P) \Leftrightarrow perf(ag(P,v),P)(v) \in \{0,1\}$;
- $\mathcal{M}, v \models do(P) \Leftrightarrow next(ag(P,v),P)(v) = 1$;
- $\mathcal{M}, v \models [P]\varphi \Leftrightarrow$ for all $w((v,w) \in R_P \Rightarrow \mathcal{M}, w \models \varphi)$.

For the dynamic operator, $[P]\varphi$ stands for "whenever P terminates, it must do so in a state satisfying φ". Because actions and their effects are not the main subject, we have "hard-wired" their performance and effects in the functions $perf$ and $nextsp$, so at each world it is determined whether a certain social plan P has just been carried out (*done*), and if so, whether it was successful or not (*succ* respectively *failed*). Also one can express that a social plan P will be carried out next (*do*).

3   Collective Attitudes

This work fits into a research program developed for a couple of years already, part of which gives a static theory of individual, social and collective attitudes within a team (compare [9, 3, 7, 10]). Below, we only give a short reminder of relevant attitudes. In our approach, teams are created on the basis of *collective intentions*, and exist as long as the collective intention between team members exists. A collective intention may be viewed as an inspiration for team activity, whereas the collective commitment reflects the concrete manner of achieving the intended goal by the team. This concrete manner is provided by planning. Thus, our approach to collective commitments is plan-based.

Collective intention and collective commitment are not introduced as primitive modalities, with some restrictions on the semantic accessibility relations. We have given necessary and sufficient, but still minimal, conditions for such collective motivational attitudes to be present.

3.1   Collective Intentions

We focus on strictly cooperative teams, which makes the definition of collective intention rather strong. In such teams, a necessary condition for a collective intention C-INT$_G(\varphi)$ is that all members of the team G have the associated individual intention INT(i, φ) towards the overall goal φ. However, to exclude the case of competition, all agents should also *intend* all members to have the associated individual intention, as well as the intention that all members have the individual intention, and so on; we call such a mutual intention M-INT$_G(\varphi)$. Furthermore, all members of the team are aware of this mutual intention, that is, they have a collective belief C-BEL$_G$(M-INT$_G(\varphi)$ about this. In [7], we introduce a formal definition which is extensively discussed and compared with alternatives such as joint intention theory and SharedPlans theory [11, 6].

3.2   Collective Commitments

We treat collective commitment as the strongest motivational attitude to be considered in teamwork. In our opinion a collective intention is a necessary but not sufficient condition for a collective commitment to be present. Our definition of collective commitment is based on a social plan.

Social Plans. Let us give a simple **example** of a social plan (see definition 2). Consider a team consisting of three agents t (theorem prover), l (lemma prover) and c (proof checker) who have as collective intention to prove a new mathematical theorem. Suppose during planning they define two lemmas, which also still need to be proved, and the following complex individual actions: $prL1$, $prL2$ (to prove lemma 1, respectively 2), $chL1$, $chL2$ (to check a proof of lemma 1, respectively 2), prT (prove the theorem from the conjunction of lemmas 1 and 2), chT (to check the proof of the theorem from the lemmas). One possible social plan they can come up with is the following. First, the lemma prover, who proves lemmas 1 and 2 in succession, and the theorem prover, who proves the theorem from the two lemmas, work in parallel, and subsequently the proof checker checks their proofs in a fixed order: $P = \langle\langle\langle\langle prL1, l\rangle; \langle prL2, l\rangle\rangle \parallel \langle prT, t\rangle\rangle; \langle chL2, c\rangle; \langle chT, c\rangle\rangle$.

The result of the whole planning process is a social plan P, and the predicate $cons(\varphi, P)$ (for "constitute"), stating that plan P ensures proper realization of goal φ. The way this predicate is constructed is discussed in section 4.3. Thus, the successful realization of P should lead to the achievement of φ:

CS $cons(\varphi, P) \rightarrow [\mathtt{conf}(succ(P))]\varphi$

Social Commitments. A social commitment between two agents is not as strong as a collective commitment among them, but stronger than their individual intentions. If an agent commits to a second agent to do something, then the first agent should have the *intention* to do that. Also, the first agent commits to the second one only if the second one is *interested* in the first one fulfilling its intention. Moreover, it is necessary that the agents are aware about the situation, i.e. about their individual attitudes. Such awareness, expressed in terms of collective belief, is generally achieved by communication. Thus, a social commitment with respect to action α is defined as follows:

$$\text{COMM}(i,j,\alpha) \leftrightarrow \text{INT}(i,\alpha) \wedge \text{GOAL}(j, done(i,\alpha))$$
$$\wedge \text{C-BEL}_{\{i,j\}}(\text{INT}(i,\alpha) \wedge \text{GOAL}(j, done(i,\alpha)))$$

The Definition of a Collective Commitment. After the team is constituted, the stage of plan generation starts, leading ultimately to a *collective commitment* between the team members. In this section, we will give a strong definition of collective commitment; for alternative definitions to be used in various types of environments and organizational structures, see [10].

A collective commitment C-COMM$_{G,P}$ is based on a social plan P and can only be established if the team has the associated collective intention. Furthermore, there is a social plan leading to the achievement of the goal, as reflected in $cons(\varphi, P)$. It is assumed here that the team is planning collectively, so that in the end the plan is completely known to all members, reflected by the conjunct C-BEL$_G(cons(\varphi, P))$. In addition, for all actions α that occur in social plan P, there should be one agent in the team who is socially committed to at least one (mostly other) agent in the team to fulfil the subgoal. Moreover, there should be a collective belief in the whole team that the plan will be entirely realised, i.e. that all actions have been adopted by committed members of the team (even if there need not be a collective belief in the team about each particular social commitment that has been made). The defining axiom reflects all these characteristics.

$$\text{C-COMM}_{G,P}(\varphi) \leftrightarrow \text{C-INT}_G(\varphi) \wedge cons(\varphi, P) \wedge \bigwedge_{\alpha \in P} \bigvee_{i,j \in G} \text{COMM}(i,j,\alpha) \wedge$$
$$\text{C-BEL}_G(cons(\varphi, P) \wedge \bigwedge_{\alpha \in P} \bigvee_{i,j \in G} \text{COMM}(i,j,\alpha)))$$

4   The Four Levels of CPS

We assume that in a dynamic system collective commitment may evolve in order to ensure the proper realization of collective intention of the group. Thus, in the first place, one should guarantee that the collective intention should last long enough. One should monitor the construction, maintenance, and realization, i.e. *evolution* of collective commitments in a dynamic system. We adopted the four-stage model of [2], containing the consecutive stages of *potential recognition*, *team formation*, *plan formation* and *team action*. The key point is to bind the appropriate individual, social and collective attitudes to these stages.

Now we specify a formal system realizing the above-mentioned consecutive stages. We assume that they are realized by complex level-associated actions, called here `PotR`, `TeamF`, `div`, `means`, and `all`. These application-dependent actions will not be refined here.

4.1   The Potential Recognition Level

Analogous to [2], we consider CPS to begin when some agent in a multi-agent environment recognizes the potential for cooperative action in order to reach its goal. The input of this stage is an agent a, a goal φ plus a finite set $T \subseteq \mathcal{A}$ of agents from whom a potential team may be formed. The output at this stage is the "potential for cooperation" $\mathrm{PotC}(\varphi, a)$ that agent a sees with respect to φ, meaning that φ is a goal of a, and there is a team G such that a believes that G can collectively achieve φ and are willing to participate in team formation; and either a cannot or doesn't desire to achieve φ in isolation, see [1] for a formal definition and extensive discussion. For now, let us assume that potential recognition stage is realized by a complex action `PotR`. Thus, in case of successful performance of this action by agent a we have:

Ps $succ(\mathtt{PotR}(\varphi, a)) \rightarrow \mathrm{PotC}(\varphi, a)$

However, the failure of `PotR`, meaning that agent a doesn't see any potential of cooperation w.r.t. φ, leads to the failure of the system as a whole.

Pf $failed(\mathtt{PotR}(\varphi, a)) \rightarrow do(\mathtt{fail}(\varphi))$

This uses the notation for results of actions inspired by dynamic logic, and stands for: potential recognition has failed, then `fail`(φ) is done, where `fail` and `succ` are realized by complex actions which will not be refined here. Their proper realization should be ensured by a system developer.

4.2   The Team Formation Level

Suppose that agent a sees the potential for cooperation to achieve φ. Somewhat different from [2], we find that during team formation agent a attempts to establish in some team G the *collective intention* C-INT$_G(\varphi)$. The input of this stage is agent a, a formula φ and sequence of potential teams as output by the potential recognition stage. The successful outcome is one team G from the sequence together with a collective intention among G to achieve φ, which includes corresponding individual intentions of all team members. Let us assume that team formation is realized by a complex action `TeamF`. Thus, in case of its successful performance:

Ts $succ(\mathtt{TeamF}(\varphi, a, G)) \rightarrow$ C-INT$_G(\varphi)$

However, the failure of execution of `TeamF`, meaning that the collective intention w.r.t. φ cannot be established among any of the teams from a sequence chosen during the `PotR` action, requires a return to the potential recognition stage to construct a new sequence of potential teams:

Tf $failed(\text{TeamF}(\varphi, a, G)) \rightarrow do(\text{PotR}(\varphi, a))$

4.3   The Plan Generation Level

The input of this stage is a team G together with collective intention C-INT$_G(\varphi)$. The successful outcome is a collective commitment of the team G based on a social plan P, somewhat different than in [2]. When building a collective commitment in the group we always assume that the team is established, and the collective intention is in place. Then, planning starts, potentially resulting in the establishment of $cons(\varphi, P)$, meaning that the planning ended up successfully. Then, a collective team activity leading ultimately to the establishment of C-COMM$_{G,P}(\varphi)$ takes place.

Construction of C-COMM$_{G,P}(\varphi)$. We see planning as a three-step process. The first step is *task division*, in which a complex task φ is decomposed into (possibly also complex) subgoals. We assume that this phase is realized by a complex action `div` and its result is described by a predicate $div(\varphi, \sigma)$ standing for "the sequence σ is a result of task decomposition of goal φ into subgoals". Here, σ is a finite sequence of propositions standing for goals. Thus, after successful realization of this stage, we have $div(\varphi, \sigma)$, otherwise not:

Ds $succ(\text{div}(\varphi, \sigma)) \rightarrow div(\varphi, \sigma)$

Df $failed(\text{div}(\varphi, \sigma)) \rightarrow \neg div(\varphi, \sigma)$

The social action $\text{div}(\varphi, \sigma)$, as well as the ones corresponding to other levels, will not be decomposed further in this paper. In fact, they are rather complex group level actions, depending on the context and the application domain, as well as communication and coordination protocols between agents.

Next follows the phase of *means-end analysis* determining means realizing ends, i.e. actions realizing particular subgoals. Again, we assume that this phase is realized by a complex action `means`, and its result is described by a predicate $means(\sigma, \tau)$ standing for "the action sequence τ is a result of means-end analysis for the subgoal sequence σ". Here, τ is a finite sequence of actions $\in \mathcal{Ac}$. This is a generalization of standard means-end analysis, which is performed for a single goal at a time. Note that to each subgoal in σ, a number of actions may be associated, so that σ and τ may have different lengths. Thus, the result of successful realization of this stage is $means(\sigma, \tau)$, otherwise not:

Ms $succ(\text{means}(\sigma, \tau)) \rightarrow means(\sigma, \tau)$

Mf $failed(\text{means}(\sigma, \tau)) \rightarrow \neg means(\sigma, \tau)$

This step is followed by *action allocation*, in which the actions resulting from means-end analysis are given to team members. It is realized by a complex action *allocation*. This results first in pairs $\langle \alpha, i \rangle$ of action α and an agent i. To make allocation complete, the temporal structure among pairs $\langle \alpha, i \rangle$ should be established. This process of constructing a social plan is described by the predicate

$all(\tau, P)$ standing for "P is a social plan resulting from allocating a sequence of actions τ to interested team members". Thus, the result of successful realization of this stage is $all(\tau, P)$, otherwise not:

As $succ(\text{all}(\tau, P)) \rightarrow all(\tau, P)$

Af $failed(\text{all}(\tau, P)) \rightarrow \neg all(\tau, P)$

The predicate $cons(\varphi, P)$ informally stands for "P is a correct social plan to achieve φ", with as formal definition:

C0 $cons(\varphi, P) \leftrightarrow \exists \sigma \exists \tau (div(\varphi, \sigma) \wedge means(\sigma, \tau) \wedge all(\tau, P))$

Note that in the predicates $div, means$ and all, it does not matter that the length n of the task sequence is not fixed in advance; one can always code finite sequences in such a way that their length may be recovered from the code.

The overall planning phase is considered as a three-step process consisting of the complex action $\text{div};\text{means};\text{all}$. In case of successful performance of this action a correct plan is constructed:

C1 $succ(\text{div}(\varphi, \sigma); \text{means}(\sigma, \tau); \text{all}(\tau, P)) \rightarrow cons(\varphi, P)$

The case of failure of plan formation will now be considered more in detail, looking carefully at which step the failure actually takes place. Thus, the failure of div, meaning that no task division for φ was found, requires a return to team formation in order to establish a collective intention in the chosen new team. It may be viewed as reconfiguration of the team together with revision of the collective intention and the respective individual attitudes.

Dd $failed(\text{div}(\varphi, \sigma)) \rightarrow do(\text{TeamF}(\varphi, a, G'))$

The failure of means, meaning that there are no available means to realize some subgoals from a goal sequence σ, requires a return to the task division level in order to create a new sequence of subgoals.

Md $failed(\text{means}(\sigma, \tau)) \rightarrow do(\text{div}(\varphi, \sigma'))$

The failure of all, meaning that some of the previously established actions cannot be allocated to agents in G, requires a return to means-end analysis for new means that could be allocated to members of the current team.

Ad $failed(\text{all}(\tau, P)) \rightarrow do(\text{means}(\sigma, \tau'))$

In the two above situations, when backtracking is considered, some partial results of earlier stages already established may be reused to achieve $cons(\varphi, P')$ for a new social plan P'. This way a sort of system conservativity is maintained (see [1] for a detailed discussion). Thus, it is assumed that the following holds:

C2 $div(\varphi, \sigma) \wedge means(\sigma, \tau) \wedge succ(\text{all}(\tau, P')) \rightarrow cons(\varphi, P')$

C3 $div(\varphi, \sigma) \wedge succ(\text{means}(\sigma, \tau'); \text{all}(\tau', P')) \rightarrow cons(\varphi, P')$

In fact, **C2** follows directly from **C0** and **As**. Now, let dial (for "dialogue") be the application-dependent complex social action realizing necessary phases of communication and information exchange, and obeying the postulate:

CTR $\text{C-INT}_G(\varphi) \wedge cons(\varphi, P) \wedge succ(\mathtt{dial}(\varphi, G, P)) \rightarrow \text{C-COMM}_{G,P}(\varphi)$

This information exchange concludes the collective part of plan generation, and the team is ready to start *team action*.

Frame Axioms for Plan Generation. We assume that the system developer takes care that all complex actions executed during plan generation, when carried out in the appropriate order, do not disturb the partial planning results created previously. For example, the result of task division stays intact during subsequent means-end analysis, action allocation and construction:

FR $succ(\mathtt{div}(\varphi,\sigma); \mathtt{means}(\sigma,\tau); \mathtt{all}(\tau,P); \mathtt{dial}(\varphi,G,P))$
$\rightarrow div(\varphi, \sigma) \wedge means(\sigma, \tau) \wedge all(\tau, P)$

4.4   The Team Action Level: Reconfiguration

During team action, all team members start executing their adequate agent-specific actions from the $\text{C-COMM}_{G,P}(\varphi)$. In terms of motivational attitudes, team action amounts to the maintenance of *social commitments* and associated *individual intentions*. The successful outcome of this stage is that all actions making up the social plan P have been carried out by the agents who were socially committed to do them, and that by the success of their actions the overall goal φ has been achieved. In the more common non-perfect case disturbances require reconfiguration of the system at some point. As this may happen at any moment, the team action level will be referred to as the *reconfiguration process*.

The successful realization of team action finishes the evolution of the team and its motivational attitudes. Before this takes place, all aspects of evolution are treated in the reconfiguration process. During this phase communication, including all types of dialogue, cooperation, and coordination take place.

5   Evolution of Commitment During Reconfiguration

Even though the definition of collective commitment is intuitive, its complexity calls for a rigorous maintenance of all motivational attitudes involved in CPS. A constantly changing environment leads to the *reconfiguration problem*: when maintaining a collective intention during plan execution, it is crucial that agents replan properly and efficiently when some members do not fulfill their delegated actions or are presented with new opportunities. The explicit model of teamwork helps the team to monitor its performance, and to replan based on the present situation. In [1] we discuss how the abstract reconfiguration algorithm helps to do this in an effective way. Here, in contrast, we concentrate on the maintenance of the collective commitments during reconfiguration.

Collective commitment is the attitude needed to start team action. Once the process is underway, the collective commitment may evolve, so that the collective intention (which persists during plan realization) is finally achieved, if possible. More precisely, the evolution of collective commitment may be connected with the evolution of collective intention, in the sense that the team involved in collective intention may evolve, though the overall goal remains the same.

This section is built on the reconfiguration algorithm, which distinguishes several cases that can occur during plan execution. These cases are based on an analysis of different kinds of failure and success of individual actions, i.e. on strictly technical aspects of team action. Agents' awareness of their situation is left aside. Here we aim solely at formulating a *minimal* set of properties ensuring a reconfiguration process to be correct.

To properly deal with the variety of situations the reason of disturbances has to be recognized. We say that the execution of an action α fails for an *objective reason* R, denoted as $objective_G(R, \alpha)$, if R implies logically that α is not realizable by anybody in the present team G in the current state of the world, i.e. that nobody has the ability and opportunity to do it. The needed information may be achieved in different ways, depending on the problem solving domain and the organizational structure of the team. In this context, the objectivity is of course an idealization.

Moreover, the complex social actions `fail` and `succ` are introduced. Again, like in the case of level-associated actions, they are context-dependent and will not be decomposed here. In terms of motivational attitudes, they are interpreted as the failure and the success of collective intention, respectively. The failure of collective intention is equivalent to the failure of the reconfiguration algorithm.

In short, during plan execution a number of different cases is treated by the reconfiguration algorithm, all of them leading to changes in the agents' attitudes. It may be helpful to keep in mind the analogue of backtracking. In the successful case, all agents successfully perform the actions to which they socially committed, leading to `system-success` (see case 1 below). Otherwise, the unsuccessful case 2 is split into a number of subcases, according to the reasons of failure and the possibility of action reallocation:

- A new action allocation succeeds (case 2a)
- A new action allocation fails, and
  - A failed action blocks achieving the collective intention (case 2b), or
  - No failed action blocks achieving the collective intention, and
    * a new means-end analysis, followed by action allocation, succeeds (case 2c), or
    * a new means-end analysis, followed by action allocation, fails, and
      · a new task division, followed by means-end analysis and action allocation, succeeds (case 2d), or
      · a new task division, followed by means-end analysis and action allocation, fails.

Thus, if some actions failed but no action failed for an objective reason, first a new `all` is attempted. This new action allocation, in which failed tasks are assigned to other team members, may be successful (case 2a). If `all` fails, on the other hand, we consider two cases: either the failed action was necessary for achieving the collective intention; i.e. there is an objective reason R for the failure of the action, that implies that the overall goal φ will never be achieved by the current team, leading to system-failure (case 2b).

If the overall goal is not blocked in this way, a new means is attempted for the current sequence of subgoals of φ. This new means-end analysis, followed by a new all, may be successful (case 2c). If it fails, however, a new div is attempted for the overall goal of the system, followed by means and all. This may be successful (case 2d). If not, on the other hand, a return is made to the level of *team formation* in order to establish a new team realizing the overall goal φ of the system (see 4.2). Now we are ready to treat the cases of evolution of the collective commitment according to the reconfiguration algorithm.

We will make use of properties for complex actions, that follow immediately from correct construction of the function *perf* and the definition of conf:

Lemma 1. *In all Kripke models $\mathcal{M}$ and worlds w, and social plans P_1, P_2, we have:* $\mathcal{M}, w \models succ(P_1; P_2) \rightarrow succ(P_2)$ *and* $\mathcal{M}, w \models [\text{conf}(\psi)]\chi \leftrightarrow (\psi \rightarrow \chi)$

We will illustrate all cases with the theorem proving example that first appeared in subsection 3.2. Here follow some more details:

Running Example: The team $G = \{t, l, c\}$ have created a collective intention to overall goal $\varphi=$"theorem T has been proved". During task division they created the subgoal sequence $\sigma = \langle \sigma_1, \sigma_2 \rangle$, with $\sigma_1 = $ "lemmas leading to T have been proved" and $\sigma_2 = $ "theorem T has been proved from lemmas". During means-end analysis, complex actions have been found to achieve these subgoals, namely $\tau = \langle prL1, prL2, chL1, chL2, prT, chT \rangle$. During action allocation the team divided these actions and created a temporal structure, resulting in social plan P of subsection 3.2. They collectively made sure that their plan was correct ($cons(\varphi, P)$) and publicly established pairwise social commitments.

Case 1: The Successful Case. In this case, everything goes right after the establishment of the collective commitment. Thus at the level of action execution, all agents carry out the actions making up social plan P according to the given temporal structure and the action allocation.

Property: The Successful Case. If a collective commitment C-COMM$_{G,P}(\varphi)$ holds and P has just been successfully executed, then φ holds. In other words, for all Kripke models $\mathcal{M}$ in which the teamwork axioms hold, and all worlds w,

$$\mathcal{M}, w \models \text{C-COMM}_{G,P}(\varphi) \rightarrow [\text{conf}(succ(P))]\varphi$$

Proof. Suppose $\mathcal{M}, w \models$ C-COMM$_{G,P}(\varphi)$. Then, using the definition of collective commitment, $\mathcal{M}, w \models cons(\varphi, P)$. Finally, by axiom **CS**, $\mathcal{M}, w \models [\text{conf}(succ(P))]\varphi$.

Case 2: An Action Failed. In the next four subcases, at a certain moment during action execution an action fails. We treat the change of collective commitment according to the differentiation of reasons for failure given in the reconfiguration algorithm. However, independently on the reasons of failure the "old" collective commitment has to be dropped, because the social commitments with respect to the failed actions from C-COMM$_{G,P}(\varphi)$ do not exist anymore. On the other hand, after an action failed, the situation is not a priori hopeless: the collective commitment may evolve accorging to the four subcases of varying difficulty.

Case 2a: Reallocation Possible. If there are other agents that can realize the previously failed actions, that is, action reallocation is possible, a new plan P' can be established, as well as a new collective commitment based on it.

Property: Reallocation Possible. Suppose there is an $(i, \alpha) \in P$ such that $failed(i, \alpha)$ but no failed action failed for an objective reason, then for the current action sequence τ and a new social plan P' we have for all Kripke models $\mathcal{M}$ in which the teamwork axioms hold, and all worlds w,

$$\text{C-INT}_G(\varphi) \wedge div(\varphi, \sigma) \wedge means(\sigma, \tau) \rightarrow$$
$$[\texttt{conf}(succ(\texttt{all}(\tau, P'); \texttt{dial}(\varphi, G, P')))]\text{C-COMM}_{G,P'}(\varphi)$$

The proof is similar to the proof of 2d below.

The Example. Suppose that l does not succeed in proving lemma 1, and in fact believes that he cannot as he misses some knowledge about elliptic curves, which t does have. After t communicates that she will pitch in for l, COMM$(l, t, prL1)$ (and thus the old collective commitment) is dropped, and a new social plan is devised, e.g.: $P = \langle\langle\langle prL2, l\rangle \parallel \langle\langle prL1, t\rangle; \langle prT, t\rangle\rangle\rangle; \langle\langle chL1, c\rangle; \langle chL2, c\rangle; \langle chT, c\rangle\rangle$

Finally, a new collective commitment is constructed, containing the social commitment COMM$(t, l, prL1)$.

Case 2b: Some Failed Action Blocks the Goal. In this case at least some action α that was *necessary* for achieving the goal failed for an objective reason R in a strong sense, where R implies that nobody will ever succeed in executing α. This is the most serious negative case, generally leading to system-failure.

To formalize this case and prove consequences, a more extended language is needed than the dynamic one used in this paper.

The Example. Suppose that, while checking t's proof of the theorem from the lemmas, c discovers that not only the proof is wrong, but that there is a counterexample to the theorem itself. Indeed, this reason for failure of checking the proof blocks the overall goal, and the disillusioned team disbands.

Case 2c: New Means-End Analysis Possible. When action reallocation is not possible, but no failed action blocks the overall goal, this means that for every relevant social plan P', allocation with respect to the current action sequence τ fails. In this situation, the old collective commitment is dropped again, but its evolution is possible if a new means-end analysis yields new actions realizing the failed subgoals, followed by a new allocation.

Property: New Means-End Analysis Possible. Suppose that there is an $(i, \alpha) \in P$ such that $failed(i, \alpha)$ and no failed α blocks φ. Then for the current task sequence σ and action sequence τ, and for every social plan P', there are τ' and P'' such that the following holds for all Kripke models $\mathcal{M}$ in which the teamwork axioms hold, and all worlds w:

$$\text{C-INT}_G(\varphi) \wedge div(\varphi, \sigma) \rightarrow [\texttt{conf}(failed(\texttt{all}(\tau, P')))]$$
$$[\texttt{conf}(succ(\texttt{means}(\sigma, \tau'); \texttt{all}(\tau', P''); \texttt{dial}(\varphi, G, P'')))]\text{C-COMM}_{G,P''}(\varphi).$$

The proof is similar to the proof of 2d below.

The Example. As in case 2a, suppose that l does not succeed in proving lemma 1, but now t and c do not believe they can prove it, either. The team does a new means-end analysis based on the old subgoal sequence, and comes up with some other lemmas (say 3 and 4) that together hopefully imply the theorem. This gives rise to new action sequence $\tau' = \langle prL3, prL4, chL3, chL4, prT, chT \rangle$. They allocate the actions in a similar way as before, creating a social plan P'':

$$P'' = \langle\langle\langle\langle prL3, l\rangle; \langle prL4, l\rangle\rangle \parallel \langle prT, t\rangle\rangle; \langle\langle chL3, c\rangle; \langle chL4, c\rangle; \langle chT, c\rangle\rangle\rangle.$$

Finally, by public communication they establish new social commitments, resulting in a new collective one.

Case 2d: New Task Division Possible. When neither action reallocation, nor a new means-end analysis is possible for the failed actions, meaning that for the current τ, allocation with respect to τ fails to deliver any social plan P'; and then means-end analysis with respect to the current σ fails to deliver any action sequence τ'. But the evolution of the collective commitment is still possible, if task division for the overall goal (φ) is executed, in order to establish a new task sequence σ', followed by new rounds of means-end analysis, establishing a new action sequence τ'', and allocation, to create a new social plan P''.

Property: New Task Division Possible. Suppose that there is an $(i, \alpha) \in P$ such that $failed(i, \alpha)$ and no failed α blocks φ. Then for the current task sequence σ and action sequence τ, and for every social plan P' and action sequence τ', there are σ', τ'' and P'' such that:

$$\text{C-INT}_G(\varphi) \rightarrow [\text{conf}(failed(\text{all}(\tau, P')))][\text{conf}(failed(\text{means}(\sigma, \tau')))]$$
$$[\text{conf}(succ(\text{div}(\varphi, \sigma'); \text{means}(\sigma', \tau''); \text{all}(\tau'', P''); \text{dial}(\varphi, G, P'')))]\text{C-COMM}_{G, P''}(\varphi).$$

Proof. Suppose $\mathcal{M}, w \models \text{C-INT}_G(\varphi)$. By the second property in lemma 1, it suffices to show that if

$$\mathcal{M}, w \models succ(\text{div}(\varphi, \sigma'); \text{means}(\sigma', \tau''); \text{all}(\tau'', P''); \text{dial}(\varphi, G, P''))) \quad (3)$$

then $\mathcal{M}, w \models \text{C-COMM}_{G, P''}(\varphi)$; so suppose (3). It immediately follows by axiom **FR** that $\mathcal{M}, w \models div(\varphi, \sigma') \wedge means(\sigma', \tau'') \wedge all(\tau'', P'')$. This implies by axiom **C0** that $\mathcal{M}, w \models cons(\varphi, P'')$.

On the other hand, by lemma 1 $\mathcal{M}, w \models succ(\text{dial}(\varphi, G, P''))$. Thus we have $\mathcal{M}, w \models \text{C-INT}_G(\varphi) \wedge cons(\varphi, P'') \wedge succ(\text{dial}(\varphi, G, P''))$, so by postulate **CTR** we conclude $\mathcal{M}, w \models \text{C-COMM}_{G, P''}(\varphi)$.

The Example. Suppose after the theorem has been divided into lemmas several times, and all these times it turned out to be impossible for the team to prove some essential lemma. They may conclude that they cannot prove the theorem by defining lemmas to be proved. Then they may come up with a completely different task division, e.g. $\sigma' = \langle \sigma_3, \sigma_4 \rangle$ where $\sigma_3 =$ "a theorem 'isomorphic' to T has been found in a different area of mathematics" and $\sigma_4 =$ "a suitable translation between the two contexts has been defined". Now means-end analysis and action allocation will result in a social plan P'' very different from P!

If task division is not successful, the story of the team is completed and a return to team formation is made to initiate a brand new story of a new team.

6   Discussion and Conclusions

This paper falls within a larger research program, an important part of which presents a *static* characterization of CPS with collective commitment as a central notion [7], constituting a complete theory of motivational attitudes in teamwork. This theory is built incrementally starting from individual intentions, through social commitments, leading ultimately to collective level of intentions and commitments. These notions play a crucial role in practical reasoning. As they are defined in multi-modal logics their semantics is clear and well defined; this also enables to express subtle aspects of CPS like various connections between agents.

The present paper deals with the *dynamic* use of the above theory in a dynamic and unpredictable environment. Discussions of reconfiguration in the MAS literature (see e.g. [12]) do not give specific attention to the dynamics of attitude revision in a team. In this paper, we have started to fill this gap. Our definition of collective commitment ensures efficiency of reconfiguration in two ways. Firstly, different from [2], the motivational attitudes occurring in the definition are defined in a non-recursive way, allowing straightforward revision. Secondly, because only social commitments to individual actions appear, it is often sufficient to revise some of these and not to involve the whole team in re-planning. This way the pragmatic power of the definition is enhanced: agents can take the whole process of building and revising collective commitments into their own hands. The dynamic language allows to precisely describe the results of relevant complex actions needed during reconfiguration. Let us stress the novelty of using dynamic logic to describe the dynamics of collective attitudes in BDI-systems.

The static definitions of relevant motivational attitudes and dynamic properties given express solely vital aspects of CPS, leaving room for case-specific extensions. This set of *teamwork axioms* constitutes a definition of motivational attitudes in BDI systems, as well as a specification of their evolution in a dynamic environment. This way they may serve a system designer as a specification to create a correct and complete system, as well as to verify a system. Recently, at Institute of Informatics of Warsaw University a platform DORCAS enabling a user to build BDI systems containing collective motivational attitudes has been created. Moreover, an interesting instantiation of the reconfiguration algorithm dealing with emergency situations on a boat is already implemented.

The presented analysis of dynamic aspects of social and collective attitudes in teams of agents assumes a rather high level of idealization: solely strictly cooperative teams are considered. This leads to a strong definition of collective intention, based on agents' mutual intentions, and then to a plan-based collective commitment. Even though in [10] we introduced a general tuning mechanism to calibrate the strength of collective commitments fitting to a variety of circumstances, an essential ingredient of these definitions — agents' awareness — is formalized by means of a strong notion of common belief. We agree with Cristiano Castelfranchi that after investigating and formalizing this basic case, it is time to relax some of the strong assumptions underlying this research in order to take a closer look on weaker and more distributed forms of cooperation.

Also, this normal modal framework, like any logic based on standard Kripke semantics, suffers from well-known problems related to logical omniscience. Agents are supposed to know and intend all tautologies; moreover, they are supposed to know all logical consequences of their knowledge, and to intend all logical consequences of their intentions. This is clearly unrealistic. For epistemic logic, several solutions to the omniscience problem have been proposed, mostly based on non-normal modal logics ([4, Ch. 9]). Similar solutions were proposed for individual intentions. For future research, we plan to design a non-normal multi-modal logic suitable to solve logical omniscience problems for our framework characterizing collective motivational attitudes.

Acknowledgements

This research is partly supported by the Polish Special KBN Grant supporting the EU funded ALFEBIITE++ Project.

References

[1] Dunin-Kęplicz, B., Verbrugge, R.: A reconfiguration algorithm for distributed problem solving. Electronic Modeling **22** (2000) 68–86   107, 108, 113, 115, 116
[2] Wooldridge, M., Jennings, N.: Cooperative problem solving. Journal of Logic and Computation **9** (1999) 563–592   107, 112, 113, 114, 121
[3] Dignum, F., Dunin-Kęplicz, B., Verbrugge, R.: Creating collective intention through dialogue. Logic Journal of the IGPL **9** (2001) 145–158   107, 110
[4] Fagin, R., Halpern, J., Moses, Y., Vardi, M.: Reasoning about Knowledge. MIT Press, Cambridge, MA (1995)   110, 122
[5] van Linder, B., van der Hoek, W., Meyer, J.J.C.: Formalising abilities and opportunities of agents. Fundamenta Informaticae **34** (1998) 53–101   110
[6] Wooldridge, M.: Reasoning About Rational Agents. MIT Press, Cambridge, MA (2000)   110, 111
[7] Dunin-Kęplicz, B., Verbrugge, R.: Collective intentions. Fundamenta Informaticae **51(3)** (2002) 271–295   110, 111, 121
[8] Harel, D., Kozen, D., Tiuryn, J.: Dynamic Logic. MIT Press, Cambridge, MA (2000)   110
[9] Dunin-Kęplicz, B., Verbrugge, R.: Collective commitments. [13] 56–63   110
[10] Dunin-Kęplicz, B., Verbrugge, R.: Calibrating collective commitments. In V.Marik, J., Pechoucek, M., eds.: Proceedings of the 3rd International Central and Eastern European Conference on Multi-Agent Systems. Volume 2691 of LNAI., Berlin, Springer Verlag (2003) 73–83   110, 112, 121
[11] Grosz, B., Kraus, S.: Collaborative plans for complex group action. Artificial Intelligence **86(2)** (1996) 269–357   111
[12] Tambe, M.: Teamwork in real-world, dynamic environments. [13] 361–368   121
[13] Tokoro, M., ed.: Proceedings Second International Conference on Multi-Agent Systems. In Tokoro, M., ed.: Proceedings Second International Conference on Multi-Agent Systems, Menlo Park (CA), AAAI-Press (1996)   122

Privacy-Aware Mobile Agent:
Protecting Privacy in Open Systems
by Modelling Social Behaviour of Software Agents

André P. Meyer

TNO FEL, Command & Control
PO Box 96864, 2509 JG Den Haag, Netherlands
a.p.meyer@fel.tno.nl

Abstract. In distributed problem solving with multi-agent systems it is assumed that collective behaviour emerges from interaction among rational agents. The dissemination of mobile agents will lead to open systems. Emergent behaviour in open systems must fulfil common goals based on goals of individual agents. Therefore, goals and tasks need to be coordinated in such a way that the desired collective behaviour emerges. At the same time, the autonomy of agents must be restricted by imposing norms on the system in order to prevent misuse and undesired effects of potential emergent behaviour. The European Privacy Directive is a collection of normative principles that can be implemented in a multi-agent system. A model for enabling emergent and normative behaviour based on social interaction paradigms is presented in this paper.

1   Introduction

Today's complex computing systems require distributed problem solving in order to reduce complexity and increase efficiency. A global and centralised approach is replaced by completely distributed systems. Such interacting systems should be open [9] to allow for communication with remote agents and allow these (mobile) agents to enter other multi-agent systems (MAS [15]). This should not happen without care for security and privacy. Distributed problem solving is based on collaboration among goal-oriented rational agents that results in emergent behaviour [2, 8, 13, 14]. The overall behaviour of an open system results from the interaction among relatively simple agents.

The emergent behaviour, obviously, can become very complex and is by nature not predictable. This is a desired effect, but the space of potential emergent system behaviours is very large and includes instances in which the global behaviour creates undesired effects. In such cases, norms can be imposed in order to limit the autonomy of agents such that undesired behaviour can be prevented and desired behaviour stimulated.

A. Omicini, P. Petta, and J. Pitt (Eds.): ESAW 2003, LNAI 3071, pp. 123-135, 2004.
© Springer-Verlag Berlin Heidelberg 2004

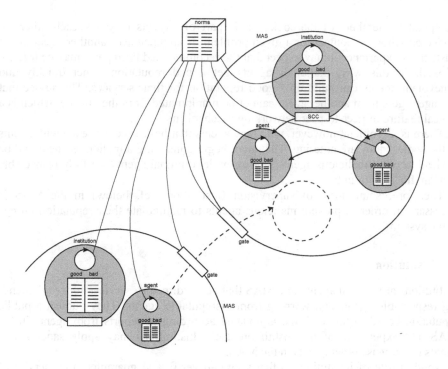

Fig. 1. Reference model for open systems

2 Reference Model

In this section we present a reference model for dealing with emergent and normative behaviour in open systems. Figure 1 shows an overview of this reference model. It shows that agents from various multi-agent systems (i.e., platforms) can interact and allow agents from one system to enter another system.

Gatekeepers collaborate to ensure that only benevolent agents can enter another system. Free access to societies in open systems is not desirable, because no guarantees can be given about the behaviour of agents in a society and the society (or the platform, respectively) itself can be harmed.

Per definition, each multi-agent system contains a multitude of agents. These agents follow different goals (or desires) and may need assistance from each other to achieve their goals. Therefore, they need to communicate with each other to co-ordinate their actions. In open systems agents do not know each other a priori, so there must be a means to confirm trust in others. There are two ways in our model in which trust can be achieved by means of reputation: communities and institutions.

2.1 Communities

In a community, trust is created by reputation over time. Each agent interacts with others and keeps a record of its partner agents where it remembers respectable and disreputable members of the society it is part of. Agents may ask each other for advice on whom to contact for a given problem. If an agent asks another agent that it trusts from experience it may expect that the recommended third party may be trusted, as well. In this way, malicious agents get a bad reputation rather quickly and benevolent agents can build up a good reputation for their services. The advice that one agent gets from another agent cannot be manipulated from the outside, which is a typical feature of peer-to-peer networking mechanisms.

There is a problem, however, with new agents that have no experience with agents in the society they are entering. They may begin contacting a malicious agent and be mislead to other malicious agents. For example, criminal agents are fully respectable in a "mafia" community.

Therefore, some form of supervision (institutions, cf. below) in the MAS is necessary in order to prevent malicious agents to manipulate their reputation ratings in the system.

2.2 Institutions

Institutions are special agents in a MAS that act as directory services for recommending respectable agents and warning from disreputable agents. They publish a public reputation board to this end that is updated according to reports from agents in the MAS and experience of the institution itself. Institutions may apply sanctions to agents that misuse other agents in the MAS.

Another role of institutions is that they can verify and guarantee[1] the identity of agents (and their owners, respectively). In this way, agents cannot pretend to have someone other's personality.

Agents may communicate directly if they trust each other or they may choose to use the secure communication channel (SCC) of institutions for their communications. The SCC provides a means for the agents to guarantee the application of the norms of the society (cf. below) to the communication under consideration.

Nevertheless, it is important that trusted communication can occur directly in a completely distributed way (without the SCC), because the SCC would form a bottleneck, otherwise.

3   Norms for Privacy

Norms [3, 5, 6] can be applied to all communication and reasoning processes inside the MAS, but are located outside of the MAS itself, because norms are more general than a specific agent society. Additionally, a society may define specific norms that are valid only in its particular context.

Norms are defined much like ontologies and have a lot in common with them. However, norms are *prescriptive* by nature, unlike ontologies, which are *descriptive*. An example of applying norms can be found in the privacy principles that we have

---

[1] Institutions take the role of a trusted third party that distributes and verifies agent certificates.

implemented [12]. In this example, the legal privacy principles were translated to social norms and related to a domain-specific ontology.

Furthermore, norms need to be defined on various levels, relating to the context to which they apply: sensorial, individual, social, and cultural. Norms on these levels have different time scales and stability. This is comparable to (dynamic) ontological modelling. Again, institutions play an important role in maintaining the norms as they are defined, applied and eventually modified.

3.1 Processing Personal Data and the Privacy Principles

Data protection legislation within the Member States of the European Union (EU) is based on the EU Directive 95/46/EC on 'the protection of individuals with regard to the processing of personal data and on the free movement of such data', the so-called 'Data Protection Directive' (DPD [4]).

In legal terms, 'personal data' means any piece of information regarding an identified or identifiable natural person. Whether we can talk of 'personal data' or personal identifiable information (PII), depends on a number of elements of which, within the scope of this document, 'identification' is the only significant element. Article 2 of the EU Directive 95/46/EC prescribes the requirements for any processing of personal data. In article 2d of the data protection directive the *'controller'* is defined as the legal entity responsible for the processing of the personal data. This controller has to make sure that the processing is done conform the privacy legislation. The privacy requirements that follow from the directive can be translated into the following nine privacy principles [11]:

- *V 1. Intention and Notification*: The processing of personal data must be reported in advance to the Data Protection Authority or a personal data protection official, unless processing has been exempted from notification.
- *V 2. Transparency*: The person involved must be able to see who is processing his personal data and for what purpose.
- *V 3. Finality*: Personal data may only be collected for specific, explicit and legitimate purposes and not further processed in a way incompatible with those purposes.
- *V 4. Legitimate ground for Processing*: The processing of personal data must be based on a foundation referred to in national legislation, such as permission, agreement, legal obligation, justified interest and such like. For special data, such as health, stricter limits prevail.
- *V 5. Quality*: The personal data must be as correct and as accurate as possible, sufficient, to the point and not excessive.
- *V 6. Data subject's rights*: The data subjects involved have the right to take cognisance of and to improve their data as well as the right to raise objections.
- *V 7. Security*: Providing appropriate security for personal data held within IT-systems is one of the cornerstones of the DPD. Measures of technical and organisational nature suitable and proportional to the sensitivity of the personal data and the nature of possible risks have to be taken potential harm should the PII be misused or disclosed in an unauthorised matter.

- *V 8. Processing by a processor*: If processing is outsourced to a processor, it must be ensured that he will observe the instructions of the person responsible.
- *V 9. Transfer of personal data outside the EU*: In principle, the traffic of personal data to a country outside the EU is permitted only if that country offers adequate protection.

In principle, any software agent that receives personal data should conform to all these privacy principles. Since the agent cannot be held responsible for the processing of the personal data, it cannot be a controller. The question arises who is responsible for the processing of personal data by an agent. In the PISA [12] project we concluded that it has to be the '*provider*' of the agent who is the controller. We define the provider of the agent as the legal entity who makes the agent available for usage by *data subjects*.

3.2 Consent, Privacy Policies and Preferences

One of the key issues of privacy legislation is the consent the data subject must give for processing his PII. The required consent of the data subject potentially conflicts with the autonomy of the agents in an agent system. If the agent has to ask for consent from its user for every action it intends to perform, the agent can hardly be autonomous. This can be solved if the data subject can specify in advance what can be done with the personal data he submits to an agent. The data subject can do this by attaching his privacy preferences to the personal data.

It is often useful for agents to transfer personal data to other agents. The agent that sends the personal data (the 'sender') should make sure that the receiving agent (the 'receiver') would also respect the privacy preferences of the data subject. The sender can determine this if the receiver can send him a privacy policy that states what he will do with the personal data he receives (the purpose(s)). For this reason every agent should have an Agent Practices Statement (APS, cf. Fig. 2.) that contains the privacy policy of the agent. An APS consists of two items: the privacy policy of the receiving agent as specified by its controller and the identification of this controller. The identification of the controller is available as readable text and can be used by the data subject or an auditor in case misuse of the PII by the agent is detected. The privacy policy needs a format that can be interpreted by agents. The APS will be digitally signed.

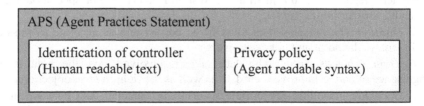

Fig. 2. The agent practices statement (APS) contains the privacy policy of the agent and a human readable identification of the controller

By using this approach of using privacy preferences of data subjects and an APS for each agent, consent will be built into every agent. Both the APS and the privacy preferences must contain the purpose(s) of the data processing by the agent. If the user for example enters the data of his CV, he also has to specify the purpose(s) for which this CV can be used. This is considered to be the explicit consent the data subject gives. Transfer to a successor agent is only allowed if the APS specified purpose(s) of this successor agent are in exact conformity with the user specified purpose(s); A data subject must be able to specify different preferences for different groups of information. In this way the data subject could specify stricter preferences for his CV than for a list of his hobbies.

The user will have to state his privacy preferences for personal data before submitting this personal data to the first agent in the sequence of agents to perform the task. Before any PII will be transferred to a successor, i.e. a receiving agent:

- The APS of the receiving agent will have to be collected, read and interpreted by the sending agent. If the privacy policy matches the privacy preferences of the data subject then the PII can be transferred to the receiving agent;
- The agent privacy policy (APP) of agents within the EU should be on the EU level. This is the responsibility of the controller and thus the agent provider of the agent. In practice, agents can be confronted with APS that provide less protection than EU standards or no APS at all;
- The terminology of privacy policy and privacy preferences is inspired by the P3P development of W3C. However, as long as P3P is not on the EU level of privacy protection, P3P cannot be used as such;
- For a processor a Service Level Agreement (SLA) (article 17 paragraph 2 of DPD [4]) indicating the APS of the controller will be required.

3.3 Levels of Personal Data

It is well recognised that security measures may differ depending on the nature of the PII. For this purpose the PISA Demonstrator the term 'Level n PII' is introduced. The following three levels of Personal Data are distinguished:

- **Level 1, 'Deal Closing Information':** This group of personal data is transferred at the very end of the scenario. In the job market case[2] the Level 1 may contain items like: Name and Address information, telephone number, and e-mail address. It is irrelevant whether one uses a real identity or a pseudo-identity. The sole use one can make of this data is to end the communication between the data subject and the company so they can get in direct contact. For this reason this type is sometimes referred to as 'contact information'. In another MAS application, for instance an agent looking for a special MP3 file, Level 1 may be the credit card number of the data subject to be debited for the MP3 file to be downloaded.
- **Level 3, 'Special Legal Categories':** Personal data as defined in Directive 96/46/EC Article 8 paragraph 1. Level 3 personal data are only to be processed under the conditions specified in Article 8 paragraph 2 through 7 of the Directive.

---

[2]   The job market case is used as the scenario for the PISA demonstrator.

- **Level 2, 'Not Level 1 and 3':** All others items of personal data.

Level 1 and level 3 Personal Data will only be transferred to other agents if it is strictly necessary. Level 2 can be used more frequently, for example to get in contact with other agents via the use of brokers or other service agents.

4   Privacy Ontology

The privacy ontology (cf. figure 3) follows the legal privacy principles. It comes as no surprise, thus, that the ontology starts from the concept of a privacy principle (PrivacyPrinciple, in the centre).

Both privacy preferences and privacy policies refer to a principle. The generic abstract principle concept is detailed for each included principle (transparency, finality, data subject rights, legal processing and transfer). For each of the principles a statement can be given in order to specify the requirements or provisions (with respect to preferences and policies, respectively) that are specific to the given principle.

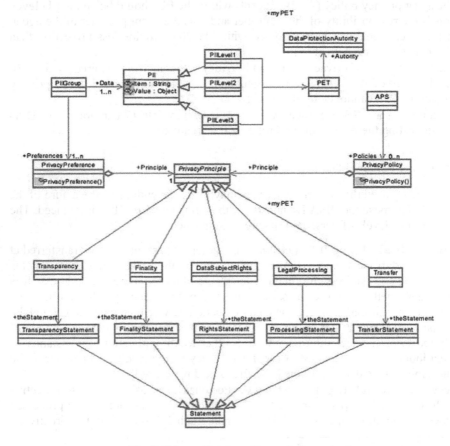

Fig. 3. Privacy Ontology Concepts (overview)

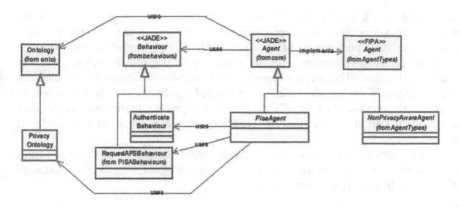

Fig. 4. Usage of the Privacy Ontology and the privacy related behaviours by the Pisa Agent

All statements are sub-concepts of a generic statement concept. Depending on the principle, the statements can have different values as its content. The content of the statements is evaluated and preferences are compared to policies using the privacy transfer rules.

Fig. 4. shows how the knowledge on the Privacy Ontology and the usage of the privacy-related behaviours are implemented by the PISA agent. Thus, all PISA agents inherit this knowledge on the privacy ontology and the usage of the privacy related behaviours.

The specification of the location of the agent poses a difficulty in the above approach, since the agent provider constructs the APS before the agents are even instantiated. This is because in some cases the agent provider can't know beforehand where the agent will be instantiated. The problem becomes even bigger if the agent is a mobile one and can travel from one host to another. Specifying the location in the certificate of the agent instead of in the APS can solve this problem. This will even solve the problem for mobile agents if mobile agents get a new certificate each time they arrive at a new agent platform, which seems a logical approach since the certificate is provided by a platform agent.

Interaction protocols specify the privacy communication types between agents in the PISA demonstrator. Interaction protocols are extensions to UML sequence diagrams and serve as patterns for agent communication.

5   Interaction Protocols and Transfer Rules

The interaction protocols show how the communication among senders and receivers in the multi-agent system is organised. The protocols will need to be combined for execution of given tasks. The basic protocols related to the transfer rules and data subject rights are explained below. Transfer rules apply the privacy norms based on the ontology to the interaction among agents by implementing the constraints on communication.

The sender of personal identifiable information (PII) must be able to determine whether or not the PII can be sent and for this purpose it needs both information on the agent that would receive the PII and privacy meta-data on the PII. From the receiver it must know the privacy policy and the meta-data of the PII because these refer to the privacy preferences of the data subject. The sender of the PII must compare the privacy preferences with the privacy policy using the privacy transfer rules as stated below. The privacy transfer rules consist of one or more rules per privacy principle. If the transfer rules are evaluated positively and the PII is sent to the receiver, the meta-data on the PII containing the privacy preferences of the data subject must be sent along with the PII. This way the receiver can act as a sender of PII in its turn.

The expressions that are evaluated positively (true) in the processing of the rules result in an agreement for transfer. All parts of all principles must be matched with positive results before information is sent.

T = true (positive result)
F = false (negative result)

5.1 Principle 2: Transparency

The data subject can specify in his privacy preferences whether he requests transparency or not (Y/N). The receiver can offer no transparency (N) or the legally required transparency applicable in the EU (Y). If the data subject requests transparency the receiver must offer it, otherwise it doesn't matter, thus three out of four possible combinations return a positive result.

t^{pref}/t^{pol}	N	Y
N	T	T
Y	F	T

5.2 Principle 3: Finality Principle

The principle of finality has two aspects: purpose binding and retention period.

Purpose Binding

The data subject can specify in his privacy preferences for what purpose information may be used. The receiver may not use the information for any purpose that is not specified by the data subject. Thus, all the purposes that are specified in the receiver's policy must also be specified in the data subject's preferences.

$P_{pref} = \{p_1, ..., p_n\}, n>0$ data subject's preferences for purposes (required)
$P_{pol} = \{q_1, ..., q_m\}, m>0$ receiver's policy for purposes (provided)

$$\underset{1\le i\le n, 1\le j\le m}{\forall} q_j \exists p_i : p_i = q_j$$

Retention Period

The data subject can specify a deadline in his privacy preferences by which the information must be deleted (retention period t_{pref}). The receiver's retention period (t_{pol}) must be shorter or equal than what the data subject requests.

$$t_{pref} \geq t_{pol}$$

5.3 Principle 4: Legitimate Ground of Processing

The data subject can specify in his privacy preferences for what other processing his PII may be used[3]. The receiver may not use the information for any processing not specified by the data subject.

$P_{pref} = \{p_1, ..., p_n\}, n>0$ data subject's preferences for processing (required)
$P_{pol} = \{q_1, ..., q_m\}, m>0$ receiver's policy for processing (provided)

$$\forall_{1 \leq i \leq n, 1 \leq j \leq m} q_j \exists p_i : p_i = q_j$$

5.4 Principle 6: Data Subject's Rights

The data subject can specify in his privacy preferences, which rights he wants to execute on his PII. The receiver (R_{pol}) must provide all the rights that the data subject requests (R_{pref}). There are five rights defined by the privacy legislation. Three out of four possible combinations return positive results.

r_i^{pref} / r_j^{pol}	N	Y
N	T	T
Y	F	T

r_1 = access, r_2 = rectify, r_3 = erase, r_4 = block, r_5 = object

$$R_{pref} = \{r_1^{pref}, r_2^{pref}, r_3^{pref}, r_4^{pref}, r_5^{pref}\}$$

$$R_{pol} = \{r_1^{pol}, r_2^{pol}, r_3^{pol}, r_4^{pol}, r_5^{pol}\}$$

$$\forall_{1 \leq i \leq 5} r_i^{pref}, r_i^{pol} : (\neg r_i^{pref} \wedge \neg r_i^{pol}) \vee (r_i^{pref} \wedge r_i^{pol}) \vee (\neg r_i^{pref} \wedge r_i^{pol})$$

5.5 Principle 9: Transfer of Personal Data Outside the EU

The data subject can specify in his privacy preferences whether his PII may be transmitted outside of the European Union member states (EU). The specification

---

[3]   e.g., internal or external marketing, list brokering.

indicates the boundary of transmission as either EU-only, EU-compliant[4] or non-EU. The receiver specifies his location with respect to these boundaries. The receiver must reside within the boundary specified by the data subject.

NB: non-EU *policy* excludes EU-only and EU-compliant, while non-EU *preference* includes the others!

t^{pref} / t^{pol}	EU-only	EU-compliant	non-EU
EU-only	T	F	F
EU-compliant	T	T	F
Non-EU	T	T	T

6 Experimental Environment

Research & Development on privacy protection with agents has to be carried on with combinations of different techniques: using anonymous and/or pseudonym mechanisms, privacy and security cryptographic tools, act according the privacy norms and user preferences, and trust and reputation systems. Therefore, the platform in figure 5 is used for experiments.

7 Conclusions

The emergence of clustering and adaptation behaviour could be confirmed in the simulation. The application of norms has been implemented, but not yet verified in real open systems, because we only have a simulation without real content so far. Normative behaviour with respect to privacy has proved to be a very important issue and an architecture and demonstrator have been defined to this end.

On the other hand, many limitations of current technology get in the way of true evaluation. For example, measuring the presence and activity of users or recognising multiple users' speech concurrently is far from trivial. This limits the possibilities for context-awareness.

Although the emergence of clustering and adaptation behaviour could be confirmed, the current system includes only very limited reasoning. This is subject to further investigation.

---

[4] The EU-compliant countries: Personal data can flow freely from the fifteen EU MS and three EEA member countries (Norway, Liechtenstein and Iceland) to that third country without any further safeguard being necessary. The Commission has so far recognised Switzerland, Hungary and the US Department of Commerce's Safe Harbour Privacy Principles as providing adequate protection.

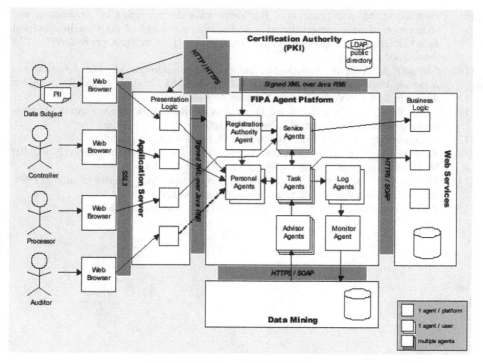

Fig. 5. Experimental PISA Platform

References

[1]   Bellifemine, F., Poggi, A., Rimassa, G., *JADE – A FIPA-compliant agent framework*, in Proceedings of PAAM'99, London, April 1999, http://jade.cselt.it/

[2]   Brooks, R.A.: Intelligence without representation. Artificial Intelligence 47, 139-159, 1991

[3]   Conte, R., Castelfranchi, C., Dignum, F., *Autonomous Norm Acceptance*, In J. Muller, M. Singh and A. Rao, editors, *Intelligent Agents V*, (LNAI-1555), pages 319-334, Springer-Verlag, 1999

[4]   Directive 95/46/EC of the European Parliament and of the Council of 25 October 1995 on the protection of individuals with regard to the processing of personal data and on the free movement of such data (Official Journal L 281, 23/11/95, p.31-50)

[5]   Hales, D., *Group Reputation Supports Beneficent Norms*, Journal of Artificial Societies and Social Simulation vol. 5, no. 4, 2002, http://jasss.soc.surrey.ac.uk/5/4/4.html

[6]   Dignum, F., Kinny, D., Sonenberg, E., *Motivational Attitudes of Agents: On Desires Obligations and Norms*, Proceedings of the second international workshop of central and eastern europe on multi-agent systems, Eds. B. Dunin-Keplicz, E. Nawarecki, Krakow, Poland, pages: 61-70, 2001

[7]   FIPA – Foundation for Intelligent Physical Agents, http://www.fipa.org/

[8]   Franks, N.G., *Army Ants: A Collective Intelligence*, American Scientist, 77, 139-145, 1989

[9]   Fredriksson, M. and Gustavsson, R., Methodological principles in construction and observation of open computational systems, in Proceedings of the First International Joint Conference on Autonomous Agents and Multi-Agent Systems, pp. 692–693, ACM Press, 2002

[10]   Georgeff, M., Pell, B., Pollack, M., Tambe, M., Wooldridge, M., *The Belief-Desire-Intention Model of Agency*, in Muller, J. P., Singh, M., Rao, A. (editors), *Intelligent Agents V*, Springer-Verlag Lecture Notes in AI Volume 1365, 1999

[11]   Leerentveld, J. P., van Blarkom, G. W., WBP Raamwerk Privacy Audit. Samenwerkingsverband Audit Aanpak, The Hague 2000

[12]   Privacy Incorporated Software Agents (PISA), http://www.pet-pisa.nl/

[13]   Resnick, M., Turtles, Termites, and Traffic Jams: Explorations in Massively Parallel Microworlds (Complex Adaptive Systems), MIT Press, 1994

[14]   Resnick, M., Silverman, B., *Exploring Emergence. An "Active Essay"*, 1996, http://llk.media.mit.edu/projects/emergence/contents.html

[15]   Weiss, G. (Editor), *Multi-Agent Systems*, MIT Press, Cambridge, 2000

Interaction Monitoring and Termination Detection for Agent Societies: Preliminary Results

Tshiamo Motshegwa and Michael Schroeder

Department of Computing
City University London
{ad225,msch}@soi.city.ac.uk

Abstract. For large-scale and complex societies of agents monitoring and control are important to both agent designers and society administrators. Specifically, interaction monitoring and termination detection are of importance in optimising performance of a system and keeping users up-to-date on progress. Both monitoring and termination detection are well-studied problems for distributed object systems. In this paper, we investigate how these approaches can be applied to agent systems. We present a novel algorithm, which takes advantage of a monitor's additional information on partial behaviour specifications of the agents to derive observable termination criteria. We sketch an implementation and qualitatively compare our novel algorithm to the existing distributed systems approaches and propose future experimental work.

1 Introduction

From an *AI* perspective agents are communicative, intelligent, rational and possibly intentional entities. From the *computing* perspective, they are autonomous, asynchronous, communicative, distributed and possibly mobile processes [1] and multiagent systems or societies of agents are *modular* distributed systems and have *decentralized* data. Agents in a society have *incomplete information* or capabilities, and typically there is no *global system control*. The model of computation is *asynchronous* [2]. In this paper, we will specify agent behaviour through protocols. This means that agents are merely observed from the outside and thus our agent definition is in line with [3], which require that a piece of software "*is* a software agent if, and only if, it communicates correctly in an agent communication language" such as KQML [4] and FIPA-ACL [5].

In this paper, we address the problem of interaction monitoring and termination detection in a society of agents. There are two aspects to this problem: Formal verification of behaviour at compile-time and monitoring and control at run-time. Regarding the former, there has been some work on the verification of agent communication languages [6]. But overall verification is difficult, as in general the specification of correct usage of speech acts in agent communication

A. Omicini, P. Petta, and J. Pitt (Eds.): ESAW 2003, LNAI 3071, pp. 136–154, 2004.
© Springer-Verlag Berlin Heidelberg 2004

languages requires access to the internal state of the agent besides the messages being exchanged. It is worth noting though that there has been some attempts, [7] to enable the verification of compliance to ACL semantics that does not require access to internal states of agents, but in general formal verification of interacting agents is not yet satisfactorily solved to be deployed in systems[8].

We set ourselves the main goal of the development of an interaction monitor for a practical and operational system, and we focus on monitoring and control at run-time rather than on compile-time verification.

For monitoring and control two perspectives need to be addressed:

- Agent Designer: Depending on the nature of tasks assigned to agents (urgency, potential risks, etc.), the owner may need to be made aware of what his agent engages in, whom it interacts with, what stage in the execution of tasks it is at, current levels of resources initially allocated, whether the strategies it is currently employing are delivering etc. In addition, the owner may require to perform various control tasks including, returning, terminating or dynamically updating his agents. While it can be argued that some or all of this functionality can, and should be embedded in the agent itself, it still needs to be investigated what can be delegated to the infrastructure and what tradeoffs there are to be made. This balance when struck will enable the implementation of less complex agents without compromising this key autonomy feature that all agents must by definition exhibit, at the same time guaranteeing confidence in deployed agent based systems.
- Society administrator: For the node hosting the agents, key interests are in the techniques that will deliver timely, automatic, transparent and pervasive resource management and scheduling mechanisms aimed at facilitating optimal and efficient running of the system. In particular, management of registries through timely automatic garbage collection tied to end of interactions phases, agent persistence, and robust agent location mechanisms, supporting mobility of entities for example.

To address the above needs, the paper presents a deliberative mechanism for detecting termination of agent interactions in a society of agents. The work discussed here is part of a larger work addressing the problem of deriving a global view in a system of agents given individual agents' partial local views. Multiagent systems by definition lack a *global perspective*, data and control. The mechanisms proposed while intended for determining a global state such as termination, can also be used to improve system visibility for management and control purposes. The approach advocated is motivated by the existing work in distributed termination detection in distributed systems based on the process model. The qualitative evaluation suggests that the approach advocated has advantages over ad-hoc methods. The paper also poses the question that, given that agents are higher level entities (compared to objects) engaging in complex interactions using protocols, what *additional* information can they reveal or make available to an outside observer to aid the timely determination of global states such as termination? The approach we adopt here is that of abstracting away from internal agent processes and the development of an architecture that introduces an external monitor to ascertain termination.

The paper is organised as follows: Section 2 provides motivational scenarios and section 3 introduces agents and the problem of termination detection and the associated existing solutions. Agents are identified as different from the underlying object model assumed in these solutions in that agents make use of protocols when engaging in interactions in pursuit of their goals. The section discusses termination detection for protocols and provides a number of definitions such as *Termination Path*, *Unique Termination Path*, *Shortest Unique Termination Path* and *Observables*, which form the basis for the algorithm developed.

Section 4 discusses the advocated approach and the proposed framework for termination detection and various detection mechanisms, namely pure polling, polling incorporated with full knowledge of the protocol and finally monitoring with knowledge of minimal partial protocol. It sketches the proposed algorithm, and this is followed by a description of the prototype implementation.

Section 5 discusses desirable experiments to evaluate the framework and some initial results.

Section 6 discusses related work, in particular work done on detecting termination of distributed quiescence in a multiagent negotiation using as a basis a standard termination detection algorithm. A qualitative evaluation is also presented here together with future planned work. Finally a summary is given in section 7.

2   Agents and Termination Detection

Before we develop our approach to termination detection, let us consider two scenarios:

Example 1: Computational Resource Marketplace. Consider an auction hosting thousands of agents. Typically participants maintain varying valuations of goods and bid to those upper bounds according to adopted private strategies. Inevitably most participants drop off early from the game. Typically in real applications, these entities would stay on longer than need be consuming system resources. In most applications this is not a concern. But where scalability and resource consumption is an issue, a deliberative mechanism for identifying and timely garbage collecting defunct agents is a necessity. In this work we consider a market place hosting a continuous double auction populated by servers offering computational resources (spare capacity to perform computations) and clients who wish to acquire resources to execute some tasks, in a GRID [1] like setting. A *continuous double auction* is one in which many individual transactions are carried on at a single moment and trading does not stop as each auction is concluded, [9].

---

[1] http://www.gridforum.org

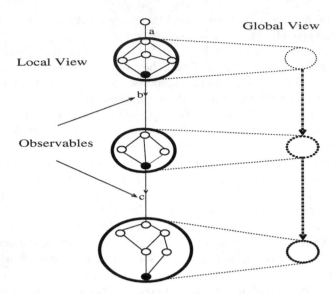

Fig. 1. Mapping local states to global states

Example 2: Business Processes. Consider a business process, with internal processes, transitions and stages. The outside observer, for example a manager, does not need to know the details of the internal processes, but would need to keep track of *deliverables*. This can be achieved by reporting or by maintaining a list of *checkpoints* or *observables*, actions marking "stage" transitions. The external entity would then keep track of particular terminal states marking end of a stage and transitions from them leading to the next phase in the process.

A cluster of local states and transitions separated by designated terminal states and checkpoints or observables can be viewed as an aggregate that can map to a "state" in the partial global view, and this view maybe what is required by an external entity to infer progress in the underlying process. Figure 1 below illustrates this process.

In both scenarios, a monitor needs to follow the progress of the agents. To do so, it requires some partial global knowledge of the protocols the agents are executing. Within the protocols the monitor can identify terminal states, which if identified upon execution, trigger the termination of the agent and the freeing of the resources it consumed.

Termination Detection in Distributed Systems: There exist a body of work on distributed termination detection in distributed systems research. A very informal problem statement can be formulated as follows: Given a network of N nodes, implement a distributed termination detection algorithm. Each node can be either in *active* or in *passive* state. Only an active node can send messages to other nodes; each message sent is received after some period of time later. After having received a message, a passive node becomes active; the receipt of a message is the only mechanism that triggers a passive node's transition to activity. For each node, the transition from the active to the passive state may occur *spontaneously*. The state in which all nodes are passive and no messages are on their way is *stable*: the distributed computation is said to have *terminated*. The purpose of the algorithm is to enable one of the nodes, say node 0, to detect that this stable state has been reached. [10] offers the following definition for termination: *"A distributed Computation is considered globally terminated if every process is locally terminated and no messages are in transit. Locally terminated can be understood to be a state in which the process has finished its computation and will not restart unless it receives a message"*.

Distributed algorithms have been used to provide solutions to the termination detection problem. These algorithms are designed to run on a distributed system where many processes cooperate by solving parts of a given problem in parallel [11]. Processes have to exchange data and synchronise their actions. Communication and synchronisation is solely done by message passing, there are no shared variables, and usually the processes do not have access to a common clock, [11]. Since message transmission times cannot be ignored, no process has immediate access to the global state. Hence control decisions must be made on partial and often outdated view of the global state which is assembled from information gathered gradually from other processes, [11].

It is also worth pointing out that the termination detection problem is related to the more general problem of detection of global predicates, a fundamental problem in debugging and monitoring [12].

Termination Detection Algorithms: Termination detection algorithms generally fall into two categories:

1) Tracing Algorithms: A tracing algorithm relies on knowledge of the set of initially active nodes. Dijkstra and Scholten's algorithm [13] is an example. Because all activity of the computation originates from these nodes by message chains, the algorithm assumes that initially exactly one node is active (root node) [14].

In the Dijkstra-Scholten algorithm, the underlying computation is augmented with construction and maintenance of a spanning tree. The tree is rooted at source node, the node with the initial input and the tree construction allows the tree to grow and shrink repeatedly. The algorithm is as follows:

When a non source node receives the first computation message, it sets the sender as parent and no acknowledgement is sent. Subsequent messages are acknowledged and the source acknowledges all messages. When any node is in a *quiescent* (silent) state and all its messages have been acknowledged, it sends an acknowledgement to its parent and deletes itself from the tree. If the deleting node is source then termination is announced.

2) Probe Algorithms: Probe algorithms repeatedly scan the entire network for active nodes and computation messages; algorithms are based on the principle laid out by Dijkstra, Feijen and Van Gasteren [15]. A special node called the *controller* is envisaged [14] to coordinate detection. The process model is adopted in the analysis of these algorithms, where processes send and receive messages via channels asynchronously.

3   Agents, Protocols, and Termination Detection

Agents and Objects: The termination problem can also be considered in the context of agents albeit that it will need to be reformulated to factor in agent characteristics and address issues pertinent to agents. It can be argued that this has to be done because agents are different from objects in many respects. Agents are higher level entities. Agents have *behaviour specifications* and through the execution of *protocols*, agents engage in possibly complex interactions while in pursuit of their goals.

As it is, the description of the termination detection problem abstracts away from the purpose and operations of the computation in question, but concentrates on the aspects relevant to termination, and all the proposed algorithms consider a very simple model for the underlying application programs. Clearly, direct application of these principles without substantial modification to suite high level entities like agents engaging in potentially complex interactions is not possible. In addition, agents may have *additional knowledge* they can reveal to aid termination detection. The work discussed here considers timely detection of termination of agent interactions using as a basis the existing work but considering it on its own right. The focus here is on the narrower problem of detecting termination of a protocol, to serve as a basis for subsequent work on a much broader and more complex problem of detecting when an agent or agent system has terminated and related problems such as automatic garbage collection.

Protocols: Protocols represent the allowed interactions among communicating agents, and they regulate the interactions. They can also be viewed as specifications of these interactions [16]. Agents participate in different protocols by appropriately interacting with each other, for example, by responding to messages, performing actions in their domain, or updating their local states. Protocols can thus be taken as specifying policies that agents would follow with regard to their interactions with other agents. These policies would for example, determine the conditions under which a request will be acceded to or permissions issued or statement believed, [16].

We require that protocols be labelled state transition systems with a set of terminal states, which have no outgoing transitions.

Definition 1 (Protocol).
A protocol is a tuple $(S, \longmapsto, L, T)$, *where* S *is a set of states,* L *is a set of labels,* $\longmapsto \subseteq S \times L \times S$ *is a set of transitions and* $T \subseteq S$ *is set of terminal states, where* $T \neq \emptyset$ *and* $\forall t \in T \; \nexists s \in S, l \in L$ *such that* $s \neq t$ *and* $(t, l, s) \in \longmapsto$. *We will sometimes write* $s \overset{l}{\longmapsto} s'$ *instead of* $(s, l, s') \in \longmapsto$.

Example 1 (CNP). Consider a Contract-Net protocol, the protocol can be represented by the state transition system as shown in Figure 2 below. The protocol

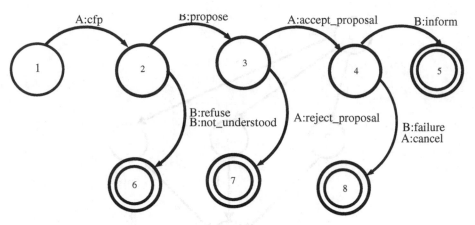

Fig. 2. Contract Net protocol adapted from [1]

shown is being executed by two agents. In this example
$S = \{1, 2, 3, 4, 5, 6, 7, 8\}$; $T = \{5, 6, 7, 8\}$; $L = \{cfp, propose...\}$ and $\longmapsto$ is as
shown in the Figure 2.

The larger problem, part of which is addressed in this work is formulated below.

Termination Detection for Protocols. By executing a protocol, an agent engages
in potentially complex interactions. Each agent participating in the protocol
undergoes various internal state transitions. Each agent has a partial local view
of interactions it engages in. The larger problem posed here is that of deriving
a global view of system of interacting agents given individual agent partial local
views.

   As part of addressing this problem, the discussion here centers on the narrower problem of determining when individual agents have reached *terminal
configurations* in the protocols they are executing. The discussion also considers
the issue of what additional information agents can avail to aid this process while
preserving autonomy and not introducing too much central control.

   To detect termination of a protocol, we can define a *termination path*, i.e.
a sequence of state transitions labelled by observable messages which end in
a terminal state.

Definition 2 (Termination Path).
*Let $P = (S, \longmapsto, L, T)$ be a protocol, then a path p of length n is a sequence
$(s_1, \ldots, s_n)$ where $s_i \in S$ for $1 \leq i \leq n$ and $s_{j-1} \overset{l_j}{\longmapsto} s_j$ for $1 < j \leq n$. The
labels of path p are defined as a sequence $(l_2, \ldots, l_n)$. Furthermore, if $s_n \in T$,
then p is a termination path.*

Example 2. Given the protocol P in Figure 3 below, then for example, the path
$p = (1, 2, 5)$ is a valid termination path with labels (b, c).

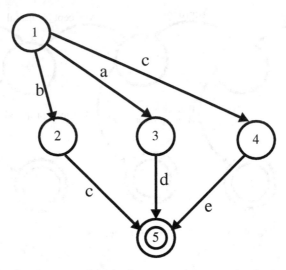

Fig. 3. A protocol with shortest unique termination path

Definition 3 (Unique Termination Path).

Let $P = (S, \longmapsto, L, T)$ be a protocol, then a termination path p with labels $(l_1, \ldots, l_n)$ is unique, if there is no path $p' \neq p$ with labels $(l_1, \ldots, l_n)$.

Example 3. Consider the protocol in Figure 3 on the left. The path $(2, 5)$ is a termination path, but as both paths $(1, 4)$ and $(2, 5)$ have labels (c) $(2, 5)$ is not a unique termination path. On the other hand $(1, 2, 5)$ is a unique termination path, as there is no other path with labels (b, c).

Definition 4 (Shortest Unique Termination Paths, Observables).

Let $P = (S, \longmapsto, L, T)$ be a protocol and TP the set of shortest unique termination paths, then the set of observables O is the union of all labels in any path $p \in TP$.

Example 4. In Figure 3 above, the set of observables is $O = \{b, c, d, e\}$. Note that "a" is not element of the set O because the shortest unique path between states 1 and 5 is $(3,5)$ with label "d".

Also Consider Figure 4. There is not always a shortest unique termination path

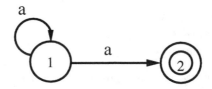

Fig. 4. A protocol with no shortest unique termination path

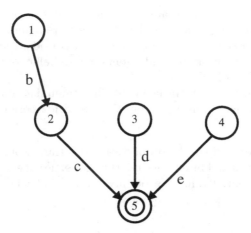

Fig. 5. Shortest unique termination paths

(e.g. $s \xmapsto{a} s$, $s \xmapsto{a} s'$, where s' is a termination state, does not have a shortest unique termination path. The reason is that it contains a circle. If we limit ourselves to directed acyclic graph, then this problem does not occur.

In summary, given an arbitrary protocol, such as that given in Figure 3, the minimal information (sub-protocol) that the monitor really needs to keep to ascertain termination is the shortest unique termination paths. For this example these are depicted in Figure 5 overleaf.

4   Approach and Proposed Framework

We define a deliberative framework that has a similar philosophy to *probe-based* distributed termination detection algorithms (see section 1), but which factors in execution of protocols by agents. In particular the mechanisms we study are based on monitoring or polling agents for additional information to detect termination.

In the setup we propose, agents communicate information about protocols and their execution when queried by a monitor, the querying mechanism is driven by a control mechanism based on polling. The monitor (if required) can reconstruct a global view or deduce termination based on information provided by individual agents.

Assumptions. We make the following assumptions explicit:

1. All protocols used in the MAS are known. This is not a far fetched assumption given that it is widely accepted that protocols be made public and individual agent strategies are normally private.
2. Agents have incentives to communicate information regarding their protocol truthfully. This is also reasonable , as far as agents need to participate.

The market place can maintain and enforce rules of participation. Similar considerations regarding auction house rules were made in [17].

3. Related to the issue above, there could be a consideration for the monitor to forcibly terminate or suspend agents whose behaviour deviate from the rules of the protocol.
4. In principle the monitor can listen to all communication, but as discussed below a polling mechanism will be considered for periodic communication with agents.

For a more complete study of the properties of this framework, we consider three detection mechanisms and briefly discuss the properties of each before discussing the one we implement. Evaluation of these would indicate which approach is appropriate for what category of applications.

Detection Mechanisms.

1. Polling, P: Equivalent to using wave-based solutions [18] in which algorithms are based on repeated execution of a wave algorithm. At the end of each wave, either termination is detected or a new wave is started. Termination is detected if local conditions turn out to be satisfied in each process (object) [18].
2. Polling with knowledge of the full protocol, P-P: Here the interaction monitor combines polling as described above with a full knowledge of a protocol to detect termination. Given an agent's protocol subgraph the monitor checks against the full known protocol to ascertain status.
3. Monitoring and knowledge of minimal partial protocol, M-P: Here the monitor needs only to keep in memory only a part of the protocol, a set of termination paths. When an agent starts executing in any of these paths, the monitor executes an algorithm to monitor the agent for termination.

The Algorithm: Given the definitions 1 - 4, the termination detection algorithm can now be discussed.

In the basic termination detection algorithm, given a protocol graph, the agent determines the shortest unique termination paths and provides them to the monitor for termination detection. The monitor determines the observables from the termination paths and polls agents for sent messages or structure containing sent messages (compare listening to all messages being sent by the monitored agent). If a message is not an observable then it can be discarded. If it is an observable, then the monitor needs to check for each path whether the message fits into the current execution of any of the termination paths. If this is the case, then the current execution state of this path is moved one transition forward. If this brings it to its last state, it means that a terminal state has been reached and that the agent can be terminated. Otherwise, it means that the current execution of the path has to be started from the beginning again. More formally, the pseudo code for the algorithm is given as in Figure 6 below:

Algorithm for Termination Detection of Protocols

- − Given: TP be the set of shortest unique termination paths with observables O.
- − Data structures: For every $p = (s_1, \ldots, s_n) \in TP$, there is a state s_i called current execution state of p.
- − Init: For all $p = (s_1, \ldots, s_n) \in TP$ initialise its current execution state to s_1.
- − Body: While not terminated do
    - • Let l be a message sent by an agent
    - • If $l \notin O$ then for all $p = (s_1, \ldots, s_n) \in TP$ set p's current execution state to s_1.
    - • Else: For all $p = (s_1, \ldots, s_n) \in TP$ with current execution state s_i do
        - ∗ If $s_i \xrightarrow{l} s_{i+1}$, then p's current execution state becomes s_{i+1} and if $s_{i+1} = s_n$, then set terminated to true.
        - ∗ If $s_i \not\xrightarrow{l} s_{i+1}$, then set p's current execution state to s_1 or to s_2 in case that $s_1 \xrightarrow{l} s_2$.

Fig. 6. Termination detection algorithm for protocols

4.1 Prototype Implementation

Regarding the engineering of the prototype, two alternative design options were considered.

1. The first option is to assume general broadcasting of messages: In this setup the monitor sends messages and receives messages from all individual agents. This option represents the worst case scenario in terms of message complexity and to mitigate, polling can be used to reduce overheads, i.e the monitor will periodically query agents at specified a rate. [2]
2. The second option is to assume special network topologies such as token ring: In this setup, the monitor maintains and manages rings of agents. A ring topology as a practical decision can reduce message overheads associated with broadcasting to individual agents. All ring members implement interfaces with the following operations: *registration, deregistration, passToken, recieveToken, recieveRingUpdates*.
   The main issues, overheads and extra generated messages to be considered here relate to the ring maintenance, ring updates (removing defunct agents, sorting if required e.tc.), missing tokens, handling acknowledgements etc. In addition there are overheads related to updating of tokens by agents. Furthermore there is too much reliance on agents cooperation in passing on tokens and there is possible risk of exposure of information to other agents. The advantages of such a scheme would be apparent in less dynamic systems where communication is infrequent and ring updates infrequent e.g in computationally intensive applications.

---

[2] This will be the subject of experimentation and will in general be dependent of the type of application being considered, e.g. highly dynamic and less dynamic systems.

On balance, given complications and overheads of network management associated with assuming a ring topology and issues of agent cooperation, token loss and delay, the broadcasting option was taken.

Given the discussion so far, the description of the prototype implementation is then straightforward. The prototype uses the JADE [19] agent execution model. Protocol implementation is based on JADE's **FSMBehaviour** (a composite behaviour). When initialised, an agent (knowing the protocol it executes), **determines** the termination paths and **registers** these with the monitor. And as it executes a protocol the agent **updates** an internal structure with its transitions. For simplicity, a test generator generates messages that takes the agent through its state transitions to simulate an ongoing conversation.

The monitor handles the **registration** of participating agents. For every registered agent and **AgentProxy** object is created and appended to an internal structure referenced by a unique agent identifier. This proxy object maintains a set on **termination paths** associated with the agent.

The monitor periodically executes a polling mechanism to **query** the agents for a snapshot of their protocol executions, and **handles** replys within a JADE behaviour tailored for this purpose. For each reply received, a **detection** behaviour is scheduled, and an associated AgentProxy retrieved.

The proxy object provides functionality to check for termination in each termination path object it maintains. It achieves this by propagating the data structure containing the current messages received from the associated agent. The termination path objects implement the algorithm discussed above to ascertain termination.

JADE provides Sender and Receiver behaviours encapsulating send and receive actions as atomic operations [3], and these were widely used in this prototype.

5   Experiments and Initial Results

Initial experiments will focus on evaluating the framework against detection delays, scalability, consideration of performance and overheads, and information revealed by agents. All these experiments will be run in both the centralised and decentralised settings. In detail;

1. Experiment SET 1: **Detection Delays**: In general, these experiments are setup to study detection delays for various mechanisms used for detection. The parameters of importance here are quantities of time. The detection delay Δ_{detec}, relates to the time that elapses between the occurrence of termination and the detection, T_{term} and T_{detec} respectively. Given a detection mechanism $\mathfrak{M}$ with parameter $\mathfrak{P}$ (e.g polling frequency) set to some value, intuitively the delay, $\Delta\text{detec} = T_{term} - T_{detec}$

---

[3] Jade API

2. Experiment SET 2: **Scalability**: The mechanisms presented in this work are in a sense useful and of value mainly in large scale multiagent systems, where manual and adhoc methods for management are not ideal. Experiments in this category will allow a study of how increasing the size of the society affects the system and to ascertain whether these mechanisms scale up.

3. Experiment SET 3: **Performance and Overheads**: These set of experiments will test the effect of incorporating the use of detection mechanisms on system performance and assess what overheads are incurred and the likely bottlenecks introduced in the system. Experiments will study different setups and architectures, and how these influence performance.

4. Experiment SET 4: **Information Revealed** : As discussed so far, the termination detection process can be influenced (e.g improved) by what additional information the individual agents are willing to reveal to the monitor about their execution of protocols. This inevitably raises questions of security and strategic concerns. Experiments in this category will consider how these affect both detection delays, scalability etc. and qualitatively things like security and agents' incentives to reveal such information.

5.1 Centralised Setting

The execution of the above experiments is still ongoing, and those initial experiments attempted so far are experiments set 1 and set 2 (Scalability and detection delays). In those, the following setup has been adopted (representing one of the worst case scenarios):

- Single Platform hosting Agents.
- Single Monitor.
- Agents executing a single protocol.
- Monitor has complete knowledge of protocol.
- fixed polling rate.

While more work is still to be done, early results with raw data , showing minimum, maximum and average detection delays for an increasing number of agents are presented below. Degradation is clearly visible as the number of agents increases. This mainly reflects both single monitor saturation and possible underlying platform performance issues.

With this observation, efforts have been made at distribution as discussed below.

5.2 Decentralised Setting

As far as distribution is concerned, the following issued were considered:

1. Introduction of additional remote monitors.
2. A monitor to monitor registration protocol: This allows monitors to make themselves known and declare themselves active.

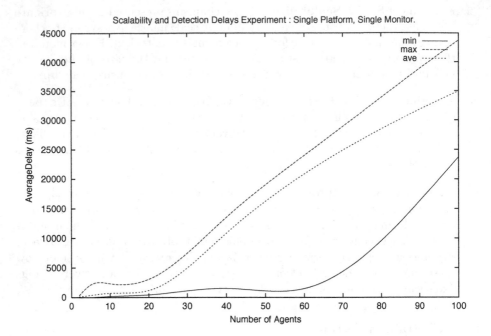

Fig. 7. Initial results for scalability and detection delay experiments

3. A protocol for allowing a remote agent to register with monitor.
4. Monitor profiles and a local load balancing scheme by each monitor, which in the future will be made adaptive.
5. Caching and persistence of information for recovery purposes

Figure 8 below shows a schematic of this setup.

Experiments assuming this setup are being conducted and in particular, a further number of issues relating to distribution are being considered, namely determination of communication delays, (related to work done in [20]) but pertaining to the work presented here. Also when regarding dealing with time measurements in a distributed setting, consideration is being made for lack of clock synchronisation.

Finally, all these initial experiments as they are, assume a closed system where we have control over the parameters of concern. For any future comparative study, issues such as local resource consumption not related to the experiments being conducted will be considered, indeed a parameter, capturing the notion of local resource utilisation, such as CPU utilisation will be factored in.

6   Discussion, Evaluation and Future Work

6.1   Related Work

Distributed termination detection algorithms have been used before in the context of agents [21]. While our approach used as a basis a polling technique,

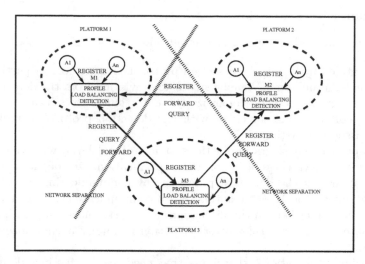

Fig. 8. Architecture for the distributed setting

(and hence falls under probe mechanisms (see section 1) in the taxonomy of distributed termination detection algorithms), [21] discusses distributed *quiescence* detection in multiagent negotiation with the solution presented there based on the Dijkstra and Scholten's algorithm (example of a tracing algorithm, see section 2). The algorithm is used a basis of a quiescence detection protocol, a protocol that operates as a layer on top of an underlying *mediated* negotiation protocol.

The first contribution of that work is a formulation of the distributed quiescence detection problem in multiagent, multi-issue negotiation. The negotiation considered there is mediated, i.e. the negotiation model comprises of agents and mediators. Mediators facilitate the negotiation by managing information flow and enforcing negotiation rules [21]. The negotiation protocol comprises two general type of messages, namely OFFER (sent by agents to mediators) and NOTIFY (sent by mediators to agents). The form and content of these messages varies according to domain specific rules enforced by mediators and negotiation policies of the agents, [21].

Applying the Dijkstra and Scholten's algorithm to the negotiation model involves requiring that agents augment their behaviors by passing and tracking ACK messages according to the detection protocol, i.e. their overall behavior is then a composition of their basic negotiation behavior with the transition diagram representing the algorithm, [21].

As a second contribution, the work identifies and discusses circumstances under which agents may have incentives to deviate from the basic protocol and discusses a modification to the negotiation framework that is argued to present limited incentive for agents to deviate, [21].

6.2   Qualitative Evaluation

We evaluate our work according to the following:

1. As identified by [21], if the detection protocol assumes correct participation by agents, a unilateral (maybe strategic) deviation from the detection protocol by any agent may jeopardize the detection process in a setup where agents compose their behavior with the detection protocol in multiagent, multi-issue negotiations.

   Our approach considers interactions at a protocol level, with the monitor having some awareness of the protocol specification. One of the ways agents can put at risk the detection process is by communicating false information about protocols, or by opting not to communicate this information. As highlighted elsewhere in the discussion, the marketplace/auction house can stipulate and enforce rules of participation to nullify agents' incentives to deviate.

2. Regarding termination, other issues that need considering include *detection delays*, the maximum time that can elapse between termination and its detection. In particular considerations have to made on how this delay can be minimized for any specific detection mechanism adopted. In our framework the parameters for polling can be adjusted. Other issues arise if agents execute multiple protocols. The set up as it is will also need to consider the fact that agents may be executing different stages of the protocol, so that generalised society wide polling frequency may not useful in minimising detection delays. Our framework can be modified to allow the monitor to maintain agent groups and associations depending on protocols used, stages in the protocol and conversation partners.

3. Another issue relates to structuring the detection mechanisms such that there is no adverse effect on the execution of underlying protocols and that no unnecessary bottlenecks are introduced in the infrastructure of the society. The framework we describe does not require that we modify the protocols, e.g. augment protocols with control messages. The main possible bottleneck is the use of a single entity, the monitor, in detecting termination. Ideas on how to decentralize this functionality will go a long in addressing this concern. Some ideas are being explored as discussed elsewhere. Indeed distribution is a general problem for most services such as directory , naming services etc. and there is exists a number of approaches and solutions to address this concern, for example distribution, hierarchical setups e.g as used in the Domain Name Service, DNS, [22], group communications [23] etc.

Finally, we argue that in addition to detecting termination, our mechanism can also be used to provide continuous visibility of the process of agent interactions. This can be used in high level management of agent societies in practical applications.

6.3   Future Work

To study the problem of termination detection in multiagent system adequately will require consideration of representative cases in the space of interactions. e.g, one to one (client server like), many to one (auction like), many to many (general).

Future work will focus first on auctions. Auctions offer an easy to implement computational mechanisms for automating negotiations in multiagent systems. Auctions are well grounded in economic theory and have been tested out and have found use in many real applications in financial trading and lately in electronic commerce and are widely used in experimental economics [24]. Future work will focus mainly on the use of auctions as a testbed for performing experiments on mechanisms for termination detection of agent interaction. This work will broadly contribute to auction mechanism design and implementation.

A number of aspects will be identified and experiments setup and executed to investigate. The evaluation of these experiments will yield insight into how to improve and best structure the management mechanisms for these large scale auction based marketplaces populated by bidding and interacting agents.

In addition to completing experiment sets above, further experiments relating to auction scenarios will be carried out: auction rules, dynamic agent relationships, auction structure (e.g centralised, decentralised).

In detail:

1. Experiment SET 5: **Auction Rules**: An auction house may stipulate a set of rules which all bidders need to abide by to be able to take part in the bidding process. A number of rules can be described. In general the auction rules may affect the dynamics of the auction. The description of the rules may include rules that ensure that the bidders have incentives to cooperate with the monitor in ways that can facilitate the monitoring process. This set of experiments are designed to investigate the effect of this rules on the dynamics of the marketplace.
2. Experiment SET 6: **Auction Structure and Distribution:** The auction service can be structured in may ways. For example multiple auctions can be hosted, the auction service can be distributed etc. Also as highlighted in the discussion, single monitor in the marketplace is a clear source of bottleneck in the system and makes the architecture susceptible to single node failure. Therefore distribution of this services is necessary. All these decisions can affect the detection mechanisms. Experiments in this category will investigate.

The discussion has so far been mainly abstract, future work will consider other aspects of protocols, not just communicative actions and exchange of messages, but time out events and physical actions (e.g performing the awarded task in contract net protocol). Also as indicated elsewhere, the discussion centered around detection termination of protocol. Clearly this is some way away from detecting termination of agents or agent systems. Future work will involve consideration of this issue, and the issue of how agents are terminated.

In addition, work presented here and elsewhere focused on termination detection. In subsequent work it will be desirable to consider the use of the monitor to drive society wide garbage collection tied to end of interactions to ensure optimal use of computational resources. Indeed it has been shown, for example by [25] that the semantics of the termination detection problem are fully contained in the garbage collection problem.

7   Summary and Conclusions

The contributions of this paper are three fold. We have suggested and presented a framework for studying determination of global states such as termination in a society of agents. Agents are higher semantic level entities that execute protocols to engage in potentially complex interactions. Our proposed framework incorporates this use of protocols by agents.

The suggested framework is motivated by probe based algorithms in standard distributed object systems. It incorporates a novel algorithm that allows a monitor to determine termination when presented additional information on partial behaviour specification by agents.

The second contribution relates to describing this additional information by presenting a number of definitions in our discussion. In addition, possible criteria for evaluation have been suggested.

Thirdly, we have also proposed future experimental work to study and identify key parameters, and aspects that can influence the termination detection service in auction based marketplaces.

References

[1] Pitt, J., Mamdani, A.: A protocol-based semantics for an agent communication language. In: Proceedings 16th International Joint Conference on Artificial Intelligence IJCAI'99, Stockholm, Sweden, Morgan-Kaufmann Publishers (1999) 486–491 136, 142
[2] Weiss, G., ed.: Multiagent Systems: A Modern Approach to Distributed Artificial Intelligence. MIT Press (1999) 136
[3] Genesereth, M., Ketchpel, S.: Software agents. Communications of the ACM **37** (1994) 48–53 136
[4] Labrou, Y., Finin, T.: Semantics and conversations for an agent communication language. In Pollack, M.E., ed.: Proceedings of the Fifteenth International Joint Conference on Artifical Intelligence (IJCAI-97), San Mateo, CA, USA, Morgan Kaufmann Publishers (1997) 584–591 136
[5] FIPA: Specification part 2 agent communication language (1997) 136
[6] Wooldridge, M.: Semantic issues in verification of agent communication languages. Autonomous Agents and Multi-Agent Systems **3** (2000) 136
[7] Venkatraman, M., Singh, M.: Verifying compliance with commitment protocols. Autonomous Agents and Multi-Agent Systems **2** (1999) 217–236 137
[8] Chaib-draa, B., Dignum, F.: Trends in agent communication language. Computational Intelligence, Volume 2, Number 5, 2002 **2** (2002) 137

[9] Friedman, D., Rust, J.: The Double Auction Market, Institutions, Theories, and Evidence. Addison Wesley Longman (1993) 138

[10] Mattern, F.: Global quiescence detection based on credit distribution and recovery. Information Processing Letters **30** (1989) 195–200 140

[11] Mattern, F.: Algorithms for distributed termination detection. Distributed Computing **2** (1987) 161–175 140

[12] Babaoglu, O., Marzullo, K.: Consistent global states of distributed systems: Fundamental concepts and mechanisms. In Mullender, S., ed.: Distributed Systems. Addison-Wesley (1993) 55–96 140

[13] Dijkstra, E., Scholten, C.: Termination detection for diffusing computations. Information Processing Letters **11** (1980) 1–4 140

[14] Tel, G.: Distributed control for AI. Technical Report UU-CS-1998-17, ICS, Information Computing Sciences, University of Utrecht,Netherlands (1998) 140

[15] Dijkstra, E.W., Feijen, W.H.J., van Gasteren, A.J.M.: Derivation of a termination detection algorithm for distributed computations. Information Processing Letters **16** (1983) 217–219 140

[16] Singh, M.: On the semantics of protocols among distributed intelligent agents. Technical Report TM-91-09, Deutsches Forschungszentrum für Künstliche Intelligenz GmbH (1991) 141

[17] Noriega, P.: Agent mediated auctions: The Fishmarket Metaphor. PhD thesis, Universitat Autonoma de Barcelona (1997) 145

[18] Tel, G.: 13. In: Introduction To Distributed Algorithms. Cambridge University Press (2000) 145

[19] Bellifemine, F., Poggi, A., Rimassa, G.: Jade: A FIPA-compliant agent framework. In: PAAM'99. (1999) 97–108 147

[20] Vitaglione, G., Quarta, F., Cortese, E.: Scalability and performance of JADE message transport system. AAMAS Workshop on AgentCities, Bologna (2002) 149

[21] Wellman, M., Walsh, W.: Distributed quiescence detection in multiagent negotiation. In: Proceedings of the 3rd International Conference on Multiagent Systems. (2000) 149, 150, 151

[22] Mockapetris, P.: RFC 1034: Domain names - concepts and facilities. Technical report, ISI, NetWorking Group (1987) 151

[23] Birman, K.: The process group approach to reliable distributed computing. Communications of the ACM **36** (1993) 37–53, 103 151

[24] Hagel, J., Roth, A., eds.: Handbook of Experimental Economics. Princenton University Press (1995) 152

[25] Tel, G., Mattern, F.: The derivation of distributed termination detection algorithms from garbage collection schemes. ACM Transactions on Programming Languages and Systems **15** (1993) 1–35 153

Competition, Cooperation, and Authorization*

Antoni Mazurkiewicz

Institute of Computer Science of PAS
Warsaw, Poland
amaz@ipipan.waw.pl

Abstract. Multi-agent systems considered in the paper consist of a finite number of agents, positions of which can be changed by system actions, and of an evaluation function which assigns to each agent a value of its current position (as e.g. the distance from the intended target). The set of all possible values is ordered; the intention of each agent is to reach a position with the minimum value. Any system action can decrease position values of some agents (the winners) and increase those of the others (the losers); consequently, an action execution can create conflicts among its participants (winners and losers); arbitrary resolutions of such conflicts can prevent some agents of reaching their goals. The present paper is aiming to formulate conditions that must be fulfilled by actions to guarantee each agent reaching its intended final situation.

Keywords: Multi-agent system, conflicts, cooperation, concurrency, non-determinism, distributed algorithms

> *For whosoever hath, to him shall be given, and he shall have more abundance; but whosoever hath not, from him shall be taken away even that he hath.* [**Mat 13:12**]

1   Introduction

One of characteristic features of multi-agent systems is a competition between agents or groups of agents. Agents may compete for resources, for access to devices, for authorization to undertake some actions, for other privileges that can be granted or refused. On the other hand, agents can cooperate, if such a cooperation can be favorable for them: some privileges can be offered only for sufficiently great number of applicants, or some resources can be allocated for a group of agents with a common purpose. Competition or cooperation among agents can vary during the system activity, and then instantaneous coalitions among agents have a dynamic character.

Agents are acting to reach their goals. To do it, they act in a rational way, evaluating their situations at any moment of the system run and try to improve

---

* Partially supported by KBN grant nr. 7 T11C 006 20 and EC Framework Program 5 IST-1999-10298 "ALFEBIITE".

A. Omicini, P. Petta, and J. Pitt (Eds.): ESAW 2003, LNAI 3071, pp. 155–167, 2004.
© Springer-Verlag Berlin Heidelberg 2004

their situation by performing a suitable action. However, an action being favorable for some agents may be unfavorable for others; the competition between agents results in choosing an action improving the situation of some agents, but at the same time worsening it for others. In effect of such a competition none of agents may reach its target: making a progress in one step, an agent can lose its gain in the next one. There is a simple strategy to avoid infinite and useless competing: an agent being in the best situation should have a chance to improve it, at the cost of others. This strategy has been already applied in some routing algorithms, e.g. in [1] and message distribution [2]. This paper is aiming to formulate precisely this strategy in an abstract framework, neglecting nonsubstantial features of multi-agent systems but retaining those enabling proper formulation of the required properties.

To grasp the essential phenomena of such a strategy, the presented set-up of the multi-agent systems is limited to the basic system components: *agents*, *states* of the system that can be transformed in effect of the system *actions*, and *evaluation* of situation of any agent at an instantaneous system state. Value of an agent situation is a measure of how far from the target the agent is.

The order of action execution as well as the choice of action is not specified; some actions with disjoint sets of participants can be executed independently of each other. Systems discussed here are uniform (no particular agent is distinguished), local (any change of state concerns only participants of the changing action, leaving positions of other agents unchanged), self-stabilizing (it can start with an arbitrary initial state), non-deterministic (there is no prescribed order in which actions are executed), and concurrent (some actions can be performed independently of each other).

In the paper the standard mathematical notions are used, with $\mathbf{N}$ denoting the set of all non-negative integers ordered in standard way. First, the description of the structure and behavior of the discussed systems is given, and next some limitations of its behavior that guarantee all agents to reach eventually their goals. Finally, some extensions and consequences of the approach is given.

2   Abstract Multi-agent Systems

An abstract multi-agent system considered here and called *ams* for short consists of a finite set of agents, a set of system states, a set of actions, and an evaluation function, which to each agent g in any state s assigns a current value $V(g, s)$ of its situation in this state; this value is called here the *position value* of agent g at state s. The set of all position values is ordered making possible their comparison. Formally, system $\mathbf{A}$ is defined as a tuple

$$\mathbf{A} = (G, S, R, V)$$

where

G is a finite set (of *agents*),

S is a set (of *states*),

$R \subseteq S \times S$ is a set (of *actions*),

$V : G \times S \longrightarrow D$, (*valuation* function),

where D is a set (of *agent position values*). Sets G, S, D are assumed to be disjoint and non-empty. Instead of $(s', s'') \in R$ write $s' \to_R s''$, or simply $s' \to s''$ if R is understood; similarly, instead $(s', s'') \notin R$ write $(s' \not\to_R s'')$ (or $(s' \not\to s'')$, resp.). Set D is totally ordered by $<$ relation; as usual, $d' \le d''$ means $d' < d''$ or $d' = d''$; $d' > d''$ means $d'' < d'$. Set D is assumed to meet the "minimum property" guaranteeing that each non-empty subset of D has the least element. The least element of the whole set D is denoted by $\mathbf{0}$. Value $V(g, s)$ will be called the *position value* of g at state s and is intended to estimate how far agent g at state s is from its goal. If $V(g, s) = \mathbf{0}$, state s is the target state for agent g. Let $r = (s' \to s'')$ be an action. Agent g is a *winner* of r, if $V(g, s') > V(g, s'')$, and is a *loser* of r, if $V(g, s') < V(g, s'')$; winners and losers in r are *participants* of r; remaining agents of the system are said to not *participate* in r. In other words, g is a winner (loser) of an action, if in effect of this action the distance from its target decreases (increases, resp.). Agent g is *dismissed* in state s, if $V(g, s) = \mathbf{0}$, and *active*, otherwise. A state is *active*, if there is at least one agent active in it, and *terminal*, otherwise. The value $V(g, s)$ will be also called the *position* or the *situation* of agent g at state s.

The intuition behind the above definition is the following. There is a group of agents that intend to reach their individual goals executing some actions. Each action concerns only its participants, i.e. some agents from the group. Actions cause change of the situation of their participants, and leave situation of remaining agents unchanged; thus, actions are local changes of agents situations. The situation of an agent is measured by its distance from its targets; distances are represented by elements of an ordered set: for any agent, the smaller is the distance from the target, the better is its situation.

System Axioms. The following axioms concerning agents and actions are assumed to hold for all states s', s'' and agents g of the system:

(A1) $s' \to s'' \Rightarrow \exists g : V(g, s') > V(g, s'')$

   (there is a winner of any action);

(A2) $V(g, s) > \mathbf{0} \Rightarrow \exists s' : s \to s' \wedge V(g, s) > V(g, s')$

   (any active agent at any state has a chance to win);

(A3) $V(g, s) = \mathbf{0} \Rightarrow \forall s' : s \to s' \Rightarrow V(g, s') = \mathbf{0}$

   (dismissal is permanent).

In other words, for any active agent in any situation there exists at least one action favorable for this agent, and the other way round: in any action there is at least one winning agent. Below we give an example of an *ams* system.

Competition and Cooperation. Depending on possible actions, agents can cooperate, compete, or be independent at some states. Agents winning an action can be viewed as cooperating, while all losers as unsuccessful competitors against the formers. The choice between two actions that are favorable for some agents causes no conflict between them; a conflict arises between winners and losers, since any loser could be a winner with another choice of action. A conflict can also arise between two agents that can win two separate actions, if a result of one action leads to a state from which the second agent has less favorable possibilities of acting. Two actions are independent, if they do not interfere with each other. Independent actions have disjoint sets of participants, executed in any sequence give the same result, making possible to treat them as a single action, with the union of participants. If two actions are independent, execution of one of them does not prevent the other from being executed. Two agents can be partners, if both of them participate in an action; allies, if both of them are winners of an action, or competitors, if one of them is a winner and the other a loser in an action. The choice of an action, which implies the choice of winning and losing agents, is non-deterministic, unless some rules of priority, called here 'authorization rules', are introduced to the agent's community. Two such rules will be formulated in the sequel.

Example 1. Let $\mathbf{E} = (G, S, R, V)$ be an *ams* system with

$$G = \{g_1, g_2\},$$
$$S = \{s_0, s_1, s_2, s_3, s_4, s_5\}$$

and with R and V given by the following tables:

Actions:

R	s_1	s_2	s_3	s_4	s_5
s_0	$\rightarrow$	$\rightarrow$	$\times$	$\times$	$\times$
s_1	$\times$	$\rightarrow$	$\rightarrow$	$\times$	$\times$
s_2	$\rightarrow$	$\times$	$\times$	$\rightarrow$	$\times$
s_3	$\times$	$\times$	$\times$	$\times$	$\rightarrow$
s_4	$\times$	$\times$	$\times$	$\times$	$\rightarrow$

Valuation:

V	g_1	g_2
s_0	3	3
s_1	2	3
s_2	3	2
s_3	1	4
s_4	4	1
s_5	0	0

States will be represented by the corresponding valuations of agents; that is, state s_0 is represented by $(3,3)$, state s_1 by $(2,3)$, ..., state s_5 by $(0,0)$. In the first table sign $\rightarrow$ (sign $\times$) in column s' and row s'' denotes $s' \rightarrow_R s''$ ($s' \not\rightarrow_R s''$, resp.); values $\{0, 1, 2, 3, 4\}$ of function V are supposed to be ordered in the natural way. It is easy to check that the above definition meets axioms $A1, A2, A3$. The winner of action $(3,3) \rightarrow (2,3)$ is g_1; the winner of action $(3,3) \rightarrow (3,2)$ is g_2; agent g_2 does not participate in action $(3,3) \rightarrow (2,3)$, agent g_1 does not participate in action $(3,3) \rightarrow (3,2)$. Both action have only one participant each, g_1 and g_2 neither cooperate, nor compete. However, actions $(3,3) \rightarrow (2,3)$ and $(3,3) \rightarrow (3,2)$ are not independent since they cannot be executed simultaneously - there is no state $(2,2)$ which could be the effect of such an execution. Agent g_2 is a loser in $(2,3) \rightarrow (1,4)$ and agent g_1 is a loser in $(3,2) \rightarrow (4,1)$. In actions transforming situation $(2,3)$ both agents compete; if the result of action is $(1,4)$, agent g_1 wins and agent g_2 loses; if the result is

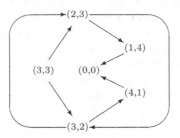

Fig. 1. The diagram of system **E**

$(3,2)$, g_2 wins, and g_1 loses. In actions transforming states $(1,4)$ and $(4,1)$ both agents cooperate, win, and become dismissed. This system can be visualized by the picture presented in Fig.1. $\qquad\square$

3 System Runs

Let $\mathbf{A} = (G, S, R, V)$ be an arbitrary agent system, fixed from now on. Call state s *live*, if there exists another state s' with $s \to s'$; denote the set of all live states of $\mathbf{A}$ by $\mathbf{L}$. Any sequence in $\mathbf{N} \longrightarrow S$ is a *run* of the system, if for all $i \geq 0$

$$s_i \in \mathbf{L} \wedge s_i \to s_{i+1} \vee s_i \notin \mathbf{L} \wedge s_i = s_{i+1}. \tag{1}$$

Run (1) is said to *terminate*, and state s to be its *last* state, if there is $k \geq 0$ such that $s = s_k \notin \mathbf{L}$. A run is *successful*, if it terminates and all agents are dismissed at its last state: $V(g, s) = \mathbf{0}$ for all $g \in G$ and for the last state s of the run in question.

Proposition 1. *Any run of ams is either successful, or non-terminating.*

Proof. In the opposite case there would be a terminating run with some agents active at its last state; then the last state would be live (by Axiom A1), contradicting the definition of runs. $\qquad\square$

Example 2. The sequence

$$(3,3) \to (3,2) \to (2,3) \to \cdots \to (3,2) \to (2,3) \to \cdots$$

is a non-terminating (hence not successful) run of the system defined in Example 1. In this run the winners alternate and no agent reaches its target (the corresponding distances are always greater than 0). However, allowing either of the two win twice gives a successful terminating run, e.g.

$$(3,3) \to (3,2) \to \cdots \to (2,3) \to (1,4) \to (0,0)$$

or, respectively,

$$(3,3) \rightarrow (2,3) \rightarrow \cdots \rightarrow (3,2) \rightarrow (4,1) \rightarrow (0,0)$$

In the above cases both agents reach their destinations (the infinite sequence of $(0,0)$ following the last state of both runs is omitted). □

4   Authorizations

Authorization is a restriction imposing some conditions on executability of system actions. Instruction $s' \rightarrow s''$ is *authorized* by condition C, if $s' \rightarrow s'' \Rightarrow C(s', s'')$; a run is authorized, if any pair of its consecutive states is authorized, and the system is authorized, if any run of it is authorized. Authorizations are introduced to prevent systems from unsuccessful runs, either nonterminating (livelocks), or terminating (deadlocks). The most liberal authorization is given by the condition identically true **T**; according to this authorization all possible runs of the system are authorized. As it is seen from the Example 2 some of runs of such systems can be non-terminating. The most restrictive authorization is given by the condition identically false **F**, i.e. by the never fulfilled condition; in this case no action is authorized and each run terminates at its first state. Clearly, all runs of such systems are terminating, but not necessarily successful. We are seeking for something in between these two extremities. In what follows we shall discuss two 'intermediate' (non-trivial) authorization conditions that guarantee all runs successful and do not admit deadlocks; moreover, they are local, i.e they refer exclusively to states of participants of the authorized action. Authorized actions do respect axioms A1 and A3, but they do not observe axiom A2 any more: not all agents active in a state can be winners.

Authorization W. The first authorization, called here **W**, is given by the following restrictions:

$$s' \rightarrow s'' \Rightarrow \exists g_0 : V(g_0, s') > V(g_0, s'') \land$$
$$(\forall g : V(g, s') < V(g, s'') \Rightarrow V(g_0, s') \leq V(g, s')) \tag{2}$$

(there exists a winner in a position not worse than any loser). Intuitively, an action is authorized by **W**, if at least one of its winners is in better or at least equal position than any of its losers. Observe that the above condition is local. We shall prove that authorization **W** prevent the system from non-terminating runs, which is the main objective of introducing authorization conditions. For any live situation (with at least one active action) there exists also at least one action enabled and authorized by **W**; it guarantees that the authorization does not cause the system deadlock, i.e. that any terminated and authorized run is successful. We prove in the sequel that any authorized run terminates.

Proposition 1 *Authorization (2) is equivalent to the following:*

$$s' \to s'' \Rightarrow \exists g_0 : V(g_0, s') > V(g_0, s'') \ \wedge$$
$$(\forall g : V(g, s') \neq V(g, s'') \Rightarrow V(g_0, s') \leq V(g, s')) \qquad (3)$$

(a participant in the best position wins).

Proof. Let (2) holds and $s' \to s''$. Then there exists a winner in a position not worse than any loser. Consequently, the participant of $s' \to s''$ in the best position is also a winner, which implies (3). Conversely, if (3) holds, then clearly there exists a winner in a position not worse than any loser. It proves the proposition. $\square$

The difference between conditions (2) and (3) is that the winner of any action authorized by (3) has the best position among *all* its participants, while in actions authorized by (2) it has a position not worse than any of losers only. In view of Proposition 1 both formulations are equivalent.

Example 3. Sequences

$$(3, 3) \to (3, 2) \to (4, 1) \to (0, 0),$$

and

$$(3, 3) \to (2, 3) \to (1, 4) \to (0, 0)$$

are successful runs of the system defined above in Example 1; they are the *only* runs starting with $(3, 3)$. Action $(3, 2) \to (4, 1)$ is the only authorized action at state $(3, 2)$, and action $(2, 3) \to (1, 4)$ is the only authorized action at state $(2, 3)$. The system $\mathbf{E}$ defined in Example 1 and authorized by $\mathbf{W}$ is presented in Fig.2. $\square$

Proposition 2 *Any terminating run of any system authorized by $\mathbf{W}$ is successful.*

Proof. If there exists any active agent at a state, then there exists an authorized action at this state, namely the action improving position of the best situated active agent. Therefore a state with a number of active agents cannot be the last one in a run. $\square$

Theorem 1 *Any run of any system authorized by $\mathbf{W}$ is successful.*

Proof. Let $\mathbf{A} = (G, S, R, V)$ be a multi-agent action system with $|G| = N$ and let $s \in \mathbf{N} \longrightarrow S$ be a run of $\mathbf{A}$ authorized by $\mathbf{W}$ with $r_i = (s_i, s_{i+1})$ for each $i \geq 0$. Define agents $g_1, g_2, \ldots, g_N$ and integers $i_1, i_2, \ldots, i_N$ as follows. Set $M_1 = \min\{V(g, s_i) \mid g \in G, i \geq 0\}$ and let agent g_1 and integer i_1 be such that $V(g_1, s_{i_1}) = M_1$. Suppose g_k, i_k have been already defined; then define $M_{k+1} = \min\{V(g, s_i) \mid g \in G - \{g_1, \ldots, g_k\}, i \geq i_k\}$ and let agent g_{k+1} and integer i_{k+1} be such that $i_{k+1} \geq i_k$ and $V(g_{k+1}, s_{i_{k+1}}) = M_{k+1}$. Since the total number of agents

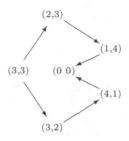

Fig. 2. System **E** authorized by **W**

of the system is equal to $N, \{g_1, g_2, \ldots, g_N\} = G$. Clearly, $i_1 \leq i_2 \leq \cdots \leq i_N$. Observe that values M_i exist due to the minimum property of set D.

Now, prove that $V(g_1, s_i) = M_1$ for all $i \geq i_1$. Indeed, by minimality of M_1, there cannot be any state s_i of the run with $i \geq i_1$ and with $V(g_1, s_i) < M_1$. Consequently, due to authorization condition (2), g_1 cannot be a winner in any action r_i with $i \geq i_1$, since otherwise g_1 should improve its own situation yielding $V(g_1, s_i) < M_1$. But also g_1 cannot be a loser of any action r_i with $i \geq i_1$, since then, by axiom A1 and the authorization condition (2), there would be a winner in r_i, say h_i, with $V(h_i, s_i) \leq M_1$, and in the effect of this action r_i it would be $V(h_i, s_{i+1}) < M_1$, again contradicting the definition of M_1. Therefore, $V(g_1, s_i) = M_1$ holds for all states s_i with $i \geq i_1$ proving g_1 not participating in any action r_i with $i \geq i_1$.

Suppose we have already proved that none of agents $g_1, g_2, \ldots, g_k$ participate in any action r_i with $i \geq i_k$ and prove $g_1, g_2, \ldots, g_k, g_{k+1}$ do not participate in any action r_i for $i \geq i_{k+1}$ either. Indeed, since $g_1, g_2, \ldots, g_k$ do not participate in any actions r_i with $i \geq i_k$, none of them can be a winner or a loser in r_i with $i \geq i_k$. By definition of i_{k+1}, M_{k+1}, we have $V(g_{k+1}, s_{i_{k+1}}) = M_{k+1}$; clearly, g_{k+1} cannot be a winner of actions r_i with $i \geq i_{k+1}$, contradicting the definition of since otherwise it would be $V(g_{k+1}, s_i) < M_{k+1}$ for some $i \geq i_{k+1}, M_{k+1}$. But g_{k+1} cannot be a loser of actions r_i with $i \geq i_{k+1}$ as well, since otherwise an agent, say h_i, out of $g_{k+2}, g_{k+3}, \ldots, g_N$ would be a winner with $V(h_i, s_i) \leq M_{k+1}$, and with $V(h_i, s_{i+1}) < M_{k+1}$, contradicting the definition of M_{k+1}. Thus, $V(g_{k+1}, s_i) = M_{k+1}$ for all $i \geq i_{k+1}$. Repeating similar arguments and taking into account inequalities $i_1 \leq i_2 \leq \cdots \leq i_N$ we prove that all agents of the system are independent of any action r_i with $i \geq i_N$. From this it follows that the length of the run is not greater than i_N, proving the run to terminate. By Proposition 2, all agents of the system are dismissed at the last state of the run.   □

Authorization S. To define this authorization, let the set of all agents be linearly ordered by $\prec$ relation. This ordering may be arbitrary, without distinguishing any agent; it can be established e.g. by a distributed enumeration procedure (see [3]), if such a procedure exists, not assuming any predefined hi-

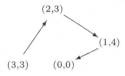

Fig. 3. System **E** authorized by **S** with $g_1 \prec g_2$

erarchy of agents (preserving uniformity of the agent's society). We shall refer to relation $\prec$ as to the "older" relation: g_1 is older that g_2 means $g_1 \prec g_2$. Then the authorization condition **S** is defined as follows:

$$s' \rightarrow s'' \Rightarrow \exists g_0 : V(g_0, s') > V(g_0, s'') \ \wedge$$
$$(\forall g : V(g, s') < V(g, s'') \Rightarrow g_0 \prec g) \tag{4}$$

(there exists a winner older than any loser). Similarly to authorization **W** we have the following property:

Proposition 3 *Authorization* **S** *is equivalent to the following:*

$$s' \rightarrow s'' \Rightarrow \exists g_0 : V(g_0, s') > V(g_0, s'') \ \wedge$$
$$(\forall g : V(g, s') \neq V(g, s'') \Rightarrow g_0 \prec g) \tag{5}$$

(The oldest participant wins).

Proof. Similar to that of Proposition 1. □

Observe that the above authorization condition, similarly to the restriction given by **W**, is local; "the oldest participant" mentioned here does not mean "the oldest agent" in the system; there can be other older agents in the system not participating in the authorized action.

Example 4. Suppose in Example 1 agent g_1 is older that agent g_2, i.e. $g_1 \prec g_2$. Then (s_0, s_1, s_3) is the only run starting with s_0 of the system **A** authorized by **B**. If it were $g_2 \prec g_1$, the only such run would be (s_0, s_2, s_3). □

Theorem 2 *Any complete run authorized by* **S** *is successful.*

Proof. The proof is also similar to that of Theorem 1. Let, as above, $\mathbf{A} = (G, S, R, V)$ be a system with $G = \{g_1, g_2, \ldots, g_N\}$, and let $g_i \prec g_j \Leftrightarrow i < j$. Let $s \in \mathbf{N} \longrightarrow S$ be a run of **A** authorized by **S** with $r_i = (s_i, s_{i+1})$ for each $i \geq 0$. If run s is terminating, then at its last state all agents must be dismissed, since otherwise any action favorable for the oldest active agent would be possible, contradicting the definition of the run. Suppose the run s is not terminating. Since the oldest agent g_1 cannot be a loser, it is either a winner or not participating in all actions of the run. Therefore, its position value cannot increase; due to the minimum property this value cannot decrease infinite number of times, hence there is $i_1 \geq 0$ such that the oldest agent does not change its value in all actions r_j with $j \geq i_1$. That is, g_1 is not participating in any action r_i for $i \geq i_1$. Suppose $g_1, g_2, \ldots, g_k$ are not participating in all actions r_i with $i \geq i_k$ for some i_k; then g_{k+1} cannot be a loser in any action r_i with $i \geq i_k$; since g_{k+1} can be a winner only finite numbers of times in sequence $(s_{k+1}, s_{k+2}, \ldots, s_{k+n}, \ldots)$, there exists $i_{k+1} \geq i_k$ such that $g_1, g_2, \ldots, g_k, g_{k+1}$ are not participating in any action r_i with $i \geq i_{k+1}$. By induction, none of actions in G are participating in any action r_i with $i \geq i_N$. It means, by its very definition, that the run is finite, a contradiction. □

Catastrophes. Sometimes it may be useful to relax Axiom A1, saying that in any action there is a winner. Let $\mathbf{A} = (S, R, G, V)$ be a system (authorized or not), in which Axiom A1 is cut out. Call action $s' \to s''$ a *catastrophe*, if for all $g \in G$ the inequality $V(g, s') \leq V(g, s'')$ holds. In other words, catastrophes are actions without winners. However, we have the following proposition.

Proposition 4 *A finite number of catastrophes occurring in runs does not prevent systems from successful termination.*

Proof. As it is seen from the system axioms for any system and any state of it there exists a successful run starting from this state. If in a run several finite number of catastrophes occur, there is a successful run starting from the state resulting from the last catastrophe. □

5   Complexity

Let $\mathbf{A} = (S, R, G, V)$ be a system authorized by $\mathbf{W}$ with N agents and with $V \in G \times S \longrightarrow \mathbf{N}$. Define the *maximum loss* in the system as the integer

$$L = \max\{V(g, s'') - V(g, s') \mid g \in G, s' \to s'' \in R\}.$$

For any run $s = (s_0, s_1, \ldots)$ of $\mathbf{A}$ let the *initial distance* of s be the integer $M = \max\{V(g, s_0) \mid g \in G\}$.

Theorem 3 *For any run of system authorized by $\mathbf{W}$ with N agents, initial distance M, and maximum loss L, the number of steps is bounded by integer S, where*

$$S = M \cdot \sum_{i=0}^{N-1} (L+1)^i. \tag{6}$$

Proof. Denote by $S(n, m)$ the upper bound of number of steps needed for reaching by n agents the terminal state of the run while starting from positions values not greater than m and assuming the maximum loss not greater than L. Since the system is authorized by $\mathbf{W}$, agents in their best positions (with the smallest position values) cannot lose; in effect, dismissing one of them requires at most m steps in which the best situated agents win. In particular, a system with only one agent and the initial distance m needs m steps to reach its terminal state. Since a success of one agent can create failures for the others, any win of an agent in its best position can increase by L position values of all remaining agents. Due to commutativity, the order of increasing and decreasing operations does not influence on the total number of system steps; hence, agents that win m times can be viewed as increasing initial distance of losing agents by $m \cdot L$. It leads to the following recursive dependency for all $n \geq 1$:

$$S(1, m) = m,$$
$$S(n, m) = m + S(n - 1, m + m \cdot L), \qquad (n > 1)$$

with the following explicit form:

$$S(n, m) = m \cdot \sum_{i=0}^{n-1} (L + 1)^i.$$

It completes the proof by setting $S = S(N, M)$. $\qquad\qquad\qquad\qquad\qquad\square$

Observe that in the above proof the most pessimistic variant of a run has been discussed, namely when a win of one agent causes the maximum lost for all agents in worse (or equal) position.

In Theorem 3 nothing has been said about the number of steps needed to dismiss a concrete agent, since it is not known *a priori* which agent reach the best position in the course of a system action. In case of systems authorized by condition **S** it is not so, as it is shown by the following theorem. Let the set of agents $G = \{g_1, g_2, \ldots, g_N\}$ be ordered by $\prec$ relation in such a way that $g_1 \prec g_2 \prec \ldots \prec g_N$ and let $\mathbf{A} = (S, R, G, V)$ be a system authorized by **S** with $V \in G \times S \longrightarrow \mathbf{N}$.

Theorem 4 *The number of steps needed to dismiss agent g_i in a run of system authorized by* **S** *is bounded by S_i, where*

$$S_i = M \cdot (L + 1)^i, \qquad\qquad\qquad\qquad (7)$$

where M is the maximum initial distance of the run, and L is the maximum loss in a single action.

Proof. The proof is similar to that of Theorem 3, but somewhat simpler. Let $S_i, i = 1, 2, \ldots, N$, be a bound for the number of steps agent g_i needs to reach its target. Clearly, $S_1 = M$, since agent g_1, according to authorization **S**, cannot lose and its distance from the goal is M. Since each win of g_1 can increase the number of steps needed for agents $g_2, g_3, \ldots, g_N$ to achieve their goals by $M \cdot L$ each, and no win of agents $g_3, g_4, \ldots, g_N$ can do the same w.r.to g_2, $S_2 = M \cdot (L + 1)$. Repeating this reasoning for the successive agents we conclude that $S_i = M(1 + L)^i$ for all $i \geq 1$. $\qquad\qquad\square$

6   Conclusions

A behavior of a finite set of agents capable to perform some (local) actions has been described. The purpose of any agent is to reach its goal; however, actions of agents may interfere with each other and an action favorable for some agents can turn out unfavorable for the others. The general question discussed in the paper is to impose some conditions on the behavior of agents that guarantee all agents reaching their targets. Any action changing situation of agents is local: it concerns only some agents, called the participants of this action. Each participant of an action is winning or losing: it wins, if the distance from its goal is decreasing, and losing if it is increasing in effect of this action. The choice of an action is non-deterministic; it can be viewed as an effect of resolution of the conflict between competing agents. Agents are competing, if at the same situation there are two actions, the first favorable for one agent and unfavorable for the other, and the second the other way round. Two agents can be viewed as cooperating in an action, if both of them are winning in this action. Observe that words "competing - cooperating" used here are related to a single action; in two different actions even their winners can be considered as competing, if they gain different values. The main objective of the paper is to formulate some conditions concerning action execution that guarantee each agent to reach its goal. Among all possible actions only those satisfying so-called authorization condition can be executed at a system state. Two such authorization conditions have been formulated and proved to meet the required properties. The following features of agent systems (either following directly from definitions or very easy to be justified) have been covered in the paper:

- locality (state changes depend on and concern participants only)
- non-determinism (there is no prescribed order of action execution)
- self-stabilization (any authorized run starting with an arbitrary initial state is successful, see [4])
- concurrency (independent actions can be executed concurrently)
- uniformity (no particular agent is distinguished, in case of **W** authorization)

The intention was to keep the described system as simple as possible, limiting introduced notions just to enable formulation and proving the basic properties. In consequence:

- Goals of agents are not specified, and in consequence, not differentiated;
- Agents have no memory i.e. they are unable to retain and use information about past experiences;
- Agents have no knowledge about the world around; they know only their own and their partners relative positions with respect to their targets.
- Agents are not intelligent; in particular, they cannot predict future consequences of their moves (they cannot look ahead more than one step forward).

It is worthwhile to make here a word of comment. In any system action there are winners which can be viewed as a "force of cooperating agents" causing the action execution. Self-stabilization property within the agent system context offers a possibility to take also into account a "force of nature", which can disturb the situation of all agents, not necessarily in a favorable manner. If such a force changes the system state in a wanton way, with worsening position values of all agents, then it cannot be viewed as a system action containing always a winner. Self-stabilization property makes possible to admit a finite number such unfavorable changes ("catastrophes"), by treating them as unexpected perturbations not preventing the system from eventual completing its task.

As possible extensions of the formalism presented in the paper one could specify the following issues:

- Partial order of position values (there can be several features with noncomparable advantages that can influence on a decision of an agent),
- Relaxing Axiom A3 by introducing reactivity (new obligation rather than dismissal); it seems possible to introduce this feature in relation to authorization **S**),
- Relative position evaluation (introducing position evaluation for collectives of agents rather than for individuals),
- Coalition authorization (introducing authorization condition concerning not single agents, but their coalitions),
- Priority negotiations (by introducing more sophisticated agents' architecture that make possible some negotiation actions).

Clearly, this list does not exhaust all possible extensions of the formalism.

Acknowledgements

Corrections, comments, and remarks of an anonymous reviewer that enable to improve the paper considerably are highly appreciated.

References

[1] Ben-Aroya, I., Eilam, T., Schuster, A.: Greedy hot-potato routing on the two-dimensional mesh. Distributed Computing **9** (1995) 3–19   156
[2] Mazurkiewicz, A., Wróblewski, D.: Messages, clocks, and gravitation. In Dunin-Keplicz, B., Nawarecki, E., eds.: From Theory to Practice in Multi-Agent Systems. Volume 2296 of LNAI. Springer-Verlag (2002) 187–196 Proceedings of CE-MAAS'01, Kraków, Poland, September 2001   156
[3] Mazurkiewicz, A.: Distributed enumeration. Information Processing Letters **61** (1997) 233–239   162
[4] Abello, J., Dolev, S.: On the computational power of self-stabilizing systems. Theoretical Computer Science **182** (1997) 159–170   166

Competent Agents and Customising Protocols

Ulle Endriss[1], Wenjin Lu[2], Nicolas Maudet[3], and Kostas Stathis[2]

[1] Department of Computing
Imperial College London
180 Queen's Gate, London SW7 2AZ, UK
ue@doc.ic.ac.uk

[2] Department of Computing, School of Informatics
City University
Northampton Square, London EC1V OHB, UK
{lu,stathis}@soi.city.ac.uk

[3] LAMSADE
Université Paris-Dauphine
75775 Paris Cedex 16, France
maudet@lamsade.dauphine.fr

Abstract. In open agent societies, communication protocols and strategies cannot be assumed to always match perfectly, because they are typically specified by different designers. These potential discrepancies raise a number of interesting issues, most notably the problem of checking that the behaviour of an agent is (or will be) conformant to the rules described by a protocol. In this paper, we argue that the ability to merely conform to a protocol is not sufficient for an agent to be a *competent* user of that protocol. We approach the intuitive idea of protocol competence by introducing a notion that considers, broadly speaking, an agent's ability to reach a particular state of the interaction and we provide preliminary results that allow us to automatically check competence in the context of a specific class of logic-based agents. Finally, we illustrate how these results can facilitate the customisation of protocols used by agents that are not fully competent.

1 Introduction

Communication is one of the key feature of societies of artificial agents [1], and standards are required to regulate the distributed decision-making involved in interactions such as, for instance, negotiation or persuasion. A *protocol* specifies the "rules of encounter" governing a dialogue between two or more communicating agents [2]. It specifies which agent is allowed to say what in any given situation. It will usually allow for several alternative utterances in every situation and the agent in question has to choose one according to its *strategy*. The protocol is *public*, while each agent's strategy is *private*. In open societies, protocols and strategies cannot be assumed to match perfectly. Protocols are typically specified by the designer of the application, whereas strategies are implemented by the designer of the agent. The potential discrepancies caused by these different points of view raise a number of interesting issues, most notably the problem

A. Omicini, P. Petta, and J. Pitt (Eds.): ESAW 2003, LNAI 3071, pp. 168–181, 2004.
© Springer-Verlag Berlin Heidelberg 2004

of checking that the behaviour of an agent is (or will be) conformant to the rules described by a protocol [3]. In this paper, we argue that the ability to merely conform to a protocol, however, is not sufficient for an agent to be a *competent* user of that protocol.

Intuitively, we understand competence with respect to a protocol as the capacity of the agent "to deal adequately" with a protocol. Surely this may involve different notions. To start with, it is clear that the agent must have the ability to understand the meaning of the messages —to put it another way, the agent must share the *ontology* used in the interaction. This means that the agent must interpret the meaning of communicative acts (the performatives and their content) properly. Another requirement is that the agent should be able to give meaningful answers within the time window specified by the protocol. Note that the problem is not whether the agent can actually give a response (a point that we shall discuss later on), but whether the answer (if given) is fully satisfactory to the agent. On top of that, the agent should be available until the protocol terminates and not leave the interaction before. In this paper, we will take for granted that agents (i) share the same ontology, (ii) have sufficient reasoning capabilities to deal with the different types of message exchanged, (iii) are available until the end of interaction. We are now in a position to give a first hint of the notion we will investigate in this paper: competence amounts to evaluating whether the agent can explore (*i.e.* reach the different states) of a given protocol.

The remainder of this paper is structured as follows: the next section describes the logic-based representation for protocols that we shall use throughout this paper. Section 3 discusses what we regard as a first requirement for an agent to be considered competent, namely that this agent should be able to give at least one legal response to any message expected as part of the protocol (exhaustive conformance). However, as we shall see, this is not a fully satisfactory notion of competence. In Section 4 we go one step further and introduce the competence of an agent as, generally speaking, its ability to reach a particular state of the interaction. We provide preliminary results that allow us to automatically check competence in the context of our logic-based agents. Section 5 introduces a notion of practical importance: the customisation of protocols in order to adapt them to agents that are not fully competent. We illustrate this idea by means of a protocol inspired by electronic transactions. Section 6 concludes.

2   Protocols for Logic-Based Agents

In this paper, we shall only consider protocols that can be represented by means of a deterministic finite automaton (DFA). This is a widely used class of agent interaction protocols (see [4] and others), but we should also point out that certain types of interaction require more expressive formalisms (for instance, where concurrent communication is required). We recall here that a DFA consists of (i) a set of states (including an initial state, and a set of final states), (ii) a set of events, and (iii) a transition function δ which maps pairs of states and events to states. Given a DFA with transition function δ, a dialogue move P is a legal

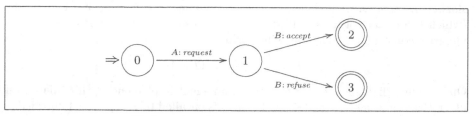

Fig. 1. A simple negotiation protocol

continuation wrt. a state S iff there exists a state S' such that $S' = \delta(S, P)$. We shall refer to *legal inputs* (respectively *outputs*) for an agent X as those legal continuations where X is the receiver (respectively the utterer) of the dialogue move. Figure 1 is an (admittedly very simple) interaction protocol for negotiation which specifies that, following a *request* made by agent A, agent B should in turn either *accept* or *refuse* this request.

This protocol, as shown below, can be translated into two sets of if-then rules corresponding to the two subprotocols used by agents A and B, respectively.

$$\mathcal{P}_A : \begin{cases} START(T) \Rightarrow request(T{+}1) \\ accept(T) \ \ \Rightarrow STOP(T{+}1) \\ refuse(T) \ \ \Rightarrow STOP(T{+}1) \end{cases} \quad \mathcal{P}_B : \big\{\, request(T) \Rightarrow accept(T{+}1) \ \vee \ refuse(T{+}1) $$

For each of the above implications, variables are understood to be implicitly universally quantified. In case we also have variables that only appear on the righthand side of an implication, these variables would be existentially quantified. This logic-based representation of protocols has been introduced in [3].

Shallow Protocols. We call protocols that permit such a straightforward translation into if-then rules, with only a single performative on the lefthand side, *shallow*. Shallow protocols correspond to automata where it is possible to determine the next state of the dialogue on the sole basis of the previous event. Of course, this is not always the case since it may be necessary to refer to the current state of the dialogue to determine the new state. In principle however, any automata-based protocol can be transformed into a protocol that is shallow in this sense (by simply renaming any duplicate transitions).

To ensure that protocols defined in such a way are well-formed, we stipulate a list of constraints that rules should meet, in particular that any dialogue move occurring on the righthand side of the first subprotocol (except *STOP*) also occurs on the lefthand side of the second one, and vice versa (*matching*). We refer to [3] for further details. The meaning of each rule which appears in a protocol is then intuitively clear: it specifies for any expected dialogue move the set of correct responses the agent may utter in reply. The set of performatives appearing on the lefthand side of the constraints defining an agent's subprotocol are called the *expected inputs* for that agent.

Agents' Strategies. Following [5], the communication *strategy* S of an agent (which forms part of its so-called *knowledge base* K) is represented as a set of integrity constraints of the following form:

$$P(T) \wedge C \Rightarrow P'(T{+}1)$$

On receiving dialogue move P at time T, an agent implementing this rule would utter P' at time $T{+}1$, provided condition C is entailed by its (*private*) knowledge base. Variables are understood to be implicitly quantified in the same way as for our protocol-rules.

3   Competence as Exhaustive Conformance

In this section, we study the notion of (exhaustive) conformance, which could be regarded as a first requirement for an agent to be considered competent. Intuitively, an agent is conformant to a given communication protocol P whenever its utterances are legal according to that protocol. Following [3], we distinguish two *levels* of conformance:

- An agent is *weakly conformant* to a protocol P iff it never utters an illegal dialogue move (with respect to P).
- An agent is *exhaustively conformant* to a protocol P iff it does utter a legal dialogue move whenever required to do so by P.

That is, an agent is exhaustively conformant to the protocol P iff (i) it is weakly conformant to P and (ii) it will utter at least *some* dialogue move whenever it is its turn (the legality of which will be ensured by the first condition). This ability to give a response to any expected input may be considered as a first requirement for an agent's competence to use a given protocol. Note that [3] also introduces a third level (robust conformance), which requires agents not only to be exhaustively conformant, but also to react appropriately to illegal moves uttered by *other* agents. In this paper, however, we are only concerned with weak and exhaustive conformance.

In general, checking *a priori* (that is, at design time) whether an agent will always behave in conformance to a given set of protocols is difficult, if not impossible. Still, as shown in [3], it *is* possible to guarantee at least weak conformance to a shallow protocol for the type of agent described in the previous section. To this end, we define the *response space* S^* of an agent with the communication strategy S based on the language L as follows:

$$\{P(T) \Rightarrow \bigvee \{P'(T{+}1) \mid [P(T) \wedge C \Rightarrow P'(T{+}1)] \in S\} \mid P \in L\} \text{ with } \bigvee\{\} = \bot$$

This is the set of protocol constraints we obtain by first dropping all conditions referring to the private knowledge of the agent in question and then conjoining implications with identical antecedents by collecting the corresponding consequents into a single disjunction. This abstraction from an agent's communicative behaviour is related to the idea of an agent automaton proposed by Singh [6]. It allows us to state a simple sufficiency criterion for weak conformance:

An agent is weakly conformant to a protocol $\mathcal{P}$ whenever that protocol is a logical consequence of the agent's response space.

This result shows that, in the case of weak conformance, it is possible to check conformance a priori by inspecting only a relatively small part of an agent's specification (namely, what we could call its "communication module"). In particular, we are *not* required to make any judgements based on the content of its (probably dynamically changing) knowledge base in general.

In the case of exhaustive conformance, the situation is rather different. To understand why, let us first take a closer look at what exhaustive conformance involves, beyond the requirements shared with the notion of weak conformance. As pointed out earlier, we can separate the property of exhaustive conformance into two parts: (i) weak conformance and (ii) the property of uttering any move at all. The latter property, which we shall simply refer to as *exhaustiveness* (of an agent) may be considered independently from a particular protocol. Sadri *et al.* [5], for instance, define the notion of exhaustiveness with respect to a given communication language (as being able to utter a response for any incoming move belonging to that language). Even for our agents, whose communicative behaviour is determined by constraints of the form $P(T) \wedge C \Rightarrow P'(T{+}1)$, it is not generally possible to guarantee exhaustiveness (be it with respect to a given protocol, language, or in general). We cannot generally ensure that one of these rules will indeed "fire" for an incoming move $P(T)$, because none of the additional conditions C may be entailed by the current state of the agent's knowledge base.

One way of ensuring exhaustive conformance would be to rely on logical truths that are independent from the (possibly dynamic) knowledge base of the agent. For a strategy $\mathcal{S}$, let $\mathrm{COND}_{\mathcal{S}}(P)$ denote the disjunction of all the private conditions that appear in $\mathcal{S}$ in a constraint together with the trigger $P(T)$:

$$\mathrm{COND}_{\mathcal{S}}(P) = \bigvee\{C \mid [P(T) \wedge C \Rightarrow P'(T{+}1)] \in \mathcal{S}\} \text{ with } \bigvee\{\,\} = \bot$$

Now, if $\mathrm{COND}_{\mathcal{S}}(P)$ is a logical theorem for every performative P appearing on the lefthand side of the relevant subprotocol of a protocol $\mathcal{P}$, then any agent implementing the strategy $\mathcal{S}$ is guaranteed to utter *some* move for any input expected in $\mathcal{P}$. Hence, we obtain a useful sufficient criterion for exhaustive conformance (again, with respect to our shallow protocols):

An agent with strategy $\mathcal{S}$ is exhaustively conformant to a protocol $\mathcal{P}$ whenever it is weakly conformant to $\mathcal{P}$ and $\mathrm{COND}_{\mathcal{S}}(P)$ is a theorem for every expected input P (for that agent, with respect to $\mathcal{P}$).

Of course, generally speaking, checking this condition is an undecidable problem because verifying theoremhood in first-order logic is. In practice, however, we would not expect this to be an issue given the simplicity of typical cases. As an example, consider a protocol consisting of only the following rule stipulating that any request by another agent X should be either accepted or refused:

$$request(X, T) \Rightarrow accept(T{+}1) \vee refuse(T{+}1)$$

An agent may implement the following simple strategy:

$$request(X,T) \wedge friend(X) \quad \Rightarrow accept(T+1)$$
$$request(X,T) \wedge \neg friend(X) \Rightarrow refuse(T+1)$$

The disjunction $\neg friend(X) \vee friend(X)$, with X being implicitly universally quantified, is a theorem. Hence, our agent would be exhaustively conformant (note that the agent is certainly going to be weakly conformant, because the protocol is a consequence of its response space —in fact, the two are even identical here). A similar idea is also present in [5], although not in the context of issues pertaining to protocol conformance.

Fulfilling the above criterion is not an unreasonable requirement for a well-designed communication strategy S that is intended to be used for interactions governed by a given protocol P. This is why, in the remainder of this paper, we are sometimes going to assume that our agents are known to be exhaustively conformant (despite the fact that, in a more general setting, such an assumption would not be justified).

We continue our discussion of exhaustiveness by observing that, in cases where we can identify a *static* part of an agent's knowledge base (beyond the set of constraints making up its communication strategy), we can give an even more general sufficiency criterion that guarantees exhaustive conformance:

> *An agent with strategy S is exhaustively conformant to a protocol P whenever it is weakly conformant to P and $\mathrm{COND}_S(P)$ is a logical consequence of the agent's knowledge base for every expected input P.*

To illustrate the idea, we slightly change our example from before an replace the agent's second communication rule with the following constraint:

$$request(X,T) \wedge enemy(X) \Rightarrow refuse(T+1)$$

That is, our agent will refuse any request by X if it considers X to be an enemy. Now our first criterion does not apply anymore; we cannot ensure exhaustive conformance. However, if the agent's knowledge base includes a formula such as $\neg enemy(X) \Rightarrow friend(X)$, expressing that anyone who is not an enemy should be considered a friend, then we can show that $friend(X) \vee enemy(X)$ is a logical consequence of that knowledge base and, thereby, that our agent will be exhaustively conformant to the protocol. Note that this agent may generate two responses for a single input, namely in cases where both $friend(X)$ and $enemy(X)$ are true. To avoid such situations (*i.e.* to ensure deterministic behaviour), we could add the formula $\neg(friend(X) \wedge enemy(X))$ to the knowledge base, resulting in the popular "you are either with us or against us" policy.

We can also use our criteria to pinpoint critical situations where a given (non-exhaustive) agent would not be able to respond appropriately. To illustrate this, suppose we remove the implication $\neg enemy(X) \Rightarrow friend(X)$ from our agent's knowledge base. When trying to establish exhaustive conformance, we would have to prove that $friend(X) \vee enemy(X)$ is —still— a consequence of the knowledge base, *i.e.* $\neg(friend(X) \land enemy(X)) \models friend(X) \lor enemy(X)$. Such a proof would be bound to fail and we could use it to construct an explicit counterexample. For instance, if we were to use *analytic tableaux*, we would attempt a refutation for a tableau initially labelled with the two formulas $(\forall X)\neg(friend(X) \land enemy(X))$ and $\neg(\forall X)(friend(X) \lor enemy(X))$, *i.e.* the (only) premise and the negated conclusion. We would soon end up with a saturated open branch containing the literals $\neg friend(a)$ and $\neg enemy(a)$, where a is the Skolem constant introduced when analysing the negated conclusion.[1] For details we refer to the literature on analytic tableaux [7, 8].

This branch gives rise to the first-order model $\mathcal{M} = (\mathcal{D}, \mathcal{I})$ with $\mathcal{D} = \{a\}$ and both $a \notin \mathcal{I}(friend)$ and $a \notin \mathcal{I}(enemy)$. This shows that our agent will fail to be exhaustively conformant as soon as it receives a request from an agent a that is neither (known to be) a friend nor an enemy. Of course, if we have additional information about the application domain, which allows us, for instance, to infer that such a situation would be impossible, then we may still be able to show exhaustive conformance. However, such methods would go beyond the purely logic-based techniques we are interested in for the purpose of the present paper.

Exhaustive conformance can only be considered a first requirement for competent agents. To illustrate this point, let us consider again the protocol of Figure 1, and assume that agent B takes part in the interaction using the following response space:

$$\mathcal{S}^* = \{ request(T) \Rightarrow refuse(T{+}1) \}$$

Even if this agent was indeed exhaustively conformant (as discussed before), it would intuitively not be competent as it could never reach state 2 (and consequently the interaction could never terminate with an accepted request). In the following section, we try to overcome this limitation by introducing a new definition of competence.

4   Competence as Reachability

In this section, we define competence as the ability of a (group of) agent(s) to reach the different stages of an interaction. In particular, from a practical point of view, we shall be especially interested in the termination of interactions.

To begin with, it is worth noting that by the condition of matching on the well-formedness of protocols, any legal (and "complete") dialogue will either end with a *STOP* move or be infinite. If a dialogue ends illegally (*i.e.* with a final move different from *STOP*) it must be the case that one of the agents is not exhaustively conformant to the protocol in operation. If both agents are known to be at least weakly conformant to the protocol (but not necessarily exhaustively conformant), then we can distinguish three situation: (i) the dialogue ends legally with a *STOP* move, (ii) the dialogue terminates illegally with a move different

---

[1] Again, due to the undecidability of first-order logic, this technique may not always be applicable, but we believe that in many practical cases it will.

from *STOP*, and (iii) the dialogue goes on forever.[2] Ideally, we would like to avoid both (ii) and (iii). In practice, we want our agents to have at least the *potential* to achieve (i). While two exhaustively conformant agents will never generate a dialogue that terminates *illegally*, they may or may not have the *competence* to generate a dialogue that does terminate at all.

For a pair of agents, having the competence to produce a legally ending dialogue amounts to these agents being able to generate a dialogue following on from a *START* move that includes (and thereby ends with) a *STOP* move. More generally, for any two dialogue moves P and P', we may ask whether a given pair of agents possesses the competence to generate a dialogue including P' once P has been uttered. Here, P' may be the *STOP* move or any other move leading to an "interesting" state in the dialogue.

> *For some protocol $\mathcal{P}$, two agents have the joint competence to reach P' from P iff they have the ability to generate a sequence of dialogue moves that are legal with respect to $\mathcal{P}$ and that include P' once P has been uttered.*

In particular, two agents have the joint competence to generate a legally terminating dialogue iff the have the joint competence to reach *STOP* from *START*.

We will now investigate how this notion of competence can be automatically checked in the context of our logic-based agents. To this end, we will make use of the notion of response space already introduced in Section 3; or more precisely of a propositional representation of these response spaces obtained by removing the reference to time as well as to any other variables (this, of course, assumes that the content of the dialogue moves is not directly relevant to our purpose).

We call the set of formulas we obtain by removing all references to variables from an agent's response space the *flattened* response space of that agent. A flattened dialogue constraint such as *request* $\Rightarrow$ *accept* $\vee$ *refuse* may be interpreted as requiring any legal dialogue that includes a *request* move to also include either an *accept* or a *refuse* move (of course, in addition to that, the *intended* meaning is that one of these moves *immediately* follows the *request* move, although this is not made explicit in this simplified representation). We note here that this kind of flattening operation would not be meaningful for protocols (and hence response spaces) that are not shallow, *i.e.* for protocols where we may have more than one trigger on the lefthand side of a protocol constraint (referring to different times in the dialogue history).

We can use the notion of a flattened response space to formulate a sufficient criterion for joint competence:

> *Two agents with flattened response spaces $\mathcal{S}_A^*$ and $\mathcal{S}_B^*$ that are exhaustively conformant to protocol $\mathcal{P}$ have the competence to reach P' from P iff $\mathcal{S}_A^* \cup \mathcal{S}_B^* \cup \{P\} \models P'$.*

---

[2] Note that we do not classify infinite dialogues as illegal. In fact, a (badly designed) protocol may even preclude agents from ending a dialogue after having have made a certain unfavourable choice (*i.e.* after having uttered some dialogue move leading to a conversational state from where there are no paths leading to a final state).

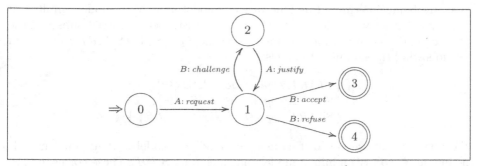

Fig. 2. A negotiation protocol with a justify/challenge loop

To see that the above is only a suitable competence criterion for agents that are exhaustively conformant, it is important to recall that $P \Rightarrow \bot$ will form part of an agent's (flattened) response space for every expected input P for which there is no rule at all in the agent's communication strategy. This means, for instance, that $STOP$ would be derivable from the union of the two response spaces together with $\{START\}$ even though, clearly, such a pair of agents would not be guaranteed to reach a final state.

To illustrate this notion of competence, we introduce an improvement of our negotiation protocol, depicted in Figure 2, which includes a justify/challenge loop inspired by argumentation-based protocols [9]. For instance, given the following flattened response spaces

$$
\mathcal{S}_A^* : \begin{cases} START & \Rightarrow request \\ challenge & \Rightarrow justify \\ accept & \Rightarrow STOP \\ refuse & \Rightarrow STOP \end{cases} \quad
\mathcal{S}_B^* : \begin{cases} request \Rightarrow accept \vee refuse \\ justify \Rightarrow accept \vee refuse \end{cases}
$$

it is easy to see that, for $P = START$ and $P' = STOP$, we indeed have

$$
\mathcal{S}_A^* \cup \mathcal{S}_B^* \cup \{P\} \models P'
$$

Intuitively, this means that termination will be reached by the agents equipped with these response spaces. In general, of course, this will not be the case. Consider for instance the following response spaces.

$$
\mathcal{S}_A^* : \begin{cases} START & \Rightarrow request \\ challenge & \Rightarrow justify \\ accept & \Rightarrow STOP \\ refuse & \Rightarrow STOP \end{cases} \quad
\mathcal{S}_B^* : \begin{cases} request \Rightarrow accept \vee refuse \vee challenge \\ justify \Rightarrow accept \vee refuse \vee challenge \end{cases}
$$

In this case, clearly, the agents can generate a legal infinite dialogue by alternating between uttering challenges and justifications.

To analyse this situation, let us consider the set of all *minimal models* of $\mathcal{S}_A^* \cup \mathcal{S}_B^* \cup \{START\}$. We identify a model with the set of propositional letters that are being interpreted as true in that model and call a model minimal iff there is no other model for which this characteristic set is a strict subset of the characteristic set of the former. In the case of $\mathcal{S}_A^* \cup \mathcal{S}_B^* \cup \{START\}$, we obtain the following three minimal models:

$$\{ \ \{START, request, accept, STOP\},$$
$$\{START, request, refuse, STOP\},$$
$$\{START, request, challenge, justify\} \ \}$$

We observe that we can distinguish two kinds of models: (i) minimal models including $STOP$, (ii) minimal models not including $STOP$. These correspond to the different sort of dialogues that can be generated from these response spaces: the two first models (including $STOP$) correspond to terminating dialogues, whereas the last model represents the infinite loop. In this case, we can only state that termination is *possible*, since there exists at least one minimal model including both $START$ and $STOP$. However, as long as there is a minimal model not including $STOP$, termination cannot be guaranteed.

But it is also noteworthy in this example that, even when the agents have entered the loop, they still have the possibility to reach termination (B can choose to utter *refuse* or *accept* after a *justify*). This is not necessarily the case in general, and we can then distinguish *good* and *bad* loops. A good loop is a loop that need not be infinite, *i.e.* at least one path to a final state is still open. A bad loop is a loop where agents have no other choice than to repeat the same sequence of utterances (that would be the case in our example if B could neither utter *accept* nor *refuse* in reply to *justify*). We now give a criterion that allows us to assess whether a given loop is good:

> *Consider the model of a loop. If for every P in that model, $\mathcal{S}_A^* \cup \mathcal{S}_B^* \cup \{P\}$ still has got at least one minimal model including STOP, then this is a good loop, otherwise this is a bad loop.*

One may be inclined to believe that bad loops only result from badly designed protocols. However, because the designer of a protocol does not know in advance the competence of the agents that will take part in the interaction, it may be the case that a protocol turns out to be problematic because it is used by agents that are not fully competent. In this case, it can be useful for the designer of the application to *customise* his protocol, in order to avoid these undesirable situations.

5   Customising Protocols

There are two ways of adapting protocols to the needs of individual agents that are not fully competent to use them in the first place. The first approach is to require an enhancement of the strategies of the agents, the second to customise the protocol itself (these two techniques are called *expansion* and *filtering* in the context of game-based interaction studied in [10]). We will now show by means

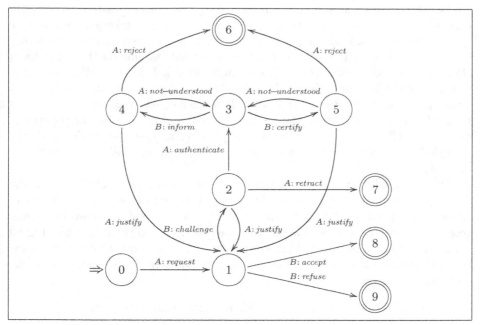

Fig. 3. A protocol for electronic transactions

of an example how the preliminary results put forward in the previous section can be used to customise protocols.

For this purpose, we will introduce a further improvement of our negotiation protocol, inspired by electronic transactions (see Figure 3). The interaction starts with a consumer (A) *request*ing a good. The seller (B) can then *accept* or *refuse* (leading to terminal states 8 or 9), or alternatively *challenge* the consumer (for instance, the seller may challenge that the consumer has the permission to purchase this good). The consumer is in a situation where he can *retract* his request, provide some *justif*ication, or himself interrogate the seller as to whether he is indeed in a position to challenge him in the first place. This is done by requiring an *auhentica*tion of the seller. This latter move leads to a sort of subprotocol starting from state 3. The protocol then assumes that the buyer could use two methods of authentication: (i) a simple method involving a text ticket simply provided by an *inform* message; or (ii) a complex method using a encryption key included in a *certif*icate. In both cases, the consumer should explicitly indicate if he cannot evaluate the response provided by the seller (*not-understood*, in which case the interaction goes back to the previous state in order to possibly use a different method of authentication). In case of a negative evaluation of the authentication provided, the buyer will *reject* and terminate the interaction (state 6). In case of a positive evaluation, the buyer should then give justification to the challenge uttered earlier. Note that this protocol is shallow.

Let us now assume that the consumer has no way to evaluate an encrypted certificate provided by the seller (*i.e.* the rule for the trigger *certify* in his response space does not include *reject*), as well as no argumentative capabilities to *justify* his claims. As far as the seller is concerned, we will assume on the other hand that only the encrypted authentication can be provided (*i.e.* the seller's response space does not include *inform*). In other words, after a *challenge*, A can only either ask B to *authenticate*, or *retract*. It is easy to observe that, if A decides to ask for an authentication, the interaction will end up in a bad loop between states 3 and 5 (that is, the consumer explaining he does not understand the provided certificate, but the seller lacking alternative methods to authenticate himself).

Our proposal in such a situation is to *customise* the protocol to prevent the participants from entering this loop by cutting this part of the protocol. This can be done systematically by (i) identifying the bad loops resulting from the agents' response spaces, as discussed in the previous section, and then (ii) removing all occurrences in the protocol of those moves of the bad loops that do not allow to reach termination. In our example, the minimal model corresponding to the bad loop would be

$$\{START, request, challenge, authenticate, certify, not\text{-}understood\}$$

which would lead to the subsequent deletion (for the period of this interaction) of *authenticate, certify, not-understood* from the protocol —indeed, none of these moves P is such that $\mathcal{S}_A^* \cup \mathcal{S}_B^* \cup \{P\}$ has got at least one minimal model including $STOP$. The resulting protocol could then be used safely by the agents (even if any challenge by the seller would immediately lead to the retraction of the request by the buyer).

In practice, we envisage this technique of customising protocols for interactions in open agent societies to be used as follows. Suppose two agents are about to enter an interaction governed by a particular protocol $\mathcal{P}$. Before starting the dialogue, they may send their respective response spaces to the authority regulating this interaction. Using the agents' response spaces, the authority can determine whether the agents would be competent users of $\mathcal{P}$. In case they are not, the authority can customise $\mathcal{P}$, using the methodology described earlier, and propose to the agents to use that customised protocol instead of the original one.

6   Conclusion

In this paper, we have argued that the ability to merely *conform* to a protocol (in the sense of not uttering any illegal dialogue moves) is not sufficient for an agent to be a *competent* user of that protocol. As a first approach to protocol competence we have further examined the concept of *exhaustive conformance* introduced in [3] and defined criteria that allow us to check whether a given agent can be expected to behave exhaustively conformant to a given protocol. While exhaustive conformance does guarantee that an agent will be able to utter at least some legal performative at any point in a dialogue, it does, for instance, still not ensure that such a dialogue will eventually terminate. Therefore, as a further step towards characterising agents that are truly competent users of a protocol, we have introduced a notion that considers, broadly speaking, an agent's ability to reach a particular state of the interaction, and we have provided preliminary results that allow us to automatically check competence in the context of the specific class of logic-based agents considered here. We have then shown how these results can facilitate the *customisation* of protocols used by agents that are not fully competent.

Whereas the notion of *competence as reachability* discussed in this paper makes reference to the group of agents involved in the interaction, it may be useful for a single agent to (even roughly) evaluate whether it is competent to use a given protocol, regardless of whom it may happen to interact with. For this purpose, we may evaluate what would happen if our agent was to interact with a *perfect* agent (that is, an agent that could provide any expected inputs, as defined by the protocol).

The notion of response space can also be used to provide a rough approximation of the individual competence of the agent: intuitively, given a protocol $\mathcal{P}$, we would expect a competent agent to have a response space that (almost) "covers" $\mathcal{P}$, namely it should have the potential to utter as many dialogue moves as the protocol allows.

In our future work, we plan to investigate whether the techniques used in this paper could help to develop a methodology for assisting in the design of *fair* protocols, in the sense that such a protocol should "treat all participants equally, or, if not, make explicit any asymmetries in their treatment" [11]. For instance, agents may assign different values to different final states of a protocol. In case a pair of agents would not have the competence to reach any of the final states rated positively by one of the agents after a particular dialogue move has been uttered, this would amount to an unfair advantage for the other agent.

Acknowledgements

We would like to thank the ESAW referees for their helpful comments. This research has been funded by the European Union as part of the SOCS project (IST-2001-32530) and has been carried out while the third author was employed at City University, London.

References

[1] Wooldridge, M.: An Introduction to Multiagent Systems. MIT Press (2002) 168
[2] Rosenschein, J., Zlotkin, G.: Rules of Encounter. MIT Press (1994) 168
[3] Endriss, U., Maudet, N., Sadri, F., Toni, F.: Protocol Conformance for Logic-based Agents. In: Proceedings of the 18th International Joint Conference on Artificial Intelligence (IJCAI-2003), Morgan Kaufmann (2003) 169, 170, 171, 179

[4] Pitt, J., Mamdani, A.: A Protocol-based Semantics for an Agent Communication Language. In: Proceedings of the 16th International Joint Conference on Artificial Intelligence (IJCAI-1999), Morgan Kaufmann (1999) 169

[5] Sadri, F., Toni, F., Torroni, P.: Dialogues for Negotiation: Agent Varieties and Dialogue Sequences. In: Proceedings of the 8th International Workshop on Agent Theories, Architectures and Languages (ATAL-2001), Springer-Verlag (2001) 171, 172, 173

[6] Singh, M.: A Customizable Coordination Service for Autonomous Agents. In: Proceedings of the 4th International Workshop on Agent Theories, Architectures and Languages (ATAL-1997). (1997) 171

[7] D'Agostino, M., Gabbay, D., Hähnle, R., Posegga, J., eds.: Handbook of Tableau Methods. Kluwer Academic Publishers (1999) 174

[8] Fitting, M.: First-order Logic and Automated Theorem Proving. 2nd edn. Springer-Verlag (1996) 174

[9] Parsons, S., Sierra, C., Jennings, N.: Agents that Reason and Negotiate by Arguing. Journal of Logic and Computation 8 (1998) 261–292 176

[10] Stathis, K.: A Game-based Architecture for Developing Interactive Components in Computational Logic. Journal of Functional and Logic Programming 2000 (2000) 177

[11] McBurney, P., Parsons, S.: Desiderata for Inter-agent Protocols. In: Proceedings of the First International Conference on Autonomous Agents and Multi-Agent Systems (AAMAS-2002), Bologna, Italy (2002) 180

Coordination and Conversation Protocols in Open Multi-agent Systems

Abdelkader Gouaich

Laboratoire, Informatique, Robotique et Micro électronique
Montpellier, France
gouaich@lirmm.fr

Abstract. This paper presents an approach to formally link a simple dependency-based coordination model to its related conversation protocol. Hence, by observing conversation among coordinating entities, an external observer is able to recognise valid conversations that do not break the established norms on coordination. This may help in building reliable autonomous agent based systems in open and untrustred environments.

1 Introduction

Technological evolutions achieved in several computing fields such as hardware, networking and software engineering have enlarged the potential use of software-based services. Hence, current and future software systems are expected to be communicative and collaborative systems defined everywhere and offering their services at anytime to help users in their daily activities. Still, both changes on expectations and technological evolutions have also implied changes on software systems properties and hypothesis previously formulated on them. Hence, current and future software systems exhibit the following properties [1] :

- Situatedness: Having local communication and local interaction properties, a software system's global functionality depends on the local context of its elementary components.
- Openness: The software system has no longer a defined clear barrier and static structure. It is permanently evolving by merging or rejecting sub-components.
- Locality in interaction: Interaction among components can be conducted locally without requiring a centralised communication infrastructure. This raises the dynamics of the software system and allows emergence of new observable functionalities defined by elementary components.
- Heterogeneity: Obviously in a large connected world several actors with different goals build software components. Hence, several heterogeneous entities have to collaborate or coordinate their actions when placed together in a certain context in order to achieve their local goals.

A. Omicini, P. Petta, and J. Pitt (Eds.): ESAW 2003, LNAI 3071, pp. 182–199, 2004.
© Springer-Verlag Berlin Heidelberg 2004

– Autonomy of the components: Autonomy of a software component is an important feature that should be remembered when designing large open distributed software systems. Hence, software components have to be considered as black boxes, and lack of knowledge on their internal structure make them behaving autonomously since their reaction to an external stimulus is not fully predictable [2].

In this context, agent-based software engineering offers an interesting approach for designing and building this class of software systems. In fact, most of the presented features have already been considered as axioms in the theoretical foundation and definition of the agency [3, 4]. This paper focuses on coordination and conversation aspects of multi-agent systems and tries to make a formal link between coordination protocols and their related conversation protocols.

2   Autonomy and Responsibility of Software Agents

An autonomous software agent is defined as a self-governed entity that decide what action to do according to its local goals and rules [5]. Starting from this autonomy interpretation and by considering communication and interaction as another fundamental feature of software agents, [2] has established the need of an automatic entity that does not modify its internal rules to achieve actual interactions among autonomous agents. In fact, the integrity of the software structure encoding the agent's computational behaviours was found as a sine qua none condition in order to implement autonomous agents without having any assumption on their internal architecture. So, to interact an agent is not allowed to modify other agents' software structure and delegate this risky action to a trusted automatic entity, namely the *deployment environment*. On the other hand, in order to meet requirements of autonomous agents and guarantee virtual agent society norms on coordination and conversation, it was found useful to consider the multi-agent system as a composition of two orthogonal components: autonomous agents and the deployment environment [2]. Autonomous agents are considered as unknown software components that interact in order to achieve their private goals. The term unknown refers to software components that hide completely the software structure implementing their behaviours. As seen above, this feature has to be considered as an axiom in large distributed systems. Besides, the deployment environment may encode the agent virtual society laws and norms independently from agents that populate it and thus establishes a referential to establish agents responsibility. For instance, interaction and conversation policies may be implemented by this entity. Since, the deployment environment is an automatic entity its internal laws are static and identifiable. Due to this property, the responsibility of the deployed unknown autonomous agents is established when their actions challenge the norms of the agent virtual society [2]. As an example of such deployment environment an algebraic model named MIC* has been introduced in [6].

2.1 {Movement, Interaction, Computation}* (MIC*):

MIC* is an algebraic structure where autonomous, mobile and interacting entities are deployed. Within this framework, all interactions are conducted by explicitly exchanging interaction objects through interaction spaces. Hence, agents
do not alter directly the deployment environment or the perceptions of other
agents, but send their attempts as interaction objects. Interaction objects are
structured: in fact, a formal addition law can compose them commutatively $+$
to represent simultaneous interactions. Furthermore, abstract empty interaction
object 0 can be defined to represent no interaction. The less intuitive part of
the structure of the interaction objects concerns negative interaction objects.
Negative interaction objects are constructed formally and may have no interpretation in the real world. However, they are useful for the internal model
definitions and implementation of the deployment environment. For instance,
the deployment environment can cancel any action, x, of the agent simply by
performing an algebraic operation, $x + (-x) = 0$, that is expressed within the
model notations. Finally, interaction objects defines a structure of a commuta-
tive group $(\mathcal{O}, +)$, where $\mathcal{O}$ represents the set of interaction objects and $+$ the
composition law. Interaction spaces, represented by $\mathcal{S}$, are defined as abstract
locations where interaction between agents holds. They are active entities that
control their local and specific interaction rules. For instance, interaction object
that are sent inside an interaction space may be altered if they violate the interaction norm. Agents, represented by $\mathcal{A}$, are autonomous entities that perceive
interaction objects and react to them by sending other interaction objects. As
said before, agents' actions are always considered as attempts to influence the
deployment environment structure. These attempts are committed only when
they are coherent with the deployment environmental rules of evolution. Having
these elementary definitions, each MIC* term is represented by the following
matrices:

- Outboxes Matrix: The rows of this matrix represent agents $A_i \in \mathcal{A}$ and
  the columns represent the interaction spaces $S_j \in \mathcal{S}$. Each element of the
  matrix $o_{(i,j)} \in \mathcal{O}$ is the representation of the agent A_i in the interaction
  space S_j.
- Inboxes Matrix: The rows of this matrix represent agents $A_i \in \mathcal{A}$ and the
  columns represent the interaction spaces $S_j \in \mathcal{S}$. Each element of the matrix $o_{(i,j)} \in \mathcal{O}$ defines how the agent A_i perceives the universe in the interaction space S_j.
- Memories vector: Agents $A_i \in \mathcal{A}$ represent the rows of the vector. Each
  element m_i is an abstraction of the internal memory of the agent A_i. Except
  the existence of such element that is proved using the Turing machine model,
  no further assumptions are made in MIC* about the internal architecture of
  the agent.

The set of all MIC* terms is represented by $\mathcal{T}$.

$$t_0 \in \mathcal{T} \xrightarrow{f_0 \in \gamma \cup \varphi \cup \mu} t_1 = f_0(t_0) \in \mathcal{T} \xrightarrow{f_1 \in \gamma \cup \varphi \cup \mu} t_2 = f_1(t_1) \in \mathcal{T} \rightsquigarrow t_{n+1} = f_n(t_n) \in \mathcal{T}$$

Fig. 1. Evolution of a MAS deployment environment starting from an initial term t_0 until t_{n+1} by following elementary transformations of type μ, φ or γ

Dynamics of MIC*: The dynamics of the deployment environment is described as a sequence of elementary evolutions: $\mathcal{T} \rightarrow \mathcal{T}$. Three main classes of evolutions were characterised in MIC*:

- Movement μ: A movement is a transformation μ, of the environment where both inboxes and memories matrices are unchanged, and where outboxes matrix interaction objects are changed but globally invariant. This means that the interaction objects of an agent can change positions in the outboxes matrix and no interaction object is created or lost.
- Interaction φ: The interaction is characterised by a transformation φ that leaves both outboxes and memories matrices unchanged and transforms a row of the inboxes matrix. Thus, interaction is defined as modifying the perceptions of the entities in a particular interaction space.
- Computation γ: An observable computation of an entity transforms its representations in the outboxes matrix and the memories vector. For practical reasons, the inboxes of the calculating entity are reset to 0 after the computation to distinguish interaction objects that were involved in different computations.

The main idea of MIC* approach is that the dynamics of the deployment environment can be modelled as a composition of evolutions that can be considered as being a movement, interaction or computation. Consequently, as presented in figure 1, any state of the deployment environment can be reached by following a path of evolutions of type μ, φ or γ. Hence, the deployment environment dynamics is no more an unknown and chaotic evolution, but a structured sequence of elementary transformation.

3   Background

3.1   Generalised Study of Coordination

Malone and Crowson in [7] have noticed that coordination among autonomous entities is common to several independent fields such as computer science, economics, operational research and organizational theory. Hence, they have tried to study it in a single framework: *the coordination theory*. According to their definition, coordination is viewed as managing dependencies between activities. Hence, entities coordinate their actions in order to manage dependencies that exist between their activities. So, to understand what is coordination, one has

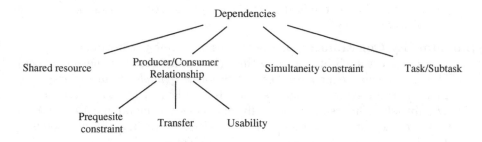

Fig. 2. Malone and Crowson [7] categorisation of common dependencies among activities

to understand and study what are the existing dependency situations among activities.

As shown in figure 2, Malone and Crowson sketch a categorisation of the dependencies among autonomous entities as follows:

Shared Resource: When several activities share some limited resource a particular *resource allocation* strategy is needed in order to handle this dependency. Several independent fields have identified this dependency and proposed some specific resource allocation strategies. For instance, computer science field has studied how available hardware and software resources are shared among computational entities. Hence, multi-threaded operating systems require allocation strategy and algorithms to share the computation units (processors, input/output devices) on a computer. Another example of limited resource dependency is the optimal sharing of available network bandwidth using a network protocol.

Producer/Consumer Relationship: This dependency represents situations when an activity produces something that is used by another activity. This relation implies the following dependencies:

Prerequisite Constraint: This dependency expresses an order that exists between the producer and the consumer.

Transfer: When the producer activity produces something that has to be used by the consumer activity, the produced object has to be transferred from the production point to the consumer point. Managing this dependency involves defining how to *transport* things between the producer and consumer activities. For instance, in case of software programs where the produced thing is information, the transfer dependency is resolved using communication protocols as a transportation mechanism.

Usability: The other dependency implied by producer/consumer relationship is the usability. In fact, the consumer should be able to correctly use the producer's products. *Standardisation* is a common way to resolve this dependency. Hence, both producer and consumer agree on what are the requirements to consider a product as consumable and try to meet these specifications. Syntax of messages and the semantics of commands are examples of standardisation when transferring information between software entities.

Simultaneity Constraint: Some activities are timely constrained, so they have to be executed at the same time (or cannot occur in the same time). This dependency expresses these situations. *Semaphores* are examples of a mechanism used in computer science to handle synchronised activities.

Task/Subtask: This relation basically expresses the hierarchical decomposition of an activity in several sub-activities. So, the main activity depends on its sub-activities and finishes when they are completed.

3.2 Models and Methodologies to Specify Coordination Protocols in Software Systems

To express coordination protocols among software components several models and notations have been introduced. This paragraph gives an overview of these models.

Software Engineering Methodologies: Usually software engineering methodologies such as MERISE and UML include in their specification model some graphical and textual descriptions to specify coordination of activities to be implemented by software programs.

Statecharts: Statecharts [8] is an extension of state transition diagrams with three elements dealing with hierarchy, concurrency and communication. This formalism is used for the specification and design of complex discrete-event systems such as distributed systems and communication protocols.

Flowchart: A flowchart system shows the overall structure of a software system by tracing the flow of information, work and by highlighting key processing and decision points. It also includes the physical media on which data are inputted, outputted and stored.

Process Algebra: This family of formal models (CSP [9], CCS [10], Pi calculus [11], Ambient [12], Join calculus [13]) implicitly expresses coordination among processes by synchronising communication and actions using algebraic operations. So, coordination mechanisms are implicitly defined in the semantics of the operators and rewriting rules. The observable result is still an ordered execution of the distributed activities. For instance, a Pi-calculus process stops its activity waiting for an incoming message on a named communication channel; when another process sends a message on this named channel, the blocked process continues its execution. This synchronisation operation implicitly defines a partial order relationship among activities and can also be viewed as a producer/consumer relation between processes where messages are the exchanged resources.

Language of Temporal Ordering Specifications (LOTOS): LOTOS   is a formal description technique standardised as ISO/IEC8807. It was developed by the International Organisation of Standardisation (ISO) to support standardisation of Open Systems Interconnections (OSI). In fact, formal description technique helps in diminishing ambiguities on OSI produced specifications that are distributed worldwide and used by several software engineering actors. LOTOS formalism is mainly based on process algebra to express the implicit order and dependencies among the activities. Besides, LOTOS allows abstract specification of data type using ACT ONE. This abstract data type specification language can be viewed as a way to resolve the usability dependency previously presented by Malone and Crowson.

Petri Nets: Petri Nets is a formal and graphical oriented language for design, specification, simulation and verification of systems in which communication, synchronisation and resource sharing are important. Examples of application areas of Petri nets are communication protocols, distributed systems, workflow analysis. The Petri Net model is a digraph composed by two classes of nodes: transitions and places representing respectively activities and perquisite relations between activities. Hence, each place contains tokens that are produced by the ancestor activities; a particular activity may be executed when all its preceding places contain tokens.

Specification and Description Language (SDL): SDL is a specification language standardised by the International Telecommunication Union (ITU) . SDL coordination mechanisms are expressed using extended finite state machines. SDL specifications include also abstract data type specifications described using ACT ONE as in LOTOS.

Extended State Transition language (ESTELLE): ESTELLE is a formal description technique standardised by ISO. It is suitable for the specification of coordination mechanisms among distributed software systems and was used to describe OSI services and protocols. An ESTELLE specification is a hierarchy of communicating non-deterministic state machines. By specifying the used type of communication, synchronous or asynchronous, both dependencies and execution order are implicitly defined between the state machines in ESTELLE.

Message Sequence Charts (MSCs) : Message Sequence Charts (MSCs) [14] are graphical and textual language for the description and specification of the interactions between different components normalised by the (ITU). They are usally used in combination with SDL specifications or used as sequence diagram in UML. MSC denotational semantics is expressed using an adaptation of process algebra formalism. This helps in defining partial order relations between events, such as message exchange and actions, occurring in the system. Another interpretation of MSC denotational semantics is done using graph grammars.

High-Level Message Sequence Charts (HMSC): They are considered as formalism to compose MSCs automatons using sequence, parallel and alternative operators. These compositions are given two different semantics within HMSC: strong composition, where all events of a scenario must hold before executing the next scenario; and weak composition where events are executed when possible. Since, MSCs semantics is defined as a partial order between events occurring in a system, the semantics of HMSC is defined as an extension of these partial order relations built following the semantics of the composition operators expressing sequential composition, alternative and iteration. HMSC denotational semantics is expressed using grammar graph that helps in studying some general properties of the system using model-checking techniques and to translate the system specification on other specification languages such as SDL, ESTELLE or Statecharts.

3.3 Software Architectures to Implement Coordination in Software Systems

Coordination (software) community has also defined some coordination architecture implementing generic coordination mechanisms such as synchronisation and producer / consumer relationships. Entities of a coordination architecture are the following: coordinables, representing entities to be coordinated; coordination media, representing the media used to coordinate the entities; and finally coordination laws that define how the coordination media reacts in response to coordinables actions. A survey of coordination architectures can be found in [15]. It categorises coordination architectures in two main categories:

Data Driven: In data-driven coordination models, the coordination media is represented by an addressable storage space shared between the coordinables. Thus coordinables interact by storing and retrieving data structures from the shared data space. Besides, the coordination laws define how these data structures are represented, stored and consumed by the coordinables.
Control Driven: In control-driven coordination models, the coordination media is represented by a set of input/output communication ports linking coordinables and enabling their interactions. In order to achieve these interactions, the coordination media considers coordinables as black boxes and check their state changes and events occurring on their communication ports. These events are then propagated to other coordinables following some specific coordination rules with no concern for their internal data and representation

3.4 Conversational Aspects of Coordination

When coordinables are distributed, coordination is necessarily achieved through communication and interaction. Hence, entities communicate by exchanging messages in order to meet the requirements of their coordination protocol. When observing these exchanged messages among coordinating entities, an external observer remarks that the structure of the conversation, defined as an ordered sequence of messages, is guided by the underlying coordination protocol. Specifying this dialogue structure is known as establishing a *conversation protocol*. Among formalisms that are used to specify conversation protocols one can find the following: finite state machines (FSM), as in works of [16, 17, 18]; state transition diagrams (STD), as in works of [19]; coloured petri nets (CPN), as in works of [20, 21].

3.5 Discussion

As presented above, several works have studied the coordination problem in computer science. These works can be classified in the following categories:

Activity Centric: Works of this category focuse on the activity part of coordination. Hence, their main goal is to know what activity to execute and when to execute it. This category is represented by the models for the specification of coordination protocols presented in §3.2.

Conversation Centric: Works of this category focus their interest on the conversational aspect of coordination. Hence, their main goal is to know what message to send and when to send it in order to coordinate distributed activities. Works of 3.4 are examples of this category.

Implementation Centric: This category of works propose generic software architectures and middlewares abstracting coordination mechanisms to easily design, implement and deploy software systems where concurrent activities have to be coordinated.

Generalisation Efforts: Works of this category sketch a general framework trying to include all aspects of coordination and linking several research fields sharing same concepts and interests. Malone and Crowson's works are an example of such generalisation effort.

By observing the literature it seems that activity centric work, conversational centric works and architecture centric constitute blocks with some synergy among them. Still, there is no established formal link between them. Malone and Crowson coordination theory is a first step to link all these works in a single framework. Hence, this paper starts from their works in order to refine a simple dependency based-coordination model expressing dependencies among activities using a directed graph as mathematical model. Having this refined coordination model some concepts such as *role*, and *role-cut* are introduced. Conversation protocols are then defined formally as a sequence of messages recognised by a rewriting grammar. This grammar is defined by the structure of the coordination model.

4   Simple Dependency-Based Coordination Model

Figure 2 presented common dependencies shared by several research fields. This categorisation is very helpful to understand why autonomous entities coordinate their actions. However, since Malone and Crowson seek for generality, they make no precise assumptions on the properties of the addressed system. Besides, some of the presented dependencies are redundant and could be expressed with other dependencies. So, by having more assumptions on the entities to be coordinated, would it be possible to define a more refined model of coordination where all dependencies are canonically expressed? To answer this question, let us first set some hypothesis on the considered systems to be coordinated:

– The considered system is a software system composed of either software or hardware autonomous and interacting components;

- The autonomy axiom implies that the internal structure of the entities is never accessible and modified by another entity. Consequently, communication and actions of the entities are asynchronous and explicitly represented as attempts of actions[2]. The autonomy axiom prevents also from knowing how entities actually behave and achieve their goals. Only observable aspects of their computation are studied.
- Communication among components is represented as an explicit exchange of data, or messages, through a communication medium and the communication process is not assumed to be synchronous.

Under these assumptions, all dependencies presented in figure 2 can be expressed canonically as producer/consumer relationships. For instance, the shared resource dependency is modelled by introducing a resource manager entity that gives authorisation to consumer to access the resource according to a particular resource management strategy. The consumers of the resource and the resource manger are obviously in a producer/consumer dependency. Similarly, simultaneity dependency is expressed as a consumer/producer dependency between a monitor and the concurrent components. Finally, task/sub-tasks dependency is also expressed as a set of producer/consumer dependency between the global task and its sub-activities. Consequently, the refined model of coordination has to express only the consumer/producer dependency with the following elements:

Activities: As said previously, coordination is defined between activities; thus, they have to be explicitly represented in the coordination model.

Transferable: According to results presented above, all common dependencies among activities can be considered as producer/consumer dependencies. A producer/consumer dependency induces both a transfer and prerequisite dependency. Notice that prerequisite dependency is also a consumer/producer dependency where the notification is considered as the thing to be transported.

Usability Dependency: According to Malone and Crowson's, each producer/consumer dependency induces a usability dependency. The usability dependency guarantees that the transferable is usable by the consumer after being produced by the producer. Consequently, for each transferable a conformity-checking function should be provided to model the usability dependency. Using Malone and Crowson's terms this function represents the standard resolving the usability dependency between activities.

Roles: Functionalities of agents in their artificial society are usually abstracted as *roles*. Roles are considered in the refined coordination model in order to situate where the activities are executed during the coordination process.

Given these elements, the coordination model can be represented as a directional graph described as follows:

- Two types of vertices are identified representing activities, graphically symbolised as boxes, and transferables graphically symbolised as circles;

- For each transferable node a usability-checking function is associated to check the conformity of the transferable according to the usability convention that was established by the producer and the consumer;
- An oriented edge links an activity to a transferable to represent a production of a transferable by that activity and a transferable to an activity to represent a consumption of a transferable by that activity. A dependency relation is then completely defined by having the producer vertex, the transferable and the consumer vertex;
- As previously mentioned, a prerequisite dependency among activities is expressed as a producer/consumer dependency with a special notification transferable noted ϵ.
- The coordination graph can be split in several connected components that are linked by transferable vertexes to represent activities associated with each role.

The above elements are captured more formally by the following definition:

Definition 1. *Let $\mathcal{O}$ be a set of interaction objects (or messages), a dependency-based coordination model is defined as a digraph $G =< A, N, T, F, V^\uparrow, V^\downarrow >$. A represents the set of activity nodes. N and T are disjoint sets where elements of $\epsilon_i \in N$ are considered as notification nodes and elements $t \in T$ are transfer nodes. Arrows of the graph are defined by $V^\uparrow$ and $V^\downarrow$, such as $V^\uparrow : A \times (N \cup T)$ and $V^\downarrow : (N \cup T) \times A$ represent respectively production and consumption arrows. $F = \{f_{t \in T} : \mathcal{O} \to \mathcal{O}\}$ is a set of functions that check for each transfer node $t \in T$ the conformity of the actual exchanged transferable considered as an interaction object.*

When a transfer node is consumed by several activities, this is interpreted as an exclusive choice. Thus, only one activity may be executed after production of the transferable. On the other hand, when an activity produces several transferables, this is interpreted as simultaneous production of resources. Roles decomposition in a dependency-based coordination digraph is viewed as a particular partitioning of the activities in the digraph. Roles have to be independent and should not share activities. In fact, without this property, actual agents implementing these roles may be in conflict on activities and consequently lose their autonomy property.

Definition 2. *Having a coordination graph $G =< A, N, T, F, V^\uparrow, V^\downarrow >$, a role decomposition d is a subset of $\mathcal{P}(A)$ where:*

$$\forall x, y \in d, x \cap y = \emptyset$$

Roles decomposition divides the global coordination graph in several sub-graphs. Hence, for each role r in a role decomposition $d \subset \mathcal{P}(A)$, the associated role sub-graphs are built by including all activities of r and inserting all production and consumption arrows that are inside r. This is more formally defined as follows:

Definition 3. *A role sub-graph* $g_r = < A_r, N_r, T_r, F_r, V_r^\uparrow, V_r^\downarrow >$ *of a role r found in a decomposition* $d \subset \mathcal{P}(A)$ *of a dependency-based coordination digraph* $G = < A, N, T, F, V^\uparrow, V^\downarrow >$ *is defined as follows:*

$$
\begin{aligned}
A_r &= r \\
N_r &= \{\epsilon \in N : \exists\, a, b \in A_r,\ (a, \epsilon) \in V^\uparrow \wedge (\epsilon, b) \in V^\downarrow\} \\
T_r &= \{t \in T : \exists\, a, b \in A_r,\ (a, t) \in V^\uparrow \wedge (t, b) \in V^\downarrow\} \\
F_r &= \{f_t \in F : t \in T_r\} \\
V_r^\uparrow &= \{(a, t) \in V^\uparrow : (a \in A_r) \wedge (t \in T_r)\} \\
V_r^\downarrow &= \{(t, a) \in V^\downarrow : (a \in A_r) \wedge (t \in T_r)\}
\end{aligned}
$$

Role sub-graphs of a complete decomposition are linked by transferables defining dependencies among these roles. This part of the graph is named a *role-cut* and represents the glue that makes roles interdependent. Still, notification objects, $\epsilon \in N$, are considered as a special transferable with a special semantics. For instance, they do not induce a usability dependency between activities and can be implemented inside the same software entity without exchanging an explicit interaction object. So, notification nodes that do not always induce an explicit exchange of messages have not to be present in the role-cut. More formally, a roles-cut is specified as follows:

Definition 4. *Roles-cut of a dependency-based coordination graph* $G = < A, N, T, F, V^\uparrow, V^\downarrow >$, *is defined as the minimal set of transferable* $c \subset T$ *that if all its elements* $x \in c$ *were removed along with there related production and consumption vertexes this would produce a digraph with more connected components than the original digraph.*

4.1 Defining Conversation Protocol Grammar from Coordination Protocol

Notations Interaction among autonomous agents has to be explicitly represented. For instance, within the MIC* model, a formal deployment environment of autonomous agents [6], interaction is conducted through explicit interaction objects represented in the set $\mathcal{O}$. This set owns at least, for the purpose of this paper, a structure of a commutative group. Hence, interaction objects found in $\mathcal{O}$ can be summed commutatively with the $+$ law. This operation has not to be misinterpreted with the non-commutative concatenation law . (dot) that will be used in order to generate ordered sequences of messages represented by $\mathcal{O}^*$. When there is no ambiguity $x.y$ is simply represented by xy. In this section $\mathcal{O}^*$ represents the free monoid generated by the interaction object set $\mathcal{O}$ with the non-commutative dot law. Intuitively this represents words where the alphabet is interaction object set. $\bar{\mathcal{O}}$ represents a marked set of interaction object defined as follows: $\bar{\mathcal{O}} = \{\bar{x} : x \in \mathcal{O}\}$. $\mathcal{O}'$ is defined as union set of $\mathcal{O}$ and $\bar{\mathcal{O}}$. $|\alpha|$ is a simple function defined on $\mathcal{O}'^* \to \mathcal{O}^*$ that retrieves marks from all marked interaction object found in a word α. The function $\pi_d : \mathcal{O}^* \to \mathcal{O}^*$, where $d \subset \mathcal{O}$ is a projection of a word on a subset alphabet. In other words, this operation simply retrieves elements found in the word that are not in the subset alphabet d. For an activity node $a \in A$ in the dependency-based coordination graph, a^+ and a^- respectively represent the set of production arrows and the consumption arrows of a. $\overset{R}{\leadsto}$ represents a path or a finite composition of a relation $\overset{R}{\rightarrow}$.

Having these notations, the grammar of the conversation protocol is defined as a rewriting system where the rewriting relation, $\overset{R}{\rightarrow}: \mathcal{O}'^* \times \mathcal{O}'^*$, is defined as follows:

$$U_0 a_1 U_1 a_2 U_2 ... a_n U_n \overset{R}{\rightarrow} U_0 \bar{a_1} U_1 \bar{a_2} U_2 ... \bar{a_i} U_i U_{i+1} ... U_n$$
$$\Rightarrow ((\textstyle\sum_{x=1}^{i} |a_x|, \sum_{x=i+1}^{n} |a_x|) \in R) \wedge (\forall j \in [1..i], a_j \notin \bar{\mathcal{O}})$$

$(a_i)_{i \in [1..n]} \in \mathcal{O}'$ are alphabet elements; $(U_j)_{j \in [0..n]} \in \mathcal{O}'^*$ are sequences belonging to the monoid.

Interpretation $R : \mathcal{O} \times \mathcal{O}$ represents the set of reduction or simplification rules. The interpretation of these rules is as follows: $(\sum x, \sum y) \in R$ means that $\sum y$ messages appear *necessarily* after $\sum x$ messages. So, this defines a partial order relationship between messages. After a reduction, messages that have been used in the left part of a reduction relation are marked to avoid confusions and ambiguities: in fact, this mechanism ensures that the left part of a reduction relation is used once.

What is missing in the previous definition is the relation $R : \mathcal{O} \times \mathcal{O}$ of simplification rules. This set is constructed from the coordination graph $G = < A, N, T, F, V^\uparrow, V^\downarrow >$ as follows:

$$\forall a \in A, (\sum_{(x,a) \in a^-} x, \sum_{(a,x) \in a^+} x) \in R_G \tag{1}$$

Having these definitions, a conversation protocol is defined as the set of message sequences recognised by the grammar defined above. This is expressed more formally as:

Definition 5. *Let $\mathcal{O}$ be the interaction objects set; a conversation protocol $P_{(x_0,G)}$ for a dependency-based coordination graph and the axiom $x_0 \in \mathcal{O}^*$ is defined as follows:*

$$U \in P_{(x_0,G)} \iff \exists U' \in \mathcal{O}'^* : U' \overset{R}{\leadsto} x_0 \wedge |U'| = U$$

The problem with the given definition is that it includes all interaction objects that are exchanged among activities. However, as said before only interaction objects exchanged through a role-cut are observable and interesting to study. So, when defining a conversation protocol for a particular roles-cut the previous definition is expressed as follows:

Definition 6. *Let $\mathcal{O}$ be the interaction objects set; A conversation protocol $P_{(x_0,G,d)}$ defined on a role-cut d found in a dependency-based coordination graph G for the axiom $x_0 \in \mathcal{O}^*$ is defined as follows:*

$$U \in P_{(x_0,G,d)} \iff \exists U' \in \mathcal{O}'^* : U' \overset{R}{\leadsto} x_0 \wedge |\pi_d(U')| = U$$

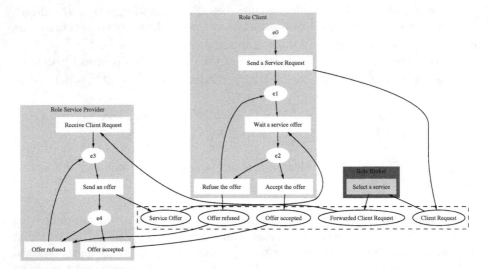

Fig. 3. Simple coordination protocol among three roles: client, broker and service provider, expressed using the dependency-based coordination graph. Activities nodes as represented as boxes and transfer nodes as circles

Thus, the projection operation ensures that only interaction objects observable on the role-cut are included in the definition of the conversation protocol.

4.2   Simple Example

Figure 3 presents a simple coordination protocol among three roles: the client, the service broker and the service provider. This coordination pattern in commonly used in both multi-agent systems and distributed systems, where the broker links clients to appropriate service providers. When connected to a client, the service provider recursively proposes offers to the client until the later accepts a good offer.

Figure 4 represents an abstracted view of the coordination protocol described in figure 3 where the roles, resources and activities are represented by abstract symbols. The roles-cut in this graph is $c_G = \{x, y, z, v, w\}$. By applying definition of equation 1, the simplification relations set, R_G, is calculated and equals to:

$$R_G = \{(e_0, x + e_1), (x, y), (e_1 + z, e_2), (e_3, z + e_4),$$
$$(e_2, e_1 + v), (v + e_4, e_3), (e_2, w), (y, e3)\}$$

Having these elements, and by applying definition 6, the conversation protocol observable at the role-cut, c_G, among the *three* roles is fully defined. e_0 is considered as the axiom the conversation protocol. Notice that the definition of the conversation protocol depends only on the role-cut, no matter how many roles are linked by this roles-cut.

Let $u = xyzvzvzw \in \mathcal{O}^*$ be an observable conversation between A, B and C

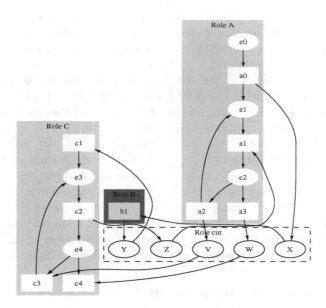

Fig. 4. Abstract view of the coordination protocol presented in figure 3

at the role-cut. This conversation is a valid conversation. In fact, by considering $\alpha_0\alpha_1\alpha_1\alpha_2$, where $\alpha_0 = e_0e_1xy$, $\alpha_1 = e_3e_4ze_2ve_1$ and $\alpha_2 = e_3e_4ze_2w$, this sequence can be reduced to the axiom e_0 as follows:

$$\alpha_0\alpha_1\alpha_1\alpha_3 \overset{R_G}{\rightarrow} \alpha_0\alpha_1\alpha_1e_3e_4z\bar{e}_2 \overset{R_G}{\rightarrow} \alpha_0\alpha_1e_3e_4ze_2v\bar{e}_1e_3e_4\bar{z} \overset{R_G}{\rightarrow} \alpha_0\alpha_1e_3e_4ze_2v\bar{e}_1\bar{e}_3$$
$$\overset{R_G}{\rightarrow} \alpha_0\alpha_1e_3\bar{e}_4ze_2v\bar{e}_1 \overset{R_G}{\rightarrow} \alpha_0\alpha_1e_3\bar{e}_4z\bar{e}_2 \overset{R_G}{\rightarrow} \alpha_0e_3e_4ze_2v\bar{e}_1e_3\bar{e}_4\bar{z} \overset{R_G}{\rightarrow} \alpha_0e_3e_4ze_2v\bar{e}_1\bar{e}_3$$
$$\overset{R_G}{\rightarrow} \alpha_0e_3\bar{e}_4ze_2v\bar{e}_1 \overset{R_G}{\rightarrow} \alpha_0e_3\bar{e}_4z\bar{e}_2 \overset{R_G}{\rightarrow} e_0\bar{e}_1xye_3\bar{e}_4\bar{z} \overset{R_G}{\rightarrow} e_0\bar{e}_1xy\bar{e}_3$$
$$\overset{R_G}{\rightarrow} e_0\bar{e}_1x\bar{y} \overset{R_G}{\rightarrow} e_0\bar{e}_1\bar{x} \overset{R_G}{\rightarrow} \bar{e}_0$$

and $\pi_{c_G}(\alpha_0\alpha_1\alpha_1\alpha_2) = u$. The interpretation of this conversation is quite simple, after being connected with the service by the broker; the client has refused two offers and accepted the third one. By contrast, when no path is found to reduce a conversation into the axiom, this means that the partial order of messages has been violated and consequently the coordination protocol is not respected. For instance, yxz is an invalid conversation that will not be recognised by the grammar.

5   Discussion

The presented approach aims to check conformity of agents' conversation according to coordination protocols at the runtime. Hence, the conversation protocols (or interaction protocols) are not represented explicitly like in [22] but derived from the coordination protocol. The presented model of coordination is based on producer/consumer dependency relationship. The resource dependency model among roles/agents is becoming used even in agent design methodologies like *Tropos* [23] and can be assumed to be rich enough to express complex situations founds in multi-agent systems.

Like [22] we assume that the coordination protocols and consequently the conversation protocols should be public and represents a part of the multi-agent system social norms. However, each agent has a specific internal strategy that steers its behaviour and responses to external stimulus. This assumption constrains us to check conformity of coordination protocol by an external observer: the deployment environment or the coordination media for instance.

The *mediated interaction* [24, 25] offers the opportunity to observe all actions coming from the autonomous agents and to check their conformity according to the established norms. In our approach, the *interaction mediator* will be responsible of checking the conformity of an ongoing conversation by applying results of the definition 6. For instance, the next paragraph presents an example of how conversation protocols are checked within the MIC* framework.

5.1   Conforming Interactions in MIC*:

Functionally, the conversation protocol checker can be considered as a Boolean function $f : \mathcal{O}^* \to \{\top, \bot\}$ taking as argument a sequence of interaction objects $o \in \mathcal{O}^*$ (or a conversation) and returning a value $v \in \{\top, \bot\}$. $\bot$ expresses the invalidity of a conversation while $\top$ expresses its validity. The set of conformity testing functions is noted CF. Using the approach presented in this paper, the conversation protocol checker has to reduce the conversation to the axiom by using the simplification rules obtained from the coordination protocol by applying the definition of equation 1. When the conversation can be reduced to the axiom, the conversation is considered as valid ($\top$) and invalid otherwise ($\bot$).

Interactions in MIC* (see §2.1) are defined as special evolutions of the deployment environment that modify the perceptions of agents, according to emissions of other agents in an interaction space. The goal here is to build interaction operations insuring the conformity of interactions. Hence, a conform interaction φ_f is built by the following application:

$$\varphi \times CF \to \varphi$$
$$(f, g) \mapsto f_g$$

where, f_g is defined as following:

$$\forall x \in \mathcal{O}^* : f_g = \begin{cases} f & \text{if } g(x) = \top \\ Id & \text{if } g(x) = \bot \end{cases}$$

Id expresses the identity application that does not modify the deployment environment. So, given a standard interaction operation defined on MIC* and a conversation protocol checker, a conform interaction operation is defined on MIC*. This new interaction operation does not modify the deployment environment, when the conservation is invalid, and behaves as the standard interaction operation φ otherwise. Consequently, the deployment environment is never modified by invalid interactions and these *bogus* attempts are transparently rejected and never reach agents' perceptions.

The next step of our work is to offer to the deployment environment concrete solutions and tools to check if a conversation belongs or not to a certain protocol.

6   Conclusion

This paper has presented an approach in order to link conversation protocols to their corresponding coordination protocols. Hence, the conversation protocol is seen as structured sequences of messages of interaction objects recognised by the rewriting system. This rewriting system is considered as a conversation policy that can be integrated in a coordination architecture such as MIC* in order to validate conversations in a multi-agent system. Consequently, future works have to explore how to automatically and iteratively recognise valid conservations by observing messages among the coordinating entities. This will help in implementing reliable multi-agent systems where conversation laws and consequently coordination protocols are guaranteed by a trusted observer, namely the deployment environment, which established a referential for agents responsibility in large open and untrusted software systems.

References

[1] Zambonelli, F., Parunak, H.V.D.: Signs of a revolution in computer science and software engineering. In: Agent Oriented Software Engineering Workshop at AAMAS 2002, Bologna (2002) 182

[2] Gouaich, A.: Requirements for achieving software agents autonomy and defining their responsibility. In: Autonomy Workshop at AAMAS 2003, Melbourne, Australia (2003) 183, 191

[3] Wooldridge, M., Jennings, N.R.: Intelligent agents: theory and practice. The Knowledge Engineering Review 10 (1995) 115–152 183

[4] Ferber, J.: Les Systemes Multi-Agents. InterEditions (1995) 183

[5] Castelfranchi, C.: Guarantees for autonomy in cognitive agent architecture. Intelligent Agents: Theories, Architectures, and Languages 890 (1995) 56–70 183

[6] Gouaich, A., Guiraud, Y., Michel, F.: Mic*: An agent formal environment. 7th World Multiconference on Systemics, Cybernetics and Informatics (SCI 2003) (2003) Orlando, USA 183, 193

[7] Malone, T.W., Crowston, K.: The interdisciplinary study of coordination. ACM Computing Surveys (CSUR) 26 (1994) 87–119 185, 186

[8] Harel, D.: Statecharts: A visual formalism for complex systems. Science of Computer Programming 8 (1987) 231–271 187

[9] Hoare, C.A.R.: Communicating Sequential Processes. Prentice-Hall International (1985) 187

[10] Milner, R.: Communication and Concurrency. Prentice-Hall (1989) 187

[11] Milner, R., Parrow, J., Walker, D.: A calculus for mobile processes, parts 1 and 2. Information and Computation 100 (1992) 187

[12] Cardelli, L.: Abstractions for mobile computation. Secure Internet Programming (1999) 51–94 187

[13] Fournet, C.: Le Join-Calcul: Un Calcul Pour la Programmation Repartie et Mobile. PhD thesis, Ecole Polytechnique (1998) 187

[14] ITU: Recommendation z.120: Message sequence chart (MSC). Technical Report Z.120, International Telecommunication Union (1993) 188

[15] Papadopoulos, G.A.: Models and technologies for the coordination of internet agents: A survey. In Omicini, A., Zambonelli, F., Klusch, M., Tolksdorf, R., eds.: Coordination of Internet Agents: Models, Technologies, and Applications. Springer-Verlag (2000) 25–56 189

[16] Barbuceanu, M., Fox, M.S.: COOL: A language for describing coordination in multi-agent systems. In Lesser, V., ed.: First International Conference on Multi-Agent Systems, San Francisco, California, AAAI Press/The MIT Press (1995) 17–24 189

[17] Barbuceanu, M., Lo, W.K.: Conversation oriented programming for agent interaction. [26] 220–234 189

[18] Martial, F.V.: Coordinating Plans of Autonomous Agents. Volume 610 of Lecture Notes in Artificial Intelligence. Springer-Verlag (1992) 189

[19] König, R.: State-based modeling method for multiagent conversation protocols and decision activities. In Kowalczyk, R., Müller, J.P., Tianfield, H., Unland, R., eds.: Agent Technologies, Infrastructures, Tools, and Applications for E-Services. Volume 2592 of Lecture Notes in Computer Science. (2003) 151–166 189

[20] Cost, R.S., Chen, Y., Finin, T.W., Labrou, Y., Peng, Y.: Using colored petri nets for conversation modeling. [26] 178–192 189

[21] Fallah-Seghrouchni, A.E., Haddad, S., Mazouzi, H.: Protocol engineering for multi-agent interaction. In Garijo, F.J., Boman, M., eds.: MAAMAW. Volume 1647 of Lecture Notes in Computer Science., Springer (1999) 89–101 189

[22] Endriss, U., Lu, W., Maudet, N., Stathis, K.: Competent agents and customising protocols. (2004) In this volume 196, 197

[23] Henderson-Sellers, B., Giorgini, P., Bresciani, P.: Supporting tropos concepts in agent OPEN. (2004) In this volume 197

[24] Omicini, A., Ricci, A.: MAS organisation within a coordination infrastructure: Experiments in tucson. (2004) In this volume 197

[25] Denti, E., Ricci, A., Rubino, R.: Integrating and orchestrating services upon an agent coordination infrastructure. (2004) In this volume 197

[26] Dignum, F., Greaves, M., eds.: Issues in Agent Communication. Volume 1916 of Lecture Notes in Computer Science. Springer, Lecture Notes in Computer Science (2000) 199

MAS Organization within
a Coordination Infrastructure:
Experiments in TuCSoN

Andrea Omicini and Alessandro Ricci

DEIS
Università degli Studi di Bologna
via Venezia 52, 47023 Cesena, Italy
{aomicini,aricci@deis.unibo.it}

Abstract. Organisation and coordination are strictly related issues in the engineering of agent societies, and some important issues such as security can be suitable modelled only considering their synergy. Accordingly, in this paper we show how to extend a MAS coordination infrastructure for agent-based systems (namely, TuCSoN) toward the specification and support of MAS organisation. To this end, we adopt the notion of *agent coordination context* (ACC) as a first-class abstraction that defines the organisation structures and rules, and makes them accessible and manageable at execution time. Then, we show how ACC provides the conceptual framework to model the presence of an agent inside the organisation and the environment, as well as the means to face MAS organisation, coordination, and even security issues in a coherent and uniform way.

1 Introduction

Multiagent systems (MAS henceforth) are often acknowledged to provide the suitable level of abstraction for modelling and engineering complex systems, characterised by organisation structures and coordination processes that are increasingly more articulated and dynamic. Inter-organisational workflow management systems [1], agent-based CSCW [2] and team-based cooperative military contexts [3] are prominent examples.

Facing complexity in MAS modelling and engineering requires a shift from a reductionist vision of MAS – focused on individual agents (individual intelligence) – to a systemic, holistic vision of MASs, explicitly accounting for social issues (social intelligence) [4, 5, 6, 7]. This attitude clearly emerges from several methodologies adopted in the context of agent oriented software engineering; generally, these methodologies adopt organisational models to describe and design system organisation in terms of its structure (such as the roles involved), organisational patterns (roles relationships) and rules (roles constraints) [6, 8, 9].

On the one hand, openness, complexity, dynamism of the systems modelled and engineered with MAS push more and more for *keeping the abstractions alive.*

A. Omicini, P. Petta, and J. Pitt (Eds.): ESAW 2003, LNAI 3071, pp. 200–217, 2004.
© Springer-Verlag Berlin Heidelberg 2004

This means that abstractions that are typically introduced at the design time should be supported as first-class citizens also at development and execution time, in order to adequately support the full system development cycle and in particular system corrective/adaptive/evolutive maintenance. This calls for MAS models and infrastructures allowing for their runtime management (construction, inspection, adaptation): in the case of MAS organisational abstractions, this requires the capability of supporting dynamic inspection and adaptation of the organisation. Moreover, in order to support aspects of self-reconfiguration and self-adaptation, these capabilities should be made available to humans as well as to artificial (intelligent) agents, which should be able to inspect and change autonomously the structures.

On the other hand, *organisation* and *coordination* are systemic issues that are strictly related and interdependent, and should be faced within a unique, coherent conceptual framework. Generally speaking, organisation mainly concerns the structure and the structural patterns (relations) of a system – i.e. the static issues of the agent interaction space; coordination mainly concerns the processes inside a system – i.e. the dynamic issues of the agent interaction space –, often related to roles that usually frame agents position in the structure/pattern of system organisation. The synergy between coordination and organisation approaches is required to adequately face security-related issues, at different level of abstractions, in terms of rules characterising both the static organisation structure and the dynamic government of system interaction, according to some policy.

According to the considerations above, MAS infrastructures aimed at supporting suitably organisation issues should provide:

- organisation abstractions to capture organisational structures and rules as first-class citizens also at execution time;
- services for dynamic inspection and change of these abstractions, so as to enable flexible monitoring and evolution of system organisation;
- support to humans as well as to artificial agents, and enabling their adoption for automated administrative and maintenance jobs.

Accordingly, in this paper we show how a coordination model and related infrastructure for MAS coordination – TuCSoN [10] – have been extended to support the description and enactment of organisational models. This has been possible by extending TuCSoN with the notion of *agent coordination context* (ACC henceforth), introduced in [11]. The remainder of the paper is organised as follows. section 2 describes the properties of organisational models suitable for open/dynamic systems, and introduces a model based on the ACC notion. section 3 describes how this model has been embodied in TuCSoN. A discussion about the benefits of the approach is provided in section 4. Finally, related work is discussed in section 5, and a roadmap for future work is drawn in section 6.

2 Modelling MAS Organisation

According to the results coming from different disciplines, the most effective and expressive organisational models for complex and articulated systems (human/social systems as well as artificial ones) are role-based.

The notion of role is essential in organisation theory, where it is used as the basic building block representing positions and responsibilities in human organisations, mainly focusing on collaboration and coordination issues [12]. Roles are also the basic abstraction in state-of-the-art models adopted for the security in complex software systems, in particular information systems management, and systems used in the context of workflow management and computer supported cooperative work [2]. All the above models are rooted in the RBAC (role-based-access) model [13], which better deals with access control in open and articulated systems than the classic approaches such as the discretionary access model (DAC). Role-based models have also been adopted in some Distributed Artificial Intelligence approaches, and in MAS as their modern counterpart, in particular in cooperative problem solving scenarios, where roles and related interaction protocols are typically exploited to reduce the complexity of agent interaction space [14]. Organisational models based on roles are widely adopted in agent-based software engineering (AOSE), mainly extending approaches rooted in Object Oriented Software Engineering, and providing means for analysis and design of MASs [8, 15, 9, 7, 5, 6].

Correspondingly, in the following we devise a role-based organisational model meant to reuse as many abstractions as possible from the above models, while developing them along the two basic lines drawn in the introduction: (i) keeping abstractions alive through a suitable agent infrastructure, and (ii) providing a suitable integration between coordination and organisation abstractions. The first line basically means extending the holistic approaches found in AOSE methodologies from analysis and design (model issue) to development, deployment and execution time (infrastructure issue). Abstractions description (such as the notion of group structure and related roles in [5]) and concretion (such as an active group composed by agents playing in some role), as defined by the organisational model, should be explicitly represented in structures provided by the infrastructure at execution time, in order to be inspectable, manageable and modifiable by humans (engineers and organisation administrator) and by intelligent agents as well. Along the second line, instead – the synergy between coordination and organisation – we aim at supporting runtime organisation abstractions in the context of an existing coordination infrastructure (TuCSoN in our case), by specialising coordination abstractions toward organisation. In the remainder of this section, first we describe the organisation model adopted for organisation structures and rules specification, and then its integration (and enactment) in the context of a coordination infrastructure by means of the notion of ACC.

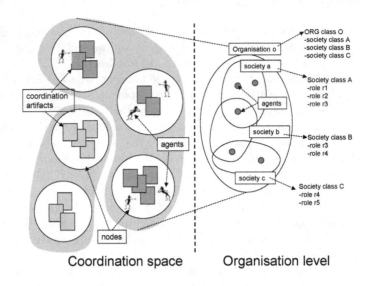

Fig. 1. The organisation viewpoint on top of the coordination space

2.1 A Model for Organisation

Following an organisation-centred perspective [5], MAS organisation can be described at two different levels: organisational (or social) level and concrete (or agent) level; at the organisational level we consider the abstractions, patterns, rules that persist when components or individuals enter or leave an organisation, i.e. the relationships that makes a whole out of an aggregate of elements [16].

In order to manage its complexity, an organisation model should provide the means for partitioning its structure. Accordingly, in our approach we consider the *society* concept (at the agent level) and the *society class* concept (at the organisational level), following the terms adopted in the SODA agent oriented software engineering methodology [17].

A society is here defined an (open) group of agents glued by some social tasks, which they can achieve collectively by exploiting some shared *coordination artifacts*, embedding coordination laws and social norms [18]. These artifacts are meant to mediate agent interaction and support their collaboration.

A society class defines a set of *roles*, as an abstract representation of a functional positions of an agent in a society. Then, a society – as a concretion of a society class – is composed (dynamically) by a set of agents playing one or multiple roles, according the structure and relationships that characterise the society.

So, in order to act inside an organisation, an agent must play a role in a society; it can play simultaneously several roles both in the same society and in different societies, according to current organisational rules. Each role is characterised by an *action/observation space*, as the set of the actions and observation that agents playing the role are allowed (forbidden) to do. In particular, in the context of a coordination infrastructure, agent actions are the basic coordination primitives to access and use the coordination artifacts provided by the organisation. An overall picture of the adopted model is provided in Fig. 1.

Following the RBAC approach [13], we distinguish two stages concerning the agent participation to an organisation:

- role admission, used to assert that an agent is admitted to play a specific role inside the organisation;
- role activation, which concerns the concrete participation of an agent to the organisation, actively playing a role within a society.

The organisational rules can be then described in terms of inter-role relationships and relationships between agents and roles, and are used to govern agent admission and role activation. This makes it possible to enact separation of duty principles, which are fundamental in the management of security in complex organisation [19]. Here we consider two types of relationships:

- **Agent-Role Relationships**. Through these relationships it is possible to specify whether a specific agent is allowed (or forbidden) to assume and then to activate a specific role inside the organisation. In the context of the RBAC model, and more generally in organisation theory, these relationships are useful to satisfy *static* separation of duty property.
- **Inter-Role Relationships**. These relationships make it possible to specify structural dependencies among the roles, so as to further define constraints on dynamic agent-role activation. By means of these relationships, it is possible to explicitly specify, for instance, whether two roles are equivalent, whether a role excludes an other one, or requires other roles to be played. These relationships make it possible to define role hierarchies and, more generally, organisational patterns. In the context of the RBAC model these relationships are useful to satisfy *dynamic* separation of duty property.

An organisation then act as a *closure* for the agent and society relationships: relationships between roles belonging to different societies can be specified in the context of the same organisation; conversely, no relationships can be defined between roles and agents belonging to different organisations.

2.2   Exploiting Agent Coordination Contexts

The notion of ACC introduced in [11] is a powerful concept to model issues that concern MAS organisation in an integrated way with coordination issues. First of all, an AC is obviously meant to represent a *context*, factorising the many meanings that emerge from the several research areas where it is commonly used (language, philosophy, logic, artificial intelligence, . . .). According to them, a context is an abstraction aimed at modelling the effect of the environment – in its most general acceptation, including the spatial and temporal interpretation

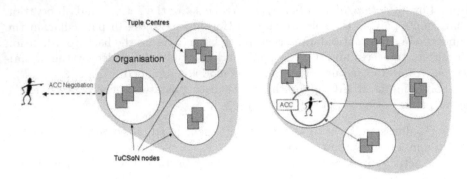

Fig. 2. ACC negotiation (left) and operating (right) stages for accessing coordination artifacts inside the organisation (in the example, TuCSoN infrastructure is considered, so the coordination artifacts are tuple centres, collected in nodes)

of the terms – on the interaction and communication occurring among active (and typically intelligent) entities, such as humans or artificial agents.

Within agent societies, the notion of context can be used as a first-class abstraction for modelling and engineering the environment. By identifying the context abstraction as the conceptual place where to set the boundary between the agent and the environment, so as to encapsulate the *interface* that enables agent actions and perceptions inside the environment, we obtain the full characterisation of ACC [11].

Then, the notion of ACC can be suitably used as the abstraction modelling the presence of an agent within an organisation, in terms of its admissible actions with respect to organisation resources and its admissible communications toward the other agents belonging to the organisation. Moreover, the ACC is meant to represent a sort of *contract* between the agent and the organisation, establishing what the agent is allowed to do but also representing agent expectations with respect to the organisation, for instance in terms of quality of service.

An ACC is meant to be created and released to an agent at beginning of each agent working session inside the organisation, and then to be destroyed when the agent quits the organisation. During a working session, the ACC acts as the interface toward the organisation (other participants and resources) for the roles the agent is going to play.

As an interface, the ACC provides the agent with the operations to interact with other agents and to access the resources hosted in the nodes of the organisation, according to the rule established for the roles which the agent is playing. Also, the ACC also provides the agent with the primitives to dynamically activate/deactivate the roles that the agent is admitted to play.

Before its creation and release, an ACC is first negotiated between a requesting agent and an organisation. ACC negotiation is meant to model the agent dynamic entrance into the organisation, for starting a working session (Fig. 2). The negotiation is engaged by the agent toward an organisation through the corresponding MAS infrastructure service when the agent aim at joining the organisation. Generally speaking, since joining an organisation is instrumental to the agent goals, the agent negotiates to obtain from the infrastructure an ACC configured in such a way that it maximise the agent chances to achieve its goals, while minimising the costs: in particular, the agent can specify which role(s) it aims at playing, and in which society of the organisation. On the other hand, the organisation aims at exploiting the agent work for its global (social) ends, while preserving its integrity and safety: so, the ACC configuration required by the agent might be not available or permitted, according the organisation rules and the dynamic state of the organisation. So, negotiation proceeds, with the infrastructure service that proposes available/permitted ACC configurations, and the agent that tries to get a configuration compatible with the achievement of its goals: negotiation may either fail or succeed, and (only) in the latter case the ACC is released to the agent, which is then enabled to join the organisation. [1]

Once the agent has joined the organisation, the ACC constrains agent actions and perception according to the policy specified for the role(s) it is playing. However, as mentioned before, the configuration of the ACC is not given once and for all once it is first released to the agent. Instead, it can be changed dynamically by the agent, negotiating with the organisation activation/deactivation of roles through the MAS infrastructure service – and again, also this negotiation process can fail or succeed.

In order to rule the ACC negotiation and role activation/deactivation stages, the agent-role and inter-role relationships defined in the organisation node are used. An agent request is then accepted only if it is either explicitly allowed or not explicitly forbidden according to the defined agent-role relationships, and if the inter-role relationships are satisfied – that is, if the agent is not already playing a role incompatible with the new one, and it is playing all the roles possibly required to be allowed to assume the new one.

2.3   Modelling Security

The integration of coordination and organisation issues provides a suitable framework to discuss and model MAS security issues.

Security in MAS concerns a multiplicity of aspects at different levels of abstraction — from traditional issues such as authentication and resource access control, up to higher level issues such as social order, electronic institutions, and agents & law [20, 21]. Agent autonomy and system openness are among the main features that make the engineering of security particularly challenging in the context of MAS. On the one hand, models and infrastructures needs to prescriptively specify and enact social norms and security policies, but without a direct and too tight control on the behaviour of the individual agent, so as

---

[1] The agent can omit to specify the role/society to activate when negotiating the ACC: in that case, a default role in a default society is activated (if the organisation constraints are satisfied). So an agent requesting an ACC with an empty configuration receives an ACC with the default role/society activated.

not hamper its autonomy. On the other hand, MAS are typically characterised by a high degree of heterogeneity and dynamism: norms and policies have to be enforced in dynamic organisation structures, where (heterogeneous) agents enter and leave the organisation at execution time. Moreover, complex scenarios call for models and infrastructures supporting runtime modifications of the security policies, in order to dynamically adapt to environment changes or new system goals.

The ACC abstraction makes it possible to extend a previous work on engineering MAS security on top of a coordination infrastructure [22] by means of RBAC models. There, two basic security issues are discussed: how agents are identified (*authentication*), and what they are allowed to do (*authorisation*).

Within the ACC framework, authentication is taken into account during the ACC negotiation stage and role activation: according to the specific application domain, an agent can be asked to demonstrate its identity in order to play a specific role inside the organisation. For the purpose, standard authentication technologies and infrastructures (such as X.509) can be exploited.

However, the most important contribute provided by the ACC abstraction is the direct support of a RBAC approach, improving on the authorisation model described in [22]. For each role inside the organisation a specific access control policy is defined. Accordingly, the ACC embeds and enacts the access control policies of the active roles that the agent owner of the ACC is currently playing inside the organisation. The access control policies can be suitably specified within the ACC by using a specific policy-oriented language with a suitable formal semantics, in order to enable in principle the formal verification of security properties [23].

Finally, during the ACC negotiation stage, other (non-functional) properties relevant for security can be specified, defining the quality of the coordination services: for instance, the possibility to encrypt the information exchanged during agent interaction.

3   Experiments in TuCSoN

As already mentioned, TuCSoN is an infrastructure providing coordination services for agent-based systems [10]. These services are embodied in *tuple centres*, that are coordination abstractions provided to agents by the infrastructure in order to enable and govern agent interaction. More precisely, tuple centres are *programmable* tuple spaces [24], that is, sort of reactive blackboards; agents interact by writing, reading, and consuming *tuples* – ordered collections of heterogeneous information chunks – to/from tuple centres via simple communication operations (*out*, *rd*, *in*) which access tuples associatively. While the behaviour a tuple space in response to communication events is fixed and pre-defined by the model, the behaviour of a tuple centre can be tailored to the application needs by defining a suitable set of *specification tuples*, which define how a tuple centre should react to incoming/outgoing communication events. The specification tuples are expressed in the ReSpecT language [24].

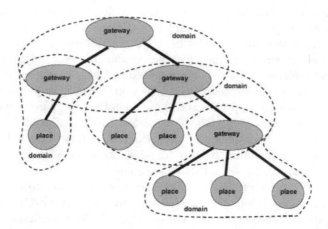

Fig. 3. Topology of the TuCSoN coordination space

So, tuple centres can be conceived as general-purpose customisable coordination artifacts, whose behaviour can be dynamically specified, forged and adapted so as to automate the co-ordination stage among agents using such artifacts [18]. Such coordination artifacts are first-class coordination abstractions that are *kept alive* from design to execution time: on the one hand, they can be used as modelling abstractions to support the design and development stage of society-oriented methodology such as SODA; on the other hand, they are exploited by agents at execution time by means of TuCSoN infrastructure.

From the topology point of view, tuples centres are hosted in TuCSoN *nodes*, distributed over the network, defining the TuCSoN coordination space [10]. In particular, the topological model of TuCSoN distinguishes the nodes in *places* and *gateways*. The former represent the nodes hosting tuple centres used for specific applications/systems need, from supporting coordination activities to hosting information or simply enabling agent communication: In a mobile agent framework, places are the nodes where mobile agents are meant to execute. The latter provide instead information for a limited set of places (a single and centralised repository is unfeasible in complex and large environments). A *domain* is the set of nodes composed by the gateway and the places for which it provides information. An overall picture of the topology is provided in Fig. 3. It is worth noting that the concepts of gateway and place do not automatically imply the definition of a unique hierarchical structure: a place can be part of different domains and a gateway can be a place in its turn. This is useful to model complex and dynamic network topologies, as those deriving from virtual organisations.

This basic model has been extended to support the specification and enactment of organisation structures and rules by embodying the notion of ACC. An organisation – in terms of its social structures, rules and resources – is mapped onto a domain (including the linked domains or sub-domains). The description of the organisation abstractions and concretions (as defined in section 2) is stored and managed dynamically in a specific tuple centre, called $ORG, which is hosted in the gateway node of an organisation. The $ORG tuple centre hosts then (dynamic) information about societies, roles, agents and related relationships (agent-role and inter-role) defined for the domain represented by the gateway and its places. Information is then represented in form of logic tuples, according to the preliminary ontology described in section 3.1. The organisation settings can be then dynamically inspected and changed both by humans as well as agents by suitably reading and modifying the tuple set content of $ORG.

The organisation structures and rules defined in a domain hold for all the places included in it, including its sub-domains. So, an ACC negotiated with the gateway of a domain holds for all its sub-domains.

Then, in order to access the tuple centres hosted by a coordination node of a place, an agent must join the organisation by entering into a suitable ACC negotiated with the gateway of the domain (Fig. 2). The configuration, properties and quality of services characterising the ACC are negotiated by the agent through the basic services provided by the infrastructure. In the case of successful negotiation, an ACC with a specific configuration is created and entered by the agent, which can then exploit its interface to access and use the tuple centres hosted by the places of the domain; basically, this interface provides the basic primitives of the ReSpecT coordination language (in, out, inp, rdp, rd, set_spec, get_spec), and enables agent access to tuple centres according to the permissions and rules defined for the roles it is playing. Also, an ACC provides the primitives to dynamically activate and deactivate roles, and to quit the ACC itself, thus ending the agent working session inside the organisation.

3.1   Organisation Structures & Rules

In the remaining part of the section the preliminary meta-model adopted for representing organisation structures and rule is presented.

Society classes and related roles available inside the organisation can be defined using the following logic tuples:

- society_class(*SocClass, AbstractContext*): a society class denoted as *SocClass* is defined in the domain. *AbstractContext* defines the *abstract context* of the society class, i.e. a set of either abstract or concrete names used as virtual references to tuple centres. These names are used in the role policy definition.
- role(*R, SocClass, Cardinality, Policy*): a role denoted as *R* is defined in the society class *SocClass*. *Cardinality* indicates the maximum number of agents that can play simultaneously the role (the inf constant can be used to specify an unlimited number). *Policy* is a pure Prolog theory shaping the action space of the agent playing the role, defining the constraints. This policy can contain both virtual and concrete references to tuple centres. Virtual references must be included in the set defined by the society class, and are resolved – i.e., bound to concrete tuple centres – only when the role is contextualised in a specific society. Details about role policies are provided in section 3.3.

Organisation structures at the agent (concrete) level, concerning societies and agents defining current concrete organisation, are expressed by the following logic tuples:

- society(*Soc, SocClass, ConcreteContext*): a society *Soc* instance of the society class *SocClass* is active in the organisation.
  The *ConcreteContext* is the *concrete context* provided by a society, in terms of the bindings linking virtual references to tuple centres (specified in the society class and used in role policies) to concrete ones.
- role_active(*AgId, R, Soc, SocClass*): the agent *AgId* is currently playing the role *R* in the society *Soc* of class *SocClass*.

Then, the relationships among agents and roles, defining the policy ruling agent entrance in the organisation, are expressed by following tuples:

- role_allowed(*AgId, R, Soc, SocClass*): an agent *AgId* is allowed to become a member of the society *Soc* of the class *SocClass* by (dynamically) assuming there the role *R*;
- role_allowed(*AgId, R, SocClass*): an agent *AgId* is allowed to become a member of any society of the class *SocClass* by (dynamically) assuming there the role *R*, unless otherwise specified by a tuple role_forbidden;
- role_forbidden(*AgId, R, Soc, SocClass*): an agent *AgId* is not allowed to (dynamically) assume the role *R* in the society *Soc* of the class *SocClass*.

Inter-role relationships, useful to refine previous agent entrance constraints, are specified by the following logic tuples:

- role_excludes(*RA, SocA, SocClassA, RB, SocB, SocClassB*): if an agent is playing the role *RA* provided by the society *SocA* (or, more generally, by the society class *SocClassA*), it cannot assume the role *RB* provided by the society *SocB* (or, more generally, by the society class *SocClassB*);
- role_requires(*RA, SocA, SocClassA, RB, SocB, SocClassB*): in order to assume the role *RA* provided by the society *SocA* (or, more generally, by the society class *SocClassA*), an agent must be playing the role *RB* provided by the society *SocB* (or, more generally, by the society class *SocClassB*).

3.2   Enactment of Organisation Rules

The rules dynamically defined in the $ORG tuple centres are enforced by the TuCSoN gateways during the negotiation of the ACC and the dynamic role activation/deactivation. The request of an agent *AgId* to activate a role *RN* into a specific society *SocN* of class *SocClassN* is satisfied if and only if the following constraints are verified:

- the agent is allowed to (dynamically) activate that role. This constraint is satisfied if a matching role_allowed/4 tuple is found that refers to the specific society, or if a role_allowed/3 tuple exists that matches the society class only, and a matching role_forbidden tuple is not found.

- pre-condition on role cardinality is satisfied. This rule is satisfied if the number of current agents playing the role (a subset of the `role_active` tuple set) is less than the cardinality specified in the `role` description tuple;
- role activation is compatible with roles currently played by the agent, according to the role relationships described the tuple centre. This rule is satisfied if

  (i) each role R currently played by the agent (recorded by tuples `role_active(AgId, R, Soc, SocClass)`) does not exclude the new role RN, i.e. no `role_excludes(R, Soc, SocClass, RN, SocN, SocClassN)` tuples are found, and

  (ii) each role R required by the new role RN (according to tuples `role_requires(RN, SocN, SocClassN, R, Soc, SocClass)`), is currently played by the agent, that is a tuple `role_active(AgId, R, Soc, SocClass)` is found.

3.3   Role Policy Specification and Enactment

In current model a role policy is expressed as a pure Prolog theory, and contains the rules defining if an action is allowed or not. Since an ACC is meant to support multiple active roles played in the same session by an agent, the overall theory about action permission is obtained by composing the theories of the individual roles. Given the resulting logic theory of the ACC, an action `Action` is allowed if the goal `can_do(Action)` can be demonstrated. An action `Action` can take the form `Tid @ Node ? op(T)`, with `op` in {out, in, rd, rdp, inp}, or the form `Tid @ Node ? op_spec(Spec)`, with `op` in {set_spec, get_spec}.

Also, some agent contextual information is provided in the theory in terms of ground facts. The contextual information currently concern temporal information, such as current time and date, the ACC creation date, roles activation dates, the period elapsed since a role activation or the ACC creations, and so on. The exact definition of all the ontology is outside the scope of the paper, and will be presented in future works, along with a formal semantics of the model.

4   Discussion

The approach proposed in this paper makes it possible to maintain organisation abstractions alive throughout all the whole engineering process, thus providing a continuum from design to execution time. In particular, the abstractions defined by the SODA methodology at the design level can be naturally described, mapped, and kept alive at the development and execution stage. For instance, the societies and related roles defined in SODA at the design stage can be mapped directly as societies and roles in TuCSoN, and the permissions specified for roles can be mapped into the rules and constraints that shape the action space enforced by agent coordination contexts. We think that this can have a significant impact on the engineering process of systems, since it reduces the conceptual gap among the different engineering stages.

We propose this approach as particularly useful in the context of intelligent agents, aiming at forms of self-configuration and self-adaptation of the systems. By reifying the description of the organisation structure and rules as knowledge encapsulated in a runtime inspectable and modifiable coordination abstraction, our approach enables the observation and construction/adaptation of the organisation settings at execution time. These features seems to be essential for any approach meant to fully exploit the potential of agent intelligence, and to promote automated reasoning on organisation dynamics: intelligent agents should be suitably supported by the infrastructure, which should in particular guarantee for the consistency of the inspected organisation information, and for the effectiveness of their changes on the whole MAS system as well. On the one hand, encapsulation of organisation knowledge makes its inspection, management, maintenance and evolution easier. On the other hand, the adoption of a tuple centre as a means of encapsulation – and so, the adoption of logic tuples to represent such knowledge – opens the inspection, management, maintenance and evolution of the organisation to (artificial) agents, which are part of the organisation.

Finally, the synergy between coordination and organisation amplifies the range of the intelligent services that are amenable to support. In particular, the coordination laws defining the behaviour of the tuple centre $ORG as a coordination artifact could be in principle extended, either statically or dynamically, to provide further services for the organisation, and to support and promote agent reasoning. For instance, it is easy to add coordination laws to log main organisation events – e.g., agents joining and leaving the organisation –, by reifying them as logic tuples stored in the tuple centre. In this way, we can easily get a consistent history of the organisation dynamics, which can then be inspected by intelligent agents in order to reconstruct the causes of possible organisation problems, to create model describing the organisation/society global behaviour, and to make predictions about the future behaviour of the organisation.

5   Related Work

Abundant research literature can be found about organisational meta-models and models for MAS. However, most of this literature is mainly focused on the analysis and design stages [9, 8, 6, 7, 25]. Our work aims at modelling MAS organisation at the infrastructure level, so as to support organisational issues from design down to development and execution time in a uniform way.

This focus on infrastructures can be devised also in [26]: according to the last development of this approach, roles are mapped directly from an XML specification to Java classes dynamically linked to agent's code (which must be necessarily based on Java) [27]. Among the others, our approach is quite different for two main reasons: first, our model is not linked to any specific agent computational model, and can be applied in the context of a heterogeneous MAS, with agents built upon heterogeneous models and languages. Then, in our approach we explicitly consider the modelling and enactment of organisation rules, governing at execution time role activation/deactivation and agent access to resources.

The meta-model presented in this articles follows the reference work of Ferber at al. with the AGR model [5], in particular for the distinction between the abstract and the concrete description level of the organisation structures. The main differences between our approach and the AGR model can be summarised as follows:

- *Integration with coordination issues.* In our approach, organisation and coordination are considered in synergy: our notion of society can be related to notion of group in the AGR model, but oriented toward the explicit support of coordination activities. In fact, societies (as defined in our model) are groups that explicitly share and exploit some coordination artifacts, which characterise society rules and norms;
- *Runtime inspection and change of the organisation.* In our approach the (infrastructure) support for dynamic inspection and change of organisation structures and rules is an important issue, explicitly modelled;
- *Role based access control.* In our approach the ACC infrastructure concept makes is possible to model and enact the constraints on agent access to resources (coordination artifacts) according to their role(s).

Our notion of Agent Coordination Context have some similarities with the notion of *controller* as found in the Law Governed Interaction (LGI) model [28]. Generally speaking, LGI is a message-exchange mechanism that allows an open group of distributed agents to engage in a mode of interaction governed by an explicitly specified and strictly enforced policy, the interaction law of the group. Law enforcement is decentralised, and carried out by a distributed set of controllers, one for each member of the community. As the LGI controller, the ACC enforces rules constraining the action/perception space of the agent exploiting it, enabling the enactment of policy that are local to the agent. Global coordination policies instead – meant to model laws concerning the society as a whole, not related to specific agent actions but to the global agent interaction space – are embedded and enforced by the coordination artifacts (tuple centres), which are independent abstractions that are non-local from the agent viewpoint. As a result, with respect to agents, the ACC framework features ACCs as local individual abstractions, and tuple centres as global social abstractions: two sorts of abstractions with different but related purposes, both necessary to an expressive and equilibrate modelling / engineering of the agent interaction space. This is one of the main difference with respect to LGI, which aims instead at capturing all the coordination issues by means of the rules applied by the (local) controllers.

Also, in the TEAMCORE model [29], agents are equipped with STEAMs (a sort of local *proxies*), which not only enforce local rules on agent action, but interact with each other pro-actively in order to enact coordination activities – according to a BDI model. In our case, ACC rules can be applied with no prior knowledge of the dynamic state of the other ACC and of the system in general, since they only deal with (the history of the) agent actions/observations:

this makes ACCs purely local abstractions, also from an engineering point of view. Global coordination is instead delegated to the tuple centres working as coordination artifacts.

6   Future Work

The integration of organisation issues upon a coordination infrastructures opened several issues that will be investigated to improve the basic model proposed in this paper. In particular:

- *ACC language and formal semantics.* We need to further investigate the best language for ACCs, for specifying role policies and their composition. Ongoing work is focusing on the adoption of process algebras for ACC syntax and semantics [23];
- *Improvement of role model.* We are investigating on how to improve our basic role model according to the research works on role algebra [15], in particular for extending the basic set of inter-role relationships. Also, we are investigating the adoption of a formal model for specifying role model semantics; for the purpose, the approach used in the RBAC context could be useful [19];
- *Electronic Institutions.* We think that the ACC abstraction and the related infrastructure could work very effectively to engineer and support at runtime the concept and functionalities of electronic institutions [21]. For this purpose, we need to further investigate how to frame some important notions in the ACC framework, such as delegation and obligations.

As a testbed, we plan to deploy the infrastructure in the context of Workflow Management Systems, collaborative environments for Virtual Organisation, and Pervasive Computing, which are application domains that we have already considered but focusing only on the coordination aspects [30].

Acknowledgements

The authors are grateful to the many people whose work and remarks have helped in conceiving and shaping the material that has been used in this paper. Also, we would like to thank all the attendants that contributed to the ESAW 2003 workshop, and the authors of the other articles of this book, which provided us with so many suggestions and contributions on how to improve this work.

This work has been partially supported by MIUR – Project COFIN 2003 (ex 40%) "Fiducia e diritto nella società dell'informazione" –, by MIPAF – Project SIPEAA "Strumenti Integrati per la Pianificazione Eco-compatibile dell'Azienda Agricola" –, and by the EC – FP6 Coordination Action "AgentLink III".

References

[1] Divitini, M., Hanachi, C., Sibertin-Blanc, C.: Inter–organizational workflows for enterprise coordination. In Omicini, A., Zambonelli, F., Klusch, M., Tolksdorf, R., eds.: Coordination of Internet Agents: Models, Technologies, and Applications. Springer-Verlag (2001) 369–398 200

[2] Tripathi, A., Ahmed, T., Kumar, R., Jaman, S.: A coordination model for secure collaboration. In Marinescu, D., Lee, C., eds.: Process Coordination and Ubiquitous Computing. CRC Press (2002) 1–20 200, 202

[3] Giampapa, J.A., Sycara, K.: Team-oriented agent coordination in the RETSINA multi-agent systems. In: 1st International Joint Conference on Autonomous Agents and Multiagent Systems (AAMAS 2002), Bologna, Italy, ACM Press (2002) Proceedings 200

[4] Ciancarini, P., Omicini, A., Zambonelli, F.: Multiagent system engineering: the coordination viewpoint. In Jennings, N.R., Lespérance, Y., eds.: Intelligent Agents VI — Agent Theories, Architectures, and Languages. Volume 1767 of LNAI., Springer-Verlag (2000) 250–259 200

[5] Ferber, J., Gutknecht, O., Michel, F.: From agents to organisations: an organizational view of multi-agent systems. In: 2nd International Joint Conference on Autonomous Agents and Multiagent Systems (AAMAS 2003), Melbourne, Australia, ACM Press (2003) Proceedings 200, 202, 203, 213

[6] Zambonelli, F., Jennings, N.R., Wooldridge, M.: Organisational rules as an abstraction for the analysis and design of multi-agent systems. International Journal of Software Engineering and Knowledge Engineering **11** (2001) 303–328 200, 202, 212

[7] Parunak, H.V.D., Odell, J.: Representing social structures in uml. In Wooldridge, M., Weiß, G., Ciancarini, P., eds.: Agent-Oriented Software Engineering II, Second International Workshop, AOSE 2001, Montreal, Canada, May 29, 2001, Revised Papers and Invited Contributions. Volume 2222 of LNCS., Springer-Verlag (2002) 1–16 200, 202, 212

[8] Kendall, E.A.: Role modelling for agent systems analysis, design and implementation. IEEE Concurrency **8** (2000) 34–41 200, 202, 212

[9] Ferber, J., Gutknecht, O.: A meta-model for analysis and design of organizations in multi-agent systems. In: 3rd International Conference on MultiAgent Systems (ICMAS'98), IEEE Computer Society (1998) 128–135 Paris, France, 3–7 September 1998. Proceedings 200, 202, 212

[10] Omicini, A., Zambonelli, F.: Coordination for Internet application development. Autonomous Agents and Multi-Agent Systems **2** (1999) 251–269 Special Issue: Coordination Mechanisms for Web Agents 201, 207, 208

[11] Omicini, A.: Towards a notion of agent coordination context. In Marinescu, D., Lee, C., eds.: Process Coordination and Ubiquitous Computing. CRC Press (2002) 187–200 201, 204, 205

[12] Biddle, B.J., Thomas, E.J.: Role Theory: Concepts and Research. Krieger Publishing Company (1979) 202

[13] Sandhu, R.S., Coyne, E.J., Feinstein, H.L., Youman, C.E.: Role-based access control models. IEEE Computer **29** (1996) 38–47 202, 204

[14] Durfee, E.H.: Practically coordinating. AI Magazine **20** (1999) 99–116 202

[15] Karageorgos, A., Thompson, S., Mehandjiev, N.: Semi-automatic design of agent organisations. In: 2002 ACM Symposium on Applied Computing (SAC 2002), ACM Press (2002) 306–313 Madrid, Spain, 11–14 March 2002, Proceedings. 202, 214

[16] Mintzberg, H.: The Structuring of Organizations. Prentice Hall (1979) 203

[17] Omicini, A.: SODA: Societies and infrastructures in the analysis and design of agent-based systems. In Ciancarini, P., Wooldridge, M.J., eds.: Agent-Oriented Software Engineering. Volume 1957 of LNCS., Springer-Verlag (2001) 185–193 203

[18] Ricci, A., Omicini, A., Denti, E.: Activity Theory as a framework for MAS coordination. In Petta, P., Tolksdorf, R., Zambonelli, F., eds.: Engineering Societies in the Agents World III. Volume 2577 of LNCS. Springer-Verlag (2003) 96–110 203, 208

[19] Ferraiolo, D.F., Sandhu, R., Gavrila, S., Kuhn, D.R., Chandramouli, R.: Proposed NIST standard for role-based access control. ACM Transactions on Information and System Security (TISSEC) 4 (2001) 224–274 204, 214

[20] Castelfranchi, C.: Engineering social order. In Omicini, A., Tolksdorf, R., Zambonelli, F., eds.: Engineering Societies in the Agents World. Volume 1972 of LNAI., Springer-Verlag (2000) 1–18 206

[21] Noriega, P., Sierra, C.: Electronic institutions: Future trends and challenges. In Klusch, M., Ossowski, S., Shehory, O., eds.: Cooperative Information Agents VI. Volume 2246 of LNCS., Springer-Verlag (2002) 14–17 6th International Workshop (CIA 2002), Madrid, Spain, 18–20 September 2002. Proceedings 206, 214

[22] Cremonini, M., Omicini, A., Zambonelli, F.: Multi-agent systems on the Internet: Extending the scope of coordination towards security and topology. In Garijo, F.J., Boman, M., eds.: Multi-Agent Systems Engineering. Volume 1647 of LNAI., Springer-Verlag (1999) 77–88 9th European Workshop on Modelling Autonomous Agents in a Multi-Agent World (MAAMAW'99), Valencia (E), 30 June – 2 July 1999. Proceedings 207

[23] Omicini, A., Ricci, A., Viroli, M.: Formal specification and enactment of security policies through Agent Coordination Contexts. In Focardi, R., Zavattaro, G., eds.: Security Issues in Coordination Models, Languages and Systems. Volume 85(3) of Electronic Notes in Theoretical Computer Science. Elsevier Science B. V. (2003) 207, 214

[24] Omicini, A., Denti, E.: From tuple spaces to tuple centres. Science of Computer Programming 41 (2001) 277–294 207

[25] Dignum, V., Meyer, J.J., Weigand, H., Dignum, F.: An organization-oriented model for agent society. In: International Workshop "Regulated Agent-Based Social Systems: Theories and Applications" (RASTA'02). (2002) AAMAS 2002, Bologna, Italy, 16 July 2002. Proceedings 212

[26] Cabri, G.: Role-based infrastructures for agents. In: 8th IEEE Workshop on Future Trends of Distributed Computing Systems (FTDCS 2001), IEEE Computer Society (2001) 210–214 Bologna, Italy, 31 October – 2 November. Proceedings 212

[27] Cabri, G., Ferrari, L., Leonardi, L.: Enabling mobile agents to dynamically assume roles. In: 2003 ACM Symposium on Applied Computing (SAC), ACM (2003) 56–60 Melbourne, FL, USA, 9–12 March 2003, Proceedings 212

[28] Minsky, N.H., Ungureanu, V.: Law-governed interaction: a coordination and control mechanism for heterogeneous distributed systems. ACM Transactions on Software Engineering and Methodology (TOSEM) 9 (2000) 273–305 213

[29] Tambe, M., Pynadath, D.V., Chauvat, N., Das, A., Kaminka, G.A.: Adaptive agent architectures for heterogeneous team members. In: 4th International Conference on MultiAgent Systems (ICMAS 2000), Boston, MA, USA (2000) 301–308 213

[30] Ricci, A., Omicini, A., Denti, E.: Virtual enterprises and workflow management as agent coordination issues. International Journal of Cooperative Information Systems **11** (2002) 355–379 Special Issue: Cooperative Information Agents – Best Papers of CIA 2001 214

Adaptability Patterns of Multi-agent Organizations

Oguz Dikenelli and Rıza Cenk Erdur

Ege University
Department of Computer Engineering
35100, Bornova, İzmir, Turkey
{erdur,oguzd}@staff.ege.edu.tr

Abstract. A multi-agent organization operating in an open environment has to adapt itself at run-time when the global knowledge of the organization changes unpredictably at run-time. In this paper this problem is named as organizational adaptability and two new patterns called as Ontology Perception and Society Merging are introduced to provide generic and reusable organizational solutions to this problem. Each pattern first defines a unique situation that causes a change in the organizational global knowledge then models the organizations' behavior in terms of responsibilities and collaboration of participating agents to solve this problem.

1   Introduction

It has been widely recognized that integration of multi-agent system (MAS) and semantic web ontology languages will change the way of engineering the information systems of the future. Today the infrastructure of this integration has been already developed such as standard ontology languages of semantic web (e.g. DAML+OIL [12], [7]), MAS standards (e.g. FIPA [8]) and agent development frameworks (e.g. JADE [2], FIPA-OS [14]). But developers still need industrial strength methodologies to develop MASs operating on the distributed, open and adaptive environment of the semantic web.

In the last few years, several methodologies have been proposed for MAS development. Some of these methodologies such as Gaia [17], MaSE [15], consider only closed MAS organizations where the organizational structure of the system is static and do not change at run-time. On the other hand, some recently proposed methodologies such as SODA [13], Tropos [4], ADALFE [3] and the one proposed by Zambonelli, Jenning and Wooldridge [18] explicitly take the agent environment into account to the model MAS organizations operating on the open environment like semantic web. Especially, Tropos is the first methodology that applies well-known organizational patterns [11], [16] such as broker, matchmaker and embassy directly during architectural design phase of the modeling. Since these patterns handle the openness of the organization, Tropos creates an open agent organization by directly applying them. But none of these methodologies focuses on the adaptability characteristic of the organization. Although Tropos considers the adaptability problem as a soft-goal during the modeling, it cannot handle the organizational adaptability since the patterns used by Tropos are not designed to solve this problem.

A. Omicini, P. Petta, and J. Pitt (Eds.): ESAW 2003, LNAI 3071, pp. 217–227, 2004.
© Springer-Verlag Berlin Heidelberg 2004

In this paper, we introduce two new patterns to handle organizational adaptability. But first of all, we have to define the concept of organizational adaptability. Organizational adaptability can be defined as the capability of the organization to handle dynamic and unpredictable changes in the organization's global knowledge. Since agent organizations depend on the global and explicit ontologies (especially in semantic web environment), any unpredictable change in the global knowledge affects the functionality of the agent organization, unless the agents of the organization are capable of adapting themselves to the environment. It is clear that MAS developers need a different modeling approach than the previous methodology proposals, to develop adaptable agent organizations. The key activity of this approach is the prediction of the possible changes of the organization's knowledge that may occur during operation. Then developers have to identify which agents will be affected from the predicted situation and define the necessary behaviors to make them adaptable. It is obvious that this approach cannot be easily applied and the best way to support developers is to provide them well-defined adaptability patterns. Existence of the adaptability patterns make it possible for developers to understand the organizational adaptability problem, then to select and to apply the right pattern (s) based on their organizational characteristic.

In general, adaptability patterns introduced in this paper identify the situations that cause a change in organizational knowledge then define behaviors and interactions of the participating agents to handle this situation. It is clear that, the most obvious situation that affects the organizational knowledge is the occurrence of any change in the structure of the global ontology managed by an explicit ontology agent. The first pattern called as " Ontology Perception " focuses on this situation and models the necessary agent responsibilities and interactions to handle this situation. The second situation occurs when two different agent organizations try to collaborate with each other. In this case, each organization has to learn the global ontology of the others and adapt itself to this new ontology. The second pattern called as " Society Merging " handles this critical situation.

The rest of the paper is organized as follows: Section 2 defines the mandatory elements of an high level multi-agent architecture to establish a common base and understanding for pattern modeling. The Ontology Perception pattern is introduced in Section 3. This introduction follows a pattern identification template in which intent of pattern, motivation behind the pattern, interactions and responsibilities of the participating agents are defined consequently. In Section 4, Society Merging pattern is introduced using the same template. Last section concludes the paper and outlines the main contribution.

2   Defining an Abstract MAS Architecture

Naturally, adaptability patterns are modeled using the well-known services of a multi-agent organization. Hence, we first need to define a high level architectural view of a multi-agent organization. This view will provide a common base to model the patterns in terms of standard services and roles of the high-level architecture. Such an architectural view has been defined by the FIPA organization and called as Abstract

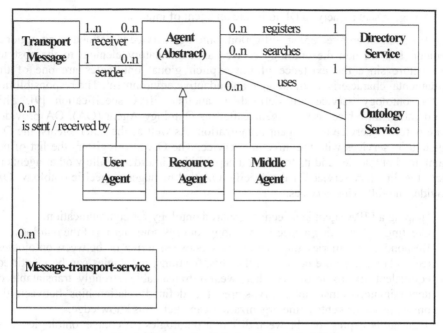

Fig. 1. High level architectural view of a MAS

Architecture Specification [8]. In this paper, we will extend the FIPA's Abstract Architectural Specification by considering the requirements of the adaptive organization. This extended architecture is shown in Fig.1 using the UML notation.

The original FIPA specification defines only one abstract agent class as a part of the abstract architecture. But we add three concrete agent types in our version by extending the abstract agent class as shown Fig.1. The responsibilities of these types are defined as follows; user agent type assists the user to communicate with the agent organization, resource agent type opens the knowledge of a resource to the organization and middle agent type handles the rest of the functionality of the organization. Our interpretation is that each real agent of the MAS plays the role (s) of the one those concrete agent types. So, we believe that the inclusion of these concrete types to the abstract architecture establishes the required infrastructure to define any type of the organizational pattern in terms of the standard abstract architecture specification.

The directory service provides a shared information repository, in which agents may publish their capabilities and in which they may search for other agents of interest. We accept the directory service as a mandatory element of the abstract architecture as in the FIPA specification since this service is the heart of any agent organization running in an open environment. A special agent usually called as Directory Facilitator (DF) Agent handles the responsibilities of the directory service in the agent organization and provides the following services to the organization:

- An agent may register a directory-entry via DF.
- An agent may modify a directory-entry that has been registered via DF.
- An agent may request a directory-entry deletion from DF.

– An agent sent a query to DF to locate an agent of interest.

In FIPA abstract architecture specification, ontology service is defined as an optional element. But we add the ontology service as a mandatory element to the abstract architecture since the existence of the explicit global ontologies are one of the fundamental characteristics of an open and adaptive environment. The responsibilities of the ontology service are defined in another FIPA specification [9]. This specification introduces a new agent called as Ontology Agent (OA). OA provides some ontology service to an agent organization. As well as the other agents, the OA registers its services with the directory service. The OA also registers the list of the maintained ontologies and its translation capabilities, in order to allow other agents to query the directory service for the specific OA that manages a specific ontology. OA provides the following services:

– Helping a FIPA agent in selecting a shared ontology for communication.
– Creating and updating a specific ontology, or only some terms of the ontology.
– Responding to queries for relationships between terms or between ontologies. (Six relationships are defined in the specifications: ontologies can be identified, equivalent, extension of the other, weakly-translatable, strongly–translatable or approximately-translatable. OA stores the defined relationships between the ontologies and agents in the organization can query this knowledge.
– Translating expressions between different ontologies (of course, ontologies must be translatable and translation rules must be defined by an authority.)

It is certain that one of the main contributions of the FIPA standardization effort is the definition of a standard agent communication language (ACL) specification. In a FIPA compliant agent organization, each agent communicates using this well-defined ACL standard. Hence, FIPA Abstract Architecture Specification defines the message-transport-service as a mandatory element of the architecture to indicate the importance of standard ACL usage. For the completeness of the architecture, we also add this service to our architecture. But, message-transport-service is not explicitly used during the pattern modeling process since any FIPA compliant framework implements this service as a part of agent's internal structures.

As a conclusion, the high level MAS architecture defined in this section accepts Ontology Service and Directory Service as mandatory elements with same responsibilities defined in FIPA specification and introduces three concrete agent types. These elements will be used with same name and defined responsibilities during pattern modeling in the following sections.

3   Ontology Perception Pattern

To document adaptability patterns, we use a simple template that is similar to the one used for design patterns [10], but has some small differences for agent-orientation. Following the template, first the intent of the pattern, then the motivation behind the pattern identification is introduced. Finally, the interaction mechanism and the responsibilities of the participating agents are defined consecutively.

3.1 Intent

Ontology Perception pattern defines how agent organization adapts itself when the structure of the global ontology changes or a new ontology is added to the organization at run-time.

3.2 Motivation

To be able to understand the motivation behind the Ontology Perception pattern, we should first acknowledge the following two characteristics as the basic characteristics of an adaptive environment;

–   In an adaptive environment, domain dependent global ontologies may change at run-time.
–   At any time, new ontologies may be added to the organization or some existing ontologies may be removed from the organization.

In such an environment, there is some obvious problems such as how the resource agents will be queried using the concept in terms of the new or changed ontologies or how the user agents will provide new interfaces for these ontologies. Of course, one possible approach to solve these problems is to stop the agents that require modifications, make these modifications and then reactivate the organization. But this is not a realistic solution for MASs operating in an open environment since there can be hundreds of agents distributed over the net and those possibly managed by more than one organization. Also new agents may join the organization at any time unpredictably. Hence, we should design the agent of the organization in a way that they should be capable of sensing the ontological changes and adapting themselves to those changes at run-time. Ontology Perception pattern introduces a generic and reusable solution by defining necessary responsibilities for each agent type and collaboration between these agent types to make agent organization adaptable to the ontological changes.

3.3 Interaction Mechanism and Responsibilities

Interaction Mechanism defines the collaboration between the agents to solve the problem at hand. The interaction mechanism of the Ontology Perception pattern is illustrated in Fig.2 using the collaboration diagram notation of the Agent-UML [1].

Ontology Agent initiates the information flow when it is informed about an ontological change or addition of a new ontology. Then, the messaging between the participating agents occurs as described below:

1.   Ontology agent requests the directory facilitator agent to find the agents that support the changed ontology. In case of new ontology addition, it requests all active agents of the organization.
2.   Directory facilitator sends the list of requested active agents to the ontology agent.
3.   Ontology agent informs each agent that there is a new ontology in the system.

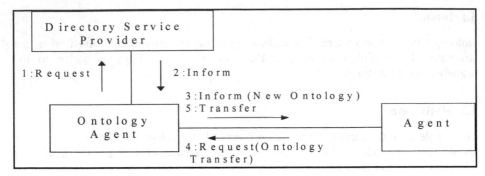

Fig. 2. Interaction mechanism of the "Ontology Perception" pattern

4.   Interested agents send a request to the ontology agent for ontology transfer.
5.   Ontology agent transfers the ontology to the interested agents.

As seen from Fig.2, we try to use standard FIPA communication acts (such as Inform, Request) during collaboration modeling. But, ontology agent needs a special communication act to indicate the ontology transfer. This new communication act is named as "transfer" and used as in Fig.2.

Of course, each incoming message to a particular agent creates a new responsibility for this agent. Also, some internal responsibilities may be required for each agent to generate the required behavior of the Ontology Perception pattern. Hence, we need to document the responsibilities of each agent to simplify the implementation of the pattern. Responsibility Catalog that is shown in Fig.3 is used for this purpose. The Responsibility Catalog indicates the required responsibilities of each participating agent to fulfill the general behavior of the Ontology Perception pattern.

One can notice that "Localize the new ontology" responsibility of abstract agent type is written in italic in Responsibility Catalog of Ontology Perception pattern as shown in Fig.3. This italic notation indicates an abstract responsibility that may be

ONTOLOGY PERCEPTION	
Agent Type	Responsibilities
Directory Facilitator	Handle the request coming from the OA Search the agents that use the ontology of interest Inform OA about the availability/unavailability of the requested agents
Ontology Agent	Understand ontological changes Query DF for agents that support ontology of interest Inform the related agent(s) about the new ontology Package and transfer the new ontology to the related agent
Agent	Build a request for ontology transfer Handle the new ontology coming from the OA *Localize the new Ontology*

Fig. 3. Responsibilities of participating agents for ontology perception pattern

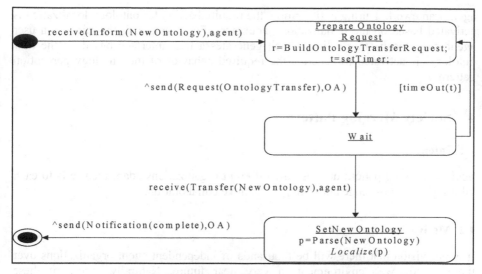

Fig. 4. Concurrent task diagram of the agent role

implemented diffrently in each concreate agent type of the abstract architecture. For example, an resource agent implements it by defining a mapping between the transferred ontologies and its local knowledge. On the other hand, an user agent implements it to create user interfaces for the transferred ontology.

These responsibilities are executed in order by each agent depending on the state of agent to generate overall behavior of the pattern. Naturally, an agent requires a separate plan to generate the required behavior of the pattern. Sometimes, it can be helpful for developers to represent these internal plans using a separate diagram. We suggest to use Concurrent Task Diagrams proposed in MaSE [15] for representing complex plan(s). For example, behavior of the agent role is represented using the concurrent task diagram as shown in Fig.4. In this diagram, agent plan is initiated when it receives an "Inform(NewOntology)" message from the OA. Then, in the "PrepareOntologyRequest" state, the agent builds the ontology transfer request message, sends it to the OA and waits for the incoming message. When it receives the "Transfer(NewOntology)" message, it enters to the new state and localizes the ontology.

It is certain that multi-agent systems are developed using the agent development frameworks. Hence, the necessary responsibilities required by the adaptability patterns have to be included in these frameworks. We have developed such an agent framework [5], [6] that supports adaptability patterns and we believe that it will be helpful to briefly introduce its software architecture to make the adaptability patterns idea implementable. The developed framework supports DAML ontology representation language. Hence, first of all, we have solved the problem of transporting DAML ontologies within the FIPA-ACL message format. Our solution is based on FIPA RDF content language, in which we transport the DAML ontologies in the content part of the message using the RDF/XML syntax. We have then implemented all the required plans of the adaptability patterns as default plans of the agent framework. During initialization, the required action for ontology localization is activated based on the initialization parameters. For example, if the agent is a user agent, then localization action, which generates a user interface based on the new ontology, is activated to generate the required behavior of the ontology perception pattern.

4   Society Merging Pattern

4.1 Intent

Society Merging pattern defines how different organizations adapt themselfs to each other's global knowledge at run-time to achieve collaboration.

4.2 Motivation

It is our vision that there will be thousands of independent agent organizations over the semantic web environment in very near future. Naturally, many of these organizations provide similar services in the same domain, but using different organizational ontologies. Conspiciously, each organization may gain additional benefits by using the services and user base of similar organizations. But, to be able to collaborate with each other, these organizations should understant the existance of the similar organizations and adapt themselfs to the organizational knowledge of the others at run-time. Society Merging pattern focuses this organizational adaptibility problem and provides a generic solution.

4.3 Interaction Mechanism and Responsibilities

Before beginning to define the interaction mechanism of the Society Merging pattern, we have to extend the abstract architecture defined in section 2 to provide an infrastructure for the society merging.   The extended version of the abstract architecture is shown in Fig.5.

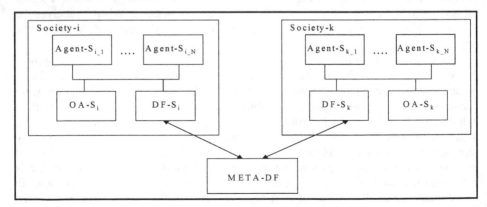

Fig. 5. Extended high level architectural view

As seen in Fig.5, there is two societies (we use the concept of organization and society interchangebly) named as Society-i and Society-k and architectural elements of each society are labeled with Si and Sk to indicate the society they belong. Extended abstract architecture introduces a new architectural element called as META-DF. META-DF is responsible of managing a meta ontology about societies. DF of each society advertises the capabilities of the society (such as its domain and high level services it provides) to the META-DF. Then, META-DF can be queried by any agent to find the societies that provide a specific service in a specific domain. As a summary, META-DF establish the necessary infrastructure for society searching and locating.

Based on the extended abstract architecture, interaction mechanism of the Society Merging pattern is shown in Fig.6.

Information flow is initiated by META-DF when DF of society-i (DF-Si) advertise its capability to it and proceeds as follows:

1. META-DF informs the DF's of each society of the same domain about the new society entry by sending the DF address of the new society.
2. Each interested DF request the address of the OA from the DF of the new society.
3. DF of new society send the address of its OA to the interested DFs.
4. Each DF informs its OA about the new society by sending the OA address of the new society.
5. Each OA request the ontology transfer from the OA of the new society.
6. OA of the new society transfer the ontology of the new society to the corresponding OAs.

At the end of the Society Merging interactions, OA of each interested society transfers the ontology of the new society and initiates the Ontology Perception pattern since the new ontology addition triggers the Ontology Perception. Execution of the Ontology Perception following the Society Merging makes agents of the society adaptable to the global knowledge of the new society.

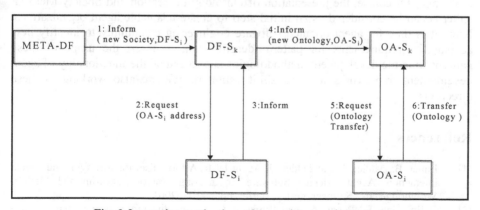

Fig. 6. Interaction mechanism of the society merging pattern

SOCIETY MERGING	
Agent Type	Responsibilities
META-DF	Manage the meta ontology Search the societies that provide the requested capability Inform the related DFs about the entry of a new society
DF	Advertise the capability of the society to META-DF Request the adress of teh OA from other DF Inform the address of own OA to the requested DFs Inform the OA about the new society
OA	Build a request for ontology transfer Package and transfer the own ontology Handle the coming ontology Localize the coming ontology

Fig. 7. Responsibilities of participating agents for society merging pattern

Examining the interaction mechanism and the general requirements of the Society Merging pattern, following responsibilities are identified for each participating agent as shown in Fig.7.

5   Conclusion

In this paper, we introduce two new patterns for organizational adaptability, which is one of the most important requirements of MAS development that is often overlooked. These patterns define generic organizational solutions for specific situations that cause a change in organizational global knowledge. Hence, they inform the developers about adaptability problems of the future during the development and assist them to implement the necessary generic agent behaviors to solve these problems. Of course, the presentation of Ontology Perception and Society Merging patterns can be considered as an initial step to create adaptable agent organizations. Now, it is time for agent oriented software engineering community to identify new adaptability requirements for pattern identification, to insert the usage of these patterns in to the development methodologies and to extend the functionality of agent development frameworks for adaptability support. We are also working in these directions.

References

[1]   Bauer, B., Müller, J.P. and Odell, J. Agent UML:A formalism for specifying multiagent interaction. Agent Oriented Software Engineering, Paolo Ciancarini and Michael Wooldridge eds., Springer-Verlag, Berlin, pp.91-103, 2001.

[2]   Bellifemine, F., Poggi, A., and Rimassa, G. Developing multi-agent systems with a FIPA- compliant agent framework. *Software Practice. and Experience*, 31:103-128, 2001.

[3]   Bernon C., Gleizes MP., Peyruqueou S., Picard G. ADELFE, a Methodology for Adaptive Multi-Agent Systems Engineering, Third International Workshop Engineering Societies in the Agents World. ESAW02, Madrid, Spain, September 2002.

[4]   Castro J., Kolp M. and Mylopoulos J. A requirement-driven development methodology. In   Proc. of the 13th Int. Conf. on Advanced Information Systems Engineering, CaiSE'01, Interlaken, Switzerland, June 2001.

[5]   Erdur, R. C. and Dikenelli, O. A FIPA-compliant agent framework with an extra layer for   ontology dependent reusable behaviour, LNCS 2457:283-292, Springer-Verlag, 2002.

[6]   Erdur, R. C,. and Dikenelli, O., A standards-based agent framework for instantiating adaptive agents, AAMAS'03, Melbourne, Australia.

[7]   Fensel, D., Horrocks, I., Van Harmelen, F., Decker, S., Erdmann, M. and Klein, M. OIL in a nutshell. In the proceedings of the workshop on applications of ontologies and problem   solving methods, 14th European Conference on Artificial Intelligence, Germany, 2000.

[8]   FIPA(a). FIPA XC00001I: FIPA abstract architecture specification. http://www.fipa.org.

[9]   FIPA(b). FIPA XC00086C: FIPA ontology service specification. http://www.fipa.org.

[10]   Gamma, E., Helm, R., Johnson, R. and Vlissides J. Desing patterns. Addison Wesley, Reading (MA), 1995.

[11]   Hayden, S., Carrick C. and Yang Q. Architectural design patterns for multiagent coordination. In Proc. of 3rd Int. Conf. on Autonomous Agents, Seattle, USA, May 1999.

[12]   Hendler, J. and McGuiness, D. The DARPA agent markup language. IEEE Intelligent Systems, 15, No.6:67-73, 2000.

[13]   Omicini, A. SODA: Societies and infrastructures in analysis and design of agent-based systems. In Ciancarini, P. and Wooldridge, M. (eds). Proc. 1st Int. Workshop on Agent-Oriented Software Engineering (AOSE 2000), Limerick, Ireland, June, 2000. Volume 1957 of LNCS, Springer-Verlag, Berlin, 2001.

[14]   Poslad, S., Buckle P., and Hadingham, R. The FIPA-OS agent platform: open source for open standards. in the Proceedings of the 5th International Conference and Exhibition on the Practical Application of Intelligent Agents and Multi-agents, 2000 UK. Available at http://www.fipa.org/resources/byyear.html.

[15]   Wood, M., DeLoach, S.A. and Sparkman, C. Multiagent system engineering. International Journal of Software Engineering and Knowledge Engineering, 2001.

[16]   Woods S. and Barbacci M. Architectural evaluation of collaborative agent-based systems. Technical Report CMU/SEI-99-TR-025, Carnegie Mellon University, Pittsburgh, USA, 1999.

[17]   Wooldridge, M., Jennings, N.R. and Kinny, D. The Gaia Methodology for agent oriented analysis and design. Journal of Autonomous Agents and Multi-Agent Systems, 3(3):285-312, 2000.

[18]   Zambonelli, F., Jennings, N., and Wooldridge, M. Organisational rules as an abstraction for the analysis and design of multi-agent systems. Int. Journal on Software Engineering and Knowledge Engineering.

Integrating and Orchestrating Services
upon an Agent Coordination Infrastructure

Enrico Denti[1], Alessandro Ricci[2], and Rossella Rubino[1]

[1] DEIS, Università degli Studi di Bologna
viale Risorgimento 2, 40136 Bologna, Italy
[2] DEIS, Università degli Studi di Bologna
via Venezia 52, 47023 Cesena, Italy

Abstract. The adoption of Multi-Agent Systems for system engineering often requires legacy and human-oriented services to be integrated into agent societies. In turn, this aspect impacts the engineering of interactive systems that involve the cooperation of agents and (human) actors – such as, for instance, workflow management systems. In this context, the coordination model adopted by the multi-agent system infrastructure strongly conditions the design, development and exploitation of available services.

In this work we address the issue of composing and coordinating services upon a suitable agent coordination infrastructure. First, we discuss how the infrastructure's metaphors and coordination artifacts can be exploited to support service integration, and illustrate the envisioned scenarios making specific reference to the TuCSoN coordination infrastructure. Then, we discuss in detail the issue of the engineering of (possibly heterogeneous and legacy) services: the case study of e-mail, file transfer, and web browsing services is finally presented.

1   Introduction

When developing agent-based systems, the ability to exploit 'standard' services is a critical issue, in particular when accessing legacy services such as mail systems, file transfer systems, database access systems. Although such services are typically exploited by human users, enabling agents to access them is a necessary step for both process automation and workflow automation in complex interactive systems.

Solving the problem *ad hoc*, building each time a specific agent that embeds the required skill and knowledge about the communication protocol, is clearly unsatisfactory. A better approach, often adopted in agent infrastructures, is based on constructing building blocks, wrapping each legacy service into an agent that may be reused in different contexts.

In this case, the adopted agent infrastructure, and in particular its *interaction model*, significantly impact the design, development and deployment of agent-based services [1]. In this work, we assume the TuCSoN infrastructure as the reference model and technology. Because it adopts a mediated interaction

A. Omicini, P. Petta, and J. Pitt (Eds.): ESAW 2003, LNAI 3071, pp. 228–245, 2004.
© Springer-Verlag Berlin Heidelberg 2004

model, the design, development and fruition of services is quite different from a conventional direct agent interaction model, usually based on some agent communication language such as KQML or FIPA ACL.

Our aim is to explore how to compose and coordinate both standard and legacy services into an integrated coordination-based framework, so as to *(i)* allow such services to be accessed in a straightforward way, with no need to know any service-specific technical detail, and *(ii)* enable some intrinsically new, higher-level services, made possible by this integrated scenario. The first goal follows from the choice of making all agents interact (only) via the TuCSoN coordination media (*tuple centres*): any request to perform a service should then be expressed as inserting / retrieving a suitable logic *tuples*, into / from the proper tuple centre. As a specific case study, we will focus on e-mail, file transfer, and web browsing services: so, any communication action, such as sending an e-mail, downloading a file, etc. will be triggered, and indirectly performed, via some tuple-centre operation. The second goal comes from the fact the TuCSoN tuple centres are *programmable* coordination artifacts, which can be exploited to express the desired coordination policies: in our case, these will be the rules needed to coordinate and orchestrate the single services so as to form new, higher-level services.

The paper is therefore structured as follows. Section 2 addresses the issue of engineering services in a mediated interaction model, also outlining the basics of the TuCSoN model. Then, in Section 3 we present our approach to service composition and orchestration, while the design of some specific services – email, FTP and HTTP – is addressed in 4, where we make explicit reference to TuCSoN coordination artifacts (tuple centres). Conclusions, related works and open issues are discussed in Section 5, discussing in particular the perspectives endorsed by the integration of Web services into our architecture.

2   Service Engineering in a Mediated Interaction Model

2.1   From Direct Approaches to Coordination Media

Since our aim in this paper is not to present a service model and discuss it in general, including issues like semantic interoperability, but, rather, discuss how the availability of a coordination model and infrastructure can impact the service design, the key question is: what does "designing a service" actually mean?

In an interaction model based on direct (peer-to-peer) interaction, each service is typically embedded into a wrapper agent, which is then directly asked to perform the service (Figure 1, left picture). Direct communication couples the interacting entities with each other, in terms of naming rules (who the partners are), space control (where the partners are) and time control (when to interact). Such a strict coupling limits both scalability and flexibility [1].

In order to face (at least some of) these problems, *mediator agents*, also called *middle-agents* [2], were introduced. Provided by infrastructure, these special-purpose agents mediate between service providers and users (Figure 1, right

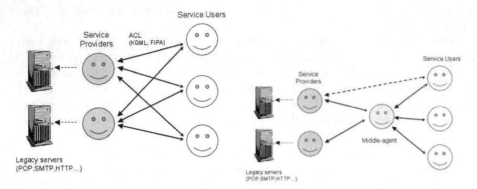

Fig. 1. Integrating services by means of a direct-interaction model (*left*), and of middle-agents model (*right*)

picture) in helping agents to locate service providers, giving support for processing agent capabilities, service descriptions, and semantic inter-operation between agents and systems.

Instead, infrastructures adopting a *tuple-based* coordination model – the most relevant instance of mediated interaction – feature a different approach, which is particularly suited for the coordination of Internet agents [1]. There, agents interact indirectly, via one or more *tuple spaces* – blackboard-like abstractions that also become run-time entities – that agents exploit to communicate, synchronise and cooperate by depositing, retrieving, and reading *tuples* associatively.

Tuple-based coordination infrastructures exploit the coordination model as a middleware to enable interactions between service users and providers: here, service providers are special-purpose agents that wrap legacy services in order to enable other agents to access the tuple spaces in a mediated, ruled fashion (Figure 2, left picture). A notable example of these systems is PageSpace [3].

By intrinsically decoupling service users from service providers both temporarily and spatially, this approach points out the need to explicitly model not only agents, but also the medium that makes interaction possible – the *coordination medium*. The infrastructure is then asked to play a central role, since it is now responsible for dynamically supporting and handling the tuple spaces as fundamental run-time abstractions.

2.2   From Coordination Media to Coordination Artifacts

Programmable coordination media constitute the evolution of the above approach towards the notion of *coordination artifacts*, that is, run-time entities specifically designed to provide the designed coordination services [4]. A coordination artifact is set up by the infrastructure and programmed so as to embed the coordination laws and the constraints needed by the agent society to share

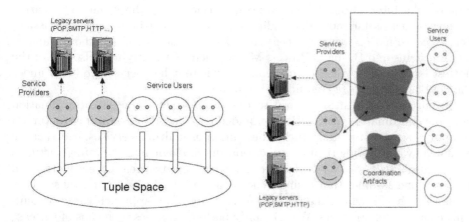

Fig. 2. Integrating services via a tuple-based model (*left*), and via a model based on coordination artifacts (*right*)

and concurrently use it to perform the required social tasks, so that the agent collectivity can accomplish its global goals.

Indeed, mediated interaction and artifacts for supporting coordination activities are fundamental notions in several disciplines and theories concerning cooperative work in complex societies, such as CSCW and Activity Theory [4]: our bet is that they should be effective also for managing coordination complexity in agent societies. *Tuple centres*, described more in detail below when presenting the TuCSoN infrastructure, are a typical example of programmable coordination medium – and, therefore, of coordination artifact.

Coordination artifacts represent the physical embodiment that make it possible to interact with the environment in order to achieve a given goal: in the service-oriented context of this paper, the goal is to access services. Such artifacts are not only access enablers – that is, 'bridges' between service users and providers: they also embed the 'social intelligence' that can rule and amplify how service users exploit services (Figure 2, right picture). Depending on the model expressiveness, these approaches allow the coordination burden to be spread and dynamically balanced in a flexible way: in particular, moving such burden from service providers onto coordination artifacts, where it conceptually belongs. Moreover, encapsulating specific coordination laws inside artifacts leads to engineering advantages in the management of coordination policies – both in terms of incremental evolution and refinement, dynamism (if artifacts are dynamically modifiable), and reuse.

3   Service Integration and Orchestration upon TuCSoN

Engineering services upon an agent coordination infrastructures leads to face one of the most challenging issues in service-oriented computing: service coordination. In fact, the engineering of a service-based complex system typically requires the integration of heterogeneous services into the same coordination context, which is far more demanding than just facing interoperability issues. Service coordination has long been studied in the context of Workflow Management Systems and Business Process Management: currently it is also one of the hottest issues in the Web Services context, where it has been introduced under the notions of *choreography* and *orchestration*.

In our approach, it is natural to design and develop service coordination onto the coordination abstractions provided by a coordination infrastructure: a composite service, requiring the orchestration of multiple services, can then be obtained by embedding the necessary coordination logic into the infrastructure's coordination artifacts. So, in this Section we present two reference architectural patterns: one assumes that a single coordination artifact is used for all services, while the other discusses the possible advantages of an approach based on multiple coordination artifacts. We exemplify both approaches by means of the case study presented in the following Subsections. Since, for the sake of concreteness, we refer to the TuCSoN coordination infrastructure, some fundamentals about TuCSoN coordination artifacts (tuple centres) are first given.

3.1   The TuCSoN Agent Coordination Infrastructure

TuCSoN is an infrastructure providing services for the specification and enactment of coordination in Multi-Agent Systems (MAS) [5]. Services are embodied in tuple centres, that are design / runtime coordination abstractions made available by the infrastructure in order to enable and govern agent interaction [6].

Tuple centres are *programmable* tuple spaces – sort of reactive, logic-based blackboards – that agents access by writing, reading, and consuming *tuples* – ordered collections of heterogeneous information chunks – via simple communication operations (*out, rd, in*), which access tuples associatively. While the behaviour a tuple space in response to communication events is fixed, the behaviour of a tuple centre can be tailored to the application needs by defining a set of *specification tuples* expressed in the ReSpecT language [6], which define how a tuple centre should react to incoming/outgoing communication events. Tuple centres can then be seen as general-purpose customisable coordination artifacts, whose behaviour can be dynamically specified, forged and adapted so as to automate the co-ordination stage among agents [4]. Moreover, from the topology viewpoint, tuple centres are collected in TuCSoN coordination nodes, spread over the network.

So, coordinating services upon the TuCSoN infrastructure means to exploit tuple centres both to represent service requests and result (as well as any related parameter, argument, or request-related data) as suitable logic tuples, and to embed the coordination rules needed to glue services together and build the new integrated services. The rest of this Section discusses some case studies.

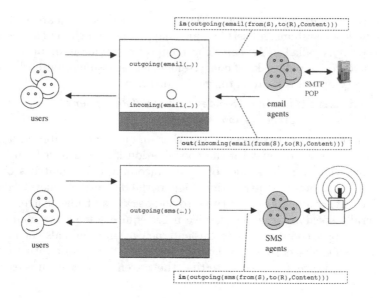

Fig. 3. The email and SMS services discussed in the reference case study

3.2   The Reference Case Study

The reference case study considers two independent services, an email service and an SMS message service. The email service is built around a tuple centre and two agents responsible for sending and receiving emails, respectively: to do so, they exploit the usual infrastructures and protocols. Analogously, the SMS service refers to its tuple centre and exploits an agent for sending SMS away (SMS reception is not considered): again, such an agent performs its task exploiting existing infrastructures and protocols.

In order to highlight service orchestration, let us keep technical details to a minimum, assuming that an email message is represented by a tuple such as `email(from(S),to(R),Content)`, incoming mails as `incoming(email(...))`, and outgoing mails as `outgoing(email(...))`; analogously, short messages could be represented as `sms(from(S),to(R),Content)`.

TuCSoN agents can then send an email or a short message by just emitting a suitable `outgoing(...)` tuple in the proper tuple centre, and read incoming mails by consuming `incoming(...)` tuples from such tuple centre (see Figure 3 for a sketch of the architecture). The following composite service, despite its simplicity, enables us discuss two architectural patterns that apply also in more complex and general cases:

"Send a short message to a given number X
each time an agent/user A receives an email from B"

3.3   Case A: One Tuple Centre for All Services

In this first architectural pattern (Figure 4), which is adequate to small and relatively-closed systems, all services are mapped onto a single tuple centre: let us suppose it is called `services`. The composite service is mapped onto such tuple centre, too: for the sake of concreteness, let us assume that each automatic SMS delivery option is represented by a tuple like

automatic_sms(from(*MailSender*), to(*SMSRecipient*),
number(*PhoneNumber*))

Now, composing these two services together amounts at suitably programming the tuple centre behaviour with the coordination law shown in Figure 4 (*top*): as a result, whenever the sender of a new incoming email matches one of the registered *MailSender*s, the reaction triggers the delivery of a new SMS, adding a suitable `outgoing(sms(...))` tuple to the `services` tuple centre.

Generally speaking, the new service may require some extra computational task, beyond pure coordination: to this end, new agents could also be introduced, along with suitable coordination laws to integrate their work with the existing system. For instance, let us suppose that the system specification is extended as follows:

"Send a short message to a given number X each time an agent/user A receives from B an email *whose content concerns information C*"

To match this requirement, a new *Content Checker* agent can be assumed to be added to the system, to check mail content: we assume that the `match` tuple is added to the tuple centre only if the check is positive. Consequently, the automatic SMS delivery option can be now represented by a tuple like:

ext_automatic_sms(from(*MailSender*), to(*SMSRecipient*),
Content, number(*PhoneNumber*))

The corresponding reaction (Figure 4, *bottom*), therefore, now activates such an agent, which in turn reacts by inserting a new `outgoing(sms(...))` tuple when appropriate.

3.4   Case B: Multiple Tuple Centres for Multiple Services

The second architectural pattern maps each service onto a separate tuple centre (which can possibly belong to a different TuCSoN node): accordingly, the new composite service can be mapped onto one further tuple centre, separate from the tuple services used to represent the single services. This raises the problem of how to link the individual services (and tuple centres) with the tuple centre that embeds the coordination rules. Two main possibilities exist for this purpose:

– exploiting the *linkability* property of ReSpecT tuple centres, i.e. the capability of relating the coordination flow of distinct coordination artifacts without interposing agents;

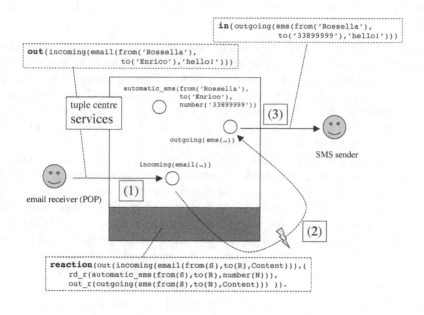

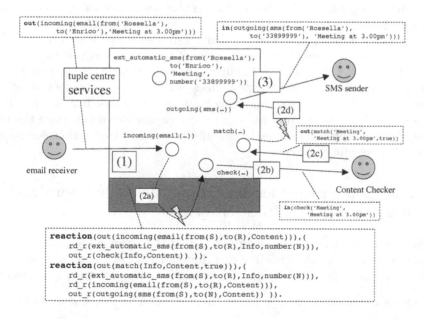

Fig. 4. Integrating and coordinating email and SMS services *(top)* and extending the coordinated service *(bottom)*. Details are given in the text

– generalising the above simple architecture by including new agents acting as bridges between the tuple centre used for service coordination and the individual services.

As shown in Figure 5 (*top*), the reference case study now maps onto three tuple centres: one for each individual service (email_service and sms_service), and another (services) for gluing the composite service. In this context, the linkability property – achieved by means of the out_tc ReSpecT primitive, which enables a reaction in tuple centre *TcA* to emit a tuple into another tuple centre *TcB* – is exploited to notify a 'target' tuple centre about an event occurred in a separate 'source' tuple centre, by means of a reaction chain.

The email_service tuple centre is then programmed so that, whenever a tuple is inserted in email_service, a suitable incoming tuple is also emitted in the services tuple centre. In turn, the behaviour of the services tuple centre is extended (beyond the reactions already discussed in the previous Subsection) with a new reaction that inserts a suitable outgoing(sms(...)) tuple in the sms_service tuple centre whenever an incoming tuple appears in services.

An alternative architecture (Figure 5, *bottom*) could instead exploit agents as bridges, avoiding the need to extend the behaviour of the two tuple centres of individual services. In this case, the link among tuple centres would be achieved by two agents: one to reify the arrival of a new email (read from the email_service tuple centre) by producing a suitable tuple in the services tuple centre, another to transfer the request of sending a short message (the tuple outgoing(sms(...))) from tuple centre services to the tuple centre sms_service.

Generally speaking, this second architecture seems well suited to situations where, for whatever reason, the behaviour of the single services' tuple centres should not be altered; otherwise, the first approach seems to offer a more natural way to model the system, in that it does not force the introduction of new agents for the sole purpose of managing coordination issues. Indeed, this choice promotes a clean architecture from the coordination viewpoint, since the rules to be added are specifically aimed at manifesting some coordination aspects into some other coordination flow.

4   Case Study: Engineering Some Messaging Services upon the TuCSoN Infrastructure

Given the coordination framework defined in the previous Sections, we now discuss more in detail the design of each individual service upon a set of agents and a TuCSoN tuple centre. Quite clearly, the following are basic requirements:

– agents encapsulate the specific competence and tasks required to perform the service;
– the tuple centre works on the one side, as the user interface to access the service; on the other side, as the coordination artifact gluing together the single agent activities that realise the service.

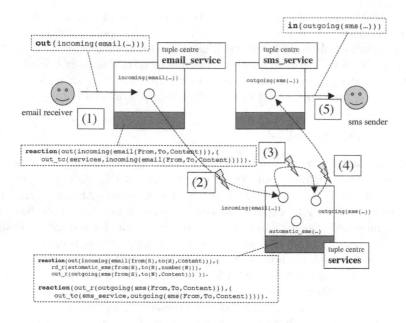

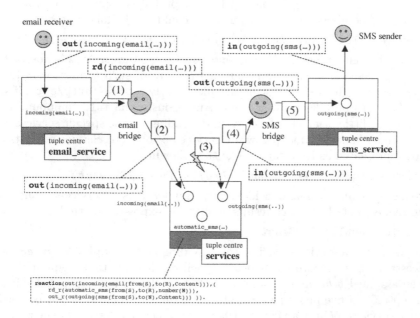

Fig. 5. Coordination with multiple tuple centres: using reaction linkability *(top)* and agents acting as bridges *(bottom)*

The service is designed as a social task, where agents are responsible for the individual activities that the coordination artifact glues together, trying to pursue the service goal. Also, as the user interface to access the service, the tuple centre can be used also to embed and enact the coordination policy ruling possible dependencies among multiple users, such as their concurrent access.

So, designing service users and providers means to define their behaviour in an information-driven way, in terms of action sequences to add, remove, read (logic) tuples to/from tuple centres, according to a pre-defined ontology.

4.1   The Service Model

Enabling each agent to trigger any kind of service by just adding/removing the proper information to/from some tuple centre implies the ability to perform the service indirectly, transparently to any service-specific technical detail. This makes it easier not only to exploit the single services, but also to orchestrate them in an integrated fashion. However, it obviously calls for a common design approach with respect to *(i)* how to represent user information, service requests and service results, and *(ii)* how to actually trigger service execution.

In order to represent user-related information, an effective approach consists of introducing the notion of *profile*. A profile is conceptually a named record of coherent information, which provides all the necessary information for accessing a given service, and possibly other complementary information regarding preferences and similar items. In our context, a profile is represented as a tuple; a structure general-enough for our purposes could be the following:

    user_profile(*ServiceName*, *ProfileName*, info(...))

where, in the general case, all arguments are Prolog terms. At this abstraction level, we prescind from the actual inner structure of such terms: for instance, *ServiceName* might well be a structure like 'mail/pop' or 'http/get', if sub-protocols are to be taken into account. Analogously, the info compound term could include little or much information, depending on the specific service: typical items may be user name, password, service options, etc. Service requests can also be represented as logic tuples, like the following:

    service_request(*ServiceName*, *ProfileName*, ID, *What*)

where ID is a unique numeric identifier, and *What* is a service-specific term giving request details. Service results could then expressed by tuples like:

    service_result(ID, *Result*)

where *Result* is a service-specific term providing result details. *ServiceName* is unnecessary, since ID already associates each result tuple to its request.

The assumed *behavioural ontology* – that is, the correct agent behaviour – is conceptually a five-phase process, although some of them may not be needed for some services: *(1)* get a new identifier for the new request, *(2)* deposit in the proper tuple centre all the information needed to perform the desired service – once again, represented as suitable logic tuples, *(3)* manifest the request by depositing a suitable `service_request` tuple, *(4)* retrieve the result by consuming the corresponding `service_result` tuple, and *(5)* read the new information possibly generated as a side effect of the service. Translating these steps into tuple centre operations, we get:

```
in(service_request_id(ID))
... series of out operations ...
out(service_request(ServiceName, ProfileName, ID, What))
in(service_result(ID, Result))
... series of rd/in operations ...
```

In the first operation, *ID* is a Prolog variable, which is bound each time to a new unique identifier, automatically generated by the infrastructure (a suitably programmed tuple centre) in response to this kind of *in* operation.

4.2   The Mail Service

The user profile for the mail service must provide the information to enable the service agent to log into the SMTP or the POP server: so, its `info` term should include at least the user name and password, and possibly other relevant options. Since the mail service actually consists of two sub-services – the SMTP service for mail sending, and the POP service for mail check – the user profile pattern could be specialised as follows:

```
user_profile(mail/pop, ProfileName,
             info(host(Host), user(User), pwd(Pwd),
             options([...]) ))
user_profile(mail/smtp, ProfileName,
             info(host(Host), user(User), pwd(Pwd),
             options([...]) ))
```

This enables a user to define multiple profiles in order to access different accounts, perhaps on different hosts, and/or with a different set of preferences.

In the perspective of easing the definition of message elaboration rules, which can easily involve header fields such as sender, receiver, subject, etc., representing a whole message as a single tuple could be counterproductive. So, we decided to separate information, using two tuple templates – one for message headers, and another for the corresponding message bodies. The correspondence between header and content is maintained by the same unique identifier that links request tuples with the corresponding response tuples. As a result, tuples representing a check mail request could be:

```
service_request(mail, ProfileName, ID, check_mail(TargetTC))
```

and analogously for mail sending:

```
service_request(mail, ProfileName, ID, send_mail(TargetTC))
```

where *TargetTC* is the tuple centre for storing the checked messages, or taking the messages to be sent, respectively.

According to the behavioural ontology, before outputting such a tuple, the necessary information must be inserted into the proper tuple centre. For mail check, no such information is needed, so step *(2)* of the agent behaviour is void; for mail sending, instead, the necessary information consists of the message header and body. Conversely, sending mail produces no specific information other than the operation's own result, so step *(5)* of the agent behaviour is void, while mail check does produce information – the retrieved messages – again calling for a suitable representation of message headers and bodies.

Since the very nature of a message is the same for both mail check and mail send, a single and uniform representation of header and body is advisable, and could take the following form:

```
mail_header(ID, MsgID, sender(Sender), recipient(Recipient),
            subject(Subject), cc(RecipientList))
mail_body(ID, MsgID, 'content-type'(MIMEtype), content(Content))
```

Here, *MsgID* is used to uniquely identify each message inside a single check mail operation: it has no special meaning for mail sending. If desired, however, the retrieved messages could be enriched with extra information, such as the original message time-stamp, priority, or other. So, the agent awaiting such messages should perform something like:

```
TargetTC ? rd(mail_header(ID, MsgID, ...))
TargetTC ? rd(mail_body(ID, MsgID, ...))
```

The above fields intentionally correspond to the XML tags defined by the XML Mime Transformation Protocol (XMTP) for mail handling [7], so as to ease future mappings towards an XML-based representation and to follow the current standards. Here is an example of a checked mail message:

```
mail_header(23, 1, sender('goofy@hotmail.com'),
       recipient('me@here.org'), subject('Here I am!'),
       date('Wed Oct 23, 2002'), cc(none))
```

while the corresponding typical content tuple could be:

```
mail_body(23, 1,
       'content-type'('text/plain; charset=us-ascii'),
       content('Hello World!'))
```

Special care is needed for MIME-multipart messages, whose content is not pure text, but may include attachments. Following the above principles of separation of concerns and information decoupling, such messages are represented by two distinct content tuples, identified by the same numeric identifier and different content types: the tuple whose `'content-type'` field is `'text/plain'` reports the message text, while the other describes the attachment in terms of its content-type and name of the file where it has been stored; by convention, the `content` field in this tuple is set to the constant atom `file`.

It should be noted that, unlike any other information, the decoded attachment is *not* stored in tuple centres, both because they currently do not support persistency and because users typical expect to find the attached filed stored somewhere on their disk. We plan, however, to provide a file system-like abstraction in TuCSoN in the future. Such a 'hybrid' solution is common to the

FTP services described below, too: currently, attachments are stored in the interface agent's working folder. For instance, a typical message with an attached image is represented by the two content tuples below:

```
mail_body(18, 3, content-type('text/plain'),
    content('See this') )
mail_body(18, 3,
    content-type('application/octet-stream; name="Flower.gif"'),
    content(file) )
```

Generalising, N attachments imply N tuples of the second type, one for each attached file, and one single tuple of the first type.

As an aside, it should be noted that, apart from the checked mail case, no date or time fields are included: in fact, a distributed system can not have a universally-valid clock, so only the tuple centre that stores a given service request or service result tuple can assign a meaningful time stamp.

4.3   The File Transfer Service

The file transfer service follows analogous design criteria. Service request can now be specialised as follows:

```
service_request(ftp, ProfileName, ID,
    transfer(from(Host1, FileName1), to(Host2, FileName2),
    priority(Priority)))
```

These tuples provide an abstract specification of the desired file transfer: in principle, *Host1* and *Host2* can be *any* host where the TuCSoN-based messaging services are available, thus allowing the specification of remote-to-remote file transfers, that do not include the local host. In this context, file *upload* from the local host, and file *download* to the local host are special cases, which can be easily obtained by setting either *Host1* or *Host2* to localhost, respectively. *FileName1* and *FileName2* are then the local / remote absolute names of the transferred file in case of uploading, and the remote / locale names when downloading, respectively.

The drawback of such a high abstraction level is that, having only the 'file transfer' notion, there is no explicit representation of the FTP concepts of *getting* and *putting* a file, which makes it impossible to define specialised user profiles for these sub-protocols. If this is a desired feature, the following representation could be alternatively adopted:

```
service_request(ftp, ProfileName, ID,
    get(from(Host, FileName), as(LocalFileName),
    priority(Priority)))
```

which allows a user profile such as:

```
user_profile(ftp/get, ProfileName,
            info(host(Host), user(User), pwd(Pwd))
```

and the same for **put**. Of course, the price is that remote-to-remote file transfers can no longer be specified. Whatever the choice, the service result tuple may have

Result bound either to a suitable `error` term, or to something representing the operation success. Secure FTP (SFTP) requests could be handled in the same way, too. For instance, assuming that the file `llncs.dem` is stored on the Springer site in the `/pub/tex/latex/llncs/latex2e` folder, the request to download it as `llncs_demo.txt` could be expressed as follows:

```
service_request(ftp, myProfile, 13,
    transfer(from('ftp.springer.de',
                  '/pub/tex/latex/llncs/latex2e/llncs.dem'),
             to(localhost, '/llncs_demo.txt'), priority(high))
```

When the request is served, the following tuple would be further added:

```
service_result(13, ok)
```

Analogously, the request tuple for requesting the upload of the image file `Map.jpg`, currently in `C:\temp`, to the `pub` folder of the FTP site `deis127`, calling the uploaded file `Italy.jpg`, would look like:

```
service_request(ftp, 22,
    transfer(from(localhost, 'C:\temp\Map.jpg'),
             to('deis127.deis.unibo.it', 'pub/Italy.jpg'),
    priority(low))
```

Since supporting remote-to-remote file transfer implies a higher complexity, our current prototype adopts the second approach for service requests and user profiles; as for the mail service, the downloaded files are stored in the download agent's working folder, which also works as the base folder for file uploads.

4.4   The Web Browsing Service

The Web browsing service is very similar to the file download, and so are the tuple formats: the only difference is that information about the host and the document name is embedded in the URL, instead of being given as a (*Host, Path*) pair. So, the service request specialises as:

```
service_request(http, ProfileName, ID,
    browse(url(URL, to(LocalFileName))
```

For instance, browsing (the default page of) `www.deis.unibo.it`, calling the file locally `deis.html`, is expressed as:

```
service_request(http, myProfile, 345,
    browse(url('www.deis.unibo.it'), to('/deis.html')))
```

As for the FTP service, HTTPS requests could be handled in the same way, too; again, our current prototype stores the downloaded HTML documents as files in the downloading agent's working folder. However, an interesting alternative would be to consider the browsed documents like incoming mail messages, emphasising their content, rather than their file-based nature: such a scenario could easily be applied by simply replacing the http agent's current behaviour with a mail agent's-like behaviour, introducing a new tuple template, such as `web_content`, for HTML documents' body.

5   Conclusions and Perspectives

In this paper we discussed the characteristics and properties of service-oriented architectures for agent societies engineered on top of the TuCSoN coordination infrastructure: in particular, we focussed on how to exploit the infrastructure services to support service coordination.

The integration of MAS/legacy and the 'agentification' of services are relevant issues in the agent literature, in particular with respect to interoperability aspects (see for instance the FIPA standard effort and the Agent/Semantic Web effort [8]). To our knowledge, agent-based coordination of services has not been considered that deeply, except for some work on basic architectural patterns [9], and recent proposals about Web Service orchestration [10]. Here we discussed these issues in the context of the TuCSoN agent coordination infrastructure, focussing on the impact of its availability on the engineering of services and their coordination.

The availability of coordination artifacts capable to encapsulate and enforce the coordination laws and rules also makes the engineering approach quite different from tuple-space-based approaches and their event-oriented extensions, such as JavaSpaces [11] or TSpaces [12]. In fact, since such approaches do not provide for balancing the coordination burden between agents and coordination media by need, most of the coordination activity must be enacted by the agents themselves.

Our future work will proceed along four main directions:

- *Services use & reuse* – The available services will be exploited and put to test in the context of existing TuCSoN-based systems, such as Workflow Management Systems [13]. We also plan to extend the set of supported services, compiling a catalogue of available agents (services), and test their use in different contexts, so as to evaluate the proposed methodology and architectures.
- *Service organisation* – As described in an article included in this volume [14], TuCSoN has been recently extended to support organisation and control access issues, in synergy with coordination. The extension makes it possible to structure a MAS in terms of organisation, societies and roles, and support infrastructure service to manage these structures at runtime. An agent can then participate to an organisation and exploit its resources – whose access is always mediated by tuple centres – by playing some role inside it. The roles define the access control policy with respect to the organisation resources, that is, the actions that agents are allowed to perform, their perceptions, the interaction protocols they are allowed to adopt, etc. Such an extension impacts also the service-oriented architecture discussed in this paper, since it offers the possibility to model service organisation and access control. Part of our future work will then be focussed on integrating the basic service model presented here with the role-base support provided by the infrastructure; in this way, we mean to exploit the access control capability provided by the infrastructure to model and enact some forms of access control to services, which is an important security issue of service-oriented computing [15].

— *Web service integration* – Web services play a fundamental role as a standard technology in service-oriented architectures. Accordingly, current work is also being devoted to interfacing TuCSoN with Web Services, making it possible for TuCSoN agents to access any Web Service by simply interacting with a tuple centre, following the philosophy of our approach: a prototype implementation, limited to web services using only primitive types as their invocation arguments, is already available.

— *Web service orchestration* – The integration of Web Services with our architecture opens the interesting possibility of exploiting the coordination approach discussed in this paper for supporting Web Service choreography and orchestration [16]. In particular, tuple centres can be naturally used to implement orchestration engines, which are the core components of Web Orchestration architecture, responsible for Web services coordination: in fact, high-level specification used to describe Web services coordination, such as BPEL4WS or BPML, can be automatically translated into a suitable ReSpecT specification and enacted by tuple centres. A similar approach proved also effective in the context of Workflow Management Systems, where tuple centres have been used to model workflow engines [13]. So, since organisation, coordination and security are hot research issues in the Web services context, we plan to explore the integration of these aspects, which are uniformly supported by the TuCSoN infrastructure, also in a standard and mainstream technology such as Web services.

In our vision, the above investigations and extensions are the base to design a collaborative working environment involving humans as well as agents and (legacy) services, framed in the same organisation / coordination / security context.

References

[1] Ciancarini, P., Omicini, A., Zambonelli, F.: Coordination technologies for Internet agents. Nordic Journal of Computing **6** (1999) 215–240 228, 229, 230

[2] Decker, K., Sycara, K., Williamson, M.: Middle-agents for the internet. In: Proceedings of the 15th International Joint Conference on Artificial Intelligence, Nagoya, Japan (1997) 229

[3] Ciancarini, P., Tolksdorf, R., Vitali, F., Rossi, D., Knoche, A.: Coordinating multiagent applications on the www: a reference architecture. IEEE Transaction on Software Engineering **24** (1998) 362–375 230

[4] Ricci, A., Omicini, A., Denti, E.: Activity Theory as a framework for MAS coordination. In Petta, P., Tolksdorf, R., Zambonelli, F., eds.: Engineering Societies in the Agents World III. Volume 2577 of LNCS. Springer-Verlag (2003) 96–110 230, 231, 232

[5] Omicini, A., Zambonelli, F.: Coordination for Internet application development. Autonomous Agents and Multi-Agent Systems **2** (1999) 251–269 232

[6] Omicini, A., Denti, E.: From tuple spaces to tuple centres. Science of Computer Programming **41** (2001) 277–294 232

[7] Borden, J.: XML MIME Transformation Protocol. www.openhealth.org (1998) 240

[8] Hendler, J.: Agents and the semantic web. IEEE Intelligent Systems (2001) 243
[9] Hayden, S., Carrick, C., Yang, Q.: Architectural design patterns for multi-agent coordination. In: Proc. Int'l. Conf. on Agent Systems – Agents'99. (1999) 243
[10] Paolucci, M., Srinivasan, N., Sycara, K., Nishimura, T.: Towards a semantic choreography of web services: from WSDL to DAML-S. In: Proceedings of the International Conference on Web Services, ICWS '03, June 23 - 26, 2003, Las Vegas, Nevada, USA, CSREA Press (2003) 243
[11] Various: JavaSpaces 2.0 Home Page. wwws.sun.com/software/jini/ (2003) 243
[12] Wyckoff, P., McLaughry, S. W., Lehman, T. J., Ford, D. A.: T Spaces. IBM Journal of Research and Development **37** (1998) 454–474 243
[13] Ricci, A., Omicini, A., Denti, E.: Virtual enterprises and workflow management as agent coordination issues. International Journal of Cooperative Information Systems **11** (2002) 355–379 Special Issue: Cooperative Information Agents – Best Papers of CIA 2001 243, 244
[14] Omicini, A., Ricci, A.: Integrating organisation within a MAS coordination infrastructure (2004) In this volume 243
[15] Bhatti, R., Joshi, J. B. D., Bertino, E., Ghafoor, A.: Access control in dynamic xml-based web-services with x-rbac. In Zhang, L. J., ed.: Proceedings of the International Conference on Web Services, ICWS '03, June 23 - 26, 2003, Las Vegas, Nevada, USA, CSREA Press (2003) 243–249 243
[16] Peltz, C.: Web Service Orchestration and Choreography. IEEE Computer (2003) 46–53 244

Formalizing the Reusability of Software Agents

Federico Bergenti

AOT Lab
Parco Area delle Scienze 181/A, 43100 Parma, Italy
bergenti@ce.unipr.it

Abstract. Since its conception, software engineering has been proposing various techniques and technologies addressing the problem of maximizing the reusability of software. The leading edge of such a research is component-based software engineering. This paper reviews agents and multiagent systems from the point of view of reusability and it provides a formalization of reusability that exploits some very basic agent-oriented concepts. In particular, we move from the lesson learned in component-based software engineering and we define a topmost level of reusability in terms of two long-debated concepts: semantic composability and semantic extensibility. Then, we formally define such concepts through goal delegation, and finally we discuss how a concrete, yet simple, agent model can approximate them.

1 Introduction

Agent-Oriented Software Engineering (AOSE) [[13]] has long been advocated as a revolutionary discipline capable of improving significantly the quality of various aspects of the software development process (see, e.g., [[23]]), thus bringing valuable improvements to the software itself. Adaptability and flexibility are just two classic examples of the benefits that agents would bring to the development of complex software systems. Unfortunately, there is a general feeling that AOSE and agent-based technologies are still confined in research departments and that deployed agent-based systems are rare exceptions. We believe that one reason for this is that there is not yet an agreement on what are the concrete advantages of agent-based technologies over more mature technologies like, e.g., distributed objects. In this paper we show formally the advantages in terms of reusability of agent-based technologies. This does not represent the final answer to the question of understanding the advantages of the use of agent-based technologies; nevertheless it provides a concrete principle for choosing agents when reusability is a desired feature.

Since the first public release of FIPA specifications [[8]], researchers clearly saw the possibility of using agents as an advanced form of software components capable of exhibiting interesting characteristics, e.g., automatic reasoning and goal-directed behavior. In addition, the transport mechanism that FIPA choose to support interoperability between agents, i.e., a CORBA interface, emphasized the strong relationship between agents and software components. This relationship suggests that

A. Omicini, P. Petta, and J. Pitt (Eds.): ESAW 2003, LNAI 3071, pp. 246–257, 2004.
© Springer-Verlag Berlin Heidelberg 2004

agents could be adopted as reusable units of software and the reasonable expectation is that they should exhibit, at least, the same properties of software components.

Reusability can be seen from different perspectives because there are a number of different types of artifact that developers would like to reuse. In the ideal world, any artifact that the developer realizes during the development of a complex software system could be reused within the same system or within other (similar) systems. For example, the classic GoF patterns [[10]] are instances of reusable pieces of architectures. In this paper we are mainly interested in reusing a particular type of artifact that the developer always has to deal with during the realization of any software system: units of executable code. It is quite common for a developer to try to reuse units of executable code that s/he developed, and from a rather superficial point of view, the meaning of the word reusability is associated only with the reuse of units of executable code. This is the case, e.g., of dynamically linked libraries or, more generally, of software components. Actually, there is no agreed definition of what a software component is, but all available definitions explicitly connect components with the intent of building reusable units of executable code.

This restriction of the broad meaning of reusability is not yet sufficient to deal easily with the reusability of agents because, generally speaking, an agent is a complex part of a software system, and it is not clear if and how it is associated with units of executable code. In this paper we take the following (somehow interrelated) assumptions to provide a generic connection between agents and units of executable code:

1. The agent is the unit of reuse, i.e., agents are the atomic parts of an executable system that are meant to be reused;
2. The agent model that we adopt for our study is minimal, i.e., all of its characteristics are justified taking into account reusability only.

Under these assumptions, we can assume a sort of one-to-one mapping between agents and units of executable code, and this is sufficient to allow for a study of the intrinsic properties of reusability of agents and for a direct comparison between agents and software components. To achieve these objectives, we first address the problem of understanding which is (if any) the topmost level of reusability that we might expect from a development technology. Then, we show that agents approximate such a topmost level better than components.

The rest of this paper is organized as follows: the following section formalizes the two key concepts of reusability that we already mentioned, i.e., composability and extensibility. Section 3 shows how such concepts can be approximated in a concrete agent model, and finally section 4 outlines some discussions our results.

2 Semantically Reusing Agents

Since the beginning of computer science, reusability has been considered one of the main properties of a development technology. First procedures, and then classes, were a direct response to the need of creating reusable units of executable code to, e.g.,:

1. Speed-up the realization of new systems;
2. Ensure the quality of systems that are realized though the composition of a number of readymade units.

Component-based software engineering (CBSE) [[20]] proposes extensions of objects, e.g., JavaBeans [[21]], .NET components [[7]] and CORBA components [[18]], as a final answer to the need of reusable units of software. Such components are the units of reuse that the developer assembles to realize a complete system. They are interoperable across networks and (possibly) languages and operating systems, to give the developer the maximal freedom on the deployment of his/her systems.

The long-pursued dream of CBSE is about the following ideas:

1. Commercial Off-The-Shelf (COTS) components, i.e., components that are available in a public market and that are assembled to create a value-added system. The quality and the cost of the system basically depend on the quality and costs of each single COTS component. Market forces should help decreasing costs while increasing the quality of available components.
2. Automatic assembly, i.e., the possibility of lowering the cost of the process of assembly of components through the use of automatic techniques. The quality and cost of the assembly process directly depend on the quality and cost of the available technologies for automatic assembly.

The use of COTS components combined with automatic assembly can lower the cost of a component-based system down to the direct investments related to each single component, summed with the cost of the technology for automatic assembly. Similarly, the quality of the system increases accordingly to the quality of each single component and of the technology for automatic assembly.

CBSE has already explored most of the peculiarities related to building a system in terms of assembled components, and it identified three concepts that any technology meant to improve extensibility and composability should take into account: semantic interoperability, semantic composability and semantic extensibility. We review such concepts here and we exploit some very basic agent-oriented concepts to provide a formal definition to them. It is worth noting that a formal definition of such concepts is lacking in the literature on CBSE.

The assumptions we mentioned in the introduction of this paper provides the very basic starting point for reviewing such three concepts from an agent-oriented standpoint. Moreover they allow shifting the focus from a general (but ungrounded) problem of maximizing reusability of agents toward a more specific (and grounded) problem of maximizing extensibility and composability of agents. We follow the results obtained in CBSE, and we assume that maximal reusability can be obtained through maximal:

1. Composability of agents, i.e., maximal possibility of composing agents freely (and possibly automatically);
2. Extensibility of agents, i.e., maximal possibility of extending the features of an agent without breaking the reusability of the multiagent system that contains it.

Concentrating on composability and extensibility rather than on a more general and abstract problem of reusability is not a limitation because modeling a system in terms of extensible and composable units is always preferable [[22]]. Moreover, this gives us the possibility of comparing the result of our work with similar results obtained in CBSE.

2.1 Semantic Interoperability

The literature on software components have explored the problem of semantic interoperability in many ways, and recently also the agent community has begun investigating the subject. For example, the recent work on the characterization of the capabilities of Web Services [[15]] draws along the lines of established results (see, e.g., [[12]]). Strangely enough, there is no agreed definition on what semantic interoperability is and some variants of this concept are available in the literature with different names, even if this name has already been around for a while [[11]].

The idea of semantic interoperability comes from a reasonable extension of syntactic interoperability, i.e., the sort of interoperability that CORBA and specifications with similar aims (e.g., DCOM and Java RMI) provide. These specifications allow components to exchange messages and they provide an agreed syntax for such messages. The semantics of the exchanged messages is implicit; e.g., the semantics of a call to a method of a CORBA interface is implicitly defined as: the call to the method actually causes the execution of body of the method (even if we recognize that the meta-object protocol can come into play here [[14]]). Nothing is said on the concrete outcome of the call, i.e., what will happen to the world surrounding the object that executed the body of the method after such an execution is completed. This outcome is considered application specific and it relies completely on the developer, whose responsibility is to read the documentation of the interface for deciding when and how to call the method.

Syntactic interoperability inhibits automatic assembly of components because a client component has no means to reason on the effects of the calls it may decide to perform on the methods of a service provider. Semantic interoperability is about extending the interface of a component with an explicit formalization of the outcome of a call to a method in order to allow a client autonomously deciding when and how to invoke each method of this interface.

What we have just described can be applied to agents if we concur that invoking a method on a component is somehow similar to asking to an agent to perform an action. Under this assumption, we can exploit the characteristics of agents to go deeper into the subject and we can formalize semantic interoperability in more general terms. Formally, we can define semantic interoperability as follows:

Definition (Semantic Interoperability, Client Standpoint) Given two agents C and $S \in acquaintance_C$, they are said to be semantically interoperable if and only if:

$$\forall g : G_Cg, G_Cdone(delegate\_to(C, S, g)) \Rightarrow K_SG_Cdone(delegate\_to(C, S, g))$$

where $delegate\_to(C, S, g)$ is a sort of abstract action of C whose outcome is: K_CG_Sg.

This definition states that if (at some point in time) an agent C wants to achieve g, and it wants to delegate such a goal to S, then S will know of such a desire. In this way we can easily capture the lack of information loss which is the core of semantic interoperability: if an agent has a goal then it can transmit such a goal to a service provider without any loss of precision. It does not really matter how the goal is communicated, the only important result of the communication is the delegation of the goal to the service provider.

This definition of semantic interoperability takes the client standpoint because C is the actual originator of g and nothing is said about S wanting to provide its services to a set of possible clients. A similar definition is obviously possible taking the server standpoint, but such a definition is basically equivalent to the one we showed and its discussion would not bring much to the aims of this paper.

An interesting consequence comes from this definition of semantic interoperability: if we consider a multiagent system where agents are only intended to interoperate semantically, then a very basic Agent Communication Language (ACL) containing the *achive* performative only is sufficient for supporting communication. This is not strange at all, because it easily generalizes the available work on ACLs. Let's take the FIPA ACL as an emblematic example: it defines performatives together with feasibility preconditions and rational effects. When an agent receives a message, it can assert that the feasibility precondition holds for the sender and that the sender is trying to achieve the corresponding rational effect. This is basically a rather knotty way to let the receiver know that the sender wanted the receiver to know that the feasibility precondition holds for it and that it is actually bringing about the rational effect. The advantage of using a structured ACL instead of a more natural exchange of representations of goals is that it simplifies the development complex interactions with obtuse agents. Such obtuse agents, i.e., agents with no reasoning capabilities at all, can exploit the performatives of the ACL to trigger the state machine of the interaction protocol that underlies a communicative act. This is what JADE [[2]] and similar platforms provide and basically it falls the communication back to syntactic interoperability.

Achieving semantic interoperability in the technology for implementing multiagent systems is not only a way for improving reusability, it is also a way for possibly promoting optimization. With everyday syntactic interoperability, agents achieve their goals asking to other agents to perform actions, i.e. exploiting task delegation [[6]] in the attempt to achieve their goals. Semantic interoperability exploits goal delegation, which is a more general mechanism. Actually, task delegation is a special case of goal delegation: the delegated goal has the form $done(a)$, i.e., my goal is that, at some time in the future, action a would be completely performed. Task delegation may inhibit cross-optimizations between actions as shown in the following example. Let's consider an agent C with a goal g that needs agent S to perform a_1 and a_2 to achieve it; C would ask to S to perform a_1 and then it would ask to perform a_2. The two requests are not coupled though the underlying idea that C is trying to achieve g, and therefore S could not exploit any possible cross-optimization between a_1 and a_2. If C and S would be semantically interoperable, then, C would simply delegate goal g to S and then S would decide autonomously the way to go, e.g., it would decide to perform a_1 and then a_2. This approach couples a_1 and a_2 through g thus enabling S to perform cross-optimizations between a_1 and a_2.

2.2 Semantic Composability

The assembly of agents to realize a multiagent system is not only a matter of enabling agents communicating in the best way. Another basic need is allowing them to find each other. Semantic interoperability requires $S \in acquaintance_C$, and therefore we need to extend this concept somehow to achieve full semantic composability.

Semantic composability has been studied for quite a long time in the literature of CBSE, starting from well-known results on the composability of objects that researchers that are now active in the community of aspect-oriented programming obtained [[1]]. The basic idea behind semantic composability is that a component should be free to compose the services provided by a set of service providers with no constraints deriving from the problem of locating the right service providers or from any possible mismatch between the interfaces of such service providers and the interfaces that the client expected.

This concept has already been extended to agents [[19]], and we can make it more formal exploiting the same technique that we used for semantic interoperability. We can say that two agents are semantically composable if no constraint is imposed on the way agents delegate goals, or more formally, we can define semantic composability as follows:

Definition (Semantic Composability) Given a set of n agents $MAS = \{A_1, A_2, ..., A_n\}$, they are said to be semantically composable if and only if:

$$\forall C \in MAS, \ \forall g : G_C g, \ \exists A \in MAS : solves_A(g),$$
$$G_C done(delegate(C, g)) \Rightarrow \exists! S \in MAS : solves_S(g), K_S G_C done(delegate\_to(C, S, g))$$

where $solves_A$ are the goals that A can solve and $delegate(C, g)$ is a sort of abstract action of C whose outcome is: $K_C(\exists B \in MAS : G_B g)$.

This definition states that if an agent C has a goal and there is at least an agent A available in the multiagent system capable of achieving such a goal, then if C wants to delegate such a goal, it can perform such a delegation to an agent S with no loss of precision caused by communication. In this way we can capture the lack of information loss that semantic interoperability requires, without the need of requiring C to know S and to desire to delegate its goal to that S. It does not really matter how or to who the goal is communicated, the ultimate result of the composition is that an agent of the multiagent system would achieve the goal for C.

This definition does not require the client to know the service provider prior to the delegation, and it does not guarantee that the chosen service provider would be known after the delegation. This is not incompatible with the common approach of explicitly choosing the service provider: the two approaches are both captured by the definition because the client can identify the service provider of choice in its goal. For example, if an agent C wants S to achieve goal j for it, then the goal that C is bringing about is actually $g=K_SG_CG_Sj$.

It is worth noting that if our agents have an explicit and public representation of G_A and $solves_A$, then semantic composability is just a matter of passing a goal from a client to a service provider, and, in the most general case, this is just a matter of communication. We can exploit a matchmaker agent capable of connecting a client with a service provider, or we can rely on the middleware infrastructure for this. In this last case, e.g., we could exploit a tuple space forwarding all goals from possible clients to possible service providers, or we could rely on a direct message passing that the programmer of the client hardcoded in the program of the client itself.

2.3 Semantic Extensibility

Taking the literature on CBSE into account, we see that reusability is pursued not only by means of composing reusable components, but also by making such components extensible [[5]]. Extensibility provides mainly two possibilities of reuse:

1. Implementation of new components as extensions of available components;
2. Substitution of an existing component with a different one with (possibly) no changes to the rest of the system.

The first approach is traditionally considered the base of object-oriented programming: it supports the creation of new classes of objects by means of inheritance and polymorphism. While this is still a good way to bring about reusability, nowadays the second approach is preferred because it allows reusing entire systems and not only single classes. This so called *framework reusability* relies on the possibility of substituting a component with another component without the rest of the system being aware of such a substitution.

Object-oriented and component-based paradigms achieve framework reusability by means of inheritance and polymorphism as they require that if two components belong to the same class, i.e., if they are of the same type, then they are substitutable. This is obviously not enough and some extensions to such an approach have been already proposed [[16]]. In particular, the main problem of approximating substitutability with type equivalence is that two classes may provide the same methods, but the semantics of such methods, i.e., what they do on the world after their complete execution, may be completely different. In other words, two classes may be structurally identical, but semantically different [[9]].

The idea behind semantic extensibility is that we want to have the possibility of substituting a component with another component extending the features provided by the first component, while preserving the semantics of the operations that clients were able to perform before the substitution. This is a generalization of ordinary type-based inheritance that is everyday practice in class-based programming language like Java.

Taking the agent-oriented mindset and exploiting the formalisms that we have introduced previously in this paper, we can formally define semantic extensibility as follows:

Definition (Semantic Extensibility) Given two agents B and D, we can say that D is a semantic extension of B if and only if:

$$\forall g : solves_B(g) \Rightarrow solves_D(g)$$

This definition states that (at each point in time), what B can solve is also solved by D, i.e., from the point of view of any possible client interested in the services that B may provide, they are substitutable.

Semantic extensibility together with semantic composability maximizes the reusability of agents, at least if we adopt the assumption of considering agents as the atomic units of reuse. Agents are composed freely on the basis of their goals and they can be substituted with other agents with extended capabilities with a guaranteed full reuse of the multiagent system surrounding substituted agents.

3   Approximating the Ideal Model

We believe that agentware [[3]], i.e., software realized through the composition of interacting agents, might bring significant improvement to everyday software practice from the point of view of reusability. In the ideal world, agents are taken from a repository of COTS agents and the multiagent system is composed and reconfigured on the fly to cope with varying conditions and requirements. Unfortunately, the definitions that we introduced in the previous section show that semantic composability and semantic extensibility are asymptotic properties of the development technology and they can only be approximated. In particular, such definitions rely on two sets, $goals_A$ and $solves_A$, that are not computable in the most general case and that seem hard to compute in restricted situations also. A technology for implementing reusable agents and reusable multiagent systems should provide a good way for the developer to approximate such sets. Just as an example, we discuss how the *PARma Agent Development Environment* (*ParADE*) [[4]] implements such approximations.

ParADE is a development framework that we developed to support the realization of reusable agents in Java. Ideally, this framework allows the assembly and reconfiguration of multiagent systems through the use of agents that are taken from a repository of (possibly COTS) agents. Agents are known to the multiagent system by means of a unique identifier and their state is characterized through beliefs and intentions. In detail, a ParADE agent has an internal mental state maintained in terms of:

1. A set of beliefs: closed propositions that the agents beliefs;
2. A set of intentions: open propositions that the agent is bringing about;
3. A set of (add/remove) deduction rules: used to generate and remove entries in the set of beliefs;
4. A set of (add/remove) intention rules: used to generate and remove entries in the set of intentions.

ParADE agents perform actions and each action is associated with an internal representation of pre- and post-conditions, i.e., open propositions that the agent uses internally for bring about its intentions. The means-end reasoning is performed though a simple and non-deterministic planning engine.

In addition to a unique identifier and a mental state, a ParADE agent has capabilities. These are described in terms of what the agent can do, i.e., the possible outcomes of its actions, and how the agent can interact with other agents, i.e., the interaction protocols it supports and the possible roles it can play in the its interaction protocols. Each agent publishes a description of itself to the matchmaker agent that ParADE provides for each multiagent system. This description contains the unique identifier of the agent and the list of its capabilities, i.e., the subset of public actions that the agent can perform together with their pre- and post-conditions.

Agents in a ParADE multiagent system communicate through an ACL and communication allows them to exchange representations of theirs and others beliefs, intentions and capabilities. To this extent, ParADE introduces a FIPA-like ACL with minimalist semantics. Such a language provides an operational means for agents to exchange representations of beliefs, intentions and capabilities. The semantics of the performatives that such a language contains are modeled as the effect that the sender wishes to achieve when sending the message, e.g., the semantics of an agent S informing an agent R of p is: $I_S B_R p$.

The communication between ParADE agents is never explicit, i.e., the programmer has no APIs for sending and receiving ACL messages. Messages are sent exploiting the semantics of the ACL only in response to a new intention. For example, if we recall the semantics of the inform message that we have just shown, agent S sends an *inform* message to agent R with a content p to bring about the goal of making R believe p. This implicit approach to communication has the advantage of decoupling the need, i.e., the intention, with the means, i.e., the act of sending the message, with obvious advantages in terms of reusability.

Isolated messages are not sufficient to allow agents to communicate fruitfully. The classic example is the case of an agent requesting another agent to perform an action. The first problem is that messages are asynchronous: there is no guarantee that the receiver would act in response to a message, i.e., there is no guarantee that the receiver would actually perform the requested action. The second problem is that the semantics of a single message might not be sufficient to express application-specific constraints. The semantics of request message does not impose the receiver to communicate to the sender that the requested action has been actually performed. The sender might hang indefinitely waiting for the receiver to tell it that the action has been performed completely.

In order to support fruitful communication, ParADE provides interaction laws. These are rules that an agent decides to adopt to govern its interactions with other agents. The interaction laws that an agent decides to follow are part of its capabilities and they are published. The interaction laws than an agent may adopt are connected to the possible roles it can play in the multiagent systems, and they may vary over time. With the introduction of precondition and termination condition, interaction laws become an elegant and flexible way to describe interaction protocols.

The ParADE agent model exploits communication in the planning process: if an agent cannot solve a goal on its own, it asks to the matchmaker to find an agent capable of solving the goal for it. If a possible service provider is found, then the action of delegating the goal is scheduled, and an *achieve* message will be sent from the client to the chosen service provider. More formally, ParADE enforces the following behavior rule for any agent $C \in MAS$:

$$\forall g : I_C g, \exists A \in MAS : capable_A g, \exists! S \in MAS : capable_S g \Rightarrow B_S I_C I_S g$$

where $capable_A g$ are the post-conditions that A published to the matchmaker agent that contain g.

The classic approach to implementing rational agents that ParADE exploits is sufficient to approximate semantic composability and semantic extensibility. In particular, let's consider the following approximations:

1. $B_A \approx K_A$: we approximate the knowledge of the agent with what the agent beliefs, i.e., what it deduced from its knowledge of the world;
2. $I_A \approx G_A$: we approximate the set of goals of an agent with the set of the intentions that it calculated from its knowledge of the world and from its rules;
3. $capable_A \approx solves_A$: we approximate the set of goals an agent can solve with the set of post-conditions of its feasible actions.

Such approximation together with the behavior rule that ParADE enforces show how ParADE enforces a reasonable approximation to semantic composability.

ParADE approximates also semantic extensibility because the matchmaker agent hides the identity of service providers and the choice of the right service provider to serve a particular request is performed on the basis of the sets capabilities of each agent in the multiagent system.

4 Conclusions

The creation and further development of AOSE in the last decade has promoted agents as a viable new way to develop complex software systems. AOSE gives to the developer all the flexibility and the expressive power of agents and it helps with the management of the software lifecycle in the attempt to improve the quality of the resulting software products. Exploiting the set of tools that AOSE provides, agents are increasingly being used as atomic building blocks of complex software systems thus emphasizing the strong relation between agents and software components. Even if the AOSE community has not yet found a general agreement on a criterion assisting developers in choosing agents instead of components, the general feeling is that:

1. Agents are more easily tractable than components because, in some way, they are the core of a new system level [[17]] that comprises high-level abstractions and metaphors [[3]];
2. Agents are atomic building blocks that are intrinsically more reusable than components.

Both such topics are of equally remarkable importance to judge on the quality of agents as a development technology. In particular, the importance of the first topic seems somehow obvious today. People started enumerating the benefits of working at a high level of abstraction in the early days of computer science. When computers could only be programmed in assembly language, people felt the urge of higher-level abstractions, e.g., types and procedures. Today, the component-based approach provides high-level abstractions, e.g., messages and events, and any further increase of the level of abstraction seems a significant result. Taking Booch's words into account: *"at any given level of abstraction, we find meaningful collections of entities that collaborate to achieve some higher level view [[5]],"* we can see how the meaningful collection of agent-oriented entities, e.g., beliefs, goals and capabilities, are closer to the human intuition than their component-based counterparts.

Also the importance of the second topic is trivial if we want our agents to be adopted in the realization of real-world systems. Nevertheless, its correctness does not seem so obvious. This is the reason why this paper addresses the problem of understanding the properties of reusability of agents. For this study we adopted the approach of CBSE because it obtained significant result in the past few years and because nowadays it is almost completely accepted. In particular, we constrained the problem of reusability under the assumption that reusability can be obtained in terms of composability and extensibility. This required expressing extensibility and composability in terms of typical agent-oriented concepts and this also gave us the possibility of providing a formal definition to such ideas in terms of goal delegation. It is worth noting that these very basic agent-oriented concepts allowed us to give formal definitions to concepts that were not formally defined yet, mostly because CBSE does not comprise metaphors, like knowledge and goal, with a sufficient expressive power. This suggests that the agent-oriented approach is more suited to discuss these concepts than the more traditional component-based one.

The result of our investigation in the characteristics of reusability of agents is that agents are potentially more reusable than components, even if such an improvement may come at a cost: performances. The use of goal delegation instead of task delegation requires means-end reasoning and therefore we have to deal with the reasonable possibility of implementing slow agents. Fortunately the performances of agents degrade gracefully: we can choose how much reasoning, i.e., how much loss of speed, we want for each and every agent. In particular, we may use reasoning for agents that are likely to be reused in order to exploit semantic composability as much as we can, while we can fallback on reactive agents when we have an urge for speed. This decision criterion seems sound because the more an agent is complex and value-added, the more we want to reuse it and compose it with other agents. Moreover, reactive agents are perfectly equivalent to components and we do not loose anything using the agent-oriented approach instead of the component-based approach.

References

[1]   Aksit, M., Wakita, K., Bosch, J., Bergmans, L., Yonezawa, A.: Abstracting Object-Interactions using Composition-Filters, in Guerraoui, R., Nierstrasz, O., Riveill, M. (Eds.), Object-based Distributed Processing, Springer-Verlag, (1993)

[2]   Bellifemine, F., Poggi, A., Rimassa, G.: Developing Multi-agent Systems with a FIPA-Compliant Agent Framework. Software Practice and Experience 31 (2001) 103–128

[3]   Bergenti, F.: A Discussion of Two Major Benefits of Using Agents in Software Development, Engineering Societies in the Agents World III, LNAI 2577, (2003) 1–12

[4]   Bergenti, F., Poggi, A.: A Development Toolkit to Realize Autonomous and Inter-
        operable Agents. Procs. 5th Int'l. Conf. on Autonomous Agents, (2001) 632–639
[5]   Booch, G.: Object-Oriented Analysis and Design with Applications. Addison-Wesley
        (1994)
[6]   Castelfranchi, C.: Modelling Social Action for AI Agents. Artificial Intelligence 103(1)
        (1998)
[7]   European Computer Manufacturer's Association: Standard ECMA-335, Partition II
        Metadata Definition and Semantics. Available at http://www.ecma.ch
[8]   Foundation   for   Intelligent   Physical   Agents.   Specifications.   Available   at
        http://www.fipa.org
[9]   Fankhauser, P., Kracker, M., Neuhold, E. J.: Semantic vs. Structural Resemblance of
        Classes. ACM SIGMOD RECORD 20(4) (1991) 59–63
[10]   Gamma, E., Helm, R., Johnson, R. and Vlissides, J.: Design patterns, Addison-Wesley,
        1997
[11]   Heiler, S.: Semantic Interoperability. ACM Computing Surveys, 27(2) (1995) 271-273
[12]   Jeng, J-J., Cheng, B. H. C.: Specification Matching for Software Reuse: A Foundation,
        in Procs. ACM SIGSOFT Symposium Software Reusability, ACM Software
        Engineering Note, Aug. 1995
[13]   Jennings, N. R.: On Agent-Based Software Engineering. Artificial Intelligence, 117
        (2000) 277–296
[14]   Kiczales, G., des Rivières, J., Bobrow, D.G.: The Art of the Metaobject Protocol. MIT
        Press (1991)
[15]   McIlraith, S., Martin, D.: Bringing Semantics to Web Services, IEEE Intelligent
        Systems, 18(1) (2003) 90–93
[16]   Meyer, B.: Object-Oriented Software Construction. Prentice-Hall (1997)
[17]   Newell, A.: The Knowledge Level. Artificial Intelligence, 18 (1982) 87–127
[18]   Suhail, A.: CORBA Programming Unleashed. Sams (1998)
[19]   Sycara, K., Widoff, S., Klusch, M., Lu, J.: LARKS: Dynamic Matchmaking among
        Heterogeneous Software Agents in Cyberspace. Int'l. J. Autonomous Agents and Multi-
        Agent Systems, 5, (2002) 173–203
[20]   Szyperski, C.: Component Software: Beyond Object-Oriented Programming. Addison
        Wesley (1998)
[21]   Sun   Microsystems: JavaBeans   Specification: Version   1.1.   Available   at
        http://java.sun.com
[22]   Wegner, P.: Why Interaction is More Powerful than Algorithms. Communications of the
        ACM 40(5) (1997) 80–91
[23]   Wooldridge, M. J., Jennings, N. R., Kinny, D.: The Gaia Methodology for Agent-
        Oriented Analysis and Design. Int'l. J. Autonomous Agents and Multi-Agent Systems 2
        (1) (2000)

A Design Complexity Evaluation Framework
for Agent-Based System Engineering Methodologies

Anthony Karageorgos and Nikolay Mehandjiev

Department of Computation
UMIST
Manchester, M60 1QD, UK
{karageorgos, mehandjiev}@acm.org

Abstract. Complexity in software design refers to the difficulty in understanding and manipulating the set of concepts, models and techniques involved in the design process. Agents are sophisticated software artefacts, associated with a large number of features and therefore Agent-Based System (ABS) engineering methodologies involve considerable design complexity. This paper proposes a framework to evaluate ABS engineering methodologies against a number of criteria related to design complexity. The framework is applied to a number of representative ABS engineering methodologies. The strengths and weaknesses of each methodology with respect to the framework aspects are discussed within the context of a case study of a virtual enterprise combining manufacturing and logistics services. The evaluation results are used to motivate and guide further work in the area.

1 Introduction

Agent-Based Systems (ABSs) can currently be designed based on ad-hoc methodologies, formal methodologies or informal but structured methodologies. In addition, design can be done either statically, before the ABS is deployed, or dynamically on run-time. All existing methodologies have certain weaknesses and involve considerable difficulty in understanding and manipulating the concepts and models needed for the detailed ABS design. This is referred to as *design complexity*.

The term complexity has been given many definitions in the literature and the majority of them are based on the Oxford English dictionary definition, referring to "difficulty in understanding". Software engineering complexity relates to how difficult it is to implement a particular computer system [17]. It is considered that high software complexity results in low software quality [10]. In this work, the focus is on ABS engineering complexity and in particular on that related to ABS design.

The sophisticated structure and properties of software agents increase the complexity inherent in ABS design. For example, designing agents to operate in dynamic and open environments and carry out non-trivial tasks that require maximisation of some utility payoff function involves high design complexity [33].

Decreasing software complexity results in reduced time and cost for development and maintenance, fewer functional errors and increased reusability. Therefore, software metrics researchers often try to predict software qualities based on

A. Omicini, P. Petta, and J. Pitt (Eds.): ESAW 2003, LNAI 3071, pp. 258–274, 2004.
© Springer-Verlag Berlin Heidelberg 2004

complexity metrics [17]. Furthermore, certain factors are associated with lower complexity. For example, reusing design knowledge reduces design complexity allowing designers to work with concepts of larger granularity at higher abstraction levels [1].

Traditional software engineering methodologies have proven unsuitable for engineering ABSs, and this has spawned new methodologies specifically targeting ABSs. These new methodologies involve different degrees of design complexity because of differences in modelling concepts and techniques used. For example, the technique of semi-automating the design process results in lower design complexity [14]. Work on reducing ABS design complexity would therefore benefit from a systematic assessment of ABS engineering methodologies with respect to design complexity, which can lead to identifying issues that would need further improvement. To this end, a framework for evaluating ABS engineering methodologies with respect to design complexity is proposed in this paper.

There are only a few attempts to systematically evaluate ABS engineering methodologies. Evaluations are typically done in the context of a case study in order to identify issues that would justify extending a particular methodology as is the case in [13]. However, such evaluations concentrate only on a small number of issues of interest. In other cases, a systematic framework is proposed, which typically focuses on specific parts of the methodologies, for example the expressiveness [7], or trying to provide a high-level overall evaluation of the methodologies as is the case in [8]. Furthermore, a detailed evaluation framework for comparing ABS engineering methodologies, accompanied with references to existing relevant work, is proposed in [26]. However, none of the existing works focuses on assessing the difficulty involved in designing an agent-based system using a particular methodology, which is the focus of this paper.

To demonstrate the evaluation framework proposed in this paper, seven representative ABS engineering methodologies were evaluated: RAPPID [23], DESIRE [4], Gaia [34], MESSAGE/UML [5], Tropos [6], the Zeus methodology [21] and KARMA [27]. The evaluation results reveal that the majority of the methodologies examined involve high design complexity as they do not consider organisational settings and collective behaviour as first class design constructs, they do not provide systematic support for design heuristics and non-functional aspects, they do not allow work at a high abstraction level and do not support automating parts of the design process. Therefore, further work is required in this direction.

The contents of the paper are as follows. The proposed framework is described in Section 2. Section 3 discusses the results of applying the framework to evaluate a number of representative ABS engineering methodologies. Some issues concerning further research are highlighted in Section 4. Finally, Section 5 concludes the paper.

2   An Evaluation Framework for ABS Design Complexity

The proposed framework was inspired by attempts to discuss the issues involved in ABS design in a systematic manner [11] and it is based on similar work concerning evaluation of object-oriented software engineering methodologies [29], comparison of ABS toolkits [24] and measurement of software complexity [10].

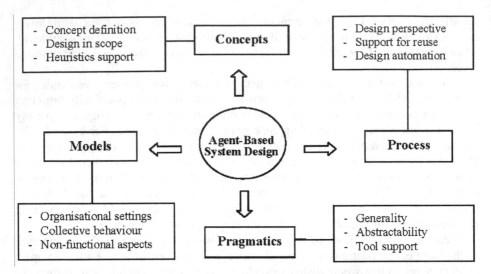

Fig. 1. A framework for assessing the design complexity of ABS engineering methodologies

The framework examines ABS engineering methodologies from four different views, Con*cepts*, *Models*, *Process* and *Pragmatics*, which are summarised in Fig. 1. Each view represents a set of conceptually linked aspects and examines ABS engineering methodologies from a different perspective. For example, the implementation language and the use of standard notations are both related to implementation and hence they should be associated with an implementation-related view.

When assessing an ABS engineering methodology using the proposed framework, a ranking scheme for each aspect is applied. The ranking is based on subjective, qualitative values, for example, low, medium, high. The possible ranking values are discussed together with the different aspects of the framework below. Where appropriate, examples referring to relevant ABS engineering methodologies are provided.

2.1 Concepts

The concepts view concentrates on which modelling concepts are used in each methodology to represent the ABS behaviour. It includes the following aspects:

1. *Concept Definition:* This aspect refers to restrictive premises concerning the agent architecture and the type[1] of agents that can be produced with the methodology. Based on this criterion, an ABS engineering methodology can be characterised as *open, bounded* or *limited (highly bounded)*. A methodology is open if it does not consider a particular agent architecture and does not produce specific agent types, such as Gaia [34]. An example of a methodology bounded to a particular agent architecture is Tropos [6], which assumes only BDI agents.

---

[1]   An agent type is a class of agents with similar capabilities and purpose.

Finally, a methodology limited to specific agent types is RAPPID [23], which considers only *Component Agents* that represent humans and *Characteristic Agents* that represent parts of a product design system. An open methodology is preferable as it can directly produce different agent types which are most appropriate for different application domains and allows implementation using the programming language or agent toolkit of choice. This results in lower design complexity.

2. *Design in Scope:* This aspect refers to whether a methodology includes specific steps and guidelines for the design phase of the ABS engineering lifecycle and can be *true* or *false*. For example, MESSAGE/UML [5] covers only the analysis phase while Tropos [6] covers analysis, design and also part of the implementation. Explicitly supporting the design phase results in lower design complexity.

3. *Heuristics support:* This aspect refers to the explicit support for applying heuristic guidelines and tips when designing the ABS and can be *true* or *false*. Explicit heuristics support involves providing formal techniques that can be used to ensure application of the design heuristics. For example, in KARMA [27] heuristics can be specified as constraints in the STEAM specification language. In contrast, in RAPPID [23] there is no rigorous way for ensuring that design heuristics have been applied. Formal heuristics support results in lower design complexity.

2.2 Models

The *Models* view refers to the models that are used to represent different parts of the ABS or issues of particular interest and the techniques that are used to create and manipulate those models. The *Models* view includes the following aspects of interest:

1. *Organisational settings:* This framework aspect concerns whether organisational settings are considered as first-class design constructs and can be *true* or *false*. For example, in the ABS engineering methodology associated with the Zeus agent toolkit [21] organisational settings are represented by explicit role models in contrast to DESIRE [4] where they are implied by the agent behaviour. Organisational settings should be considered as first class design constructs [22], [35], enabling work in higher abstraction levels and thus lowering the design complexity.

2. *Collective Behaviour:* This aspect refers to whether an approach includes appropriate first-class modelling constructs to represent collective agent behaviour and it can be *true* or *false*. Representation of collective behaviour can be implicit via the individual agent behaviour such as in RAPPID [23]. In can also be explicit, for example, in the Zeus methodology collective behaviour is represented by role models [21]. Collective behaviours should be considered as first class design constructs enabling reasoning at a high abstraction level [15] and hence resulting in lower design complexity.

3. *Non-functional aspects:* This aspect refers to whether non-functional aspects are explicitly considered in the methodology and can be *true* or *false*. Non-functional aspects can be explicitly represented by appropriate modelling constructs, such as

in Tropos [6], or they can be implicitly modelled within individual agent behaviour such as in Gaia [34]. Explicitly modelling non-functional aspects enables work at a higher abstraction level and results in lower design complexity.

2.3 Process

The process view concentrates on the steps that are executed to construct the models discussed in the *Models* view and on techniques that support and assess those steps. In particular, this view is concerned with the following aspects:

1. *Design Perspective:* This aspect refers to the perspective from which each methodology views the ABS design. The perspective can be *top-down, bottom- up* or *both* (top-down and bottom-up), depending on how the design of the ABS progresses. In the top-down perspective, the design models are constructed by refining high-level models of the agent organisation, such as in Gaia [34]. In the bottom-up perspective, design models are progressively composed from existing finer-grain models thus enabling reuse [15]. Supporting both perspectives, as in MESSAGE/UML [5], can help to reduce design complexity.

2. *Support for Reuse:* This aspect refers to whether the methodology supports using previous knowledge in designing an ABS and can be *true* or *false*. Support for reuse involves modelling constructs, techniques and guidelines for the identification, representation, testing and application of reusable knowledge. For example, in the Zeus toolkit methodology [21] there are guidelines for creating, storing and reusing negotiation strategies when specifying agent interactions, whilst in RAPPID [23] there are not such facilities. Support for reuse is a fundamental step towards achieving lower design complexity [1].

3. *Design Automation:* This aspect refers to whether there are formal underpinnings in the specification models of the methodology enabling automation of the design process to a certain extent. Some process steps should definitely be carried out based on the judgement of the human designers, for example the selection of roles in the analysis phase in Gaia [34]. However, other steps could be automated and carried out by a software tool, for example based on formal model transformations [25]. The degree to which the process steps are automated can be characterised as *true* or *false*. For example, the DESIRE [4] design process can be automated, as many steps are formally defined using mathematical techniques, in contrast to RAPPID [23] where there are no formal underpinnings. Automating the design process results in lower design complexity and reduces development effort and errors [1].

2.4 Pragmatics

This view focuses on the pragmatics of each ABS engineering methodology. In other words, this view refers to how practical the methodology is for the design of real-world agent systems. It is concerned with the following aspects:

1. *Generality:* The generality of a methodology refers to the existence of restrictive premises concerning the environment and the application domain that affect the applicability of the methodology and can be characterised as *high, medium* or *low*. High generality means that the methodology can be applied without any significant restrictions, such as Tropos [6]. The generality is medium when there are considerable restrictions but the applicability of the method is still wide. For example, Gaia [34] assumes closed ABSs and small numbers of cooperating agents. In contrast, RAPPID [23] is limited since it can only be applied to design ABSs that will be used to support industrial product design and, therefore, its generality is low. High generality results to lower design complexity since it is easier to apply the methodology in various application domains.

2. *Abstractability:* This aspect refers to whether there is support to enable work at different levels of abstraction which is one of the main factors affecting design complexity [1] and it can be *true* or *false*. For example, role-based methodologies, such as [15], support abstractability since agent behaviour can be specified at both the level of roles and at the level of role characteristics. In contrast, in Tropos [6] this is done only at the agent level and hence Tropos does not support abstractability.

3. *Tool support:* This aspect is concerned with whether there are tools supporting the realisation of the methodology. For example, the Zeus methodology [21] is supported by the Zeus agent building toolkit, which assists the users in designing ABSs. On the other hand, there is no tool support for the Gaia approach [34] and the engineer is responsible for manually creating all the relevant models. The tool support of an approach can be characterised as *true* or *false.* It is preferable for an approach to be supported by CASE tools since this reduces development effort and development errors [17] and automates repetitive tasks [20] increasing the usability of the methodology and resulting to lower design complexity.

It must be noted that some aspects are interrelated. For example, low or limited concept definition is likely to be combined with low or medium generality, as is the case in RAPPID [23]. However, this is not always the case, For example, Tropos [6] is bounded to only BDI agents and it is still applicable in many application domains.

3 A Motivating Case Study Example

To better illustrate the different aspects of the framework we consider a case study involving providing support for cross-organisational business process management in virtual enterprises using agent technology (Fig. 2). An example of such an effort is the MABE research project [28]. The requirements imposed by this case study are used to illustrate the strengths and weaknesses of the seven ABS engineering methodologies evaluated in Section 4.

For the needs of this example we can assume a Virtual Enterprise (VE) consisting of manufacturers, suppliers and logistic service providers, all dispersed throughout the world. Each VE partner operates its business in different local economic, cultural and political conditions, uses various types of legacy systems and software technologies and has different business interests. However, after becoming members of the VE all partners comply with the VE business rules and operational regulations.

The software enabling such interoperation is based on agent technology. All interacting parties including the VE partners plus various VE establishment and administration bodies are associated with appropriate agent components capable of carrying

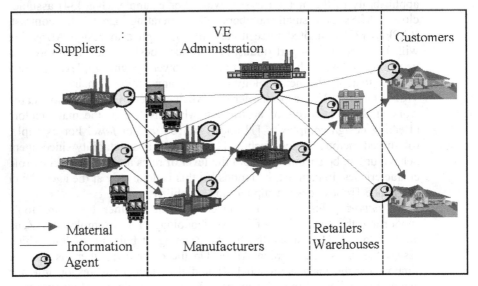

Fig. 2. Agent support for manufacturing and logistics virtual enterprises

tasks in a distributed and autonomous manner. The agent components are backed by a software infrastructure complementing the agent functionality, for example providing user interfaces to agents, linking agents with external web-services and other information sources and assisting agents in knowledge discovery by implementing data mining and knowledge management algorithms. The only requirement for each VE partner is to install agent software capable of interoperating with that of the existing VE partners and the main VE administration body. Furthermore, the VE partner software will have to comply with the functional specifications designated by the VE establishment body and implement the minimum required functionality.

It can be assumed that the agent software is built according to FIPA standards, for example agents communicate using a FIPA compliant communication language. Furthermore, discovery of agent services could be done using a central agent service registry providing white and yellow page information to the eligible agents as is currently done in the Agentcities project [31]. The VE administration body exercises control on the operation of the VE and interacts with all the agents in the VE.

The underlying philosophy in this case study is that the agent system design will be done once by the VE establishment body and the relevant parts will become available to each new VE partner after it has been accepted to join the VE. The new

VE partner will have to either develop the necessary software according to the given specifications or purchase it from other partners or software vendors.

In designing the agent-based system certain authority relationships need to be ensured between the main VE agents and the VE member agents. For example, main VE agents should be able to exercise control on VE member agents with respect to providing information about transactions, pricing quotes and service details. Furthermore, several widely used patterns of interacting agent behaviour such as the mediator pattern [18] need to be applied for security and privacy reasons. For similar reasons, a number of heuristics have to be followed in the design, for example, all financial transactions for each VE member should be carried out by an authorised agent, which is recognised by the main VE financial controller agent. Furthermore, since the resulting agent system is large and complicated, a design which allows black-box re-use of different components is to be preferred. Finally, this complex agent system design exercise would be significantly facilitated if a software tool could carry out certain routine but tiresome and error-prone design steps, such as automatically combining known design patterns and imposing constraints on the design product.

4   Comparative Evaluation of ABS Engineering Methodologies

ABS engineering methodologies can be classified as ad-hoc, formal, informal and structured, and dynamic (see Fig. 3). Ad-hoc methodologies involve designing an ABS in an application domain specific manner, while formal approaches are based on the use of formal methods. Informal and structured methodologies originate from knowledge engineering and software engineering and are predominantly extensions of object-oriented analysis and design methodologies. Finally, dynamic methodologies involve defining the structure of an ABS and the behaviour of the individual agents dynamically on run-time. All classes have advantages and disadvantages with informal and structured methodologies being regarded as more practical for numerous real-world applications.

A representative methodology of each class (RAPPID [23], DESIRE [4], Gaia [34], MESSAGE /UML [5], Tropos [6], Zeus methodology [21] and KARMA [27]) has been evaluated using the evaluation framework described in Section 2. A summary of the results is presented in Table 1. A more detailed discussion of this classification scheme and a review of the above ABS engineering methodologies can be found in [14].

Regarding the *Concepts* perspective, about half of the ABS engineering methodologies examined (DESIRE, Tropos and Zeus methodology) are bounded to specific agent architecture. RAPPID is the only one limited to specific agent types as well. However, based on the case study described in Section 3, it is clear that a methodology not bounded to specific agent architecture is needed. For example, some VE partners may prefer to develop the agent software using tools they are familiar with or they may want to market their software to other potential VE members. In such a case, proprietary development tools or publicly available tools which are released under a suitable licence (such as JADE [30] that comes under LGPL2) will need to be used.

Regarding the *Concepts* perspective, about half of the ABS engineering methodologies examined (DESIRE, Tropos and Zeus methodology) are bounded to specific agent architecture. RAPPID is the only one limited to specific agent types as well. However, based on the case study described in Section 3, it is clear that a methodology not bounded to specific agent architecture is needed. For example, some VE partners may prefer to develop the agent software using tools they are familiar with or they may want to market their software to other potential VE members. In such a case, proprietary development tools or publicly available tools which are released under a suitable licence (such as JADE [30] that comes under LGPL3) will need to be used.

The majority of the methodologies examined (DESIRE, Gaia, Tropos, Zeus methodology and KARMA) consider design as an explicit step in the ABS engineering lifecycle. This is an important requirement of the VE case study since otherwise it would be difficult to design such a large business system without making errors. However, only KARMA provides formal support for heuristics in the design of the ABS and as mentioned in the case study scenario, being able to apply design heuristics in a systematic manner is needed to facilitate such a complex design task. Clearly, this is a general deficiency of current ABS engineering methodologies.

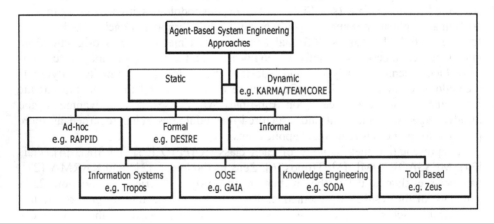

Fig. 3. Classification of Agent-Based System Engineering Methodologies

---

2 LGPL stands for Lesser General Public Licence and it allows extensions to the original software to be released under any, even commercial, licence.
3 LGPL stands for Lesser General Public Licence and it allows extensions to the original software to be released under any, even commercial, licence.

Table 1. Design complexity evaluation of ABS engineering methodologies

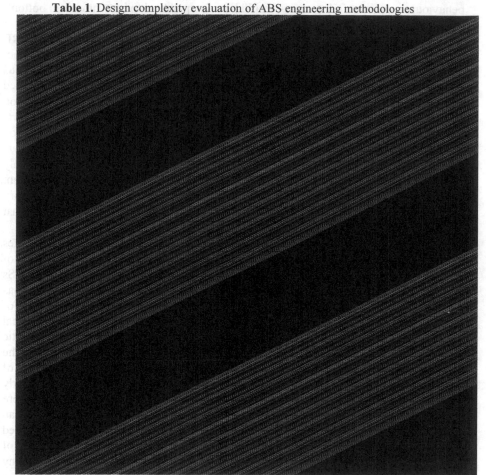

As far as it concerns the *Models* perspective, only the Zeus methodology and KARMA explicitly model organisational settings. Representing collective behaviours as first class design constructs is also not supported in most of the examined methodologies. The only exceptions are Zeus where collective behaviours can be represented by role models and KARMA where collective behaviours are modelled by appropriate team plans. The lack of support for non-functional aspects is even more pronounced. Indeed, only Tropos considers non-functional aspects in the design of ABSs. As discussed in the previous section, all three aspects are needed to efficiently design the ABS for the case study considered.

In the *Process* perspective, only MESSAGE/UML allows working in both top-down and bottom-up fashion (but the current version of MESSAGE/UML supports only the analysis phase of the ABS engineering lifecycle and hence it is not practically useful). The Zeus methodology supports bottom up design, the rest of the approaches are all supporting top-down design. In the case study considered, both top-down and bottom-up design would be needed. The VE administrative structure would be easier to be modelled in a top-down manner. On the other hand, agent behaviours supporting VE partners would be more practical to be synthesised bottom-up to better reflect the localised dependencies and requirements.

Furthermore, only two approaches explicitly provide support for reuse, DESIRE and the Zeus methodology. DESIRE includes guidelines about how the agent system designer can reuse generic task components in the design of the ABS and the Zeus methodology includes guidelines about how to reuse generic behaviours represented by role models and generic agent characteristics — for example negotiation strategies. Support for reuse is mandatory in the case study considered, as large parts of the required agent software functionality, such as contracting and negotiation mechanisms, have already broadly implemented and tested.

There is also significant lack of support for automatic design of ABSs. Only KARMA supports automatic selection of the agents that will participate in the agent organisation based on team plans specified by the designer. This is also a mandatory requirement in the case study scenario due to the size of the agent application that needs to be designed.

Regarding the *Pragmatics* perspective, approximately half of the approaches (MESSAGE, Tropos and KARMA) are general, targeting a broad range of application domains. The rest are restricted as follows: Gaia assumes closed ABSs consisting of small numbers of static, cooperating agents. The Zeus methodology has restrictions regarding the environments where the agents produced can operate. For example, Zeus agents cannot be mobile and they require a large amount of physical RAM memory to execute. DESIRE is also specific to applications requiring static agents whose behaviour can be described by a task-based hierarchy. RAPPID is the most specific approach since it targets a specific application domain; that of supporting industrial product design. The case study example considered clearly highlights the need for a general methodology. The VE is an open system where partners can dynamically join and deregister and therefore it must be supported by an open agent system. Mobility can also be useful, for example for realising ant-based coordination algorithms. Finally, the case study considered concerns the domain of manufacturing and logistics service provision and specific methodologies concerning other domains, such as RAPPID, are not applicable.

DESIRE formally supports specifying interactions among task components at different levels of abstraction, which reduces design complexity. This is the case for KARMA, which is based on the STEAM formal specification language. STEAM makes possible for the designer to work at different levels of abstraction with appropriate rigour. The rest of the tools do not support abstractability and the designer has to manually consider all the design details. This is something that would not suit the case study considered. For example, common functionality such as interactions with the VE administration and transaction handling and logging would need to be specified in detail for each agent type.

Finally, four of the methodologies examined (DESIRE, MESSAGE, Zeus and KARMA) are associated with tools that assist the designers in applying them. The assistance provided includes graphic user interfaces behaviour allocation mechanisms as well as automatic design product construction, verification and generation of the source code. Clearly, these are necessary features for the methodology selected to be applied to the design of the required in the case study considered in this paper.

5 Implications for Further Research

The above analysis has demonstrated that none of the ABS engineering methodologies examined covers all aspects of design support included in the evaluation framework introduced in Section 2. An effective approach to ABS design should therefore cover a number of outstanding issues, which are described in more detail below.

5.1 Support for Design Heuristics

Existing ABS engineering methodologies do not provide systematic and rigorous models for considering heuristics in the design of the ABS. In methodologies having formal underpinnings, such as DESIRE [4], design heuristics can be taken into account in a rigorous manner in the design but there are no guidelines and systematic techniques assisting in this task. The designer needs to manually incorporate the heuristic rules in the formal ABS specifications.

Some methodologies support informal ABS design heuristics. For example in the Zeus methodology [21] the *sphere of responsibility* and *point of interaction* heuristics are provided. The former requires the designer to partition the application resources to areas of control and represent each area with a software agent. The latter refers to representing each resource in the application domain with an agent. However, those informal heuristics cannot be easily applied to the design of large ABSs. Furthermore, it is difficult for the designer to predict the effect on design decisions when those heuristics contradict with other requirements such as non-functional requirements. Hence, new ways to support heuristics in ABS are required.

5.2 Organisational Settings

Some ABS engineering methodologies explicitly model organisational settings — for example, MAS-CommonKADS [12] and SODA [22] — and there are cases where the agent organisation is designed during a distinct design step, before the agent behaviour is completely specified [3]. However, it has been argued that even when organisational settings are explicitly modelled, the models only represent the organisational relationships between agents without considering social tasks and social laws [36]. Furthermore, organisational settings are not considered as first class design constructs apart from a few exceptions of approaches that use roles [21], [22]. Another problem concerning organisational settings is that existing approaches do not provide rigorous methodologies for combining organisational settings with application functionality. This has to be done intuitively by the designer without any assistance by a software tool.

5.3 Collective Behaviour

A similar problem exists regarding representing collective behaviour. Many authors argue that collective behaviours should be treated as first-class design constructs, namely that they should be able to be instantiated and given identity [2], [15].

However, even where this is issue is addressed, such as in the Zeus methodology [21], there is no rigorous way to reuse collective application functionality and combine it with organisational settings.

5.4 Non-functional Aspects

An issue of major concern in ABS design is the modelling and consideration of non-functional aspects such as security and performance. To the best of author's knowledge, no ABS engineering approach explicitly considers non-functional aspects in design apart from Tropos [6], In Tropos, the software system is represented as one or more actors, which participate in a strategic dependency model, along with other actors from the system's operational environment. Actors can fulfill certain goals and are progressively identified and inserted in the conceptual models by the agent system engineers. In this way, non functional aspects can be considered if engineers insert appropriate actors with goals that contribute positively to the satisfaction of non-functional requirements in the Tropos conceptual models. However, the Tropos approach to modelling non-functional aspects suffers from two main weaknesses. Firstly, it models non-functional aspects in a way that it cannot be directly reused in other ABS designs. Secondly, quantitative characterisation of non-functional aspects is not possible.

In some cases, non-functional aspects are the basis for criteria for reorganisation in dynamic approaches, as is the case in KARMA [27]. In these instances non-functional aspects are taken into account by adjusting the agent behaviour and the organisation of the ABS at run-time. However, this treatment of non-functional aspects impedes the reuse of non-functional models. It also contributes to significant consumption of resources and may cause system instability.

5.5 Automating the Design Process

In order to reduce development effort and software design errors the design process should be partially automated [16]. This view is also adopted by some ABS engineering methodologies [9], [25], [32] which are considered informal because their analysis models use informal specifications of desired systems. They nevertheless try to provide the formal underpinnings necessary for automatically designing ABSs. The common way of doing that is by progressing from analysis to design by successive formal transformations of the analysis models. The transformations used, however, focus on ensuring that the designed agent components are correctly represented in respect to the analysis models, using object-oriented software engineering concepts and techniques. For example, in [25] formal transformations are used to decide on the number of objects and concurrent threads that should be used to correctly realise the behaviour of each agent component. To the best of author's knowledge, current informal ABS engineering approaches do not provide any automatic support for actually deciding on what behaviour each agent in the ABS should have. This is not the case for dynamic approaches where the design of the agent system is done during reorganisation steps. For example, in KARMA the agent components are automatically selected based on specifications of the agent-based application requirements described in the STEAM modelling framework [27]. However, KARMA assumes that agents already exist in cyberspace, which is not generally the case.

5.6 Working at Different Abstraction Levels

There is a consensus that abstraction in software design reduces design complexity [19]. Although it has the trade-off of reducing software efficiency and performance, it may add to the reliability of the produced software as frequently used components are thoroughly tested and the design process can be automated [1].

As abstraction is a common practice in software design, a number of ABS engineering methodologies allow the designer to work at different levels of abstraction. However, not all of them provide appropriate formal support. For example, MESSAGE/UML allows modelling at levels 0 and level 1 but there is no formal description of the relations between the models of the two levels. As a result, proper use of MESSAGE/UML requires the designers to have a clear understanding and explicitly consider the links between models at levels 0 and 1, which makes the ABS design task more difficult,

The only approaches examined that provide formal support for working at different levels of abstraction are DESIRE [4] and KARMA [27]. However, their support is limited. DESIRE only supports interaction between tasks at different abstraction levels and KARMA supports teamwork at different levels of abstraction in the form of joint intentions. Agent behaviour, however, is characterised with other aspects as well. For example, coordination protocols or negotiation strategies, which the designer should specify at the lowest level of detail in those two approaches. This problem is addressed in the Zeus approach [21]. For example, in the Zeus methodology, the agent system designer can either select a predefined negotiation strategy or specify all negotiation rules in detail. Zeus models agent behaviour at different levels of abstraction based on role modelling. However, this support is informal since the relations among roles have not been given formal semantics.

6 Summary

This paper proposed a framework to assess ABS engineering methodologies with respect to design complexity they involve. Using this framework, a set of representative methodologies has been examined revealing a number of issues that would require further research.

The proposed framework suggests looking into ABS engineering approaches from four views: *Concepts*, *Models*, *Process* and *Pragmatics*. The *Concepts* view refers to the modelling concepts used to model ABSs and it concerns the generality of the concept definition, the existence of specific support for design in the ABS engineering process and the support for design heuristics. The *Models* view refers to modelling of organisational settings and collective behaviour to be used as first class design constructs and to explicit modelling of non-functional aspects. The *Process* view examines the perspective of the design process and whether it can be based on reuse and if it can be automated. The *Pragmatics* view evaluates the applicability of the approach to real-world applications by assessing the generality, the complexity handling and the tool support of the approach.

None of the methodologies examined supports all aspects of the proposed framework. Significant gaps have been uncovered to inform further work on ABS engineering methodologies, where the aim would be to decrease design complexity by providing more comprehensive support for all aspects of the framework. It is the authors' belief that using roles as behavioural modelling constructs and providing appropriate semantics for role relations and role characteristics is the most appropriate path to follow towards achieving this goal.

References

[1]   Alagar, V.S., Periyasamy, K.: *Specification of Software Systems*. New York: Springer-Verlag, 1998.

[2]   Andersen, E.P. *Conceptual Modelling of Objects: A Role Modelling Approach*. PhD Thesis. Oslo, Norway: University of Oslo, 1997.

[3]   Barber, K.S., Liu, T.H., Han, D.C. *Agent-Oriented Design*. Austin, TX, USA: University of Texas at Austin, 1999, http://powerlips.ece.utexas.edu/pubs/techReports/1999/TR99-UT-LIPS-AGENTS-01.pdf.

[4]   Brazier, F.M.T., Dunin-Keplicz, B., Jennings, N., Treur, J.: *DESIRE*: Modelling Multi-Agent Systems in a Compositional Formal Framework. *International Journal of Cooperative Information Systems, Special Issue on Formal Methods in Cooperative Information Systems: Multi-Agent Systems*, 5, 1 (June 1997), 67-94.

[5]   Caire, G., Coulier, W., Garijo, F., Gomez, J., Pavon, J., Leal, F., Chainho, P., Kearney, P., Stark, J., Evans, R., Massonet, P. Agent Oriented Analysis Using Message/UML. In Wooldridge, M.J., Weis, G., Ciancarini, P. (eds.), *Agent-Oriented Software Engineering II, Second International Workshop, (AOSE 2001), Montreal, Canada*. Berlin: Springer Verlag, 2002, 151-168.

[6]   Castro, J., Kolp, M., Mylopoulos, J.: Towards requirements-driven information systems engineering: the Tropos project. *Information Systems*, 27, 6 (September 2002), 365-389.

[7]   Cernuzzi, L., Rossi, G. On the Evaluation of Agent Oriented Methodologies. *OOPSLA 2002 Workshop on Agent-Oriented Methodologies*. 2002.

[8]   Dam, K.H., Winikoff, M. Comparing AgentOriented Methodologies. *Fifth International Bi-Conference Workshop on Agent-Oriented Information Systems (AOIS-2003)*. Malbourne, Australia, 2003.

[9]   Depke, R., Heckel, R., Kuster, J.M. Agent-Oriented Modelling with Graph Transformation. In Ciancarini, P., Wooldridge, M. (eds.), *Agent-Oriented Software Engineering I, First International Workshop (AOSE 2000), Limerick, Ireland*. Berlin: Springer-Verlag, 2001, 106-119.

[10]   Fenton, N., Pfleeger, S.L.: *Software Metrics: A Rigorous and Practical Approach*. Boston, MA, USA: PWS Publishing Co., 1997.

[11]   Iglesias, C.A., Garrijo, M., Gonzalez, J.C. A Survey of Agent-Oriented Methodologies. In Muller, J., Singh, M.P., Rao, A.S. (eds.), *Proceedings of the 5th International Workshop on Intelligent Agents {V}: Agent Theories, Architectures, and Languages (ATAL-98)*. Heidelberg, Germany: Springer-Verlag, 1999, 317-330.

[12] Iglesias, C.A., Garijo, M., Gonzalez, J.C., Velasco, J.R. Analysis and Design of
      Multiagent Systems   using MAS-CommonKADS. In Singh, M.P., Rao, A.S.,
      Wooldridge, M.J. (eds.), *Intelligent Agents IV: Agent Theories, Architectures, and
      Languages (ATAL '97)*. Berlin, Germany: Springer Verlag, 1998, 313-326.
[13] Juan, T., Pearce, A., Sterling, L. ROADMAP: Extending the Gaia Methodology for
      Complex Open Systems. *Autonomous Agents and Multi-Agent Systems (AAMAS 2002)*.
      Bologna, Italy: ACM Press, 2002.
[14] Karageorgos, A. *Using Role modelling and Synthesis to Reduce Complexity in Agent-
      Based System Design*. PhD Thesis. Manchester, UK: University of Manchester Institute
      of Science and Technology, 2003.
[15] Kendall, E.A.: Role models - patterns of agent system analysis and design. *BT
      Technology Journal*, 17, 4 (October 1999), 46-57.
[16] Lowry, M.R., McCartney, R.D. (eds.). *Automating Software Design*. Menlo Park, CA:
      AAAI Press, 1991.
[17] MacDonell, S.G.: Determining delivered functional error content based on the
      complexity of CASE specifications. *New Zealand Journal of Computing*, 5, 1 (July
      1994), 57-65.
[18] Maturana, F., Norrie, D.H.: Multi-agent mediator architecture for distributed
      manufacturing. *Journal of Intelligent Manufacturing*, 7, 257-270.
[19] Metzger, A., Quelns, S. A Reuse- and Prototyping-based Approach for the Specification
      of Building Automation Systems. In Schuerr, A. (ed.), *OMER-2 Workshop Proceedings*.
      Munich: University of the Federal Armed Forces, Germany, 2001, 3-9.
[20] Ng, K., Kramer, J., Magee, J.: A CASE Tool for Software Architecture Design.
      Automated Software Engineering, 3, 3/4 (1996), 261-284.
[21] Nwana, H.S., Ndumu, D.T., Lee, L.C., Collis, J.C.: Zeus: A Toolkit for Building
      Distributed Multi-Agent Systems. *Applied Artificial Intelligence Journal*, 13, 1 (January
      1999), 129 - 185.
[22] Omicini, A. SODA : Societies and Infrastructures in the Analysis and Design of Agent-
      based Systems. In Ciancarini, P., Wooldridge, M.J. (eds.), *Agent-Oriented Software
      Engineering I, First International Workshop (AOSE 2000), Limerick, Ireland*. Berlin:
      Springer Verlag, 2001, 185-193.
[23] Parunak, V.D., Sauter, J., Fleischer, M., Ward, A.: The RAPPID Project: Symbiosis
      between Industrial Requirements and MAS Research. *Autonomous Agents and Multi-
      Agent Systems*, 2, 2 (June 1999), 111-140.
[24] Silva, A.R., Romao, A., Deugo, D., Silva, M.M.d.: Towards a Reference Model for
      Surveying Mobile Agent Systems. *Autonomous Agents and Multi-Agent Systems*, 4, 3
      (September 2001), 187-231.
[25] Sparkman, C.H., DeLoach, S.A., Self, A.L. Automated Derivation of Complex Agent
      Architectures from Analysis Specifications. In Wooldridge, M.J., Weis, G., Ciancarini,
      P. (eds.), *Agent-Oriented Software Engineering II, Second International Workshop
      (AOSE 2001), Montreal, Canada*. Berlin: Springer Verlag, 2002, 278-296.
[26] Sturm, A., Shehory, O. A Framework for Evaluating Agent-Oriented Methodologies.
      *Fifth International Bi-Conference Workshop on Agent-Oriented Information Systems
      (AOIS-2003)*. Malbourne, Australia, 2003.
[27] Tambe, M., Pynadath, D.V., Chauvat, N.: Building Dynamic Agent Organisations in
      Cyberspace. *IEEE Internet Computing*, 4, 2 (March/April 2000), 65-73.
[28] The MABE Consortium. *The MaBE (Mulii-Agent Business Environement) Project*.
      2003, http://www.mabe-project.com.
[29] The Object Agency Inc. A Comparison of Object-Oriented Development
      Methodologies.   The   Object   Agency,   Inc,   (Autumn   1995),
      http://www.toa.com/pub/mcr.pdf.

[30]   TILAB - Motorola. *The   Jade   Agent   Building   Toolkit.*   2003, http://sharon.cselt.it/projects/jade/.

[31]   Willmott, S.N., Dale, J., Burg, B., Charlton, C., O'brien, P.: Agentcities: A Worldwide Open Agent Network. *Agentlink News*, 8, 13-15.

[32]   Wood, M., DeLoach, S.A. An Overview of the Multiagent Systems Engineering Methodology. In Ciancarini, P., Wooldridge, M.J. (eds.), *Agent-Oriented Software Engineering I, First International Workshop (AOSE 2000), Limerick, Ireland.* Berlin: Springer Verlag, 2001, 207-221.

[33]   Wooldridge, M.: On the Sources of Complexity in Agent Design. *Applied Artificial Intelligence*, 14, 7 (August 2000), 623-644.

[34]   Wooldridge, M., Jennings, N.R., Kinny, D.: The Gaia methodology for agent-oriented analysis and design. *International Journal of Autonomous Agents and Multi-Agent Systems*, 3, 3 (September 2000), 285-312.

[35]   Zambonelli, F., Jennings, N.R., Wooldridge, M. Organisational Abstractions for the Analysis and Design of Multi-Agent Systems. In Ciancarini, P., Wooldridge, M.J. (eds.), *Agent-Oriented Software Engineering I, First International Workshop (AOSE 2000), Limerick, Ireland.* Berlin: Springer Verlag, 2001, 235-250.

[36]   Zambonelli, F., Jennings, N.R., Omicini, A., Wooldridge, M.J. Agent-Oriented Software Engineering for Internet Applications. In Omicini, A., Zambonelli, F., Klusch, M., Tolksdorf, R. (eds.), *Coordination of Internet Agents: Models, Technologies and Applications.* Berlin Heidelberg: Springer-Verlag, 2001, 326-346.

Laying Down the Foundations
of an Agent Modelling Methodology
for Fault-Tolerant Multi-agent Systems

Sehl Mellouli, Bernard Moulin, and Guy Mineau

Department of Computer Science and Software Engineering
Laval University, G1K 7P4, Quebec, Canada
{sehl.mellouli,bernard.moulin,guy.mineau}@ift.ulaval.ca

Abstract. Multi-Agent Systems (MAS) are designed to solve problems, sometimes in unstable environments. Each agent in a MAS can play a set of roles; it may be prone to failure, which may cause a system failure. As a result, agents may become unavailable and some roles may be left unfilled (thereafter called missing roles). Unfortunately, there are not always backup agents ready to replace unavailable ones. In this case, the MAS must reorganize itself in order to achieve its objectives by assigning missing roles to the remaining agents. We propose an agent modelling methodology for Fault-Tolerant Multi-Agent Systems based on MAS reorganization. By taking into account the environment in the modelling phases of the system, we can anticipate different critical situations that could occur in the environment and that could have an impact on the MAS organization. Hence, we can propose an appropriate MAS re-organization so that the system continues to operate correctly. We know that it is impossible to consider all the different situations that can happen in the environment, but we can consider those that are predictable and critical.

1   Introduction

In an unstable environment, agents may be prone to failure that can cause system malfunctions. These failures, whenever possible, should be considered when designing a MAS so that they can be prevented or remedied. This kind of MAS is called a Fault-Tolerant Multi-Agent System; it aims at operating successfully despite failures of individual agents. In general, the proposed approach to overcome these failures is based on agent replication [9]. However, it is not always possible to benefit from the mechanism of agent replication. For example, let us consider a squadron of F-16 fighters on their way to attack a given target. One of the fighter is the *head fighter*. Suppose that during the attack, the *head fighter* is hit by a missile and crashes. Since it played some vital roles in the attack, the overall mission of the squadron is compromised. To overcome such a situation, the missing fighter should be replaced by another one so that all the key roles of the squadron are fulfilled. But unfortunately, in this context, its replacement is not possible. Somehow the squadron has to continue its mission to its target.

A. Omicini, P. Petta, and J. Pitt (Eds.): ESAW 2003, LNAI 3071, pp. 275–293, 2004.
© Springer-Verlag Berlin Heidelberg 2004

So, the MAS has to reorganize itself by assigning the missing fighter roles to the remaining agents so that the target is reached. In such contexts, we propose a MAS design methodology for *Fault-Tolerant Multi-Agent Systems* based on system reorganization that takes into account predictable critical situations that could cause system failure.

To illustrate our methodology, we will use the F-16 squadron example. Obviously, this MAS operates in a highly unpredictable environment in which many troublesome situations may arise such as an interception attempt from enemy fighters or from the enemy's air defense system. In certain situations, the fighters must reorganize themselves, as for example they may have to regroup in smaller squadrons to engage the enemy. The MAS guiding the attack must quickly react to any new situation and try to reach its target as much as possible, or retreat. There is much information that must always be shared between squadron fighters such as the number of airplanes, the number of enemy's airplanes, the positions of enemy fighters, etc. Hence, it is important to identify this information, and describe various situations of the environment that influence the behavior of the MAS. The proposed methodology is suited for Fault-Tolerant Multi-Agent Systems in which each agent in the MAS cannot be replaced by another agent.

This paper is organized as follows: Section 2 presents an overview of agent-oriented design methodologies in order to introduce our methodology. Section 3 presents the analysis phase. Section 4 presents the design phase. Section 5 concludes.

2   Agent-Oriented Methodologies

In order to build a design methodology for Fault-Tolerant Multi-Agent Systems (FTMAS), we need to take into account the common concepts used in other MAS design methodologies.

2.1   Overview of Agent-Oriented Software Engineering Methodologies

Multi-agent systems can be applied to solve problems in various domains such as the organizational [20] and web based domains [18]. We found that most of the studied methodologies have similar phases or use similar modelling techniques. Consequently, we present in this section an overview of seven agent-oriented software engineering methodologies: MAS-CommonKADS, GAIA, SODA, AALAADIN, ADELFE, MESSAGE/UML and Tropos, in order to identify their commonalities so that we can propose some guidelines to propose a design methodology for fault-tolerant MAS (Section 3).

The MAS-CommonKADS Methodology. MAS-CommonKADS [10] has three phases: the conceptualization phase, the analysis phase, and the design phase.

The Conceptualization Phase. The conceptualization phase helps developers to understand the problem to be solved. The main outputs of this phase are two models: use cases (based on actors), and MSC (Message Sequence Charts) used to describe interactions between different actors.

The Analysis Phase. The second phase is analysis. It carries out a requirement specification of the MAS through the development of five models:

1. The Agent model: it identifies agent types, describes them and determines their instances.
2. The task model: it consists of a task decomposition, goal determination, and the identification of tasks ingredients.
3. The coordination model: it describes the interactions and coordination protocols between agents. It shows the dynamic relationships between them.
4. The knowledge model: it determines the application knowledge model and the problem solving knowledge. The application knowledge model consists of the domain knowledge, the inference knowledge and the task knowledge. The problem solving knowledge specifies how the inference is carried out.
5. The organization model: it represents the organization in which the MAS will be deployed and the software organization of the MAS.

The Design Phase. The third phase is design. It carries out the design model which consists of:

1. The agent network design that determines the infrastructure of the MAS-system according to the network, knowledge and coordination facilities.
2. The agent design that consists of agents such that each agent is subdivided into modules for user-communication, agent communication (inferred from the coordination model), deliberation and reaction (from the expertise, agent and organization models), and external skills and services (from the agent, expertise and task models).
3. The platform design that is the selection of the needed software and hardware to implement the MAS.

The Gaia Methodology. The Gaia [21] methodology is applicable to a wide range of multi-agent systems in which agents are cooperative and the system is closed. It is composed of two main phases: the analysis phase and the design phase. These two phases are preceded by the requirement statement.

The analysis phase aims at collecting and organizing the system specification. It produces the following outputs: the environment model, the preliminary role model, the preliminary interaction model, and the organizational rules. The design phase aims at refining the output of the analysis phase, and defining the organizational structure of the MAS. Its outputs are: the organizational structure, the completion of the role and interaction models, the agent model, and the services model.

The SODA Methodology. The SODA [18] methodology is suited for internet-based systems. It consists of two phases, the analysis phase and the design phase. During the analysis phase, the application domain is studied and modelled, the available resources and the technological constraints are listed, the fundamental application goals and targets are pointed out. The design phase deals with the representation of the abstract models obtained during the analysis phase.

The Analysis Phase. The analysis phase generates three models that are: the role model in which the application goals are modelled in terms of the tasks to be achieved, the resource model in which the application environment is modelled in terms of the available services, and the interaction model in which the interactions involving roles are represented.

The Design Phase. The design phase enables the designer to create three models: the agent model in which individual and social roles are mapped upon agent classes, the society model in which groups are mapped onto societies of agents, and the environment model in which resources are mapped onto infrastructure classes. In the agent model, an agent class is defined as a set of one or several roles. It is characterized by the tasks, the set of permissions, and the interaction protocols associated with its roles. In the society model, each group is mapped into a society of agents. An agent society is characterized by the social tasks, the set of permissions, the participating social roles, and the interaction rules associated with its groups.

The AALAADIN Methodology. AALAADIN [4] is a generic meta-model for multi-agent systems. The core concepts of AALAADIN are roles and groups. A group is defined as a set of agents. A role is defined as an abstract representation of an agent function or a service. In AALAADIN, agents are defined by their functions in an organization, that is by their roles and the set of constraints which they must accept in order to be able to play these roles. Agents can play different roles in different groups. AALAADIN's methodological approach consists in determining first the group structure by identifying all the roles and interactions that can appear within a group, and second the MAS organizational structure, which is the set of group structures expressing the design of a multi-agent organization scheme.

The ADELFE Methodology. ADELFE [1] is suited for adaptive multi-agent systems in which the environment is unpredictable and the system is open. A strong adaptation is the ability that the system must possess in order to take into account unpredictable events and to react to evolutionary environments. In adaptive multi-agent systems, the agents are involved in cooperative interactions. ADELFE proposes three workflows: the requirements workflow, the analysis workflow and the design workflow.

The Requirements Workflow. In the requirements workflow, ADELFE provides a model composed of the target system (described by a set of keywords), and the system environment. This workflow focuses on what may be in interaction with the studied system in terms of passive or active entities or constraints. It requires a characterization of data flows and interactions between passive or active entities and the system. These interactions are expressed by collaboration and sequence diagrams [19].

The Analysis Workflow. In the analysis workflow, ADELFE proposes to first identify the agents by performing a domain analysis in order to produce a preliminary class diagram. Each agent has to be analyzed as a system. Second, it proposes to study the interactions between the different entities as a set of sequence diagrams (like in AUML [15]) and activity diagrams which explain the possible interactions between the different entities within the system at each level.

The Design Workflow. In the design workflow, ADELFE defines the agent model and the Non Cooperative Situations model (which could be considered as exceptions in classical programs). The agent model represents the relationships between agents. The non cooperative situation model deals with the non cooperative situations that are situations in which the multi-agent system cannot reach its objectives. In addition, the design phase produces the architecture of the system in terms of blocks, classes, agents and interactions.

The MESSAGE Methodology. MESSAGE [2] stands for: Methodology for Engineering Systems of Software AGEnts. It proposes five model views that are: the organization view, the goal/task view, the agent/role view, the interaction view and the domain view. The organization view (OV) shows concrete entities (agents, organizations, roles, resources) of the system and its environment, and coarse grained relationships between them (aggregation, power, and acquaintance relationships). The goal/task view (GTV) shows goals, tasks, situations and dependencies between them. The agent/role view (ARV) focuses on the individual agents and roles. In the interaction view (IV) a designer must, for each interaction taking place between agents/roles, show the initiator, the collaborators, the motivator, the relevant information supplied/achieved by each participant, the events that trigger the interaction, and other relevant effects of the interaction. The domain view (DV) shows the domain specific concepts and relations that are relevant to the system under development.

The analysis process is based on a refinement approach. The system is viewed as a set of organizations that interact with resources, actors, or other organizations. Actors may be human users or other existing agents. The modelling process starts by building the organization and the goal/task views. These views act as inputs to create agent/role and domain views. Finally, the interaction model is built using inputs from the other views.

The Tropos Methodology. The Tropos methodology [8] is based on key features that are agents, goals, and plans. The phases of the methodology are early requirements, late requirements, architectural design, detailed design, and implementation. The early requirement phase identifies actors and their goals. The late requirements introduces the system-to-be as an actor that interacts with other actors. In the architectural design more system actors are introduced and they are assigned sub-goals. The detailed design defines the system actors in further details, including specifications of communication and coordination protocols. The implementation transforms the system into code compatible with the JACK platform.

2.2   Common Modelling Concepts

In [14], we have studied the MAS design methodologies found in [1] [2] [4] [8] [10] [18] [21], and found that they have common phases related to analysis and design. In addition, most of the methodologies share common concepts such as *role, group, interaction and environment*, despite the fact that some methodologies are specialized for a particular domain applications like decision support for example.

A summary of the different models proposed in the studied methodologies is presented in [14], and are summarized in what follows:

1. MAS-CommonKDAS [10]:
   − Analysis: agent, task, coordination, knowledge, organization
   − Design: design
2. Gaia [21]:
   − Analysis: role,interaction
   − Design: agent, services, acquaintance
3. SODA [18]:
   − Analysis: role, resource, interaction
   − Design: agent, society, environment
4. AALAADIN [4]:
   − Analysis: possible roles, interactions, structure of groups
   − Design: agent organization
5. ADELFE [1]:
   − Analysis: environment
   − Design: agent
6. Message/UML [2]:
   − Analysis: organization, goal/task, agent/role, interaction, domain
   − Design: none
7. Tropos [8]:
   − Analysis: actors and their goals, the system-to-be
   − Design: actor systems

We notice that there are 48 models proposed by the different methodologies we examined. The agent model and the interaction model (interaction, communication or cooperation models) appear in all the reviewed methodologies. Moreover, the role model and the organization model appear in six methodologies. These models count for 32 models out of 48. Since we aim at developing a MAS modelling methodology that is as general as can be, we will consider them in our methodology for fault-tolerant MAS. We will also introduce the environment diagram in our methodology since two methodologies (SODA and ADELFE) use it, and we showed its importance when designing a MAS [11] [13].

But first, let us summarize the major concepts referred to by the different methodologies, and their definitions, which are presented hereafter:

- Agent: An agent is a computational process that implements the autonomous, communicating functionality of an application. Typically, agents communicate using an Agent Communication Language [6].
- Task: A task refers to a set of coherent activities that are performed to achieve a goal in a given domain [3].
- Goal: A goal is a set of states of the world that an agent is committed to achieve/maintain. Therefore, a goal is a situation, but not all situations are goals. A set of states of the world can be seen as a goal if there is an agent committed to achieving/maintaining this set of states [6].
- Interaction: The communication pattern performed by instances playing the roles to accomplish the task. [19]
- Collaboration: Collaboration deals with the interactions between agents in a multi-agent system. It is based on the relationships between the individual agents' mental structures and the system's (also seen as an agent) collective mental structure [6].
- Environment: The environment of an agent refers to all the elements that are external to the agent. One can distinguish the social environment of A (the agents that it knows) from its physical environment (the material resources that can be perceived by the agent or used by its effectors) [6].
- Organization: An organization provides a framework for activity and interaction through the definition of roles, behavioral expectations and authority relationships (e.g control) [5]. In addition, from [21] we mention that an organization is a collection of roles, that stand in certain relationships to one another, and that take part in systematic, institutionalized patterns of interactions with other roles.
- Role: The characteristic and expected social behavior of an agent. A role can interact with another role [6]. Another definition of a role is a set of tasks grouped semantically.
- Resource: a resource defines an abstract access mode, modelling the different ways in which the service it provides can be exploited by agents [6].
- Group: A group is a set of two or more agents that are related via their role assignments, such that these relationships must form a connected graph within the group. Agents and Roles are associated with Groups to provide context. [17]

All these concepts are taken into account in our FTMAS methodology as shown in the next section.

2.3 Modelling Methodology for Fault-Tolerant Multi-agent Systems

A multi-agent system interacts with its environment: we need an *environment model* model to represent the environment. In addition, each agent has one or more roles to play in the system. We need to define a *role model* to represent the different roles that will be played by the agents. Each role can interact with other roles: we need an *interaction model*[1] to represent role interactions.

Hence, the analysis phase has at least the following models:

- An environment model which describes the environment and its evolution over time. The environment model structures the environment as a set of discrete situations described by sets of predefined parameters (called critical parameters). During the analysis phase, we can identify particular situations which can lead agents to failure, and propose solutions to overcome the undesirable situations before implementation. Such an approach reduces considerably the subsequent cost of system repair (maintenance). We can also identify situations that the MAS has to reach in order to achieve its objectives. These are *goal situations*. Hence, the environment model will help us to identify particular situations that can occur during MAS operation, and lead it to a failure.
- A role model that specifies the different roles that will be played by the agents. A role can be thought of as a set of tasks [11]. Each situation associated with the environment model, that could generate an agent failure, may require a reassignment of roles between the remaining agents. This implies that the MAS organization must be dynamic. Furthermore, relationships between roles do not change, since they are defined according to the nature of the tasks composing the roles. The role model describes the tasks and the necessary interaction protocols between them; while the agent model, defined in the design phase (below), defines how the roles can be dynamically assigned to agents.
- An interaction model that specifies how roles interact with each other according to the protocols used in the interactions.

One or more roles will be assigned to each agent. Hence, we need an *agent model* to represent agents and their roles. An agent has to communicate with other agents. Hence, we need a *communication model* to represent agent communication. In addition, agents have to collaborate with each other, and we need a *collaboration model*[2] to represent agent collaborations.

Consequently, the design phase has at least the following models:

---

[1] In this paper, only the environment and role models are described. The other models will be described in forthcoming papers.

[2] In this paper, only the agent model is described. The other models will be described in forthcoming papers.

Table 1. Association between models and agent concepts

Model	Concept
environment	environment, goal
role	role, task
interaction	interaction
agent	agent, group, organization
communication	resource
collaboration	collaboration

- An agent model that shows the agents' roles and their relationships. In the agent model, we emphasize the assignment and determination of agent roles and agent relations. In a Fault-Tolerant MAS, we can sometimes use replicated agents to replace unavailable ones [9]; at other times, we cannot. To solve this problem, the agents' roles may change in order to fulfill the missing roles. We have to propose rules to decide how to assign unfilled roles to existing agents or how to modify roles so that the overall system still accomplishes its tasks. The agent model presents agent relationships partly deduced from the role model. Agent relationships may also change as a result of role reassignment. The agent model defines the MAS organization.
- A communication model that specifies the communication paths between agents,
- A coordination model that specifies the protocols used to coordinate agents' actions. These protocols can be inferred from the interaction model.

Referring to our models, we would like to point out to the reader that all concepts presented in section 2.1 are considered in our models as shown in Table 1. Moreover, we may need to enhance this methodology with other models that were not considered in the kernel so that it can be used in a wide range of applications. By doing so, we hope to propose a flexible and easily adaptable methodology. We will address this issue in a forthcoming paper. In this paper, we will only present the environment model, the role model, and the agent model.

3   The Analysis Phase

First, we would like to remind the reader that our methodology addresses Fault-Tolerant Multi-Agent Systems in which no agent replication can be used to replace faulty ones, as it is the case with the F-16 squadron example. The analysis phase that we propose is mainly based mainly on the development of use cases, and of the environment model.

3.1   The Use Case Model

The use case model captures the system functionalities. It is defined as in UML 1.4 [19] : "The use cases represent functionality of a system or a classifier, like a subsystem or a class, as manifested to external interactors with the system or the classifier". In our example, there are six system functionalities: sensing the environment, deciding what to do next, defining plans, collecting information, assisting in planning, and engaging.

3.2   The Environment Model

The MAS must have a representation or a model of its environment as explained in [1] [11] [13] [18] . In our model, the environment defines the properties of the world in which an agent will operate [16]. The world consists of the internal and external environment. The internal environment is composed of agents and their resources. The external environment is composed all objects that are not in the internal environment and that influence the MAS's organization. The environment is viewed as a set of situations. A situation is described by a set of parameters, representing environment properties, whose value changes may induce a critical state changes in the system [11]; they are referred to as *critical parameters*. The event that induces a state change defined as critical is called a *critical event* [12].

Hence, considering the environment in the analysis phase, we need to verify whether:

- the environment is dynamic;
- the changes in the environment influence the MAS's organizational structure;
- the environment's evolution can prevent the system from reaching its objectives;
- the environment is discrete. It is described by a finite set of discrete situations[3];
- the environment has initial and final states;
- the environment is deterministic. If a critical event occurs in a particular situation, we know its consequences.
- the MAS can modify its internal organization by reassigning its resources.

Formally, we define the environment structure S as <I, W, E, R, F> where I is the set of initial situations, W is the set of all identified situations ($I \subseteq W$), E is the set of all identified critical events, R is a relation that represents transitions between sets of situations with $R \subseteq \wp(W) \times E \times \wp(W)$ where $\wp(X)$ is the power set of X. R is a set of triplets $<S_i, e, S_j>$ where S_i and S_j are subsets of $\wp(W)$, and e is in E. The triplet $<S_i, e, S_j>$ means that from any situation in S_i, if event e occurs, the system will evolve to all the situations in S_j. The set F is the set of final situations that can be reached by the environment ($F \subseteq W$) (i.e. no situation can occur after reaching a situation of F) [12].

The situations and their transitions define what we call *the environment model* which is a state transition diagram representing R such that the nodes

---

[3] If there are a lot of situations, and due to complexity problem, we select the most critical ones. For the non-considered situations we can propose a generic solution. With our F-16 example, retreat could be such a generic solution.

represent elements of W. An arc e between two situations s_i and s_j in W exists if there exists two sets $S_i \subseteq \wp(W)$ and $S_j \subseteq \wp(W)$ such that $s_i \in S_i$, $s_j \in S_j$ and $<S_i, e, S_j> \in R$. Each situation is identified by a unique name and is characterized by the values of its parameters (see Figure 1).

To define the environment model, we need to identify critical parameters and critical events. To this end, we need to:

1. *Identify all the resources needed by the MAS in order to operate properly in order to achieve its goals. Identify the parameters that provide a description of each resource.* If a change in a resource state implies a MAS reorganization or failure, then this resource must be considered when describing the environment situations.

   For the F-16 example, we identify the communication means as a resource used by airplanes to communicate. If there are problems in the communication resource, the MAS definitely needs to change tactics.

2. *Identify all the parameters other than those resource-related, that can influence the agents' roles so that the MAS has to reorganize itself or can be prevented to achieve its objectives.*

   Agent states can influence the system organization. For example, if one agent is out of service, then the MAS may have to reorganize itself in order to overcome this problem. Considering our example, we need to know in which states the fighters are, what are their positions, etc. In that case, the situations are described by the following parameters : fighter states, communication media state, number of fighters in squadron, number of enemy fighters, position of enemy fighters, and number of incoming enemy missiles;

3. Along with the representation of the critical parameters, *we need to identify the different events (E) that trigger their change* (called critical events). These events are:
   - for the communication medium: {channel down || channel up} [4].
   - for the airplane states: {good, not good}.
   - for the number of fighters: {one fighter out || one fighter back}.
   - for the number of enemy fighters: {number of enemy fighters attacking}.
   - for the position of enemy fighters: {enemy fighters formation}.
   - for the number of missiles: {detection of air defence missile}.

   All agents must have sensors to detect any change in the environment and can relay this information to other fighters if the communication channels are up;

4. using the critical parameters:
   - *identify the possible initial situation(s) (I).*
     The initial situation s_0 is described by the following values:
     $$\left\{ \begin{array}{l} \text{number of fighters: 5;} \\ \text{communication media state: good;} \\ \text{fighter states: good.} \\ \text{number of enemy fighters: 0.} \\ \text{position of enemy fighters: null.} \\ \text{number of incoming missiles: 0.} \end{array} \right.$$

---

[4] Whatever the reason is: signal blocking, material breakdown, etc.

– *identify a set of final situations (F).* Final situations are situations in which the system reaches or fails to reach its objectives;

– *identify the different possible situations (W), considering the different values that can be taken by the critical parameters.*

In each situation s_i, we try to identify all the different events that can happen and all the different situations that can be reached thereafter. We then consider only situations which are evaluated as critical ones and which require a MAS re-organization.

In the F-16 example, among the different situations that can be reached from s_0, we can consider:

$$
\text{Situation } s_1:
\begin{cases}
\text{number of airplanes: 5;} \\
\text{communication media state: good;} \\
\text{airplanes states: good.} \\
\text{number of enemy fighters: 2.} \\
\text{position of enemy fighters: behind the squadron.} \\
\text{number of missiles: 0.}
\end{cases}
$$

$$
\text{Situation } s_2 \text{ can be reached from } s_1:
\begin{cases}
\text{number of airplanes: 4;} \\
\text{communication media state: good;} \\
\text{airplanes states: good.} \\
\text{number of enemy fighters: 2.} \\
\text{position of enemy fighters: behind the squadron.} \\
\text{number of missiles: 0.}
\end{cases}
$$

A part of the environment model associated with this MAS is given in Figure 1.

An agent must be flexible, which means [7]:

– Reactivity: agents are able to perceive their environment and to react to changes that occur in it;

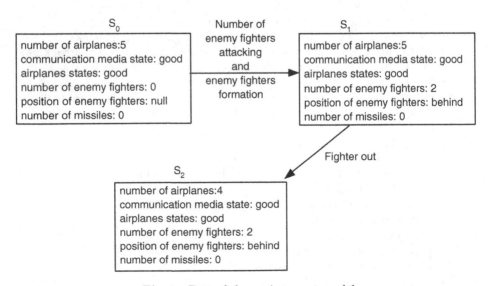

Fig. 1. Part of the environment model

- Pro-activeness: agents take initiative in order to satisfy their design objectives;
- social ability: agents interact together.

An agent must be reactive to changes that occur in the environment. Hence, an agent should have the ability to perceive these changes and to react to them. An agent should have the ability to learn which changes will harm its ability to achieve its goals. In all cases, the agent must get information about its environment in order to be able to identify changes. Agents in a MAS must take initiatives in order to satisfy their design objectives. In other words, an agent must decide which actions should be carried out next so that its objectives can be reached in a foreseeable future. This decision must be based, among other things, on the current state of the environment. Using the environment model, an agent knows the most important events to consider in order to revise its plans. To this end, the environment model provides a valuable information.

3.3   The Role Model

A Multi-Agent System is composed of a set of agents. Each agent has a set of tasks to achieve. Tasks can be grouped to form roles. In the F-16 example, the following tasks were identified in the use case model: Decide, Plan, Attack, Collect information, Sense, and Assist in planning. These tasks can be divided into three groups that are {Decide, Plan, Attack, Sense}, {Collect information, Assist in planning, Attack, Sense}, and {Attack, Sense}. These groups define three roles which are respectively: *head fighter*, *auxiliary head fighter*, and *fighter*.

The role model describes the different roles that need to be handled out to various agents of the MAS. A role is characterized by its its tasks, its required resources, and the various protocols that define role interactions [21]. The tasks determine the functionalities supporting the role [21]. The resources are the resources available to the role in order to fulfill its tasks (they were identified in step 1 of the environment model, see section 3.2). The protocols define the ways the role can interact with other roles. In addition, a role r requires a certain processing capability (noted rc) to be executed, and has a priority (noted rp) according to other roles.

From Figure 1, each situation in the environment model leads an agent to a failure. However, all identified roles must be fulfilled despite this failure, requiring a reassignment of roles between the remaining agents: this implies that the MAS organization is dynamic. Furthermore, relationships between roles do not change since they are defined according to the nature of the tasks composing the roles: we can say that they are static. Hence, the role model will describe the tasks and the necessary interaction protocols between them.

For the F-16 fighters example, the different roles are defined as follows:

- name: *Head fighter*,
- description: It makes all the decisions during the attack that it sends them to other roles, and participates in launching bombs;

- capacity: rc_1
- priority: rp_1

The *auxiliary head fighter* role is defined as follows:

- name: *auxiliary head fighter*,
- description: It collects information and helps the *head fighter* role to make decision, and participates in launching bombs;
- capacity: rc_2
- priority: rp_2

The *fighter* role is defined as follows:

- name: *fighter*,
- description: It receives orders from the *head fighter* to launch bombs.
- capacity: rc_3
- priority: rp_3

We assume that $rp_1 \geq rp_2 \geq rp_3$.

Now that the roles are identified, we have to define the relations between these roles. Several kinds of relations can be defined between roles. These relations can be grouped in the following categories:

- Control relation: that shows which role controls which other role (the *head fighter* controls the *auxiliary head fighter* and the *fighter*).
- Cooperation relation: two roles cooperate if one role offers a service to another role. For example, there is cooperation between the *head fighter* and the *auxiliary head fighter*, in the decision making process.
- Communication relation: two roles have to communicate in order to exchange information. For example, all the fighters have to exchange sensory information.
- Inheritance relation: Let us assume that role r_1 has tasks $t_1, t_2, ..., t_n$, and that role r_2 has its tasks defined as a subset of r_1 tasks. In this case, we can say that r_1 inherits from r_2. In the F-16 example, the *head fighter* role and the *auxiliary head fighter* role inherit from the *fighter* role.
- **kShare**: this relation stands for *knowledge share*. If two roles r_1 and r_2 have a *kShare* relation, this means that they share some knowledge. This relation guarantees that if an agent playing some roles is out of service, other agents that share its knowledge can fulfill its roles. For example, the *auxiliary head fighter* role shares knowledge with the *head fighter* role.

In the F-16 example, we summarize the different roles and relations as follows:

- The *head fighter* controls the *auxiliary head fighter* and the *fighter*;
- The *head fighter*, *auxiliary head fighter*, and the *fighter* cooperate together. To engage, a fighter needs a direct order from the *head fighter*. To decide whether to attack, the *head fighter* needs information gathered by the *auxiliary head fighter*. To deliver information to the *head fighter*, the *auxiliary head fighter* waits for an order from the *head fighter*;

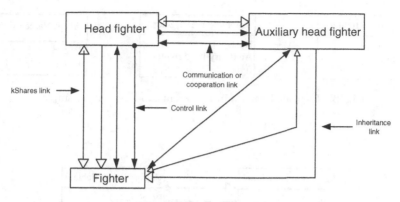

Fig. 2. The role model

- The different roles must communicate and coordinate their actions in order to achieve their objectives.
- Hence, the *head fighter* role, and the *auxiliary head fighter* role inherit from the *fighter* role;
- The three fighters share knowledge such as target position, their current position, etc. Hence, there is a *kshare* relation between the three roles.

The role model is represented in Figure 2.

Now that we have determined the different roles and their relationships, we need to assign them to actual agents. This is what the next section presents.

4   The Design Phase

4.1   The Agent Model

In the agent model, we focus on assigning roles to agents. An agent's social ability is defined in relation to its capacity to interact with other agents. Two agents cannot interact if there is no relation between them. Each agent plays one or several roles. Roles are related to each other as presented in the role model. Role relations must be handled by agents so that the agents can interact together correctly. Agent relations can be deduced from role relations. If we have an agent Ag playing role A, and an agent Bg playing role B, if the two roles A and B are related by a relation r, then agents Ag and Bg are related by the relation r.

In a Fault-Tolerant MAS, we can sometimes use replicated agents to replace unavailable agents [9]. At other time, we cannot count on replicating agents as in our F-16 example. To solve this problem, the agent roles may change in order to fulfill the missing roles.

Each agent A_i is associated with a processing unit that will handle the execution of its roles $r_{i1}, r_{i2}, ..., r_{in}$. Each processing unit has a limited capacity denoted ac_i; it may be thought of as an internal resource needed by an agent to accomplish its roles. Each role r_{ij} requires a capacity rc_{ij}. Hence, an agent can

Agent Name : fighter1
Role:
head fighter
fighter

Agent Name : fighter2
Role:
Auxiliary head fighter
fighter

Agent Name : fighter3
Role:
fighter

Fig. 3. Identified agents in the agent model of our example

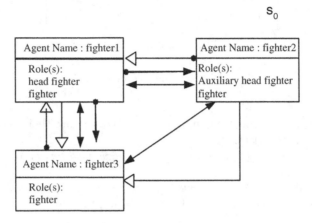

Fig. 4. Part of the agent model in situation s_0

be assigned a role only if the sum of the needed processing capacity to perform all of its assigned roles is less or equal than the agent's processing capacity.

Since a MAS must reorganize itself according to the environment model, the agent model will be associated with a situation of the environment model [11] [12] that suits the various needs of the system, providing it with an organization that maximizes its possibility to reach its objectives [5].

The agent model of the F-16 example is presented in Figure 3.

The three agents *fighter1*, *fighter2*, and *fighter3* are with respective available capacities: ac_1, ac_2, and ac_3. For each fighter, we assume that (see Section 3.3 for the definition of rc_1, rc_2, and rc_3):

- *fighter1*: $ac_1 \geq rc_1 + rc_3$
- *fighter2*: $ac_2 \geq rc_2 + rc_3$
- *fighter3*: $ac_3 \geq rc_3$

In situation s_0, the MAS organization structure (deduced from role relations of Figure 2) is given in Figure 4.

However, in situation s_1 (see Figure 1), the *fighter1* agent is down. Hence, the two roles *head fighter* and *fighter* are missing. They must be assigned to

---

[5] Agent relationships are deduced from role relations defined in the role model.

S_1

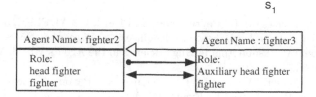

Fig. 5. Part of the agent model in situation s_1

the other agents. We notice that role *fighter* is already played by agents *fighter2* and *fighter3*. Hence, we only need to assign role *head fighter*. Agent *fighter2* has a higher priority than agent *fighter3* since *fighter2* has one role with a higher priority than all the roles of *fighter3*. Consequently, we examine whether we can assign role *head fighter* to *fighter2*. We assume that $rc_1 + rc_2 + rc_3 > ac_2$. We know that $rc_1 + rc_3 \leq ac_2$. We know also that the *head fighter* role has a higher priority than the *auxiliary head fighter* role. So, we make the decision to assign role *head fighter* to agent2. Now, we have to assign *auxiliary head fighter* role to agent *fighter3*. We assume that $rc_2 + rc_3 \leq ac_3$. So, *auxiliary head fighter* role can be assigned to agent *fighter3* as shown in Figure 5.

In summary, we propose to represent role relations in the role model instead of representing them in the agent model. In fact, roles are predefined, and their relationships are preserved independently of their assignment to agents. Meanwhile, agents can see their roles change as well as their relationships. But, agent relations can be deduced from role relations. This is why our agent model focuses on the assignment of unfilled roles to existing agents.

5   Conclusion

In this paper, we proposed guidelines to a design methodology for Fault-Tolerant Multi-Agent Systems. We dealt with the environment so that some troublesome situations can be identified at an early stage of the system design. By allowing the dynamic assignment of roles to agents in some predefined ways, we facilitate the design and implementation of a fault-tolerant multi-agent system.

As future works, we will develop an interaction model to complete the set of models. In addition, we need to specify an implementation phase to our methodology. We will possibly need to introduce probabilities in the environment model since transitions between situations are very often probabilistic. We will also propose a modal logic, tailored to our set of models, which will be useful to do model checking between particular situations and the definitions of the MAS as represented by its set of models.

References

[1] Bernon, C., Gleizes, M. P., Peyruqueou, S., Picard, G.: ADELFE, a Methodology for Adaptive Multi-Agent Systems Engineering. Workshop Notes of the Third International Workshop Engineering Societies in the Agents World. Madrid, Spain (2002) 21–34 278, 280, 284

[2] Caire, G., Coulier, W., Garijo, F. J., Gomez, J., Pavon, J., Leal, F., Chainho, P., Kearney, P. E., Stark, J., Evans, R., Massonet, P. Agent Oriented Analysis Using Message/UML. Agent Oriented Software Engineering (AOSE) (2001) 119-135 279, 280

[3] Duursma, C., Olsson, O., Ulf, S. Task Model Definition and Task Analysis Process. Technical Report KADS-II/VUB/TR/004/2.0. Esprit Project P5248, Free University Brussels and Swedish Institute of Computer Science (1994) 281

[4] Ferber, J., Gutknecht, O. A meta-model for the analysis and design of organizations in multi-agent systems. In Proceedings of the Third International Conference on Multi-Agent Systems (ICMAS98), Paris, France,(1998) 128-135 278, 280

[5] Ferber, J., Gutknecht, O., Michel, F. From Agents to Organizations: an Organizational View of Multi-Agent Systems. Third International Conference on Autonomous Agents and Multi-Agent Systems, Sydney, Australia (2003) 281

[6] FIPA Methodology Glossary:
http://www.pa.icar.cnr.it/~cossentino/FIPAmeth/glossary.htm 281

[7] Gerhard, W.:Multiagent Systems, A modern Approach to Distributed Artificial Intelligence. Weiss Gerhard Editor. The MIT Press, Cambridge, Massachussets, London, England (1999) 286

[8] Giunchiglia, F., Mylopoulos, J., Perini, A. The tropos software development methodology: processes, models and diagrams. Proceedings of the second international joint conference on Autonomous agents and multiagent systems, Bologna, Italy (2002) 35–36 280

[9] Hagg, S.:A Sentinel Approach to Fault Handling in Multi-Agent Systems. Proceedings of the Second Australian Workshop on Distributed AI, in conjunction with the Fourth Pacific Rim International Conference on Artificial Intelligence (PRICAI'96). Cairns, Australia, (1996) 275, 283, 289

[10] Iglesias C. A., Garijo, M., Centeno-Gonzalez J., Velasco, J. R. Analysis and Design of Multiagent Systems Using MAS-Common KADS. Agent Theories, Architectures, and Languages (1997) 313–327 276, 280

[11] Mellouli, S., Mineau, G., Moulin, B.: Multi-Agent Systems Design.Workshop Notes of the Third International Workshop Engineering Societies in the Agents World. Madrid, Spain (2002) 127–138 281, 282, 284, 290

[12] Mellouli, S., Mineau, G., Moulin, B.: Situation Event Logic for Early Validation of Multi-Agent Systems. 16th Canadian Conference on Artificial Intelligence (AI'2003). June, Halifax, Nova Scotia, Canada (2003) 284, 290

[13] Mellouli, S., Mineau, G., Pascot, D.:The integrated modeling of multi-agent systems and their environment. Proceedings of the first international joint conference on Autonomous agents and multiagent systems. Bologna, Italy (2002) 507–508 281, 284

[14] Mellouli, S., Moulin, B., Mineau, W. Towards an Agent Unified Modelling Methodology (AUMM). The 7th World Multiconference on Systemics, Cybernetics and Informatics. July 27-30 2003, Orlando, Florida, USA. Volume XIII. pp 14–19. 280

[15] Odell., J., Parunak., H., Bauer, B.: Extending UML for Agents. Proceedings of the Agent-Oriented Information Systems Workshop at the 17th National conference on Artificial Intelligence. (2000) 279

[16] Odell., J., Parunak., H., Fleisher., M., and Brueckner., S: Modeling Agents and their Environment. Workshop on Agent-Oriented Software Engineering. Bologna, Italy (2002) 173–188. 284

[17] Odell, J., Parunak, H., Fleischer, M. The Role of Roles. Journal of Object Technology, January-February, Vol.2, No. 1 (2003) 39–51 281

[18] Omicini, A.: SODA: Societies and Infrastructures in the Analysis and Design of Agent-Based Systems. Workshop on Agent Oriented Software Engineering. (2000) 185–193 276, 278, 280, 284

[19] UML: Unified Modelling Language. http://www.uml.org. 279, 281, 283

[20] Van Lamsweerde, A., Leiter, E. Handling Obstacles in Gaol-Oriented Requirements Engineering. IEEE Transactions on Software Engineering, Vol. 26, No. 10, October(2000) 978–1005 276

[21] Wooldridge, M., Jennings, N.R., Kinny, D.:Developing Multiagent Systems: The Gaia Methodology. ACM Trans on Software Engineering and Methodology 12(3)(2000):pp. 317–370 277, 280, 281, 287

Patterns Reuse in the PASSI Methodology

Massimo Cossentino[1], Luca Sabatucci[1], and Antonio Chella[1,2]

[1] Istituto di Calcolo e Reti ad Alte Prestazioni, Consiglio Nazionale delle Ricerche
Viale delle Scienze, 90128 Palermo, Italy
`{cossentino,sabatucci}@pa.icar.cnr.it`
[2] Dipartimento di Ingegneria Informatica, Università degli Studi di Palermo
Viale delle Scienze, 90128 Palermo, Italy
`chella@unipa.it`

Abstract. Design patterns already proved successful in lowering the development time and number of errors of object-oriented software; now, they are, candidate to play a similar role in the MAS (multi-agent system) context. In this work we describe our experiences in the identification, production and application of patterns for agents. Some patterns are described together with the classification criteria and documentation approach we adopt. Upon them, we base a pattern reuse process that can be considered one of the distinguishing elements of the design methodology (PASSI) we use to develop MAS. Patterns can be applied to an existing agent or used to produce a new one with the support of a specific web based application that can read both the JAVA source code and XMI representation of the agent design documentation. After the successful application of the desired pattern(s), the source code and the design diagrams (usually a structural and dynamic diagram) of the agent can be exported. Some experimental results are reported in order to demonstrate the utility of this approach in automatically producing an interesting percentage of code lines.

1 Introduction

In the last years, multi-agent systems (MAS) achieved an unprecedent success and diffusion; as an example, e-commerce applications are growing up quickly, they are leaving the research field and the first experiences of industrial applications are appearing. These applicative contexts require high-level qualities of design as well as secure, affordable and well-performing implementation architectures. In our research we focus on the design process of agent societies considering that this activity implies not only modeling an agent in place of an object but also capturing the ontology of its domain, representing its interaction with other agents (social aspects), and providing it with the ability of performing intelligent behaviors. Several scientific works that address this topic can be found in literature; it is possible to note that they come from different research fields: some come from Artificial Intelligence (Gaia [1]) others from Software Engineering (MaSE [2], Tropos [3]) but there are also methodologies coming directly from Robotics (Cassiopeia [4]). They give different emphasis to the different aspects of

A. Omicini, P. Petta, and J. Pitt (Eds.): ESAW 2003, LNAI 3071, pp. 294–310, 2004.
© Springer-Verlag Berlin Heidelberg 2004

the process (for example the design of goals, communications, roles) but almost all of them deal with the same basic elements although in a different way or using different notations/languages. In the following, we will pursuit a specific goal: lowering the time and costs of developing a MAS application. In order to obtain this result, we think that a fundamental contribution could come by the automation of as many steps of the process as possible (or similarly by providing a strong automatic support to the designer). In pursuing these objectives we developed a design methodology (PASSI, "Process for Agent Societies Specification and Implementation" [5]) specifically conceived to be supported by a CASE tool that automatically compiles some models that are part of the process, using the inputs provided by the designer. PASSI is a step-by-step requirement-to-code methodology for developing multi-agent software that integrates design models and philosophies from both object-oriented software engineering and MAS using UML notation. We widely applied it in the design of robotics applications [6] but it also proved successful in designing information systems [7]. In PASSI (Fig. 1), the reuse of existing patterns has a great importance. Unlike other authors (Kendall [8]), we chose to introduce a pattern definition conceived for MAS belonging to a specific architecture (the FIPA one). As a consequence, all the agents we consider in our pattern, have a similar structure and their behavior refers to a finite state machine. All of these simplifications were useful in order to create a pattern that affects all the stages of the agent development process. Our pattern is a representation and implementation of some kind of (a part of) the system behaviors that solves a recurrent problem (for example a specific type of agents' interaction). During a PASSI design process, the designers will use a Rational Rose add-in that we have specifically produced. In this procedure they move gradually from the problem domain (described in the System Requirements Model and Agent Society Model) towards the solution domain (mainly represented by the Agent Implementation Model) and, passing through the coding phase, to the dissemination of the agents in their world. It is in this progress of activities that they can identify some problems that could be profitably solved reusing the patterns of our repository. The choice of the implementation platform is postponed to the final steps of the design and in order to support the localization of our patterns in both the most diffused FIPA [9] platforms (FIPA-OS [10] and JADE [11]) we represent the models and the code of each pattern using XML. In the case of the models we use the diffused XMI representation of the UML diagrams while for the code we introduced some intermediate levels of representation in XML from which we obtain the final Java code using several XSL transformation.

The remaining part of the paper is organized as follows: section 2 describes our approach to the classification of agent patterns; section 3 provides a discussion on the process used to construct the code for a specific execution environment starting from the platform-independent pattern; section 4 discusses where patterns can be identified during the design process and their impact in it; numerical results about the amount of automatically generated lines of code are provided in section 5 and finally some conclusions are drawn in the final section.

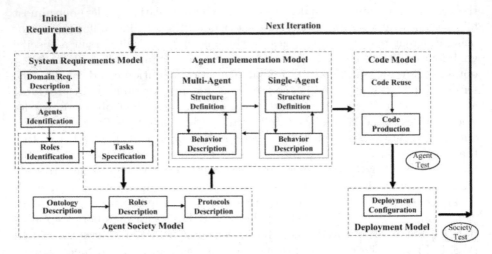

Fig. 1. The PASSI methodology

2   Patterns Classification

A classic approach to patterns classification, can be found in [12], where patterns are classified by two criteria: purpose and scope. With purpose the authors refer to what the pattern does and according to this, they enumerate creational (dealing with the process of object creation), structural (dealing with the composition of classes and objects) or behavioral (describing the interactions of classes/objects) patterns. The scope classification is directed to separate patterns that apply to classes or object. While the first category (class patterns) deal with the relationships among classes (usually structural, for example inheritance), the second one includes relationships among object (usually dynamic and established at runtime).

A different, more agent-oriented, classification is proposed by Lind in [13]. Patterns are classified in accordance to the views defined by the author in the MASSIVE methodology [14]. Categories reported in this work are: Interaction, Role, Architecture, Society, System, Task, and Environment.

Another classification can be found in [15] where patterns are clustered in the traveling (dealing with agent mobility issues), task (regarding the breakdown of agents tasks and the delegation of them from one agent to another) and interaction (dealing with agents communications) categories. Recently another possible category (adaptability patterns [16]) has been proposed by other authors.

We think that the basic duality that exists in software between structure and dynamic behavior is someway captured by the Gamma's approach but we also consider the importance of enriching it in order to fit the specific context (agents not objects). For this reasons we decided to classify the patterns of our repository using two main criteria (like in Gamma et al. [12]) and to include agent specific subcategories in them. The first criterion is the *application context*; it regards the

Table 1. The classification of the patterns in our repository. (I/P) indicates the presence of both the Initiator and Participant role patterns. Action patterns are not listed by name because of their number

		Application Context			
		Action	*Behavior*	*Component*	*Service*
Functio-nality	*Access to local resources*	53		Generic Agent, Parallel Resource Sharing, Sequential Resource Sharing, Publish-Subscribe, Resource Caching	
	Communica-tion	66	Request (I/P), Query (I/P), Inform (I/P), ContractNet (I/P)		Request, Query, Inform, Contract-Net
	Elaboration	44		Planner	
	Mobility	7			Explorer

structural aspects of the pattern, whether it is to be applied to one agent, more agents or to their composing elements (tasks/behaviors). The second criterion is the *functionality* expressed by the pattern. We enumerated four kinds of patterns in the first category:

Action patterns — They address a functionality of the system; for instance they can be implemented as a method of either an agent class or a task class.

Behavior patterns —They address a specific behavior of an agent; we can look at each of them as a collection of actions.

Component patterns — They are entire agent patterns; these patterns propose a solution composed of the entire structure of an agent together with its tasks.

Service pattern — Concerned about the collaborations between two or more agents; they can be thought as an aggregation of component patterns.

Again, looking at the functionality of the patterns, we can consider four categories:

Access to local resources — They deal with information retrieval and manipulation of data source.

Communication — They represent the solution to the problem of making two agents communicate by an interaction protocol.

Elaboration — They are used to deal with the agent's functionality devoted to perform some kind of elaboration on its knowledge.

Mobility — These patterns describe the possibility for an agent to move from a platform to another, maintaining its knowledge.

In Table 1 we can find a classification of the patterns in our repository. Some of them have proved particularly useful for building up a totally new agent (the *GenericAgent* component pattern includes the base functionalities that an agent needs in order to register to the platform and yellow pages service) or enriching the capabilities of an existing one (the *Request Initiator* behavior pattern can be applied to an agent to give it the possibility of initiating a communication with the FIPA Request interaction protocol).

3   From Design Representation to Multi-platform Coding of Patterns

Patterns can contribute to significantly enhance the quality of the software design and this is one of the reasons that justify their diffusion. In addiction to this argument, we think that under precise hypothesis, patterns can also provide another important contribution, to the development process: enhancing the amount of code produced with a CASE tool. The hypothesis we assume to achieve this goal regards the implementation domain.

If we suppose that all the agents will be implemented with a specific FIPA-compliant platform, then we define the structure of the implementation obtaining an extreme simplification. This is a very restrictive hypothesis that can be done in a specific company but it is too limiting for a wider research purpose. Therefore, we decided to study the possibility of reducing the implementation platforms to a little number in order to obtain some kind of generality for our approach. In this first phase we selected two different platforms (JADE [11] and FIPA-OS [10]) that, together represent a greater part of the installed platforms in the Agentcities EU initiative [17].

3.1   Differences in FIPA-Compliant Implementation Platforms

In order to understand how the choice of coding our patterns for the JADE and FIPA-OS platforms effects the proposed solution we will now describe the main differences of two different implementations (FIPA-OS and JADE) of the same agent. We will initially propose a FIPA-OS implementation of a simple agent that once started invokes a task (behavior in the JADE platform implementation) in order to accomplish its duty. In so doing this task uses the results provided by another one. Both the presented implementations (fig. 2 and fig. 3) are documented using a class diagram that shows the structural differences between the two agents and an activity diagram that reports the flow of control.

In fig. 2 we can see the structure of the FIPA-OS agent, it is composed of the main agent class and two task classes. Its behavior consists of:

1. The execution of the agent's constructor and *setup* methods.
2. The instantiation of the *ComponentTask1* task (a piece of behavior in the FIPA-OS terminology), invoked by the agent's *setup*. In the FIPA-OS platform at the moment of the instantiation of a new task, the execution of the

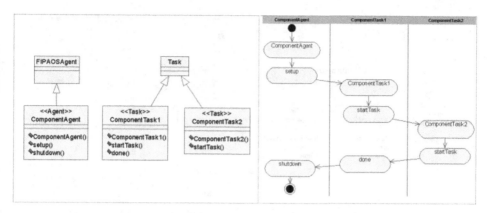

Fig. 2. A simple FIPA-OS agent (left) and its behavior (right)

constructor it is followed by the execution of its *startTask* method. While the constructor is often used to initialize variables, the *startTask* method is commonly used to actuate the specific initial behavior of the task.

3. The *startTask* method of *ComponentTask1* instantiates *ComponentTask2* (another task, for instance devoted to elaborate some kind of data). Again, after the constructor, the *startTask* method is executed.
4. The conclusion of the execution of *ComponentTask2* is stated by a *done* command in the last line of the code of its *startTask* method. The result is that the *done* event is sent to the task that invoked this one. This event is intercepted by the *done* method in *ComponentTask1*. One different *done* method is necessary, in FIPA-OS systems, in the calling task for each other invoked task (the link between the instantiated task and the related *done* method is based on the name of the method that is in fact composed by the *done* prefix and the invoked task name).

In fig. 3 we can see the JADE implementation of the agent described before. We can see that the structure is very similar (considering that task classes in FIPA-OS are named behavior in JADE). One of the differences, only formal, is in the name of the FIPA-OS *startTask* method, that is called *setup* in JADE. Another difference consists in the *done* method. In JADE we have one done method for each behavior class, its duty is related to the behavior that is hosting it, not to an invoked one. The platform scheduler verifies the value reported by the done method of each behavior and if it is true the class will not be rescheduled. There is no necessity of introducing a method in a behavior who calls another one. Another difference can be found in the *shutdown* method, present in the FIPA-OS agent that is not necessary in the JADE agent.

As we can see in fig. 2 and in fig. 3 these little differences are clearly shown in both the structural and dynamical diagrams. This fact concretely affects our work and we introduced in our patterns, a specific instrument (constraints, described in the next subsection) to deal with it.

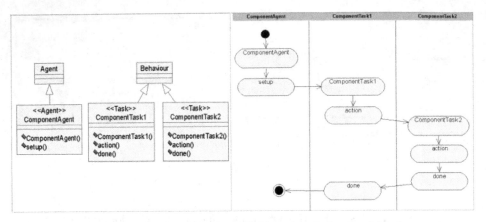

Fig. 3. A simple Jade agent (left) and its behavior (right)

3.2 Pattern Definition

These platforms use the same coding language (JAVA) and share several similarity. Starting from these working hypothesis, we produced a meta representation of all our patterns (see fig. 4) that describes the pattern not considering implementation specific issues. This meta-pattern can be derived from the repository and can be used to generate portions of the design diagrams through an XML-XMI transformation. From the same meta-pattern we instantiate the platform specific pattern and then we generate the related code. In the following sections we will briefly describe this process.

Meta-Patterns — The key element of our multi-platform implementation of patterns consists in the introduction of meta-patterns. They are platform independent and contain all the elements that are common to patterns of the different environments. For example meta-patterns refers to class constructors, mother-classes from which agents and their standard elements inherit their behavior, setup and shutdown methods and so on. Meta-patterns are described using XML and can be used to both generate portions of design diagrams and the platform-specific pattern description.

Patterns — Applying an XSL transformation we substitute the meta-level placeholders with the name used in the selected platforms and if the case the values introduced by the designer (for example the specific name of the agent or some parameters). In this XML file an agent is described inside an Agent tag. Agent properties such as attributes or tasks are represented as inner elements of the structure.

Patterns and constraints — When a pattern is applied to a project it modifies the context in which it is placed, for instance introducing new functionalities into the system. These additions need to satisfy some constraints (e.g. in FIPA-OS, when we insert a communication task pattern into an existing agent, the listener task should have a handleX method to catch performative acts of a particular type). This relationship between the pattern and

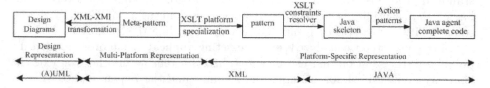

Fig. 4. The process used to obtain the platform specific pattern from its meta-representation

the existing elements could be expressed with a constraint. A constraint is a rule composed of two elements: a target and a content. The target specifies what agent/task will be influenced by the rule. The content expresses the changes to be applied when the pattern is inserted into the project; it could be an aggregation of attributes, constructors or methods. After localizing the pattern for the specific platform we apply all the constraints related to it using another XSL transformation.

Multi-platform code generation — As briefly mentioned before, XSLT application grants to export an agent described with our meta-language into a specific programming language. This is possible because the pattern at this stage intrinsically represents an implementation viewpoint. As a matter of fact, UML classes (of the design representation) correspond to Java classes, and UML attributes and methods correspond to the Java classes' attributes and methods. This allows us to look at the source code as one of the possible views of an agent: we could imagine this agent representation as an intermediate layer between agent design and agent development. The use of XSLT enables code generation for both FIPA-OS and Jade frameworks by only changing the transformation sheet. At this stage the JAVA skeleton of the agent (and it's tasks) is complete. In order to (partially) fill the skeleton with the remaining code, action patterns are applied. An action pattern is a portion of code realizing some kind of behavior, for example the registration to the DF (Directory Facilitator) service, the yellow pages of the platform. Action patterns are stored in a database of pieces of code and the correct one for each method is selected referring to the value of the *Code* tag for the specific module.

3.3 Pattern Repository Population

The process of patterns identification has been divided in two different stages. In the first one, on the basis of our previous experiences with MASs, we prepared several common use, easily identifiable patterns. Among these patterns we have the *GenericAgent* one; this implements the basic behaviors of each agent (registration with the agent platform and yellow pages service). Other patterns that we identified in this phase are the communication related ones. We produced a set of patterns to deal with communications based on the most diffused FIPA standard protocols (AIP, Agent Interaction Protocols) at different levels (a behavior that can initiate or participate to a communication, an agent with the same ability or a couple of agents interacting according the same AIP).

In the next step we analyzed several existing applications in order to identify portions of the solution that can be generalized for reusing in other contexts. In this way we identified, for example, the *Planner* and the *Explorer* pattern.

The *Planner* pattern is a component pattern (i.e. it describes an entire agent) and it implements the structure necessary to perform some kind of planning activity for reaching a goal. It partitions the system architecture in almost three levels: a superior strategic level, an intermediate planner level and an inferior actuator level. We could explain the usefulness of this pattern by applying it in a classic robotic mission, the exploration of an unknown environment. The strategic level responsibility consists in selecting the goal to pursue from a set of possible choices, in the navigational example it selects the direction to explore from all the possible alternatives. When the strategic level has selected a goal (or sub-goal), it passes this information to the planner level; this has access to the already discovered map of the environment and builds the plan. When the plan is ready the last level provides commands to some actuator agents that enable the robot movements.

The *Explorer* pattern allows the exploration of remote sites with the intent of searching for some information. A typical scenario that illustrates the scope this pattern is represented by web searching. It is a service pattern and therefore it is composed of two agents: the *base* agent and the *explorer* agent. The first one is responsible for the searching activity and can create one or more *explorer* agents that will move to the target sites. Each *explorer* is associated to a destination and when created, it moves to reach it; once there it starts the searching activity and then reports the results using a communication based on some kind of interaction protocol.

The pattern repository is actually composed (see Table 1) of five service patterns (regarding problems solved by the participation of at least two agents), six component patterns (an entire agent is involved in the problem), eight behavior patterns (including behavior-level solutions) and a consistent number of action patterns (solutions at the class method level, some of them extracted from the previous patterns).

4   Reusing Patterns

In order to better describe where we can introduce and reuse patterns with PASSI we should start defining what we mean by pattern. We accept the definition provided by Christopher Alexander [18]: "Each pattern describes a problem which occurs over and over again in our environment, and then describes the core solution to that problem". A pattern can be found (or applied) wherever a problem is present. If we consider our pattern classification we can conclude that we can reuse patterns when we face a local resource access, communication, elaboration of mobility problem. This reuse can have different scopes: a collab-

oration among two agents can be accomplished by a service pattern, a single
agent with a particular vocation can be realized applying a component pattern,
specific features of an agent can be delegated to a behavior pattern and simple actions can be done with action patterns. As the design process starts from
an high level of abstraction and step by step goes down to the more detailed
aspects of the solution we should expect that larger patterns (services, components) will be identified in the initial phases of the design while smaller ones
(behaviors, actions) could arise during the final design choices. Now we will discuss these aspects with regard to the PASSI methodology in order to describe
our experiences.

In PASSI from the functional requirements description (use case diagrams
of the Domain Requirements Description phase), we obtain the agent's responsibilities in terms of the functionalities they will provide. This happens in the
Agent Identification diagram that is an use case diagrams where packages are
used to enclose use cases that will be under the responsibility of the same agent.
Stereotypes of relationships among use cases belonging to different agents are
changed to *communicate* (not standard in UML) since they represent interactions among different active elements (agents) of the system. In this diagram we
could easily identify patterns of higher structural levels (service and component)
as described in the following scenario.

Let us consider a supply chain whose purpose is to ensure the availability
of raw materials for the production chain of some manufacturing company. In
fig. 5 we can see a part of the A.Id. diagram of this application; the scenario
we are dealing with involves the following agents (see the package name): *Stock-
Guardian*, *PurchaseAgent* and *SupplierAgent*. The *StockGuardian* is responsible
of looking at the amount of raw materials and starting the supplying process once
they go below a defined level (depending on the scheduled work). It calculates the
quantity of materials that is necessary to buy and asks to the *PurchaseAgent*
of supplying them (*SupplyingRequest* use case). The *PurchaseAgent* starts an
auction (in the proposed implementation not really an auction since the process will be based on the ContractNet interaction protocol) to buy at the best
price. The possible suppliers are selected considering the previous experiences of
the company with them (*CompileGoodSupplierList* and *SuppliersEvaluation* use
cases. Each selected supplier receives a notice and then, can post his own bids
(*IntroduceBidParameters* use case) for the auction, interacting (via web) with
the instance of the *SupplierAgent* that has been devoted to him (the access is
password protected). Suppliers achieve an highest level of security installing an
agent platform in their company. In this case the *SupplierAgent* will move to his
owner host.

Now suppose that we want to apply patterns to this diagram. We can decide to use an Explorer service pattern in order to realize the basic part of the
SupplierAgent. This pattern allows to an agent the exploration of remote agent
platforms with the intent to perform some kind of operation in them; it is composed of two agents: the base agent will create an explorer agent and will send
it to the other platform(s). The explorer agent will perform the required (and

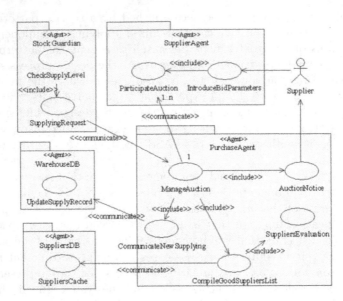

Fig. 5. Part of the Agent Identification diagram of a manufacturing plant software solution

not described in the pattern) operation and then will inform its base agent. We can apply the base agent part of the pattern to the *PurchaseAgent* and the explorer part to the *SupplierAgent*. The auction communications can be implemented by a ContractNet service pattern (the initiator part will be applied to the *PurchaseAgent* and the participant part to the *SupplierAgent*). Several communications can be identified in the diagram and these can be realized using the corresponding service pattern (for instance the Request service pattern that is a communication pattern providing the initiator and participant roles for a communication based on the FIPA Request interaction protocol).

Summarizing, in the agent identification diagram reported in fig. 5 we can identify six service patterns and one component pattern. It should be noted that many of them cannot arise from the analysis of a standard UML use case diagram; specifically, communications among agents (that are pointed out by the *communicate* relationship among use cases of different agents) are present in the A.Id. diagram since it shows a particular hypothesis of solution (an agent-based system).

4.1   Impact of Patterns in the Design

It is interesting to note how relevant can be the backlash of the previous identified patterns in the other phases of the PASSI design. In the following we will describe two different typologies of possible consequences: the guidance that the reused pattern gives to the designer in his/hers (manual) operations, and the support that can be automatically provided by a tool in reusing that pattern (some of these features are already supported by PTK, the Rational Rose add-in that we built in order to design with PASSI).

After the A.Id. phase, the designer performs the Roles Identification where he/she describes the scenarios arising from the use case diagrams using several sequence diagrams. When the scenarios involves the identified pattern, the designer receives a guidance from the sequence diagram that illustrates the collaborations of the pattern. During the exploitation of these scenarios, a first draft of the MASD (Multi-Agent Structure Diagram) is built. This is an high level representation of the agent society structure and interaction. It is a class diagram reporting each agent as a class and each agent behavior as a method of this class; relationships among agents represent their communications. The choice of reusing a pattern obviously has a direct (and tool-supported) effect on this diagram. In fact, new behavior and agents are introduced according to the pattern structure.

The Task Specification (T.Sp.) phase is the next one and this also offers an opportunity to identify behavior patterns. In this step, one different activity diagram is drawn for each agent. It represents a possible decomposition of the agent functionalities into a series of activities (that are candidate to be implemented as behaviors). As a consequence, it is possible to find behavior patterns in these diagrams. Their compilation is also strongly affected by previous introduced component and service patterns. Suppose that in the previous discussed manufacturing company scenario, we decide to introduce a *Resource caching* pattern in the *SuppliersDB* agent in order to implement a caching mechanism for minimizing accesses to the DB. In fig. 6 we can see the *Resource caching* pattern; this diagram can be largely reused in order to build the T.Sp. diagram of the *SuppliersDB* agent and PTK support this.

We have now completed the system requirements model and only minor effects we will find in the following agent society model (for example in the communication ontology description diagram we will complete the description of all the communication including the pattern supported ones).

The third PASSI model (agent implementation) is strongly related to the final coding activities and almost all of its phases receive an influence from selected patterns. This model is composed of a structural and behavioral definition of the MAS that is performed at both the multi and single agent level. As a result we have two structural diagrams and two behavioral diagrams: the multi-agent structure diagram (MASD, one unique diagram representing each agent of the society as a class and communications among agents as relationships, see fig. 7), the single-agent structure diagram (SASD, one different class diagram for each agent, reporting all the agent implementation structure, it is the nearest to the code), the multi-agent behavior diagram (MABD, an activity diagram representing the agents and their behaviors) and a single-agent behavior diagram (SABD, used to represent the algorithmic aspects of the solution). Finally the code is generated, also reusing patterns from the repository and the designer after having manually completed the agents, can deploy them.

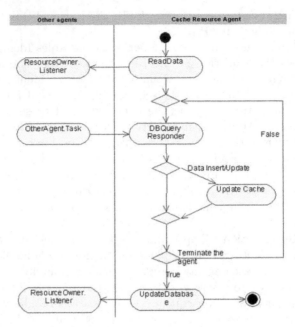

Fig. 6. The Resource cache pattern can store some data from a DB and provide it to the other interacting agents without repeatedly querying the DB

In section 5 we will report some numerical results about the contribution that the automatic code generation can give in developing the cited manufacturing application.

5   Experimental Results

In this section we will report the results obtained applying our methodology and patterns to an application built to support the production and supply chains of a manufacturing company.This is not a theoretic exercise because the introduction of this software in the real productive environment is ongoing.

Because of the large dimension of the whole application we will here describe only a part of it and specifically, we will focus on the supply chain whose purpose is to ensure the availability of raw materials to the production chain.

The initial application has been designed following the PASSI methodology [5] but without a considerable use of patterns, since their repository was almost empty at that time. Now, in our experiment we will reproduce it applying the patterns with the support of PTK and the AgentFactory tool (the pattern reuse tool we integrated in PASSI and that is also available as a standalone or an on-line application[1]). The identification of the best suited patterns will be performed on the PASSI diagrams as discussed in section 4. Then we

---

[1] Website: http://mozart.csai.unipa.it/af/

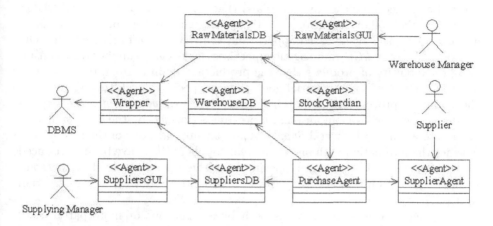

Fig. 7. A class diagram reporting the agents involved in the experiment and their relationships (communications)

will compare the number of lines of code (LOC) of the original agents with the number of lines of code obtained by the patterns application.

In fig. 7 we can see a class diagram reporting the agents involved in the experiment. Each class in the diagram represents an agent, and its relationships stand for the agent's communications. Agents' attributes (knowledge) and operations (tasks) are not reported for clarity but they are present in the original diagram that is a Multi-Agent Structure Definition diagram of the PASSI methodology.

Here is a description of the way these agents interact to provide the production chain with the necessaries supplies:

The *Warehouse Manager* interacts with the *RawMaterialsGUI* agent running on his laptop or PDA in order to describe the raw materials needed for each artifact. This data is received by the *RawMaterialAgent* (responsible for

Table 2. Statistics of the experiment

Agents	Total LOC	Automatically Generated LOC	% of Total	Methods Body LOC	% of Autom. Generated
SuppliersDB	284	162	57	85	52
Wrapper	790	66	8	35	53
RawMaterialsDB	290	144	49	78	54
SuppliersAgent	124	43	34	26	60
PurchaseAgent	304	133	43	79	59
WarehouseDB	219	162	73	87	53
StockGuardian	109	98	89	49	50
RawMaterialsGUI	71	36	50	19	52
SuppliersGUI	69	36	52	19	52
Totale	2260	880	39	477	54

everything concerning the raw materials) that registers it in the central DBMS asking for the collaboration of the *Wrapper* agent (responsible for the interactions among the agent-based application, the DBMS, and other existing OO software). The *StockGuardian* agent supervises the levels of supplies (also considering the quantity of products that the production chain is going to deal with). When the stock of some material goes under a specified level, this agent starts the supplying process with a message to the *PurchaseAgent* agent. The acquisition of new materials is an automatic process performed by the *PurchaseAgent* agent interacting with several *SupplierAgent* agents; each one of them is responsible for the interaction with one of the real suppliers that have been introduced by the *Supplying Manager* in a specific list. The agents involved in the commercial transaction interact using the standard FIPA Contract Net interaction protocol [19].

Each agent of this scenario has been built using one or more patterns. In Table 2 we summarize the results of this experiment. Globally this portion of the system is composed of about 2000 lines of code subdivided into nine agents. The result of building the agents with patterns is that we obtain a base code of 880 lines: the 43% of the entire system. In this code, automatically generated, we can separate the class skeletons (generated by several CASE tools) from the methods body (not generated by conventional CASE tools). The methods body, represents the behavior and the actions of the agents. The amount of this code is the 54% of the automatically generated one; usually this should be entered and tested manually by skilled programmers. With the use of our approach this code (already tested) is automatically generated with a minimal amount of work and this allows a remarkable saving in time and a positive effect on the overall quality.

6   Conclusions

Our conviction is that pattern reuse is a very challenging and interesting issue in multi-agent systems as it has been in object-oriented ones. However we are aware that the problems arising from this subject are quite delicate and risky. Nonetheless, we believe, thanks to the experiences made in fields such as robotics, that it is possible to obtain great results with a correct approach. In the previous sections we discussed the impact of pattern reuse in PASSI, a complete design methodology for multi-agent systems that is supported by PTK (PASSI ToolKit), an add-in for Rational Rose, and AgentFactory, a pattern reuse tool. The use of this methodology and the related tools allowed us the construction of significant projects (as an example here we reported the rebuild of part a large application) with very good results in terms of autmatically generated code. Our multi-phase approach to the representation of patterns, based on XML, allows us the generation of agents' code for two different multi-agents FIPA-compliant operating environments (FIPA-OS and JADE) starting from platform-independent design patterns. In order to cover the entire process we use different representation languages (UML, XML and JAVA for the final code) and apply several transformations. Experimental results have demonstrated the goodness of the approach that is however strongly effected by the number of patterns in the repository and the support that the tool offers to designer in terms of automatically performed operations. We are now working in order to increase the number of patterns and to enhance the functionalities of our design tool.

References

[1] Wooldridge, M., Jennings, N. R., Kinny, D.: The gaia methodology for agent-oriented analysis and design. Journal of Autonomous Agents and Multi-Agent Systems **3** (2000) 285–315 294

[2] DeLoach, S. A., Wood, M. F., Sparkman, C. H.: Multiagent systems engineering. International Journal on Software Engineering and Knowledge Engineering **11** (2001) 231–258 294

[3] Castro, J., Kolp, M., Mylopoulos, J.: Towards requirements-driven information systems engineering: The tropos project. In: To appear in Information Systems, Elsevier, Amsterdam, The Netherlands (2002) 294

[4] Collinot, A., Drogoul, A.: Using the cassiopeia method to design a soccer robot team. Applied Articial Intelligence (AAI) Journal **12** (1998) 127–147 294

[5] Cossentino, M., Potts, C.: A case tool supported methodology for the design of multi-agent systems. In: The 2002 International Conference on Software Engineering Research and Practice, Las Vegas (NV), USA, SERP'02 (2002) 295, 306

[6] Chella, A., Cossentino, M., Pirrone, R., Ruisi, A.: Modeling ontologies for robotic environments. In: The Fourteenth International Conference on Software Engineering and Knowledge Engineering, Ischia, Italy (2002) 295

[7] Burrafato, P., Cossentino, M.: Designing a multi-agent solution for a bookstore with the passi methodology. In: Fourth International Bi-Conference Workshop on Agent-Oriented Information Systems (AOIS-2002), Toronto, Canada (2002) 295

[8] Kendall, E. A., Krishna, P. V. M., Pathak, C. V., Suresh, C. B.: Patterns of intelligent and mobile agents. In Sycara, K. P., Wooldridge, M., eds.: Proceedings of the 2nd International Conference on Autonomous Agents (Agents'98), New York, ACM Press (1998) 92–99 295

[9] O'Brien, P., Nicol, R.: FIPA – Towards a standard for software agents. BT Technology Journal **16** (1998) 51–59 295

[10] Poslad, S., Buckle, P., Hadingham, R.: The FIPA-OS agent platform: Open source for open standards. In: 5th International Conference and Exhibition on the Practical Application of Intelligent Agents and Multi-Agents, Manchester, UK (2000) 295, 298

[11] Bellifemine, F., Poggi, A., Rimassa, G.: JADE - a FIPA2000 compliant agent development environment. In: Agents Fifth International Conference on Autonomous Agents (Agents 2001), Montreal, Canada (2001) 295, 298

[12] Gamma, E., Helm, R., Johnson, R., Vlissides, J.: Design Patterns Elements of Reusable Object Oriented Software. Addison-Wesley (1994) 296

[13] Lind, J.: Patterns in agent-oriented software engineering. In: AOSE Workshop at AAMAS 2002, Bologna, Italy (2002) 296

[14] Lind, J.: The Massive Development Method for Multiagent Systems. In Bradshaw, J., Arnold, G., eds.: Proceedings of the 5th International Conference on the Practical Application of Intelligent Agents and Multi-Agent Technology (PAAM

2000), Manchester, UK, The Practical Application Company Ltd. (2000) 339–354
296

[15] Aridor, Y., Lange, D. B.: Agent design patterns: Elements of agent application design. In: Autonomous Agents '98. (1998) 296

[16] Dikenelli, O., Erdur, R. C.: Adaptability patterns of multi-agent organizations. (2004) In this volume 296

[17] Agentcities.NET: http://www.agentcities.net (2001) 298

[18] Alexander, C.: The Timeless Way of Building. Oxford University Press (1979)
302

[19] Foundation for Intelligent Physical Agents: FIPA Interaction Protocol Library Specification. (2000) 308

Designing Agents' Behaviors and Interactions within the Framework of ADELFE Methodology

Carole Bernon[1], Valérie Camps[2], Marie-Pierre Gleizes[1], and Gauthier Picard[1]

[1] IRIT, University Paul Sabatier
118, Route de Narbonne, 31062 Toulouse, Cedex 4, France
{bernon,gleizes,picard}@irit.fr
[2] L3I, University of La Rochelle
Avenue M. Crépeau, 17042 La Rochelle, Cedex 1, France
vcamps@univ-lr.fr

Abstract. ADELFE[1] is a methodology devoted to software engineering of adaptive multi-agent systems. Adaptive software is used in situations in which the environment is unpredictable or the system is open; in these cases designers cannot implement a global control on the system and cannot list all situations that the system has to be faced with. To solve this problem ADELFE guarantees that the software is developed according to the AMAS (*Adaptive Multi-Agent System*) theory[2]. This theory, based on self-organizing multi-agent systems, enables to build systems in which agents only pursue a local goal while trying to keep cooperative relations with other agents embedded in the system. ADELFE is linked with OpenTool, a commercialized graphical tool which supports UML notation. The paper focuses on the extension of OpenTool to take into account AMAS theory in designing agents' behaviors. The modifications concern static aspects, by adding specific stereotypes, and dynamic aspects, with the automatic transformations from Agent Interaction Protocols into state machines. Then state machines simulate agent behaviors and enable testing and validating them.

1 Introduction

Nowadays, problems to solve in computer science are becoming more and more complex (like information search on the Internet, mobile robots moving in the real world and so on). Systems able to respond to such problems are open and complex because they are incompletely specified, they are immersed in a dynamic environment and especially it does not exist an *a priori* known algorithm to find a solution. This

---

[1] ADELFE is a French acronym for "Atelier de Développement de Logiciels à Fonctionnalité Emergente". It is a French RNTL-funded project which partners are: ARTAL Technologies (http://www.artal.fr) and TNI-Valiosys (http://www.tni-valiosys.com) from industry and IRIT (http://www.irit.fr/SMAC) and L3I (http://www-l3i.univ-lr.fr) from academia. This project was started in December 2000 and is ended till September 2003.
[2] Further information at http://www.irit.fr/SMAC.

A. Omicini, P. Petta, and J. Pitt (Eds.): ESAW 2003, LNAI 3071, pp. 311-327, 2004.
© Springer-Verlag Berlin Heidelberg 2004

solution must build itself according to interactions the system will have with its environment in runtime.

That led us to propose a theory called AMAS (*Adaptive Multi-Agent System*) theory [3], based on the use of self-organizing systems. This theory has been successfully applied to many projects: a tool to manage the knowledge required to assist a user during information retrieval training [17], an electronic commerce tool for mediation of services [12], a software tool for adaptive flood forecast [9], adaptive routing of the traffic in a telephone network...

Obtained results led us to promote the use of self-organizing systems based on the AMAS theory and to build a methodology for designing such systems. They are required both to reuse our know-how and to guide an engineer during an application design. In that sense, ADELFE, a toolkit to develop software with emergent functionality, is currently under study [1]. ADELFE is not a general methodology; it only concerns applications in which self-organization makes the solution emerge from the interactions of its parts. It also gives some hints to the designer to tell him if using the AMAS theory is pertinent to build his application. If it is proved, ADELFE will then help him to express the behavior of the agents composing the system and the behavior of the society formed by these agents.

This paper is structured as follows. First, the AMAS theory is briefly described in section 2 to understand the presentation of the ADELFE process done in section 3. Then, section 4 expounds the cooperative agent model that fits with AMAS theory requirements. Section 5 explains how a designer can express the static aspects of adaptive agents' behavior in order to let it interact with the society it is living in. Section 6 presents the dynamics aspects and the definition of a new schema type to OpenTool in order to take into account the adaptive agent concept and to enable designers to verify the coherence of an agent behavior. This section also enables the reader to understand how relations between agents can be designed using AIP (*Agent Interaction Protocols*). Finally, a brief discussion about difficulties of such a method leads us to conclusion and perspectives.

2 AMAS Theory

Problems to solve nowadays are becoming more and more complex: they need the construction of open complex systems. All the interactions the system may have with its environment cannot be exhaustively enumerated, unpredictable interactions can occur during the system functioning and the system must adapt itself to these unpredictable events. In this context, classical design approaches cannot be applied [3].

We defined the AMAS theory to help a designer confronted with such a problem. This theory gives a solution to build complex systems that are functionally adequate and for which classical algorithmic solutions do not exist. A system is qualified by an external observer as being "functionally adequate" when the system realizes the function for which it has been built.

This theory relies on the following characteristics:

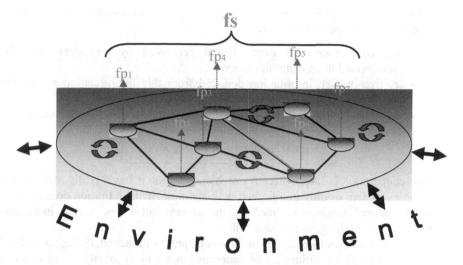

Fig. 1. Interacting agents constitute the system

- As the global function of the system cannot be clearly defined, the provided solution is then to rid ourselves of the global searched goal. We propose to build artificial systems for which the observed collective activity is not described in any agent composing it.

- This global function f_S, even if we disregard it, is the composition of partial functions f_{Pi} realized by agents making up the system (figure 1). f_S is the result of the combination of the partial functions f_{Pi}, noted by the operator "$\circ$". The combination being determined by the current organization of the parts, we can deduce $f_S = f_{P1} \circ \ldots \circ f_{Pn}$. As generally, $f_{P1} \circ f_{P2} \neq f_{P2} \circ f_{P1}$, transforming the multi-agent organization leads to the modification of the partial functions and therefore the change of the global function f_S. Therefore, this is a way to adapt the system to the environment. These modifications must be done autonomously by the system to adapt itself to the dynamic environment in which it is plunged into: such systems are called adaptive systems.

- The agents making up the system must have local criteria to initiate the modification of the relations (links) they have with others. In this sense, the AMAS theory recommends the judgment by an agent on its cooperative state. This property relies on the following theorem [11]: "*with any functionally adequate system in a given environment can be associated at least one system having a cooperative internal medium and achieving an equivalent function*". A system that has a cooperative internal medium is a system that consists of agents having cooperative relations with each other. Each agent must then have the capabilities to detect if it has cooperative relations with agents it knows.

- The cooperation searched between agents presupposes that agents are able to dynamically build a representation of other agents' capacities in order to make cooperative actions and then to interact with them in a cooperative way. An agent must act in a cooperative way (c_3) and perceive the other agents' activities as being cooperative (c_1 and c_2). Therefore, "ideal cooperation" is reached if the three following points are verified:

- c_1 (comprehension): every signal perceived by an agent must be interpreted in an unambiguous way,
- c_2 (reasoning): information deduced from this interpretation allows the agent to reason and to achieve one or more conclusion(s),
- c_3 (action): this (or these) conclusion(s) must be useful to other agents.

$$\boxed{\text{Ideal cooperation: } c_1 \wedge c_2 \wedge c_3}$$

This cooperation is "ideal" because such cooperation is never really reached in a complex system or only in a limited way and time. This definition does not rely on the global function realized by the system but relies on the individual viewpoint of each agent composing it.

When one (or several) of these conditions is (are) not reached, the agent is faced with a "cooperation failure". The concerned agent must locally act in order to suppress the failure and come back to a cooperative state.

An agent is faced up to a cooperation failure if, at least, one of the previous conditions is not verified:

- $\neg c_1$ (incomprehension): an agent does not understand a perceived signal. In this case, a cooperative agent will not ignore it but will transmit it to agents that seem (from its point of view) relevant to deal with it.
- $\neg c_2$ (unproductiveness): an agent receives an already known piece of information or some information that leads to no reasoning for it. In this case, a cooperative agent will try to find agents that could benefit of this information.
- $\neg c_3$ (uselessness): an agent can make an action that is not beneficial (according to its beliefs) to other agents. The agent is then faced with a conflict or a concurrency situation. In this case, a cooperative agent must act in order to suppress such a situation. For example, in case of a resource conflict, implicated agents must relax constraints in order to share the resource in a better way.

$$\boxed{\text{Cooperation failure: } \neg c_1 \vee \neg c_2 \vee \neg c_3}$$

According to the AMAS theory, each internal part of the system (agent) only pursues an individual objective and interacts with agents it knows by respecting cooperative techniques which lead to avoid cooperation failures (like conflict, concurrency…) that could appear during the system functioning. These cooperation failures are called Non Cooperative Situations (NCS). Faced with a NCS, a cooperative agent acts to come back to a cooperative state and permanently adapts itself to unpredictable situations while learning on others. Interactions between agents are depending on their local view and on their ability to "cooperate" with each other. Changing these local interactions reorganizes the system and thus changes its global behaviour.

The functional adequacy theorem has an important methodological impact: to design a system, designers only have to ensure that agents' behaviors are cooperative to make certain the system provides an adequate function. It also raises a main problem: "How can we design agents to obtain coherent societies?" The ADELFE methodology aims at providing an answer to these design difficulties.

3   ADELFE Overview

The ADELFE toolkit enables the development of software with emergent functionality and consists of a notation based on UML, a design methodology, a platform made up of a graphical design tool called OpenTool and a library of components that can be used to make the application development easier.

The objective of ADELFE is to cover all the phases of a classical software design from the requirements to the deployment. It is based on the RUP (*Rational Unified Process*) [15], uses UML (*Unified Modeling Language*) and AUML (*Agent-UML*) [19][20] notations and adds some specific steps to design adaptive systems. The aim is not to add another methodology but to work on some aspects not already considered by existing ones such as complex environment, dynamic or software adaptation. ADELFE is based on the view of a multi-agent system as a dynamic organization consisting of various cooperative agents. OMG's SPEM (*Software Process Engineering Metamodel*) [21] has been used to express the ADELFE process [13]. The SPEM vocabulary (WorkDefinitions (WDi), Activities (Aj) and Steps (Sk)) will be used to expound the methodology.

Only the requirements, analysis and design WorkDefinitions require modifications in order to be tailored to AMAS and are presented in the next paragraphs. Other WorkDefinitions appearing in the RUP remain the same. Any Activity and/or Step added to the RUP are/is marked with a bold font in the following description tables.

Preliminary and Final Requirements. Contrary to classical approaches, the environment of the system is central in the AMAS theory because the adaptation process depends on the interactions between the system and its environment. This characteristic has led to the addition of one Activity (A6) and one Step (A7-S2) in the "Final Requirements" WD2. To characterize the environment of the system, designers must think about it and qualify it as being accessible or not, deterministic or not, dynamic or static and discrete or continuous. These terms have been reused from [23] and represent a help to later determine if the AMAS technology is required or not to build the studied system (A11). ADELFE is only interested in "cooperative agents" that enable building AMAS. At this point, designers must also begin to think about the situations that can be "unexpected" or "harmful" for the system. These situations mainly result from interactions between the system and its environment and will probably lead to NCS at the agent level. Therefore, the determination of use cases has been modified to take this aspect into account (A7-S2), using dotted lines to specify and interaction prone to failure between the system and the external actors.

WD1: Preliminary requirements	
A1: Define user requirements	S2: Define context
A2: Validate user requirements	S3: Characterize environment
A3: Define consensual requirements	A7: Determine use cases
A4: Establish keywords set	S1: Draw an inventory of use cases
A5: Extract limits and constraints	S2: Identify cooperation failures
WD2: Final requirements	S3: Elaborate sequence diagrams
A6: Characterize environment	A8: Elaborate UI prototypes
S1: Determine entities	A9: Validate UI prototypes

Analysis. The use of AMAS theory is not a solution necessary to every application. For that reason, ADELFE provides an interactive tool (A11) to help a designer at two levels. Firstly, it helps him to decide if the use of the AMAS theory is required to implement his application. Secondly, it gives hints about the need of decomposing agents into AMAS if the skills or the representations of these agents need to evolve (see section 4.1). ADELFE does not assume that all the entities defined during the final requirements are agents; some may remain "simple" objects. Therefore, this methodology focuses on the agents identification (A12) and some guidelines are then provided to help designers to identify agents: autonomy, interaction with others, ability to negotiate, possibility to be faced up to NCS, for instance. A Step (A13-S3) has also been added concerning the study of agents relationships. Tools enabling the building of such protocols are presented in section 6.

WD3: Analysis	A12: Identify agents
A10: Analyze the domain	S1: Study entities in the domain context
S1: identify classes	S2: Identify potentially cooperative entities
S2: Study interclass relationships	S3: Determine agents
S3: Construct preliminary class diagrams	A13: Study interactions between entities
A11: Verify the AMAS adequacy	S1: Study active/passive entities relationships
S1: Verify it at the global level	S2: Study active entities relationships
S2: Verify it at the local level	S3: Study agents relationships

Design. Agents being identified and their relationships being studied, designers have now to study the way in which the agents are going to interact (A15) thanks to protocol diagrams using the AUML notation (see section 6). ADELFE also provides a model to design cooperative agents (A16). For each type of agents, designers must describe its aptitudes, its interaction language, its world representation and the NCS this agent can encounter. The global function of a self-organizing system is not coded; designers have only to code the local behavior of the parts composing it. ADELFE provides some generic cooperation failures such as incomprehension, ambiguity, uselessness or conflict. Designers must fill up a table to give the name of each NCS, its generic type, the state in which the agent must be to detect it, the conditions of its detection and what actions the agent must perform to deal with it. A new Activity (A17) of fast prototyping based on finite state machine has been added to the process (see section 6). It enables designers to verify the behavior of the built agents.

The aim of the remainder of this paper is to show how the specificities of the AMAS theory have been taken into account to modify and adapt the notations used in the ADELFE methodology.

WD4: Design	**S1**: Define skills
A14: Study detailed architecture and multi-agent model	**S2**: Define aptitudes
S1: Determine packages	**S3**: Define interaction languages
S2: Determine classes	**S4**: Define world representations
S3: Use design-patterns	**S5**: Define Non Cooperative Situations
S4: Elaborate component and class diagrams	**A17: Fast prototyping**
A15: Study interaction languages	A18: Complete design diagrams
A16: Design agents	S1: Enhance design diagrams
	S2: Design dynamic behaviors

4 Cooperative Agent Model

Self-organization is a way to design multi-agent systems that are more adaptive. Agents need local criteria to choose when to re-organize, i.e. change their own places within the organization. In this paper, we propose an agent model which uses a cooperative attitude as an engine of self-organization.

4.1 Cooperative Agents' Modules

Cooperative agents are equipped with several modules representing a partition of their « physical », « cognitive » or « social » capacities (see figure 2). Each module represents a specific resource for the agent during its « perceive-decide-act » lifecycle.

Interaction Modules. Agents' interactions are managed by two modules. The Perception Module represents the inputs the agent receives from its environment. Inputs may have different natures and types: integer, boolean for simple agents or even mail box for high level agents. The Action Module represents the outputs and the way the agent can act on its physical environment, its social environment or itself (considering learning actions for example). Similarly to perceptions, actions may have different granularities: simple effectors activation for a robot or semantically complex message sending for social agents.

Skill Module. Even if cooperative agents mainly try to avoid NCS, they have several tasks to complete. The ways to achieve their goals are expressed in the Skill Module. Skills are knowledge about given knowledge fields and allow agents to realize their partial function – as a part of a multi-agent system that produces a global function. No technical constraints are required to design and develop this module. For example, skills can be represented as a classical or fuzzy knowledge base of facts and rules on particular domains. It also can be decomposed into a lower level multi-agent system to enable learning, as in the ABROSE online brokerage application [12] in which skills were decomposed into a semantic network.

Representation Module. As for the Skill Module, the Representation Module can be implanted as a classical or fuzzy knowledge base, but its scope is the environment (physical or social) and itself. Beliefs on the other agents are considered as representations. Alike skills, representation can be decomposed into a multi-agent system when learning capabilities on representations are needed for example.

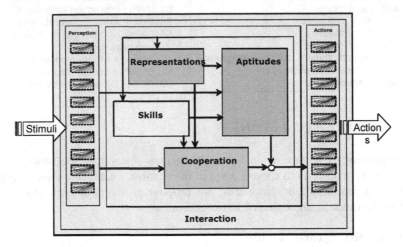

Fig. 2. The different modules of a cooperative agent

Aptitude Module. Aptitudes represent the capabilities to reason on perceptions, skills and representations – for example, to interpret messages. These aptitudes can be implemented as inference engines if skills and representations are coded as knowledge bases. Considering a given state of skills, representations and perceptions, the Aptitude Module chooses an action to do. Cases when there is zero or several proposed actions must be taken into account too (see Cooperation Module).

Cooperation Module. Cooperative attitudes of agents are implemented in the Cooperation Module. Alike the Aptitude Module, this module must provide an action for a given state of skills, representations and perceptions, *if the agent is in a NCS.* Therefore, cooperative agents must own rules to detect NCS. Several types of NCS have been identified (see 4.3). With each NCS detection rule, the Cooperation Module associates one or several actions to perform, to avoid or to solve the current NCS.

4.2 Internal Functioning

Considering the described modules, the internal behavior of a cooperative agent is defined as follows. During the perception phase of the agents' lifecycle, the Perception Module updates the values of the sensors. These data directly imply changes in the Skill and Representation Modules. Once the knowledge updated, the decision phase must result on an action choice. During this phase, the Aptitude Module computes from knowledge and proposes action(s) or not. In the same manner, the Cooperation Module detects if the agent is in a NCS or not. In the former case, the Cooperation Module proposes an action that subsumes the proposed action by the Aptitude Module. In the latter one, the only action[3] proposed by the Aptitude module is chosen. Once an action is chosen, during the action phase, the agent acts by activating effectors or changing its knowledge.

4.3 Agents' Cooperative Attitude

The AMAS theory identifies several types of NCS, resulting from the analysis of the cooperation definition: an agent is cooperative if : all perceived signals must be understood without ambiguity (c_1) and the received information is useful for the agent's reasoning (c_2) and reasoning leads to useful actions toward other agents (c_3). Therefore, a NCS occurs when $\neg c_1 \vee \neg c_2 \vee \neg c_3$. We identify seven NCS subtypes that express these conditions:

- *incomprehension* : the agent cannot extract the semantic contents of a received stimulus;
- *ambiguity* : the agent extracts several interpretations from a same stimulus;
- *incompetence* : the agent cannot derive benefit from the current knowledge state during the decision phase;
- *unproductiveness* : the agent cannot propose an action to do during the decision phase;
- *concurrency* : the agent sees another agent which is going to act to reach the same world state;
- *conflict* : the agent believes the transformation it is going to operate on the world is incompatible with the activity of another agent;
- *uselessness*: the agent believes its action cannot change the world state.

The cooperative attitude of an agent must avoid all these NCS. There are several ways to detect and process these NCS. The more visible one is the Cooperation Module that explicitly detects NCS. The manner knowledge is coded within skills or representations is another way too. The more agents are cooperative, the more the organization is effective. Cooperative agent design focuses on NCS specification – like a kind of exception-oriented programming in which designers focus on exceptions.

5 Designing Static Aspects of an Agent

ADELFE must give some notations and/or guidelines to express the particular components of cooperative agent behavior.

Two solutions were available to add the previous specificities: extending the meta-model or using a UML profile [7]. A meta-model extension is generally used when the concepts concerning a particular domain are well defined and set. However, in the multi-agent domain, the agent concept is not a uniform one; different architectures

---

[3] There is only one action possible, otherwise a NCS is detected.

may exist: cooperative ones for ADELFE, BDI for GAIA [25], etc. Several points of view on multi-agent systems also exist. For instance, ADELFE works on self-organization but other methodologies consider organizations that are known in advance, such as TROPOS [14]. It is therefore more difficult to extend the meta-model and as a result, to "dictate" an agent or a multi-agent architecture. That is why the second solution was chosen in order to be more flexible.

So, in ADELFE, nine stereotypes have been defined to express how an agent is formed and/or how its behavior may be expressed:

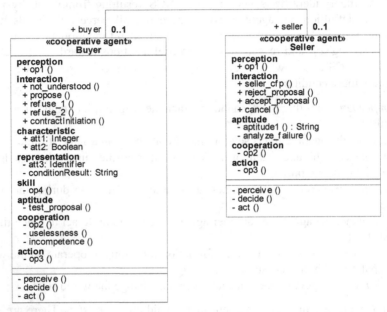

Fig. 3. A sample class diagram in which appear two classes of cooperative agents: the Buyer and the Seller

- <<cooperative agent>> expresses that an entity is an agent which has a cooperative attitude and can be used to build AMAS,
- <<characteristic>> tags an intrinsic or physical property of a cooperative agent,
- <<skill>> is used to tag specific knowledge enabling an agent to realize its own partial function,
- <<aptitude>> expresses the ability of an agent to reason both about knowledge and beliefs it owns,
- <<interaction>> tags tools that enable an agent to communicate directly or not with others or with its environment,
- <<representation>> is a mean to indicate world representations that are used by an agent to determine its behavior,
- <<perception>> expresses a mean that an agent may use to receive information from the physical or social (other agents) environment,

- <<action>>[4] is used to signal a mean for an agent to act on the environment during its action phase,
- <<cooperation>> expresses that the social attitude of an agent is implemented using rules allowing Non Cooperative Situations (NCS) solving.

In order to modify the semantics of classes and features depending on the specificities of cooperative agents these stereotypes have been included in the graphical development tool linked with ADELFE (see figure 2). This tool, called OpenTool and commercialized by our partner TNI-Valiosys, supports the UML notation to model applications while assuring that the produced models are valid. Furthermore, some rules are embedded in OpenTool/ADELFE in order to guide designers for correctly using these stereotypes and then implementing agents. All these stereotypes, except <<cooperative agent>> which must be applied to a class, can be applied to attributes and/or methods.

6 From Protocol Diagrams to Finite State Machines in OpenTool

In ADELFE, agents' dynamical behaviors are modeled as classical finite state machines or AIP protocol diagrams. For this reason, OpenTool has been enhanced to support AUML notation during the ADELFE project. Since the ADELFE process defines a Fast Prototyping Activity, OpenTool seems to be an adequate tool to simulate agents' behaviors. The simulation functionality of OpenTool enables designers to simulate objects by running their state machine from an initial collaboration diagram. This simulation enables designers to validate behaviors: it is possible to find if some deadlocks can take place within a protocol, or if some protocols are useless or inconsistent... Thus, the behavior of several agents could be judged conform (or not) to the sequence diagrams described in the analysis work definition.

Until now, OpenTool lacks an automatic process to transform protocol diagrams into state-machines to simulate them. For this reason, a proposal of transformation of protocol diagrams into state machines is discussed in this section and illustrated by an example protocol taken from [19]. This process has been implemented in OpenTool/ADELFE and is now available for academic evaluation at www.irit.fr/ADELFE.

6.1 AUML Protocols in OpenTool

OpenTool/ADELFE proposes a generic protocol diagram as specified in [19] and shown in figure 4. These protocol diagrams are extensions of classical UML generic sequence diagrams. The notion of agent roles is added to express a role an agent may have during a protocol, since an agent can have several roles at the same time.

---

[4] <<action>> stereotype is different from the Action class of the CommonBehavior package of the UML 1.4 metamodel. <<action>> only concerns features of a cooperative agent class.

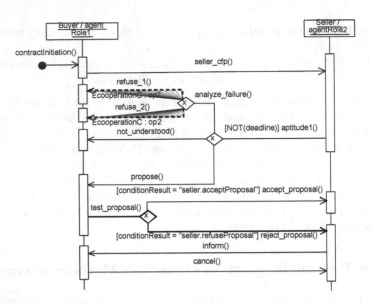

Fig. 4. An example of protocol diagram between Buyer and Seller. In this example, there are two classes of agents—Buyer and Seller—and only one role for each class. This diagram has been created with OpenTool

Some decisions have been made to take into account particularities of agents' interactions:

– The graphical representation of time has only sense during activation because AND, OR and XOR branches destroy time continuity; for example, in figure 4, refuse_1, refuse_2 and not_understood messages do not occur as a sequence but only one of them is received by the Buyer.

– A protocol diagram must begin with an initial message; in figure 3, the initial message is contractInitiation;

– The protocol must be represented as a tree from the initial message, with some exceptions.

Moreover, we added some ADELFE-specific notations to fulfill the AMAS technology requirements, such as cooperation:

– An <<interaction>>-stereotyped method must be attached to XOR and OR nodes to specify decision making of an agent; in figure 3, the analyze_failure method is attached to the first XOR node;

– A <<cooperation>>-stereotyped method can be attached to the reception of a message to react to Non Cooperative Situations; in figure 4, the op2 cooperation method is attached to the reception of the refuse_1 message. Such messages are represented by dotted arrows.

Once this notation is embedded in OpenTool/ADELFE, designers can specify dynamical behavior with protocol diagrams. The next subsection shows how to transform such a protocol diagram into a finite state machine.

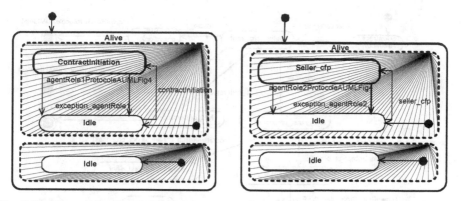

Fig. 5. The two top-level state machines corresponding to the two classes appearing in figure 1: the Buyer (left) and the Seller (right). Each class has two roles: a default one (at bottom) and a protocol role one (at top). Dotted lines are representing concurrent state-machines in OpenTool

6.2 Transformation into Finite State Machines

As previously said, to simulate agents' behavior, OpenTool requires a dynamic model (Statechart) for each simulated entity (object or agent). Nevertheless, agents' behaviors are modeled as AIP protocol diagrams. By now, there is no formal method to transform a protocol diagram (a particular generic sequence diagram) into a state-chart that OpenTool is able to simulate. Therefore, we propose a method, in terms of the previously expounded choices concerning the semantics of protocol diagrams.

As a preliminary, an initial state-machine is added to each <<**cooperative agent**>> stereotyped class. This state-machine is composed of an initial state and an **Alive** state. In the latter state, there are as many concurrent state machines as protocols associated with the agent plus at least one state-machine corresponding to standard behavior (not conformed to a protocol), as shown in figure 5.

First, a state-machine is associated with each role involved in the protocol. Figure 5 shows the two-state machines corresponding to the two classes appearing in the protocol in figure 3. Each class is composed of two concurrent state-machines: a first one corresponding to a role in the protocol (named ContractInitiation role state) and a default one (with a single Idle state).

Second, considering the particular semantics previously given to life-line, a sub-state of the role state is associated with each message reception and emission as shown in figure 6. For example, a state is created and associated with the reception of the message seller_cfp, named seller_cfp_sent. Moreover, a state Refuse_1 is added corresponding to the refuse_1 message emission.

Third, a transition between two states is created when a message is received or sent. For example, when the Buyer agent is in the seller_cfp_sent state and receives refuse_1, a transition is created between the seller_cfp_sent and the refuse_1 states. If a state does not receive or send any more messages, a final state is created and both states are linked to return to an Idle state.

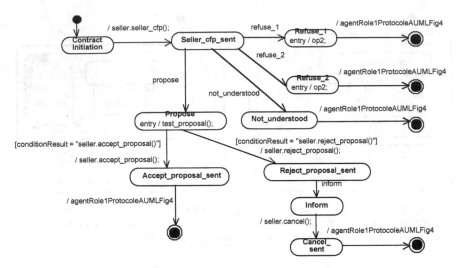

Fig. 6. The bottom-level state machine for the Buyer role

Concerning AUML-specific branches, as an <<aptitude>>-stereotyped method is associated with the decision-making process of the branch, a condition[5] is attached to the transitions in terms of the result of the <<aptitude>> method. To transform XOR branches, the attached <<aptitude>> method returns the signature of the method to activate. This latter is considered as an internal method calling and appears in this "entry" clause of the corresponding state. The signature must be stored in the conditionResult attribute. If the XOR node has n branches, it generates n transitions. In figure 5, conditions corresponding to the XOR branch of the Buyer are [conditionResult = "seller.acceptProposal"] and [conditionResult = "seller.refuseProposal"]. These conditions are attached to transitions to Accept_proposal_sent and Reject_proposal_sent states. A state is created for each AND nodes. To transform them, the transition corresponding to the AND has, as an action to do, all the events of the AND branches. The same message, sent to different instances is done in a single action. Concerning OR branches, the attached aptitude is supposed to manage the choice between the different messages, as for the XOR nodes.

Up to now, OpenTool/ADELFE automatically generates these state-machines. Designers can attach protocols to agents and then attach new concurrent state machines to simulate the agents' behavior in order to verify the consistency or to detect deadlocks; but it is not yet automated.

7   Main Difficulties

The approach discussed in this article, that consists in designing adaptive multi-agent systems within which self-organization is led by cooperation, raises some difficulties as we mentioned in section 2. More precisely, we can extract two main problems. The

---

5   This condition is expressed in the OTScript language which is a simple action language provided by OpenTool.

first one is a theoretical issue. Up to now, the cooperation efficiency has not been formally proved. Such a proof would require a more complex approach concerning system specification. Some preliminary works based on set or B specifications have been initiated last year in our team. The choice of the appropriate formalization tool seems primordial and may influence results but, unfortunately, we do not have still found the right one to tackle self-organizing systems. Nevertheless, such formalizations should produce some interesting results such as discovering new NCS types. The AMAS theory employs cooperation notion as an attribution on the generic behavior of an entity in a given world. This world is our world for example and the theory assumes the definition of cooperation as being 'universal'. Therefore, discovery of new NCS types cannot result from demonstrations, but only from observation and generalization. So, the choice of a specific formalism does not matter, which is not the case for demonstrating properties as convergence. Interesting results might be the much needed proof of convergence and efficiency. But now, as AMAS deals with emergent phenomena, the current state-of-the-art in multi-agent formalism does not seem to be adequate, even if some preliminary and interesting studies are going on in the simulation domain for example, as Jean-Pierre Müller's works [18].

The second main difficulty of AMAS design is more methodological. AMAS theory ensures the multi-agent system will produce an adequate function if all the agents composing it are cooperative. It means that designers must exhaustively list all the possible NCS. Currently, ADELFE only proposes an analysis by NCS type, state by state, for each agent. But during this analysis there is no mean to ensure the exhaustiveness of NCS enumeration – only hints and guidance... Answers to such difficulties may be formalization – once again – and real fast prototyping – or *Living Design*. The first point echoes the previous paragraph issue. The second one has been proposed in [10] as a way to shift adaptation and self-organization analysis and specification to the more living phases of the design process: test/validation, deployment and maintenance. Considering AMAS, it means studying NCS exhaustiveness during test/validation – fast prototyping – to interactively detect missing NCS detection rules. It implies adequate tools and models (in the sense of the MDA approach) to simulate agents' societies and to equip agents with minimal behaviors. ADELFE will try to focus on these two points in the future. One first milestone has been crossed by developing a preliminary fast prototyping functionality in OpenTool.

8   Conclusion and Perspectives

ADELFE is based on object-oriented methodologies, follows the RUP (*Rational Unified Process*) and uses UML and AUML notations. Some Steps have been added in the classical WorkDefinitions to be specific to adaptive MAS. ADELFE is not a general methodology such as GAIA [25] but it has a niche, which concerns applications that require adaptive multi-agent system design using the AMAS theory. ADELFE covers the entire process of software engineering like MESSAGE [8], PASSI [5] and TROPOS [4]. ADELFE is a methodology such as DESIRE [2], MASSIVE [16], INGENIAS/MESSAGE [8], MaSE [6], PASSI [5], PROMETHEUS

[22] in which modeling graphical notations are supported by tools. ADELFE differs from other methodologies because it only concerns the development of adaptive multi-agent systems.

This paper focused on designing the behavior of a cooperative agent and on the interactions within a society of agents. These static and dynamic aspects have been taken into account in ADELFE and new functionalities have been added to the graphical tool linked with ADELFE, OpenTool. First, nine stereotypes have been defined to help designers to embed the cooperative agent model. Then, the simulation capability of OpenTool has been used to test and validate the agent behavior. All these add-ons guide designers to use the AMAS technique and participate in the development process control. The first prototype is now operational, it offers some tools: a graphical one, OpenTool, the AMAS adequacy tool and an interactive tool to guide and help the designer when using ADELFE. This prototype has been evaluated during the design of two systems: a flood forecast system [9] and a bioinformatics application.

Acknowledgements

We would like to thank the support of the French Ministry of Economy, Finances and Industry as well as our partners: TNI-Valiosys Ltd., ARTAL technologies Ltd. and the IRIT software engineering team.

References

[1]   Bernon C., Gleizes M-P., Peyruqueou S., Picard G.r - ADELFE, a Methodology for Adaptive Multi-Agent Systems Engineering - *Third International Workshop "Engineering Societies in the Agents World" (ESAW-2002), 16-17 September 2002, Madrid.* Petta P., Tolksdorf R., Zambonelli F., Eds., Springer-Verlag, LNAI 2577, p. 156-169.

[2]   Brazier F.M., Jonker C. M., and Treur J., Compositional design and reuse of a generic agent model. In *Proceeding of Knowledge Acquisition Workshop - KAW'99*, 1999.

[3]   Capera D., George J-P., Gleizes M-P., Glize P. - The AMAS Theory for Complex Problem Solving Based on Self-organizing Cooperative Agents - *1st International Workshop on Theory And Practice of Open Computational Systems (TAPOCS 2003) at 12th IEEE International Workshops on Enabling Technologies (WETICE 2003), Infrastructure for Collaborative Enterprises, 9-11 June 2003, Linz, Austria.* IEEE CS, p. 383-388.

[4]   Castro J., Kolp M., and Mylopoulos J., A Requirements-driven Development Methodol-ogy, In *Proceedings of the 13th International Conference on Advanced Information Systems Engineering (CAiSE'01), Stafford, UK* - June, 2001

[5]   Cossentino M., Different Perspectives in Designing Multi-Agent System, *AgeS'02 (Agent Technology and Software Engineering) Workshop at NodE'02*, Erfurt, Germany, October 2002.

[6]   DeLoach S., Analysis and Design Using MaSE and agentTool, *12th Midwest A.I. and Cognitive Science Conference (MAICS01)*, Ohio, 2001.

[7]   Desfray P., UML Profiles Versus Metamodel Extensions: An Ongoing Debate, *OMG's UML Workshops: UML in the .com Enterprise: Modeling CORBA, Components, XML/XMI and Metadata Workshop*, November 2000.

[8]   Eurescom, Project P907-GI - *MESSAGE: Methodology for Engineering Systems of Software Agents*, Deliverable 1 - Initial Methodology, http://www.eurescom.de/~pub-deliverables/P900-series/P907/D1/P907D1.

[9]   Georgé J-P., Gleizes M-P., Glize P., and Régis C., Real-time Simulation for Flood Forecast: an Adaptive Multi-Agent System STAFF, *Proc. of the AISB'03 symposium on Adaptive Agents and Multi-Agent Systems*, Univ. of Wales, Aberystwyth, 2003.

[10]   Georgé J.-P., Picard G., Gleizes M.-P. and Glize P., Living design for open computational systems. In M. Fredriksson, A. Ricci, R. Gustavsson, and A. Omicini, editors, *International Workshop Theory And Practice of Open Computational Systems (TAPOCS) at 12th IEEE International Workshop on Enabling Technologies: Infrastructure for Collaborative Enterprises (WETICE'03)*, pages 389–394, Linz, Austria, June 2003. IEEE Computer Society.

[11]   Gleizes, M.P., Camps V., Glize P., A theory of emergent computation based on cooperative self-organization for adaptive artificial systems, Fourth European Congress on Systemic, see also http://www.irit.fr/SMAC, 1999.

[12]   Gleizes M-P., Glize P. and Link-Pezet J., An Adaptive Multi-Agent Tool For Electronic Commerce, In *The workshop on Knowledge Media Networking IEEE Ninth International Workshops on Enabling Technologies: Infrastructure for Collaborative Enterprises (WET ICE 2000)* 14-16 June 2000 Gaithersburg, Maryland.

[13]   Gleizes M-P., Millan T., Picard G., *ADELFE: Using SPEM Notation to Unify Agent Engineering Processes and Methodology*, Rapport interne IRIT n° IRIT/2003-10-R, Juin 2003.

[14]   Giunchiglia F., Mylopoulos J., and Perini A., The Tropos Software Development Methodology: Processes, Models and Diagrams, *AOSE'02*, Bologna, July 2002.

[15]   Jacobson I., Booch G. and Rumbaugh J., *The Unified Software Development Process*, Addison-Wesley, 1999.

[16]   Lind J., *Iterative Software Engineering for Multiagent Systems: the MASSIVE Method*, LNCS Vol. 1994, 2001.

[17]   Link-Pezet J., Gleizes M-P., and Glize P., FORSIC: a Self-Organizing Training System - *International ICSC Symposium on Multi-Agents and Mobile Agents in Virtual Organizations and E-Commerce (MAMA'2000)* December 11-13, 2000, Wollongong, Australia.

[18]   Müller, Jean-Pierre, Emergence of collective behaviour and problem solving, 2004. In this volume.

[19]   Odell J., Parunak H.V., and Bauer B., Representing Agent Interaction Protocols in UML, In *Agent Oriented Software Engineering*, P. Ciancarini and M. Wooldridge eds., Springer-Verlag, Berlin, pp. 121-140, 2001.

[20]   Odell J., Parunak H.V., and Bauer B., Extending UML for Agents, In *Proceedings of the Agent Oriented Information Systems (AOIS) Workshop at the 17th National Conference on Artificial Intelligence (AAAI)*, 2000.

[21]   OMG, Software Process Engineering Metamodel Specification, http://cgi.omg.org/docs/formal/02-11-14.pdf.

[22]   Padgham L., and Winikoff M. - Prometheus : A Pragmatic Methodology for Engineer-ing Intelligent Agents, *Workshop on Agent-Oriented Methodologies at OOPSLA 2002*.

[23]   Russel S., and Norvig P., *Artificial Intelligence: A Modern Approach*, Prentice Hall Series, 1995.

[24]   Wooldridge M., An introduction to multi-agent systems, John Wiley & Sons, 2000.

[25]   Wooldridge M., Jennings N.R., and Kinny D., A Methodology for Agent-Oriented Analysis and Design, In *Proceedings of the 3rd International Conference on Autonomous Agents (Agents 99)*, pp 69-76, Seattle, WA, May 1999.

Supporting Tropos Concepts in Agent OPEN*

Brian Henderson-Sellers[1], Paolo Giorgini[2], and Paolo Bresciani[3]

[1] University of Technology, Sydney, NSW 2007 Australia
brian@it.uts.edu.au
[2] Department of Information and Communication Technology
Università degli Studi di Trento, Italy
paolo.giorgini@dit.unitn.it
[3] ITC-irst, Povo, Trento, Italy
bresciani@itc.it

Abstract. The growth of interest in agent-orientation as a new paradigm has introduced the need for developing concepts, tools and techniques for modeling and engineering agent-based software systems. Object technology has been supporting the development of information systems for many years but is now slowly evolving to encompass more recent ideas relating to the concept of "agent". Integrating agent concepts into existing OO methodologies has resulted in several agent-oriented methodologies, one of which is Agent OPEN. In this paper, we evaluate the existing Agent OPEN description against ideas formulated within Tropos, an agent-oriented software development methodology.

1 Introduction

The explosive growth of application areas such as electronic commerce, enterprise resource planning and mobile computing has profoundly and irreversibly changed our views on software and Software Engineering. Software must now be based on open architectures that continuously change and evolve to accommodate new components and meet new requirements. Software must also operate on different platforms, without recompilation, and with minimal assumptions about its operating environment and its users. In addition, software must be robust and autonomous, capable of serving a naïve user with a minimum of overhead and interference. These new requirements, in turn, call for new concepts, tools and techniques for engineering and managing software.

For these reasons – and more – agent-oriented software development is gaining popularity over traditional software development techniques. While object technology has been in widespread use for the development of information systems for many years, new ideas from the agent-oriented community are beginning to be addressed by extending existing OO methodologies to support the development of agent-based information systems (e.g., [27]). This is particularly evident in the discussions regarding whether agent orientation is a brand new paradigm

---

* This is Contribution Number 03/10 of the Centre for Object Technology Applications and Research (COTAR).

A. Omicini, P. Petta, and J. Pitt (Eds.): ESAW 2003, LNAI 3071, pp. 328–345, 2004.
© Springer-Verlag Berlin Heidelberg 2004

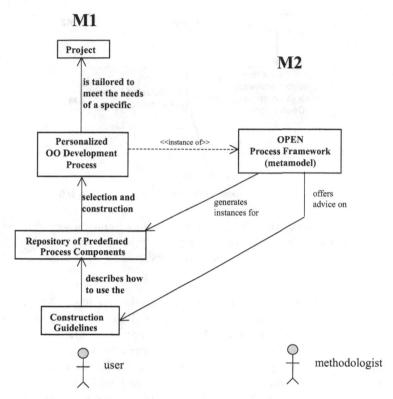

Fig. 1. The OPF metamodel generates a large number of instances from each meta-class, which are stored in a repository. Individual process components are then selected and used to construct the process

requiring a non-OO mindset or whether it can be accommodated as an extension of existing OO ideas.

In this paper, we make the (common) assumption that adding support for agent concepts into an existing object-oriented methodological approach is feasible and useful. We begin with the OO approach offered by the OPEN Process Framework or OPF [9]. Although some basic agent concepts have recently been added [6] to create "Agent OPEN", Agent OPEN still lacks the sophisticated support for agents necessary to provide complete support for agent-oriented software development (AOSD).

Although it would be possible to use a combination of methodologies (e.g., here, OPEN complemented by Tropos), it is not practical for industry, which preferably requires a single, coherent and integrated "package" to support application development. This paper reports on the first results of a project intended to ensure that Agent OPEN's repository of process components contains *complete* support for AOSD. To accomplish this, each of the major AO methodologies is analyzed in turn in order to discover agent-oriented process components cur-

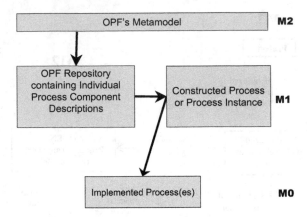

Fig. 2. Three metalevels (M2, M1, M0) that provide a framework in which the relationship between the metamodel (M2), the repository and process instances (M1) and the implemented process (M0) can be seen to co-exist

rently deficient in the OPF repository of process components — actual methodologies being constructed from these components (Figure 1) using the principles of method enginering [3]. The first AO methodology to be analyzed in this way is Tropos [2], which stresses the need for agent-orientation in early requirements engineering — topics not already addressed in the OPEN literature.

In Section 2, we present these pre-existing agent extensions in the context of the OPF itself. In Section 3 we outline the Tropos methodology and then in Section 4 we evaluate whether the OPF in its extended form [6] is adequate to support the concepts and process elements described in Tropos and, where not, what further extensions are needed. We conclude in Section 5 with recommendations and outline directions for future work.

2   The OPEN Process Framework
and its Existing Agent-Oriented Enhancements

Integrating agent concepts into existing OO methodologies has resulted in several agent-oriented methodologies, for example, [7, 4, 27, 1]. One which we will discuss is the OPEN Process Framework, or OPF [11, 17, 9], which is a little different from most others in that it offers a metamodel-underpinned framework rather than (strictly) a methodology.

Method engineering (e.g., [3, 25]) is then used to construct project-specific or "situational" methods (a.k.a. methodologies). This is possible because of the provision of a repository of method fragments (e.g., [26]) or process components (e.g., [9]).

Initially, the repository of method fragments in OPEN was aimed at providing the ability to construct methodologies in the general area of information systems development. However, as new ideas emerged over the last few years,

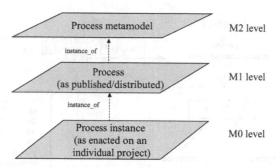

Fig. 3. For process metamodelling, we adopt a 3 layer version of the 4 layer OMG UML metamodel [19] i which every concept in layer x is an instance of a concept at level $x + 1$ (except for the self-referential top layer)

projects to extend the contents of the OPF repository have seen additions in areas such as component-based development [14], web-based development [13, 12] and organizational transition [16]. Initial extensions to agent-oriented development were formulated in [6, 15] and it is these extensions which we evaluate for completeness against the agent-oriented Tropos methodology — a comparison which is the focus of this paper.

2.1   The OPEN Process Framework

OPF consists of (i) a process metamodel or framework from which can be generated an organizationally-specific process (instance) created, using a method engineering approach [3], from (ii) a repository and (iii) a set of construction guidelines. The metamodel can be said to be at the M2 metalevel (Figure 2) with both the repository contents and the constructed process instance at the M1 level (Figure 3). The M0 level in Figure 2 represents the execution of the organization's (M1) process on a single project. Each (M1) process instance is created by choosing specific process components from the OPF Repository (Figure 1) and constructing (using the Construction Guidelines) a specific configuration — the "personalized OO development process". Then, using this method engineering approach, from this process metamodel we can generate an organizationally-specific process (instance).

The major elements in the OPF metamodel are Work Units (Activities, Tasks and Techniques), Work Products and Producers [9] — see Figure 4. These three components interact; for example producers perform work units, work units maintain work products and producers produce work products. In addition to these three metatypes, there are two auxiliary ones (Stages and Languages), which interact as shown in Figure 4.

Activity is at the highest level in the sense that a process consists of a number of Activities. Activities are large scale definitions of *what* must be done. They are not used for project management or enactment because they are at too high an abstraction level. Instead, OPEN offers the concept of Task (in agreement

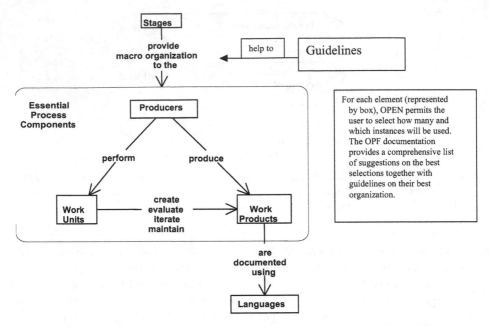

Fig. 4. The five major metatypes in the OPF metamodel (after [9])

with the terminology of the Project Managers' Body of Knowledge [8]) which is defined as being the smallest unit of work that can be project managed. Both Activities and Tasks are kinds of Work Unit in the OPF metamodel (Figure 4).

Work Products are the outputs of the Activities. These work products may be graphically or textually described. Thus, we need a variety of languages to describe them. Typical examples here are English (natural language), UML (modelling language) and C# (implementation language). Since the metamodel itself is a "design model", it is reasonable to document it with one of the available modelling languages. Here, we use the Unified Modeling Language of the OMG [19] since it is probably the most commonly used (at least in OO developments).

While it is possible to analyze the metamodel directly, in this paper we address the issue of whether the contents of the current repository for the OPF is adequate for supporting agent-oriented developments. This repository contains *instances* generated from each of the metaclasses in the metamodel. For each metaclass there are potentially numerous instances. These are documented in various books and papers, as noted earlier. The ones specific to agents are listed in Table 1 (see next section).

2.2   The Current Agent OPEN

As a consequence of the modular nature of the OPEN approach to methodology, via the notion of a repository of process components together with the

Table 1. Tasks and Techniques already proposed [6, 15] for addition to the OPF repository in order to support the development of agent-oriented systems

Tasks for AOIS	Techniques likely to be useful
Identify agents' roles	Environmental evaluation
Model the agent's environment	Environmental evaluation
Identify system organization	Environmental evaluation
Determine agent interaction protocol	Contract nets
Determine delegation strategy	Market mechanisms
Determine agent communication protocol	FIPA KIF compliant language
Determine conceptual architecture	3-layer BDI model
Determine agent reasoning	Deliberative reasoning: Plans
	Reactive reasoning: ECA Rules
Determine control architecture	Belief revision of agents
	Commitment management
	Activity scheduling
	Task selection by agents
	Control architecture
Determine system operation	Learning strategies for agents
Gather performance knowledge	
Determine security policy for agents	[topic of future research]
Undertake agent personalization	Environmental evaluation
	User model incorporation
Identify emergent behaviour	[topic of future research]

application of method or process engineering [24], it is relatively easy to add additional meta-elements and extremely easy to add additional examples of process components to the repository (as instances of pre-existing meta-elements). To extend this approach to support agent-oriented information systems, Debenham and Henderson-Sellers [6] analyzed the differences between agent-oriented and object-oriented approaches in order to be able to itemize and outline the necessary additions to the OPEN Process Framework's repository in the standard format provided in [17]. The focus of that work was primarily on instances of the meta-class WorkUnit useful for agent-oriented methodologies and processes. Table 1 lists the Tasks and Techniques so far added to the OPF repository (no new Activities were identified).

3   The Tropos Methodology

The Tropos methodology [2, 5, 10, 20] was designed to support agent-oriented systems development, with a particular emphasis on the early requirements engineering phase.

In particular, Tropos aims at two important objectives:

1. raising the conceptual level of Requirements Engineering techniques, so that formal and semiformal languages and representations can be used since the

very early stages of requirements elicitation and analysis (this means that empirical measures, tables, and transcripts or cards provided in free text form [23]) have to be transformed into more precise and more easily analyzable formats, so that transforming them into functional and non-functional requirements —to feed the Software Engineering process— results to be a more straightforward step);

2. providing and supporting the system architecture and functions definition with a set of "social-oriented" notions —to be used aside the traditional system oriented concepts— that allows for a easier mapping of the requirements provided in terms of social and organizational needs —as provided by Requirements Engineering— into the characteristics (functional, architectural, and design oriented) of the system-to-be.

Tropos aims at this objective by adopting two specific strategies:

1. It pays attention to the activities that precede the specification of the prescriptive requirements, like understanding how and why the intended system can meet the organizational goals (*Late Requirements Analysis*). Even before this phase, it is important to understand and analyze the organizational goals themselves (*Early Requirements Analysis*). In this, Tropos is largely inspired by the Eric Yu's *i**framework for requirements engineering, which offers actors, goals, and actor dependencies as primitive concepts. The *i**framework has been presented in detail in [29] and has been related to different application areas, including requirements engineering [28], business process reengineering [31], and software processes [30].

2. Tropos deals with all the phases of system requirement analysis and all the phases of system design and implementation in a uniform and homogeneous way, based on common mentalistic notions as those of *actors, goals, softgoals, plans, resources*, and *intentional dependencies*.

One of the main advantages of the Tropos methodology is that it allows to capture not only the *what* or the *how*, but also the *why* a piece of software is developed. This, in turn, allows for a more refined analysis of the system dependencies and, in particular, for a much better and uniform treatment not only of the system functional requirements, but also of its non-functional requirements.

The choice of focusing on the goals (and all the related mentalistic notions) along all the phases of the Tropos methodology, has in important impact on the overal process of software development, including the very implementation of the system, specially if, although not exclusively, an Agent Oriented Programming [18] is adopted. In particular, agent oriented specifications and programs use the same notions and abstractions used to describe the behavior of human agents and the processes involving them; thus, the conceptual gap between users' specifications (in terms of why and what) and system realization (in terms of what and how), is reduced to a minimum.

The Tropos methodology is mainly based on four phases [20, 2]:

– *Early Requirements Analysis*, aimed at defining and understanding a problem by studying its existing organizational setting;

- *Late Requirements Analysis*, conceived to define and describe the system-to-be, in the context of its operational environment;
- *Architectural Design*, that deals with the definition of the system global architecture in terms of subsystems;
- *Detailed Design*, aimed at specifying each architectural component in further detail, in terms of inputs, outputs, control and other relevant information.

In particular, in this paper we will concentrate on the Early Requirements Analysis phase of Tropos. During the Early Requirements Analysis the existing organizational setting is analyzed, in terms of *actors*, who plays some role in the organization, and of their *intentional dependencies* in the context of the organization. The output of this phase is an organizational model which includes relevant actors and their respective intentional dependencies. Actors, in the organizational setting, are characterized by having *goals* that each single actor, in isolation, would be unable —or not as well or as easily— to achieve. Intentional dependencies are used to describe this kind of relationships among actors. Goals are the the elements around which the intentional dependencies are established.

Thus, in a nutshel we can say that the stated aim of Tropos is to use agent concepts in the description and definition of the methodology rather than using agent concepts in a minor extension to existing OO approaches. Tropos takes the BDI model [22, 18], formulated to describe the *internal* view of a single agent, and applies those concepts to the *external* view in terms of problem modelling as part of requirements engineering.

It is for this reason that, in Tropos, AI derived mentalistic notions such as *actors* (or *agents*), *goals*, *soft-goals*, *plans*, *resources*, and *intentional dependencies* are used in all the phases of software development, from the first phases of early analysis down to the actual implementation. Tropos also includes descriptions of Work Products and several Techniques such as Means-End Analysis, useful in requirements engineering.

A crucial role is given to the earlier analysis of requirements that precedes prescriptive requirements specification. In particular, aside from the understanding of *how* the intended system will fit into the organizational setting, and *what* the system requirements are, Tropos addresses also the analysis of the *why* the system requirements are as they are, by performing an in-depth justification with respect to the organizational goals.

Thus, the stakeholder intentions are modelled as goals which, through a goal-oriented analysis, eventually lead to the functional and non-functional requirements of the system-to-be. In Tropos, early requirements are assumed to involve social actors who depend on each other for goals to be achieved, tasks to be performed, and resources to be furnished. Tropos includes *actor diagrams* for describing the network of social dependency relationships among actors, as well as *goal diagrams* for analyzing goals through a means-ends analysis in order to discover ways of fulfilling them. These primitives have been formalized using intentional concepts from AI, such as goal, belief, ability, and commitment [2].

An Actor Diagram is a graph, where each node may represent either an actor, a goal, a soft-goal, a task or a resource. Links, among nodes, may be used to

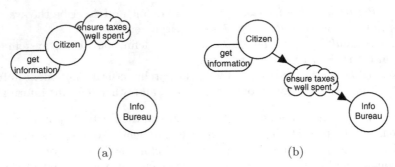

(a)   (b)

Fig. 5. (a) Example actor diagram showing goals attached to actors; (b) Example actor diagram showing an explicit dependee, depender and dependum

form paths like: *depender* → *dependum* → *dependee*, where the *depender* and the *dependee* are actors, and the *dependum* is either a goal, a soft-goal, a task or a resource. Each path between two actors indicates that one actor depends on another for something (represented by the *dependum*) so that the former may attain some goal/soft-goal/task/resource. In other terms, a dependency describes an "agreement" between two actors (the *depender* and the *dependee*), in order to attain the *dependum*. The *depender* is the depending actor, and the *dependee* the actor who is depended upon. The type of the dependum describes the nature of the dependency (and, therefore, of the implied agreement). Goal dependencies are used to represent delegation of responsibility for fulfilling a goal; soft-goal dependencies are similar to goal dependencies, but their fulfillment cannot be defined precisely (for instance, the appreciation is subjective, or the fulfillment can occur only to a given extent); task dependencies are used in situations where the dependee is required to perform a given activity; and resource dependencies require the dependee to provide a resource to the depender. As exemplified in Figure 5, actors are represented as circles; *dependums —goals, soft-goals, tasks* and *resources—* are respectively represented as ovals, clouds, hexagons and rectangles[1].

As an example of actor diagram, let us consider Figure 5 (adapted from [2]), in which the following actors have been identified:

– Info Bureau, that is a government agency, the objectives of wich include improving public information services, increasing tourism through new information services, also encouraging Internet among the citizens.
– Citizens, who want easily accessible information, of any sort, and (of course) good administration of public resources.

Thus, in Figure 5-a the Citizen is characterized by one goal (get information) and one soft-goal (ensure taxes well spent). In Figure 5-b (that represent a first, simple evolution of figure Figure 5-a), the soft-goal (ensure taxes well spent is shown as a dependency between the Citizen and the Info Bureau.

---

[1] In this paper only examples of goals and soft-goals are shown.

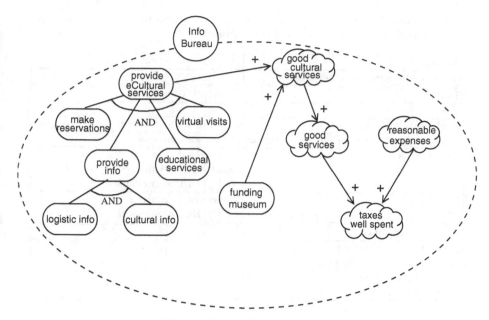

Fig. 6. Example goal diagram

Once the stakeholders have been identified, along with their goals and social dependencies, the analysis proceeds in order to enrich the model with further details. In particular, the rationale of each goal relative to the stakeholder who is responsible for its fulfillment has to be analyzed. Basically, this is done through means-end analysis and goal/plan decomposition. It is important to stress that what goals are associated with each actor is a decision of the corresponding stakeholder, not the design team.

An example of the result of such an analysis from the perspective of Info Bureau is given by the *goal diagram* depicted in Figure 6. Here, the goal analysis for Info Bureau, relative to the goal that Citizen delegates to Info Bureau as a result of the previous analysis, is given. Inside the goal diagram, soft-goal analysis is performed identifying the goals and soft-goals that contribute positively (or negatively) to the soft-goal. For example, the soft-goal taxes well spent gets positive contributions from the soft-goal good services, and, in the end, from the goal provide eCulture services too.

The goal provide eCultural services is decomposed (AND decomposition) into four subgoals: make reservations, provide info, educational services and virtual visits. As basic eCultural service, the Info Bureau must provide information (provide info), which can be logistic info, and cultural info. More in detail, accordingly with the original scenario introduced in [2], Logistic info concerns, for instance, timetables and visiting instructions for museums, while cultural info concerns the cultural content of museums and special cultural events. This content may include descriptions and images of historical objects, the description of an ex-

Table 2. Activity, Tasks, Techniques and Work Products proposed for inclusion in the OPF repository as a result of analyzing Tropos

Activity	
Early requirements engineering	
Tasks	**Related Techniques**
Model actors	
Model capabilities for actors	Capabilities identification and analysis
Model dependencies for actors and goals	Delegation analysis
Model goals	Means–End Analysis Contribution Analysis AND/OR Decomposition
Model plans	Means–End Analysis AND/OR Decomposition
Work Products	
(Tropos) actor diagram	
(Tropos) capability diagram	
(Tropos) goal diagram	
(Tropos) plan diagram	

hibition, and the history of a particular region. Virtual visits are services that allow, for instance, Citizen to pay a virtual visit to a city of the past (Rome during Cæsar's time!). Educational services includes presentation of historical and cultural material at different levels (e.g., high school or undergraduate university level) as well as on-line evaluation of the student's grasp of this material. Make reservations allows the Citizen to make reservations for particular cultural events, such as concerts, exhibitions, and guided museum visits.

4   Supporting Tropos Concepts in the OPEN Process Framework

In this section, we evaluate the existing Agent OPEN description (summarized in Section 2.2 above) against ideas formulated within the Tropos methodology, seeking any omissions or poor support of Tropos elements in the OPF. We then make recommendations for enhancements to the OPF in order that it can fully support all agent-oriented concepts formulated in Tropos.

Several new process components (method chunks) need to be added to the existing OPF repository. These are primarily Tasks and Techniques but there is also one new Activity: Early Requirements Engineering (in Tropos called the Early Requirements Analysis phase) as well as some work products. All of these are outlined below in standard OPEN format and summarized for convenience in Table 2.

4.1   Activity

An Activity in the OPF describes a coarse granular "job to be done". It describes "what" needs to be done but not "how". One new Activity is proposed here for inclusion in the OPF repository based on contributions made by Tropos.

Early Requirements Engineering. Early requirements engineering focusses on domain modeling. It consists of identifying and analyzing the relevant actors in organizations and their goals or intentions. These actors may correspond with the stakeholders but may also include other social elements (individuals, but also organizations, organizational units, teams, and so on) who do not directly share an interest in the project, but still need to be modelled in order to produce a sufficiently complete picture of the organizational domain. Each organization active element is modelled as a (social) actor that is dependent upon another (social) actor in order for them to achieve some stated goal. During Early Requirements Engineering, these goals are decomposed incrementally and finally the atomic goals can be used to support an objective analysis of alternatives.

The results of this analysis can be documented using a variety of Tropos diagrams. Goals, actors and dependencies can be depicted on an actor diagram and, in more detail, on a goal diagram. These results then form the basis for the "late requirements analysis" which in OPEN is called simply Requirements Engineering in which the system requirements are elicited in the context of the stakeholders' goals identified in this activity of Early Requirements Engineering.

4.2   Tasks

A Task in the OPF describes a granular "job to be done". As with Activities, a Task describes what is to be done but not how. However, the granularity is at an individual developer's scale, in comparison to the team scale of an Activity. In this section, we describe five new/modified Tasks in the layout style used as standard in the OPEN literature (e.g. [11]).

Task: Model Actors
Focus: People, other systems and roles involved
Typical supportive techniques: Business process modelling, Soft systems analysis
Explanation. While the concept of actors in OO systems already exists (and is supported in the original OPF), the Tropos methodology extends the OO notion of an actor beyond that of a single person/system/role interacting with a system to that of a more general entity that has strategic goals and intentionality within the system or organizational setting [2] including also, for example, whole organizations, organizational units and teams. Actors in Tropos can represent either agents (both human and artificial) or roles or positions (a set of roles, typically played by a single agent). This new Task thus considerably extends the existing concepts related to traditional OO actors. To model an actor, one must identify and analyze actors of both the environment and the system (or system-to-be).

Tropos encourages the use of this Task in the early requirements phase for the modelling of domain stakeholders and their intentions as social actors. Actors can be depicted using (Tropos) actor diagrams (see below).

Task: Model Capabilities for Actors

Focus: Capability of each actor in the system

Typical supportive techniques: Capabilities identification and analysis

Explanation. The capability of an actor represents its ability to define, choose and execute a plan (for the fulfilment of a goal), given specific external environmental conditions and a specific event [2]. Capability modelling commences after the architecture has been designed, subsequent to an understanding of the system sub-actors and their interdependencies. Each system subactor must be provided with its own individual capabilities, perhaps with additional "social capabilities" for managing its dependencies with other actors/subactors. Previously modelled goals and plans generally now become an integral part of the capabilities. Capabilities can be depicted using (Tropos) capability diagrams and plan diagrams (see below).

Task: Model Dependencies for Actors and Goals

Focus: How/if an actor depends on another for goal achievements

Typical supportive techniques: Delegation analysis

Explanation. In Tropos, a dependency may exist between two actors so that one actor depends in some way on the other in order to achieve its own goal, a goal that cannot otherwise be achieved or not as well or as easily without involving this second actor. Similarly, a dependency between two actors may exist for plan execution or resource availability [2]. The actors are named, respectively, the depender and the dependee while the dependency itself centres around the dependum. Dependencies can be depicted using (Tropos) actor diagrams and, in more detail, in goal diagrams (see below).

Task: Model Goals

Focus: Actor's strategic interests

Typical supportive techniques: Means-end analysis, contribution analysis, AND/OR decomposition

Explanation. A goal represents an actor's strategic interests [2] — Tropos recommends both hard and soft goals. Modelling goals requires the analysis of those actor goals from the view point of the actor itself. The rationale for each goal relative to the stakeholder needs to be analyzed — typical Techniques are shown in Table 2. Goals may be decomposed into subgoals, either as alternatives or as concurrent goals. Plans may also be shown together with their decomposition, although details of plans are shown in a Plan Diagram (q.v.). Goals can be depicted using (Tropos) goal diagrams (see below).

Task: Model Plans
Focus: Means to achieve goals
Typical supportive techniques: Means-end analysis, AND/OR decomposition
Explanation. A plan represents a means by which a goal can be satisfied or, in the case of a soft goal, *satisficed* [2, 29]. Plan modelling complements goal modelling and rests on reasoning techniques analogous to those used in goal modelling. Plans can be depicted using (Tropos) goal diagrams and plan diagrams (see below).

4.3   Techniques

To complement the "what" of Activities and Tasks, OPF Techniques detail "how" they are to be achieved. We have identified four new Techniques from Tropos and describe them here in the standard format for OPF Techniques [17].

Technique: Means–End Analysis
Focus: Identifying means to achieve goals
Typical tasks for which this is needed: Model goals, Model plans
Description. Means-end analysis aims at identifying plans, resources and goals as well as means to achieve the goals.
Usage. To perform means-end analysis, the following are performed iteratively:

- Describe the current state, the desired state (the goal) and the difference between the two
- Select a promising procedure for enabling this change of state by using this identified difference between present and desired states.
- Apply the selected procedure and update the current state.

If this successfully finds an acceptable solution, then the iterations cease; otherwise they continue. If no acceptable solution is possible, then failure is announced.

Technique: Contribution Analysis
Focus: Goals contributing to other goals
Typical tasks for which this is needed: Model goals
Description. Contribution analysis identifies goals that may contribute to the (partial) fulfilment of the final goal. It may be alternatively viewed as a kind of means-end analysis in which the goal is identified as the means [2]. Contribution analysis applied to soft-goals is often used to evaluate non-functional requirements.
Usage. Identify goals and soft-goals that can contribute either positively or negatively towards the achievement of the overall goal or soft-goal. Of course the focus is on identifying positive contributions, but the technique may also lead, as a side effect, to the identification of negative contributions. Annotate these appropriately (say with + or −). A + label indicates a positive, partial contribution to the fulfilment of the goal being analyzed. Contribution analysis is very effective for soft goals used for eliciting non-functional (quality) requirements.

Technique: AND/OR Decomposition

Focus: Goal decomposition
Typical tasks for which this is needed: Model goals, Model plans
Description. This is a technique to decompose a root goal into a finer goal structure.
Usage. Start with a high level goal and decompose into subgoals. These subgoals may either be alternatives (OR decomposition) or additive (AND decomposition).

Technique: Capabilities Identification and Analysis

Focus: Capabilities identification
Typical tasks for which this is needed: Model capabilities for actors
Description. For each goal introduced, we identify a set of capabilities that the responsible actor should have in order to fulfill the goal. When the achievement of the goal involves other actors, the analysis is expanded also to these actors. Capabilities for the interaction/collaboration are then identified and analyzed contextually (see [2] for more details).
Usage. Start with a goal associated to an actor and identify the capabilities needed locally. If the goal involves other actors the analysis is extended to these actors with respect to their contribution in the achievement of the goal.

Finally, we had to consider also the technique Delegation Analysis. Indeed, this technique is not new in OPF (see [17]), but its original focus is on modeling objects, possibly to create components, and it is aimed at transforming designs. In the Tropos context, instead, Delegation Analysis processes the (Tropos) Actor Diagrams, that are work products of both the Early Requirements Engineering activity ("early requirements analysis" in Tropos) and the Requirements Engineering activity ("late requirements analysis" in Tropos). An example of (Tropos) Delegation Analysis is presented in Section 4.4, as the transformation of Figure 5-a into Figure 5-b. Here, we simply recommend modification of the Delegation Analysis technique introduced in [17], in order to deal also with the agent and Tropos typical notions (i.e., actor, goal, task, resource, depender, dependum and dependee), so as to fully accommodate the Tropos process.

4.4 Work Products

OPF Work Products describe artefacts that are created, consumed and/or maintained. Some of these act as deliverables, either to other team members or to a third party client. Four new work products are identified and described here.

Work Product: (Tropos) Actor Diagram. In Tropos, the actor diagram graphically depicts actors (as circles), their goals (as ellipses and clouds) attached to the relevant actor (Figure 5-a) together with a network of dependencies between the actors (Figure 5-b). In Figure 5-a, Citizen has two goals: the hard goal to get information and the soft goal to ensure taxes well spent. However, this soft goal is best delegated to the Info Bureau actor. To show this delegation, the delegated goal is shown explicitly as a dependum (cloud symbol) connected by two line segments to the two actors (Citizen and Info Bureau) (Figure 5-b).

Work Product: (Tropos) Capability Diagram. A capability diagram is drawn from the viewpoint of a specific agent. They are initiated by an event caused by an external event. Nodes in the diagram model plans (which can be expanded through the use of a Plan Diagram (q.v)) and transition arcs model events. Beliefs are modelled as objects [2]. Each node in the capability diagram may be expanded into a Plan Diagram (q.v.). Capability diagrams in Tropos use UML activity diagrams.

Work Product: (Tropos) Goal Diagram. Figure 6 shows an example goal diagram in which the focus is that of how Info Bureau tries to achieve the delegated soft-goal taxes well spent. Providing good services with reasonable expenses, Info Bureau can contribute to spend taxes well. Good services may include good cultural services, which in turn may include services available via the web. So provide eCultural services can contribute positively in achieving the sotfgoal good cultural services. Figure 6 shows also the partial AND decomposition of the provide eCultural services goal.

Work Product: (Tropos) Plan Diagram. A plan diagram depicts the internal structure of a plan, summarized as a single node on a Capability diagram (q.v.). Plan diagrams in Tropos use UML activity diagrams.

5 Conclusions and Future Work

Based on an understanding that OO methodologies can usefully be enhanced to support agency, we report here on the first results of a project to extend the OPEN Process Framework (OPF) to include agent-oriented support found in various agent-oriented (AO) methodologies. Initial analysis of the Tropos AO methodology identifies its significant support for early requirements. It captures many aspects of agent-oriented requirements gathering not previously documented.

In analyzing the extent to which other methodological frameworks, and in particular the OPEN Process Framework, supports these ideas, many deficiencies were identified. Here, we have itemized these gaps in OPEN's repository of process components and proposed additions to the repository specifically to address activities, tasks, techniques and work products found in Tropos but, until now, not available in the OPF repository.

We intend to progress this cross-fertilization between OPEN and Tropos, specifically taking advantage of the strengths of each: the early requirements engineering and agent focus of Tropos and the full lifecycle process of OPEN together with its metamodel-based underpinning that permits it to be used for situated method engineering [3].

References

[1] Bernon, C., Gleizes, M.-P., Picard, G. and Glize, P., The ADELFE methodology for an intranet system design, Procs. Agent-Oriented Information Systems 2002 (eds. P. Giorgini, Y. Lespérance, G. Wagner and E. Yu), May 2002, Toronto, Canada 330

[2] Bresciani, P., Giorgini, P., Giunchiglia, F., Mylopolous, J. and Perini, A.: Tropos: an agent-oriented software development methodology. Journal of Autonomous Multi-Agent Systems (2003) in press 330, 333, 334, 335, 336, 337, 339, 340, 341, 342, 343

[3] Brinkkemper, S.: Method engineering: engineering of information systems development methods and tools. Inf. Software Technol. **38(4)** (1996) 275–280 330, 331, 343

[4] Caire, G., Chainho, P., Evans, R., Garijo, F., Gomez Sanz, J., Kearney, P., Leal, F., Massonet, P., Pavon, J. and Stark, J., Agent-oriented analysis using MESSAGE/UML, Procs. Second Int. Workshop on Agent-Oriented Software Engineering (AOSE–2001), Montreal, Canada, May 2001, 101–107 (2001) 330

[5] Castro J., Kolp M. and Mylopoulos J.: Towards Requirements-Driven Information Systems Engineering: The Tropos Project. *Information Systems*. Elsevier, Amsterdam, the Netherlands (2003) in press 333

[6] Debenham, J. and Henderson-Sellers, B., Designing agent-based process systems — extending the OPEN Process Framework, Chapter VIII in Intelligent Agent Software Engineering (ed. V. Plekhanova), Idea Group Publishing (2003) 160–190 329, 330, 331, 333

[7] DeLoach, S. A., Multiagent systems engineering: a methodology and language for designing agent systems, Procs. Agent-Oriented Information Systems '99 (AOIS'99), Seattle, WA, USA, 1 May (1999) 330

[8] Duncan, W. R.: A Guide to the Project Management Body of Knowledge, Project Management Institute, PA, USA (1996) 176pp 332

[9] Firesmith, D. G. and Henderson-Sellers, B.: The OPEN Process Framework. An Introduction, Addison-Wesley, Harlow, UK (2002) 330pp 329, 330, 331, 332

[10] Giorgini P., Perini A., Mylopoulos J., Giunchiglia F. and Bresciani P.: Agent-Oriented Software Development: A Case Study . Proceedings of the Thirteenth International Conference on Software Engineering and Knowledge Engineering (SEKE01), June 13-15 2001, Buenos Aires, Argentina (2001) 333

[11] Graham, I., Henderson-Sellers, B. and Younessi, H.: The OPEN Process Specification, Addison-Wesley, Harlow, UK (1997) 314pp 330, 339

[12] Haire, B., Henderson-Sellers, B. and Lowe, D., Supporting web development in the OPEN process: additional tasks, Procs. 25th Annual International Computer Software and Applications Conference. COMPSAC 2001, IEEE Computer Society Press, Los Alamitos, CA, USA (2001) 383–389 331

[13] Haire, B., Lowe, D. and Henderson-Sellers, B., Supporting web development in the OPEN process, Object-Oriented Information Systems (eds. Z. Bellahsène, D. Patel and C. Rolland), LNCS 2425, Springer–Verlag, 2002 331

[14] Henderson-Sellers, B., An OPEN process for component-based development, Chapter 18 in Component-Based Software Engineering: Putting the Pieces Together (eds. G. T. Heineman and W. Councill), Addison-Wesley, Reading, MA, USA, 2001 331

[15] Henderson-Sellers, B. and Debenham, J., 2003, Towards OPEN methodological support for agent oriented systems development, Procs. First International Con-

ference on Agent-Based Technologies and Systems (eds. B. H. Far, S. Rochefort and M. Moussavi), University of Calgary, Calgary, Canada, 14-24   331, 333

[16] Henderson-Sellers, B. and Serour, M., Creating a process for transitioning to object technology, Proceedings Seventh Asia–Pacific Software Engineering Conference. APSEC 2000, IEEE Computer Society Press, Los Alamitos, CA, USA, 2000   331

[17] Henderson-Sellers, B., Simons, A. J. H. and Younessi, H.: The OPEN Toolbox of Techniques, Addison-Wesley, UK (1998) 426pp + CD   330, 333, 341, 342

[18] Kinny, D., Georgeff, M. and Rao, A., A methodology and modelling techniques for systems of BDI agents, TR 58, Australian Artificial Intelligence Institute (1996)   335

[19] OMG: OMG Unified Modeling Language Specification, Version 1.4, September 2001, OMG document formal/01-09-68 through 80 (13 documents) [Online]. Available http://www.omg.org (2001)   331, 332

[20] Perini A., Bresciani P., Giorgini P., Giunchiglia G. and Mylopoulos J.: A Knowledge Level Software Engineering Methodology for Agent Oriented Programming. In J. P. Müller, E. Andre, S. Sen, and C. Frasson, editors, Proceedings of the Fifth International Conference on Autonomous Agents, May 2001, Montreal, Canada, 2001   333, 334

[21] Perini A., Bresciani P., Giorgini P., Giunchiglia F. and Mylopoulos J.: Towards an Agent Oriented approach to Software Engineering. In A. Omicini and M. Viroli, editors, WOA 2001 – Dagli oggetti agli agenti: tendenze evolutive dei sistemi software, 4–5 September 2001, Modena, Italy, Pitagora Editrice Bologna (2001)

[22] Rao, A. S. and Georgeff, M. P., BDI agents: from theory to practice, Technical Note 56, Australian Artificial Intelligence Institute (1995)   335

[23] Robertson, S. and Robertson, J., Mastering the requirements process. Number 0201360462 in ACM press books. Addison-Wesley (1999)   334

[24] Rupprecht, C., Fünffinger, M., Knublauch, H. and Rose, T., Capture and dissemiantion of experience about the construction of engineering processes, Procs. CAiSE 2000, LNCS 1789, Springer Verlag, Berlin, 294-308 (2000)   333

[25] Ter Hofstede, A. H. M. and Verhoef, T. F., On the feasibility of situational method engineering, Information Systems, 22, 401-422 (1997)   330

[26] van Slooten, K., Hodes, B., Characterizing IS development projects, in Proceedings of the IFIP TC8 Working Conference on Method Engineering: Principles of method construction and tool support (eds. S. Brinkkemper, K. Lyytinen, R. Welke) Chapman&Hall, Great Britain, 29–44 (1996)   330

[27] Wooldridge, M., Jennings, N. R. and Kinny, D., The Gaia methodology for agent-oriented analysis and design, J. Autonomous Agents and Multi-Agent Systems, 3, 285–313 (2000)   328, 330

[28] E. Yu. Modeling organizations for information systems requirements engineering. In Proceedings of the First IEEE International Symposium on Requirements Engineering, pages 34–41, San Jose, January 1993. IEEE   334

[29] E. Yu. Modelling Strategic Relationships for Process Reengineering. PhD thesis, University of Toronto, Department of Computer Science, 1995   334, 341

[30] E. Yu and J. Mylopoulos. Understanding 'why' in software process modeling, analysis and design. In Proceedings Sixteenth International Conference on Software Engineering, Sorrento, Italy, May 1994   334

[31] E. Yu and J. Mylopoulos. Using goals, rules, and methods to support reasoning in business process reengineering. International Journal of Intelligent Systems in Accounting, Finance and Management, 1(5), January 1996   334

Dynamic Analysis of Agents' Behaviour – Combining ALife, Visualization and AI

Pavel Nahodil[1], Pavel Slavík[2], David Rehor[2], and David Kadlecek[1]

[1]Dept. of Cybernetics, FEE, Czech Technical University in Prague
Karlovo nám. 13, 121 35, Prague 2, Czech Republic
kadlecd@rtime.felk.cvut.cz
nahodil@k333.felk.cvut.cz
[2]Dept. of Computer Science and Engineering, FEE, Czech Technical University in Prague
Karlovo nám. 13, 121 35, Prague 2, Czech Republic
{rehord,slavik}@cslab.felk.cvut.cz

Abstract. The analysis of an agent or agent communities combining advanced methods of visualization with traditional AI techniques is presented in this paper. However this approach can be used for arbitrary Multi-Agent System (MAS), it was primarily developed to analyse systems falling into Artificial Life domain. Traditional methods are becoming insufficient as MAS are becoming more complex and therefore novel approaches are needed. Our approach builds upon various techniques to deliver means for assessment on multiple levels ranging from single agent to overall properties of an agent community. Our visualization tools suite utilizes novel visualization methods together with traditional AI techniques such as sensitivity analysis and clustering. Among others it offers visualization of many agent's parameters along time, correspondence between current/previous states (of an agent community), resulting behaviour, grouping of agents based on dominant properties etc. This transparent approach emphasizes MAS dynamics through automatic discovery of its tendency. Agent position inside virtual environment together with overview over the whole time interval adds strong contextual information to analysis. Position in our understanding is not limited to geometrical meaning, but covers also the space of dynamically changing constraints for action selection. A simulated artificial life environment with intelligent agents has been used as a test bed. We have selected this particular domain because our long-term goal is to model life as it could be so as to understand life, as we know it.

1 Introduction

Agent organizations are an emergent area of MAS that relies on the notion of openness and heterogeneity of MAS and poses new demands on traditional MAS models. These demands include the integration of organizational and individual perspectives and the dynamic adaptation of models to organizational and environmental changes. . Organizational self-design will play a critical role in the development of larger and more complex MAS. As systems grow to include hundreds or thousands of agents, we must move from an agent-centric view of coordination and control to an organization-centric one. Practical applications of agents to

A. Omicini, P. Petta, and J. Pitt (Eds.): ESAW 2003, LNAI 3071, pp. 346-359, 2004.
© Springer-Verlag Berlin Heidelberg 2004

organizational modelling are being widely developed but formal theories are needed to describe interaction and organizational structure. Furthermore, it is necessary to get a closer look at the relation between organizational roles and the agents that fulfil them.

The overall problem of analysing the social, economic and technological dimensions of agent organizations, and the co-evolution of agent and human social and personal structures in the organization, provide theoretically demanding, interdisciplinary research questions at different levels of abstraction.

Current Multi-Agent Systems (regardless of their domain)are getting complex and thereby hard to assess and analyse. This is due to:

- Agents becoming more complex with many dynamic properties
- Multi-agent system consists of many objects and agents
- Agents usually have diverse, not very transparent architectures
- Many possible deployment domains (different actuators and sensors etc.)
- Environment is becoming more complex and time varying.

These facts have resulted in an increasing effort dedicated to development of new approaches to MAS analysis. The main streams of this analysis include: different levels of agent behaviour classification, agents' interaction, negotiation and contracting, various communicative acts, quality of service, action selection of one agent, knowledge representation and derivation by one agent, learning and adaptation, and finally global characteristics of MAS.

2   State of Art

The questions in MAS analysis are both global-to-local and local-to-global, i.e.: how the environment and inter-agent negotiations influence individual agents and how strategies and states of individual agents influence the global behaviour of the system [1]. There are currently various approaches. The MAS analysis using visualization is one of them. A lot of effort in agent technology in conjunction with visualization has dealt with information systems, intelligent user interfaces and modelling [2]. Special area of research of agent visualization is directed to virtual environments and embodied agents [3]. Different approaches have been developed for visualization of agent gestures, moods and behaviour. Schroeder [4] states, that research area of agent visualization has two different aspects (i) visualization of a single agent and (ii) visualization of MAS. However the visualization of internal structures and behaviour of MAS systems for purposes of design, debugging and analysis has not been largely addressed yet. Common problem is analysis of agents' behaviour and large number of agents with many properties.

3   Multiple Levels of Detail

To work-around the differences among internal architectures embodied by agents together with the fact that they have different purpose and goals, we have had to unify agent architectures on some level. The highest level of universality can be achieved by considering agents as black boxes; however this approach must not avoid loss of potentially important information. We have discovered that we can make a good compromise without loosing necessary information for analysis purposes and still be very universal.

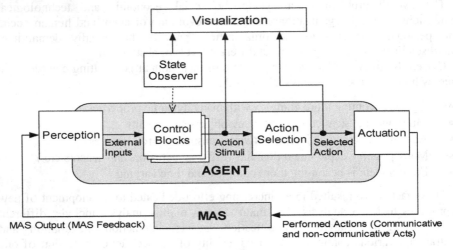

Fig. 1. The approximation of agents' internal architectures for the analysis purposes

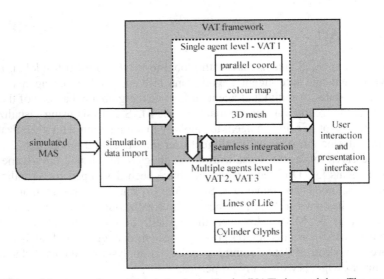

Fig. 2. The architecture of our Visual Analysis Tools (VAT) is modular. The sources of visualized data are the simulations of various multi-agent systems scenarios. The data is loaded through the simulation data input module. Its basic function is to parse an XML file and build internal representation of the analysed MAS. This representation is stored independent of any visualization method. We consider every visualization method as a view on the data. These views (VAT1, VAT2, ...) hold additional contextual data structures for visualization (colours, geometry, ...). This allows us to seamlessly switch among different VATs - different views of the analysed MAS

Regardless of their purpose, agents have perception layer, which transforms feedback (information) from MAS (other agents, objects, ambient environment) to their internal representation and actuation layer that transforms agent's internal representation of actions to physical actions. These physical actions may be considered as communicative or non-communicative acts. There is also a set of control blocks, which take perceived inputs and make motivations for an agent to make decision. These motivations (action stimuli) are combined in ASM (Action Selection Mechanism), where the best action is selected in order to maximize progress towards agent's (time varying) goals. Information we use for analysis are agent's state (selected properties of its control blocks) gathered via state observer, motivations (action stimuli) and selected actions. This is shown in Fig. 1.

It is obvious that looking on a system of agents from one point of view doesn't provide enough information for the analysis. Multiple views and various levels of detail becomes a necessity, which is reflected in our approach. Our research has resulted in development of several integrated Visualization Analysis Tools (VATs) for seamless analysis on various levels of detail and from various views as depicted in Fig. 2.

3.1 Problem Analysing – Key Concepts

The power of our tools lies in utilization of the following key concepts:

1. VAT is specialized on discovering of important features within very complex MAS space and consequently their deeper analysis.
2. Visual Analysis Tools (VAT) allow representing of many agents (or many agent's properties) all at once and within long time interval. The collection of agent's as well as properties to be displayed is configurable (i.e. only small number of interesting entities may be displayed for isolation of dependencies)
3. Position of an object (agent) in virtual MAS space provides strong context information to any analysed feature. Our understanding of *position* covers the common *space of dynamically changing behaviours*. The simulator records agents' positions within this space and gives important proximity issues (important objects and agents). Newly, positions in the space of behaviour constraints are computed and visualized by presented VAT tools.
4. *MAS dynamics* is provided in VAT within the *whole time interval* with additional inter-linked views, which supply additional details about particular time interval.
5. Individual views are fully *interactive* with virtual trackball used for rotation and zooming and panning support. Interactive seeking through the time interval provides instant relevant details in the linked views.
6. *Sensitivity* and *cluster analysis* with interactive manipulation of their constraints and parameters provide solid framework for analysis and their results are visualized by diverse methods. The result of the sensitivity function is *mapped into a colour palette* consisting of up to 32 distinct colours. Mapping is linear and the colours may be selected upon user's will.
7. VAT views are interlinked together to easily find causalities - correspondence between current or previous state of an agent, community or environment and resulting behaviour.

8. The key information to understand MAS lies in identifying changes in its tendency – changes in behaviour of single agents, community or environment.
9. Our Visual Analysis Tools run on the Microsoft Windows platform, they are implemented in C++ language and use the OpenGL API for 3D graphics.

Sensitivity Analysis. The concept of sensitivity analysis [5] has proven to us to be a valuable approach to parameter reduction. In our application we have selected a simple weighting mechanism. The sensitivity function for each agent is computed as follows:

$$fn_j(t) = \sum_i p_{ji}(t) \cdot w_i \qquad (1)$$

where p_{ji} is the i-th parameter of agent j, w_i is the weight of i-th parameter and t is time. Weight w_i is common to parameter i of every agent in the system. The weights can be manipulated interactively.

Cluster and Sensitivity Analysis. Input parameters for clustering in VAT are granularity (number of groups to be created) and agent's parameters. User selects interesting agent's parameters (money, hunger, thirst, fear etc.) and the system automatically divides agents into groups based on selected granularity. The "closest" agents are grouped together using classical cluster analysis approaches with Euclidean metrics. User is usually moving with the granularity parameter and views the analysed MAS to see how particular granularity and parameters influence splitting into groups. Different granularity of the agent system becomes immediately apparent (Fig. 3.)

Agents can be divided into groups based for example on their happiness and hunger or goals and likewise. Fig. 4 depicts a demo situation where agents were automatically divided into three groups: happy ones (smiling), sad ones (frowning) and confused ones (with question mark). Clustering is supplemented by sensitivity analysis, which allows setting parameters used for grouping and also changing their priority. User can thus view an agent community with different granularity and also see correspondence between particular parameters and the result of grouping. Only particular parameters can be set to be used for sensitivity – for example setting all parameters except one off allows seeing results of sensitivity analysis, where only this one parameter is being taken into account.

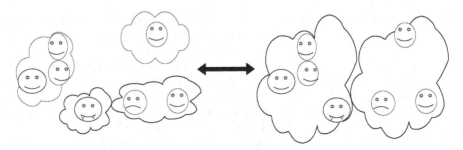

Fig. 3. Changing number of groups

Fig. 4. Arbitrary grouping of agents

3.2 Single Agent - Level of Detail 1

On this level a selected agent is being analysed with high level of granularity. Two main inter-linked VAT views are used: 3D mesh[1] and parameter curves with colour map. The first visualizes agent's parameters (gathered by state observer – see Fig. 1), the second visualizes action selection mechanism with contextual information to see correlations between agent's parameters and action selection.

Agent's Internal State (Agent's Parameters). VAT level 1 combines two main visualization approaches – *method of parallel coordinates* [6] and *Colour map* [7]. The original method of parallel coordinates is used to visualize the agent's internal state. During the execution of MAS, selected agent's parameters are observed by State Observer and recorded to an external XML file (for each time step). This data are later imported into VAT for visualization.

Parameters are visualized as poly-lines (each parameter has its own axis). The individual poly-lines are stacked behind each other along the time axis to produce a mesh (Fig. 5). A semitransparent cutting plane represents current time slice. It can be interactively moved along the time axis of the mesh.

The mesh has several important features: (i) represents the dynamics of parameter progression, (ii) keeps inter-parameter context, (iii) the characteristics of agent parameter changes are of such nature, that this mesh forms continuous and easily recognizable "peaks and valleys" – local parameter minima and maxima. Current time slice represents reference values of each parameter. The mesh can be coloured in two ways: first, colour represents relative difference of each slice in relation to current slice, and second, colour expresses the gradient of parameter change between particular slices, which is particularly useful for inflection point detection.

---

[1] The term *mesh* is used in computer graphics to describe 3D objects composed of triangles like a net.

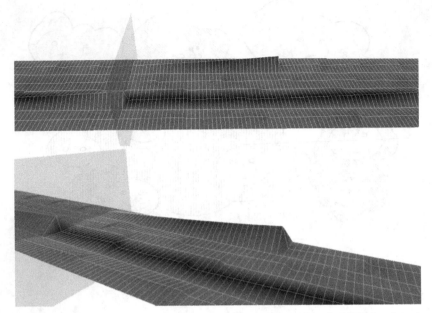

Fig. 5. Two screenshots of the *3D mesh* from different viewpoints in VAT level 1: Agent's parameters – 3D mesh with "peaks and valleys"

Agent's Action Selection Mechanism (ASM). Stimuli coming from various architectural components (motivations) of an agent function as inputs for action selection (action stimuli in Fig. 1). Embedded ASM computes action preferences from these stimuli (preference to select particular action) based on agent's actual state and its surrounding environment. Every time step at least one most preferred action is selected and consequently executed by proper actuator (send message, go forward, eat etc.). A special approach has been chosen to visualize action preferences - the *Colour map*. It is partially similar to ThemeRiver [8] or an unwrapped pie chart. The *Colour map* works as follows: in every time step preference is computed for each action by the ASM. The preferences are normalized to 1. The relative value of action preference in relation to other actions is more important than the actual preference value. In the *Colour map*, each action has its own coloured stripe. The thickness of the stripe represents normalized action preference. Stripes of all available actions are stacked onto each other to produce a *Colour map*. Under the *Colour map* there are several lines of colour bars, which represent actions selected by the ASM and performed by actuators in the corresponding time step.

Mutual Relations. The real power of these methods lies in their tight integration. Agent's internal state influences its action selection mechanism. The *Colour map* thus shows an evolution of agent's action preferences together with its physically performed actions during agent's life. In order to analyse mutual correspondence between agent parameters and preferred actions, the *Colour map* is directly linked to parameter curves (Fig. 6) and thus to the parameter mesh (Fig. 5). This enables us to see important dependencies between parameters and actions undertaken by the agent.

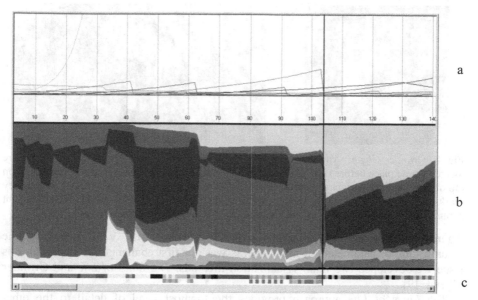

Fig. 6. Agent's parameters in relation to action preferences: the upper part (a) shows the development of selected agent's parameters in time, part (b) is the *Colour map* and part (c) shows coloured bars, which represent selected actions. The vertical black line denotes the current time slice – a synchronization facility among the interconnected views. This particular screenshot shows an agent, which has just fed itself and its preference of the eat act and its hunger parameter has dramatically fallen. This combination of views provides valuable direct relation between parameter value and action preference

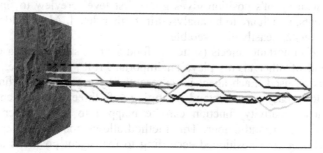

Fig. 7. *Lines of life* with a textured current time slice cutting plane. Each line depicts the path of an agent through the environment. Each line segment is coloured according to the result of a sensitivity analysis function

3.3 Multiple Agents – Level of Detail 2

Single agent does not reflect the behaviour and characteristics of the whole multi-agent system, which is our primary goal to visualize. Several difficulties are arising: many agents, parameters and actions, dynamic system, inter-agent communication and reciprocal popularity etc. All these features influence both the behaviour of the whole agent community (local-to-global) and every single agent (global-to-local) as well.

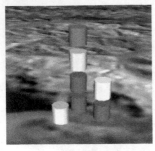 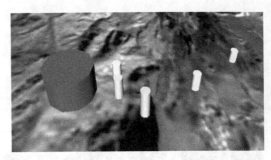

Fig. 8. *Cylinder Glyphs*: The left screenshot shows a common start-up scenario – agents are located at one place before they take a run into various directions. The cylinders are stacked on top of each other. The right screenshot shows a situation in the virtual ecosystem – scared prey (dark thick cylinder) hunted by hungry predators (bright thin cylinders). In this scenario agent parameter *fear* was mapped to cylinder radius, *hunger* to height and *thirst* to colour

Agents' Parameters Visualization – VAT Level 2 and VAT Level 3. The visualization of parameters of many agents was our first challenge. To deal with this issue we developed two main visualization methods: *The Lines of Life* and *Cylinder Glyphs*[2] [9].

The Lines of Life approach provides the topmost level of detail to the other visualization methods. Path through the environment (sequence of agent's physical coordinates in 2D) is recorded for each agent during simulation. The sequence of positions produces a 3D poly-line, which represents the travel of a particular agent through the environment during its life (Fig. 7). Each line segment is coloured according to the result of a sensitivity analysis function. The Method provides good general overview of agent population evolution. Single sensitivity function value in combination with agent's position gives good first level preview to find interesting clusters of agents, which are to be analysed in further detail. Also, sudden changes in agent's parameters are easily discoverable.

Proximity of important objects (water or food source, shelters in case of a virtual ecosystem) and of other agents plays an important role. In this case, the *Cylinder Glyphs* method is used. Each agent is represented by a glyph – a cylinder (Fig. 8). Cylinders allow easy-to-understand mapping of three independent sensitivity functions. Each sensitivity function can be mapped to one independent feature: cylinder radius, height and colour. This method allows good proximity information overview. Cylinders are positioned according to real agent positions and thus it is possible to analyse how their environment influences agent's parameters. Cylinders are stacked on top of each other if many agents share the same coordinates.

VAT level 3 deploys cluster analysis to identify specific groups within an agent community. The grouping is based again on parameters gathered from agents (Fig. 1)

Agents can be for example divided into groups based on their physical coordinates or even other parameters like their internal needs, goals or mood. The result of cluster analysis is mapped to cylinder colour; the other two properties are used for two independent sensitivity functions.

---

[2] In computer visualization the term *glyph* is used to describe any graphical entity that data points map to. The various attributes of the glyph such as size, shape, and color are controlled by the values of the data point in different dimensions.

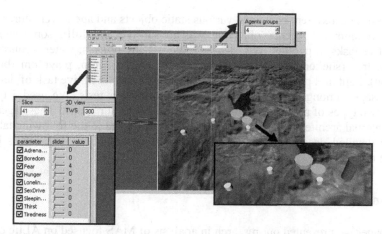

Fig. 9. Screenshot with *Cluster* and *Sensitivity Analysis* implemented in VAT3: left detail depicts sensitivity analysis panel where one can select parameters to be considered (with preferences), top right detail depicts panel where number of agent groups can be selected and bottom right detail depicts agents as they are divided into groups (distinguished by colours)

4   Case Study Based on Artificial Life Simulator

As a testing MAS we have used Artificial Life Simulator (ALS) [10] developed at CTU, Department of Cybernetics, Prague. This Java based MAS allows to set up a complex environment inhabited by agents with arbitrary internal architecture. ALS has been used for numerous simulations; most of them fall into the Artificial Life domain. ALS records agents' activity together with various characteristics and exports this data via XML to be later used in a visualization tool. ALS is depicted in the following Figure.

Fig. 10. Artificial Life Simulator used as a test bed for visualization

Our testing ecosystem contained various static objects and agents (creatures) living in the environment. Agents' objective was to survive and fulfil some subsidiary deliberative tasks in parallel. We used 8 types of static objects: water resource, food resource, tree (shelter), flower (increase agent's interest), trap, playroom (boredom reduction), light and post office (for agents performing deliberative task of delivering post messages among post offices and agents) during our tests. We used 3 types of agents: two types of prey agents (blue and red) and predator agents. These agents had CZAR internal architecture. ALS configuration is described in the following tables.

More detailed description of our ecosystem is described in [10], but is beyond scope of this paper.

5 Conclusion

In this paper we presented our research in analysis of MAS focused on ALife domain. Our approach is largely inspired by Biology, and more specifically by the field of Ethology, which attempts to understand the mechanisms, which animals use to demonstrate adaptive and successful behaviour. However common definition of agent is used within this research [11] and also results of this research can be generally used across many MAS domains.

Table 1. Static objects used in the ecosystem

STATIC OBJECTS – these objects don't change their position		Num. of objects
Water/Food	Unlimited/limited water or food source. Used to feed prey agents. Water is for both prey and predator agents.	2 water, 3 food
Trees and flowers	Functions like a shelter; agents can hide from predators. Predators can't see them if they are sheltered.	8
Trap	An agent is injured when caught to a trap. His life variable is reduced and pain drive increased.	3
PlayStation	Agents can avoid boredom here.	2
Day light	Agents can perceive daylight. This stimulus influences agents to feel more sleepy in the night.	X
PostOffice	Some agents perform deliberative task of delivering post messages. If an agent is going to send message to another one without meeting him, he can put his message to a PostOffice. Another agent responsible for delivering messages picks up these messages and deliver them to appropriate agents.	2

Table 2. Agents in the ecosystem

AGENTS – creatures		Num. of agents
Prey (blue color)	Male or female. Can mate with both blue and red agents but prefer blue agents.	10
Prey (red color)	Male or female. Can mate with both blue and red agents without any preference.	5
Predator	Male or female. Predator agents are hunting blue and red agents.	4

Table 3. Agent's Internal Architecture

AGENTS' INTERNAL ARCHITECTURE
Actuators – Acts
Agents are capable of the following actions:
Eat(subject or agent), Drink(subject), Step Left/Right/Forward/Backward, Use(item), Mate(agent), Hobnob(agent), Sleep, Attack(agent)
Perception
Agents can perceive the following meta-information:
Recognize(subject), Recognize(agent), Recognize(direction), feel(temperature), feel(smell), perceive(day time)
ISM (Internal State Model)
Listed are all agents' internal state variables:
Energy, Water, Alcohol, Fear toxin, Immunity level, Anabolic steroid, Endorphin, Testosterone, Estrogen, Sex drive, Adrenaline, Life, Injury, Stress, Pain, Hunger, Coldness, Hotness, Tiredness, Sleepiness, Loneliness, Crowdedness, Fear, Boredom, Anger, Reward and Punishment.
ASM (Action Selection Mechanism)
The following activities are considered in ASM
Eat, Drink, Step Left/Right/Forward/Backward, Use, Mate, Hobnob, Sleep, Attack, Reproduce, Cooperate, Approach, Explore, Need, Avoid Hazard, Avoid Predator, Flee, Fight
Additional Control Components
3 specific modules embodied by agents are:
Map generation, Object evaluation, Sequencer
Adaptation and Learning Capabilities
Agents have the following adaptation and learning capabilities:
1. Intergeneration Improvement - Parameters of the internal state model equations are adjusted. (Genetically from parents to offspring)
2. Individual Adaptation – Agents evaluate static objects and other agents, create map of the environment.

To support analysis, we have developed visualization tools that are integrated together to allow seamless iterative analysis on various levels of MAS. Three levels of analysis are considered in our approach. Level 1 focuses on detailed analysis of a single agent and visualizes agent's internal state, visualization of its action selection mechanism and relationships (or correspondence) between agent's state and resulting actions – agent's behaviour. Level 1 leverages two methods: Method of *parallel coordinates* and *colour map*. Used approach allows handling large amount of rapidly changing parameters, which is always problem in MAS. This method is effective up to 15-20 parameters.

Level 2 focuses on analysis of multiple agents. *The Lines of Life* and *Cylinder Glyphs* work together with the sensitivity analysis function to bring overview of agents over the whole time interval, as well as means for discovering changes in MAS and interesting agent clusters. These methods present agent's state in context to its position, other agents, and surrounding environment. Theoretically, it supports up to several hundreds of agents.

Level 3 focuses on visualization of agent groups. *Clustering together with sensitivity analysis* is used here. Combination of clustering and sensitivity analysis brings significant contribution to the analysis, especially when large amount of agents are being analysed. Splitting into groups based on arbitrary parameters brings another dimension into analysis. We can analyse agent community in more abstract way such as in terms of mood and emotions and others. The sensitivity analysis allows changing importance of particular parameters to identify those ones that influence particular splitting into groups.

We see the following key aspects of our methods: utilization of modern visualization approaches together with standard AI techniques, namely sensitivity analysis and clustering, position of an agent in the virtual ecosystem, system *dynamics* in the *whole time interval,* fully *interactive views.* Important is also that VAT views are linked together in such a way to easily find causalities. Key information to understand MAS lies in identifying changes in its tendency – changes in behaviour of single agents, community or environment [12], [13].

We have identified the following shortcomings of our approach: Even though our approach allows displaying of many parameters and agents at the same time, it was shown in praxis that analysis looses its transparency for more than 20 parameters (confusing tangle of lines in VAT 1 or overcrowded 3D environment in VAT3). This shortcoming is caused by limited computer performance and its display device resolution. Analysis can be performed only offline and thus analysis results cannot be used on ad hoc basis to change MAS settings during its run. Our approach has been tested on autonomous agents in the ALife domain only. We believe that our approach is universal and applicable across many domains incorporating small changes. This has not been fully tested yet, however we have recently received requests for cooperation and utilization of our approach in other domains from several research groups. This research is partially related to the activities of the Computer Graphics Group towards visualization in specific environments [14]. The results of our simulations are backed by collaboration with important ethology, biology and sociology research groups in the Czech Republic [15].

Analysis of MAS is not an easy task. In the near future we are going to add level 4 to our analysis – to provide overall metrics of the MAS itself, do more investigation in visualization of connections among agents (i.e.: communication, inter-agent preferences.) Automatic classification of correspondence among levels of analysis is also being considered. Extensive methodology tests are to take place in the near future to evaluate our tools in many different agent scenarios and domains.

References

[1]   Szekely, P., Rogers, C., M.: Interfaces for Understanding Multi-Agent Behavior, Proc. ACM Conf. on Intelligent User Interfaces, Santa Fe New Mexico USA (2001) 161-166.

[2]   Beneš, B., Espinosa, E.: Modeling Virtual Ecosystems with Proactive Guidance of Agents, to appear In IEEE Computer Animation and Social Agents, New Bruncwick USA (2003).

[3]   Allbeck, J., Badler N.: Toward Representing Agent Behaviors Modified by Personality and Emotion, Workshop on Embodied Conversational Agents, Bologna, Italy (2002).

[4]   Schroeder, M., Noy, P.: Multiagent Visualisation Based on Multivariate Data, Proc. 5th International Conf. on Autonomous Agents, Montreal Canada (2001) 85-91.

[5]   Chatterjee, S., Hadi, A. S.: Sensitivity Analysis in Linear Regression, New York: John Wiley & Sons (1988).

[6]   Inselberg, A., Dimsdale, B.: Parallel Coordinates: A Tool for Visualizing Multivariate Relations (Plenum Publishing Corporation), New York (1991).

[7]   Havre, S., Hetzler, E., et all.: ThemeRiver: Visualizing Thematic Changes in Large Document Collections, IEEE Trans. on Visualization and Computer Graphics, 8(1), (2002).

[8]   Nahodil, P.,Kadlecek, D., Rehor, D., Slavík, P.: Transparent Visualization of Multi-Agent Systems, Proc. 4th International Carpathian Control Conference, High Tatras Slovakia (2003) 723-727.

[9]   Rehor, D., Kadlecek, D., Slavík, P., Nahodil, P.: VAT – An Approach to Multi-Agent System Vizualization. IASTED International Conference on Visualization, Imaging and Image Processing. Benalmadena Spain (2003) 849-854.

[10]   Kadlecek, D., Nahodil, P.: New Hybrid Architecture in Artificial Life Simulation. Advances in Artificial Life. - Lecture Notes in AI No 2159, Springer Verlag, Berlin, (2001) 143-146.

[11]   McFarland, D., and Bosser, U.: Intelligent Behavior in Animals and Robots. MIT Press, Cambridge, MA (1993).

[12]   Ferber, J.: Multi Agent Systems. An Introduction to Distributed Artificial Intelligence. Addison-Wesley (1999).

[13]   Kadlecek, D., Rehor, D., Nahodil, P., Slavík, P.: Analysis of Virtual Agent Communities by Means of AI Techniques and Visualization. In Intelligent Virtual Agents, Heidelberg, Germany. Heidelberg: Springer Verlag, (2003), 274-282.

[14]   Slavík P., Míkovec Z., Hrdlicka F.: Special Problems of Visualization in a Specific Environment, In: East-West-Vision 2002. Wien: Österreichische Computer Gesellschaft, (2002), 269-270.

[15]   Nahodil, P., Petrus, M.: Behaviour Co-ordination in Multi-Robot Group. In *Proceedings of the International IASTED Conference MIC, 18. - 21. February 2002 Innsbruck, Austria.* Calgary: ACTA Press, (2002), 464-468.

Advancing Profile Use in Agent Societies

Penny Noy and Michael Schroeder

Department of Computing, City University
Northampton Square, London EC1V 0HB, UK
{p.a.noy,msch}@soi.city.ac.uk

Abstract. Ubiquitous, persistent and pervasive computing systems and their modelling and engineering as agent societies suggest much potential for the application of personal and task profiles. Increasing quantities and types of profiling data are also becoming available. This paper discusses the use of profiles in this context and suggests a new form of profile employment to ease the use of profile data, by increasing convenience and privacy. Familiar dimension reduction techniques map the high dimensional profile to a position in a reduced dimension profile space. However, in this method, each profile owner calculates their position with respect to a number of reference vectors. This method avoids third party involvement and keeps the profile details private. Empirical studies indicate that calculating the whole set iteratively by this method compares favourably with respect to abstraction error when compared to direct calculation.

1 Introduction

The rapidly emerging scenario of ubiquitous, persistent and pervasive computing presents challenges of complexity in presenting us with quantities of information and interactions that we can now only imagine. From access by a single application to computing power and resources on a world scale, to innumerable sensors cooperating and interacting at a particular locality, uses of profile data immediately suggest themselves for efficiency, personalization and presence. Agent-oriented computation is considered by many to have a leading role to play in the engineering of the new computing systems (e.g. [1]) and provides a vision of electronic, agent societies embedded within our own human ones [2]. At the same time, agent technology looks set to expand both to include agents that we use as extensions of ourselves, as well as those that we interact with embedded within a large number of devices and applications [3]. The consideration of the extension of ourselves has been described as *cognitive prosthetics* [4]. Agents as separate, differentiated individuals or extensions of ourselves or possessing the ability to change between the two (for instance in emergencies) implies different levels of autonomy and human-agent collaboration [5].

What is the relevance of profile data to the engineering of agent societies? A number of factors indicate that the relationship between profiles and the interaction mechanisms and structures in agent societies looks set to expand and needs to be explored. Consider the following:

A. Omicini, P. Petta, and J. Pitt (Eds.): ESAW 2003, LNAI 3071, pp. 360–375, 2004.
© Springer-Verlag Berlin Heidelberg 2004

- Profiles of many kinds are central to human society. A factor that is at the core of human activity should not be sidelined in agent societies.
- There is an abundance of data available with which one can construct many kinds of profiles - the environment is naturally *profile rich.*
- The role of search is expanding as we move towards the point where a single application (or agent) can access the computing power and data resources of the entire world via the (semantic) Web [6].
- In general, the similarity of correspondents (agent/human/interface) can be related to the *semantic thickness* or *depth* of the communication channel between them. The costs and benefits of increasing semantic depth of communication channels have implications for agent systems.
- Agent societies are expected to increase in terms of complexity and scope, and become ubiquitous in the new computing environments.

The first of these points is an intuitive view that profile data are important to the engineering of agent societies, because interactions and mechanisms of interaction in human societies are tightly bound up with profiles consisting of data about ourselves, our desires and intentions. Together we humans can achieve a great deal, but how do we get together? We develop the ability to recognize profiles in others, by many subtle signs based upon body language, accent, style of expression, context etc. This recognition is based upon our experience of life and represents embedded information with which we compare ourselves, or our requirements. We have developed structures to help elicit information and compare (or test against other) profiles. For instance, an interview is used to find the right person for a job, to check profiles and hence compatibility with the interviewer and the post requirements. Human managers arrange sessions at work for people to get to know each other better, to see where common interests lie. We value bonding and often important decisions are made on this basis. We build teams of people with complementary profiles. We match a profile of a task with the suitability of a service and so on. We progressively reveal our profile to another person as we develop trust and a sense of shared interests and opinions. One cannot imagine human society without profiles. Thus, intuitively, profiles have an important part to play in differentiating between and enhancing relationships in agent societies and at the human/agent and agent/application boundaries and thus in the engineering of such scenarios.

Yet agent societies are not the same as human societies. For instance, we humans cannot carry with us a vector one thousand elements long and measure it, in a millisecond, against another similar vector carried by a friend, though a software agent can. We do the equivalent by using subtle indicators based upon our experience and senses. This emphasizes that engineering agent societies is partly about creating equivalent mechanisms that use the strengths of the computational medium, as well as being open to new mechanisms that arise directly from different capabilities.

Perhaps the most important factor from the list above is the expansion of the role of search. The expansion of available information and the reduction in human cost of search will ensure that the role of search, in its most general sense, will expand in the new computing environments. Searching for resources, people, products, information, 'something new', excitement, love . . . Every second that passes witnesses millions of people searching via a myriad of means. Increasingly such means and media employed are electronic. Many people are seeking similar information and work on similar problems. Software agents carrying our profile can meet with the representatives of others and exchange important information or provide introductions. These agents may provide real-time search responses or background information monitoring. The concepts are embodied in many search and classification applications. These may be ordinary searches, not explicitly involving other agents (or agents at all), but agents may assist in improving precision and speed. Precision, because a profile can assist in returning a more relevant subset of returns from a query, and speed, because similar agents can exchange information and thus search more quickly. The agents may be looking for products, services or pieces of information. They may be looking for similar people (or agents) working on similar problems, like-minded people in general or someone within a specific organization who might know the answer to a question they have. Such an agent may also be an entity in its own right, not simply our representative.

The vision of agents, extensions of ourselves or their own masters, freely roaming to find like minds (other agents) and information and engaging in commerce, encounters numerous obstacles. Leaving aside the question of agent mobility, consider the following: the degree to which information is searchable (i.e. specified according to agreed ontologies); the accuracy of the metrics in matching seeker with sought; the willingness of humans to allow an agent to carry their profile (and the security issues involved); privacy of information. On this last point, there are powerful civil liberties questions involved. For this reason (and others) there are calls for the ownership and management of electronic profile data and preferences to remain with the consumer [7]. Yet currently there is little use of profiles under the control of users; it is more common for server side applications to build profiles of a user from user interaction (e.g. the building of user profiles by on-line bookstores such as Amazon). However, the inexorable move in the direction of personal data collection, combined with the desire to pursue links and knowledge should see more techniques for users to take charge and use their own profiles.

Consider how profiles might be exchanged electronically. Assume that an agent (electronic or human) has an appropriate profile and that this agent meets with another entity (agent or application), which also possesses a profile. They now want to measure their similarity in an appropriate manner and may prefer not to reveal their profile details in the process. Some of our earlier work looked at proximity data and multivariate data (these terms are described in Section 3) in the agent domain and explored possible metric choices for visualization [8, 9]. It occurred to us that it might be useful to take this idea of an agent's position in a transformed space, which we used for visualization, to give the agents a lightweight version of their profile which would protect the details of their profile. The agent could also be given a 'map' of the terrain of this space to have some idea of the overall community (for human or agent personal profiles) or the different product or service specifications (for product or service specification profiles).

This paper first gives some background covering ways in which profiles have been used in agent systems, then outlines profile definition and similarity measurement. The use of a transformed position profile, as raised in the previous paragraph, is described. This expands work begun in our use of visualization to define like-minded agents [10, 11]. The two key aspects of accuracy (dimension reduction algorithms create approximate solutions to the layout in a reduced dimension space) and security (under what conditions, if any, is it possible to retrieve the original profiles) are examined.

2   Background

The task of *matching seeker with sought* may involve a user profile or a profile of a task or desired piece of information. It is in this general sense that the word profile is used here. To compare profiles a means of measuring the difference between two profiles, a *metric* is needed. Examples of metrics used in this work are given in Section 4. There are examples of the use of metrics in various types of agent systems. For instance: Faratin et al use the maximum value distance in making negotiation trade-offs [12]; the Yenta system uses correlation to determine user interests and then a direct comparison to find a common joint interest [13]; Somlo and Howe use incremental clustering for profile maintenance in information gathering web agents based on term vectors of documents the user has shown interest in [14]; GRAPPA (Generic Request Architecture for Passive Provider Agents) is a configurable matchmaking framework which includes demand and supply profiles and has been applied to matching multidimensional profiles of job applicants to vacancies [15]; Ogston and Vassiliadis use minimal agents working without a facilitator to match services and providers [16]. The many possible application areas divide broadly into two areas - matchmaking (eg matching services to clients, service discovery, people connecting) and search. The general topic lies within organizational concepts in multi-agent systems and improving learning with communication [17]. The *finding* and *remembering* of agents or services can be centralized, left as a diffusion process or engineered in a computational ecology sense [18, 13, 16]. The mechanism of finding, as in agent and service discovery, is not the focus of this work, which concentrates on the matching of entities, tasks and so on. Though profile data could be used in creating entries in yellow page directories, or in the form those entries take. Similarity is also possible within logic, a form of fuzzy reasoning described as *similarity reasoning* captures the notion of interpolation inside a logical setting (e.g. [19]). This paper excludes the wider discussion of comparing agents' logical profiles (such as for BDI agents), for simplicity.

3   Defining Profiles

The creation of the profile itself may be quite straightforward, as in the case of a specification for a required product, or it may be a challenging matter, as in the case of the construction of personal profiles. Examples of the latter are: the learning and revising of user profiles using Baysian classifiers and their use to more accurately predict World Wide Web sites of interest to the user [20], the Yenta system [13] and many examples of relevance feedback (these generate a certain type of profile, but, in general, do not start from the use of a multidimensional profile). There are also a number of Microsoft projects that record and analyze user behaviour (e.g. Lumiere [21]). For this discussion, the derivation of the profile is not included, the profile is taken as given.

For illustration, an agent's profile is considered to be a vector of interests and behaviours (a feature list) or a similarity measure or sets and/or combinations of these [8, 9]. It is considered thus for simplicity, but this analysis relates equally to other types of profiles, such as where the profile is of a specification or task an agent is carrying for negotiation, matchmaking or search purposes. A set of n agent interest vectors, each p elements long, forms an nxp matrix (or *pattern* matrix) of data often described as *multivariate data*. Where the data is the measure of dissimilarity between each pair of the n agents, it results in an nxn *proximity* matrix and the data is described as *proximity data*. In visualizing proximity data *dissimilarity* equates with *distance*, so that entities are close in distance because they are similar. Data may originate in the form of (dis)similarity data, such as where the number of messages exchanged between agents is used as a measure of their similarity, but it is also possible to transform multivariate data to proximity data by using metrics. Metrics define measures of difference between the vectors of the pattern matrix. Metrics used in this paper are described in Section 4. The aim of our work in visualization was to find layouts (in 2D or 3D) for these data either by using mathematical transformations or novel representations (eg colour maps, hierarchical axes, parallel co-ordinates [22]). Mathematical transformation can be achieved directly, for example by means of Principal Components Analysis (PCA), or indirectly by first creating a proximity matrix using a metric and then finding a layout which approximates (usually) the pairwise distances of the proximity matrix. The finding of a layout for proximity data is described as *multidimensional scaling* (MDS), two common methods of MDS are Principal Coordinates Analysis (PCoA) and spring embedding [23]. Self-organizing Map (SOM)[24] is another method of reducing the dimensions of multivariate data for visualization. PCA expresses the nxn matrix in an equivalent form which allows truncation of the matrix, removing dimensions that contribute the least information. The resultant visual representations may provide meaningful clusters or reveal patterns from which knowledge can be gained, despite the fact that they are often great abstractions of the original data. In the normal use of similarity metrics, the complete profiles have to be known, since all the data is required to make the calculations. For agent applications where privacy is an issue, they must be submitted to a trusted third party or encrypted and given to a special algorithm that can operate without exposing the decrypted profile to the user [25]. In this paper, we suggest, instead, that the mathematically transformed profiles (of the discussion above) are carried by the agents. Thus they use xy or xyz co-ordinates as the profile. This avoids revealing the profile. The implication is that there must be a central entity which will do the calculation (and thus that one needs to reveal one's profile to) and then give the agent its co-ordinates and the bounds of the space (so that it can judge relative similarity). Also this does not deal easily with dynamic situations (i.e. reflecting changing profiles), as it would require a periodic return to base to profile updating. A possible alternative is to calculate one's own co-ordinates with respect to a number of reference points, i.e. calculate one's proximity to the reference points and then find a position in space to satisfy this reduced set of distances. For instance for a feature list of length 5, consisting of a set of five possible agent interest areas and interest values in the range 0 to 1 (say), the following is an indication of the bounds of the space.

	A	B	C	D	E
agent1	1	0	0	0	0
agent2	0	1	0	0	0
agent3	0	0	1	0	0
agent4	0	0	0	1	0
agent5	0	0	0	0	1

It may be unwise to base the position on a computation that satisfies the similarity measures to all of these vectors (since this increases the inaccuracy of the layout), but the agent could carry the set of co-ordinates for certain bounds (or other reference vectors) and profile position, having the calculations made back at base. In higher dimensional spaces there is an interesting observation [26] that there exist in a high-dimensional space a much larger number of almost orthogonal vectors than orthogonal vectors, so that vectors having random directions might turn out to be close to orthogonal. The two methods of using the mathematically transformed profiles are illustrated in Section 5 and their accuracy and security examined in Sections 6 and 7 respectively.

4   Choosing a Metric

Assuming the profile values have been identified, the next issue is to specify the variables to be used in describing the profile and the ways in which pairwise similarities can be derived from the matrix formed by the set of profiles. Many different measures of pairwise similarity have been proposed [27, 28]. Some are closely related to one another. Measures are usually presented that are particularly relevant for comparing objects that are described by a single type of variable. This discussion restricts itself to quantitative data type for brevity. Let x_{ik} denote the value that the kth quantitative variable takes for the ith object $(i = 1, \ldots, n; \; k = 1, \ldots, p)$. The Minkowski metric defines a family of dissimilarity measures, indexed by the parameter λ.

Minkowski metric

$$d_{ij} = (\sum_{k=1}^{p} w_k^{\lambda} |x_{ik} - x_{jk}|^{\lambda})^{1/\lambda} \ (\lambda \geq 1)$$

where $w_k (k = 1, \ldots, p)$ are non-negative weights associated with the variables, allowing standardization and weighting of the original variables. Values of λ of 1 and 2 give the two commonly used metrics of this family.

City block

$$d_{ij} = \sum_{k=1}^{p} w_k |x_{ik} - x_{jk}| \tag{1}$$

Euclidean distance

$$d_{ij} = (\sum_{k=1}^{p} w_k^2 (x_{ik} - x_{jk})^2)^{1/2} \tag{2}$$

5   Position as Profile

The pictures of information spaces as maps or terrains derived from multivariate data using self-organizing maps [24] provide us with a compelling image of the profile or topic space we are exploring. The metrics discussed above generate similar conceptual spaces when visualized. Yet this is a misleading image, since the data are high dimensional and it is impossible to represent their similarities accurately in 2 or 3D space (direct mapping methods for multivariate data, such as colour maps and parallel co-ordinate plots, are not included in this comment). Nevertheless, as an approximation and as a representation, an overview perhaps, of a large body of entities, it is being found useful (see eg [29]). Suppose we assume the validity of the layout and propose that the agent carries with them their xy (or xyz) co-ordinates and uses them as their profile. When meeting a fellow agent they can ask for the agent's xy co-ordinates and compute the Euclidean distance (Equation 2), say, to calculate their similarity. This would be more efficient than carrying a potentially long profile vector and enable them to use their profile without revealing details or requiring encryption. To illustrate this approximate profile method, consider a small matrix of 7 agents with certain levels of interest (of 0 to 10) in 7 topics. Again, note that this data could also relate to the specification of tasks, products or information.

$$
\begin{array}{l|ccccccc}
\text{Agent1} & 9 & 3 & 4 & 6 & 5 & 5 & 5 \\
\text{Agent2} & 1 & 10 & 10 & 1 & 7 & 2 & 0 \\
\text{Agent3} & 4 & 1 & 6 & 8 & 0 & 5 & 7 \\
\text{Agent4} & 2 & 7 & 8 & 4 & 0 & 2 & 0 \\
\text{Agent5} & 3 & 6 & 4 & 7 & 1 & 10 & 6 \\
\text{Agent6} & 1 & 7 & 6 & 5 & 0 & 2 & 0 \\
\text{Agent7} & 8 & 1 & 7 & 1 & 2 & 5 & 9 \\
\end{array}
$$

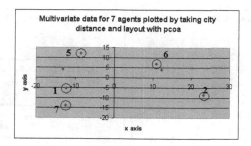

Fig. 1. Illustration of base plot, the three reference agents (5,6 and 7) and the two of interest in this measurement (1 and 2) are circled

Suppose Agent1 and Agent2 want to compare their profiles without exchanging them. Here we propose that they are given positions in the plot in 2D produced by reducing the dimensions of this matrix. The position can be derived in two ways: by base calculation or on-the-fly.

5.1   By Base Calculation

The agents both have the calculations done at a base point and periodically return for updates. Here the error will be that of the layout itself and the agent would be able to have details of the mean error and variance supplied with its co-ordinates, so that it can take this into account. Figure 1 shows the layout after City distance (Equation 1) and PCoA of the seven agents of randomly generated data from above. The City distance is first calculated between each pair of agents based on Equation 1 (with weights, $w_k(k = 1, \ldots, p)$, all equal to 1) resulting in a 7x7 symmetric proximity matrix. A two-dimensional layout that approximately satisfies this proximity matrix is then found using PCoA. PCoA takes the proximity matrix as input and creates a corresponding multivariate matrix, finds an equivalent form and allows truncation to two dimensions (in a manner similar to PCA) resulting in the set of xy co-ordinates plotted in Figure 1. Thus, if Agent1 meets Agent2 they can compare co-ordinates, ((-12.30, -5.20),(23.27,-8.44)), to calculate the Euclidean distance to give them the distance they are apart in this map.

5.2   By Calculation on the Fly

Here the agent calculates its position with respect to a number of reference vectors (either dynamically or at an earlier point in time) and then compares with another agent's position calculated similarly. Using the seven agent random data again, the reference vectors are chosen to be agents 5,6 and 7. Three reference agents are the minimum since only two will create two possible arrangements when agents 1 and 2 overlay their positions. Agents 1 and 2 separately calculate their City distances to the three reference vectors and subsequently lay out these distances with PCoA as shown in Figure 2.

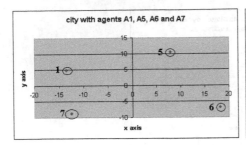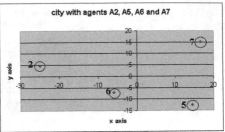

Fig. 2. Illustration of plots calculated individually by agents 1 (left) and 2 (right) with respect to the three reference agents (5,6 and 7) as circled and numbered

They now have xy co-ordinates, but in order to compare them they must be scaled (the Euclidean distance between 5 and 6 is used here), centered (here Agent 5 is placed at 0,0) and finally rotated to bring the agents 5,6 and 7 into position. Now the co-ordinates of the agent's position are in a form that they can use for comparisons. The results of the base calculation and on-the-fly calculation of the difference between agents 1 and 2 are given in the table below. (Since these are normalized with respect to the distance between agents 5 and 6, a value of 1 would indicate that they were the same distance away from each other as agents 5 and 6 are)

original city dist	base dist	on-the-fly dist
1.64	1.77	1.57
exact	8%err	-4%err

This iterative version of the transformation has the same time complexity as the direct method, since, given n entities with d dimensions, PCA has $O(nd^2)$, whereas, in the case of 3 reference vectors, the calculation is done for 4 entities, iteratively n times, which requires a time n times PCA for $n = 4$ with dimensions, d, which is also $O(nd^2)$. Also the iterative version has transformed the process into one which can allow the addition of entities and the change in attributes of an existing entity, *without re-calculation of the whole set*, which would be necessary with direct PCA. The implication of this is also that the iterative version is less affected by missing or erroneous values, though these will still potentially affect the standardization procedure. (The standardization procedure may, as in the empirical testing of section 6 employ the range of each variable across the whole dataset, other methods may use the mean. Thus the existence of erroneous zero values - sometimes used as a way of dealing with missing values - or outliers will alter the range or mean considerably.)

6   Empirical Accuracy Examination

The aim of this series of experiments was to examine the accuracy of using a position-as-profile version of the profile, both using base calculation and on-the-fly calculation. The Euclidean metric was used to give a measure of distance

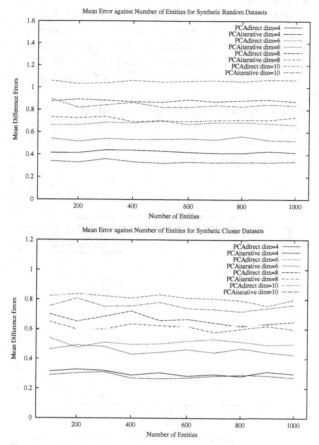

Fig. 3. Mean Error against Number of Entities for Synthetic Random Datasets (top) and Cluster Datasets (bottom)

between the original profiles. The corresponding distances were calculated for the transformed profiles, for base calculation and on-the-fly. The distance errors obtained were then calculated and averaged to give an average difference in distance error, d_{avg}, where, as in Equation 2:

$$d_{ij} = \left(\sum_{k=1}^{p} (x_{ik} - x_{jk})^2\right)^{1/2}$$

and

$$d_{avg} = 1/p^2 \sum_{i,j=1}^{p} d_{ij}$$

Two different types of synthetic datasets were used - random and clustered. For each of these datasets, the number of entities, n, and the number of dimensions, d, were varied and for each d and n, 30 runs were executed (i.e. 30 datasets of that type and size created), d_{avg} for each taken and the 30 values averaged. In each case, for convenience, 3 reference vectors were chosen from within the datasets and used to align the transformed sub matrices as described in section 5. n was varied between 100 and 1000, d between 4 and 40. Standardization with individual ranges of variable was used [27]. PCA was used for the matrix transformations.

The results given in Figures 3 and 4 show that the error is largely independent of the number of entities. The error increases with increasing dimensions, but iterative PCA outperforms direct PCA. In the clustered datasets, the variance increases significantly for increasing dimension.

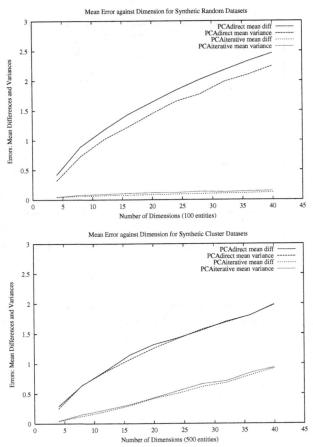

Fig. 4.   Mean Error against Dimension for Synthetic Random Datasets (top) and Cluster Datasets (bottom)

7 How Secure is the Transformation?

When we use either method, PCA direct or iterative, the resultant distance calculated between two agents is approximate, due to the abstraction of the dimension reduction. As before, let x_{ik} denote the value that the kth quantitative variable takes for the ith object ($i = 1, \ldots, n$; $k = 1, \ldots, p$). Using either PCA direct or iterative, the ith object now possesses a two-dimensional vector $\tilde{x}_i$. Consider now that entities i and j are agents Alice and Bob, and that they meet. Alice knows her own values (x_i), but not Bob's values (x_j). Is it possible for Alice to deduce Bob's original profile? Alice can exchange position vectors $\tilde{x}$ with Bob and calculate the Euclidean distance $\tilde{d}_{ij}$ between their positions, according to Equation 2. This distance in the transformed position space is an approximation of the original Euclidean distance d_{ij}. Thus:

$$(\sum_{k=1}^{p}(x_{ik} - x_{jk})^2)^{1/2} \approx \tilde{d}_{ij}$$

Squaring and replacing (x_i) with constants $c_{i1}, \ldots, c_{ip}$
(since entity i, Alice, knows these values):

$$\sum_{k=1}^{p} x_{jk}^2 + \sum_{k=1}^{p} c_{ik} - 2\sum_{k=1}^{p} c_{ik}x_{jk} \approx \tilde{d}_{ij}^2 \qquad (3)$$

Consider now that Alice procures other similar equations, either by repeatedly posing as another entity (with a different profile) or by sharing information with other entities or, in the use of iterative PCA, (which allows the use of a dynamically changing profile) by the natural development of her own profile (though in this case, for the sake of this argument, it is assumed that Bob's profile does *not* change). Alice now possesses a set of equations of the form of Equation 3. If she collects p of these equations and subtracts one from another in pairs (to remove the squared terms), the result is a set of p linear equations of the form:

$$2\sum_{k=1}^{p}(c_{i_{2k}k} - c_{i_{2k-1}k})x_{jk} \approx \tilde{d}_{i_{2k-1}j}^2 - \tilde{d}_{i_{2k}j}^2 + \sum_{k=1}^{p} c_{i_{2k-1}k} - \sum_{k=1}^{p} c_{i_{2k}k}$$

where c_{i_1k} is the kth variable value of i's first profile example. These equations can be solved to find values for x_j, but the values obtained will be approximate. Thus, it is possible to retrieve an approximation of the original profile vector of an entity that is met, assuming that sufficient distances to this entity in the reduced profile space are available.

Without extra information of the form collected by Alice posing as other agents (or otherwise), there are many possible vectors that would map to the point occupied by j in the transformed space. To illustrate this, consider the example of 2D reduced to 1D shown in Figure 5. Two reference vectors, R1 and R2 lie on the x and y axes respectively, vectors A and B will become the same

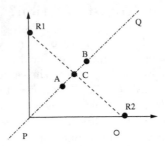

Fig. 5. Reduction from 2D to 1D. R1 and R2 are reference vectors, in transforming to 1D points A and B move to the single point C. The mapping back of point C is to a locus of points along PQ

point, C in 1D and $d_{AB} = 0$, since they collapse onto the principal axis R1R2. This would be true for positions of A and B along the locus PQ, up to a point at which their position alters the principal axis. Thus, given a distance of zero in the reduced dimension space, there is no way of retrieving the original locations.

8   Conclusions and Future Work

This paper has illustrated the use of a lightweight reduced dimension profile which also keeps the details of the profile private. This differs from the standard use of metrics in two ways: by the use of the transformed profile in agent/agent (or other) interactions; by using a method of transforming the profile without third party involvement. Tests with random and clustered datasets show that the error involved in the transformation is not affected by increasing number of entities, but does increase sharply for increasing dimensions. The results for calculation *on-the-fly* (using a form of iterative PCA with respect to three random reference vectors) are slightly better than those for *base* calculation (direct PCA). In this case, using PCA, the time complexity is not altered, which means that the iterative form of PCA could be used to avoid recalculating the whole set, and be useful where values are missing or erroneous, the entity that possesses this problematic data will be affected, but not the rest.

A means by which an approximation to the original profile of an entity can be obtained has been demonstrated under the condition that another entity is able to procure a set of distances from that entity to other entities of known value. Even if it is possible to obtain such a set, the approximation is very high so that only the general area of the original profile can be derived.

Further work needs to be done on the examination of error associated with different dimension reduction techniques and types of dataset. The usefulness of the transformed profile needs to be examined within applications of different kinds, to demonstrate its use in practice and to assess its behaviour compared to use of the full profile. We have described two scenarios for use within the socio-cognitive grids [30] context [31] involving personalization and for meeting people. For implementation, one approach would be for the participating parties - services, users, agents, interfaces - to subscribe to a profiling service. The profiling service would provide a template for the profile vector production and the reference vectors (if required). A participating party receives, from the service, software to obtain a profile from their raw data (e.g. for a personal profile - email and data files on their pc; for a product or task specification - a textual description) or for constructing the profile explicitly (for instance, by filling in a form or from scratch). For the on-the-fly method, the participants require information, from the service provider, of the bounds of each of the profile spaces and, for clients and peers, the reference vectors with which to calculate their position in the profile spaces. If it is required that the calculation is done centrally, the profile service can do this. Thus when two parties meet, one can ask the other whether they subscribe to a certain profile service and, if they do, proceed to exchange profiles, or in the case of interactions with an interface, the client may proceed to load their profile.

The paper has underlined the potential of profile use in agent societies due to the abundance of personal data, resources and information, the increase in the role of search and the expected growth in scale and complexity of agent oriented systems on a world scale. Such an environment is thus propitious for the advancement of profile use.

Acknowledgements

This work is supported by the EPSRC and British Telecom (CASE studentship - award number 99803052).

References

[1] Zambonelli, F., Van Dyke Parunak, H.: Signs of a revolution in computer science and software engineering. In: Proceedings of Engineering Societies in the Agents World ESAW 2002, Madrid, Spain (2002) 360

[2] Pitt, J., Mamdani, A., Charlton, P.: The open agent society and its enemies: A position statement and programme of research. Telematics and Informatics **18** (2001) 67–87 360

[3] Gershenfeld, N. A.: When Things Start to Think. Henry Holt and Company, New York (1999) 360

[4] Ford, K. M., Glymour, C., Hayes, P.: Cognitive prostheses. AI Magazine **18** (1997) 104 360

[5] Bradshaw, J. M., Sierhuis, M., Acquisti, A., Feltovich, P., Hoffman, R., Jeffers, R., Prescott, D., Suri, N., Uszok, A., Van Hoof, R.: Adjustable autonomy and human-agent teamwork in practice: An interim report on space applications. In Hexmoor, H., Falcone, R., Castelfranchi, C., eds.: Agent Autonomy. Kluwer (2003) in press 360

[6] Berners-Lee, T., Hendler, J., Lassila, O.: The semantic web. Scientific American (2001) 361

[7] Shearin, S., Maes, P.: Representation and ownership of electronic profiles. In: CHI 2000 Workshop Proceedings: Designing Interactive Systems for 1-to-1 E-commerce, The Hague, Netherlands (2000) 362

[8] Schroeder, M.: Using singular value decomposition to visualise relations within multi-agent systems. In: Proceedings of the third Conference on Autonomous Agents, Seattle, USA, ACM Press (1999) 362, 364

[9] Schroeder, M., Noy, P.: Multi-agent visualization based on multivariate data. In: Proceedings of Autonomous Agents2001, Montreal, Canada, ACM press (2001) 362, 364

[10] Noy, P., Schroeder, M.: Defining like-minded agents with the aid of visualization. In: Proc. of First International Joint Conference on Autonomous Agents and Multiagent Systems, Bologna, Italy, ACM press (2002) Poster 363

[11] Noy, P., Schroeder, M.: Defining like-minded agents with the aid of visualization. In: ECML/PKDD Workshop Proceedings, Helsinki, Finland, University of Helsinki, Department of Computer Science, Report B-2002-4 (2002) 363

[12] Faratin, P., Sierra, C., Jennings, N. R.: Using similarity criteria to make negotiation trade-offs. In: Proc. of 4th Int. Conf. on Multi-Agent Systems ICMAS-2000, Boston, USA, IEEE Computer Society (2000) 119–126 363

[13] Foner, L.: Yenta: a multi-agent, referral-based matchmaking system. In: The First International Conference on Autonomous Agents, Marina del Rey, California, ACM press (1997) 363, 364

[14] Somlo, G., Howe, A.: Incremental clustering for profile maintenance in information gathering web agents. In: Proceedings of Autonomous Agents2001, Montreal, Canada, ACM press (2001) 363

[15] Veit, D., Muller, J., Schneider, M., Fiehn, B.: Matchmaking for autonomous agents in electronic marketplaces. In: Proceedings of Autonomous Agents2001, Montreal, Canada, ACM press (2001) 363

[16] Ogston, E., Vassiliadis, S.: Matchmaking among minimal agents without a facilitator. In: Proceedings of Autonomous Agents 2001, Montreal, Canada, ACM press (2001) 363

[17] Weiss, G., ed.: Multiagent Systems. MIT Press (1999) 363

[18] Foner, L.: Clustering and information sharing in an ecology of cooperating agents. In: AAAI Spring Symposium '95 on Information Gathering in Distributed, Heterogeneous Environments, Palo Alto. (1995) 363

[19] Dubois, D., Prade, H., Esteva, F., Garcia, P., Godo, L.: A logical approach to interpolation based on similarity relations. International Journal of Approximate Reasoning 17 (1997) 1–36 363

[20] Pazzani, M. J., Billsus, D.: Learning and revising user profiles: The identification of interesting web sites. Machine Learning 27 (1997) 313–331 364

[21] Horvitz, E., Breese, J., Heckerman, D., Hovel, D., Rommelse, K.: The Lumiere project: Bayesian user modeling for inferring the goals and needs of software users. In: Proceedings of the Fourteenth Conference on Uncertainty in Artificial Intelligence, Madison, WI, Morgan Kaufman (1998) 256–265 364

[22] Card, S. K., Mackinlay, J. D., Shneiderman, B.: Readings in Information Visualization: Using Vision To Think. Morgan Kaufmann (1999) 364

[23] di Battista, G., Eades, P., Tamassia, R., G.Tollis, I.: Graph Drawing: Algorithms for the Visualization of Graphs. Prentice Hall (1999) 364

[24] Kohonen, T.: Self-organising maps. 2nd edition edn. Springer-Verlag (1997) 364, 366

[25] Foner, L.: Yenta (2000) http://foner.www.media.mit.edu/people/foner/yenta-brief.html 365

[26] Hecht-Nelson, R.: Context vectors: General purpose approximate meaning repre-
      sentations self-organized from raw data. In Zurada, J. M., Marks, R. J., Robinson,
      C. J., eds.: Computational Intelligence: Imitating Life. IEEE Press, Piscataway,
      New York (1994) 43–56   365
[27] Gordon, A. D.: Classification. 2nd edn. Chapman and Hall / CRC (1999)   365,
      370
[28] Webb, A.: Statistical Pattern Recognition. Arnold, London (1999)   365
[29] WEBSOM: Self-Organizing Maps for Internet Exploration. (1999)
      http://websom.hut.fi/websom/   366
[30] de Bruijn, O., Stathis, K.: Socio-cognitive grids: The Net as a universal human
      resource. In: Proceedings of Tales of the Disappearing Computer. (2003) To appear
      373
[31] Noy, P., Schroeder, M.: Approximate profile utilization for finding like minds and
      personalization in socio-cognitive grids. In: Proceedings of 1st International Work-
      shop on Socio-Cognitive Grids: The Net as a Universal Human Resource. (2003) In
      conjunction with Tales of the Disappearing Computer 1-4 June, Santorini, Greece
      373

A Computational Framework for Social Agents in Agent Mediated E-commerce

Brendan Neville and Jeremy Pitt

Imperial College London
Electrical and Electronic Engineering Department, SW7 2BT London, UK
{brendan.neville,j.pitt}@imperial.ac.uk

Abstract. Agents that behave maliciously or incompetently are a potential hazard in open distributed e-commerce applications. However human societies have evolved signals and mechanisms based on social interaction to defend against such behaviour. In this paper we present a computational socio-cognitive framework which formalises social theories of trust, reputation, recommendation and learning from direct experience which enables agents to cope with malicious or incompetent actions. The framework integrates these socio-cognitive elements with an agent's economic reasoning resulting in an agent whose behaviour in commercial transactions is influenced by its social interactions, whilst being motivated and constrained by economic considerations. The framework thus provides a comprehensive solution to a number of issues ranging from the evolution of a trust belief from individual experiences and recommendations to the use of those beliefs in market place level decisions. The framework is presented in the context of an artificial market place scenario which is part of a simulation environment currently under development. This is planned for use in evaluation of the framework, and hence can inform design of local decision making algorithms and mechanisms to enforce of social order in agent mediated e-commerce.

1 Introduction

Malicious or incompetent agents are a potential hazard to open distributed e-commerce systems which have some features of delegation, autonomy and commercial transaction. Object-oriented software engineering methods based on increased security, testing and standards only offer a partial solution because of the unmoderated, dynamic and unpredictable nature of such a system. If however, we design the system as a society we can use social theories such as trust, reputation, recommendation and learning from direct experience to increase the system's protection from such undesirable behaviour. For example Conte [6] argues that reputation plays a crucial role in decentralised mechanisms for the enforcement of social order. In this paper we advance this argument by developing a computational socio-cognitive framework where the actions of agents in market-level interactions are influenced by their relationships on a social level. Therefore the agents' social interaction acts as a means to provide accountability

A. Omicini, P. Petta, and J. Pitt (Eds.): ESAW 2003, LNAI 3071, pp. 376–391, 2004.
© Springer-Verlag Berlin Heidelberg 2004

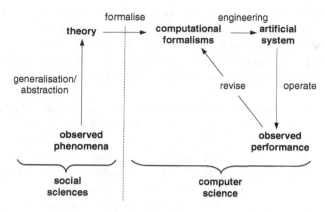

Fig. 1. Adapted Synthetic Method [11]

to market level actions and thus discourages malicious behaviour and isolates incompetent agents. We argue the framework would also increase consumer information regarding potential sellers and therefore the efficiency of the market.

Integrating this framework with an agent's economic rationale, results in an agent whose behaviour in commercial transactions is influenced by its social interactions, whilst being constrained by economic considerations. By simulating a system composed of such agents and observing the outcome, we aim to tailor the formalisms to achieve the desired performance and hence have an agent design that is applicable both socially and economically for a distributed agent mediated market. This process is illustrated by the *Adapted Synthetic Method* shown in Fig. 1 and is explained in more detail in [11]. It is our intent to evaluate the performance of the applied models based on the efficiency, fairness and dynamics of the resulting e-commerce communities. By giving particular attention to the suitability of the economic models employed, we hope to ensure that the results of our future simulation work will accurately portray the behaviour of an actual distributed multi-agent system (DMAS) market.

The distinctive features of our computational framework are:

- Both economic and social factors are utilised in the agents decision to trust.
- The framework represents recommendation as a generic task, as a result evaluating trust in recommenders and recommending recommenders requires no special formalisms or protocols.
- Our functions for determining the certainty measure associated with a belief are based on the age, source and quantity of information used to form the belief.
- The formation of experiences though the agent's actions in the commercial arena, provides positive feedback to the socio-cognitive elements of the framework.
- The framework's numerical formalisms are amenable to immediate computational implementation.

Therefore our framework provides a comprehensive solution to issues ranging from the evolution of trust beliefs from individual experiences and recommendations to the use of those beliefs in market place level decisions. Which is compatible with our aim of creating an artificial system to test what formalisms and parameters will provide desirable system performance in diverse real world applications.

In this paper we present the work from the first two stages of Fig. 1, namely our computational formalisms of social theories and the specification of an artificial retail market scenario. The paper is organised as follows. In Section 2, we present a brief specification of our market scenario. In Section 3, we describe an economic model for producer/seller agents. In Section 4, we detail the socio-cognitive framework and the economic rationale of the consumer agents. Finally Section 5 concludes with a summary of the paper, discusses related work and addresses our future research direction.

2   Retail Market Scenario

To address issues pertaining to agent e-commerce using simulation methods, we first need to specify a suitable market based scenario. There are many possible types of market that could be used, however we have chosen to focus on software agent mediated e-commerce within a manufacturing retail market place [20]. In these markets agents buy and sell information goods or services such as multimedia products, content hosting or information retrieval. This decision follows the precedent of online retail outlets such as Amazon[1] and distributed on-line market places like e-bay[2]. The market model comprises two groups of agents, one group represents the producers of a service or product the other its consumers. Consumers having selected the product or service they require then communicate their order to the producer, on receipt of payment the producers supply the product to the consumer.

Effectively the role of the producer agents in our proposed simulation environment will be to the test the ability of the consumer agents' socio-cognitive framework to protect against malicious or incompetent behaviour. Hence the producer agents will be implemented with both an economic model and a character type, some of these characters will aim to defraud the consumer agents. Given that the market mechanism proposed, inherently protects the producer agents from risk they are not simulated as socio-cognitive. We intend to address this simplifying assumption in future work, as the producers could benefit greatly from knowing their own reputation and those of their competitors. The consumer agent model presented is both socio-cognitive and economic, socio-cognitive in the sense that it forms a social network of peers with which it communicates its opinions as well as receiving and reasoning about the opinions of others. Its behaviour is economic in that consumer agents aim to maximise their owner's utility.

---

[1] www.amazon.com

[2] www.ebay.com

3   The Producer Agent

In this section we define both our economic model of a producer and the determinants of the producer agent's behaviour. A producer agent's goal is the maximisation of their owner's profit. We define profit as the difference between the business agents' revenue and the total cost of producing its product, $Profit = TotalRevenue - TotalCost$. It is thus necessary that the agents have a model of their total costs.

The total cost (TC) of producing a good is the sum of the total variable cost (TVC) and total fixed cost (TFC) of production. Dynamic behaviour of the total variable cost is the result of increasing returns to scale as the quantity produced increases, followed by diminishing returns to scale. The agents' cost function is best represented as a cubic polynomial, the coefficients of which are experimental parameters. A possible producer cost function for use in the simulation is shown in Fig. 2.

Total revenue (TR) is the product of the quantity of goods demanded and at what price, this said the quantity of good demanded is itself dependent on the price of the product. In our simulation environment the producer agents are responsible for setting the price at which they sell their wares for that time period. The consumers then decide whether or not to purchase the product at that price and how much to order. Producers are expected to supply the quantity demanded by the consumer. Kephart et al use this *dynamic posted pricing* mechanism in [12]. For the producer to maximise its profit they must optimally set the price of their goods and services. This method represents only one possible pricing mechanism, examples of others would include the many different types of auction. Auctions require the opposite set of decisions, as the

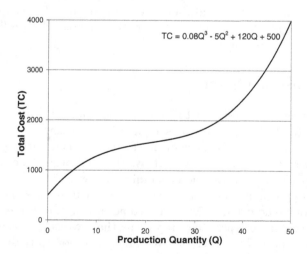

Fig. 2. Example producer cost curve

producer decides the quantity of product and the consumers set the price they are willing to pay.

To set their price the agents employ the derivative-follower algorithm from Greenwald and Kephart [9]. In each time period the derivative follower increments its price. It does this until its profit in that time period drops below the profit in the previous round it then reverses the direction of its price increments. The effect of this is to ascend the gradient to a local maxima in the profit. In addition the agent needs to decide upon an initial price at which to start its search for the maximum. In the case where there is already a market for competing products the agent aims to undercut the competition in its first time period. However when there are no competing producers we assume that the owner of the producer agent is capable of providing a suitable first price.

So far we have described the characteristics of a totally reliable, honest and cooperative producer agent acting within a error free environment. Whats missing is the malice or incompetence of some agents and the unreliability inherent in multi-agent system (MAS) environments and real-world applications. To model this environment, each producer has an associated competence level and character type. The competence variable is defined as the probability the producer agent will succeed in its task given that it attempts to do so. If the agent tries to supply the consumer but fails due to incompetence then it still incurs the cost of that action. Its character type determines if the agent attempts to supply the consumer. We have decided to model the following producer character types:

- *The Altruist*: always attempts to supply goods or services even if that action will not maximise its profit.
- *The Profiteer*: will only attempt to supply the good if the cost of suppling the product is less than or equal to the price gained for it.
- *The Skimmer*: does not attempt a certain percentage of orders, this is an attempt to mask theft beneath an acceptable degree of incompetence.
- *The Skimming-Profiteer*: the characteristics of both the profiteer and the skimmer rolled into one agent.

4   The Consumer Agent

The consumer agent is designed to be an integration of economic rationality and sociality. In this section we present a brief overview of these social and economic components and the mechanisms for fusing their outputs. Throughout this section we refer to Fig. 3, which portrays the relationships between the main elements of the socio-cognitive and economic framework.

Given the opportunity to trust a peer, the agent uses its economic model to calculate the outcome utilities. These outcome utilities are the economic influence on the decision to trust, they represent the payoffs of accepting the risk of relying on the peer. The other variable in the decision to trust is the agent's trust belief, this being the agent's subjective evaluation of the probability of a successful outcome of trusting the peer. The agent's trust belief, is computed from the combination of the agent's belief about its direct experiences and the

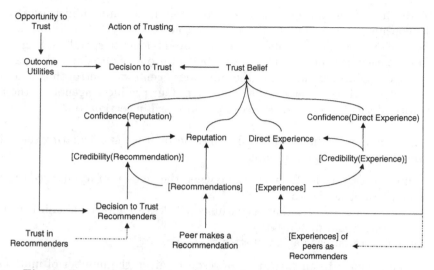

Fig. 3. Economic and Socio-cognitive elements of the Consumer Agent

reputation of the potential trustee. The relative influence of these beliefs on the trust belief is determined by the agent's confidence in their respective accuracies. Direct experience represents a distillation of its set of prior first hand interactions with the trustee into one belief. Likewise the agent's opinion of the reputation of the potential trustee is informed by the recommendations of its peers. The credibility assigned to an experience or recommendation and hence its weight of influence during the distillation process, is a function of the currency of the belief and it is also dependent upon the agents decision to trust the source of the belief. This opportunity to trust a peer as a source of recommendations is handled in the same manner as defined here for the generic case. The agent will look to its experiences of the peer as a recommender and at what its peers recommend about them as recommenders. We will assume that the agent can trust itself not to lie about or distort it's own experiences.

In the cases where the resultant trust belief is enough to decide to trust the potential trustee, and given there are no better opportunities available, the agent will act upon its decision. The resultant experience of the trustee is added to the agents set of prior experiences. Experiences are also formed about those agents that have made recommendations referring to the trustee and subsequently the agents that recommended them and so on.

4.1 Consumer Economic Rationale

Our economic model of the consumer agent focuses on estimating the utility gained by the consumer from consuming the goods and services it purchased. In addition the consumer agent estimates the utility lost in the event that a producer fails to supply those products to the consumer. These utility measures are employed in the integration of socio-cognitive and economic influences as part of the consumer agent's decision to trust a producer.

Each of our consumer agents have a designated budget to spend on the generic resource in each time period. The agent's budget is one of our simulation parameters. By changing the budgets of the consumer agents we control the monetary value of the markets demand for the resource. Our producer agents set the per unit price of their goods and services (as addressed in section 3).

The key factors which need to be taken into account when calculating the value of a purchase to the consumer are:

- A unit of resource is of highest value when the amount of resource consumed is equal to or near zero.
- The more of a resource that is consumed the less an additional unit is valued (diminishing marginal utility).
- More of a resource is always better than less.

The value assigned to an extra unit of resource given the number of units currently consumed (in this time period) is given by the derivative (1). This addresses the key factors outlined above, the constants in the derivative are used to tailor the valuations to a specific consumer's profile. The constant ξ is the value of an extra unit resource when the quantity already consumed is zero and γ determines the rate at which the value of an extra unit decreases as the amount consumed increases. Fig 4 shows formula (1) for $\xi = 500$ with diminishing utility at a rate of $\gamma = 0.1, 0.2$ and 0.3. Given the price per unit resource, the consumer can maximise its utility by consuming $S1$ units where $S = S1$ solves the marginal utility function (1) equal to the price per unit. If it consumes more than $S1$ the utility gained by consuming the additional units will be less than what it has paid for them where as consuming less than $S1$ units would be sub-optimal. Sometimes the consumer will be unable to maximise its utility as it cannot afford $S1$ units ($S1 > Budget/Price$), in which case it will do best to purchase as much as it can afford ($S1 = Budget/Price$). To calculate the utility of a successful purchase we integrate (1) from zero to the number of units in the proposed purchase (consumption $S1$), we then subtract the cost of the purchase giving us (2). In the case of an unsuccessful outcome the achieved consumption $S1$ is zero and so (2) reduces to (3), the utility lost is the money paid. The significance of these results and especially how they inform the socio cognitive model are explained in the following section.

$$\frac{dU(\textbf{Success})}{dS} = \frac{\xi}{e^{\gamma S}} \tag{1}$$

$$\begin{aligned} U(\textbf{Success}) &= \int_0^{S1} \frac{\xi}{e^{\gamma S}} dS - (Price \times S1) \\ &= \frac{\xi}{-\gamma} \left(e^{-\gamma S1} - 1 \right) - (Price \times S1) \end{aligned} \tag{2}$$

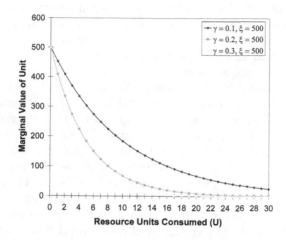

Fig. 4. $\frac{\mathrm{dU}}{\mathrm{dS}} = \frac{\xi}{e^{\gamma S}}$ for $\xi = 500$, and $\gamma = 0.1, 0.2$ and 0.3

$$\mathbf{U}(\mathbf{Failure}) = -(Price \times S1) \tag{3}$$

4.2 Consumer Socio-Cognitive Model

Our socio-cognitive modeling is based on social theories of trust, reputation, recommendation and learning from direct experience. Specifically we follow Castelfranchi [3, 5] by defining trust not only as a truster's evaluation of a trustee (its trust belief), but also as the decision to and the action of trusting. This section outlines our conceptualisation of an agent's trust belief and a mechanism by which this belief and the agent's utility evaluations influence its decision to trust. We go on to introduce our method for subjectively evaluating the trustworthiness of a peer from its direct experiences and peer testimony.

Our computational representation of an agent's trust belief is based on the formal model of Castelfranchi and Falcone [4, 7]. The essential conceptualisation is as follows: the degree to which Agent A trusts Agent B about task τ in (state of the world) Ω is a subjective probability $\mathbf{DoT}_{A,B,\tau,\Omega}$. This is the basis of agent A's decision to rely upon B for τ. Our method incorporates this stance, and defines trust as the resultant belief of one agent about another, born out of direct experiences of that other party and/or from the testimonies of peers (i.e. reputation). Although the formal model outlined above identifies the trustworthiness of an agent and an agent's beliefs as being dependent upon the state of the world, we omit the Ω parameter in subsequent descriptions for reasons of simplicity. It should also be noted that the socio-cognitive framework is generic and can be widely applied to many interpretations of the task τ. In the case of our e-commerce scenario this task is considered to be the provision of a service or information good. In the specific case of peer recommendations $\tau = srec$

indicates that the task τ is for the peer to act as a reliable "source of recommendations". For purposes of readability throughout the rest of the paper we assign the following agent identities and roles. Agent A is our consumer agent, agent B is a peer consumer and agent C is a producer agent.

In defining the mental state of trust Gambetta [8] refers to the decision to trust, as an evaluation 'that the probability that he will perform an action that is beneficial or at least not detrimental to us is high enough for us to consider engaging in some form of cooperation with him.'. He goes on to note that this assessment is based on both the degree of trust and the perceived risk. Indicating that as the risk associated with an interaction increases, the degree of trust needed to trust (decide to rely upon) also increases. We have implemented a decision to trust function (4) which is guided by this theory. The function takes the form of predicting the expected utility of the action of trusting. With bi-polar outcomes of trustee success or failure, the calculation is straight forward. The agent estimates the utility of the successful scenario ($\mathbf{U}(\mathbf{Success})_{A,C,\tau}$) where its trading peer Agent C cooperates and succeeds at task τ and conversely its losses ($\mathbf{U}(\mathbf{Failure})_{A,C,\tau}$) in the event its trading partner fails. The trust belief ($\mathbf{DoT}_{A,C,\tau}$) of the agent is the probability of the successful scenario occurring and its distrust ($1 - \mathbf{DoT}_{A,C,\tau}$) the probability of failure. Knowing the payoffs of each outcome in advance and having an estimate of their probabilities of occurrence, the agent can calculate the expected utility of trusting its peer. If the expected utility is positive then the agent estimates that it can benefit from trusting its peer and so should make the decision to trust. The expected outcome method captures the intuition that as the cost of failure increases the degree of trust needed to decide to trust increases and vice versa. Markets may provide a choice of a number of trading partners, in this case the agent takes the action of trusting the partner with the highest positive expected utility.

$$\mathbf{Expected\ Utility} =$$
$$\mathbf{DoT}_{A,C,\tau} \times \mathbf{U}\,(\mathbf{Success})_{A,C,\tau} + (1 - \mathbf{DoT}_{A,C,\tau}) \times \mathbf{U}\,(\mathbf{Failure})_{A,C,\tau} \tag{4}$$

The agent having delegated a task τ to Agent C, evaluates the outcome of trusting Agent C about τ at time t. This outcome evaluation ($\mathbf{Experience}_{C,\tau,t}$) is heavily application dependent, for instance when forming an experience of a peer as a recommender the evaluation takes the form of a continuous variable ($\mathbf{Experience}_{C,\tau,t}$ valued between -1 and 1) which represents a degree of accuracy or similarity measure. In other cases such as contractual scenarios the outcome can be characterised by a discrete bipolar evaluation i.e. Success or Failure to meet the agreed to contractual obligations ($\mathbf{Experience}_{C,\tau,t} = $ -1 or 1).

Recommendations are the testimonies by which the agents share their experiences with their peers. They are integral in informing the reputation of agents and therefore in applying pressure for agents to act honestly and ethically. A recommendation by agent B regarding its experience of an agent C about a task τ which is received at time t is represented by $\mathbf{Recommendation}_{B,C,\tau,t}$. Only the most current recommendation from each peer is maintained by the agent, e.g. $\mathbf{Recommendation}_{B,C,\tau,t_2}$ replaces $\mathbf{Recommendation}_{B,C,\tau,t_1}$ for $t_2 > t_1$.

Recommendations take the form of a continuous variable in the range [0-1]. It should also be noted that chained recommendations are not implicitly catered for by this representation. Chained recommendations occur where agent B informs agent A that agent D recommends agent C to do a task τ. Instead the third party (agent B) can first introduce the recommendation's source (agent D) and secondly agent B can recommend agent D as a source of recommendations. Now agent A can query agent D regarding agent C and using agent B's recommendation about agent D decide whether to trust agent D's recommendation.

The credibility attached to a belief is defined as its quality and power to elicit belief, we view this credibility as being a function of the agents trust for the beliefs source and how long ago the assertion was made (its currency). It must be proportional to the agents trust in the source of the belief (which may be itself or a peer) and inversely proportional to the age of the belief Δt. Functions (9) and (10) are examples of suitable functions for deriving the credibility of **Recommendation**$_{B,C,\tau,t}$ and **Experience**$_{C,\tau,t}$ respectively.

The first term of each function determines the rate by which a belief is discredited with age, $e^{-\alpha \Delta t} = 1$, for $\Delta t = 0$ i.e. the belief is current and its credibility is judged purely by the agents trust in its source. As $\Delta t \Rightarrow \infty$ the term is asymptotic to the x-axis. The constant α governs the rate of decay of credibility with age. The trust belief, the second term in functions (9) and (10) is the degree of trust Agent A has in Agent B as a "source of recommendations". For function (10) we assume that the agent implicitly trusts itself as a source of outcome evaluations (source of experiences abbreviated to sexp) and so **DoT**$_{A,A,sexp} = 1$ [3]. Fig. 5 plots the credibility assignment of a belief against the age of that belief, for different values of α and assuming **DoT**$_{A,B,sbeliefs} = 1$.

Earlier we argued that the agent must decide to trust a peer given both its trust belief in that peer and the perceived risk of trusting them. This is also the case when deciding to trust a peer as a source of beliefs. We argue that the risk of trusting a peer's recommendation is a function of the risk of trusting the recommendations target about the task τ to which the recommendation refers. Rearranging function (4) gives us a formula for **ReqDoT**$_{A,C,\tau}$ (function (5)) this represents the minimum required trust belief needed for Agent A to decide to trust Agent C about τ given the outcome evaluations. If Agent B's **Recommendation**$_{B,C,\tau,t}$ is greater than or equal to **ReqDoT**$_{A,C,\tau}$ then Agent B is effectively recommending that Agent C be trusted about τ. In this case the outcome of trusting Agent B's recommendation is to trust Agent C about τ, therefore the outcome evaluations (and hence the required degree of trust) of trusting Agent B as a source of recommendations is equal to those for trusting Agent C about τ. Conversely, if Agent B's **Recommendation**$_{B,C,\tau,t}$ is less than **ReqDoT**$_{A,C,\tau}$ then its recommendation is to not trust Agent C about τ. In this case the outcome of trusting Agent B's recommendation is to decide not to trust Agent C about τ, if trusting Agent B's recommendation is a success

---

[3] This is not to say that for the general case **DoT**$_{A,A,\tau} = 1$ or that **DoT**$_{A,A,\tau} \geq$ **DoT**$_{A,B,\tau}$ in fact a number of hypothetical scenarios can be envisioned where **DoT**$_{A,A,\tau} <$ **DoT**$_{A,B,\tau} \leq 1$.

then Agent A has saved the cost $\mathbf{U}(\mathbf{Failure})_{A,C,\tau}$ by Agent C, and if Agent B was wrong then Agent A has lost the successful outcome $\mathbf{U}(\mathbf{Success})_{A,C,\tau}$ of trusting Agent C about τ. These two cases are summarised by the equations (6) and (7) which provide outcome utilities for trusting Agent B as a recommender these are used by equation (8) to calculate the minimum required trust belief needed to decide to trust Agent B's recommendation about Agent C. There exists a set of equations of the same structure as (6), (7) and (8) to calculate $\mathbf{ReqDoT}_{A,A,sexp}$.

For both equation (9) and (10) we assign a condition that if $\mathbf{DoT}_{A,B,sbeliefs} < \mathbf{ReqDoT}_{A,B,sbeliefs}$ then the credibility of the evidence and correspondingly its influence on the decision to trust Agent C about τ is set to zero. These conditions act as the agents decision to trust a peer or itself as a source of beliefs.

$$\mathbf{ReqDoT}_{A,C,\tau} = \frac{\mathbf{U}\,(\mathbf{Failure})_{A,C,\tau}}{\mathbf{U}\,(\mathbf{Failure})_{A,C,\tau} - \mathbf{U}\,(\mathbf{Success})_{A,C,\tau}} \tag{5}$$

$$\mathbf{U}\,(\mathbf{Success})_{A,B,srec} =$$
$$\begin{cases} \mathbf{U}\,(\mathbf{Success})_{A,C,\tau}, & \text{if } \mathbf{Recommendation}_{B,C,\tau,t} \geq \mathbf{ReqDoT}_{A,C,\tau} \\ -\mathbf{U}\,(\mathbf{Failure})_{A,C,\tau}, & \text{if } \mathbf{Recommendation}_{B,C,\tau,t} < \mathbf{ReqDoT}_{A,C,\tau} \end{cases}$$
$$\tag{6}$$

$$\mathbf{U}\,(\mathbf{Failure})_{A,B,srec} =$$
$$\begin{cases} \mathbf{U}\,(\mathbf{Failure})_{A,C,\tau}, & \text{if } \mathbf{Recommendation}_{B,C,\tau,t} \geq \mathbf{ReqDoT}_{A,C,\tau} \\ -\mathbf{U}\,(\mathbf{Success})_{A,C,\tau}, & \text{if } \mathbf{Recommendation}_{B,C,\tau,t} < \mathbf{ReqDoT}_{A,C,\tau} \end{cases}$$
$$\tag{7}$$

$$\mathbf{ReqDoT}_{A,B,srec} = \frac{\mathbf{U}\,(\mathbf{Failure})_{A,B,srec}}{\mathbf{U}\,(\mathbf{Failure})_{A,B,srec} - \mathbf{U}\,(\mathbf{Success})_{A,B,srec}} \tag{8}$$

$$\mathbf{Credibility}(\mathbf{Recommendation}_{B,C,\tau,t}) =$$
$$\begin{cases} e^{-\alpha\Delta t} \times \mathbf{DoT}_{A,B,srec}, & \text{if } \mathbf{DoT}_{A,B,srec} \geq \mathbf{ReqDoT}_{A,B,srec} \\ 0, & \text{if } \mathbf{DoT}_{A,B,srec} < \mathbf{ReqDoT}_{A,B,srec} \end{cases} \tag{9}$$

$$\mathbf{Credibility}(\mathbf{Experience}_{C,\tau,t}) =$$
$$\begin{cases} e^{-\alpha\Delta t} \times \mathbf{DoT}_{A,A,sexp}, & \text{if } \mathbf{DoT}_{A,A,sexp} \geq \mathbf{ReqDoT}_{A,A,sexp} \\ 0, & \text{if } \mathbf{DoT}_{A,A,sexp} < \mathbf{ReqDoT}_{A,A,sexp} \end{cases} \tag{10}$$

We define agent A's direct experience of agent C about task τ ($\mathbf{Exp}_{C,\tau}$), as the belief agent A has about the trustworthiness of agent C based purely on its first-hand interactions of agent C. By this we refer to the subset of the agent's experiences consisting specifically of the agent's experiences of agent C about τ. Experimentally, we impose a maximum size on the subset, when the subset reaches its maximum the addition of further experiences results in the oldest being deleted. Function (11) calculates the direct experience belief by summing

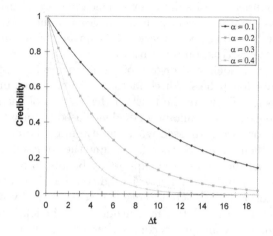

Fig. 5. Belief Credibility vs $\mathbf{\Delta t}$, for $\mathbf{DoT}_{A,B,sbeliefs} = 1$ and $\alpha = 0.1, 0.2, 0.3$ and 0.4

the agents most recent experiences each of which weighted by their assigned credibilities, $E_{C,\tau}$ denotes the set of times at which the agent had experiences of agent C about τ, the constants in the formula bound the result to within [0-1].

$$\mathbf{Exp}_{C,\tau} = \frac{0.5 \times \sum_{t \in E_{C,\tau}} \mathbf{Experience}_{C,\tau,t} \times \mathbf{Credibility}(\mathbf{Experience}_{C,\tau,t})}{\sum_{t \in E_{C,\tau}} \mathbf{Credibility}(\mathbf{Experience}_{C,\tau,t})} + 0.5 \tag{11}$$

In our agent system, reputation is defined as the collectively informed opinion held by an agent about the performance of a peer agent within a specific context. Agents form a belief about an agent's reputation from the recommendations of their peers. However, the received testimonies may be affected by existing relationships and attitudes. Thus, reputation is also a subjective concept which we define as a belief held/derived by one agent. Equation (12) formulates subjectively, from the perspective of agent A the reputation $\mathbf{Rep}_{C,\tau}$ of an agent C about a task τ. The reputation is the weighted sum of the recommendations of its peers, weighted by the credibility measure assigned to each of those recommendations (equation (9)). The set $R_{C,\tau}$ contains the identifiers of agents b whom made recommendations of C about τ.

$$\mathbf{Rep}_{C,\tau} = \frac{\sum_{b \in R_{C,\tau}} \mathbf{Recommendation}_{b,C,\tau,t} \times \mathbf{Credibility}(\mathbf{Recommendation}_{b,C,\tau,t})}{\sum_{b \in R_{C,\tau}} \mathbf{Credibility}(\mathbf{Recommendation}_{b,C,\tau,t})} \tag{12}$$

Earlier we defined the trust belief $\mathbf{DoT}_{A,C,\tau}$ as being a subjective evaluation based on the agent's experiences and reputation. In this section we describe the final stage in determining the agent's degree of trust by addressing the combination of the agent's direct experience and reputation beliefs. Intuitively an agent with strong confidence in its direct experience belief and little confidence in the accuracy of its reputation beliefs should rationally choose to calculate its trust belief primarily from its direct experiences. Conversely an agent with little experience should base its trust on reputation.

To achieve this we associate a degree of confidence with both our direct experience and reputation beliefs. Three factors are important in determining this confidence measure. They are the trust in the sources of the evidence, the currency of the evidence and the amount of evidence used to form the belief. The first two of these factors are addressed when determining the credibility of the individual evidences themselves. We therefore define the confidence in the beliefs $\mathbf{Exp}_{C,\tau}$ and $\mathbf{Rep}_{C,\tau}$ as the sum of the supporting beliefs respective credibility measures (equations (13) and (14)). The weighted combination of the two beliefs takes the form of function (15), where the result is scaled to between [0-1] by the denominator. We see that the relative magnitude of the beliefs influence on the trust belief is determined by an agent's confidence in their respective accuracies.

$$\mathbf{Confidence}(\mathbf{Exp}_{C,\tau}) = \sum_{t \in E_{C,\tau}} \mathbf{Credibility}(\mathbf{Experience}_{C,\tau,t}) \qquad (13)$$

$$\mathbf{Confidence}(\mathbf{Rep}_{C,\tau}) = \sum_{b \in R_{C,\tau}} \mathbf{Credibility}(\mathbf{Recommendation}_{i,C,\tau,t}) \qquad (14)$$

$$\mathbf{DoT}_{A,C,\tau} = \frac{\mathbf{Confidence}(\mathbf{Exp}_{C\tau}) \times \mathbf{Exp}_{C\tau} + \mathbf{Confidence}(\mathbf{Rep}_{C\tau}) \times \mathbf{Rep}_{C\tau}}{\mathbf{Confidence}(\mathbf{Exp}_{C\tau}) + \mathbf{Confidence}(\mathbf{Rep}_{C\tau})} \qquad (15)$$

5   Summary and Further Work

In this paper, we have presented a specification for an agent framework that we argue will act as a decentralised mechanism for enforcing honest and competent behaviour in a distributed agent mediated market place. This enforcement is integral to building global trust in DMAS market places and therefore in establishing them as profitable environments to carry out commercial transactions. The application of this framework is not limited to retail market places. Other scenarios for the use of socio-cognitive and economically rational agents can be found in the domains of digital rights management [16], on-line auctions(e.g. ebay), contractual agreements and virtual enterprises [15].

The key features of our agent model are based on the cross-fertilisation of two social sciences, namely sociology and economics. In the economic sense we have harmonised the agents goals with those of their potential owners e.g. the maximisation of profit or utility. Our consumer agents' economic model of utility is based on the theory of diminishing marginal utility. It also allows for the parameterisation of the consumer economic model to fit their individual owners utility evaluations and income. The key concepts in the specification of the producer agents' economic models relate to the cost function which describes their individual owners' cost structure. We have based this cost function on the actual concepts which govern total costs in real world producers, such as fixed costs, increasing and decreasing returns to scale. In reference to sociology we have generated a computational socio-cognitive framework which comprises formalisms of social theories of trust, reputation, experience, recommendation and credibility. We have shown how the agent derives its trust belief from both its own experiences and the recommendations of its peers. The agent's trust belief is the key output of the socio-cognitive framework and is combined with the agent's utility evaluations in its decision to trust. Thus both economic and social factors influence the agents' actions in the distributed market place.

5.1   Related Work

Marsh [14, 13] define trust as a computational concept for use in agent systems to facilitate decisions of a social nature, such as trading partner selection. Marsh's research like ours, is grounded heavily in the social sciences. Abdul-Rahman and Hailes [1] aims to simplify [13], for example by representing trust in discrete values. They also extend it in terms of its social interactions to include recommendation and reputation mechanisms. We are however not only interested with the formalisation of social theories but in the operation of the systems created with these social concepts in mind. Witkowski [19] simulates a trading environment of supplier and consumer agents, the agents selected partners to trade with on the basis of trust. This trust being based purely on the truster agents direct experiences, and was updated simply by a trust update function [10]. The iterated prisoners dilemma (IPD) and its many variants are used extensively in simulations of social phenomena not least by Axelrod [2]. Yao and Darwen [21] also uses an IPD, and in addition to this applies genetic algorithms to explore the effects of game length and reputation on the evolution of cooperative strategies. Sen et al [18, 17] shows how in a group of self-interested agents, reciprocal behaviour can promote cooperation and increase global performance.

5.2   Further Work

Our future goal is to show through simulation that social order in competitive multi-agent systems can be created and supported by the introduction of the socio-cognitive framework in support of the agent's economic reasoning. We aim to demonstrate that the framework benefits benevolent members of the agent-mediated market place and hence the human society in which they are embedded. In response to this goal we are currently engaged in developing an agent simulation environment, to provide tools facilitating the specification of agents, control of the specified market economic factors, data logging, results analysis, demonstration and visualisation. We will also develop a set of consumer agent characters to provide simulation of dishonest consumers whom for instance might spread inaccurate recommendations in an attempt to reduce demand for reliable producers services and hence drive down prices. Our simulation package will be used to provide experimental verification for the framework in a number of scenarios, by simulating heterogeneous groups of producer and consumer agents.

Acknowledgements

This work has been undertaken in the context of two EU-funded projects, the ALFEBIITE Project (IST-1999-10298) and the ICECREAM Project (IST-2000-28298). We have also benefited from Cristiano Castelfranchi and Rino Falcone's contributions on defining and representing social theories of trust.

References

[1] Alfarez Abdul-Rahman and Stephen Hailes. A distributed trust model (extended abstract), 1997. 389

[2] R. Axelrod. The evolution of cooperation, 1984. 389

[3] C. Castelfranchi. Modeling social action for agents. *Artificial Intelligence*, 103:157–182, 1998. 383

[4] C. Castelfranchi and R. Falcone. Social trust: A cognitive approach. In C. Castelfranchi and Y.-H. Tan, editors, *Trust and Deception in Virtual Societies*, page 5590. Kluwer Academic Press, 2000. 383

[5] C. Castelfranchi and Tan. Introduction. In *Deception, Fraud and Trust in Virtual Societies*. Kluwer Academic Press, 2000. 383

[6] R. Conte. A cognitive memetic analysis of reputation. Technical report, Alfebiite Deliverable, URL: http://alfebiite.ee.ic.ac.uk/docs/Deliverables/D5D6.zip., 2002. 376

[7] Rino Falcone, Munindar P. Singh, and Yao-Hua Tan, editors. *The socio-cognitive dynamics of trust: Does trust create trust?*, volume 2246 of *Lecture Notes in Computer Science*. Springer, 2001. 383

[8] Diego Gambetta. Can we trust trust? In Diego Gambetta, editor, *Trust: Making and Breaking Cooperative Relations*, chapter 13, pages 213–237. Basil Blackwell, New York, NY, 1988. 384

[9] Amy R. Greenwald and Jeffrey O. Kephart. Shopbots and pricebots. In *Agent Mediated Electronic Commerce (IJCAI Workshop)*, pages 1–23, 1999. 380

[10] C. M. Jonker and J. Treur. Formal analysis of models for the dynamics of trust based on experiences. In F. J. Garijo and M. Boman, editors, *Multi-Agent System Engineering, Proceedings of the 9th European Workshop on Modelling Autonomous Agents in a Multi-Agent World*, volume 1647 of *Lecture Notes in AI*, pages 221–232. Springer Verlag, 1999. 389

[11] L. Kamara, B. Neville, and J. Pitt. Simulating socio-cognitive agents. In J. Pitt, editor, *Open Agent Societies*. Wiley, 2003. 377

[12] Jeffrey O. Kephart, James E. Hanson, and Amy R. Greenwald. Dynamic pricing by software agents. *Computer Networks (Amsterdam, Netherlands: 1999)*, 32(6):731–752, 2000. 379

[13] S. Marsh. Formalising trust as a computational concept, 1994. 389

[14] Stephen Marsh. Trust in distributed artificial intelligence. In *Modelling Autonomous Agents in a Multi-Agent World*, pages 94–112, 1992. 389

[15] D. O'Leary, D. Kuokka, and P. Plant. Artificial intelligence and virtual organisations. *Communication of the ACM*, 40(1):52–59, 1997. 388

[16] Bill Rosenblatt, Bill Trippe, and Stephen Mooney. Digital rights management: Business and technology, 2001. 388

[17] S. Sen, A. Biswas, and S. Debnath. Believing others: Pros and cons, 2000. 389

[18] Sandip Sen. Reciprocity: A foundational principle for promoting cooperative behavior among self-interested agents. In Victor Lesser, editor, *Proceedings of the First International Conference on Multi–Agent Systems*. MIT Press, 1995. 389

[19] M. Witkowski, A. Artikis, and J. Pitt. Experiments in building experiential trust in a society of objective-trust based agents. In R. Falcone, M. Singh, and Y.-H. Tan, editors, *Trust in Cyber Societies*, LNAI 2246, pages 110–132. Springer, 2001. 389

[20] M. Witkowski, B.Neville, and J. Pitt. Agent mediated retailing in the connected local community. *Interacting with Computers*, 15(1):5–32, 2003. 378

[21] Yao and P. J. Darwen. How important is your reputation in a multi-agent environment. In *IEEE Conference on Systems, Man, and Cybernetics*. IEEE Press, 1999. 389

You've Got Mail From Your Agent:
A Location and Context Sensitive Agent System

Guoqiang Zhong[1], Satoshi Amamiya[1], Ken'ichi Takahashi[1],
Tadashige Iwao[2], Kazuya Kawashima[3], Takayuki Ishiguro[3],
Tatsuya Kainuma[3], and Makoto Amamiya[1]

[1] Kyushu University, Fukuoka, Japan
{zhong,roger,tkenichi,amamiya}@al.is.kyushu-u.ac.jp
[2] Fujitsu Laboratories, Tokyo, Japan
iwao@flab.fujitsu.co.jp
[3] Fujitsu Prime Software Technologies, Nagoya, Japan
{kawashima,guro,kainuma}@pst.fujitsu.com

Abstract. The best way to evaluate a new technology such as the agent-oriented programming paradigm is to test it in the real world. In this article, we illustrate how multiagent systems can be deployed to analyse, design and implement a location- and context-dependent information system in a shopping mall. Our goal in this application was to help people by making personalised information available where and when it is needed in a way that disturbs them as little as possible and protects their privacy as much as possible. By employing the VPC communication framework on the KODAMA agent platform, we were able to build a shopping-support system as a collection of interacting, autonomous, flexible agents, with support functions capable of dynamically adapting services to client location and preferences as well as environment changes. Here we will give a close view of the system, examine application scenarios and discuss the pros and cons that emerged from the results of a large-scale experiment.

1 Introduction

Advances in mobile telecommunications, wireless networking, processor speed, device miniaturisation and many other technologies have propelled our lives and work into an era of *ubiquitous computing* that Mark Weiser foresaw nearly a decade ago [1]. Following on — but not limited to — his vision, numerous research efforts are underway that aim to create *smart environments* from home to office[1] and from health [2] to entertainment [3].

Together with Fujitsu Kawasaki Laboratories and Fujitsu Prime Software Technologies (PST), we were interested in both the technical and commercial aspects of a shopping-support system. Our goal in creating one was to foster ad hoc interaction and deliver the latest, customisable information to individual

---

[1] Some examples include MIT's *House_n* project and *Oxygen* project, INRIA's *SmartOffice* project and Stanford's *Interactive Workspaces* project.

A. Omicini, P. Petta, and J. Pitt (Eds.): ESAW 2003, LNAI 3071, pp. 392–409, 2004.
© Springer-Verlag Berlin Heidelberg 2004

visitors in a convenient and 'smart' way, while taking privacy and shopping habits into consideration. This particular scenario is only one among many others [4] along the road towards environments rich in *Ambient Intelligence* (AmI) [5], environments which potentially comprise thousands of embedded and mobile devices (or software artefacts) interacting to support human-centered goals and activity [6]. A system like ours involves the convergence of several present-day computing trends, and its key characteristics are that it is: ubiquitous, location- and context-aware, interactive, scalable and dynamically configurable, human-centered, and secure [7].

Based on our previous work on the KODAMA[2] project [8], we took an agent-based approach, believing that agent-oriented approaches are well suited for coping with the inherent uncertainty, dynamism and complexity in modern applications such as ubiquitous systems. Although this paper will not argue why agent-oriented approaches are widely studied and adopted, there is a substantial literature on this topic. Recent contributions include Jennings [9, 10], Wooldridge [11] and Luck *el al.* [6].

With core concepts (the notions of agent, society and interaction) inherited from the basis of *multiagent systems* (MAS), the Kodama agent platform introduced a multi-layer model to build full-scale network-aware MAS in which application-level logic can be separated from agent-level logic, which in turn can be separated from network-level logic. The platform itself concentrates on generic network-level logic and agent-level logic, such as communication and agent society support, but leaves to application developers application-level logic, such as which agents should be in one group, which agent communication language (ACL) should be used, and so forth.

The VPC (Virtual Private Community) communication framework [12], which we have also used, defines a *push* and *pull* model for ad hoc interaction and cooperation between agents. In this framework, agent attributes are divided into those belonging to a *public profile* — which can be exposed, and those belonging to a *private profile* — which can not be exposed. Thus services are offered through interaction between agents by pushing the public profile to service agents and pulling available services back. These services are in turn evaluated locally according to the private profile.

By integrating the VPC communication framework into the KODAMA agent platform, we were able to build a shopping-support system as a collection of interactingagents, which deliver adapting services to individual visitors depending on their location and preference but without compromising their privacy. In the remainder of this article, our experiences in designing, implementing, deploying and experimenting with the system are presented: Section 2 describes the background. Section 3 examines implementation issues, system integration, and application scenarios. Section 4 discusses experiments and experimental results. We then outline, in Section 5, some future work that will be needed to refine the introduced approach, and in Section 6, offer some concluding remarks.

---

[2] Kyushu University Open & Distributed Autonomous Multiagent

2   Background

2.1   Related Work

Established in 1995 as a non-profit organisation, FIPA (Foundation for Intelligent Physical Agents) began its work on standards for agent systems. With the participation of many major companies, FIPA has been working on specifications that range from agent architecture for the support of agent-to-agent communication to communication languages and content languages for expressing those messages (FIPA ACL), and interaction protocols with a scope ranging from single messages to complete transactions [13]. By December 2002, 23 experimental specifications were promoted to the status of standards [14]. There are many different FIPA-compliant agent platforms. Agent Development Kit, FIPA-OS, Grasshopper, JACK Intelligent Agents, JADE, Java specification request for Agent Services, LEAP and ZEUS [15] are some examples.

To date, agents have found application in almost all areas of computing from control systems to *e-commerce* and the *Web*, and from human-computer interfaces to simulation and information systems. As the hardware environments for ubiquitous computing are becoming a reality, it has been argued that MAS are the right metaphor for managing the dynamism and complexity of communications in ubiquitous systems [16]. *MyCampus*, for example, is an ambitious project at Carnegie Mellon University that aims at leveraging the power of recent *Semantic Web* concepts in support of mobile, context-aware services. Users of MyCampus can pull individual copies of task-specific agents into their personal environments — PDAs in the experiment — in which access to personal preferences and contextual attributes are controlled. The power and scalability of the MyCampus project directly derives from a set of ontologies for describing contextual attributes, user preferences and web services, making it possible to easily accommodate new task-specific agents and new Web services [17].

2.2   KODAMA Agent Platform

The Kodama agent platform was not designed from scratch. Following on the previous work on MAS [18, 19, 20, 21], its emphasis was on agent methodologies for building industrial-strength, network-aware MAS, which — we hope — are not simply add-ons but a productive integration and extension of the existing network, distributed computing and agent technologies.

Proceeding from a study of MAS, we identified the elementary question of *what, when* and *how* to interact with *whom* as the key question of many challenging issues raised in agent interaction. We argued, in [22], that the higher-level problem of *what, when* and with *whom* to interact can be separated from the low-level problem of *how* to interact.[3] It soon turned out that the higher-level problem can be further divided into application-dependent and application-independent

---

[3] In the *FIPA abstract architecture specification*, in contrast, the agent directory facilitator (yellow pages), agent management system (white pages) and agent communication channel are all types of agent [23].

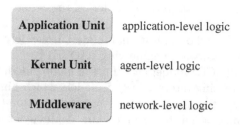

Fig. 1. The three-layer model of the KODAMA agent platform

problems [24]. By detaching data exchange activities (i.e. network-level logic) from agent programmes and detaching application context (i.e. application-level logic) from common agent context (i.e. agent-level logic), it is possible to build a generic agent platform, providing convenient abstraction and sufficient transparency for the modeling and building of network-aware MAS.

Such a principle of separation can be best summarised by a three-layer model, as illustrated in Figure 1. With this model, a *plug-and-play* standard and a *middleware* layer have been deployed. The plug-and-play mandates that an agent be made up of a *kernel* unit (KU), which encapsulates the common modules, and an *application* unit (AU), which encapsulates the application-dependent modules [22]. The middleware layer, on the other hand, seeks primarily to hide the underlying network's complexity by insulating agents from explicit protocol handling, network faults and parallelism [25, 26]. Once agent messages are passed from agents — who may reside anywhere and talk with anyone at anytime — to the middleware layer, they are delivered to their destination without further interaction with agents. The main purpose in having the kernel unit layer and middleware layer is to integrate a set of common services that forms a uniform development platform on which various applications can be built with inherent support for common network and agent functions.

2.3   Portal Agent Model

Multiagent systems are considered as an emerging programming paradigm, characterised by organisation structures and interaction that are more and more articulated and dynamic in complex distributed applications. This paradigm implies a shift from traditional computing — focused on algorithm and individual intelligence — to next-generation computing — focused on interaction and social intelligence [27].

With this perspective, it has been argued in [28] that multiagent systems can be described by three inter-related concepts: *role*, *interaction* and *organisation*. At the micro level, roles are the basic building blocks representing generic agent behaviors that can interact mutually. At the macro level, an organisation is composed of a set of role-play agents and their interactions. Agents, on the one hand, are specified as active communicative entities which play roles. The behavior of a multiagent system as a whole, on the other hand, is the result of the roles playing by agents.

Accordingly, role-based organisational models are widely adopted in the context of agent-oriented software engineering (AOSE) [29, 30], such as the *agent coordination context* (ACC) model [31] and the *holon*[4] model [33]. Among those models, there is increasing interest in the models which aim at supporting the concepts of agent-oriented decomposition and organisation [9] as first class citizens from analysis and design to development, deployment and runtime (which Andrea Omicini argued as *keeping the abstractions* alive [31]). Both the ACC model and the holon model are such examples.

Our organisational model, that is the *portal agent* model [22], is based on the *role-interaction-organisation* (RIO) methodology [28] mentioned above. To manage organisation complexity and dynamism, the portal agent model defines the following principle for partitioning agent organisations:

> *There is one and only one portal agent in one community which allows all agents in the community to be treated as one single normal agent — the portal agent itself — outside the community.*

As this principle stipulates, a portal agent has its role limited in a community, and the portal agent itself is managed by another high-level portal agent as a normal agent. A community here is defined as a group of agents, which achieve collectively some social tasks by exploiting their roles and interaction. In addition, this model employed the concepts of *agent hiding* and *agent message filtering*. If an agent wants to be hidden from outside, it can ask its portal agent to act as its proxy so that messages can be processed, sometimes filtered, through the portal agent. Outside a community, however, the only difference between a portal agent and an ordinary agent is that a portal agent can have child agents whereas an ordinary agent cannot. This observation, in fact, is consistent with another observation made in holonic organisations: an agent that appears as a single entity to the outside world may in fact be composed of several agents [33].

2.4   VPC Communication Framework

Developed at Fujitsu Laboratories, the VPC framework facilitates ad hoc interaction and cooperation between agents by pushing agent public profiles to service agents and pulling back *policy packages*, which are evaluated locally depending on agent private profiles [34]. As mentioned earlier, the public profile consists of those attributes that can be sent out whereas those of the private profile cannot. Policy packages are used to pack together services (which are described as roles), assignment rules of roles (which are described in a rule base), and service contents. The structure of policy packages is as follows:

---

[4] The term *holon* was originally introduced in 1967 by the Hungarian Philosopher Arthur Koestler [32] to refer to natural or artificial structures that are neither wholes nor parts in an absolute sense.

```
<policy package> ::= <rules> <roles> <contents>
<rules>          ::= <rule> | <rule> <rules>
<rule>           ::= <condition> <role names>
<role names>     ::= <role name> | <role name> <role names>
<condition>      ::= ''TRUE''
                   | ''and'' <condition> <condition>
                   | ''not'' <condition>
                   | ''eq'' <attribute>
                   | ''<'' <attribute>
<attribute>      ::= <variable name> <value>
<roles>          ::= <role> | <role> <roles>
<role>           ::= <role name> <programme name> <init description>
<contents>       ::= <content> | <content> <contents>
<content>        ::= <programme name> <programme path>
```

Public and private profiles are stored as pairs of variable and value, or as digital certificates with Public Key Infrastructure (PKI). They can only be accessed by a specific *profile manager*. Meanwhile, policy packages are evaluated by a specific *policy evaluator*. Once an agent gets a policy package, its policy evaluator deduces roles by evaluating rules in the policy package through the following:

```
1.  function Policy-Package-Evaluation
2.  input: a~policy package  p
3.    for each rule in  p
4.       check conditions through a~profile manager
5.       if TRUE
6.          load role programme with name and path
7.          initialise role programme
8.          start role
9.       endif
10.   endfor
11. end function Policy-Package-Evaluation
```

An agent may get no role if its internal state, represented by its public and private profiles, is not appropriate for any role.

In this way, the VPC framework enables agent services to be described and delivered as policy packages, manages public profiles and private profiles differently, and deduces appropriate services for agents according to specific service descriptions and attributes.

3   The Shopping-Support System

As a part of an academe-industry (Kyushu University, Fujitsu Kawasaki Laboratories and Fujitsu PST) joint research project we had an opportunity to make a location- and context-aware shopping-support system and perform a large-scale experiment in the Osu shopping mall in Nagoya, Japan. In this section, we first take a quick look at the location sensing system, and then discuss agent society, ad hoc agent interaction and the system integration. Finally, we outline two application scenarios.

Fig. 2. An RF beacon transmitter (left) and receiver (right)

3.1 Location Sensing

Advances in data acquisition and access technologies are enabling more and more location-sensing mechanisms, which vary significantly in their capabilities and infrastructure requirements [35]. The Global Positioning System (GPS) is the most widely known system today. However it does not work indoors and GPS receivers are not yet widespread. An alternative solution for limited range and usage is to use a wired infrastructure with base stations that define cells of wireless coverage around them.

For our use, we deployed an active RF beacon system with a resolution of 3 to 4 meters. This system comprises many key-holder-like RF beacon transmitters (the left side of Figure 2), which move freely and transmit identifying signals, as well as some fixed RF beacon receivers (the right side of Figure 2), which receive the transmitters' signals and send them to a specified server in the network. The position of a transmitter can be calculated from the position of the receivers (at least three) that get its ID signals. Among the RF beacon receivers, an ad hoc and secure wireless backbone network was built using Fujitsu's proprietary Snownet [36] technology.

3.2 Agent Society

A computational agent society was designed and implemented, in which both individual visitors and shops in the real world have agents corresponding to them in the computing world. Responding to a visitor's location, the user agent interacts with nearby shops' agents, retrieves live data from the shops based on a personal profile and if valuable information is found, sends notification email to the visitor. Consequently, we have implemented four kinds of agents and two kinds of agent communities (see Figure 3) as follows:

user agent. One user agent represents one person who visits the shopping mall. At first, it is initiated in the user agent community by a creator agent. Then it may move among different shopping-mall communities and retrieve valuable shop information on behalf of its owner.

shop agent. One shop agent represents one shop in the shopping mall. Unlike user agents, shop agents are initialised when the system is set up and cannot be created dynamically. Shop agents are not mobile.

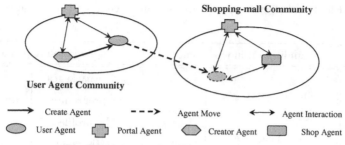

Fig. 3. An overview of the agent society

creator agent. A creator agent is used in the registration and de-registration of user agents. When a new person becomes involved with the system, the creator agent initiates a new user agent with the person's profile, which will be active in the agent society till the person leaves. The creator agent is not mobile.

portal agent. As mentioned earlier, one agent community has one portal agent, which is the local root of the community. By de-registering and registering with portal agents, user agents can move from one community to another community. Portal agents are not mobile.

user agent community. This community is the starting and ending place for all user agents. Also, it is the default community for user agents when they do not belong to any shopping-mall communities. The community consists of a portal agent, a creator agent and user agents, if any.

shopping-mall community. One shopping-mall community represents one shopping mall in the real world which needs to be treated separately in the application. Cooperation among different agents in different communities is carried out through portal agents.

It worth noting that we chose a relatively simple implementation for the agent society in this application. That is, only user agents are allowed to be dynamically created, deleted and move in the society. Although capable of being configured dynamically, portal agents, the creator agent and shop agents need to be initialised when the system is set up.

3.3   Ad Hoc Interaction

Reflecting the nature of their real-world counterparts, agents are social computational entities not only in the sense that they need to interact, but in the sense that they rely on others, and that each of them has its own role in an agent society. More importantly, agent roles are no longer hard-wired, but frequently change for two reasons. First, agents may join, move within or leave the agent society at any time, thus requiring updating of their roles. Second, changes in the state or interaction patterns of agents can result in changes in their behavior.

In accordance with the elementary question of *what, when* and *how* to interact with *whom*, Table 1 outlines, in the shopping-support system, the challenging

Table 1. Challenging issues of agent interaction and their solution

	application independent		application dependent	
what	agent messages (ACL) content language	kernel unit layer, portal agent	policy packages role programme public profiles advertisement	appli-cation unit layer, VPC, sensing, system configu-ration
when	transaction-protocols		location update	
whom	interaction patterns social relationship agent directory (yellow pages)		rules private profiles	
how	agent name resolution (white pages), agent message delivery, QoS, mobile computing support, and network faults, protocols, security			
	Kodama middleware layer			

issues in agent interaction as well as how they are solved by the VPC communication framework and the Kodama agent platform separately.

3.4   System Integration

The integration of the VPC framework and the Kodama platform was realised by implementing an application unit with a profile manager and a policy evaluator installed. In accordance with the plug-and-play standard of the Kodama platform, user agents, shop agents and portal agents are made from VPC-enabled application units and already-implemented kernel units. The creator agent does not need a VPC-enabled application unit because it does not participate in the VPC communication framework.

Agents alone are not sufficient for building the system. They need, for example, non-agent components through which they can perceive and then act on the outside real world. In a highly abstracted view, Figure 4 shows how agents and non-agent components fit together. The four subsystems behind agents are the (de)registration Web interface, location sensing, email, and advertising subsystems.

Making use of Java Server Pages (JSP), the (de)registration Web interface is a browser-friendly interface for creating, updating and removing specified data for

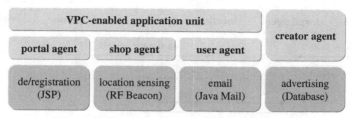

Fig. 4. The application component structure

the creator agent and shop agents. The creator agent uses one instance of this interface to get necessary data such as user ID and profile to create new user agents or delete inactive user agents. Meanwhile, shop agents use another instance to keep their advertising message database up-to-date. The location sensing subsystem keeps sending location information to user agents repeatedly so that they know their physical position and can decide whether or not they should move their logical position in the agent society to another community or get a list of shop agents. Furthermore, user agents rely on the email subsystem (which uses the Java Mail package internally) to send email to their owners. Developed by Fujitsu PST, the advertising subsystem is actually a proprietary database whose contents are managed by shop agents through the (de)registration Web interface, and which provides personalised advertising messages to user agents.

3.5   Application Scenarios

To understand how the whole system works, we look at two application scenarios in this subsection: a normal scenario of information notification and a special scenario of cooperation. As shown in Figure 5, a user agent retrieves valuable information on behalf of a visitor through a sequence of ad hoc interactions between agents as follows:

1. A shop agent joins a shopping-mall community by sending a notification message to the portal agent, which then sends an acknowledgment to the shop agent.
2. The location sensing system receives an RF beacon transmitter's identifying signals of a visitor, calculates and sends position information to a user agent.
3. Based on the position, the user agent joins the shopping-mall community by sending a notification message to the portal agent, which then sends an acknowledgment and an agent name list for nearby shops.
4. The user agent sends notification messages and its public profile to the agents on the list. Based on the received public profile, the shop agents send policy packages to the user agent.
5. The user agent evaluates the policy packages with its private profile locally. If any roles are found, the user agent will load and execute the role programme. If something interesting is found, it will send advertising email to the visitor.

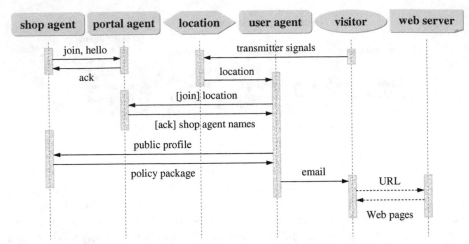

Fig. 5. Location- and context-aware information notification

The specific email delivered by user agents depends on the registered visitor profiles and the location of visitors and shops. Following the URLs embedded in the email, visitors can see detailed and customised information on the Web. For example, an electric product store might have two pages, a washing machine page for women and a shaver page for men. When a visitor is a 25-year-old man, he may see a message for an electric shaver filtered by the following rules in a VPC policy package.

```
<rules>
  <rule> <condition> <and>
    <condition type=''not <'' age=''20''/>
    <condition type=''eq'' gender=''MALE''/>
    </and> </condition>
    <role name=''shaver''/> </rule>
  <rule> <condition> <and>
    <condition type=''not <'' age=''20''/>
    <condition type=''eq'' gender=''FEMALE''/>
    </and> </condition>
    <role name=''washing machine''/> </rule>
</rules>
```

In this example, the age information can be protected by storing the 25-year-old attribute in the private profile but the twentysomething attribute in the public profile.

Even if very simply, we simulated actual cooperation between real shops by implementing virtual cooperation between their computational counterparts — shop agents. As shown in Figure 6, two shop agents in two shopping-mall communities can cooperate to provide integrated services through inter-community interactions as follows:

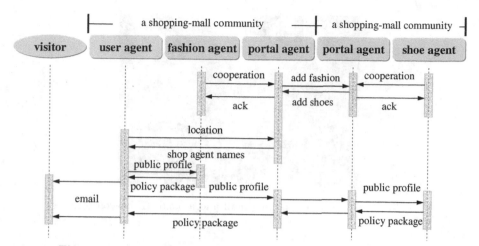

Fig. 6. Cooperation between two shop agents in two communities

1. A fashion shop agent and a shoe shop agent send cooperation notification to their portal agents, say portal agent a and portal agent b, respectively.
2. Portal agent a and portal agent b exchange a cooperation notification with each other, then add the shoe or fashion shop agent name.[5]
3. A user agent sends its position to portal agent a, and then receives an agent name list. The fashion shop agent is included because of its position, while the shoe shop agent is included because of the cooperation relationship established in previous steps.
4. Between the fashion shop agent and the user agent, Step 4 and Step 5 in the previous scenario are carried out.
5. Meanwhile, the user agent sends its public profile to the shoe shop agent, if and only if the user agent is allowed to do so.
6. Based on its filtering policy and the established cooperation conditions, portal agent a sends the public profile to portal agent b.
7. In a similar way, portal agent b sends the public profile to the shoe shop agent.
8. Based on the received public profile, the shop agent sends a policy package to the user agent through portal agent b and portal agent a.
9. Step 5 in the previous scenario is then carried out by the user agent.

4   Experiments and Results

4.1   Experiments in the Shopping Mall

From March 8th to April 30th 2003, a large-scale experiment was conducted with full collaboration of the Osu shopping mall and its staff. The Osu shopping mall

---

[5] We suppose that both portal agents allow such cooperation. Otherwise, messages will not be set out of the communities.

Fig. 7. A view of Osu shopping mall and a fixed RF beacon receiver

(see Figure 7) is about 450m x 400m in size and consists of three smaller shopping malls, called Osu PC shop, Nioumon and East Nioumon. The experiment aimed to examine how well a ubiquitous system can help shops and visitors and also to evaluate our agent-based approach to designing and implementing such systems.

Cell phones are chosen as the portal devices that users should employ during the experiment. (More than eighty-one million people, 63.7% of the population, in Japan own call phones, and all providers support email and Web access.) Ordinary visitors join/quit this experiment through the registration center when they enter/leave the mall. The experiment works as the followings.

1. In the registration center, a participant has his cell phone's email address, shopping interests, preference of receiving messages from shops, age and several other personal data registered. Then he is given an RF transmitter.
2. The registered profile is divided into a public profile and a private profile, with which the creator agent creates a user agent in the user agent community.
3. As the participant is moving through the Osu shopping mall, the location sensing system (see Section 3.1) sends his position data to the user agent every seven seconds.
4. The user agent, shop agents and portal agents work on either scenario presented in Section 3.5.
5. Repeat Step 3 and Step 4, till the participant leaves the Osu shopping mall and returns the RF transmitter to the registration center and quits the experiment.[6]

Most roles we employ in the experiment only have one simple task: sending an advertising email of a shop to a potential buyer if his public profile and private profile show a certain intent to the shop. An example of advertising email is as follows:

---

[6] Participants have to register again the next time they join the experiment. We know it is tedious, but we do not have an alternative because we have to collect and distribute those RF transmitters repeatedly.

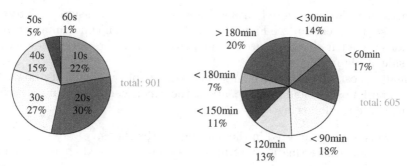

Fig. 8. Percentage of participants per age (left) and participation time (right)

```
Subject: On sale! Dozens Roses --- Only £ 5.00
Content:  some simple advertising messages
          http://.../ShowAd?no=XX&id=XX
```

4.2   Results and Discussion

In total, 56 shops and 901 people (631 men and 270 women) participated in the experiment. The system delivered 10579 email messages and 1625 URLs embedded in the email were visited. The left side of Figure 8 shows the breakdown of the participants by age. Only 605 persons returned their RF transmitters immediately before leaving. Among them, the average participation time was 1 hour and 44 minutes. The right side of Figure 8 shows the breakdown of participation time in increments of 30 minutes.

Fig. 9. Participants' response to the system in general

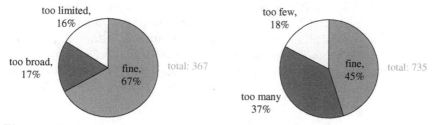

Fig. 10. Survey results: location sensitivity (left) and message quantity (right)

Participants were surveyed during the experiment to measure their response to the system in general (see Figure 9), and their opinion concerning sensitivity to location (see left side of Figure 10), and the number of received messages (see right side of Figure 10).

Finally, most of the participants very kindly told us or wrote down their feelings, both positive and negative, about the experiment. Some of the common comments are the following:

- I became more interested in the offerings of the shops.
- It was very interesting because up-to-date email created chances for me to talk with the clerks.
- Most of the information I got was useful, but some of it was useless.
- It was fun. I could find new shops that I had never entered before.
- The email messages were too brief. They should be richer in content so that I do not have to check the embedded URLs.

5   Future Directions

Several topics in both ubiquitous, context-aware systems and MAS deserve additional research and development. On the commercial front, we are encouraged to develop a second-generation prototype. Besides many suggested enhancements, there is an urgent demand to add orientation-sensing (determining the direction of mobile objects) and simultaneous use of multiple portable devices such as bluetooth-enabled, IEEE 802.11-enabled and infrared-enabled devices. On the research front, both the VPC framework and the Kodama platform may take advantage of the emerging Web services infrastructure. Making use of SOAP (communication), WSDL (description) and UDDI (discovery) promises better application-to-application interaction than the tailor-made counterparts that we implemented in this application. For rich coordination between independently implemented MAS, we are interested in the standardisation effort in the agent community (particularly FIPA), and in particular in enabling the Kodama agent platform to cooperate with FIPA-compliant platforms.

6   Conclusions

We believe that the challenging issues in agent research include not only theoretical issues but also methodological and software engineering issues. Through our work, we illustrated how the initial agent-based approach can be used for a real-world application in a shopping mall environment. Although preliminary, the results of the large-scale experiment performed in the Osu shopping mall were positive, and generated a lot of feedback suggesting further developments and improvements.

Acknowledgements

We thank the rest of the team: Makoto Nishino at Fujitsu PST; Lusheng Ji at Fujitsu Laboratories of America; (who designed, implemented and setup the SNOWNET); Hideki Nagino, Masatak Kushigemachi at Fujitsu Network Technologies (who designed and implemented the RF beacon sensing system) for their support and efforts. The experiment in the Osu shopping mall was funded by a grant from the Telecommunications Advancement Organisation (TAO) of Japan.

References

[1] Weiser, M.: The computer for the 21st Century. Scientific American **265** (1991) 94–104   392
[2] Stanford, V.: Using Pervasive Computing to Deliver Elder Care. IEEE Pervasive Computing **1** (2002) 10–13   392
[3] Margaret Fleck and Marcos Frid and Tim Kindberg and Eamonn O'Brien-Strain and Rakhi Rajani and Mirjana Spasojevic: From informing to remembering: Ubiquitous systems in interactive museums. IEEE Pervasive Computing **1** (2002) 13–21   392
[4] Ducatel, K., Bogdanowicz, M., Scapolo, F., Leijten, J., Burgelman, J. C.: Scenarios for Ambient Intelligence in 2010. Technical report, IST Advisory Group (2001) 393
[5] Shadbolt, N.: Ambient Intelligence. IEEE Intelligent Systems **18** (2003) 2–3   393
[6] Luck, M., McBurney, P., Preist, C.: Agent Technology: Enabling Next Generation Computing (A Roadmap for Agent Based Computing). Technical report, AgentLink (2003)   393
[7] Bellavista, P., Corradi, A., Stefanelli, C.: The Ubiquitous Provisioning of Internet Services to Portable Devices. IEEE Pervasive Computing **1** (2002) 81–87   393
[8] Zhong, G., Takahashi, K., Amamiya, S., Mine, T., Amamiya, M.: KODAMA Project: from Design to Implementation of a Distributed Multi-Agent System. In: Proceedings of Autonomous Agents and Multi-Agent Systems. (2002) 43–44 393
[9] Jennings, N. R.: On agent-based software engineering. Artificial Intelligence **117** (2000) 277–296   393, 396
[10] Jennings, N. R.: An agent-based approach for building complex software systems. Communications of the ACM **44** (2001) 35–41   393
[11] Wooldridge, M.: An Introduction to MultiAgent Systems. John Wiley & Sons, Chichester England (2002)   393
[12] Iwao, T., Okada, M., Kawashima, K., Matsumura, S., Kanda, H., Sakamoto, S., Kainuma, T., Amamiya, M.: Large Scale Peer-to-Peer Experiments with Virtual Private Community (VPC) Framework. In: Proceedings of Cooperative Information Agents. Volume 2442 of LNAI., Springer Verlag (2002) 66–81   393
[13] O'Brien, P., Nicol, R.: FIPA — towards a standard for software agents. BT Technical Journal **16** (1998) 51–58   394
[14] www.fipa.org/resources/pr0004.html: FIPA Specifications voted to Standard Status (2002)   394
[15] www.fipa.org: The foundation for intelligent physical agents (1996)   394

[16] Mathieu, P., Routier, J., Secq, Y.: Ubiquitous computing: vanishing the notion of application. In: Proceedings of the Workshop on Ubiquitous Agents on embedded, wearable, and mobile devices. (2002) 394

[17] Sadeh, N. M., Chan, E., Van, L.: MyCampus: An Agent-Based Environment for Context-Aware Mobile Services. In: Proceedings of the Workshop on Ubiquitous Agents on embedded, wearable, and mobile devices. (2002) 394

[18] Gasser, L.: Agents and concurrent objects. IEEE Concurrency **6** (1998) 74–77, 81 Interviewed by Jean-Pierre Briot 394

[19] Gasser, L.: MAS Infrastructure Denitions, Needs, and Prospects. In: Proceedings of the Workshop on Scalable MAS Infrastructure. (2000) 394

[20] Weiss, G., ed.: Multiagent Systems: A Modern Approach to Distributed Artificial Intelligence. MIT Press, Cambridge, USA (2000) 394

[21] Ricordel, P. M., Demazeau, Y.: From Analysis to Deployment: A Multi-Agent Platform Survey. In: Proceedings of Engineering Societies in the Agents World: First International Workshop. Volume 1972 of LNAI., Berlin, Springer Verlag (2000) 93–105 394

[22] Zhong, G., Amamiya, S., Takahashi, K., Mine, T., Amamiya, M.: The Design and Implementation of KODAMA System. IEICE Transactions on Information and Systems **E85-D** (2002) 637–646 394, 395, 396

[23] http://www.fipa.org/: FIPA standard specification: FIPA Abstract Architecture Specification (2002) 394

[24] Zhong, G., Takahashi, K., Amamiya, S., Matsuno, D., Mine, T., Amamiya, M.: From computer Networks to Agent Networks. In: Proceedings of the 36th Hawaii International Conference on System Sciences, IEEE press (2003) 395

[25] Geihs, K.: Middleware Challenges Ahead. IEEE Computer **34** (2001) 24–31 395

[26] Raatikainen, K., Christensen, H. B., Nakajima, T.: Application requirements for middleware for mobile and pervasive systems. ACM SIGMOBILE Mobile Computing and Communications Review **6** (2002) 16–24 395

[27] Wegner, P.: Why Interaction Is More Powerful Than Algorithem. Communications of the ACM **40** (1997) 80–91 395

[28] Hilaire, V., Koukam, A., Gruer, P., Müller, J. P.: Formal Specification and Prototyping of Multi-Agent Systems. In: Proceedings of Engineering Societies in the Agents World: First International Workshop. Volume 1972 of LNAI., Berlin, Springer Verlag (2000) 114–126 395, 396

[29] Kendall, E. A.: Role Modeling for Agent System Analysis, Design, and Implementation. IEEE Concurrency **8** (2000) 34–41 396

[30] Zambonelli, F., Jennings, N. R., Wooldridge, M.: Organizational Rules as an Abstraction for the Analysis and Design of Multi-agent Systems. Journal of Knowledge and Software Engineering **11** (2001) 303–328 396

[31] Omicini, A., Ricci, A.: Integrating Organisation within a MAS Coordination Infrastructure. In: Proceedings of the 4th workshop Engineering Societies in the Agents World. (2003) 165–172 396

[32] Koestler, A.: The Ghost in the Machine. Hutchinson (1967) 396

[33] Rodríguez, S., Hilaire, V., Koukam, A.: Towards a Methodological Framework for Holonic Multi-Agent Systems. In: Proceedings of the 4th workshop Engineering Societies in the Agents World. (2003) 179–185 396

[34] Iwao, T., Wada, Y., Yamasaki, S., Shiouchi, M., Okada, M., Amamiya, M.: Collaboration among Agents in Logical Network of Peer-to-Peer Services. In: Proceedings of SAINT, IEEE (2002) 6–7 396

[35] Patterson, C. A., Muntz, R. R., Pancake, C. M.: Challenges in Location-Aware Computing. IEEE Pervasive Computing **2** (2003) 80–89 398

[36] Ji, L., Agre, J., Mishra, A.: Secure Nomadic Wireless Networks (SNOWNET). Technical Report FLA-PCRTM03-01, Fujitsu (2003) 398

Author Index

Lecture Notes in Artificial Intelligence (LNAI)

Vol. 2843: G. Grieser, Y. Tanaka, A. Yamamoto (Eds.), Discovery Science. XII, 504 pages. 2003.

Vol. 2842: R. Gavaldá, K.P. Jantke, E. Takimoto (Eds.), Algorithmic Learning Theory. XI, 313 pages. 2003.

Vol. 2838: N. Lavrač, D. Gamberger, L. Todorovski, H. Blockeel (Eds.), Knowledge Discovery in Databases: PKDD 2003. XVI, 508 pages. 2003.

Vol. 2837: N. Lavrač, D. Gamberger, L. Todorovski, H. Blockeel (Eds.), Machine Learning: ECML 2003. XVI, 504 pages. 2003.

Vol. 2835: T. Horváth, A. Yamamoto (Eds.), Inductive Logic Programming. X, 401 pages. 2003.

Vol. 2821: A. Günter, R. Kruse, B. Neumann (Eds.), KI 2003: Advances in Artificial Intelligence. XII, 662 pages. 2003.

Vol. 2807: V. Matoušek, P. Mautner (Eds.), Text, Speech and Dialogue. XIII, 426 pages. 2003.

Vol. 2801: W. Banzhaf, J. Ziegler, T. Christaller, P. Dittrich, J.T. Kim (Eds.), Advances in Artificial Life. XVI, 905 pages. 2003.

Vol. 2797: O.R. Zaïane, S.J. Simoff, C. Djeraba (Eds.), Mining Multimedia and Complex Data. XII, 281 pages. 2003.

Vol. 2792: T. Rist, R.S. Aylett, D. Ballin, J. Rickel (Eds.), Intelligent Virtual Agents. XV, 364 pages. 2003.

Vol. 2782: M. Klusch, A. Omicini, S. Ossowski, H. Laamanen (Eds.), Cooperative Information Agents VII. XI, 345 pages. 2003.

Vol. 2780: M. Dojat, E. Keravnou, P. Barahona (Eds.), Artificial Intelligence in Medicine. XIII, 388 pages. 2003.

Vol. 2777: B. Schölkopf, M.K. Warmuth (Eds.), Learning Theory and Kernel Machines. XIV, 746 pages. 2003.

Vol. 2752: G.A. Kaminka, P.U. Lima, R. Rojas (Eds.), RoboCup 2002: Robot Soccer World Cup VI. XVI, 498 pages. 2003.

Vol. 2741: F. Baader (Ed.), Automated Deduction – CADE-19. XII, 503 pages. 2003.

Vol. 2705: S. Renals, G. Grefenstette (Eds.), Text- and Speech-Triggered Information Access. VII, 197 pages. 2003.

Vol. 2703: O.R. Zaïane, J. Srivastava, M. Spiliopoulou, B. Masand (Eds.), WEBKDD 2002 - Mining Web Data for Discovering Usage Patterns and Profiles. IX, 181 pages. 2003.

Vol. 2700: M.T. Pazienza (Ed.), Extraction in the Web Era. XIII, 163 pages. 2003.

Vol. 2699: M.G. Hinchey, J.L. Rash, W.F. Truszkowski, C.A. Rouff, D.F. Gordon-Spears (Eds.), Formal Approaches to Agent-Based Systems. IX, 297 pages. 2002.

Vol. 2691: V. Mařík, J.P. Müller, M. Pechoucek (Eds.), Multi-Agent Systems and Applications III. XIV, 660 pages. 2003.

Vol. 2684: M.V. Butz, O. Sigaud, P. Gérard (Eds.), Anticipatory Behavior in Adaptive Learning Systems. X, 303 pages. 2003.

Vol. 2671: Y. Xiang, B. Chaib-draa (Eds.), Advances in Artificial Intelligence. XIV, 642 pages. 2003.

Vol. 2663: E. Menasalvas, J. Segovia, P.S. Szczepaniak (Eds.), Advances in Web Intelligence. XII, 350 pages. 2003.

Vol. 2661: P.L. Lanzi, W. Stolzmann, S.W. Wilson (Eds.), Learning Classifier Systems. VII, 231 pages. 2003.

Vol. 2654: U. Schmid, Inductive Synthesis of Functional Programs. XXII, 398 pages. 2003.

Vol. 2650: M.-P. Huget (Ed.), Communications in Multiagent Systems. VIII, 323 pages. 2003.

Vol. 2645: M.A. Wimmer (Ed.), Knowledge Management in Electronic Government. XI, 320 pages. 2003.

Vol. 2639: G. Wang, Q. Liu, Y. Yao, A. Skowron (Eds.), Rough Sets, Fuzzy Sets, Data Mining, and Granular Computing. XVII, 741 pages. 2003.

Vol. 2637: K.-Y. Whang, J. Jeon, K. Shim, J. Srivastava, Advances in Knowledge Discovery and Data Mining. XVIII, 610 pages. 2003.

Vol. 2636: E. Alonso, D. Kudenko, D. Kazakov (Eds.), Adaptive Agents and Multi-Agent Systems. XIV, 323 pages. 2003.

Vol. 2627: B. O'Sullivan (Ed.), Recent Advances in Constraints. X, 201 pages. 2003.

Vol. 2600: S. Mendelson, A.J. Smola (Eds.), Advanced Lectures on Machine Learning. IX, 259 pages. 2003.

Vol. 2592: R. Kowalczyk, J.P. Müller, H. Tianfield, R. Unland (Eds.), Agent Technologies, Infrastructures, Tools, and Applications for E-Services. XVII, 371 pages. 2003.

Vol. 2586: M. Klusch, S. Bergamaschi, P. Edwards, P. Petta (Eds.), Intelligent Information Agents. VI, 275 pages. 2003.

Vol. 2583: S. Matwin, C. Sammut (Eds.), Inductive Logic Programming. X, 351 pages. 2003.

Vol. 2581: J.S. Sichman, F. Bousquet, P. Davidsson (Eds.), Multi-Agent-Based Simulation. X, 195 pages. 2003.

Vol. 2577: P. Petta, R. Tolksdorf, F. Zambonelli (Eds.), Engineering Societies in the Agents World III. X, 285 pages. 2003.

Vol. 2569: D. Karagiannis, U. Reimer (Eds.), Practical Aspects of Knowledge Management. XIII, 648 pages. 2002.

Vol. 2560: S. Goronzy, Robust Adaptation to Non-Native Accents in Automatic Speech Recognition. XI, 144 pages. 2002.

Vol. 2557: B. McKay, J. Slaney (Eds.), AI 2002: Advances in Artificial Intelligence. XV, 730 pages. 2002.

Vol. 2554: M. Beetz, Plan-Based Control of Robotic Agents. XI, 191 pages. 2002.

Vol. 2543: O. Bartenstein, U. Geske, M. Hannebauer, O. Yoshie (Eds.), Web Knowledge Management and Decision Support. X, 307 pages. 2003.

Vol. 2541: T. Barkowsky, Mental Representation and Processing of Geographic Knowledge. X, 174 pages. 2002.

Vol. 2533: N. Cesa-Bianchi, M. Numao, R. Reischuk (Eds.), Algorithmic Learning Theory. XI, 415 pages. 2002.

Vol. 2531: J. Padget, O. Shehory, D. Parkes, N.M. Sadeh, W.E. Walsh (Eds.), Agent-Mediated Electronic Commerce IV. Designing Mechanisms and Systems. XVII, 341 pages. 2002.